THE CONTINENTAL ARMY

THEY SCRAMBLED UP THE PARAPET

Military professionals launched this bayonet attack on Redoubt 10 during the siege of Yorktown. Only an army with thorough training, sophisticated organization, esprit de corps, and courage could have attempted this assault. The Continental Army had become such an army. The hastily assembled group that gathered at Lexington in the spring of 1775 evolved by the fall of 1781 into the effective force shown here. Howard Pyle's modern masterpiece captures this "spirit of victory."

ARMY LINEAGE SERIES

THE CONTINENTAL ARMY

by
Robert K. Wright, Jr.

MILITARY INSTRVCTION

CENTER OF MILITARY HISTORY
UNITED STATES ARMY
WASHINGTON, D.C., 1983

Library of Congress Cataloging in Publication Data

Wright, Robert K., 1946–
  The Continental Army.

  (Army lineage series)
  Bibliography: p.
  Includes index.
  1. United States. Continental Army—History.
2. United States—History—Revolution, 1775-1783—Campaigns and battles.
I. Title. II. Series.
UA25.W84   1983   355.3'0973   82-16472

CMH Pub 60-4

First Printing

For sale by the Superintendent of Documents, U.S. Government Printing Office
Washington, D.C. 20402

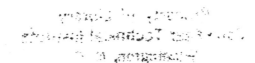

ARMY LINEAGE SERIES

David F. Trask, General Editor

Advisory Committee
(As of 1 January 1982)

James C. Olson
University of Missouri

Maj. Gen. Quinn H. Becker
Deputy Surgeon General, U.S.A.

Maj. Gen. John B. Blount
U.S. Army Training and
Doctrine Command

Brig. Gen. Dallas C. Brown, Jr.
U.S. Army War College

Richard D. Challener
Princeton University

Col. Roy K. Flint
U.S. Military Academy

Arthur L. Funk
University of Florida

Joseph E. Harris
Howard University

John H. Hatcher
The Adjutant General Center

Morten Jay Luvaas
Allegheny College

James O'Neill
National Archives and Records Service

John Shy
University of Michigan

Col. William A. Stofft
U.S. Army Command and General
Staff College

Betty M. Unterberger
Texas A&M University

U.S. Army Center of Military History

Brig. Gen. James L. Collins, Jr., Chief of Military History

Chief Historian
Chief, Histories Division
Editor in Chief

David F. Trask
Col. James W. Dunn
John Elsberg

Foreword

This volume completes the Center of Military History's trilogy of special studies on the War of American Independence (the Revolution). As part of the Army's contribution to the Bicentennial, the center undertook three separate but related projects to produce significant monographs on previously unexplored aspects of the Revolutionary War. Dr. Mary C. Gillette's *The Army Medical Department, 1775–1818* was published in 1981 as was Dr. Erna Risch's *Supplying Washington's Army*. Each has increased the information available on the war by detailing the support furnished to the fighting man. *The Continental Army* now directs us to the basic military organization used during the war and to the forming of the Army's traditions and first tactical doctrine. This book traces the birth of the Army and its gradual transformation into a competent group of professionals and emphasizes for the first time the major influences of eighteenth century military theorists on that transformation. It should join the other two volumes as a basic reference on the military history of the Revolution.

The Continental Army is the first volume of the Army Lineage Series published under a revised format. Hereafter, lineage volumes will include lengthy, footnoted narratives, along with lineages and bibliographies. In a sense, a study of the Continental Army, the forerunner of today's Regular Army, is a fitting choice for beginning a new series. Later volumes will detail the development of specific branches of the army from those early days to the present. The U.S. Army Center of Military History regards this series as essential to its mission of helping today's Army prepare for tomorrow by better understanding its past. In addition, the narratives herein make accurate information available to those in the Army as well as the general public. Furthermore, the lineages should help to foster unit *esprit-de-corps*. We hope that this volume with its new format will prove as popular as earlier volumes in the series.

Washington, D.C.
1 May 1982

JAMES L. COLLINS, JR.
Brigadier General, USA
Chief of Military History

The Author

Robert K. Wright, Jr., received a B.A. degree in history from the College of the Holy Cross in 1968 and M.A. and Ph.D. degrees in early American history from the College of William and Mary in 1971 and 1980, respectively. He served with the Army on active duty from 1968 to 1970, first as a radio-teletype operator in Germany and then in the 18th Military History Detachment. During the latter assignment, he recorded the combat operations of the 25th Infantry Division in the former Republic of Vietnam for 1969 and 1970. Before returning to graduate school, Dr. Wright attained the rank of sergeant. He joined the Organizational History Branch, U.S. Army Center of Military History in 1974. In 1982 he was commissioned as a captain in the Virginia Army National Guard. Dr. Wright is also the author of many articles related to the War of American Independence and to unit history.

Preface

Past historical accounts of the War of American Independence have largely ignored two areas which I find fundamental to evaluating campaigns and generalship. The basic concepts of military organization within units and in the larger realm of command and staff determine an army's capabilities. These concepts, for example, can insure that an army will be unable to cope with irregular opponents in difficult terrain. An army's doctrine—a theory on employing force which is taught to the army and is based on carefully worked out principles—in turn reveals how well that army's leaders understand their own organization and the situation in which they intend to fight. This monograph treats the organization and doctrine used in the Continental Army during the War of American Independence.

This book is not, however, a comprehensive account of the Revolution. Militia and regular state troops gave invaluable service during the war, but other historians have already dealt with these forces' contribution. This volume does not address logistical and medical support within the Continental Army because other volumes of the U.S. Army Center of Military History have covered those subjects in detail. Also, this volume does not discuss actual operations. Instead, *The Continental Army* provides a background for other historians to better evaluate campaigns through understanding how the Continentals and their adversaries organized and deployed their troops.

The present volume grew out of a proposal in January 1975 to produce a shorter, special volume in the Army Lineage Series for the Bicentennial. We then assumed that the Continental Army's organizational history was simple, that we could produce a short narrative relatively quickly, and that the book would serve primarily as a reference tool by including lineage (outline histories) of the approximately 200 regiments and smaller units which made up that Army. However, actual research soon revealed an untold story. The Continental Army actually underwent a complex evolution which greatly affected the military, political, and social history of the Revolution. Our discovery of Revolutionary leaders' decision to adopt many then contemporary European, and especially French, military theorists' concepts justified transforming a short narrative into the present footnoted monograph. Yet we have retained the original plan to include all 177 unit lineages and have added extensive bibliographies. I hope that the military and academic communities will accept this volume as a serious, scholarly treatment of a very important subject. I also expect it to be useful as a reference for professional and amateur historians and for genealogists interested in a specific unit's services. Nevertheless, practical considerations mandated including only selective bibliographies and publishing the lineages without footnotes. Those interested in more extensive bibliographies or in sources for a particular lineage entry may write to the U.S. Army Center of Military History, ATTN: DAMH-HSO, Washington, D.C. 20314 for additional information.

Many contributed to the success of this project. Cols. Walter McMahon, William F. Strobridge, and Robert N. Waggoner, successive Chiefs, Historical Services Division, lent their support. As Chief, Organizational History Branch, and later as supervisory historian of that division, Mr. Stanley R. Connor read the manuscript and shared his expertise. Ms. Janice E. McKenney, the current branch chief, contributed many valuable suggestions which improved both the narrative and the lineages. Past and present coworkers in the branch asked critical questions, endured frequent monologues, and reminded me to step down from my soapbox.

Dr. Robert Coakley served as this book's midwife during his tenure as deputy chief historian. He patiently read each draft and provided countless suggestions, corrections, and words of encouragement. Mr. Detmar Finke loaned me numerous rare volumes, saving long hours of research time. Mr. Howell C. Brewer prepared the superb maps and charts, and Mr. Arthur S. Hardyman, Chief, Cartographic Branch, reviewed them and suggested placing the state maps within the lineage section.

The polish of the finished product is due in no small measure to the skill of several editors: Mr. John W. Elsberg, Mrs. Sara Heynen, and Mrs. Ann Conley. They patiently worked with me to turn my rough prose into a readable book. Typing support came from Mrs. Reda Robinson, the division secretary, and from the members of the center's Word Processing Unit, especially Mrs. Elizabeth Miles and Mrs. Joycelyn Bobo.

I cannot list all of the archivists and librarians who extended courtesies to me during my research. Several, however, merit special thanks: Carol Anderson and Joseph Mosley of the center's library, John Slonaker and Phyllis Cassler of the Military History Institute, Penny Crumpler of the Corps of Engineers Library, Ronald Gephart of the Library of Congress, Stewart Butler and Charles Shaughnessy of the National Archives, John Kilbourne of the Anderson House Museum of the Society of the Cincinnati, and Thomas Dunning of the New-York Historical Society. Professors Richard Kohn, Russell Weigley, and Charles Royster read parts of the manuscript and deserve commendation for their insights. Mr. Nicholas D. Ward and Col. Joseph B. Mitchell of the American Revolution Round Table of the District of Columbia allowed me to read chapters before their group and to benefit from that organization's critical skills.

Every historian is the product of his teachers. I want to acknowledge the contributions of some of the more influential men who helped to mold my career: Professors Edward F. Wall and James F. Powers of the College of the Holy Cross; Richard M. Brown, now of the University of Oregon; John Selby, Ludwell H. Johnson, and Thomas F. Sheppard of the College of William and Mary; and an extra thanks to Dr. Bruce T. McCully, formerly of the latter institution.

One group actually contributed more to this book than any other: my family. My parents and brother sacrificed innumerable vacations to my eccentricities and allowed me to walk over many of the battlefields and encampment areas of the Revolution. Insights gained then gave me an edge in dealing later with documentary sources. My sons Robbie and Michael endured abandonment many evenings and weekends to let me put in the hours necessary to meet deadlines and to compensate for unavoidable interruptions during normal duty hours. Marcia, my wife, put me through graduate school, brewed the oceans of coffee to keep me going, and gave me remedial spelling lessons.

In spite of the best efforts of so many, some errors may have gone undetected. I am fully responsible for them.

Washington, D.C.   ROBERT K. WRIGHT, JR.
1 May 1982

Contents

Tables

Charts

Maps

Illustrations

The following color illustrations appear between pages 187 and 194:

The Battle of Bunker Hill

The Death of General Warren at Bunker Hill

Death of General Montgomery in the Attack on Quebec

The Retreat Through the Jerseys

Capture of the Hessians at Trenton

The Death of General Mercer at the Battle of Princeton

Attack Upon the Chew House

The Surrender of General Burgoyne at Saratoga

The Meeting of Greene and Gates

Guilford Court House, 15 March 1781

Thomas Shubrick

Morgan Lewis

Jacob Kingsbury

Jacob Reed, Jr.

Henry Henley Chapman

John Taliaferro Brooke

Surrender of Lord Cornwallis at Yorktown

Frederick Wilhelm Augustus von Steuben

Illustrations courtesy of the following sources: p. 135 from the Star-Spangled Banner Flag House Association; pp. 138 and 162 from the Historical Society of Pennsylvania; p. 101 from the Permanent Collection, the Berkshire Museum, Pittsfield, Mass.; p. 63 from the American Philosophical Society; pp. 43 and 88 from the Art Commission of the City of New York; p. 97 and between pp. 187 and 194 from the Anderson House Museum of the Society of the Cincinnati (photographs by Sgt. Jim Moore, 50th Military History Detachment); the frontispiece and between pp. 187 and 194 from the Delaware Art Museum, Howard Pyle Collection; pp. 9, 12, 23, 24, 27, 28, 37, 52, 54, 61, 74, 76, 79, 80, 103, 111, 115, 116, 117, 123, 129, 130, 133, 140, 148, 155, 164, 166, 168, 169, 171, 173, and between pp. 187 and 194 from the Independence National Historical Park Collection; and p. 86 and between pp. 187 and 194 are copyright the Yale University Art Gallery. The documents on pp. 31, 33, 34, 77, 96, 124, 144, 172, 174, and 185 are from Record Group 93, National Archives. Illustrations on pp. 30, 64, and between pp. 187 and 194 are from the Army Art Collection. The line art on pp. 328, 334, and 344 is by William S. Ballou, Typography and Design Division, U.S. Government Printing Office.

THE CONTINENTAL ARMY

CHAPTER 1

The Army of Observation:
New England in Arms

On 19 April 1775 local Massachusetts militiamen and regular British troops began the War of American Independence at Lexington and Concord. The New England colonists reacted to this news by raising four separate armies. Each jurisdiction formed its force according to its particular experience in earlier wars and its individual interpretation of European military developments over the previous century. The speed of the American response stemmed from a decade of tension and from the tentative preparations for possible armed conflict that the colonists had made during the preceding months. The concentration of four separate armed forces at Boston under loose Massachusetts hegemony as a de facto regional army paved the way for establishing a national Continental Army.

Warfare in the Eighteenth Century

The Continental Army was the product of European military science, but like all institutions developed by the American colonists, its European origins had been modified by the particular conditions of American experience. A proper appreciation of that Army in the context of its own times thus requires an understanding not only of the general developments in the military art of western civilization during the seventeenth and eighteenth centuries, but also of the particular martial traditions and experiences of the English colonists in North America.

In the seventeenth century Europeans developed a new range of weapons and gradually introduced them into their armies. At the same time a wave of dynastic wars in western Europe led to the creation of increasingly larger forces serving nation-states. Commanders and leading military theoreticians spent most of the eighteenth century developing organizational structures and tactical doctrines to exploit the potential of the new weapons and armies. The full impact of these changes came at the end of that century.[1]

---

[1]The basic sources for this section are as follows: David Chandler, *The Art of Warfare in the Age of Marlborough* (New York: Hippocrene Books, 1976); Christopher Duffy, *The Army of Frederick the Great* (New York: Hippocrene Books, 1974); Robert S. Quimby, *The Background of Napoleonic Warfare: The Theory of Military Tactics in Eighteenth Century France* (New York: Columbia University Press, 1957); Richard Glover, *Peninsular Preparation: The Reform of the British Army, 1795–1809* (Cambridge: Cambridge University Press, 1963); and Oliver Lyman Spaulding, Jr., Hoffman Nickerson, and John Womack Wright, *Warfare: A Study of Military Methods From the Earliest Times* (New York: Harcourt, Brace, and Co., 1925).

During the seventeenth century, the firearm replaced the pike as the basic infantry weapon. The original firearm, a heavy matchlock musket, suffered from several serious defects as a military weapon: it was cumbersome; reloading was long and complicated; the chance of misfire was extremely high, particularly in damp weather; and the lit match required to ignite the gunpowder charge betrayed positions in the dark. These defects, particularly at close quarters, required a proportion of each unit to carry pikes for defense against an attack by enemy cavalry or pikemen.

A technological breakthrough occurred in the second half of the century with the introduction of a new firing mechanism. It relied on the spark produced by a piece of flint striking a steel plate to touch off the propellant charge. Although still susceptible to moisture, the flintlock musket was lighter and more wieldy than its predecessor, had a higher rate of fire, and was easier to maintain. Late in the century, development of the socket bayonet complemented the flintlock musket. The bayonet, a foot-long triangular blade which slipped around the muzzle of the musket without blocking it, transformed the firearm into a pole weapon. The transition to the musket and bayonet combination gradually eliminated the need for defensive pikemen, who disappeared from most western European armies by the end of the first decade of the eighteenth century. Standardized flintlocks appeared shortly thereafter.

Whether produced at government arsenals or by private contractors, all eighteenth century muskets were inaccurate. Weighing over ten pounds and with a barrel over a yard long, they were difficult to aim. Flints tended to wear out after only twenty rounds, and even under ideal conditions the effective range of these smoothbore weapons, which fired one-ounce balls (two-thirds to three-quarters of an inch in diameter), was only about one hundred yards. An average soldier under the stress of combat could fire three rounds a minute for short periods, but he required considerable training to accomplish this feat. Since care in reloading was a major factor influencing accuracy, only the first round loaded before combat began was completely reliable.

New tactical formations and doctrine between 1688 and 1745 took advantage of these new weapons. The emergence of the infantry as a major factor on the battlefield gained momentum from the growing importance of firepower. Beginning with the War of the Spanish Succession (1702–14), generals sought literally to blast the enemy off the field with concentrated fire delivered at close range. They moved away from the massed formations which had characterized the era of the pike and adopted a deployment in long lines (linear tactics); by mid-century infantrymen in nearly every army stood three-deep to bring a maximum number of muskets into play. The critical firefight took place at ranges of between fifty and one hundred yards.

These weapons and tactics required adjustments in organization. Since the sixteenth century the regiment had formed the basic component of an army, providing administrative and tactical control over a group of companies. The need for better fire control in battle led to many complicated experiments. Ultimately, every army turned to a more manageable subelement, the platoon, whose fire could be controlled by a handful of officers and noncommissioned officers. Coordinating the actions of a number of these basic elements of fire (normally eight) produced the battalion, the basic element of maneuver. Most regiments were composed of two or more battalions, except in the British Army, where the regiment and battalion were normally synonymous. The relationship between the company (an administrative entity) and the platoon varied, but by the end of the century most armies were making them interchangeable.

Filled with rank and file trained to fire in unison at areas rather than individual targets, these units constituted the latest advances in organization at the time of the Seven Years' War (1756-63).

A second development during the eighteenth century was improved handling of armies on the battlefield. At the beginning of the century, armies marched overland in massed formation and took hours to deploy into line of battle. A commander who felt at a disadvantage refused battle and marched away or took refuge in fortifications. Engagements normally occurred when both generals wanted to fight. Several reforms were introduced to force battle on an unwilling opponent. The cadenced march step and standardized drill maneuvers sought to reduce the time needed to deploy and the confusion associated with forming a line of battle. These changes also allowed a commander to adjust his formations to the changing flow of a battle without risking total disruption of his ranks. Brigades and divisions controlled the movements of several battalions and increasingly became semipermanent.

Mobile field artillery also emerged in the eighteenth century. While heavy cannon continued to be important for fortresses and sieges, lighter guns were introduced to give direct support to the infantry. Standardized calibers eased administrative and logistical problems. Ballistics experts and metallurgists reduced the weight of the tubes, while others improved carriages. The French emerged with the best of the new artillery after reforms in 1764 by General Jean Baptiste de Gribeauval, an experienced combat officer and able theoretician. The new mobility enabled tacticians to consider artillery as a supporting arm whose function was firing at enemy personnel instead of engaging in artillery duels. In nearly every European army the artillery became a separate armed service, legally distinct from the infantry and cavalry.

The army which naturally exercised the greatest influence on the American colonies was the British. Great Britain enjoyed a unique status among the great powers during this period because its strong navy gave it security from attack by its neighbors. One consequence was that the British Army at first lagged behind the other European armies in adopting the reforms of the seventeenth and eighteenth centuries, but by the time of the Seven Years' War, it had adopted the major ones. In fact, it had led the way in introducing many techniques of infantry fire control. Its slow and ad hoc growth as an institution, however, had produced an inefficient and extremely complex administrative and logistical superstructure. Authority and responsibility were divided between two major Army commands (the British and Irish Establishments), between the Army proper and the Ordnance Department (controlling artillery, engineers, and munitions), and between the civilian Secretary at War and the military Commander in Chief (when that office was filled). Strategic direction was shared by two or three civilian Secretaries of State. At times the various individuals responsible for these chains of command cooperated, and the system functioned well. However, when breakdowns occurred, the British Army appeared leaderless and inept.[2]

Colonial Military Experience

English military institutions formed part of the cultural inheritance which the first colonists brought to America. Immigrants and occasional contact with the British

[2]Glover, *Peninsular Preparation*, pp. 2, 12.

Army kept the colonists informed about newer developments. The most important of the inherited institutions was the militia, which dated back to Anglo-Saxon times, but the specific conditions of colonial settlement produced important modifications. Other variations crept in as the defensive needs of the colonies began to outstrip the capabilities of the militia.

The Tudors had revived the English militia in the sixteenth century as an inexpensive alternative to a large permanent army. They used the traditional universal obligation to serve in the defense of the realm as a basis for sustaining a body of voluntary "trained bands." The members of the general population acted as a reserve force through their possession of arms, and various fines levied on them in relation to their obligations furnished financial support for the trained bands. The county lords lieutenant provided organization, geographical identity, and central direction.[3]

The first settlements in Virginia, Plymouth, Massachusetts Bay, and Connecticut all recruited professional soldiers to act as military advisers. The colonists recognized from the beginning that both the Indians and England's European rivals posed potential threats. The Jamestown trading post organized itself into a virtual regimental garrison, complete with companies and squads. Plymouth, on the advice of Miles Standish, organized four companies of militia within two years of its founding. The Massachusetts Bay Colony profited from the experiences of the earlier settlements. In 1629 its first expedition left England for Salem with a militia company already organized and equipped with the latest weapons.

During the course of the seventeenth century the colonists adapted the English militia system to meet their own particular needs. Several regional patterns emerged. In the Chesapeake Bay area a plantation economy took root, leading to dispersed settlement. Virginia and Maryland formed their militia companies from all the residents of a particular area. In New England religion and a different economy led to a town-based residential system. Each town formed one or more militia companies as soon as possible after establishing its local government. South Carolina had a plantation economy, but its settlers came from Barbados and brought a large slave population with them. Its militia followed the example of Barbados and placed a heavy emphasis on controlling the slaves. Pennsylvania, on the other hand, did not pass a law establishing a mandatory militia until 1777. The differences in the militia establishments among these colonies in part explain later variations in organizing units for the Continental Army in 1775–76.

Growth in each colony soon led to innovations. In Massachusetts, for example, an excess of noncommissioned officers over European norms allowed for forming subordinate elements, or "demi-companies," which received a field test in a 1635 punitive expedition against Indians on Block Island. When the colony then grouped its fifteen

---

[3]Unless otherwise noted, this section is based on the studies of colonial militias listed in the bibliography and on the following: Darrett B. Rutman, "A Militant New World, 1607–1640: America's First Generation, Its Martial Spirit, Its Tradition of Arms, Its Militia Organization, Its Wars" (Ph.D. diss., University of Virginia, 1959); Patrick Mitchell Malone, "Indian and English Military Systems in New England in the Seventeenth Century" (Ph.D. diss., Brown University, 1971); John W. Shy, "A New Look at Colonial Militia," *William and Mary Quarterly*, 3d ser., 20 (1963):175–85; Timothy Breen, "English Origins and New World Development: The Case of the Covenanted Militia in Seventeenth-Century Massachusetts," *Past and Present* 57 (1972):74–96; Douglas Edward Leach, *Arms for Empire: A Military History of the British Colonies in North America, 1607–1763* (New York: Macmillan Co., 1973); and Howard H. Peckham, *The Colonial Wars, 1689–1762* (Chicago: University of Chicago Press, 1964).

companies into three regional regiments in December 1636, it became the first English-speaking government to adopt permanent regiments. Other colonies followed: Maryland and Plymouth in 1658, Virginia in 1666, and Connecticut in 1672. Standing regiments appeared in the English Army only in the 1640's.

Another modification of the European heritage occurred in the choice of weapons. Wilderness conditions accentuated the flintlock musket's advantages. By 1675 nearly every colony required its militiamen to own flintlocks rather than matchlocks: American armies thus completed this transition a quarter of a century before European armies. Many colonists hunted, but few had ever fought in a formal line of battle. Militia training consequently stressed individual marksmanship rather than massed firing at an area, which had been the norm in the Old World. A specific byproduct of this emphasis was the refinement of the rifle—a hunting weapon with German roots—by gunsmiths in Pennsylvania. The Pennsylvania rifle was longer than the standard musket but had a smaller bore (usually .45-caliber). Grooves, or rifling, cut into the barrel imparted spin to the ball and allowed a trained marksman to hit targets at up to 400 yards. As a military weapon the rifle was effective in skirmishing, but its slow rate of fire and lack of a bayonet placed riflemen at a disadvantage in open terrain.

By the eighteenth century the colonial militia, like the English trained bands, was armed with flintlocks and was organized geographically. The southern colonies with one regiment per county were closest to the "shire" system; the more densely populated northern colonies normally formed several regiments in each county. Most colonies gave both administrative and command responsibilities to the colonel of each regiment and dispensed with the office of county lieutenant. Local elites in both the mother country and America dominated the militia officer positions, whether elected or appointed, just as they controlled all other aspects of society. Ultimate responsibility for the militia was a function of the Crown. In England it was exercised for the Crown by the county lords lieutenant; in America, by the governor. The financial powers of the elective lower houses of the colonial legislatures, however, placed major limits on a governor's prerogatives.

The biggest difference between the English trained bands and the colonial militia was the latter's more comprehensive membership. Few free adult males were exempted by law from participating: the clergy, some conscientious objectors, and a handful of other special groups. This situation was the result of the first settlers' immediate need for local defense, a need absent in England since the days of the Spanish Armada. But in the late seventeenth and early eighteenth centuries, the danger to the more settled regions subsided. Although a militia structure based on an area's total male population was an admirable goal for local defense, taking the men for military service disrupted a colony's economy during extended crises or lengthy offensives. As other institutions emerged, the militia was left as "a local training center and a replacement pool, a country selective service system and a law enforcing agency, an induction camp and a primitive supply depot."[4]

As early as the 1620's in Virginia and in the 1630's during the Pequot War in New England, temporary detachments were drawn from the militia companies for field operations against the Indians. Volunteers or drafted quotas formed the detachments. This expedient practice minimized economic dislocation and concentrated field lead-

---

[4]Louis Morton, "The Origins of American Military Policy," *Military Affairs* 22 (1958):80.

ership in the hands of the most experienced officers. But even the detachments were seen as disrupting community life too much, and eventually they were employed primarily as garrisons. A different type of force emerged in the 1670's. Hired volunteers ranged the frontiers, patrolling between outposts and giving early warning of any Indian attack. Other volunteers combined with friendly Indians for offensive operations deep in the wilderness where European tactics were ineffective. The memoirs of the most successful leader of these mixed forces, Benjamin Church, were published by his son Thomas in 1716 and represent the first American military manual.[5]

During the Imperial Wars (1689–1762) against Spanish and French colonies, regiments completely separated from the militia system were raised for specific campaigns. These units, called Provincials, were patterned after regular British regiments and were recruited by the individual colonial governors and legislatures, who appointed the officers. Bounties were used to induce recruits, and the officers enjoyed a status greater than that of equivalent militia officers. Although new regiments were raised each year, in most colonies a large percentage of officers had years of service. Provincial field officers tended to be members of the legislature who had compiled long service in the militia. The company officers, responsible for most of the recruiting, were drawn from popular junior militia officers with demonstrated military skills.[6] The most famous Provincial units were formed by Maj. Robert Rogers of New Hampshire during the French and Indian War. His separate companies of rangers were recruited throughout the northern colonies and were paid directly by the British Army. They performed reconnaissance for the regular forces invading Canada and conducted occasional long-range raids against the French and their Indian allies.

The French and Indian War was different from earlier wars in one very important way. Formerly Great Britain had been content to leave fighting in North America to the colonists and had furnished only naval and logistical aid. William Pitt's ministry reversed that policy, and the regular British Army now carried out the major combat operations. The Provincials were relegated to support and reserve functions. Americans resented this treatment, particularly when they saw British commanders such as Edward Braddock and James Abercromby perform poorly in the wilderness. At the same time, Britons formed a negative opinion of the fighting qualities of the Provincials. British recruiting techniques and impressment of food, quarters, and transport created other tensions. The resulting residual bitterness contributed to the growing breach between the colonies and the mother country during the following decade.

The Coming of the Revolution

During the years following the Seven Years' War, the central government in London adopted a series of policies which altered the traditional relationship between England and the American colonies. The colonists, whose political institutions were rapidly maturing, resented English intervention in what they viewed as their internal

[5]Benjamin Church, *The History of the Great Indian War of 1675 and 1676, Commonly Called Philip's War. Also, The Old French and Indian Wars, From 1689 to 1704*, ed. Samuel G. Drake (Hartford: Silas Andrus & Son, 1854).
[6]Ranz E. Esbenshade, "Sober, Modest Men of Confined Ideas: The Officer Corps of Provincial New Hampshire" (Master's thesis, University of New Hampshire, 1976).

TIMOTHY PICKERING *(1745–1829), author of a military manual and commander of a regiment of Essex County, Massachusetts, militia, served the Continental Army as adjutant general, quartermaster general, and member of the Board of War. (Portrait by Charles Willson Peale, 1792.)*

affairs. Many different issues led to a growing alienation. By 1774 there was a real potential for armed confrontation.[7]

A change in British military policy was a catalyst for the controversy. After the 1763 Peace of Paris, London decided to create an American Establishment and to tax the colonists to pay for it. In the eyes of London planners, this army, patterned on a similar garrison stationed in Ireland for nearly a century, would serve several useful ends. It would enable the British Army to retain more regiments in peacetime than it could have otherwise. The regiments in America were to secure the newly won territories of Canada and Florida from French or Spanish attack and also to act as a buffer between the colonists and the Indians. The Americans felt that these troops served no useful purpose, particularly when the majority moved from the frontier to coastal cities to simplify logistics. As tensions rose, the colonists became more suspicious of British aims and increasingly saw the regular regiments as a "standing army" stationed in their midst to enforce unpopular legislation.

Political leaders cited the American Establishment in their rhetoric as an example of the British government's corruption and unconstitutional policies. Threats to use the troops in New York City to enforce the Stamp Act and to act as police during later land unrest in the Hudson River Valley caused initial concern. A major affront in American eyes came when Britain transferred several regiments to Boston in the immediate aftermath of protests over taxes imposed by the Townshend Act. To Americans this pattern paralleled the actions of the Stuarts in England in the late seventeenth

---

[7]Basic sources for this section are the following: Alan Rogers, *Empire and Liberty: American Resistance to British Authority, 1755–1763* (Berkeley: University of California Press, 1974); John Shy, *Toward Lexington: The Role of the British Army in the Coming of the American Revolution* (Princeton: Princeton University Press, 1965); and David Ammerman, *In The Common Cause: American Response to the Coercive Acts of 1774* (Charlottesville: University Press of Virginia, 1974).

century. In 1770 the Boston Massacre proved this point to a large body of the American people.[8]

Other American leaders moved beyond rhetoric to counter force with force. For instance, the Sons of Liberty emerged in New York in 1765–66 as a paramilitary organization in direct response to British troop movements. Even more intense reactions came in Massachusetts, the center of opposition to British policy. Although most troops withdrew from Boston in 1771, a garrison remained. Local politicians began agitating for serious militia reforms to create a force capable of offering opposition to the British Army if it returned in strength. A number of individuals who later occupied important positions in the Continental Army, such as Timothy Pickering ("A Military Citizen") and William Heath ("A Military Countryman"), contributed articles to the Massachusetts press advocating such reforms. Others organized voluntary military companies for extra training.[9]

When British troops returned to Boston in far greater numbers after the Boston Tea Party of 1773, the final phase of tension began. If Americans needed any further proof of British intent, this action and Parliament's punitive "Coercive Acts" furnished it. Military preparations quickened throughout New England, and the First Continental Congress met at Philadelphia in September to direct a concerted effort to secure a redress of American grievances. New Englanders removed militia officers known to be loyal to the Crown and increased the tempo of training. By the autumn of 1774 calls arose for forming a unified colonial army of observation that could take the field if hostilities erupted.[10] Similar trends, although less pronounced, existed in the middle and southern colonies.

Interest in the militia was matched during 1774 and early 1775 by a concern for war supplies. Adam Stephen, later a major general in the Continental Army, spoke for many in 1774 when he warned Virginia politicians that artillery, arms, and ammunition were in short supply in the colonies. His suggestions to encourage domestic production and importation from Europe were echoed by others who agreed with his statement that if enough arms and ammunition were available, "individuals may suffer, but the gates of hell cannot prevail against *America*."[11] Imports of arms and powder

[8]John Todd White, "Standing Armies in Time of War: Republican Theory and Military Practice During the American Revolution" (Ph.D. diss., George Washington University, 1978), pp. 1–111; Lawrence Delbert Cress, "The Standing Army, the Militia, and the New Republic: Changing Attitudes Toward the Military in American Society, 1768 to 1820" (Ph.D. diss., University of Virginia, 1976), pp. 80–128.

[9]Ronald L. Boucher, "The Colonial Militia as a Social Institution: Salem, Massachusetts, 1764–1775," *Military Affairs* 37 (1973):125–26; Stewart Lewis Gates, "Disorder and Social Organization: The Militia in Connecticut Public Life, 1660–1860" (Ph.D. diss., University of Connecticut, 1975), pp. 35–38; Roger Champagne, "The Military Association of the Sons of Liberty," *New-York Historical Society Quarterly* 41 (1957):338–50.

[10]David Richard Millar, "The Militia, the Army, and Independency in Colonial Massachusetts" (Ph.D. diss., Cornell University, 1967), pp. 284–88; Peter Force, ed., *American Archives: A Collection of Authentic Records, State Papers, Debates, and Letters and Other Notices of Public Affairs*, 9 vols. (Washington: M. St. Clair Clarke and Peter Force, 1839–53), 4th ser., 1:739–40, 787–88; J. Hammond Trumbull and Charles C. Hoadley, comps., *The Public Records of the Colony of Connecticut*, 15 vols. (Hartford, 1850–90), 14:296, 308–9, 327–28, 343–46 (hereafter cited as *Conn. Records*); John Russell Bartlett, ed., *Records of the Colony of Rhode Island and Providence Plantations in New England*, 9 vols. (Providence, 18–64, 7:247, 257–71 (hereafter cited as *R.I. Records*); Nathanael Greene, *The Papers of General Nathanael Greene*, ed. Richard K. Showan et al. (Chapel Hill: University of North Carolina Press, 1976–), 1:68–76; *Historical Magazine*, 2d ser., 7 (1870):22–26.

[11]Force, *American Archives*, 4th ser., 1:739–40.

grew by October 1774 to such a degree that British officials became alarmed. Individual colonial governments began to move existing stores beyond the reach of British seizure and to encourage domestic manufacturers. Massachusetts took the lead in collecting munitions, as it did in reforming the militia.[12]

The First Continental Congress rejected a proposal by Richard Henry Lee of Virginia to form a nationwide militia but did adopt a plan for concerted economic protest. The plan provided for a boycott of British goods after 1 December 1774 and authorized forming enforcement committees which quickly became de facto governments at the colony and local levels. The committees also secured political control over the countryside, a control which British authorities were never able to shake. This political control included leadership of the militia, and that institution became an instrument of resistance to the British. Instead of being intimidated by Britain's Coercive Acts of 1774, the colonists were moving toward armed resistance.

Thus in the years immediately before 1775, tensions built to the point that the leaders in each colony foresaw the possibility of violence. They reacted by gathering war materials and restoring the militia (or volunteer forces) to a level of readiness not seen since the early days of settlement. British officers in America were aware of the colonists' actions but dismissed them as "mere bullying."[13] Given these attitudes, the presence of Maj. Gen. Thomas Gage's garrison in Boston, and the advanced state of preparation in Massachusetts, it is not surprising that war began in that colony.

Massachusetts Acts

The Massachusetts Provincial Congress met as a shadow government and on 26 October 1774 adopted a comprehensive military program based on the militia. It created the executive Committees of Safety and of Supplies and gave the former the power to order out the militia in an emergency. It also directed the militia officers to reorganize their commands into more efficient units, to conduct new elections, to drill according to the latest British manual, and to organize one-quarter of the colony's force into "minute companies." The minutemen constituted special units within the militia system whose members agreed to undergo additional training and to hold themselves ready to turn out quickly ("at a minute's notice") for emergencies. Jedediah Preble, Artemas Ward, and Seth Pomeroy, three politicians who had served in the French and Indian War, were elected general officers of the militia. A month later two younger general officers were added: John Thomas (a veteran of the French and Indian War) and William Heath (a militiaman with a reputation as an administrator). During periods of congressional recess, the Committee of Safety and the Committee of Supplies collected material and established depots.[14]

---

[12]Ibid., pp. 746, 841–45, 858, 881, 953, 1002, 1022, 1032, 1041–42, 1066, 1077, 1080, 1143–45, 1332–34, 1365–70; Paul H. Smith et al., eds., *Letters of Delegates to Congress, 1774–1789* (Washington: Library of Congress, 1976–), 1:266–71, 298–301.

[13]Hugh Earl Percy, *Letters of Hugh Earl Percy From Boston and New York 1774–1776*, ed. Charles Knowles Bolton (Boston: Charles L. Goodspeed, 1902), pp. 35–37; see also W. Glanville Evelyn, *Memoir and Letters of Captain W. Glanville Evelyn, of the 4th Regiment ("King's Own") From North America, 1774–1776*, ed. G.D. Scull (Oxford: James Parker and Co., 1879), pp. 31–37.

[14]Unless otherwise noted, this section is based on Force, *American Archives*, 4th ser., 1:830–53, 993–1008, 1322–69; 2:461, 524, 609–10, 663, 742–830, 1347–1518.

ARTEMAS WARD *(1727–1800) of Massachusetts became the Continental Army's senior major general and first commander of the Eastern Department. (Portrait by Charles Willson Peale, ca. 1794.)*

After new elections were held, the Provincial Congress reconvened in February 1775. It clarified the Committee of Safety's powers, reappointed the five generals, and added John Whitcomb, another politically active veteran, as a sixth general.[15] The Congress also altered its basic military policy. In the face of increased tension, it took steps to augment the militia with a more permanent force patterned after the earlier Provincials. Regulations for this "Constitutional Army" were adopted on 5 April.

The Provincial Congress made a momentous decision three days later. By a vote of 96 of 103 members present, a report on the "State of the Province" was approved. The report stated that "the present dangerous and alarming situation of our publick affairs, renders it necessary for this Colony to make preparations for their security and defence by raising and establishing an Army." The projected volunteer force was to include more than just Massachusetts men, and delegates were sent to the other New England colonies to urge their participation. On 14 April the Committee of Safety was instructed to begin selecting field officers for Massachusetts' contingent. These officers, in turn, were to assist the committee in selecting captains, who would appoint subalterns. Minuteman officers were given preference. Officers selected would then raise their regiments and companies, as the Provincial officers had done.

After initiating its plans for a New England army, the Provincial Congress adjourned on 15 April. It reassembled on the 22d after the events at Lexington and Concord. The first order of business was accumulating testimony to prove to the English people that Gage's troops had been the aggressors.[16] The congress then turned its attention to forming a volunteer army from the men who had massed around Boston. The Committee of Safety had already taken tentative steps in this direction. On 21 April

---

[15]The age of some of the generals raises some doubt about their ability to take to the field: Pomeroy was 68, Preble 67, Whitcomb 61, Thomas 50, Ward 47, and Heath 37.

[16]The testimony collected was published as *A Narrative of the Excursions and Ravages of the King's Troops. . .* (Worcester: Isaiah Thomas, 1775).

TABLE 1—INFANTRY REGIMENTS, 1775

Colony	Field					Staff			Each Company									Aggregate					
	Colonel	Lieutenant Colonel	Major	Adjutant	Quartermaster	Surgeon	Surgeon's Mate	Chaplain	Number of Companies	Captain	Lieutenant	Ensign	Sergeant	Corporal	Drummer	Fifer	Privates	Officers	Staff Officers	Noncommissioned Officers	Drummers and Fifers	Privates	Total Strength
Massachusetts....	1	1	1	1	1	1	2	1	10	1	2	0	4	4	1	1	46	33	6	80	20	460	599
New Hampshire ..	1	1	1	1	1	1	1	1	10	1	2	0	2	4	1	1	53	33	5	60	20	530	648
Rhode Island.....	1	1	1	1	1	1	1	0	10[a]	1[b]	1[b]	1	3	3	1	1	49	33	4	60	20	490	607
Connecticut......	1[c]	1	1[c]	1	1	1	2	1	10	1[d]	2	1	4	4	1	1	90[e]	40	6	80	20	900[e]	1,046[e]
New York........	1	1	1	1	1	1	1	1	10	1	2	0	3	3	1	1	64	33	5	60	20	640	758

[a]One regiment only nine companies.

[b]Three companies in each regiment with captain-lieutenant instead of captain.

[c]Where colonel was general officer two majors authorized.

[d]Three companies without captain.

[e]7th and 8th Connecticut Regiments had only 65 privates per company.

the committee had approved an enlistment format; 8,000 effectives were to serve until 31 December in regiments consisting of a colonel, a lieutenant colonel, a major, and 9 companies. The committee planned to have each company consist of 3 officers, 4 sergeants, a drummer, a fifer, and 70 rank and file, though it subsequently reduced the latter figure to 50. The pre-Lexington plan had been to form an army by apportioning quotas of men on the various towns, a traditional colonial device. The committee decided instead to have the generals survey the men at the siege lines at Boston to persuade them to remain. Its decisions were preliminary since final authority rested with the Provincial Congress. As confusion spread, on 23 April General Ward, the commander of the siege, suggested that the congress use smaller units to retain a maximum number of officers.

The Provincial Congress incorporated Ward's suggestions into a comprehensive plan that it adopted the same day. It called for a New England army of 30,000 men, of which Massachusetts would furnish 13,600. The regimental organization adopted for the infantry called for 598 men: a colonel, a lieutenant colonel, a major, an adjutant, a quartermaster, a chaplain, a surgeon, 2 surgeon's mates, and 10 companies. Each company was to have a captain, 2 lieutenants, an ensign, and 55 enlisted men. On 25 April, following additional discussions with the Committee of Safety, this structure was confirmed with one change: it also accepted the committee's suggestion that each regiment headed by a general officer have two majors. (*Table 1*) Finally, after some discussion, it approved pay scales for the new force.

The Massachusetts plan called for artillerymen as well as infantry regiments. As early as 23 February the Committee of Safety, planning to train artillery companies, had distributed field guns to selected militia regiments. On 13 April the Provincial Congress had directed the committee to form six companies for the planned volunteer army. On 6 May congress adopted an organization of 4 officers, 4 sergeants, 4 corporals, a drummer, a fifer, and 32 matrosses, or privates, for each company. Four days

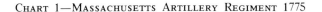

CHART 1—MASSACHUSETTS ARTILLERY REGIMENT 1775

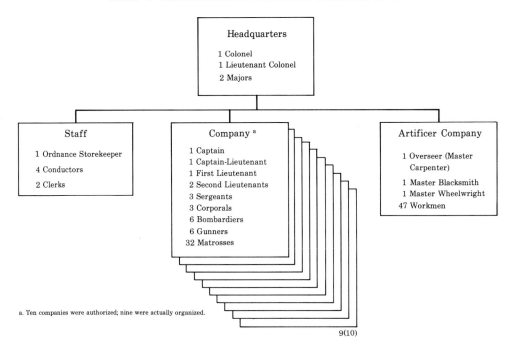

Headquarters

1 Colonel
1 Lieutenant Colonel
2 Majors

Staff

1 Ordnance Storekeeper
4 Conductors
2 Clerks

Company [a]

1 Captain
1 Captain-Lieutenant
1 First Lieutenant
2 Second Lieutenants
3 Sergeants
3 Corporals
6 Bombardiers
6 Gunners
32 Matrosses

Artificer Company

1 Overseer (Master Carpenter)
1 Master Blacksmith
1 Master Wheelwright
47 Workmen

a. Ten companies were authorized; nine were actually organized.

9(10)

later it rescinded that organization and sent a committee to confer with Richard Gridley on the propriety of organizing a full artillery regiment. Gridley, hero of the 1745 capture of Louisbourg, was the colony's leading expert on artillery. Following the talks, on 12 May the Provincial Congress authorized a ten-company regiment. (*Chart 1*) Four days later it gave Gridley the command.

The regiment formed in June. Neither Gridley nor William Burbeck, his assistant, could concentrate on it since they had also been appointed the colony's two engineers on 26 April. In June the Committee of Safety added a logistical staff and an organic company of artificers (skilled workmen) to do maintenance. The important post of ordnance storekeeper went to Ezekiel Cheever. The company officers came largely from the several Boston militia artillery companies, particularly Adino Paddock's which had received extensive training from British artillerymen in the 1760's and was composed mostly of skilled artisans and Sons of Liberty. Two of its members, John Crane and Ebenezer Stevens, had moved to Providence, Rhode Island, in 1774 after the closing of the port of Boston. Their close ties enabled the Rhode Island artillerymen to merge easily with the regiment in 1776.[17]

In spite of careful preparations, Massachusetts entered the war in a state of chaos. The Provincial Congress and the Committee of Safety frequently found themselves working at cross-purposes. Confusion over the size and configuration of the army created duplication of effort, and prospective officers were recruited under a variety of authorities. The minutemen and other militia who had responded to Lexington by

[17]John Austin Stevens, "Ebenezer Stevens, Lieut. Col. of Artillery in the Continental Army," *Magazine of American History* 1 (1877):588–92; Asa Bird Gardner, "Henry Burbeck: Brevet Brigadier-General United States Army—Founder of the United States Military Academy," ibid., 9(1883):252.

besieging Boston, moreover, were not prepared to remain in the field for an extended period, although later arrivals were more inclined to serve a full term (until 31 December).

Order began to emerge in May when formats for commissions and oaths were codified. Mustermasters were appointed to examine enlistment rolls at Cambridge and Roxbury so that the Committee of Safety could certify officers for commissioning. Regiments emerged with a geographic basis, drawing their precedence from that of the militia which furnished the majority of their men. Since all commissions were dated 19 May 1775, the touchy matter of seniority remained to be settled later. By the end of June twenty-six regiments had been certified, plus part of a regiment whose status as a Massachusetts or New Hampshire unit was unresolved.

During early June 1775, the Massachusetts army achieved a relatively final form. The Provincial Congress decided on 13 June to retain in service a force of one artillery and twenty-three infantry regiments. This limit was altered ten days later when the raising of troops specifically for coastal defense released Edmund Phinney's Cumberland County regiment from that mission to join the army. The Congress also resolved the status of the generals. Ward retained the overall command he had exercised since the outbreak of hostilities. John Whitcomb, William Heath, and Ebenezer Frye were designated major generals.[18]

Formation of a New England Army

With remarkable speed, committees of correspondence spread the traumatic news of Lexington and Concord beyond the borders of Massachusetts. By 24 April New York City had the details and Philadelphia had them by the next day. Savannah, the city farthest from the scene of the engagement, received the news on 10 May.[19] Massachusetts' call for a joint army of observation was answered by the three other New England colonies—New Hampshire, Rhode Island, and Connecticut. Each responded in its own way. Within two months three small armies joined the Massachusetts troops at Boston, and a council of war began strategic coordination. This regional force paved the way for the creation of a national institution, the Continental Army.

New Hampshiremen responded as individuals and in small groups to the news of Lexington. On 25 April, anticipating formal aid from New Hampshire, the Massachusetts Committee of Safety directed Paul Dudley Sargent of Hillsborough County to raise a regiment from these individuals.[20] Four days earlier the New Hampshire Provincial Congress had convened in emergency session. After considering a copy of Massachusetts' plan for a New England army, the New Hampshire body sent three of its members to confer with the Massachusetts Provincial Congress, but deferred further action until it could mobilize public support and make adequate financial plans.[21]

---

[18]The coast defense troops remained in state service instead of becoming Continentals. Joseph Warren, who was to have been senior major general, was killed at Bunker Hill before he received his commission.

[19]Frank Luther Mott, "The Newspaper Coverage of Lexington and Concord," *New England Quarterly* 17 (1944):489–505.

[20]When New Hampshire did not accept responsibility for Sergent's regiment, Massachusetts did.

[21]This section on New Hampshire is based on the following: Force, *American Archives*, 4th ser., 2:377–79, 401, 429–30, 519–24, 639–60, 745, 868, 1005–7, 1022–23, 1069–70, 1092, 1176–86, 1529; 4:1–20; John Sullivan, *Letters and Papers of Major-General John Sullivan, Continental Army*, ed. Otis G. Hammond, 3 vols. (Concord: New Hampshire Historical Society, 1930–39), 1:58–60; and Chandler Eastman Potter, *Military History of New Hampshire, From Its Settlement, in 1623, to the Year 1861*, 2 vols. (Concord: Adjutant General's Office, 1866), 1:263–272.

On 18 May the full Provincial Congress resolved to raise men "to join in the common cause of defending our just rights and liberties." Legislation on 20 May created a Committee of Safety and authorized a 2,000-man quota for the New England army. This figure included those New Hampshiremen already in service at Boston. The initial plan called for regiments organized on the same pattern as those in Massachusetts, but two days later, on 22 May, the Congress adopted a more specific plan. (*See Chart 1.*) It created three regiments and dispatched two officials to Cambridge to muster the volunteers who had gone to Massachusetts as one of those regiments. The volunteers had already elected John Stark, a veteran of Rogers' Rangers, as their colonel.

On 23 May the Provincial Congress appointed Nathaniel Folsom as the general officer to command the colony's forces, and the Committee of Safety began to nominate officers for the three regiments. On 24 May Enoch Poor of Exeter received command of the second of the regiments with an order to organize it immediately. On 1 June the congress appointed the officers of the 3d New Hampshire Regiment, the command going to James Reed of Fitzwilliam. Reed raised it in Strafford and Rockingham counties. Two days later the congress designated the regiment at Boston the 1st, or "eldest," Regiment, and confirmed Stark and its other field officers.

Folsom initially received the rank of brigadier general with duties similar to those of such officers in Massachusetts, except that he had no regimental command. On 6 June the Provincial Congress reaffirmed his authority as the commanding general, under General Ward, of all New Hampshire forces, and at the end of the month it promoted him to major general. Jealousy by the volunteers at Boston limited his authority for a time. When Reed assembled his 3d New Hampshire Regiment at Boston on 14 June, he received two of Stark's surplus companies to round out the unit. Poor's 2d New Hampshire Regiment was detained to defend the colony from possible British attack, but it was ordered to Cambridge on 18 June. Its last company arrived in early August. Although Folsom had wanted an artillery company to support his regiments, New Hampshire had no officers qualified to command one. The best the Provincial Congress could do was to send artillery pieces for the Massachusetts men to use.

Meeting in emergency session in response to the news of Lexington, the Rhode Island Assembly on 25 April decided to raise 1,500 men "properly armed and disciplined, to continue in this Colony, as an Army of Observation; to repel any insults or violence that may be offered to the inhabitants; and also, if it be necessary for the safety and preservation of any of the Colonies, that they be ordered to march out of this Colony, and join and cooperate with the Forces of our neighbouring Colonies."[22] It deferred substantive action until the regular May session. In the interim the commander of the Providence County militia brigade offered Massachusetts the services of his three battalions; other individuals went off to Boston as volunteers.

At the regular May session, the Rhode Island Assembly created an "Army of Observation" and a Committee of Safety. Because Governor Joseph Wanton remained loyal to the Crown, the colony's secretary signed the commissions. Deputy Governor Nicholas Cooke soon replaced Wanton. Rhode Island organized its contingent as a balanced brigade under Brig. Gen. Nathanael Greene, thus adopting a different ap-

---

[22]Force, *American Archives*, 4th ser., 2:390. For Rhode Island see the following: ibid., 431, 590, 900; Bartlett, Rhode Island Records 7:308–61; *Greene Papers*, 1:78–85; and Rhode Island Historical Society *Collections*, 6:108–9.

proach than that of the other New England colonies. (*See Chart 1.*) Greene's staff included a brigade adjutant and a brigade commissary responsible for logistics. The troops formed three regiments (two with eight companies and one with seven) and a company of artillery.[23] Greene, Cooke, and the Committee of Safety arranged the officers; since all commissions were dated 8 May, seniority was resolved by drawing lots. The three regiments rotated posts of honor to avoid establishing a system of precedence. One regiment was raised in Bristol and Newport Counties by Thomas Church; another was raised by Daniel Hitchcock in Providence County. A business associate of Greene's, James Mitchell Varnum, was given command of the regiment from King's and Kent counties, while John Crane, formerly of Boston, became captain of the artillery company.

Companies left for Boston as quickly as possible. Hitchcock's and Church's regiments had assembled there by 4 June, the date that Greene opened his headquarters. The artillery company, armed with four field pieces and escorting a dozen heavy guns, also arrived in early June. Varnum's regiment arrived several weeks later. The Rhode Island Assembly reconvened on 12 June and remained in session until 10 July. During this period it settled various logistical and disciplinary matters and added a secretary, a baker, and a chaplain to the brigade's staff. It also raised six new companies, two for each regiment. Greene was given the power, in consultation with the field officers, to fill vacancies, and he was placed under the "command and direction" of the Commander in Chief of the "combined American army" in Massachusetts.[24]

On 21 April representatives from Massachusetts met with the Connecticut Committee of Correspondence in the home of Governor Jonathan Trumbull at Lebanon. Trumbull sent his son David to inform Massachusetts that a special session of the Connecticut assembly would meet as soon as possible. While some Connecticut militia units marched to Boston on hearing of Lexington, most followed the advice of the governor to wait until the assembly could act. The wisdom of this course was confirmed by news that although Israel Putnam had asserted a loose hegemony over the volunteers, a formal command structure was needed before they would become effective.[25]

The special session convened at Hartford on 26 April, and the next day the Connecticut Assembly ordered that six regiments be raised, each containing ten companies. (*See Chart 1.*) Officers were appointed on 28 April and arranged on 1 May. At the time the assembly believed that these 6,000 men represented 25 percent of the colony's militia strength; they were obligated to serve until 10 December. The companies were apportioned among the several counties according to population. Connecticut's regimental structure followed a somewhat older model than that chosen by the other colonies and was considerably larger. Connecticut placed generals in direct command of regiments, as Massachusetts did, but followed Rhode Island's example in having field officers command companies. This left generals filling three roles at the same

---

[23]The artillery company consisted of a captain (later major), captain-lieutenant (later captain), 3 lieutenants, a conductor, 2 sergeants, 2 bombardiers, 4 gunners, 4 corporals, 2 drummers, 2 fifers, and 75 privates.

[24]Some pieces of legislation stated that troops were to serve until 1 December; others, until 31 December. The latter date became official.

[25]This section on Connecticut is based on the following: *Conn. Records*, 14:413-40; 15:1-109; Force, *American Archives*, 4th ser., 2:370-73, 383-84, 423-24, 731, 1000-1002, 1010; and Wladimir Edgar Hagelin and Ralph A. Brown, eds., "Connecticut Farmers at Bunker Hill: The Diary of Colonel Experience Storrs," *New England Quarterly* 28 (1955):84-89.

time—that of general, colonel, and captain. Rather than assigning an extra lieutenant to each field officer's company, as Rhode Island did, Connecticut merely designated the senior lieutenant in each colonel's company as a captain-lieutenant. On the other hand, the Connecticut organization called for each company to contain four officers rather than the three the other New England jurisdictions provided. The assembly appointed Joseph Spencer and Israel Putnam brigadier generals and David Wooster major general. It assigned supply responsibilities to Joseph Trumbull, another of the governor's sons, by appointing him commissary general.

After a recess the assembly reconvened on 11 May and remained in session for the rest of the month, passing legislation that resolved a number of logistical, administrative, and disciplinary problems. It defined the regimental adjutant as a distinct officer. It also appointed Samuel Mott as the colony's engineer, with the rank of lieutenant colonel, and ordered him to Fort Ticonderoga. This session created a Committee of Safety, also known as the Committee of Defense or the Committee of War, which served for the rest of the war as the governor's executive and advisory body. The assembly considered, but rejected, reorganizing the six regiments into eight to bring the size of these units more into conformity with that of the regiments from the other colonies. Another special session (1–6 July) added two more regiments, but these were smaller than the earlier ones. The assembly reduced the number of privates in these regiments by nearly a third, while retaining their same organization and superstructure, and then ordered both to Boston.

Deployment of the Connecticut regiments followed a pattern established during the colonial period. In the Imperial Wars the colony had been responsible for reinforcing its neighbors, supporting New York on the northern frontier around Albany and assuming primary responsibility for the defense of western Massachusetts. In 1775 Spencer's 2d and Putnam's 3d Connecticut Regiments, raised in the northeastern and northcentral portions of the colony, naturally marched to Boston. Samuel Parsons' 6th, from the southeast, followed as soon as the vital port of New London was secure. Benjamin Hinman's 4th, from Litchfield County in the northwest, went to Fort Ticonderoga, where the county's men had served in earlier wars. The 1st under Wooster and the 5th under David Waterbury, from Fairfield and New Haven Counties, respectively, in the southwest, prepared to secure New York City.[26] News of the battle of Bunker Hill led Governor Trumbull to place the men in Massachusetts temporarily under the command of General Ward. At the same time the 1st and 5th regiments were ordered into New York, subject to the orders of the Continental Congress and the New York Provincial Congress.

Although the three other New England colonies, in responding to Massachusetts' plan for a joint army, experienced delays in fielding their regiments, these delays turned out to be a blessing. The regiments were formed in a rational manner that avoided the confusion that had plagued Massachusetts' efforts. Only the 1st New Hampshire Regiment, organized from the volunteers at Boston, experienced the same organizational troubles the Massachusetts regiments did.

---

[26]Richard H. Marcus, "The Connecticut Valley: A Problem in Intercolonial Defense," *Military Affairs* 33 (1969):230–42; Marcus A. McCorison, "Colonial Defense of the Upper Connecticut Valley," *Vermont History*, n.s., 30 (1962):50–62. Some companies were diverted to sectors other than their regiment's to meet immediate needs.

For all these New England troops, however, arms and ammunition were in short supply even though efforts had been made to accumulate them. The available weapons were mostly English military muskets—known colloquially as Tower or Brown Bess muskets—left over from earlier wars, and domestically manufactured hunting weapons. The scarcity of gunpowder, lead (for musket balls), and paper (for cartridges) was severe. These shortages were immediate and severely limited the operations of the New England troops. It would take years for the domestic arms industry to become established despite the best efforts of local governments. In the interim, imports from France, other European nations, and Mexico City were needed.[27]

Summary

The New England army that assembled around Boston in the aftermath of Lexington and Concord reflected, in its modifications of European military institutions, nearly two centuries of American colonial experience. Its emergence was a microcosm of the evolution of colonial military institutions. The common colonial heritage explains why the four colonies adopted organizational patterns that were very similar; particular experiences and individual backgrounds account for the variations.

The initial American response to the possibility of armed confrontation with British authorities had been a strengthening of the militia. Each colony took steps to replace aged or unreliable leaders and to reorganize units for greater efficiency. Training was increased. By 1775 most colonies were able to restore the militia to a degree of defensive competence not seen for a century or more. As the crisis worsened, American leaders moved beyond the basic militia. They began to prepare provisional militia units that could muster at short notice and remain in the field for longer periods. Whether volunteer companies or minutemen, these units were a response to the same need to minimize economic disruption that seventeenth century colonists had faced. The New England army that came into being at the instigation of Massachusetts moved a step beyond the minutemen. Like its Provincial model, this regional force was composed of regiments standing apart from the militia system, although drawing heavily on it for its recruits.

The Massachusetts Provincial Congress had set the minimum force needed to meet the British threat at some 30,000 men. By July a substantial portion of that total had assembled around Boston.[28] Not counting artillery and several regiments that had not reported to Boston, the New England force consisted of 26 infantry regiments from Massachusetts and 3 each from New Hampshire, Rhode Island, and Connecticut. On paper these units had 99 field officers, 866 company and 144 staff officers, and 18,538 enlisted men. This total was more than 2,500 men below authorized levels. More importantly, it included 1,600 sick and almost 1,500 on furlough or detached duty. These regiments were still only partially organized. Only nine from Massachusetts had

[27]David Lewis Salay, "Arming for War: The Production of War Material in Pennsylvania for the American Armies of the Revolution" (Ph.D. diss., University of Delaware, 1977), pp. 165–204; James Allen Lewis, "New Spain During the American Revolution, 1779–1783: A Viceroyalty at War" (Ph.D. diss., Duke University, 1975), p. 52; Orlando W. Stephenson, "The Supply of Gunpowder in 1776," *American Historical Review* 30 (1925):271–81; and Neil L. York, "Clandestine Aid and the American Revolutionary War Effort: A Re-Examination," *Military Affairs* 43 (1979):26–30.

[28]Record Group (RG) 93, National Archives (general return, main army, 19 July 1775).

reached a paper strength of 95 percent; five were below 80 percent of their authorized levels and were, therefore, of questionable combat value.

These deficiencies were due in part to the lack of any centralized control over the army, or, rather, the collection of separate armies. The forces raised by each of the New England colonies in response to Massachusetts' call for assistance arrived piecemeal and were assigned positions and responsibilities around Boston according to the needs of the moment. The only coordination was furnished by a committee form of leadership. The Massachusetts commanders established a council of war on 20 April, and senior officers from the other colonies joined it as they arrived. Although it worked closely with the Massachusetts civil authorities, the council did not really command; it merely worked out consensus views. In practice this arrangement not only prevented effective planning but blocked the individual regiments from making their needs known. Incomplete information proved to be a major problem in the early months of the Boston siege.[29]

On 17 June the regional army fought its first engagement, a battle which revealed its weaknesses and its strengths. The council of war decided to apply pressure on the Boston garrison by occupying dominating hills on Charlestown Peninsula. It did not prepare an adequate plan, committing units piecemeal without sufficient ammunition or a clearly delineated chain of command. The British decided to launch a frontal assault in the hope of demoralizing the New Englanders. From the security of hasty fieldworks the defenders shattered two attacks with accurate musketry. A third assault drove them from the peninsula. Sir William Howe, staggered by a 42 percent casualty rate, realized he could not afford to let the colonists again fight from prepared positions since that advantage compensated for many of their weaknesses. He reported to his superiors in London after the battle: "When I look to the consequences of it, in the loss of so many brave Officers, I do it with horror—The Success is too dearly bought."[30]

The New England army had been defeated, although it had inflicted heavy losses on the enemy. The colonists had to find solutions to the problems highlighted by the battle, but it was already clear that these solutions required a national army. The search turned to Philadelphia where the Continental Congress was in session.

[29]William Henshaw, *The orderly book of Colonel William Henshaw, of the American army, April 20–September 26, 1775* (Boston: A. Williams, 1881), pp. 13–39.
[30]John Fortescue, ed., *The Correspondence of King George the Third from 1760 to December 1783*, 2d ed., 6 vols. (London: Frank Cass & Co., 1967), 3:220–24.

CHAPTER 2

The Continental Army: Washington and the Continental Congress

Formation of a New England army in the first months after Lexington marked the first phase in the military struggle with England, but even as the regional army gathered before Boston, a significant step in the creation of a national force was being taken in Philadelphia. The Continental Congress convened there on 10 May 1775 to resume its coordination of the thirteen colonies' efforts to secure British recognition of American rights. It faced the fact that four colonies were already in a state of war. News arrived a week later that Ethan Allen and Benedict Arnold had captured Fort Ticonderoga, an event which expanded the dimensions of the conflict and largely ended hopes of a swift reconciliation with Britain. The Continental Congress reluctantly moved to assume direction of the military effort. Thus far the organization of forces had followed colonial precedents, but to establish an army representing all thirteen colonies, Congress had to break new ground.

Adoption of the Army

The New England delegations immediately tried to secure congressional support for armed opposition to Great Britain. They argued that New England was merely protecting itself from British aggression, and that in so doing it was acting to defend all the colonies. Their goal was the adoption by Congress of the troops at Boston, an action which would both remove the objection that the war was a regional issue and broaden the base of support for the military effort.[1]

The first step in this direction came on 15 May when James Duane of New York introduced a letter from the New York City Committee of One Hundred. That body, concerned with a rumor that British troops were on their way to the city, requested congressional advice. Congress recommended that the British regulars be left alone as long as they committed no overt actions, but it urged the New Yorkers to prevent the troops from erecting fortifications and to defend themselves if attacked. Congress used

---

[1]Edmund C. Burnett, *The Continental Congress* (New York: Macmillan Co., 1941), pp. 64-75; Jonathan Gregory Rossie, *The Politics of Command in the American Revolution* (Syracuse: Syracuse University Press, 1975), pp. 2-15; H. James Henderson, *Party Politics in the Continental Congress* (New York: McGraw-Hill Book Co., 1974), pp. 34-54, 72-89, 102-8.

this occasion also to appoint a committee to consider the general defensive needs of that colony. The committee included Virginia delegate George Washington.[2]

On the next day Congress formed itself into a Committee of the Whole to "take into consideration the State of America."[3] This important parliamentary maneuver reflected the fact that Congress although unsure of its objectives, was absolutely convinced of the importance of presenting an appearance of unanimity to the world. As the Committee of the Whole, the delegates could freely debate in secret and arrive at a consensus without placing any disagreements into the record.[4] Congress successfully used this formula for the next month.

The first business brought before the Committee of the Whole was a motion on 16 May by Richard Henry Lee of Virginia that Congress raise an army. The motion received some support from all elements of the political spectrum, but it also faced opposition. The delegates knew of the Massachusetts plan for a regional army, but they assumed that the force at Boston amounted to only nine or ten thousand men. Although no action was taken on Lee's motion at this time, it was clear that there was congressional support for a defensive military posture.[5]

The impact of the capture of Fort Ticonderoga was evident in the deliberations on 18 May. Information from Ticonderoga now led Congress to assume that the British planned to use troops stationed in Canada against the colonies. Congress instructed the local committees in Albany and New York City to move military supplies to safety and to call on New England for assistance in defending Ticonderoga.[6] On the next day the report of the study committee that had been established following Duane's motion was referred to the Committee of the Whole for consideration.[7] On 21 May John Adams referred to the fact that many delegates had become convinced that the British were hostile when he wrote to colleagues in Massachusetts, "I can guess that an Army will be posted in New York, and another in Massachusetts, at the Continental Expense."[8] Other delegates also expected formal action to confirm "Continental" or "American" armies for Boston and New York.

On 25 May the Committee of the Whole delivered a report on three specific measures to be recommended to New York. Two currently undefended strategic points needed fortification: King's Bridge, which linked Manhattan to the mainland, and the Hudson Highlands, a zone some forty miles above New York City where the Hudson River narrowed between hills. The committee also recommended that the colony's militia be brought to a state of readiness and that the New York Provincial Congress raise up to 3,000 men to serve, under terms similar to those of the men at Boston, until 31 December 1775. They would garrison Ticonderoga and the other posts. Congress unanimously approved these recommendations on 26 May after adding a preamble

---

[2]Worthington C. Ford, ed., *Journals of the Continental Congress, 1774-1789*, 34 vols. (Washington: Government Printing Office, 1904-37), 2:49-53 (hereafter cited as *JCC*); Smith, *Letters of Delegates*, 1:351, 353.

[3]*JCC*, 2:53-54.

[4]Smith, *Letters of Delegates*, 1:465.

[5]Ibid., pp. 351, 356, 366-69.

[6]Ibid., pp. 356, 358, 362-63, 369-70; *JCC*, 2:55-56.

[7]*JCC*, 2:57. On 1 June another committee, established on 27 May (including Washington, Philip Schuyler, and Thomas Mifflin), reported on ways and means to procure arms: ibid., pp. 67, 74.

[8]Smith, *Letters of Delegates*, pp. 364, see also pp. 442-43, 445-46, 464-65.

JOHN ADAMS *(1735–1826), a delegate to the Continental Congress from Massachusetts, played a key role in establishing the Continental Army and in its early direction, despite his lack of military experience. (Portrait by Charles Willson Peale, ca. 1791.)*

emphasizing that Congress hoped for reconciliation but had to defend the colonies. Actually, the only debate came over the size of the New York force.[9]

On 31 May Congress received a report from Benedict Arnold that indicated British forces were massing at St. John's (St. Jean, Quebec) at the northern end of Lake Champlain. Congress asked Connecticut to send troops to help defend Ticonderoga from them. The delegates deliberately left vague the number of men to allow freedom of action to the Connecticut authorities, who were closer to the scene. In actuality, this request amounted to Congressional approval for movement of the 4th Connecticut Regiment (approximately 1,000 men). The delegates felt the need to act swiftly. Connecticut's men were already organized; the New York Provincial Congress, on the other hand, had not yet raised its troops.[10]

Decisive action came on 14 June when Congress adopted "the American continental army" after reaching a consensus position in the Committee of the Whole. This procedure and the desire for secrecy account for the sparseness of the official journal entries for the day. The record indicates only that Congress undertook to raise ten companies of riflemen, approved an enlistment form for them, and appointed a committee (including Washington and Schuyler) to draft rules and regulations "for the government of the army."[11] The delegates' correspondence, diaries, and subsequent actions make it clear that they really did much more. They also accepted responsibility for the existing New England troops and the forces requested for the defense of the various points in New York. The former were believed to total 10,000 men; the latter, both New Yorkers and Connecticut men, another 5,000.[12]

[9]*JCC*, 2:59–61, 64–66; Smith, *Letters of Delegates*, 1:407, 409–10.
[10]*JCC*, 2:73–74; Smith, *Letters of Delegates*, 1:422–24, 429–31, 449–50.
[11]*JCC*, 2:89–90; Smith, *Letters of Delegates*, 1:488–90, 503–4, 507–8, 515–16, 526–27.
[12]*JCC*, 2:95, 99; Smith, *Letters of Delegates*, pp. 486–90, 498–500, 502–4, 507–8, 515–16, 519–21, 526–27, 539–40.

OTHO HOLLAND WILLIAMS *(1749–94) joined the Continental Army in 1775 as a first lieutenant in Price's Maryland Rifle Company and rose to the rank of brigadier general. From 1780 to 1782 he served as deputy adjutant general in the Southern Department. (Portrait by Charles Willson Peale completed after the Revolution.)*

At least some members of Congress assumed from the beginning that this force would be expanded. That expansion, in the form of increased troop ceilings at Boston, came very rapidly as better information arrived regarding the actual numbers of New England troops. By the third week in June delegates were referring to 15,000 at Boston.[13] When on 19 June Congress requested the governments of Connecticut, Rhode Island, and New Hampshire to forward to Boston "such of the forces as are already embodied, towards their quotas of the troops agreed to be raised by the New England Colonies," it gave a clear indication of its intent to adopt the regional army.[14] Discussions the next day indicated that Congress was prepared to support a force at Boston twice the size of the British garrison, and that it was unwilling to order any existing units to be disbanded. By the first week in July delegates were referring to a total at Boston that was edging toward 20,000.[15] Maximum strengths for the forces both in Massachusetts and New York were finally established on 21 and 22 July, when solid information was on hand. These were set, respectively, at 22,000 and 5,000 men, a total nearly double that envisioned on 14 June.[16]

The "expert riflemen" authorized on 14 June were the first units raised directly as Continentals. Congress intended to have the ten companies serve as a light infantry force for the Boston siege. At the same time it symbolically extended military participation beyond New England by allocating 6 of the companies to Pennsylvania, 2 to Maryland, and 2 to Virginia. Each company would have a captain, 3 lieutenants, 4 sergeants, 4 corporals, a drummer (or horn player), and 68 privates. The enlistment period was set at one year, the norm for the earlier Provincials, a period that would expire on 1 July 1776.[17]

[13]Smith, *Letters of Delegates*, 1:515–17, 543–44.
[14]*JCC*, 2:99; see also Smith, *Letters of Delegates*, 1:518–22, 539–40.
[15]*JCC*, 2:100–101; Smith, *Letters of Delegates*, 1:561, 569, 585–86.
[16]Ibid., 2:202, 207; Smith, *Letters of Delegates*, 1:662–64.
[17]*JCC*, 2:89–90; Smith, *Letters of Delegates*, 1:313–15. On 12 June 1776 the organization of a rifle company was amended to include both a drummer and a fifer: *JCC*, 5:432.

Responsibility for recruiting the companies was given to the three colonies' delegates, who in turn relied on the county committees of those areas noted for skilled marksmen. The response in Pennsylvania's western and northern frontier counties was so great that on 22 June the colony's quota was increased from six to eight companies, organized as a regiment. On 25 June the Pennsylvania delegates, with authority from the Pennsylvania Assembly, appointed field officers for the regiment. Since there was no staff organization, company officers and volunteers performed the necessary duties. On 11 July delegate George Read secured the adoption of a ninth company that his wife's nephew had organized in Lancaster County. In Virginia Daniel Morgan raised one company in Frederick County, and Hugh Stephenson raised another in Berkeley County. Michael Cresap's and Thomas Price's Maryland companies were both from Frederick County. All thirteen companies were organized during late June and early July. They then raced to Boston, where their frontier attitudes created disciplinary problems.[18]

Selection of Commanders

The inclusion of troops from outside New England gave a continental flavor to the army at Boston. A desire to broaden the base of support for the war also led John Adams to work for the appointment of a southerner as the commander of "all the continental forces, raised, or to be raised, for the defense of American liberty."[19] On 15 June Congress unanimously chose George Washington. Washington had been active in the military planning committees of Congress and by late May had taken to wearing his old uniform. His colleagues believed that his modesty and competence qualified him to adjust to the "Temper & Genius" of the New England troops. Washington was given the rank of General and Commander in Chief.[20]

Congress clearly respected Washington, for it granted him extensive powers which combined functions of a regular British commander with the military responsibilities of a colonial governor. His instructions on 20 June told him to proceed to Massachusetts, "take charge of the army of the united colonies," and capture or destroy all armed enemies. His was also to prepare and to send to Congress an accurate strength return of that army. On the other hand, instructions to keep the army obedient, diligent, and disciplined were rather vague. The Commander in Chief's right to make strategic and tactical decisions on purely military grounds was limited only by a requirement to listen to the advice of a council of war. Within a set troop maximum, including volunteers, Washington had the right to determine how many men to retain, and he had the power to fill temporarily any vacancies below the rank of colonel. Permanent promotions and appointments were reserved for the colonial governments to make.[21]

Although sectional politics were involved in Washington's selection, in strictly military terms, he was in fact the best-qualified native American. He had begun his

[18]*JCC*, 2:103–4, 173; *Pennsylvania Archives*, 9 series (Philadelphia and Harrisburg, 1852–1925), 2d ser., 10:3–43; Smith, *Letters of Delegates*, 1:491–92, 598–99, 621–25.

[19]*JCC*, 2:91.

[20]Smith, *Letters of Delegates*, 1:416–17, 486–99, 507–9, 515–17; Henderson, *Party Politics*, pp. 53–54; *JCC*, 2:91–93, 96–97.

[21]*JCC*, 2:92–93, 96–97, 100–101.

military career in 1752 in the Virginia militia as one of four regional adjutants responsible for training. During the first phase of the French and Indian War, he served
with gallantry as Edward Braddock's volunteer aide at the battle of the Monongahela,
and later as the commander of Virginia's two Provincial regiments defending the colony's frontiers. In 1758 he commanded a brigade composed of Virginia, Maryland,
and Pennsylvania units on John Forbes' expedition against Fort Duquesne. Washington was the only American in that war to command so large a force. The experience of
these years taught him the importance of discipline, marksmanship, and professional
study. Exposure to Forbes' ideas on adapting European tactics to the American wilderness also contributed significantly to his military education. Above all, he came to
the conclusion that only unyielding commitment to hard work and attention to administrative detail could keep troops in the field.[22]

On 16 June, the day after Washington's appointment, Congress authorized a variety of other senior officers for its new army. Details were again settled by the Committee of the Whole. Positions for five major staff officers were established: an Adjutant
General, a Commissary of Musters, a Paymaster General, a Commissary General,
and a Quartermaster General. These officers were expected to assist the Commander
in Chief with the administration of the "grand army." The forces allocated to New
York already were considered a separate department and were authorized their own
deputy quartermaster general and deputy paymaster general. A military secretary
and 3 aides for Washington, a secretary for the separate department, and 6 engineers
(3 for each force) completed the staff. Congress also created the ranks of major
general and brigadier general. The number of generals remained uncertain for several
days as Congress debated. Between 17 and 22 June it finally decided on 4 major generals, each having 2 aides, and 8 brigadier generals. These totals allowed each colony
raising troops to have a share of the patronage. Congress then took steps for issuing
paper money to finance the army, and on 30 June it adopted the Articles of War.[23]

Selection of the subordinate generals and senior staff officers led to political maneuvering as delegates sought appointments for favorite sons. On 17 June Congress
elected Artemas Ward and Charles Lee as the first and second major generals and
Horatio Gates as the Adjutant General. Ward received seniority because he was in
command at Boston and because Massachusetts had furnished the largest contingent
of troops. Ward was a Harvard graduate with many years of political experience.
After two years of active duty as a field officer in the French and Indian War, he had
compiled an excellent record as a militia administrator. Lee and Gates were professional
English officers in their forties who were living in Virginia on the half-pay (inactive)
list. Both had served in the French and Indian War and were associates of politicians
in England and America who opposed British policies. Lee had also seen service in
Portugal and in the Polish Army. Gates had ended the Seven Years' War as a major
in the Caribbean. His appointment as Adjutant General (with the rank of brigadier

---

[22]In addition to the standard biographies, the following works provide key insights into Washington's
military background: George Washington, *The Writings of George Washington from the Original Manuscript Sources, 1745-1799*, ed. John C. Fitzpatrick, 39 vols. (Washington: Government Printing Office,
1931-44) 1:148-50, 331-36, 466-71, 490-91; 2:6-19, 295-98 (hereafter cited as Fitzpatrick, *Writings*);
Oliver L. Spaulding, Jr., "The Military Studies of George Washington," *American Historical Review* 29
(1924):675-80.

[23]*JCC*, 2:93-94, 97, 99, 102-4, 106, 111-22; Smith, *Letters of Delegates*, 1:503, 509, 518-22, 525-30,
533, 535-36, 539-42, 547-48; Henderson, *Party Politics*, pp. 53-54.

HORATIO GATES *(ca. 1728–1806) was a former British officer living in Virginia when selected in 1775 as the first adjutant general. As a major general he won glory at Saratoga and suffered humiliation at Camden. (Portrait by Charles Willson Peale, 1782.)*

general) reflected Congress' hope that his staff experience would enable him to provide Washington with strong administrative assistance.[24]

On 19 June two more major generals were appointed to satisfy other colonies' contributing large troop contingents. Philip Schuyler, a New York delegate with close ties to Washington, was expected to take command of the troops in his colony. A member of one of New York's leading families, the 42-year-old Schuyler had been a major in the French and Indian War, specializing in logistics. His experience, political connections, and extensive business interests in Albany were particularly valuable in his new command. Connecticut's delegation could not agree on a nominee for that colony's major general. In the end Israel Putnam's status as a folk hero outweighed consideration of seniority, and he received the appointment. Putnam, at 57, had seen extensive service in the French and Indian War, rising to the rank of lieutenant colonel. He had also been an early, vocal leader of the Connecticut Sons of Liberty.[25]

The process of selecting brigadier generals on 22 June was the product of a compromise. Congress allotted these appointments in proportion to the number of men contributed by each colony and followed the recommendations of the colony's delegates in the actual selection. Congress, however, created problems by ignoring seniority and status. When it elected Massachusetts' Seth Pomeroy, William Heath, and

[24]Smith, *Letters of Delegates,* 1:503–4, 507–8, 529–30, 533, 537; Charles Martyn, *The Life of Artemas Ward, the First Commander-in-Chief of the American Revolution* (1921; reprint ed., Port Washington, N.Y.: Kennikat Press, 1970); John R. Alden, *General Charles Lee, Traitor or Patriot?* (Baton Rouge: Louisiana State University Press, 1951); Paul David Nelson, *General Horatio Gates: A Biography* (Baton Rouge: Louisiana State University Press, 1976).

[25]Smith, *Letters of Delegates,* 1:442–43, 521–22, 529–30, 535, 539–40, 542–43, 555–56, 626–27; Martin H. Bush, *Revolutionary Enigma: A Re-appraisal of General Philip Schuyler of New York* (Port Washington, N.Y.: Ira J. Friedman, 1969); Don R. Gerlach, *Philip Schuyler and the American Revolution in New York, 1733–1777* (Lincoln: University of Nebraska Press, 1964); Increase N. Tarbox, *Life of Israel Putnam ("Old Put"), Major-General in the Continental Army* (1876; reprint ed., Port Washington, N.Y.: Kennikat Press, 1970). Putnam's election was the only unanimous one other than Washington's.

NATHANAEL GREENE *(1742–86) emerged from a Quaker background to become one of the Continental Army's most brilliant strategists and commander of the Southern Department. (Portrait by Charles Willson Peale, 1783.)*

John Thomas as the first, fourth, and sixth brigadier generals, respectively, Thomas felt he had been slighted. The situation was resolved when Pomeroy declined the appointment, citing age, before Washington handed out the commissions. Congress then made Thomas the first brigadier general, although it did not fill the vacancy created by Pomeroy's withdrawal. Thomas, a surgeon, militiaman, and former Provincial born in 1724, had gained combat experience primarily in medical roles. Heath, thirteen years younger, was strictly a product of the militia.[26]

Richard Montgomery of New York became the second ranking brigadier general. Born in Ireland in 1738 and educated at Dublin's Trinity College, he had entered the British Army in 1756. After combat service in North America and in the Caribbean, he resigned in 1772 when he failed to receive a promotion to major. He moved to New York, married into the powerful Livingston family, and in 1775 won election to the New York Provincial Congress. Montgomery's appointment was intended to complement Schuyler's logistical and administrative skills with combat experience. David Wooster and Joseph Spencer of Connecticut became the third and fifth brigadier generals. Born in 1711 and educated at Yale, Wooster had served in Connecticut's navy during King George's War. He later commanded a regiment in the French and Indian War. Spencer, three years younger, had also served in both wars. The two men initially refused to serve under Putnam, disputing his seniority, and had to be coaxed into accepting their commissions. Delegate John Sullivan of New Hampshire, a 35-year-old lawyer, became the seventh brigadier general instead of Nathaniel Folsom. Nathanael Greene of Rhode Island completed the list.

In retrospect, the June 1775 decision of the Continental Congress to create the Continental Army seems remarkably free from political strife. Delegates of all shades of opinion supported each step, and arguments largely concerned technical details.

---

[26]*JCC*, 2:103–4, 191; Smith, *Letters of Delegates*, 1:525–30, 542–43, 651–53, 662–64; Rossie, *Politics of Command*, pp. 16–24; Fitzpatrick, *Writings*, 3:465–67; Force, *American Archives*, 4th ser., 3:1107–8.

Unanimity resulted from a conviction that British actions required defensive measures and from carefully worded compromises. Those individuals committed to the ideal of the citizen-soldier saw Congress' adoption of the short-term New England force as an acceptance of a yeoman army. Others, remembering practical lessons of the colonial wars, believed that they were forming an army based on the Provincial model. Officer selection was another area of compromise; the fact that Washington and Schuyler were given blank commissions from Congress to distribute to the regimental officers confirmed local selections while retaining a nominal national level of appointment.[27]

Washington Takes Command

Washington and Schuyler left Philadelphia on 23 June to take up their new responsibilities. The Commander in Chief reached Cambridge late in the evening on 2 July and formally opened his headquarters the next day. His mission was to turn the various armed forces assembled around Boston into a unified army. Three major needs required his attention: a tactical and administrative organization above the regimental level; a centralized special staff; and a unified system of discipline. Washington was guided in this work by Congress' general directions and by the model provided by the British Army. Although the troops were still drawn primarily from the five northernmost colonies at the end of 1775, a national control over them was clearly emerging.

Regiments from the different New England colonies arrived at Boston in 1775 in a piecemeal fashion and occupied positions dictated by the terrain and the road network. Washington imposed greater rationality and control by introducing divisions and brigades as echelons between his headquarters and the regiments. He also adapted his organization to the specific geographical conditions and personalities at Boston. On 22 July, after some hesitancy because of problems of rank and precedence and lack of guidance from Congress, Washington assigned his available generals to command three divisions and six brigades.[28]

Each general defended a sector of the siege lines. The British occupied two peninsulas in Boston harbor connected to the mainland by narrow necks. Ward, with brigades under Thomas and Spencer, guarded the southern, or right, wing opposite Boston Neck. Lee manned the left wing, shutting off Charlestown Peninsula with Sullivan's and Greene's Brigades. The third division remained in the central area of the lines as a reserve force under Washington's close supervision. Putnam commanded Heath's Brigade and the sixth brigade. The latter was under the temporary command of the senior colonel because Pomeroy's vacancy had not been filled. This arrangement was retained throughout the siege. Each brigade, normally six regiments, defended its own sector, while the specialized riflemen and the artillery remained directly under Washington's headquarters.

Congress had begun creating a staff structure on 16 June, but it had filled only one

[27]Henderson, *Party Politics*, pp. 53–54; White, "Standing Armies," pp. 95–97, 109–10, 112, 119; Cress, "The Standing Army, the Militia, and the New Republic," pp. 114–38.

[28]Fitzpatrick, *Writings*, 3:349, 354–56, 396–97. The printed version of the General Orders for 22 July is incomplete.

BOSTON, JULY 1775. *H. Charles McBarron's modern painting shows Generals Washington and Ward and an aide examining plans of the siege lines. Infantry units in the background illustrate the lack of standard uniforms during this period.*

post immediately, appointing Gates as Adjutant General.[29] The primacy Congress accorded the post of Adjutant General is evident also in the general officer rank that Gates received. In the British Army the Adjutant General, working closely with the civilian Secretary at War, had responsibility for discipline, compilation of rolls and rosters, and supervision of drills and clothing. The specific model for the Continental Army's Adjutant General, however, was the temporary staff adjutant general that the British appointed for each major expeditionary force. This officer, whose position was relatively new, handled guards, details, paperwork (including the transmission of orders), and the formation of the infantry into the line of battle. A brigade-level officer, the brigade major, assisted him, plus a detail of sergeants who acted as messengers.

Washington let Gates have a free hand in establishing administrative procedures, a task Gates performed efficiently. The difficulties Gates experienced in compiling the first strength returns, a major portion of his job, led to the introduction of printed forms and regularized procedures.[30] His authority extended to lower echelons through brigade majors and adjutants. British brigade majors were captains selected by a brigade commander to serve as his link between the expeditionary adjutant general and the regiments. The brigade major also supervised the daily working and guard parties of the brigade. His office was temporary since in the British Army a brigade was a

[29]General background on the duties of staff officers is contained in the following: George Smith, *An Universal Military Dictionary* (London: J. Milan, 1779); S. G. P. Ward, *Wellington's Headquarters: A Study of the Administrative Problems in the Peninsula, 1809–1814* (Oxford: Oxford University Press, 1957), pp. 10–31; Clifford Walton, *History of the British Standing Army, AD 1660 to 1700* (London: Harrison and Sons, 1894), pp. 615–29, 637–47.

[30]George A. Billias, "Horatio Gates: A Professional Soldier," in George A. Billias, ed., *George Washington's Generals* (New York: William Morrow and Co., 1964), pp. 82–84; Fitzpatrick, *Writings*, 3:318–19, 328, 335; Charles H. Lesser, ed., *The Sinews of Independence: Monthly Strength Reports of the Continental Army* (Chicago: University of Chicago Press, 1976), pp. *xii–xxviii*. RG 93, National Archives, contains weekly returns that were maintained as a separate system from the monthly returns to provide a check on the latter's accuracy.

GENERAL RETURN, MAIN ARMY, 19 JULY 1775. *Adj. Gen. Horatio Gates compiled this first strength return of the Continental Army at the siege of Boston. This return established a general format for returns used throughout the war, i.e., a list of units, with a detailed accounting of officers, non-commissioned officers, and privates present or in various duty categories. It normally indicated how many enlisted men each unit still needed to recruit to reach its full authorization. Washington received weekly and monthly returns, which were prepared separately, and special returns. He used these in planning.*

transitory formation. The adjutant paralleled the brigade major on the regimental level. In the British Army a junior company officer customarily was assigned this duty in addition to his normal tasks. He assisted the major, who retained nominal responsibility for the regimental's staff work. In the Continental Army both the brigade major and the adjutant initially were modeled after these British precedents but were normally established as separate staff officers. In addition, on 14 September Congress confirmed the New York Provincial Congress' selection of Edward Fleming as deputy adjutant general for the New York Department with the rank of colonel.[31]

On 27 June Massachusetts had appointed William Henshaw as adjutant general for Ward's troops and Samuel Brewer for its other major concentration of troops commanded by General Thomas. When Washington informed Congress of his command organization on 10 July, Congress assumed correctly that he had established three geographic centers, and it, therefore, authorized three brigade majors. Washington accepted Massachusetts' two adjutants general and Rhode Island's brigade major as de facto brigade majors and requested Congress to authorize three more, one for each of the army's six brigades. When Congress failed to reply, he acted in August on his own authority. He appointed David Henley, John Trumbull, and Richard Cary and confirmed Daniel Box of Rhode Island, Brewer, and Alexander Scammell, who had succeeded Henshaw. As the war continued, Congress normally delegated authority to appoint brigade majors to either the Commander in Chief or the territorial department commanders, who in turn deferred selection of specific individuals to the brigade commanders.[32]

In the weeks following 16 June Congress and Washington selected the remaining administrative staff, again following British precedents. Their intention was to use the Paymaster General, the disburser of funds, to consolidate Continental control over finances. Two important politicians, James Warren of Massachusetts and Jonathan Trumbull, Jr., of Connecticut, were elected on 27 and 28 July as the Paymaster General and the deputy paymaster general (for the New York Department). At the end of the siege of Boston, Warren declined to move with Washington and the Main Army to New York. Congress replaced him on 27 April 1776 with William Palfrey, a Boston merchant who had been John Hancock's business manager and Charles Lee's aide.[33] This staff department would always be relatively small and unimportant. In the British Army, where regiments were the property of their colonels, the Paymaster General served as the channel through which funds were transmitted to the regiment's commercial agent to purchase needed items. Since most of these items were issued directly in the Continental Army, the agent system never developed, and the Paymaster General concentrated particularly on disbursing funds for salaries.

The British Commissary General of Musters (or Mustermaster General) was the

[31]*JCC*, 2:220–23, 249; Force, *American Archives*, 4th ser., 2:1803; 3:549, 564; Smith, *Letters of Delegates*, 1:631; 2:19–20. Fleming was actually a third choice after William Duer and Robert G. Livingston had declined the post.

[32]Force, *American Archives*, 4th ser., 2:581, 783, 1451–52; *JCC*, 2:190; Smith, *Letters of Delegates*, 1:662–64; 2:42; Fitzpatrick, *Writings*, 3:320–29, 352–53, 390–99, 425, 427, 456, 461–63; Edmund C. Burnett, ed., *Letters of Members of the Continental Congress*, 8 vols. (Washington: Carnegie Institution of Washington, 1921–36) 3:262–63; Henshaw, *Orderly Book*, p. 13.

[33]Fitzpatrick, *Writings*, 3:346–52; 4:470–73; 5:11–12; *JCC*, 2:93, 209–12; 4:42–44, 296, 314–16; Smith, *Letters of Delegates*, 1:667–68, 682; Henderson, *Party Politics*, p. 54.

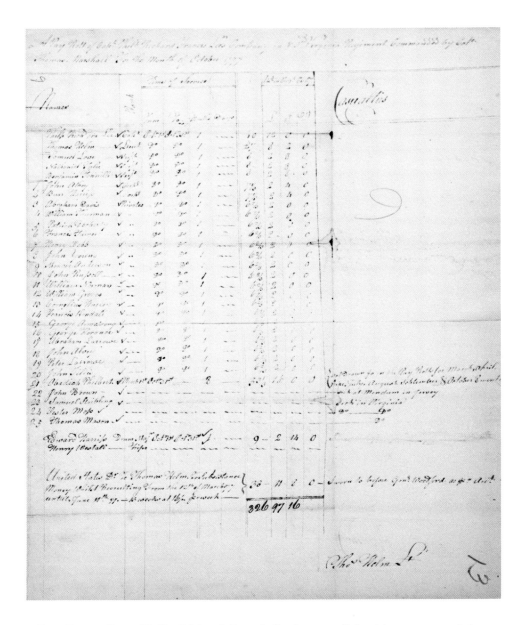

PAY ROLL. *Capt. Philip Richard Francis Lee's pay roll for his company of the 3d Virginia Regiment for October 1777 is typical of this type of document. It lists all the company's members, their ranks, that part of the month each actually served, the pay due each, and any casualties or changes which took place during the month. The senior officer present when the roll was submitted had to attest to its accuracy and sign it. Captain Lee raised this company in Prince William County, Virginia, in 1776.*

A Muster Roll of Capt. Valentine Peyton's Company of the 3d Virga. Regiment commanded by Col. Thomas Marshall for the Month of November 1777

Commissiond Officers

Valentine Peyton Capt.
John Gullime Lieut.
Neariless Bull Ens.

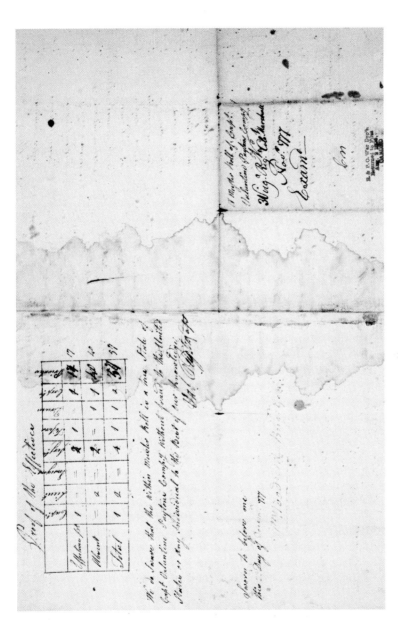

MUSTER ROLL. *The monthly muster roll, shown here on two pages, was one of the most important documents kept by the Continental Army. It listed all officers and men in a company; their dates of enlistment, rank, and promotion; their length of enlistment; and the status of each on the day the company was officially inspected by the Mustermaster's Department. The roll was drawn up by the company commander and signed by him and by the inspecting officer. This roll for November 1777 is for Capt. Valentine Peyton's company of the 3d Virginia Regiment. The company was originally raised in 1776 in Fauquier County by Capt. John Ashby.*

official watchdog who ensured that regimental commanders actually furnished the men and equipment they claimed payment for. Massachusetts had appointed two mustermasters as early as 6 May 1775. Congress included a Mustermaster General in the first set of staff officers it authorized and delegated the selection to Washington. He chose Stephen Moylan, a wealthy merchant from Philadelphia, one of the earliest volunteers from outside New England. Congress authorized a deputy for the New York Department on 29 July.[34]

Commanders' personal staffs of aides and military secretaries completed the Army's 1775 administrative structure. Following British precedent, the Commander in Chief and the major general selected these individuals for their personal connections as well as their abilities. The aides acted as messengers; the military secretaries performed most of the correspondence duties. During 1775 Washington's "family," as these individuals on his personal staff were collectively known, consisted of various important young politicians and members of influential families. This talented group included at different times Thomas Mifflin (a Philadelphia merchant and member of the First Continental Congress) and Joseph Reed of Pennsylvania, John Trumbull of Connecticut, and Edmund Randolph, George Baylor, and Robert Hanson Harrison of Virginia.[35]

British logistical practices divided supervisory responsibilities between a civilian Commissary General of Stores and Provisions, concerned with foodstuffs and the procurement and storage of general supplies, and a military Quartermaster General, responsible for transportation, forage, camps, and the movement of troops. A separate logistical branch handled munitions. When Washington arrived at Boston, he reviewed the supply measures undertaken by the several colonies. He was particularly impressed by the work of Joseph Trumbull of Connecticut, the colony that Washington expected would furnish most of his supplies. On his recommendation, Congress appointed Trumbull Commissary General on 19 July. Washington appointed Thomas Mifflin as Quartermaster General on 14 August. In addition, three days later he appointed Ezekiel Cheever as Commissary of Artillery. He had persuaded Congress to create that office to handle the ordnance branch's special needs. Cheever had performed that role for Massachusetts. Realizing the practical difficulties of consolidating logistics for widely separated armies, Congress created a parallel logistical organization of deputies for Schuyler's force.[36]

At this stage of the war Congress largely left the development of the logistical apparatus to the judgment of the local commanders, who relied on British precedents. The most important official in the daily life of the troops was the regimental quartermaster. In the Continental Army his position was elevated from additional duty to permanent status. He was responsible for distributing rations, clothing, and ammunition within the regiment, for assigning quarters, and for pitching camp. A daily duty detail of about six privates, known as the camp color men, assisted him. The Com-

---

[34]*JCC*, 2:93, 190, 220–23; Force, *American Archives*, 4th ser., 2:750, 790, 793, 795; Fitzpatrick, *Writings*, 3:320–29, 414; Charles Lee, *The Lee Papers*, 4 vols., New-York Historical Society *Collections* for 1871–74, 1:199–200.

[35]Fitzpatrick, 3:309–11, 342, 352, 354, 368–69, 419, 425–26, 450–54; 4:68; Berthold Fernow, "Washington's Military Family," *Magazine of American History* 7 (1881):81–87.

[36]*JCC*, 2:93, 190; Fitzpatrick, *Writings*, 3:309, 320–29, 378–79, 419, 427–28, 514–15; Smith, *Letters of Delegates*, 1:521–22, 529, 632, 641–43, 662–64.

THOMAS MIFFLIN *(1744–1800), a wealthy Quaker merchant from Philadelphia and member of the First Continental Congress, joined the Army in 1775 as Washington's aide and later served as the quartermaster general and a brigade commander. He broke with Washington in late 1776, and in early 1778 was a leader in the movement to supersede Washington. (Portrait by Charles Willson Peale, 1784.)*

missariat had numerous civilian functionaries. They included such specialists as conductors, storekeepers, clerks, laborers, and skilled craftsmen.[37]

Medical care drew attention very early in the war. The regimental surgeon and one or two assistants (mates) provided basic care in the Continental and British Armies. Washington, drawing on his French and Indian War experience, bolstered their efforts by trying to convince the soldiers of the importance of sanitation and diet. Congress followed the lead taken by Massachusetts and on 27 July 1775 created a centralized hospital organization and medical supply system. Dr. Benjamin Church, a Massachusetts political leader, was appointed as the first Director General and Chief Physician. In the autumn of that year, Church was revealed as a British spy and was replaced by the noted Dr. John Morgan of Philadelphia. Under Morgan, a major step toward central control was instituted when regimental medical personnel were required to pass competency examinations. Congress gave the New York Department a similar hospital corps under Dr. Samuel Stringer, an Albany politician and Schuyler's personal physician.[38]

New England, a region with a strong religious tradition, naturally provided for the spiritual as well as physical welfare of its troops. Chaplains had served on all major New England expeditions since the Pequot War of 1637, and the clergy in those colonies had been politically active in the prewar period. In 1775 Connecticut and New Hampshire authorized a chaplain for each regiment, while Rhode Island allowed one

[37]For a detailed treatment of the Continental Army's logistical services, see Erna Risch, *Supplying Washington's Army* (Washington: Government Printing Office, 1981), and Victor L. Johnson, *The Administration of the American Commissariat During the Revolutionary War* (Philadelphia: University of Pennsylvania, 1941).

[38]*JCC*, 2:209–11, 249; 3:297; Fitzpatrick, *Writings*, 3:440–41, 449–50; 4:2–3, 345–46; 5:125–26; Smith, *Letters of Delegates*, 1:558–59, 662–64; Philip Cash, *Medical Men at the Siege of Boston, April, 1775–April 1776: Problems of the Massachusetts and Continental Armies* (Philadelphia: American Philosophical Society, 1973); Richard L. Blanco, "The Development of British Military Medicine, 1793–1814," *Military Affairs* 38 (1974):4–10.

for its brigade. However, difficulties arose in Massachusetts. On 20 May the colony dropped a plan to provide one chaplain for each regiment and instead accepted the offer of the Congregational synod to provide clergymen on a rotating basis. Congregationalism was the colony's officially supported denomination. Within two weeks this plan was discarded as unworkable, and the colony's generals and field officers selected nine official chaplains. This method of letting the units select chaplains, rather than assigning them, became standard in every colony except the Carolinas and Georgia.[39]

Regimental organizations also contained an important specialist category whose function was technically not considered a staff one. Companies included a drummer and, in most cases, a fifer as well. Unlike modern musicians, these individuals, who commonly massed behind the regiment during a battle, were concerned with signaling rather than with morale. The eighteenth-century drum produced a sound that could carry several miles, and in groups its pounding was audible over the din of combat. Standard beats regulated the routine of camp life and transmitted orders during battle. Drummers and fifers also administered corporal punishment, maintained the regimental guard room, and assisted the surgeon and quartermaster in evacuating casualties. As early as 1777 these musicians began to carry arms, and their combat functions became more important than their musical skills as the war progressed. In 1776 fife and drum majors were added to the regimental staff as performing musicians responsible for instructing the fifers and drummers.[40]

Later in the war the "field music" provided by the fifers and drummers was supplemented by that of "bands of music." These were true bands and normally contained up to eight musicians equipped with woodwinds and horns. Unlike European armies, the Continental Army did not hire civilians as bandsmen; instead, it allowed soldiers to perform in a band as an additional duty. The bands, which only a few regiments maintained, were legally the property of the regimental officers who had pooled their funds to purchase instruments and who paid the musicians. Washington had to ask officers' permission to use a band at an unofficial dance or even at a formal Continental Army ceremony.

The type of staff officer that proved most difficult to obtain was the military engineer. Many civilian occupations required skills which could be applied to the Army; merchants, for example, were able to step into various logistical assignments. Military engineering was a highly technical field. American engineers knew a great deal about civil construction and could erect a simple fieldworks, but their skills were not on a par with those of formally trained European military engineers. Congress had authorized Washington and Schuyler each to have one chief engineer and two assistants, but at Boston, Washington had to make do with a handful of men who were at best gifted amateurs: Col. Richard Gridley and Lt. Col. William Burbeck of the Artillery Regiment, Jeduthan Baldwin, and Rufus Putnam. This group created a ring of earthworks which the British chose not to attack, but the engineers could not press a formal siege of the town. Their lack of skill turned operations into a mere blockade, a

---

[39]Force, *American Archives*, 4th ser., 2:766, 815–16, 876, 1384; Eugene Franklin Williams, "Soldiers of God: Chaplains of the Revolutionary War" (Ph.D. diss., Texas Christian University, 1972).

[40]Fitzpatrick, *Writings*, 8:181–82; 9:124–27; 11:335–36, 366–67; 14:293–94; Simon Vance Anderson, "American Music During the War of Independence, 1775–1783" (Ph.D. diss., University of Michigan, 1965); Raoul F. Camus, *Military Music of the American Revolution* (Chapel Hill: University of North Carolina Press, 1976).

fact that strongly influenced Washington's tactical organization, since it dictated trying to lure the British into costly frontal attacks.[41]

Finally, turning the force at Boston into an army also involved creating special staff officers to maintain discipline.[42] Obedience and internal control were absolute necessities for the linear warfare of the eighteenth century. New England's military and civil law both grew from English roots, but the disciplinary system the New England colonies created for their armies was less draconian than Great Britain's. Massachusetts approved its Articles of War on 5 April 1775. Connecticut and Rhode Island adopted similar versions in May, and New Hampshire implemented Massachusetts' code on 29 June. Derived from British articles in force since 1765, the fifty-three clauses adopted by each colony defined crimes, punishments, and legal procedures. Minor offenses were punishable by summary action of the regimental commander, intermediary crimes were subject to a regimental court-martial, and the most serious were tried at a general court-martial. Most infractions were handled with fines or corporal punishment (up to a maximum of thirty-nine lashes); desertion in combat and betraying the password to the enemy were the only offenses subject to the death penalty.

The Continental Articles of War adopted by Congress on 30 June added sixteen clauses to the basic Massachusetts text. The extra articles covered applicability of the system, administrative forms, pardons, sutlers, and disposition of the personal effects of deceased soldiers. This material, contained in the British articles, had been omitted by the New Englanders. The Continental text was distributed at Boston on 10 August. Following a conference between a congressional committee and Washington's staff, Congress adopted sixteen changes on 7 November, expanding the list of capital crimes. The revision, prompted by the realization that under existing articles treason was not a punishable offense, went into effect on 1 January 1776. Since it also resolved lingering doubts about the legal applicability of the Continental Articles to men enlisted prior to 14 June, Washington now began serious efforts to enforce them.

Although Washington relied heavily on British precedents and the unofficial legal advice of William Tudor, a Harvard graduate who had studied law under John Adams, he recognized the importance of a permanent legal staff to assist him. Congress approved his plan to appoint a judge advocate to advise him and a provost marshal to enforce camp discipline. Tudor was appointed on 30 July as the "Judge Advocate of the Continental Army." His principal function was supervising trials. The general supervision of discipline, however, remained a function of the Adjutant General. William Marony became provost marshal for the Main Army on 10 January 1776. The provost's functions were identical to those of the post in the British Army: maintaining the camp jail and supervising the guards furnished daily by line regiments in rotation. The office suffered from a heavy personnel turnover throughout the war, largely

[41]Fitzpatrick, *Writings*, 3:340–41; Force, *American Archives*, 4th ser., 2:767–68, 1436; *Lee Papers*, 1:199–200; Jeduthan Baldwin, *The Revolutionary Journal of Col. Jeduthan Baldwin, 1775–1778*, ed. Thomas William Baldwin (Bangor: De Burians, 1906), pp. 17–29. The British Army began formal military engineer training in 1741 with the founding of the Royal Military Academy at Woolwich.

[42]The following discussion is based on: *JCC*, 2:111–22, 220–23; 3:331–34; Force, *American Archives*, 4th ser., 1:1350–56; 2:564–70, 1145–46, 1180; 3:411–12, 1164; 5th ser., 1:576; Smith, *Letters of Delegates*, 1:517, 558–59, 584–85; Fitzpatrick, *Writings*, 3:320–29, 346–52, 378, 411; 4:7–13, 22–25, 206–7, 220, 224, 232–33, 527; Robert Harry Berlin, "The Administration of Military Justice in the Continental Army During the American Revolution, 1775–1783" (Ph.D. diss., University of California at Santa Barbara, 1976); Maurer Maurer, "Military Justice Under General Washington," *Military Affairs* 28 (1964):8–16.

because the provost was required also to serve as executioner. Washington normally selected a sergeant and conferred on him the temporary rank of captain.

By mid-October 1775 Washington had made great progress in organizing, staffing, and disciplining his army, although his correspondence indicates that he still was not satisfied. The Main Army actually exceeded the 22,000 men Congress had agreed to support.[43] In addition to the artillery, the riflemen, and a handful of separate companies, it included 27 infantry regiments from Massachusetts, 5 from Connecticut, and 3 each from New Hampshire and Rhode Island. Although each colony's units had different authorized strengths, all the regiments were at least 90 percent full on paper except for 11 from Massachusetts. Of the latter, 8 were between 80 and 90 percent complete, and 3 were below 80 percent. The individual regiments in the army averaged 474 rank and file total, ranging between 364 and 816. The total infantry rank and file strength of the Main Army was 19,497. There were also 690 drummers and fifers, 1,298 sergeants, 934 company officers, 163 regimental staff officers, and 94 field officers. Of the total rank and file strength, nearly 2,500 were sick, 750 were on furlough, and 2,400 were detached on various duties.

Four of the six brigades each contained approximately 2,400 men in combat strength. Sullivan's Brigade was slightly larger with 2,700 men. The largest brigade was Spencer's (3,200) because it contained two of the large Connecticut regiments and several separate companies. The relative strengths of the divisions reflected their defensive responsibilities. Ward's had the most men (5,600), and Lee's was only 400 smaller. The reserve division under Putnam was the smallest (4,800), while the 700 riflemen remained outside the divisional alignment.

This total force was substantial. Equipped with a staff organization and a disciplinary system, it was grouped in a tactical arrangement which suited its location and mission. On the other hand, the British had not tested it in battle. Washington finished 1775 unsure of the combat potential of his army and eager to resolve some of the remaining issues relating to its internal organization.

The War Spreads to Canada

Congressional control was not limited to Washington's main army in eastern Massachusetts. The American seizure of Fort Ticonderoga on 10 May 1775 had played an important role in persuading Congress to take military action, but the irregulars who had taken the fort under the leadership of Ethan Allen of the Green Mountain Boys and Benedict Arnold, a Connecticut volunteer acting under a Massachusetts commission, quickly melted away. The fort and its valuable cannon required more security than the Albany County (New York) Committee of Correspondence could provide with

---

[43]General Return, Main Army, 17 Oct 75; RG 93, National Archives. Interpretation of Continental Army strength returns requires an understanding of the categories used by the staff. Officers and noncommissioned officers were counted if present in camp but not if on detached duties. More complete information was furnished for rank and file (privates and corporals). Sick were classified as either "present" (with their unit) or "absent" (in hospital or on convalescent leave). The category "on command" included all men on detached duty, either in the immediate vicinity of camp or at a distance. A true picture of the combat strength of a unit would include not only the rank and file "fit for duty" but also a significant percentage of those on command (men who could be recalled on short notice) and those of the sick who were present (men capable of bearing arms in a defensive situation). Officers in company grades and sergeants also were part of the combat force. A variation of this return is printed in Lesser, *Sinews*, pp. 8–9.

the handful of volunteer companies at its disposal. Congress stepped in when it not only directed New York to raise 3,000 troops but also assumed responsibility for the 4th Connecticut Regiment sent to protect the area from British counterattack.

Washington and Schuyler, commander of the troops in New York, discussed plans on their trip north from Philadelphia. Washington gave his instructions to Schuyler on 25 June when they parted company at New York City. The Commander in Chief emphasized organization and the importance of creating a logistical apparatus. He also told his subordinate to follow any instructions that came directly from Congress. On 20 July Congress formalized Schuyler's territorial department as one of the basic command elements of the Continental Army when it instructed Schuyler: "to dispose of and employ all the troops in the New York department in such manner as he may think best for the protection and defense of these colonies,...subject to future orders of the commander in chief."[44] Schuyler's little army in the New York Department (known for most of the war as the Northern Department) contained the 4th Connecticut Regiment, the 1st and 5th Connecticut Regiments near New York City, and the planned force of 3,000 New Yorkers. His subordinate generals, Montgomery and Wooster, reflected the two-colony origin of his command.[45]

The New York Provincial Congress, for a variety of reasons, did not approve a plan for organizing and recruiting its quota until 27 June. The selection of officers took another three days. The four regiments it fielded fell between the extremes of the New England regiments in size. (*See Chart 1.*) Each contained ten companies; a company included 3 officers and 72 enlisted men. The companies were apportioned among the various counties, whose committees of correspondence supervised recruiting. This apportionment gave the regiments a geographical basis, and their numerical designations reflected the militia precedence of the counties which furnished the bulk of the men in a particular regiment.[46]

Alexander McDougall commanded the 1st New York Regiment, which was raised in New York City. He had no military experience but was a leader in the city of the Sons of Liberty. A substantial proportion of his officers had backgrounds either in the French and Indian War or in the city's elite volunteer militia battalion. The 2d Regiment was assigned to the northern portion of the colony and to Albany, the other urban area in the colony. Its commander, Col. Goose Van Schaick, was the son of a former mayor, and many of the other officers also came from the Dutch segment of the population. The 3d and 4th Regiments divided the rest of the colony, roughly along the line of the Hudson River. James Clinton, a militant leader in Ulster County, commanded the 3d. James Holmes and Philip Van Cortlandt, more conservative leaders from Westchester and Dutchess Counties, respectively, became colonel and lieutenant colonel of the 4th. The officers of each regiment represented the prevailing political sentiments of their portion of the colony. The recently established Committee of Safety also decided to form an artillery company, and on 17 June it appointed John

[44]*JCC*, 2:194.

[45]Fitzpatrick, *Writings*, 3:302-4; Force, *American Archives*, 4th ser., 2:1667-68. Schuyler's first monthly report to Washington, dated 15 July, includes the department's first return, dated 1 July.

[46]Force, *American Archives*, 4th ser., 2:1259, 1267, 1275, 1280, 1314-28, 1334-35, 1719-20, 1796; 3:23-25, 525, 532, 1268-69; James Sullivan and Alexander C. Flick, eds., *Minutes of the Albany Committee of Correspondence, 1775-1778*, 2 vols. (Albany: University of the State of New York, 1923-25), 1:120-21, 140-42.

Lamb, another New York City Son of Liberty, as its commander. Raised in the city, the company was organized on the same pattern as the companies of artillery at Boston.[47]

The Continental Congress authorized the formation of a special unit in Schuyler's army as a reward for Ethan Allen's role in the seizure of Ticonderoga. His Green Mountain Boys were a quasi-independent group in the area known as the Hampshire Grants (today's Vermont). Congress recognized that they possessed special skills in wilderness fighting, but it also knew that they were fiercely independent. It, therefore, instructed Schuyler and the New York Provincial Congress, which deferred to Schuyler, to allow Allen's men to organize seven companies and to elect their own officers. They were formed into a regiment with the same company structure and terms of enlistment that the New Yorkers had, but they were commanded by a lieutenant colonel rather than a colonel. To Allen's disgust, his men elected Seth Warner, a veteran of Rogers' Rangers of the French and Indian War, to the command.[48]

Schuyler, following congressional instructions, launched an invasion of Canada on 31 August. Montgomery received the primary tactical responsibility for the offensive. Governor Guy Carleton attempted to halt the Americans at St. John's, but Montgomery drove him back toward Quebec City before winter weather restricted American movements. The regiments of Schuyler's army were supplemented during this offensive by French-Canadians and by three companies of rangers commanded by Maj. Timothy Bedel. New Hampshire had raised these companies as state troops during the summer to guard the Connecticut River valley; on Washington's advice, the colony had offered them to Schuyler when it had become clear that the region was not in immediate danger.[49]

Washington launched a second invasion directly from Boston. This maneuver not only complicated Carleton's defensive problems but also enabled Washington to send reinforcements to Montgomery by the most direct route. On 11 September he gave Benedict Arnold, who had returned to Boston, command of a special force of 1,100 men drawn from the main army. Three rifle companies (Daniel Morgan's from Virginia and Mathew Smith's and William Hendricks' from the Pennsylvania Rifle Regiment) and two provisional five-company infantry battalions of New Englanders reached the banks of the St. Lawrence River on 9 November after an epic trek through the wilderness of Maine. Lacking the strength to attack the city of Quebec alone, Arnold had to wait for Montgomery, who had paused at Montreal to regroup his disease-riddled ranks. The two forces linked outside Quebec on 1 December. Although Montgomery was able to persuade some of his troops to extend their enlistments beyond 31 December 1775, many more indicated that they would leave for home at the start of the new year. Carleton could not be bluffed into surrendering, and Lamb's field guns

[47]Force, *American Archives*, 4th ser., 2:1140, 1791, 1811–13; 3:445, 563; *Historical Magazine*, 1st ser., 7 (1863):194–95; Roger J. Champagne, *Alexander McDougall and the American Revolution in New York* (Schenectady: New York State American Revolution Bicentennial Commission, 1975), pp. 90–95; Isaac Q. Leake, *Memoir of the Life and Times of General John Lamb* (Albany: Munsell, 1850). Rich insight into the creation of these first New York units comes from the papers of McDougall and Lamb; both collections are in the New-York Historical Society.

[48]Force, *American Archives*, 4th ser., 2:1339; 3:529–30, 570–71, 1268–69; *JCC*, 2:105; Smith, *Letters of Delegates*, 1:541.

[49]*JCC*, 2:109–10; Force, *American Archives*, 4th ser., 2:655–57, 1183, 1767; 3:60, 697, 779; Sullivan, *Letters and Papers*, 1:65–68, 71–72; Fitzpatrick, *Writings*, 3:370–71, 436–39.

MARINUS WILLETT *(1740–1830) was a veteran of the French and Indian War, the New York City volunteer militia, and the Sons of Liberty when he became a captain in the 1st New York Regiment in 1775. He rose to the rank of lieutenant colonel and led the New York State troops from 1781 to war's end. (Portrait by John Trumbull, 1808).*

were ineffective against the city's walls. Deciding to gamble on storming the works, Montgomery made his attempt on the night of 30–31 December under cover of a snowstorm. He was killed, and the attack was repulsed. A wounded Arnold, with only a handful of men, continued to blockade the city as 1776 began.

Summary

By the end of 1775 control over the war had passed from the individual northern colonies to the Continental Congress. Acting as a national government, that body had appointed general officers, had initiated the development of staff and disciplinary systems, had accepted financial responsibility for existing units, had authorized the creation of other units, and had formed two major operational commands under two of its members. Unanimously chosen as Commander in Chief, Washington took charge of the main army, which was penning the British into Boston. Philip Schuyler accepted responsibility for the smaller force that was created to defend New York but which was then employed in a preemptive invasion of Canada.

Various conditions prevented Congress and Washington from imposing a fully rational arrangement during the first months of the war. They had to accept existing military forces and react to the flow of events. More importantly, any action which Congress took had to be supported by delegates representing every shade of political opinion. The rhetoric of protest against British policy had strongly denied the need for a large "standing army" of regular soldiers in America on the grounds that the colonial militia forces, composed of virtuous citizen-soldiers, were perfectly adequate for local defense. The outbreak of hostilities in Massachusetts did not change this attitude. Lexington, Concord, and Bunker Hill only seemed to confirm the validity of that assumption.

To secure a broad base of support, Congress carefully stressed that it was acting only out of self-defense. The modest size of the forces at its command and the short period of enlistment directly reflected the American opposition to the notion of a standing army. These features also stemmed from American experiences in raising troops during earlier colonial wars. In 1775 the American units resembled the Provincials of the French and Indian War, which had been raised for a specific term to counter a clearly identified enemy regular force. Since most of the Continental forces had been raised and organized by the governing bodies of the individual colonies, assisted by local committees of correspondence or safety, they were ideologically viable because they could still be considered responsible to "the people." Indeed, except for the rifle companies, the men technically remained enlisted in the service of the various colonial governments which had turned the units over to Congress.

The first Continental officers, like the officers who had commanded the Provincials, were drawn from the leaders of individual communities. They were products of the militia system, chosen for their experience, for their ability to raise men, and especially for their political reliability. That these leaders mirrored the socio-political elites of their respective colonies is not surprising. American society in the eighteenth century was "deferential." Leadership in every sphere of life was entrusted to men of merit and wealth on the grounds that they had the greatest stake in society. In return, the leaders, according to this theory, were obligated to serve society to the best of their abilities.

Despite the various factors involved in their selection, the senior officers of the Continental Army turned out to have a remarkable amount of practical military experience, largely gained as captains and field officers during the French and Indian War. This experience was comparable to that of their opponents. In 1775 few of the junior officers in the British regiments in America had ever heard a shot fired in combat, and most of the senior officers had little combat experience beyond the lower field grades. The Continental commanders had an advantage in their more flexible approach to the art of war. Aware that they had much to learn, they tended to approach problems with a less rigid attitude. In effect, they "grew into their jobs."

Washington, in cooperation with Congress, worked during 1775 to impose unity and cohesion on the several armies he found at Boston. His task was made somewhat easier by the relative homogeneity of the New England colonies and by their long tradition of military cooperation. He made progress in creating a functional staff. Brigades, divisions, and separate territorial departments would form the pattern of Continental Army command organization throughout the war; all three echelons emerged in 1775. At the end of the year he was concerned particularly to continue fostering a sense of common identity and to standardize regimental organization. He also now turned to the task of reenlisting his soldiers directly under Continental auspices and reorganizing them into a genuinely Continental institution.

CHAPTER 3

The Continental Regiments of 1776: Boston and Quebec

In 1775 the four New England colonies had raised their own armies in the aftermath of Lexington, and New York followed suit with encouragement from the Continental Congress. Lack of centralized direction allowed each colony to base its regimental organization on its own particular experience in the earlier Imperial Wars. Congress accepted responsibility for the troops in June when it established the Continental Army. The enlistments of most of the soldiers composing the field armies besieging the British strongholds of Boston and Quebec expired on the last day of December. Congress, George Washington, and his senior officers used the reenlistment of those troops as a vehicle for transforming the Continental Army into a unified national force. In the process they emphasized lessons derived from the French and Indian War.

Washington's Unified Reorganization

In his first week at Boston in 1775 George Washington had identified several organizational problems, and his earliest letters to Congress suggested solutions. During the summer individual delegates visited the Main Army, and in the fall a special congressional committee held extensive discussions with the military leaders and with representatives of the New England governments. Based on that committee's report and Washington's recommendations, a number of major reforms were introduced for 1776.

Washington's first concern was the weakness of so many of the Massachusetts regiments. Calling out militia to supplement the Main Army did not appear to be a viable policy. The generals unanimously agreed "that no Dependence can be put on the Militia for a continuance in Camp, or Regularity and Discipline during the short time they may stay."[1] Washington attempted to fill the strength deficiencies locally, but he privately doubted that he would succeed, and as early as 10 July he suggested to Congress that it recruit in areas outside New England. In time Washington decided that some incompetent officers also were undermining the quality of his army. He blamed this problem on defects in the methods of selecting officers used by Massachusetts and urged Congress to retain sole control over commissions. This policy would have the additional advantage of broadening the geographical base of the officer corps. In addition, he complained that the differences in the New England regimental organizations hampered efficient operations.[2]

[1]Fitzpatrick, *Writings*, 3:327.
[2]Ibid., pp. 320–31, 390–400, 433, 450–54, 456–57, 505–13. On 10 July, the date Washington submitted his first report to Congress, he began a policy of sending personal letters to individual members of Congress. He used these letters to express opinions which would have been impolitic in official dispatches and to solicit the recipients to act as his agents in securing legislation he desired.

During Congress' August recess several members traveled to Massachusetts for a personal view of Washington's army. After Congress reconvened, the delegates decided that to begin a reorganization now would only cause needless discord since enlistments would expire before any changes could become effective. Promising to make improvements in the future, they requested Washington to send specific proposals. On 29 September Congress established a special committee to confer with Washington, his senior advisers, and officials of the New England governments. None of the committee members (Thomas Lynch, Benjamin Harrison, and Benjamin Franklin) came from New England, but all favored a vigorous military effort. This fact-finding committee arrived at headquarters on 15 October with instructions to persuade the Connecticut troops to remain until 31 December rather than 10 December as their enlistments specified. They also conveyed a message that Congress hoped that Washington could attack Boston before the end of the year. The committee's basic task, however, was to prepare a report for Congress on specific measures needed to reorganize the Continental Army, including Schuyler's army, for an additional year's service. Committee members were instructed to discuss the projected total cost, the rates of pay and the size of the ration, the need for additional regulations, and the implementation of a uniform regimental organization; they were also to recommend a plan for raising troops that would provide for the retention of as many veteran officers and men as possible.[3]

Washington prepared for these meetings by collecting written opinions from his generals and the heads of the staff departments; he also held a Council of War on 8 October. The consensus reached at this meeting reflected Washington's personal views. The officers wanted the new Main Army to consist of at least 20,000 men organized in 26 standard infantry regiments and separate units of riflemen and artillery. Each regiment was to be reduced from ten to eight companies. Each company was to have a captain, 2 lieutenants, an ensign, 4 sergeants, 4 corporals, a fifer, a drummer, and 76 privates. Each regiment would then have a total strength of 728 officers and men. Eight companies lent themselves to better tactical deployment than ten companies in linear warfare. The new organizations would have stronger companies than those of most of the existing regiments and would save money. The generals avoided the question of how to select the officers because of its "delicacy."[4]

These findings and the written staff reports formed the basis for frank discussions with the congressional committee and New England civil leaders from 18 to 24 October. The committee promised Washington that his Main Army would be reinforced before it was made responsible for the defense of New York City, and the committee (exceeding its authority) allowed him to begin reenlisting his men, for a year ending on 31 December 1776. Congress began debating the committee's report on 2 November and completed the reorganization in a month. It was clearly impressed by the unanimity reported by the committee, and it approved the recommendations of

[3]*JCC*, 3:265-67, 270-72; Smith, *Letters of Delegates*, 2:26-27, 64-65, 79-86, 112-13. For a general discussion of Congress' role in the 1776 reorganization, see the following: Burnett, *The Continental Congress*, pp. 101-8; Donald John Proctor, "From Insurrection to Independence: The Continental Congress and the Military Launching of the American Revolution" (Ph.D. diss., University of Southern California, 1965), pp. 141-43, 151-83.

[4]Fitzpatrick, *Writings*, 4:7-13; Force, *American Archives*, 4th ser., 3:1039-44. Other topics discussed included pay, rations, terms of enlistment, regulations, and enlistment of Negroes.

CHART 2—INFANTRY REGIMENT 1776

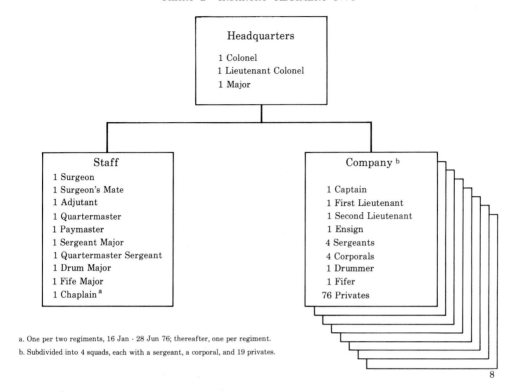

a. One per two regiments, 16 Jan - 28 Jun 76; thereafter, one per regiment.

b. Subdivided into 4 squads, each with a sergeant, a corporal, and 19 privates.

Washington and the other military leaders with little change. The committee thus served as the vehicle for transmitting the Main Army's ideas to Congress.[5]

On 4 November Congress approved the reorganization of the infantry into 26 regiments, each with the structure recommended by the generals. (*Chart 2*) It also accepted their plan for implementing the reorganization.[6] Congress ordered that uniforms were to include brown coats with different colored facings (collar, lapels, cuffs, and inside lining of the coattails) to distinguish the regiments, a system borrowed from the red-coated British Army. Each regiment contained 3 field officers (who could not be generals or captains), a small staff, and 8 companies. Each company had 4 officers and 2 musicians, plus 8 noncommissioned officers and 76 privates evenly divided into 4 squads.[7] At full strength the regiment deployed 640 privates and corporals—the soldiers who stood in the ranks with muskets—or 88 percent of its total of 728. The 32 officers and 32 sergeants provided a favorable ratio of one supervisor to ten rank and file for maintaining company-level control.

A comparison of this Continental regiment with its British counterpart reveals

[5]Force, *American Archives*, 4th ser., 1155-67; Smith, *Letters of Delegates*, 2:233-38, 243-44, 298, 337-38; Fitzpatrick, *Writings*, 4:22-23, 45-47; *JCC*, 3:313-14, 318.

[6]*JCC*, 3:321-25, 399. Compared to the regimental structure established in October for units from Pennsylvania and New Jersey, the new structure added a lieutenant, a fifer, a drummer, and eight privates to each company: ibid., pp. 285-86, 291.

[7]Fitzpatrick, *Writings*, 4:213-14.

CHART 3—BRITISH INFANTRY REGIMENT 25 AUGUST 1775

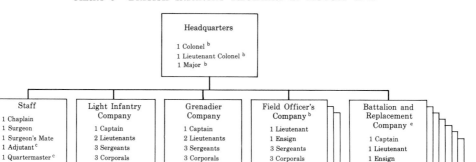

a. Exceptions to this organization were a handful of regiments organized with more than
   one battalion and certain units raised after France entered the war.
b. Field officers were also nominal captains of these companies.
c. Performed by subalterns.
d. Including 3 fictitious "contingent men."
e. Five battalion companies, one replacement company in England and one replacement company in Ireland.

some basic philosophical differences and sheds light on their relative strengths and weaknesses, although it must be remembered that both sides habitually operated with units well below full strength. The basic single-battalion British infantry regiment (*Chart 3*) was far less formidable than the Continental regiment despite an aggregate strength of 809. It also had three field officers on its rolls, but the colonel was a titular officer, the lieutenant colonel often served as a brigadier, and he or the major were frequently detailed to special duties. Staff organization was identical to that of the Continental regiment, but British chaplains and medical personnel were absent to a greater extent. Each British regiment had 12 companies, but 2 were recruiting depots (one each in England and Ireland). Two were "flank" companies: the grenadier company, composed of the largest men, served as the heavy strike force on the right (honor) flank of the regiment, while the light infantry, selected for agility, held the left flank or served as skirmishers. By the era of the Revolution, however, the British normally detached the flank companies from their regiments and formed provisional grenadier and light infantry battalions from them. This practice deprived a regiment of its best men; in addition, the remaining line, or "battalion companies," had to supply replacements to the flank companies.[8]

The British companies all had the same basic organization: 3 officers, 3 sergeants, 3 corporals, 2 drummers (actually a fifer and drummer), and 56 privates. Both flank companies had two lieutenants rather than a lieutenant and an ensign. Three of the line companies lacked a captain since the field officers commanding them nominally

[8]Headquarters Papers of the British Army in America, Colonial Williamsburg Foundation, nos. 27–29 (Sec at War Barrington to Gage, 31 Aug 75, with enclosure); 206 (Barrington, Circular to Colonels, 26 Aug 75); 288 (Barrington to Howe, 10 Jun and 18 Oct 76); 660 (Sec of State Germain to Howe, 1 Sep 77); 3181–82 (Sec at War Jenkinson to Clinton, 5 Dec 80); 3343 (Clinton, General Orders, 26 Oct 80); Edward E. Curtis, *Organization of the British Army in the American Revolution* (New Haven: Yale University Press, 1926), pp. 1–4, 23–24; Eric Robson, "The Raising of a Regiment in the War of American Independence," *Journal of the Society for Army Historical Research* 27 (1949):107–15.

were also captains. The grenadier company had two additional fifers, slots used for the regimental fife and drum majors. Three of the privates in every company were "contingent men," fictitious names carried on the regiment's rolls. Their pay was used as a special regimental fund for the care of widows and orphans. These exceptions plus normal detachments and details greatly reduced the fighting strength of the regiment. A British lieutenant colonel could deploy a maximum of only 514 men, 63 percent of the theoretical total; only 448 were musketmen. Such full-strength figures, moreover, were rarely seen during the Revolution.

Although a common heritage produced many apparent similarities in the eight-company battle formations of the Continental and British battalions, Washington planned to make his much more powerful. The American battalion contained nearly 50 percent more musketmen (640 to 448) without sacrificing any control. The British had a similar theoretical ratio of roughly one supervisor (21 company officers and 24 sergeants) for every ten fighters, but Washington normally enjoyed a higher ratio of officers to men than his opponents because so many British officers were absent.[9] Shortages of enlisted men plagued both armies, but the additional problems of trans-atlantic communications made the procurement of replacements particularly trouble-some for the British.[10]

The differences in British and American regimental organizations reflected delib-erate doctrinal differences. Britain, influenced by Frederick the Great and its own ex-perience in the Seven Years' War, produced a regiment tailored to formal European battle. It deployed its battalion companies in three ranks to achieve the density needed for a bayonet charge.[11] The Continentals turned instead to their colonial tradi-tion of aimed fire and to the lessons of the French and Indian War for inspiration. They adopted a formation using only two ranks, with a frontage more than twice the size of that of a British battalion (320 men to 150). In the American volley all 640 shots counted. The fire of a third rank was so ineffective that a British volley only hoped for 300 shots.

The regimental staff expanded during 1776. Original plans assumed that it would consist of a chaplain, a surgeon, and a surgeon's mate, with the functions of adjutant and quartermaster being additional duties for subalterns. Congress formally ap-proved the surgeon's position on 8 December 1775 and the mate's on 30 March 1776. The hospital staff screened all candidates since Washington considered it "a matter of too much importance, to intrust the Wounds and Lives of Officers, and Soldiers, to un-skilled Surgeons."[12] At Washington's request Congress added five specialists on 16 July.

---

[9]British Headquarters Papers, nos. 371 (Germain to Howe, 14 Jan 77); 411 (Barrington to Howe, 24 Feb 77); 552 (Howe to Barrington, 1 Jun 77).

[10]Ibid., nos. 496, 530, 660 (Germain to Howe, 19 Apr, 18 May, and 3 Sep 77); 1031 (Germain to Clin-ton, 21 Mar 78); 2993, 3181 (Jenkinson to Clinton, 5 Sep 80 and 5 Dec 81).

[11]Ibid., no. 1999 (Clinton to Germain, 14 May 79); Glover, *Peninsular Preparation*; pp. 112–22; J. F. C. Fuller, *British Light Infantry in the Eighteenth Century* (London: Hutchinson & Co., 1925), pp. 79–92, 124–57, 193; Sir William Howe, *General Sir William Howe's Orderly Book at Charlestown, Boston, and Halifax, 17 June 1775, to 26 May 1776*, ed. Benjamin Franklin Stevens (1890; reprint ed., Port Washing-ton, N.Y.: Kennikat Press, 1970), pp. 132, 145–46, 294. By 1778 the British shifted to two ranks to com-pensate for endemic shortages and a lack of firepower: William B. Willcox, ed., *The American Rebellion: Sir Henry Clinton's Narrative of His Campaigns, 1775–1782. With an Appendix of Original Documents* (New Haven: Yale University Press, 1954), p. 95n.

[12]Fitzpatrick, 4:345.

The drum and fife majors supervised musicians; the sergeant major assumed administrative responsibilities as the adjutant's enlisted assistant; and the quartermaster sergeant became the quartermaster's helper. The creation of these four enlisted positions merely formalized de facto specialties. A paymaster relieved the combat officers of financial bookkeeping.[13]

Washington wished to attract more capable chaplains by improving their status. He recommended raising salaries and assigning each chaplain to minister to two regiments, and Congress approved. When this arrangement proved unmanageable during the course of the year, Congress authorized a chaplain for each regiment. The deteriorating battlefield situation, however, limited actual appointments. The chaplains' duties remained the same throughout the war: providing moral, spiritual, and political guidance, plus assisting the surgeon. The chaplains corps was notable for its freedom from denominational friction. A Roman Catholic priest, for example, became an Army chaplain; this appointment would have been unthinkable in 1774.[14]

While Congress dealt with the new regimental organization and related matters, Washington began the reorganization of the Main Army. Acting on preliminary instructions from the congressional committee, he surveyed his officers to find out how many planned to remain in service. By 1 November Adjutant General Gates had compiled preliminary statistics. (*Table 2*) The overall response was encouraging: 751 of the authorized 1,465 officers intended to stay. Among 1,286 combat officers, 641 (78 field grade and 563 company grade) made positive responses. Twenty-six regiments required 78 field officers and 832 company officers. Thus only minor adjustments were necessary to account for a full complement of field officers. Massachusetts had an excess of candidates, while the other colonies had some shortages. In terms of company officers, the creation of a second lieutenant position caused some problems since most colonies had not had this rank in 1775. At the same time, there was a surplus of captains.[15]

Washington and his generals selected the field officers on 2 November. Because a more detailed evaluation was required to choose the remaining officers, those selections were delegated to groups composed of the brigadier general and field officers of each brigade. Washington retained the right to review all arrangements. To make up the shortages in the company-officer ranks, he instructed the groups to consider officers who had originally indicated that they would not remain but who had since changed their minds, officers who had been absent from camp at the time of the survey, and qualified sergeants. Washington reluctantly abandoned his desire to mingle officers from all colonies in each regiment when the idea proved extremely unpopular. The arrangements were gradually completed, and the officers began reenlisting men on 13 November. Recruiting parties, promises of liberal furloughs, and elimination of arrears in pay all were employed in an unsuccessful effort to fill the regiments before 1 January.[16]

[13]Ibid., 5:238, 337, 410, 441; *JCC*, 3:416; 4:242–43; 5:418, 479, 563; 6:862; 8:426–27.

[14]*JCC*, 4:61; 5:522; 6:891; Fitzpatrick, *Writings*, 4:197–98, 205, 307–8; 5:192–93, 244–45; Williams, "Soldiers of God," pp. 69, 95–101, 111–33.

[15]Fitzpatrick, *Writings*, 4:36–37, 43–45, 58–59, 145–47; the returns are in RG 93, National Archives. The riflemen were not included in the statistics since their service did not expire until 1 July 1776.

[16]Fitzpatrick, *Writings*, 4:73, 77, 81–88, 94–96, 99–103, 108–11, 116, 120–23, 145–49, 153–54; Smith, *Letters of Delegates*, 2:96; Force, *American Archives*, 4th ser., 3:1333–34.

TABLE 2—1775 OFFICERS WILLING TO SERVE IN 1776

Colony	Colonels	Lieutenant Colonels	Majors	Captains	First Lieutenants	Second Lieutenants	Ensigns
Rhode Island							
Willing To Serve	2	2	3	12	12	0	11
Authorized for 1775	2	2	2	16	16	16	16
New Hampshire							
Willing To Serve	3	2	2	14	14	0	17
Authorized for 1776	3	3	3	24	24	24	24
Connecticut							
Willing To Serve	4	2	3	24	22	15	10
Authorized for 1776	5	5	5	40	40	40	40
Massachusetts							
Willing To Serve	15	20	20	145	140	30	97
Authorized for 1776	16	16	16	128	128	128	128
Totals:							
Willing To Serve	24	26	28	195	188	45	135
Unwilling To Serve	4	5	5	112	107	63	92
Absent	4	5	4	53	60	16	37
Vacant	5	1	1	13	21	6	31
Grand Totals:							
Officers From 1775	37	37	38	373	376	130	295
Authorized for 1776	26	26	26	208	208	208	208

Source: Table was compiled from the following: Return of the Commissioned Officers in the Army of the United Colonies Who Incline To Serve for One Year From the 31st Day of Decr 1775, Dated 1 November 1775; Return . . . Who Decline Serving for the Ensuing Year, same date; Return of the Commissioned Officers Absent . . . , same date; and Return of the Commissioned Officers Vacant . . . , same date. All in Record Group 93, National Archives.

Washington implemented the reorganization of the Main Army on 1 January 1776. General Orders announced:

This day giving commencement to the new army, which, in every point of View is entirely Continental, . . . His Excellency hopes that the Importance of the great Cause we are engaged in, will be deeply impressed upon every Man's mind, and wishes it to be considered, that an Army without Order, Regularity and Discipline, is no better than a Commission'd Mob.[17]

Each infantry regiment was assigned a numerical designation based on its colonel's relative seniority. New Hampshire's three regiments of 1775 under Cols. James Reed, John Stark, and Enoch Poor, for example, became the 2d, 5th, and 8th Continental Regiments with only minor modifications. Promotions and some new appointments filled the officer ranks; the colony's support, such as exempting soldiers from the poll tax, helped recruiting.[18]

Rhode Island retained a quota of 1,500 men, organized into two instead of three regiments. Brig. Gen. Nathanael Greene, working closely with his brother Jacob (a member of the colony's Committee of Safety) and Governor Nicholas Cooke, used the reduction as an opportunity to purge the officer corps. James Varnum's and Daniel

[17]Fitzpatrick, *Writings*, 4:202.
[18]Force, *American Archives*, 4th ser., 4:8, 633–46; 5th ser., 3:1035–38; Fitzpatrick, *Writings*, 4:202–7; William F. Goodwin, ed., "Journal of the Congress of the Colony of New Hampshire," *Historical Magazine*, 2d ser., 4 (1868):147.

JAMES MITCHELL VARNUM *(1748–89), a close friend of General Greene, raised a regiment in Rhode Island in 1775 and later commanded the Rhode Island Brigade and served in the Continental Congress. (Portrait by Charles Willson Peale.)*

Hitchcock's regiments were retained as the 9th and 11th Continental Regiments. Thomas Church's was disbanded because Greene judged its officers poor disciplinarians; a handful of the latter, such as Maj. Henry Sherburne, were used to fill the two Continental regiments or were placed in units from other colonies.[19]

Connecticut had sent five regiments to Boston in 1775 and three to Canada. Since the colony's quota for 1776 was five regiments, the cadres at Boston were used to form the 10th, 17th, 19th, 20th, and 22d Continental Regiments. All had slightly modified geographical bases. Some sergeants became ensigns, and several other individuals, particularly veterans of the four companies that had been sent to Boston when their regiments went to Canada, received promotions to round out the officer complement.[20]

Massachusetts had particular problems in making the transition. Washington assigned it a quota of 11,648 men, about 2,000 less than the colony had set for itself in 1775, to be divided into 16 regiments instead of the existing 27. Officers were selected on the basis of competence and in proportion to the number of men their 1775 regiments furnished. Where a regiment could be reorganized from an existing one, it was held together. In most cases, however, a single regiment could not furnish eight full companies; therefore, companies from several regiments were merged, with the field officer assignments reflecting the proportions from each. Massachusetts furnished the 3d, 4th, 6th, 7th, 12th, 13th, 14th, 15th, 16th, 18th, 21st, 23d, 24th, 25th, 26th, and 27th Continental Regiments.

The reorganization involved New England's artillerymen as well as its infantry, combining Richard Gridley's regiment from Massachusetts and John Crane's Rhode Island company into a single regiment. On 17 November Congress named Henry Knox, a Boston bookseller whose volunteer service had impressed Washington, to re-

[19]Rhode Island Historical Society *Collections*, 7 (1867):117–18; Greene, *Papers*, 1:124, 134–37, 147–48, 154–65.
[20]Force, *American Archives*, 4th ser., 3:1110–11.

CHART 4—ARTILLERY REGIMENT 1776

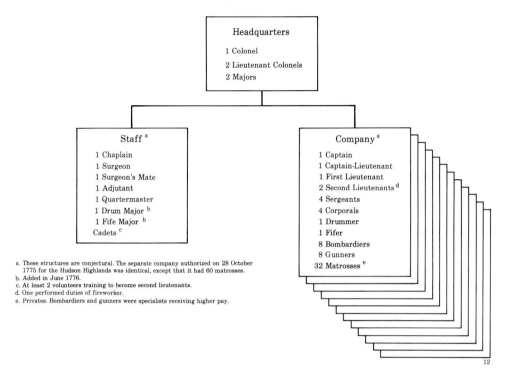

Headquarters

1 Colonel

2 Lieutenant Colonels

2 Majors

Staff [a]

1 Chaplain

1 Surgeon

1 Surgeon's Mate

1 Adjutant

1 Quartermaster

1 Drum Major [b]

1 Fife Major [b]

Cadets [c]

Company [a]

1 Captain

1 Captain-Lieutenant

1 First Lieutenant

2 Second Lieutenants [d]

4 Sergeants

4 Corporals

1 Drummer

1 Fifer

8 Bombardiers

8 Gunners

32 Matrosses [e]

a. These structures are conjectural. The separate company authorized on 28 October 1775 for the Hudson Highlands was identical, except that it had 60 matrosses.
b. Added in June 1776.
c. At least 2 volunteers training to become second lieutenants.
d. One performed duties of fireworker.
e. Privates. Bombardiers and gunners were specialists receiving higher pay.

place Colonel Gridley as the artillery commander. After debate, Congress confirmed William Burbeck and John Mason as lieutenant colonels and Crane and John Lamb, commander of New York's artillery company, as majors. Burbeck and Mason had been Gridley's field officers in 1775. Congress ruled on 2 December that the regiment should consist of these five officers and twelve companies but left further organizational details to Washington and his advisers. (*Chart 4*) The regiment's staff was similar to that of an infantry regiment except that it included cadets undergoing on-the-job training. Each company contained 5 officers and 58 enlisted men. Eight noncommissioned officers, 8 bombardiers, 8 gunners, and 32 matrosses were allowed, but Knox followed a policy of filling those positions in proportion to the real strength of each company. Bombardiers, gunners, and matrosses were all privates, but the gunners and bombardiers were specialists who received higher pay.[21]

The Royal Artillery was technically a separate armed service, but Washington deliberately avoided this British precedent. The Royal Artillery consisted of a single regiment organized as four 8-company (increased in 1779 to four 10-company) battalions. In peacetime each company contained 5 officers and about 50 men; in wartime it expanded to 6 officers, 4 sergeants, 4 corporals, 9 bombardiers, 18 gunners, 2 drummers, and 73 matrosses. Both the battalion and the company were administrative

[21]*JCC*, 3:359, 399; Fitzpatrick, *Writings*, 4:74, 120, 140–41, 158, 161, 460; 5:34–35; Force, *American Archives*, 4th ser., 4:633–34; Artillery Returns for 1776, RG 93, National Archives. The separate company in the Hudson Highlands had the same organization except that it had sixty matrosses in deference to the added needs of detached duty: *JCC*, 3:309.

HENRY KNOX *(1750–1806), the Boston bookseller who created the Continental Army's superlative artillery arm, succeeded Washington as the senior officer of the Army. He later became the first secretary of war. (Portrait by Charles Willson Peale, 1783.)*

units. Tactical flexibility was provided by the use of provisional artillery "brigades" with crews for eight to ten guns.[22]

Knox's companies were smaller than the British ones on a wartime footing, but their composition was more symmetrical. Like its British counterpart, the regiment was an administrative unit. Although he did not adopt the British "brigade" style, Knox distributed his companies in 1776 to man specific fortifications or batteries and had them camp with nearby infantry brigades. During the later stages of the campaign, detachments of one or two officers and crews for several guns were assigned to infantry brigades to furnish direct field artillery support. Shortages of trained artillerymen were a serious problem by summer. Knox prepared a plan to form a second regiment, and Congress approved it on 24 July. The events of the campaign, however, prevented any action to fill the regiment.[23]

The Pennsylvania Rifle Regiment and the four associated Virginia and Maryland companies were not reorganized at the beginning of 1776 because their enlistment terms did not expire until 1 July 1776. The regiment, however, assumed a new designation to conform with those of the infantry regiments; in recognition of the fact that the riflemen were the first Continentals, the regiment was given primacy as the 1st Continental Regiment. Washington continued to employ it as a special reserve force. Two of its nine companies had been sent to Quebec, but attachment of the remaining Virginia company and the two Maryland companies enabled it to perform its mission. Washington and Congress began planning its reorganization in the spring of 1776,

[22]Curtis, *Organization of the British Army*, pp. 6, 33–50; Horatio Rogers, ed., *Hadden's Journal and Orderly Books* (Albany: Joel Munsell's Sons, 1884), pp. 110, 154–59, 178–82, 216–20, 250–54; British Headquarters Papers, no. 5597 (Capt. John Stewart, "Disposition of Three Heavy Brigades of Field Brass Artillery," 13 Sep 82).

[23]Force, *American Archives*, 4th ser., 6:920–21; 5th ser., 1:502; 2:1096–97; 3:873; *JCC*, 5:606–7; Fitzpatrick, *Writings*, 5:38, 134–35, 322–24, 406–7.

and Congress ordered reenlistment for a two-year term on 17 June. Combat operations, however, slowed the reorganization.[24]

The planning phase of the Main Army's reorganization in 1775 was short and smooth. Congress, Washington, and his senior officers agreed on both general policy and specifics, but a real crisis occurred when Washington started to reenlist the New Englanders on 13 November. Indeed, he became so upset by the slow progress that on 4 January 1776 he complained to Congress:

> It is not in the pages of History perhaps to furnish a case like ours. To maintain a post within musket shot of the Enemy...and at the same time disband one Army and recruit another within that distance of twenty odd British regiments, is more than probably ever was attempted: But if we succeed as well in the latter, as we have hitherto in the former, I shall think it the most fortunate event of my whole life.[25]

New England's civil and military leaders had been very confident in October that their troops would rapidly reenlist, but by 30 December only 9, 649 men had signed up, an average of less than 1,400 a week. Another 2,808 enlisted by 3 February, less than 600 a week during the first five weeks of the new year. The Commander in Chief urged the New England governments to institute a form of a draft to fill their regiments, and on 16 January Congress removed the restriction on reenlisting free Negroes. The extent to which unit commanders opened their ranks to this new source of recruits depended on their personal attitudes.[26]

During the transition period, Washington filled the gaps in his lines with militiamen called up for limited periods by the New England colonies. New Hampshire and Massachusetts furnished about 4,000 men during late December 1775 when Washington anticipated that Connecticut's regiments might depart. On 16 January he called for full regiments of militia organized on the Continental pattern and for a longer period of service (until 1 April). New Hampshire had General Sullivan organize a regiment from companies already at Boston. Connecticut furnished four regiments, and Massachusetts provided six by calling on quotas from towns close to Boston.[27]

Another crisis was the discovery in December that many firearms were not suited for sustained military use. Washington paraded the Connecticut units on 9 December, the day before their original enlistments expired, so that he could confiscate sound weapons from owners he feared would depart. He bombarded the New England governments with requests for any available arms, particularly British Brown Besses, and sent letters to Schuyler and Montgomery begging for captured materiel. This shortage, plus problems of ammunition supply, persisted during early 1776, but the crisis passed by the summer.[28]

[24]Fitzpatrick, *Writings*, 4:501–2; 5:109, 501; *JCC*, 4:188, 284; 5:452; Force, *American Archives*, 4th ser., 4:633–34; 5:1433; Greene, *Papers*, 1:336–38. On 31 August the regiment was provisionally grouped with elements of the Pennsylvania Flying Camp to offset losses.

[25]Fitzpatrick, *Writings*, 4:208.

[26]Ibid., 4:172–74, 210–11, 227, 240–51; General Return of the Troops of the Continental Army Inlisted Upon the New Establishment, n.d., RG 93, National Archives; *JCC*, 4:60; Fitzpatrick, *Writings*, 4:193–95; Smith, *Letters of Delegates*, 2:67; David O. White, *Connecticut's Black Soldiers, 1775–1783* (Chester, Conn.: Pequot Press, 1973).

[27]Fitzpatrick, *Writings*, 4:189–91, 227–28, 246–51, 257–58; Force, *American Archives*, 4th ser., 4:7, 221, 932–33, 1233–34, 1272–1312, 1410–68; 5:14–17; Sullivan, *Letters and Papers*, 1:129–34, 165–87.

[28]Fitzpatrick, *Writings*, 4:150–53, 231, 235–39, 242, 246–51, 264, 325–27, 345–47. A 24 June 1776 return for 17 regiments at New York City (about 9,100 men) showed that 76 percent had arms rated good and that only 9 percent lacked arms. Shortages were concentrated in two regiments (1st and 3d New York Regiments) that had not yet completed organization and in one (20th Continental Regiment) whose colonel (Benedict Arnold) had never been present; Force, *American Archives*, 4th ser., 6:1121–22.

By March the regiments at Boston had passed through the period of greatest danger associated with the reorganization. Excluding artillery, Washington had 27 Continental regiments. They contained 828 officers, 694 sergeants, 365 drummers and fifers, and 12,510 rank and file. Militia reinforcements added 400 more officers and 6,500 enlisted men. The Main Army was roughly back to its 1775 strength in raw numbers. Just under 3,000 of the Continentals were sick at that time, although only 10 percent of these were hospitalized. Thirteen hundred more, including the entire 14th Continental Regiment, were on detached duties. All of the 25 reorganized infantry regiments on the siege lines were over half-strength. One had recruited over 90 percent of its rank and file goal, 10 others were at least three-quarters full, and only 5 were below 60 percent. In terms of real combat strength, half the regiments were over the 400-man level; only one was below 300. The regiments were not yet full, but they had made considerable progress.[29]

Washington, however, had been profoundly disturbed by the reorganization. On 9 February he summarized his view for Congress:

To go into an enumeration of all the Evils we have experienced in this late great change of the Army...would greatly exceed the bounds of a letter....I shall with all due deference, take the freedom to give it as my opinion, that if the Congress have any reason to believe, there will be occasion for Troops another year...they would save money, and have infinitely better Troops if they were [to enlist men] for and during the war....The trouble and perplexity of disbanding one Army and raising another at the same Instant, and in such a critical situation as the last was, is...such as no man, who has experienced it once, will ever undergo again.[30]

The Canadian Department

The congressional committee sent to Cambridge in the fall of 1775 to discuss reorganization was instructed to deal with the troops in the Northern Department as well as those in eastern Massachusetts. With Washington's approbation, however, they limited their talks to the Main Army, realizing that the two field forces faced unique problems. In fact, Philip Schuyler's reorganization difficulties dwarfed Washington's. Rather than being concentrated in a small area, his troops faced a number of different situations. Congress sent a special committee to his headquarters to begin the reorganization, but events left the northern area in a state of flux until July 1776.

On 11 October 1775 Congress instructed Schuyler to encourage the Canadians to join the Revolution. It particularly stressed a guarantee of religious freedom for Roman Catholics, a major concession for American Protestants. Schuyler was even authorized to organize a Continental regiment from Canadians who were willing to join his army. He was also to confer with his senior officers and to determine how to raise the troops needed to defend Canada and the Lake Champlain forts during the coming winter. After receiving additional reports, Congress formed a committee to visit Schuyler. Three New Englanders were selected on 2 November: Robert Treat Paine,

---

[29]General Return, Main Army, 2 Mar 76, RG 93, National Archives (also printed in Lesser, *Sinews*, pp. 17–18).

[30]Fitzpatrick, *Writings*, 4:315–18. At this point in the war duration enlistments probably were not feasible.

John Langdon, and Eliphalet Dyer. When Dyer fell ill, New York's Robert R. Livingston, General Montgomery's brother-in-law, replaced him.[31]

Because the need for action was immediate, this committee's instructions included fairly broad powers. It took specific steps to encourage the Canadians to enlist and to solve logistical problems. Its primary purpose, however, was to collect data about the garrison needed for Canada and the forts in northern New York. It brought Schuyler information about the regimental organization and rates of pay that Congress had just approved, blank commissions for the Canadian regiment, and instructions to reenlist as many of the department's men as possible and to raise in New York or New England as many others as he might need to complete the conquest of Canada. The committee set out on 12 November and reached Ticonderoga on 28 November after inspecting the fortifications in the Hudson Highlands. It discovered that Schuyler and Montgomery, who had been promoted to major general on 9 December, had already begun the reorganization. The committee approved their actions, gathered information, and on 23 December submitted its report to Congress.[32]

Congress acted on the report on 8 January 1776, before it learned of Montgomery's defeat at Quebec. The committee had accepted Schuyler's opinion that 3,000 men were needed for the winter; it recommended raising three regiments, including a Canadian regiment. Taking note of some of the negative aspects of the report, including the news that Seth Warner's and Timothy Bedel's men had gone home and that the other units had suffered heavy attrition, Congress approved an even larger garrison of nine regiments (about 6,500 men). Three were the units recommended by the committee: the regiment of Canadians and two regiments from Schuyler's veterans of 1775. They were to be reinforced by six new organizations. Congress requested New York, New Hampshire, and Connecticut each to raise a regiment for Canadian service. The remainder of the garrison was to come from regiments being formed in New Jersey and Pennsylvania. All nine would have the same structure as Washington's twenty-six reorganized infantry regiments.[33]

The two veteran regiments were not formed until 15 April 1776. In November Montgomery had regrouped his forces for the drive on Montreal, keeping only those of his men who would extend their enlistments from December until mid-April. His New York regiments remained nominally intact, but he partially refilled the 1st Connecticut Regiment by disbanding the 4th and 5th Connecticut Regiments and transferring their personnel who extended. When the extended enlistments expired, the two new regiments came into being. As Washington had initially hoped to do, Schuyler wanted to mix officers from several colonies in each regiment. One was to have 5 companies from New York and 3 from Massachusetts, and the other was to have 4 from New Hampshire, 3 from Connecticut, and 1 from New York. General Wooster expressed what became the consensus that this scheme was impractical. Instead, one regiment was made up from New York veterans under Maj. John Nicholson of the old

[31]*JCC*, 3:284–85, 298, 312, 317–18, 339; Smith, *Letters of Delegates*, 2:161–63, 281; Burnett, *Continental Congress*, pp. 108–12.

[32]*JCC*, 3:339–41, 350, 418, 446–52; Smith, *Letters of Delegates*, 2:326, 327n, 368, 377–79, 397–98, 407–8, 411–13.

[33]*JCC*, 4:39–44. Smith, *Letters of Delegates*, 3:60, 71–73, 77–79, 85–86, 88–89. See Chapter 4 below for background on the Pennsylvania and New Jersey units.

3d New York Regiment. Lt. Col. Samuel Elmore, who had been transferred from the old 4th to the old 1st Connecticut Regiment, commanded the other new Continental regiment, which was composed of Connecticut men and other New Englanders. Both regiments were assigned to light duty in the Mohawk Valley later in the year.[34]

The organization of the other regiments in the north followed a slightly different course than Congress had planned. Schuyler had begun reorganizing the 2d New York Regiment, an Albany-based unit, as soon as he had learned of Montgomery's death, and he and its commander, Colonel Van Schaick, were able to assemble it swiftly at Albany as the regiment requested from New York.[35] Washington received Schuyler's report of the Quebec defeat on 18 January and immediately convened a Council of War. Without knowing of the 8 January congressional action, the council recommended diverting to Canada three planned militia regiments that had been allocated to reinforce Boston: one each from Connecticut, New Hampshire, and Massachusetts. Washington wrote to these colonies the next day, recommending that they raise the regiments not as short-term militia units but for a full year as Continentals. Congress accepted the first two as the regiments authorized on 8 January and later accepted the Massachusetts unit as well.[36]

The three New England colonies recruited the regiments, as Washington had recommended, in areas close to Canada and filled them fairly rapidly. Connecticut formed its regiment in Litchfield County, which had a tradition of sending men to serve at Lake Champlain. A handful of officers were veterans of the old 4th Connecticut Regiment, but most, including Col. Charles Burrall, now entered Continental service for the first time. Capt. John Bigelow's company was equipped as artillery rather than infantry.[37] New Hampshire assembled its regiment at Coos (Haverhill) and marched it overland instead of waiting for the spring thaw to open Lake Champlain to water transport. Timothy Bedel became colonel in recognition for his ranger service. In May Maj. Isaac Butterfield ignominiously surrendered most of the regiment to an inferior force at The Cedars. He and Bedel were court-martialed for cowardice and banned from ever serving again, but Bedel successfully appealed and later served on the northern frontier.[38] Col. Elisha Porter, a popular western Massachusetts leader, filled that colony's regiment by using town quotas to raise five companies in Hampshire County and three in Berkshire County. Local politicians and the field officers selected the staff and company officers. This expedient hastened organization but created administrative difficulties.[39]

[34]*JCC*, 5:472, 615; Fitzpatrick, *Writings*, 5:362–63, 386–87; Force, *American Archives*, 4th ser., 4:1216–19; 5:549–50; 5th ser., 1:1083, 1153; 2:857–58; Thomas Jefferson, *The Papers of Thomas Jefferson* (Princeton: Princeton University Press, 1950–   ), ed. Julian P. Boyd, 1:436–47; Lt. Col. Rudolphus Ritzema to Col. Alexander McDougall, 19 Nov 75; McDougall Papers; Wooster to Congress, 10 Apr 76, Papers of the Continental Congress, RG 360, National Archives; Berthold Fernow, ed., *New York in the Revolution*, 2 vols. (Albany: Weed, Parsons and Co., 1887), 1:52, 74.

[35]Schuyler to McDougall, 25 Jan 76, McDougall Papers; *JCC*, 4:43; Smith, *Letters of Delegates*, 3:300–301; Force, *American Archives*, 4th ser., 4:1094; 5:294, 301, 312, 330–31, 1467–69.

[36]Fitzpatrick, *Writings*, 4:254–61; *JCC*, 4:99–100.

[37]*Conn. Records*, 15:225–27, 406–7; Force, *American Archives*, 5th ser., 3:1174–75.

[38]Fitzpatrick, *Writings*, 4:302–3; Force, *American Archives*, 4th ser., 4:14–18, 810–11; 5th ser., 1:167–69, 747–48; Sullivan, *Letters and Papers*, 1:169–72, 271–77, General Gates to Bedel, 4 Mar 78, Gates Papers, New-York Historical Society.

[39]Force, *American Archives*, 4th ser., 4:1270–75, 1298–99, 1404–8; Fitzpatrick, *Writings*, 4:324–25; General Ward to Congress, 3 Feb 76, RG 360, National Archives; Elisha Porter, "The Diary of Colonel Elisha Porter of Hadley, Massachusetts," ed. Appleton Morgan, *Magazine of American History* 30 (1893): 185–206.

On 19 November 1775 Montgomery had directed his kinsman James Livingston to begin raising the regiment of Canadians authorized by Congress. Livingston, a New Yorker, had married a woman from Montreal and had settled at Chambly. He formed the regiment at nearby Pointe Olivier and moved it up to Quebec in December.[40]

Several Canadians who had been expelled from Quebec by the British also began to recruit men, although only the partnership of Edward Antil and Moses Hazen proved successful. When Antil, son of a former chief justice of New Jersey, carried the news of Montgomery's death from Quebec to Congress, he used the opportunity to recommend Moses Hazen as a popular local leader. Hazen was a New Hampshire native who had served as a captain in Rogers' Rangers during the French and Indian War. Although he had been allowed to purchase a lieutenancy in the British 44th Foot, he had been forced into retirement in 1763 and had settled in Canada. After marrying a French-Canadian, he became an economic and social leader in the Richelieu Valley. Hazen arrived in Philadelphia shortly after Antil. On 20 January 1776 they secured authorization to raise a second Canadian regiment. Unlike Livingston's the new unit was patterned after French regiments in Europe during the Seven Years' War. Its 1,000 rank and file were organized in four battalions, each with five 50-man companies.[41]

Colonel Hazen and Lieutenant Colonel Antil returned to Canada and on 10 February organized the 2d Canadian Regiment, primarily in the Richelieu and St. Lawrence Valleys. Many French veterans of the French and Indian War who had remained as settlers in Canada in 1763 joined the unit, but only half the regiment was recruited before the pro-American sympathies of the Canadian populace subsided. Hazen's personal financial backing during this period gave the regiment a special status. Since Congress did not reimburse Hazen, it allowed him to retain a proprietary interest in the regiment. As a result the unit retained its unique four-battalion organization throughout the war.[42]

Although both Canadian regiments drew heavily on French-Canadians for their enlisted strength, most of the officers came from the small English-speaking community. A majority of this segment of the population had been born in America, including the two colonels, and were ardent supporters of the Revolution. The influential French clergy, however, supported the British Crown. Bishop Briand of Quebec excommunicated Catholic Canadians who supported the Americans, including Francois-Louis Chartier de Lotbiniere, a Recollet priest who served as Livingston's chaplain. The evacuation of Canada in the summer of 1776 then added exile to this spiritual hardship for the men of the regiments and their families. Both regiments had to be

[40]Montgomery to Schuyler, 19 Nov and 5 Dec 75, and Arnold to Congress, 11 Jan 76, RG 360, National Archives.

[41]Arnold to Congress, 12 Jan 76, RG 360, National Archives; Force, *American Archives*, 4th ser., 5:550; *JCC*, 4:75, 78, 223, 238–39; Smith, *Letters of Delegates*, 3:112–13, 122–24, 146–48, 154, 161, 167, 459. Valuable sources for the formation of the Canadian regiments include the following: George Francis Gilman Stanley, *Canada Invaded, 1775–1776* (Toronto: Hakkert, 1973); Gustave Lanctot, *Canada and the American Revolution, 1774–1783*, trans. Margaret M. Cameron (Cambridge: Harvard University Press, 1967); and Allen S. Everest, *Moses Hazen and the Canadian Refugees in the American Revolution* (Syracuse: University of Syracuse Press, 1976).

[42]*JCC*, 5:811–12; 6:900; 8:589; 19:427–29; Force, *American Archives*, 4th ser., 5:751–53; *Pennsylvania Archives*, 1st ser., 8:17–20; Board of War Report, 28 Jun 81, RG 360, National Archives; Gates to (probably Congress), October 1778, and Hazen to Gates, 28 Jan 79 and 12 Dec 82, Gates Papers.

withdrawn from the front lines to reorganize—Livingston's in the Mohawk Valley and Hazen's at Albany.[43]

Congress had reacted swiftly in January 1776 to news of the disaster at Quebec. In addition to officially adding the 2d Canadian Regiment and Colonel Porter's regiment to the Canadian garrison, it asked Washington to transfer one of his regiments and a general officer from Boston. On 17 January Congress clarified the command situation by transforming the invasion force into a separate territorial department. Since it believed that Schuyler did not want the Quebec assignment and that Wooster was "too infirm," Congress ordered Schuyler to shift his headquarters to New York City and instructed Charles Lee to go to Canada and to organize a department staff. Before Lee could set out, however, Congress reassigned him. On 6 March it then promoted John Thomas to major general as Lee's replacement; Thomas formally assumed command at Quebec on 2 May. Congress ordered Schuyler to remain at Albany and supervise logistical support for Canada in addition to his other duties.[44]

During January Congress also considered the non-Canadian portion of the old New York Department. On the 19th of that month New York was again authorized to raise four regiments to defend itself. The colony's Provincial Congress allocated company quotas to the various counties on 15 February and submitted nominations for field officers to the Continental Congress in March. Three of the regiments were assembled from 1775 veterans. Alexander McDougall's 1st New York Regiment continued to be principally a New York City unit. Since Colonel Van Schaick had already reorganized the 2d for service in Canada, the old 3d and 4th were redesignated the 2d and 3d, respectively. James Clinton continued to command the former, drawn primarily from Ulster County and Long Island. Dutchess and Westchester Counties furnished the bulk of the 3d, while a new 4th was raised in Albany and other northern counties. Schuyler only gradually released the New York cadres remaining in Canada, a policy which retarded recruiting but which was a compromise with tactical considerations. The 1st assembled at New York, the 4th at Albany, and the 2d and 3d in the Hudson Highlands. Schuyler retained the 4th in northern New York, while the 2d assumed garrison responsibilities in the Highlands, and the 1st and 3d served at New York City.[45]

Canada continued to attract Congress' attention. Knowing that the spring thaw would open the St. Lawrence River to the British, Congress and Washington ordered additional reinforcements to the north. Brig. Gen. William Thompson arrived in mid-May with the 8th (New Hampshire), 15th, 24th, and 25th (all Massachusetts) Continental Regiments, but they were immediately disabled by an outbreak of smallpox. Brig. Gen. John Sullivan reached St. John's on 31 May with a second force con-

[43]JCC, 5:645; Force, American Archives, 5th ser., 1:797–800, 977, 1143–44, General Orders (After Orders), 21 Jul 76, Gates' Orderly Book, New-York Historical Society; Hazen to General Steuben, 11 and 24 Feb 80, Steuben Papers, New-York Historical Society.

[44]JCC, 4:70–71, 73, 99–100, 157–58, 186–87, 240–41; Smith, Letters of Delegates, 3:108–9, 116–17, 122–27, 163–64, 267–71, 275–76, 282, 288–89, 310, 336–37, 341–42, 346–47, 350–51; Lee, Papers, 1:251–53, 271–72, 343–44.

[45]JCC, 4:69, 190, 238; Smith, Letters of Delegates, 3:80, 100–102, 116–17, 121–24, 300–301, 346–47, 355–56, 381–83, 459; Fitzpatrick, Writings, 5:7–11; Sullivan and Flick, Minutes of the Albany Committee of Correspondence, 1:343–48; Force, American Archives, 4th ser., 4:1081–82; 5:251–53, 267–80, 301, 314–18, 946–47, 968, 1439–40, 1467–69, 1498–99; Historical Magazine, 1st ser., Supplement 4 (1866), pp. 110–11.

PHILIP VAN CORTLANDT *(1749–1803) was the son of New York's deputy governor and first joined the Army in 1775 as the lieutenant colonel of the 4th New York Regiment. He rose to the rank of colonel and served in Congress from 1793 to 1809. (Portrait attributed to James Sharples, Sr.)*

sisting of the 2d and 5th (New Hampshire) Continental Regiments, the 2d New Jersey Regiment, and the 4th (less some elements) and 6th Pennsylvania Battalions. He found that Thomas himself had been stricken with smallpox on 21 May and had temporarily relinquished command to Thompson. When Thomas died on 2 June, Sullivan inherited command of the department.[46]

The arrival of a British relief force under Maj. Gen. John Burgoyne, consisting of regulars from Britain, Brunswick, and Hesse-Hanau, forced the Continentals to abandon the siege of Quebec in early May 1776. After a slow withdrawal, the main body of Sullivan's troops arrived back at Crown Point on 1 July. American hopes of making Canada the fourteenth colony had ended in failure. The effort probably had been beyond the Continental Army's logistical capability; it certainly had ruined many regiments. A dispirited Sullivan complained that "I am Sufficiently mortified and Sincerely wish I had never seen this fatal country."[47]

Congress had reacted to the deteriorating situation in Canada before Sullivan's withdrawal. A special diplomatic mission to Canada—delegates Benjamin Franklin and Samuel Chase and two leading Maryland Catholics, Charles and John Carroll—had conducted extensive discussions with American military leaders there in the late spring. Their report led to major command changes. On 17 June Congress appointed Horatio Gates as the new commanding general of "the Troops of the United Colonies in Canada" and endowed him with extensive emergency powers to reorganize the department staff and suspend incompetent officers. His selection was based both on his reputation as an organizer and administrator and on various political considerations reflecting the increased role of New England forces in a region initially considered

[46]*JCC*, 4:236, 302; Fitzpatrick, *Writings*, 4:495–97, 500, 519–21, 526, 531; 5:15, 132–33; Sullivan, *Letters and Papers*, 1:212–14.

[47]Sullivan, *Letters and Papers*, 1:242–43, 250–54, 271–77; Bush, *Revolutionary Enigma: A Re-appraisal of General Philip Schuyler*, pp. 56–62.

New York's responsibility. Gates arrived at Crown Point on 5 July and relieved Sullivan. Since Gates commanded a territorial department that no longer existed, on 8 July Congress ruled that he came under Schuyler's command.[48]

Schuyler allowed Gates a large measure of autonomy by keeping his own headquarters at Albany and concentrating on logistics and affairs in the Mohawk Valley. Gates' "Northern Army" contained the majority of the department's combat troops and had the task of developing a fortress complex in the Ticonderoga area. Benedict Arnold and David Waterbury, who had commanded ships as civilians, commanded the Lake Champlain naval squadron. On 20 July Gates created a brigade structure for the units at Ticonderoga. Following the advice of his senior officers and relying on his own experience at Boston, he organized his four brigades by grouping units from the same or adjacent colonies to minimize friction. Arnold, the only brigadier general, commanded one brigade. The others were under three senior colonels: James Reed (replaced later by John Paterson), John Stark, and Arthur St. Clair.[49]

Congress also formed two new units for the Northern Department from veterans of 1775. On 21 June 1776 it ordered New York to raise another regiment. Unlike earlier units, this regiment was enlisted for three years' service. Maj. Lewis Dubois of John Nicholson's regiment received the command, but disputes over the appointment of officers and seniority prevented the regiment from becoming fully operational. Congress authorized the second regiment, also for three years, on 5 July. Its cadre, Seth Warner's Green Mountain Boys, had begun reorganizing in early February. A shortage of cash limited Warner's recruiting until November.[50]

Knox's Artillery Regiment was designed to support only the Main Army. Separate companies performed the same mission for Schuyler. The remnants of John Lamb's 1775 company voluntarily reenlisted under Lt. Isaiah Wool. They were reinforced in the spring by Ebenezer Stevens' and Benjamin Eustis' companies of Knox's regiment, Capt. John Bigelow's company (in Burrall's regiment), and a Pennsylvania company. That colony had misinterpreted a congressional resolution and had directed Bernard Romans, an engineer, to recruit an artillery company for service in Canada. Congress accepted it, however, and it marched north under Capt.-Lt. Gibbs Jones. New York also raised two new artillery companies in New York City, nominally in support of Schuyler. Sebastian Bauman's was a Continental unit created to garrison the fortifications in the Hudson Highlands. Alexander Hamilton's company of state troops spent most of 1776 under Knox's operational control, and on 17 March 1777 it formally transferred to the Continental Army.[51]

[48]*JCC*, 4:151-52, 215-19, 233; 5:436, 448-53, 526; Burnett, *Letters of Congress*, 1:486-87; 2:16-17, 29-34; Fitzpatrick, *Writings*, 5:173-75, 547-51; Sullivan, *Letters and Papers*, 1:280-82. The political problems resulting from the appointment of Gates are discussed in Rossie, *Politics of Command*, pp. 97-134, and Henderson, *Party Politics in the Continental Congress*, pp. 112-17.

[49]Fitzpatrick, *Writings*, 5:222-24, 257; Gates, General Orders for 20 Jul and 11 Aug 76, Gates' Orderly Book; Gates to Hancock, 16 and 29 Jul and 6 Aug 76, and Colonel Hartley to Gates, 10 Jul 76, Gates Papers.

[50]*JCC*, 4:177; 5:471-72, 479, 481, 518-19, 761; Burnett, *Letters of Congress*, 1:506-7, 510-13; Force, *American Archives*, 4th ser., 4:588-89, 852-53, 1131; 5th ser., 1:717, 1390-99; Nathan Clark to Schuyler, 16 Jul 76, and Warner to Gates, 26 Apr 77, Gates Papers.

[51]*JCC*, 3:309; 4:74, 99; Force, *American Archives*, 4th ser., 3:1289-90, 1315-16; 4:1026, 1058, 1068, 1567-69; 5:303, 316, 378, 389-90, 536, 730-32, 1416, 1436; 6:1336, 1339, 1412; 5th ser., 1:660-61, 1509; W. T. R. Saffell, *Records of the Revolutionary War*, 3d ed. (Baltimore: Charles E. Saffell, 1894), pp. 178-81; Alexander Hamilton, *The Papers of Alexander Hamilton*, ed. Harold C. Syrett and Jacob E. Cooke (New York: Columbia University Press, 1961-   ), 1:187-88, 199-200.

BENJAMIN FRANKLIN *(1706–90) became famous as a scientist, diplomat, philosopher, and politician. He also sponsored the careers of two very important Continental Army generals: Anthony Wayne and Frederick von Steuben. (Portrait by Charles Willson Peale, 1772.)*

The Northern Department finally stabilized during the pause in operations caused by the contest for naval control of Lake Champlain. In January 1776 Congress had planned a forward Canadian Department with nine regiments (6,500 men), supported by the Northern Department's four regiments (2,900 men) defending the area from New York City to Lake George. By August the Canadian Department no longer existed, and the Northern Department's responsibilities stopped just south of Albany. Its troops remained divided into two major groups: Gates' field army garrisoning the Ticonderoga complex and Schuyler's rear echelon sustaining communications and controlling the Mohawk Valley.[52]

Gates commanded a force, exclusive of artillery, of fifteen Continental infantry regiments and one separate rifle company, plus six regiments of militia. It contained 386 officers, 333 sergeants, 143 drummers and fifers, and 6,262 rank and file, a total roughly equivalent to the number Congress originally had intended for Canada. True combat strength was about 4,000 continentals, including the detachment manning the fleet on Lakes Champlain and George, because nearly 2,200 were sick, another 1,000 were on detached duties, and 185 were on furlough. Only three of the Continental regiments were over three-quarters full even on paper, and ten were between half and two-thirds complete. This shortage significantly reduced their effectiveness in open battle, but it was less of a problem in garrison. The militia added about 200 officers and over 3,500 enlisted men, most of whom were still fit.

In terms of the division of forces in the north, Gates had the six strongest regiments of those originally assigned to the Canadian garrison or added by Congress in January 1776. He also had the four regiments sent north under Thompson and five of the six that had accompanied Sullivan. Schuyler retained the four regiments which had served longest in Canada and which consequently were in the worst shape. He

---

[52]General Return, Northern Department, 24 Aug 76, Gates Papers. This return contains complete data only for the units directly under Gates.

SECOND EMBARKATION, NEW LONDON, 1776. *H. Charles McBarron's modern painting illustrates the complexity of logistical support in the Continental Army. Particularly involved were long moves by large units.*

also had the two regiments raised by New York in the Albany region (Van Schaick's and the 4th New York Regiment), the 3d New Jersey Regiment from Sullivan's force, and the two new regiments just beginning their organization. Three militia regiments supplemented his troops. Schuyler had only three Continental regiments that were even reasonably effective. They certainly contained less than the 3,000 effectives he had originally been promised, but they were sufficient for his reduced defensive responsibilities.

Summary

Congress and the Continental Army's leaders worked closely together during the autumn of 1775 to prepare for the coming year. They hoped to eliminate problems revealed during the preceding months and to make the transition smooth. The cornerstone of the effort was Congress' approval of a standard infantry regiment designed by Washington and his generals to be a very powerful force with a streamlined organization. Unlike the British Army, which had been heavily influenced by the Seven Years' War in Europe, the Continental Army reflected Anglo-American experiences in the French and Indian War. The standard regiment's high ratio of officers to enlisted men recognized the greater need for control under American conditions than under European. The organization and use of the two-rank battle formation emphasized American faith in musketry rather than shock action.

Adoption of the standard regiment solved one problem revealed during 1775, but reorganization raised new difficulties. Both Washington and Schuyler hoped to emphasize national identification by mingling personnel from several colonies in each regiment. Opposition from officers and men alike ended that concept. A far greater source of trouble was that regiments in 1776 fell short of their authorized strength. Few regiments ever reached their legal maximum size, and many took a long time to achieve minimum efficiency.

Washington's Main Army at Boston was able to survive the crisis created by slow enlistments by calling on a sizable militia contingent. Slow but steady recruiting raised his army by March to a level where it could begin to apply pressure on General Howe in Boston. British evacuation of the town on 17 March gave the Commander in Chief his first victory. By contrast, defeat marked the American military effort in Canada during the first half of 1776. Reinforcements of continentals were dispatched several times, but Governor Carleton's British and German regulars still drove the field army of the Canadian Department all the way back to Ticonderoga. In addition, many of the units sent north were badly weakened by attrition and disease. The main focus of events now shifted back to the Main Army.

CHAPTER 4

An Army Truly Continental: Expanding Participation

While the Continental Army in the north took shape in 1776, the colonies to the south also turned to military preparations. The process began, much as it had in New England, with the formation of forces by revolutionary governments to oppose British threats in the immediate vicinity of each colony. Congress brought these forces into the Continental establishment and raised others not in accord with a general plan but in response to circumstances, although it did attempt to introduce some order by establishing separate Middle and Southern Departments for administration and command and for expansion of the staff. By the time of the signing of the Declaration of Independence, Continental regiments represented every state. When the British then mounted a massive invasion against New York, Washington moved most of his Main Army from Boston and augmented it, under congressional direction, with new Continental units and short-term militia. As units from the south arrived to meet this crisis, the Continental Army began to take on the character of a genuine national force.

The Southern Colonies

Virginia, the Carolinas, and Georgia began 1775 without significant British garrisons. They were under British governors, however, and regular troops were nearby in Florida. Like their northern neighbors, the southern colonies soon replaced their Royal governments with new political bodies. The new governments raised troops as soon as the deposed governors posed a military or naval threat. Because these early colonial efforts were undertaken with minimal supervision by the Continental Congress, a diversity of regimental organizations emerged. That diversity was wider in the south than it had been in New England and New York because the southern colonies were less homogeneous and had accumulated more varied experiences in the colonial wars. During 1776 Congress moved to provide the type of unified central control that it had already established in the north.

The aggressiveness of Governor John Murray, the Earl of Dunmore, led Virginia to act first. When it organized an extra-legal assembly in March 1775, the more radical element led by Patrick Henry was unable to persuade the colony to raise regular troops. The news of Lexington and Concord, however, had produced a change in attitude when the Virginia Convention reconvened in July. Although there was general agreement on the need to take military action, debates over actual measures lasted until 21 August. Proposals for an armed force of 4,000 men were scaled down to three 1,000–man regiments, but they still could not gain approval. The final compromise divided the colony into sixteen regional districts: fifteen on the mainland and another on the peninsula between the Atlantic and Chesapeake Bay. Each district established a committee of safety to raise one company of regular, full-time troops for one year's service and to form a ten-company battalion of minutemen within the militia system to provide a better trained local defense force. The minutemen replaced volunteer companies formed in 1774 and 1775. The Eastern Shore district did not form a regular company, but it received authorization for a somewhat larger minuteman regiment. The convention also created a Committee of Safety and adopted Articles of War and the current British drill manual.[1]

After reporting to Williamsburg, the fifteen regular companies (about 1,020 men) were organized on 21 October into two regiments. The 1st Virginia Regiment under Patrick Henry contained 2 rifle companies and 6 musket companies; the 2d Virginia Regiment under William Woodford also had 2 rifle companies but only 5 musket companies. The rifle companies—intended as light infantry—came from the frontier districts; the musketmen, from more settled regions. Each had a captain, 2 lieutenants, an ensign, 3 sergeants, a drummer, a fifer, and 68 rank and file. The district committees selected the company officers, while the convention appointed three field officers for each regiment. Regimental staffs contained a chaplain, an adjutant, a paymaster who doubled as mustermaster, a quartermaster, a surgeon with two mates, and a sergeant major. Because Henry was the senior officer, the 1st also had a secretary. The officers of Virginia's two regiments carried impressive credentials: all were political leaders, and four had significant combat experience. The captains were prominent in local affairs, although most were too young to have served in the French and Indian War.

The compromise which created the two regiments also included five independent companies to garrison strategic frontier posts. They were under the overall command of Capt. John Neville, who established his headquarters at Fort Pitt (Pittsburgh). Four were rather large: a captain, 3 lieutenants, an ensign, 4 sergeants, 2 drummers, 2 fifers, and 100 rank and file; the fifth had only a single lieutenant and 25 enlisted men. Two of the large companies manned Fort Pitt while the small one garrisoned Fort Fincastle at the mouth of the Wheeling River. These three companies were recruited in the West Augusta District, a partially organized region on the northwest frontier. Another company, from Botetourt County, defended Point Pleasant, and the last defended its home county of Fincastle. The use of independent companies followed the British Army's practice of sending separate units to remote colonial garrisons.[2]

Skirmishes with Lord Dunmore's forces in the Hampton Roads area during the late fall culminated in a minor battle at Great Bridge. The Virginia Convention reacted by passing legislation on 11 January to raise 72 more companies of regulars. It

[1]William J. Van Screevan et al., eds., *Revolutionary Virginia: The Road to Independence* (Charlottesville: University Press of Virginia, 1973–), 3:319–43, 392–409, 427–29, 450–59, 471–72; 497–504. William Waller Henning, comp., *The Statutes at Large; Being a Collection of All the Laws of Virginia*, 14 vols. (1821; reprint ed., Charlottesville: Jamestown Foundation, 1969), 9:9–50; George Mason, *The Papers of George Mason, 1725–1792*, ed. Robert A. Rutland, 3 vols. (Chapel Hill: University of North Carolina Press, 1970), 1:245–57; *The Virginia Gazette* (ed. Alexander Purdie), 25 Aug 75; Brent Tarter, ed., "The Orderly Book of the Second Virginia Regiment, September 27, 1775–April 15, 1776," *Virginia Magazine of History and Biography* 85 (1977):170–71.

[2]Van Screevan, *Revolutionary Virginia*, 3:343, 404; Reuben Gold Thwaites and Louis Phelps Kellogg, eds., *The Revolution on the Upper Ohio, 1775–1777* (Madison: Wisconsin Historical Society, 1908), pp. 12–17.

TABLE 3—REGIMENTS, 1776

Colony	Field			Staff									Each Company									Aggregate					Total Strength
	Colonel	Lieutenant Colonel	Major	Adjutant	Quartermaster	Surgeon	Surgeon's Mate	Chaplain	Sergeant Major	Quartermaster Sgt.	Fife and Drum Major	Paymaster	Number of Companies	Captain	Lieutenant	Ensign	Sergeant	Corporal	Drummer	Fifer	Privates	Officers	Staff Officers	Noncommissioned Officers	Drummers and Fifers	Privates	
Continental........	1	1	1	1	1	1	1	1	1	1	2	1	8	1	2	1	4	4	1	1	76	35	6	68	16	608	733
Virginia...........	1	1	1	1	1	1	2	1	1	1	1	0	10[a]	1	2	1	4	4	1	1	64	43	6	83	20	640	792
South Carolina Rifle..	1[b]	1	1	1	1	1	0	0	1	1	0	1	7[b]	1	2	1	4	4	0	0	92	31	4	58	0	644	737
Southern Ranger.....	0	1	1	0	0	1	0	0	0	0	0	1	10	1	2	0	2	0	0	0	50	32	2	20	0	500	554
Pennsylvania State Musket..........	1	1	1	1	1	1	1	1	1	0	0	0	8	1	1	1	2	2	1	1	52[c]	27	5	32	16	420	500
Pennsylvania State Rifle[d]............	1	2	2	2	1	2	2	1	0	0	0	0	12	1	3	0	4	4	1	1	68[e]	53	8	96	24	819	1,000
Rhode Island State ..	1	1	2	1	1	1	1	0	0	0	0	0	12	1	1	1[f]	4	4	1	1	50	39	4	96	24	600	763
Maryland...........	1	1	2	1	1	1	1	0	0	1[e]	0	0	9	1	2[f]	1[f]	4	4	1	1	60[f]	40	4	73	18	544	679
Maryland Separate Cos.	0	0	0	0	0	0	0	0	0	0	0	0	7	1	3	0	4	4	1	1	92	28	0	56	14	736	806

[a] In most regiments seven musket and three rifle companies.
[b] The 6th South Carolina Regiment had no colonel and only five companies.
[c] Some companies authorized one additional private.
[d] Two battalions.
[e] Clerk.
[f] Light infantry company had three lieutenants, no ensign, and four more privates.

expanded the 1st and 2d Virginia Regiments to ten companies each, added a sergeant to each company, and somewhat increased the regimental staff. (*Table 3*) The convention also established six new regiments of the same size, each with seven musket and three rifle companies, plus a ninth regiment with only seven companies to replace the minutemen on the Eastern Shore. Protection of the western coast of the Chesapeake Bay was provided by pairs of regiments assigned to sectors separated by the James, York, and Rappahannock Rivers. The 8th Virginia Regiment was unique in that the convention intended to raise it from the German-Americans of the Shenandoah Valley and, therefore, exempted it from having a fixed ratio of riflemen to musketmen. The Committee of Safety assembled the other new regiments on a regional basis, although it continued to draw the rifle companies from frontier counties. The new companies were raised by individual counties, and the men were enlisted to serve until 10 April 1778. The new field officers, like the earlier set, were an experienced group: six of the seven colonels had served with Washington in the French and Indian War. Company officers and many of the enlisted men came from the minutemen battalions.[3]

The nine regiments, like the frontier companies, were raised as state troops for the defense of Virginia and its neighbors. That fact, the ten-company organization, and the short enlistments made the regiments similar to the earlier Provincials. The financial burden of such a large force, however, soon led the colony to ask that the regiments be transferred to the Continental Army. On 28 December 1775, Congress, which was already moving to broaden the geographical base of the Continental Army, authorized six Virginia regiments. The Virginia delegates engaged in prolonged negotiations before Congress accepted all nine regiments. The 1st and 2d retained seniority by being adopted retroactively; the others came under Continental pay when they were certified as full. Virginia did not alter its regimental organization to conform to Continental standards, and the transfer did not alter the terms of enlistment. It did require the officers to exchange their colony commissions for Continental ones, and a few refused and resigned. When Virginia requested Congress to appoint general officers to command these troops, Washington objected to Henry's lack of military background and successfully blocked his appointment. In the end, two men who had served under Washington were appointed brigadier generals: Andrew Lewis on 1 March 1776 and Hugh Mercer on 5 June.[4]

The Virginia Convention had authorized an artillery company on 1 December 1775 consisting of a captain, 3 lieutenants, a sergeant, 4 bombardiers, 8 gunners, and 48 matrosses. On 13 February the Committee of Safety selected James Innis as captain and Charles Harrison, Edward Carrington, and Samuel Denney as lieutenants. Congress adopted the company on 19 March, and soon after instructed Dohicky Arundel, a French volunteer, to raise another artillery company in Virginia. When Innis transferred to the infantry, Arundel attempted to merge the two companies, but

[3]Henning, *Statutes at Large*, 9:75–92; Force, *American Archives*, 4th ser., 4:78–83, 118; Van Screevan, *Revolutionary Virginia*, 4:467–69, 497–99; William P. Palmer, ed., *Calendar of Virginia State Papers and Other Manuscripts*, 11 vols. (Richmond: Virginia State Library, 1875–93), 8:75–149. The 9th expanded to ten companies on 18 May: Force, *American Archives*, 4th ser., 6:1528, 1556; Henning, *Statutes at Large*, 9:135–38.
[4]*JCC*, 3:463; 4:132, 181, 235; 5:420, 466, 649; Force, *American Archives*, 4th ser., 4:116–17; 5th ser., 1:719–22; Fitzpatrick, *Writings*, 4:379–84; Jefferson, *Papers*, 1:482–84; Van Screevan, *Revolutionary Virginia*, 4:421–22, 470–71; Smith, *Letters of Delegates*, 3:100–102, 123–24, 240, 245–46, 248–49, 252, 316n, 440; Burnett, *Letters*, 2:31–32.

he was killed on 12 July while experimenting with a mortar. The companies retained separate identities although they worked closely with each other.[5]

In May 1776 the colony reorganized the frontier defense companies, for the most part retaining their large size. Reenlistments at Fort Pitt and Point Pleasant filled one company from each place. A third was organized in Botetourt County for duty at Point Pleasant. New, smaller companies (3 officers, 3 sergeants, a drummer, a fifer, and 50 rank and file) were raised in Hampshire and Augusta Counties to garrison Wheeling (Fort Fincastle) and a post on the Little Kanawha River. All were under Neville, who was promoted to major. The same legislation ordered reenlistment of the men of the 1st and 2d Virginia Regiments for three years.[6] Virginia's regular forces were more than a match for Lord Dunmore, and the British soon withdrew to New York.

North Carolina's revolutionary leadership was less sure than Virginia's of its popular support and consequently turned to outside assistance sooner. The colony contained many recent Scottish immigrants who were still loyal to the Crown, and old grievances left the backcountry's willingness to follow Tidewater planters in doubt. On 26 June 1775 the North Carolina delegates secured a congressional promise to fund a force of 1,000 men. This support enabled the colony's leaders to act.[7]

Aside from raising the Continental force, North Carolina organized six regional military districts and instructed each to raise a ten-company battalion of minutemen. At the same time, the colony disbanded its volunteer companies to remove any obstacles to recruiting. The minutemen had the same organization as the colony's Continental companies: 3 officers, 3 sergeants, and 50 rank and file. This structure was quite similar to that of the Virginia minutemen. On 1 September the colony's 1,000 continentals were arranged in 2 regiments, each consisting of 3 field officers, an adjutant, and 10 companies. The companies assembled at Salisbury beginning in October. The colony's total response was a compromise. Eastern interests received the two regular regiments to defend the coastline from naval vessels supporting former Governor Josiah Martin. Less threatened areas relied on the less expensive minutemen.[8]

On 28 November 1775 the Continental Congress ordered both North Carolina regiments reorganized on the new Continental eight-company structure. It went on to authorize a third regiment on 16 January 1776 and two more on 26 March. Colonial concurrence was required to raise the new regiments. However, the Provincial Congress was receptive and on 9 April approved raising the three new regiments for two and a half years. The Continental Congress had already rewarded North Carolina's prompt actions in 1775 by promoting Cols. James Moore and Robert Howe to brigadier general on 1 March 1776. The Provincial Congress had second thoughts, however, and on 13 April it ordered that its regular forces be reorganized as six instead of five regiments. Five new companies were raised by each of the six military districts, and

[5]Henning, *Statutes at Large*, 9:75–92; *JCC*, 4:212, 364. *Virginia Gazette* (Purdie), 16 Feb and 12 Jul 76; Charles Campbell, ed., *The Orderly Book of That Portion of the American Army Stationed at or Near Williamsburg, Va., Under the Command of General Andrew Lewis From March 18th, 1776, to August 28th, 1776.* (Richmond: privately printed, 1860), pp. 26–27, 36–37; Lee, *Papers*, 1:367–68, 416–17, 440–43, 477–80; Smith, *Letters of Delegates*, 3:102n, 108–9, 168–69, 397, 469–70, 570–72.

[6]Henning, *Statutes at Large*, 9:135–38; Force, *American Archives*, 4th ser., 6:1532, 1556, 1568; Henry Read McIlwaine et al., eds., *Journals of the Council of the State of Virginia*, 4 vols. (Richmond: Virginia State Library, 1931–67), 1:97, 108, 148, 173.

[7]*JCC*, 2:107; 3:330; Smith, *Letters of Delegates*, 1:545.

[8]Force, *American Archives*, 4th ser., 2:255–70; 3:181–210, 679, 1087–94.

the remaining two were organized in the colony at large. The staff of these units deviated from the Continental model by omitting the fife major and adding a commissary of stores, an armorer, and a wagonmaster. The Continental Congress accepted the 6th North Carolina Regiment on 7 May (retroactively) and subsequently adopted three troops of light horse and an artillery company which the colony had raised during the summer.[9]

Meanwhile, continued concern for the security of the coast had led to a proposal to add another regular regiment, with six companies. General Moore persuaded the Provincial Congress to modify this plan on 29 April. Instead of a seventh regiment, five independent companies of state troops were authorized to defend specific points. Two were standard-sized companies, but the other three each had only sixty privates. On 3 May a 24-man company was added to garrison a frontier fort.[10]

South Carolina's situation in 1775 was somewhat similar to North Carolina's. Again there was lingering tension between the Tidewater and backcountry, but the colony's leaders were more secure. Like Virginia, the colony decided to supplement the militia with regular state troops rather than turn immediately to the Continental Congress. The Provincial Congress adopted a regional compromise on 4 June. Two 750-man regiments of infantry were authorized to defend the Tidewater from possible attack by regular British troops. The "upcountry" received a third regiment of 450 mounted rangers to counter potential Indian raids. Since there was no immediate danger, the Provincial Congress limited expenses by restricting the companies to cadre strength when it issued recruiting orders on 21 June. The infantry regiments were authorized ten 50-men companies each, a structure similar to that selected by North Carolina and Virginia in 1775. The nine ranger companies were allowed thirty men each. Competition for commissions was intense, and a minor mutiny occurred in some companies of the ranger regiment when the spirit of the regional compromise was violated by the assignment of a Tidewater militia officer as the regimental commander.[11]

During the winter the South Carolina Provincial Congress expanded its forces. An artillery regiment, small but highly specialized, was established to man the fortifications at Charleston. (*Chart 5*) The 4th South Carolina Regiment drew its cadre from Charleston's elite militia artillerymen. A separate artillery company authorized at this time to defend Fort Lyttleton at Port Royal was not raised. On 22 February 1776 the three original regiments were finally allowed to recruit to full strength, and shortly thereafter two rifle regiments were added. (*See Table 3.*) The 5th South Carolina Regiment had seven companies, recruited in the Tidewater. The 6th had only five companies; Thomas Sumter raised this regiment along the northwestern frontier where many of the inhabitants were former Virginians. Each rifle company contained four

[9]*JCC*, 3:387–88; 4:59, 181, 237, 331–33; 5:623–24; 8:567; Smith, *Letters of Delegates*, 3:18–19, 42–44, 100–103, 123–24, 315–18, 448; Burnett, *Letters*, 1:448; Force, *American Archives*, 4th ser., 4:299–308; 5:68, 859–60, 1315–68; 6:1443–58.

[10]Force, *American Archives*, 4th ser., 5:1330–31, 1341–42, 1348.

[11]Force, *American Archives*, 4th ser., 2:897, 953–54; William Moultrie, *Memoirs of the American Revolution, So Far As It Related to the States of North and South Carolina and Georgia*, 2 vols. (New York: David Longworth, 1802), 1:64–65; John Drayton, *Memoirs of the American Revolution, From Its Commencement to the Year 1776, Inclusive*, 2 vols. (Charleston: A. E. Miller, 1821), 1:249, 255, 265, 286–88, 323, 352–53; R. W. Gibbes, ed., *Documentary History of the American Revolution*, 3 vols. (Columbia and New York: Banner Steam-Power Press and D. Appleton & Co., 1853–57), vol. A, pp. 104–5.

CHART 5—SOUTH CAROLINA ARTILLERY REGIMENT 12 NOVEMBER 1775

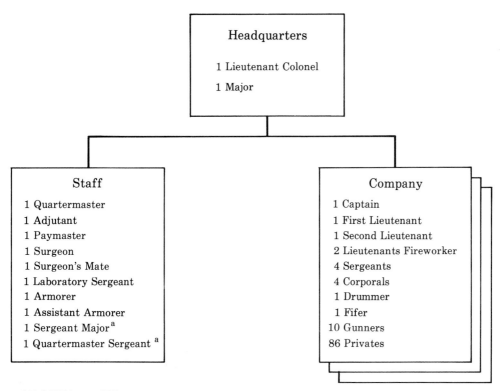

a. Added 22 February 1776.

officers and one hundred men. At the same time, artillery companies were allocated for Fort Lyttleton (100 men) and Georgetown (60).[12]

On 4 November 1775 the Continental Congress had directed South Carolina to raise three Continental regiments with the standard Continental infantry organization. A second act, on 25 March 1776, increased the quota to five regiments. The colony did not immediately transfer its units to the Continental Army but tried simply to delegate operational control over them. Congress did not accept that alternative. On 18 June it decreed that all of the regiments except the rangers had been adopted by the earlier acts. As a major concession, however, it promised not to send more than one-third of the troops outside South Carolina without prior notice. The rangers and a similar Georgia mounted unit were adopted on 24 July with a special organization and a requirement that they serve on foot as well as on horseback. (*See Table 3.*) Congress restored seniority by other legislation.[13]

[12]Force, *American Archives*, 4th ser., 4:27–76; 5:561–615; Moultrie, *Memoirs*, 1:93, 126–27; Gibbes, *Documentary History*, vol. A, pp. 246–48.

[13]*JCC*, 3:325–27; 4:235; 5:461–62, 606–7, 760; Smith, *Letters of Delegates*, 3:440; Moultrie, *Memoirs*, 1:141; Force, *American Archives*, 5th ser., 1:631–32; Lee, *Papers*, 2:10–12, 37–39, 57, 173, 199–202, 251, 254; Thomas Pinckney, "Letters of Thomas Pinckney, 1775–1780," ed. Jack L. Cross, *South Carolina Historical Magazine* 58 (1957):29–30.

THOMAS SUMTER *(1734–1832), "the Game-cock," organized the 6th South Carolina Regiment and commanded it until he re-tired in 1778. Later in the war he became one of the most effective southern leaders of irregulars. The famous fort in Charleston harbor is named for him. (Portrait by Rem-brandt Peale.)*

Georgia, like North Carolina, waited for congressional support before risking military action. It had only 3,000 males of military age and was the most exposed colony. When Congress authorized South Carolina's three regiments on 4 November 1775, it also directed Georgia to raise a standard infantry regiment. Because communications with the colony took so long, its Provincial Congress was allowed to appoint all officers, not just those of company-grade. After factions within the Provincial Congress fought for control of the regiment, a compromise gave command to Lachlan McIntosh, the leader of the Scottish element in the colony. Two representatives of the Savannah mercantile interests were named as the other field officers. Most of the company positions went to sons of the planters who constituted the "Country Party." The Provincial Congress and the state government that succeeded it caused continual troubles for senior Continental officers by asserting a right to retain an interest in the regiment's affairs.[14]

McIntosh began raising the regiment in February 1776, arming one of the companies with rifles. He correctly anticipated that limited resources would hamper his efforts: two months later the regiment had reached only half strength. Maj. Gen. Charles Lee supported the colony's efforts to have Congress raise six additional regiments elsewhere and to station them in Georgia. Before this recommendation arrived, Congress voted to have Georgia raise two additional regiments (one of which was to be composed of riflemen) and two artillery companies to garrison Savannah and Sunbury. On 24 July Congress adopted the colony's horse troops and expanded them into a regiment as well.[15]

---

[14]*JCC*, 3:325–27; Allen D. Candler, ed., *The Revolutionary Records of the State of Georgia*, 3 vols. (Atlanta: Franklin-Turner Co., 1908), 1:77–78, 273; Lee, *Papers*, 2:216–29, 254; Force, *American Archives*, 4th ser., 2:1553; 6:1159–60; Lachlan McIntosh, "The Papers of Lachlan McIntosh, 1774–1799," ed. Lilla M. Hawes, *Georgia Historical Quarterly* 39 (1955):53.

[15]*JCC*, 5:521, 606–7; Lee, *Papers*, 2:48–49, 107–17, 241–45, 249; Candler, *Revolutionary Records*, 1:124, 194–99; Force, *American Archives*, 4th ser., 4:1159–61; 5:1106–9.

McIntosh made little progress in organizing the new units despite receiving permission from Virginia and North Carolina to recruit within their borders. Low bounties, year-long enlistments, and a fear in colonies to the north that Georgia's climate was fatal discouraged enlistments. Although the ranger regiment under his brother William did better than the infantry regiments and was on duty by late October, the colony was fortunate that British pressure was minimal.[16]

In many respects the first year of military preparations in the south resembled New England's efforts in 1775. Each colony raised a separate force independently or with congressional encouragment. Regimental structures varied, although a 10-company, 500-man formation had some regional appeal. These forces gradually were adopted as part of the Continental Army. Two key differences set the south apart. The region, with little manpower to spare from a plantation economy, turned rapidly to enlisting men for long terms, typically two years. Many of the colonies also resisted surrendering full control over their troops to the national government in distant Philadelphia. All refused to comply completely with the standard eight-company structure for Continental infantry regiments.

The 1776 military effort in the south culminated on 28 June with the repulse of a British attack on Charleston, South Carolina. A return for the forces in that state shortly after the event shows that all six South Carolina regiments were there along with the 8th Virginia Regiment; the 1st, 2d, and 3d North Carolina Regiments; and a troop of North Carolina horse. Excluding the artillery and cavalry, the concentration of continentals at Charleston included 239 officers, 30 staff officers, 209 sergeants, 86 drummers and fifers, and 3,158 rank and file. About 500 were sick, and almost another hundred were absent on furlough. The force was thus well below authorized levels. The three North Carolina regiments were about half full; the 8th Virginia Regiment about three-quarters full. The three senior South Carolina regiments averaged about 350 men apiece, but the newer 5th and 6th Regiments were both still under 300.[17]

In addition to the concentration at Charleston, by July sizable Continental forces were on hand in all the southern states. Georgia had one infantry regiment nearing full strength and a partially organized mounted regiment. Two other infantry regiments and two artillery companies were beginning to recruit. North Carolina was held by three regiments, two troops of horse, and an artillery company. In Virginia, where Governor Dunmore was preparing to depart, eight infantry regiments defended the Tidewater area while five companies were on the frontier.

Even before the decisive victory at Charleston, Virginia had bested Governor Dunmore; North Carolina had crushed a Loyalist uprising at Moore's Creek Bridge; and Georgia had chased off the forces of its former governor. Joint operations had silenced Cherokees in the interior. The fact that militia or minutemen had played a major role in defeating the Loyalists and Indians, however, led to difficulty in recruiting for the Continental regiments since their success had reinforced colonial leaders' belief that militia forces were adequate for local defense. These southern leaders consequently did not give the Continental units the same support that their northern counterparts did. When General Lee left the south in the autumn of 1776, he feared that "it is not

[16]Ibid., 5th ser., 1:6–8; McIntosh, "Papers," 38 (1954):161–66, 253–57; Candler, *Revolutionary Records*, 1:213; "Letters Colonial and Revolutionary," *Pennsylvania Magazine of History and Biography* 42 (1918):77–78.
    [17]Monthly Return, Forces in South Carolina, July 1776, Force, *American Archives*, 5th ser., 1:631–32.

LACHLAN McINTOSH (1725–1806) was Georgia's ranking Continental officer. He raised the 1st Georgia Regiment and later commanded the Western Department as a brigadier general. He is best known, however, as the man who killed Button Gwinnett—one of Georgia's signers of the Declaration of Independence—in a duel. (Postwar portrait by Charles Willson Peale.)

impossible that the late repulse of the Enemy may be fatal to us [for] we seem now all sunk into a most secure and comfortable sleep."[18]

The Middle Colonies

New Jersey, Pennsylvania, Delaware, and Maryland also participated in Congress' expansion of the military effort in 1776. Like the south, these middle colonies were more diverse in their origins and ethnic composition than New England. On the other hand, the area was much closer to the national authority in Philadelphia. Proximity simplified communications and enabled the governments of these colonies to coordinate their efforts with Congress and to avoid the variety of unit structures of the other colonies. By waiting to raise troops until they had instructions from Congress, they also reduced their expenses.

Aside from the original 1775 riflemen, the first troops that Congress requested from the middle colonies were two regiments from New Jersey. Anticipating that the British would attack New York City, Congress on 9 October 1775 asked that colony's Provincial Congress to replace the New York regiments that had marched to Canada. New Jersey asserted that it should name all the officers because, knowing its own citizens, it was in the best position to select the most effective men. Delegates in Congress who were committed more to local interests than national ones supported the colony, but the resulting debate was won by other delegates who hoped to strengthen Congress' role as a national government. In practice Congress would follow a compromise by commissioning individuals from those nominated by the governments of the respective colonies.[19]

[18]Lee, *Papers*, 2:105–6.
[19]*JCC*, 3:285–89, 305, 335, 429; Smith, *Letters of Delegates*, 2:147–48, 155–56, 171, 253, 489–90; Force, *American Archives*, 4th ser., 3:1050–51, 1224–25, 1240; William Livingston to Lord Stirling, 8 Nov 75, William Alexander Papers, New-York Historical Society (hereafter cited as Stirling Papers); Rossie, *Politics of Command*, pp. 26–30, 61–74.

COMMISSION OF ALEXANDER SPOTSWOOD. *This commission as colonel of the 2d Virginia Regiment is typical of Continental Army commissions used throughout the war. An officer was required to carry his commission at all times. The commission was a printed form showing the person's rank, unit, and date of rank. It was signed by the president of the Continental Congress and certified by the Congress' secretary.*

During succeeding months the delegates resolved most of the other questions relating to appointment of officers and seniority. Congress strengthened its authority by ruling that officers elected on the same day took seniority according to the order in which their names appeared in the minutes of Congress. Promotions made to fill a vacancy were considered effective on the date that the vacancy occurred. Congress also steadfastly maintained a right to promote officers without regard for seniority in cases of exceptional merit. Delegates from the middle and southern colonies were aware that strict adherence to seniority would allow New England to dominate Army leadership.[20]

Congress appointed the field officers that the New Jersey Provincial Congress had recommended. Lord Stirling of the 1st New Jersey Regiment and William Maxwell of the 2d were veterans of the French and Indian War, militia colonels, and important politicians. The Provincial Congress raised sixteen companies by apportioning them among the counties according to their respective militia strength. The composition of regiments reflected the territorial subdivisions of the colony. East Jersey, the north-

---

[20]*JCC,* 4:29, 342; 6:864; Burnett, *Letters,* 2:14.

eastern portion, filled the 1st, while West Jersey, the southwestern area, furnished the 2d.[21]

New Jersey delegate William Livingston secured authorization for a third regiment when Congress ordered the 2d to Canada. Its commander, Elias Dayton, had the same military and political credentials as the two other colonels. This regiment was raised on a colony-wide basis during the early spring of 1776. The provincial Congress disbanded its minutemen at the same time. It also created two companies of artillery. These companies, one for East Jersey and one for West Jersey, were regular state troops designed to support the militia. On 1 March 1776 Congress rejected New Jersey's effort to have them adopted as Continentals and its offer to raise two more regiments.[22]

On 7 March 1776 Lt. Col. William Winds replaced Lord Stirling as commander of the 1st New Jersey Regiment. Matthias Ogden, who had gone to Boston as a volunteer, became the new lieutenant colonel. The 1st and 3d went to New York, although two companies of the latter were briefly diverted to protect Cape May. Washington later sent the 1st to join the 2d in Canada and the 3d to serve in the Mohawk Valley.[23]

Pennsylvania, like New Jersey, was relatively untouched by operations in 1775. Because it lacked a compulsory militia, the Quaker-dominated colony relied on volunteers, known as associators. The Pennsylvania Assembly assumed responsibility for supervising the associators on 30 June 1775. Under the leadership of Benjamin Franklin, the colony's Committee of Safety then began vigorous preparations; by the end of September, it had expended large sums and had drafted rules and regulations for the associators. For the benefit of the large German-speaking minority, the committee printed the regulations in German as well as in English.[24]

On 12 October 1775 Congress authorized the colony to raise a regiment. The assembly appointed company officers and began recruiting almost immediately, but it did not nominate field officers until November. The companies, recruited across the colony, assembled in the capital on 11 January 1776. At that point the officers objected to the appointment of Col. John Bull as commander and forced his resignation. John DeHaas, veteran of the French and Indian War, replaced Bull. The regiment, with eight companies in conformity with the Continental model, reached Quebec in time to participate in the closing moments of the siege.[25]

On 9 December 1775 Congress authorized Pennsylvania to raise four more regiments. Congress appointed field officers in early January following the Committee of Safety's recommendations. Companies were raised by counties and grouped into regiments on a geographical basis. Pennsylvania did not call its units regiments but rather designated them as the 1st through 5th Pennsylvania Battalions. Cumberland County's local committee of safety petitioned the Committee of Safety to allow it to

[21]Force, *American Archives*, 4th ser., 3:1234-44; 4:164-66, 288, 294-95. American-born William Alexander's claim to the Earldom of Stirling had been recognized in Scotland but rejected by the British House of Lords.

[22]*JCC*, 4:47, 123, 181n; Smith, *Letters of Delegates*, 3:77, 80, 120-21, 158, 219, 306, 311, 318-19; Force, *American Archives*, 4th ser., 4:664, 1391, 1580-1624.

[23]Stirling to Samuel Tucker, 3 Mar 76, and Tucker to Stirling, 7 Mar 76, Stirling Papers; Stirling to Congress, 5 and 19 Feb 76, RG 360, National Archives; *JCC*, 4:188, 204, 291. Fitzpatrick, *Writings*, 4:526.

[24]Force, *American Archives*, 4th ser., 2:1771-77; 3:496, 501-11, 870-71; *Pennsylvania Archives*, 1st ser., 4:639-42; 8th ser., 8:7245-47, 7351-52, 7369-80, 7384.

[25]*JCC*, 3:291, 370; *Pennsylvania Archives*, 8th ser., 8:7306-8, 7314, 7324-25, 7345, 7356. As in the case of the first two New Jersey regiments, the initial strength of the Pennsylvania regiment was slightly increased to conform to the standard organization adopted for Washington's regiments.

ANTHONY WAYNE (1745-96) raised the 4th Pennsylvania Battalion in 1776 and commanded the Pennsylvania Division as a brigadier general during most of the war. In 1792 he replaced Arthur St. Clair as the senior officer of the United States Army and led the Army to victory in the battle of Fallen Timbers three years later. His nickname, "Mad Anthony," did not become popular until after the Revolution. (Portrait attributed to James Sharples, Sr., 1795.)

raise a full regiment, and Congress rewarded this enthusiasm on 4 January 1776 by directing Pennsylvania to raise a sixth regiment there. Congress appointed officers for it according to the county's wishes. One company of every regiment except the 1st Pennsylvania Battalion was armed with rifles, although Congress attached Capt. John Nelson's independent rifle company to the 1st for most of 1776. Congress had accepted that company, organized by the Berks County committee of safety, on 30 January.[26]

Pennsylvania hoped to retain a voice in the use of its regiments through having them serve as a unified brigade.[27] Such a course would also allow it time to train the junior officers, who were considered "pretty generally men of some Education, capable of becoming good officers, [and] willing to do their duty."[28] The Canadian crisis, however, prevented any such systematic deployment. Congress quickly ordered north the 1st, 2d, and 4th (under Benjamin Franklin's protege Anthony Wayne). A shortage of arms delayed the movement of the other regiments and led Congress to toy with the idea of arming Robert Magaw's 5th with pikes instead of muskets. The 6th later reached Canada, but the 3d and 5th went only as far as New York City.[29]

During the summer of 1776 Congress authorized Pennsylvania to raise two more regiments for special missions. In the first instance Congress became concerned with preserving the neutrality of Indians on the frontier. On 11 July it ordered General Schuyler to raise a regiment to garrison several key points in New York and Pennsylvania. Seven of the companies were raised in Westmoreland County and the eighth in adja-

[26]*Pennsylvania Archives*, 1st ser., 4:693-94, 711; Force, *American Archives*, 4th ser., 4:501, 507-11; Smith, *Letters of Delegates*, 3:27-28, 31, 60, 80, 123-26, 167; *JCC*, 3:29, 101-2, 207, 418; 4:23-24, 29-31, 47-48. The 5th Pennsylvania Regiment absorbed Nelson's company in 1777.

[27]William Thompson to unknown, 25 Jan 76, *Pennsylvania Magazine of History and Biography* 35 (1911): 304-6.

[28]Lee, *Papers*, 1:303-8.

[29]*JCC*, 4:163, 204, 215; 5:431; Force, *American Archives*, 4th ser., 5:435-36; 6:664; Smith, *Letters of Delegates*, 3:376, 420.

WILLIAM SMALLWOOD *(1732–92) became the first commander of the 1st Maryland Regiment after leading his colony's opposition to British policies. He rose to the rank of major general and became governor of Maryland after the Revolution. (Portrait by Charles Willson Peale, ca. 1782.)*

cent Bedford County. Westmoreland County had already organized an independent company of 100 men under Capt. Van Swearingen to protect its frontier. On 16 June the Pennsylvania Assembly had accepted this company as a state unit and had stationed it at Kittaning. Swearingen's company became part of the new regiment. Aneas Mackay, a former British officer living in Westmoreland County, was appointed colonel on 20 July, but a food shortage prevented concentration of the regiment until mid-December.[30]

Mackay's regiment was not responsible for defense of the colony's northern border (Northumberland and Northampton Counties), and Congress authorized a second regiment to secure that region on 23 August. Commanded by Lt. Col. William Cook, it contained only six companies, and it did not complete organization in time to participate in the operations of 1776. By having Cook's unit cooperate with two separate companies from the Wyoming Valley, Congress intended in effect to provide a full regiment to defend the frontier. The valley was claimed by both Pennsylvania and Connecticut, but the latter colony exercised effective control and organized the companies under Capts. Robert Durkee and Samuel Ransom.[31]

Delaware responded promptly when Congress assigned it a single Continental regiment on 9 December 1775. It appointed company officers on 13 January, and six days later Congress approved the field officers. The regiment assembled at Dover in March and began training under the tutelage of Thomas Holland, the adjutant, who was a former British captain. Several companies skirmished with British landing

[30]Force, *American Archives*, 4th ser., 6:1284; 5th ser., 2:7–9; *Pennsylvania Archives*, 1st ser., 5:92–93, 135; 8th ser., 8:7535–36; *JCC*, 5:542, 562, 596, 759–60.

[31]*JCC*, 5:699, 701; 6:1024; *Pennsylvania Archives*, 1st ser., 5:84–85; Force, *American Archives*, 5th ser., 2:16, 28, 35, 60; Charles J. Hoadley et al., eds., *The Public Records of the State of Connecticut*, 11 vols. (Hartford: various publishers, 1894–1967), 1:7. The Wyoming Valley is now part of Pennsylvania.

parties from the frigate *Roebuck*, but most of the regiment lacked weapons until July. It obtained muskets in Philadelphia, and in August the regiment set out to join the Main Army at New York City.[32]

Maryland was not in any immediate danger in 1775. On 14 August it merely reorganized the militia and established forty minutemen companies. Lord Dunmore's activity in Chesapeake Bay, however, caused the Maryland Convention to reconsider the colony's defenses. On 1 January 1776 the convention approved the concept of raising regular troops. Two weeks later it disbanded the minutemen and replaced them with a force of state troops. (*See Table 3.*) Maryland formed one regiment of nine companies from the northern and western parts of the colony and organized it along lines similar to those of the Continental Army except for the addition of a second major and a light infantry company. The light company, armed with rifles, had a third lieutenant instead of an ensign. It had 64 privates, 4 more than the line companies. The total number of privates in the regiment was the same as in a regiment with eight 68-man companies. The convention also formed 7 separate companies of infantry with 92 privates each, plus 2 artillery companies with the same organization to defend Annapolis and Baltimore.[33]

The regiment's officers came from the colony's political leadership. Col. William Smallwood, Lt. Col. Francis Ware, and four captains had been members of the Maryland Convention. Both majors had prior service: Thomas Price had commanded one of the Continental rifle companies in 1775, and Mordecai Gist had organized the first Maryland volunteer company in 1774. The regiment and three of the separate infantry companies reached New York on 9 August. The remaining four infantry companies under Thomas Price did not join them until 19 September, after they had been released from coastal defense. When Congress formally assigned Maryland a quota of two Continental regiments on 17 August 1776, the colony simply transferred the regiment and independent infantry companies (equivalent to two regiments) to the Continental establishment without providing a second regimental staff.[34]

Two other regiments raised during the summer of 1776 drew their manpower primarily from the middle colonies. When the British introduced German auxiliaries, American propagandists condemned them as "Hessian mercenaries," but Congress responded by mobilizing the German-American population. On 25 May Congress authorized the German Battalion. Men of German descent and immigrant Germans were recruited in Maryland and Pennsylvania for three-year terms. Each colony furnished four companies. Congress appointed Maj. Nicholas Hausegger of the 4th Pennsylvania Battalion as colonel; Capt. George Stricker of Smallwood's Maryland light company, as lieutenant colonel; and Ludowick Weltner of Maryland, as major. All three were leaders in the German community. On 17 July Congress authorized a ninth company to be raised in Pennsylvania as a direct result of Washington's recommenda-

[32]Force, *American Archives*, 4th ser., 5:745–46, 814–15, 1173; 5th ser., 1:739–41; 2:881–82; *JCC*, 3:418; 4:68–69, 251; 5:520, 596, 631; Enoch Anderson, *Personal Recollections of Captain Enoch Anderson*, ed. Henry Hobart Bellas (Wilmington: Historical Society of Delaware, 1896), p. 7.

[33]Force, *American Archives*, 4th ser., 3:108–12; 4:728–35, 744–53; 5:1528; *Muster Rolls and Other Records of Service of Maryland Troops in the American Revolution, 1775–1783, Archives of Maryland*, vol. 18 (Baltimore: Maryland Historical Society, 1900), pp. 4–20.

[34]Force, *American Archives*, 4th ser., 6:1474, 1507; 5th ser., 3:87; Fitzpatrick, *Writings*, 5:416; 6:72; *JCC*, 5:665–66.

tion of John David Woelper, a lieutenant in the 3d Pennslyvania Battalion who had served in the French and Indian War.[35]

Congress authorized another joint unit on 17 June as the Maryland and Virginia Rifle Regiment. Like the 1st Continental Regiment, on which it was modeled, its cadre came from the Continental rifle companies of 1775. Daniel Morgan's Virginia company had been captured at Quebec, but the men of the other Virginia rifle company and of both Maryland companies were at New York and were reenlisted on the same terms as those of the 1st Continental Regiment. Four additional companies were raised in Virginia and three in Maryland, all in the northwestern parts of each colony. Capts. Hugh Stephenson, Moses Rawlings, and Otho Holland Williams became the regimental field officers, retaining their relative seniority. Some of the companies had still not joined the regiment before it was captured at Fort Washington, New York, in November.[36]

During late 1775 and 1776 Congress thus called on the four middle colonies to raise over 11,000 men for the common military effort. New Jersey, Pennsylvania, and Delaware formed ten regiments. Maryland organized the equivalent of two more regiments as state troops, but when Congress asked, it transferred them to the Continental Army. Four other regiments were added during the summer of 1776, two through joint recruiting efforts. Like the first units of other colonies, these regiments attracted men of talent, influence, and experience as officers. Except for Maryland, which behaved more like Virginia than like the other middle colonies, each concentrated on improving its militia and turned to regular troops only at the request of Congress. That fact eliminated most of the variation in organization that had been a problem in the north in 1775 and that was still complicating the southern military effort. As soon as the issue of authority in appointing field officers was resolved, the middle colonies' regiments blended smoothly into the Army. Seven went north, and the equivalent of six others joined Washington's Main Army at New York City.

The Departments and the Main Army

The addition of Continental regiments from the southern and middle colonies raised a new issue of command. Congress reacted by extending the territorial concept that it had implemented with the New York and Canadian Departments. On 13 February it appointed a committee "to consider into what departments the middle and southern colonies ought to be formed, in order that the military operations...may be carried on in a regular and systematic manner."[37] Following the committee's recommendations, Congress created two new territorial departments on 27 February 1776. Virginia, the Carolinas, and Georgia became the Southern Department. New Jersey, Pennsylvania, Delaware, and Maryland joined New York as Schuyler's Middle Department. Three days later Congress placed Charles Lee in command of the former and elected six new brigadier generals as subordinate commanders for the new departments. John Armstrong of Pennsylvania, Andrew Lewis of Virginia, and North

[35]JCC, 4:392; 5:487–88, 526, 571, 590, 825–26; Force, American Archives, 4th ser., 6:1508; 5th ser., 1:124, 186–87, 1289, 1293, 1334–36.
[36]Force, American Archives, 5th ser., 1:31–32, 183, 251, 1335–37, 1343; JCC, 5:452, 486, 529, 540, 740–46; Fitzpatrick, Writings, 5:202, 216; 6:128; Burnett, Letters of Congress, 1:518.
[37]JCC, 4:132–33.

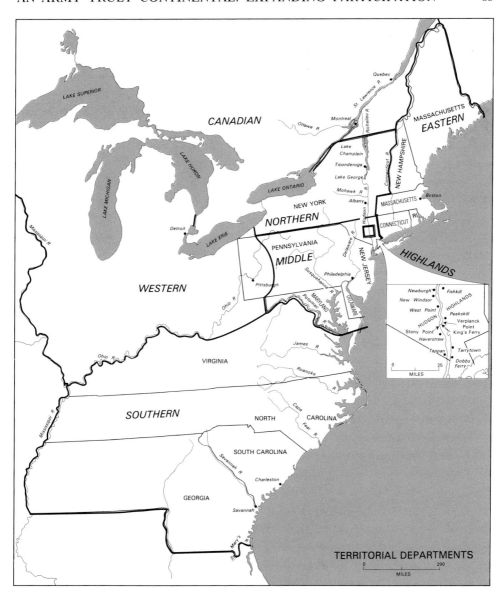

TERRITORIAL DEPARTMENTS

Carolina's James Moore and Robert Howe went to the Southern Department, while William Thompson of Pennsylvania and Lord Stirling of New Jersey became Schuyler's subordinates.[38]

Washington remained as Commander in Chief and held command in the "Military District" of New England. Congress intended each of the four territorial departments (Southern, Middle, Northern, and Canadian) to have a major general and two

[38]Ibid., 174, 181, 187, 236, 241, 243, 331-32, 364-65; Smith, *Letters of Delegates*, 3:252, 270-71, 275-76, 288-89, 310-11, 315-19, 346-47, 459, 606-7.

brigadier generals. Lee received two additional brigadier generals because his department included such a large area and because Congress believed that it was in immediate danger. Events, however, would doom this symmetry. More immediately, there was a series of transfers and resignations. One of the resulting new appointments was the election of Frederick de Woedtke, on 16 March, as a brigadier general for the Canadian Department. He was the first foreign volunteer elevated to the rank of general, largely on the basis of his claim that he had served as a Prussian general.[39]

Washington's Main Army retained its organization of three divisions and six brigades in January 1776. The average size of a brigade remained the same, although each now contained only four or five of the larger 1776 regiments. By early March, Henry Knox had accumulated enough heavy artillery to allow Washington to occupy dominant positions on Dorchester Heights, forcing the British to evacuate Boston. Washington correctly guessed that General Howe intended to attack New York and began sending units to that city on 14 March. The regiments went overland to Norwich, Connecticut, where they embarked and sailed the rest of the way along Long Island Sound. He opened his new headquarters at New York on 14 April, and the last of his units arrived three days later.

The shift of the Main Army to New York brought Washington into the area of Schuyler's Middle Department. In the subsequent adjustment of responsibilities, Washington assumed control of the Middle Department and Schuyler reverted to a more limited command over a reorganized Northern Department. The change allowed the latter to concentrate on furnishing logistical support to the Canadian Department which remained as a separate command. New England reverted to the status of a territorial department (the Eastern Department) under Maj. Gen. Artemas Ward. He had wanted to resign, but Congress persuaded Ward to remain at Boston until a suitable replacement could be spared. His forces included an artillery company and five Continental regiments from Massachusetts that Washington had left behind. The 8th, 16th, 18th, and 27th Continental Regiments protected Boston. The 14th occupied the naval base at Marblehead.[40]

The Main Army in New York now gained some of the new regiments from the middle colonies to compensate for the five left in Massachusetts. Shortly thereafter Washington had to transfer the equivalent of two brigades to the north. In April he regrouped his regiments under the one major general and four brigadier generals he had available for command assignments. Each of the four resulting brigades contained four or five regiments and defended a specific area or terrain feature; the artillery remained outside the brigade formations, although Washington placed the riflemen in the brigades manning the most advanced positions.[41] These units formed the nucleus of the Continental forces that would defend New York in August against the onslaught of Howe.

Meanwhile, state units were taking shape in New England to take over the burden of local defense. Washington's policy, established in 1775 and maintained throughout

[39]*JCC*, 4:47, 186, 209–20; Smith, *Letters of Delegates*, 3:315–17, 336–37, 342–43, 350–51, 384–85, 387, 406, 440, 633–35; Fitzpatrick, *Writings*, 4:221–23, 374, 381–82.

[40]Ward to Congress, 22 Mar 76, RG 360, National Archives; *JCC*, 4:300; 5:694; 6:931; Fitzpatrick, *Writings*, 4:467–70; 5:1–4; Burnett, *Letters*, 1:450–52, 505–6; C. Harvey Gardiner, ed., *A Study in Dissent: The Warren-Gerry Correspondence, 1776–1792* (Carbondale: Southern Illinois University Press, 1968), pp. 16–19; Samuel Adams, *The Writings of Samuel Adams*, ed. Henry Alonzo Cushing, 4 vols. (New York: G. P. Putnam's Sons, 1907), 3:290–91.

[41]Fitzpatrick, *Writings*, 4:512–13, 535–36; 5:36–37.

the war, left local defense to "the Militia, or other Internal Strength [state troops] of each province."[42] The New England governments initially filled their particular military needs by raising short-term independent companies to protect key harbors. On 31 October 1775 Rhode Island took a different course and began raising a 500-man regiment of state troops under Col. William Richmond. On duty since 22 December, Richmond's regiment was expanded in January to 763 men in 12 companies, while Henry Babcock raised a second regiment of the same size. (*See Chart 6.*) The resulting brigade freed Ward's continentals from a large part of their defensive responsibilities.[43]

When the New England delegates became quite concerned with the adequacy of the Continental forces under Ward, they produced a study in May 1776 which recommended a New England garrison of 6,000 men. Congress responded first by ordering Ward's five regiments to recruit to full strength. On 11 May it also retroactively accepted the two Rhode Island regiments, which remained in their home state until September, and on 14 May it authorized the other three New England colonies to raise new Continental regiments: two in Massachusetts and one each in Connecticut and New Hampshire.[44] New Hampshire's regiment was intended as a garrison for Portsmouth, but chaos resulted from an attempt to use state troops as a cadre, and Col. Nicholas Long made no recruiting progress until August. In Connecticut Andrew Ward recruited his regiment with more success in the Hartford area and in the northeastern part of the state, but on 1 August Washington ordered it to New York. Connecticut also raised two regiments of state troops under Benjamin Hinman and David Waterbury, former Continental colonels, to take over the burden of local defense. Massachusetts did not raise its regiments but placed three existing regiments of state troops under Ward's control with the provision that they could not be sent out of the state. The net result, in terms of the Continental establishment, was an addition of 4 regiments: 2 from Rhode Island, 1 from New Hampshire, and 1 from Connecticut. On the other hand, the Connecticut and Massachusetts state troops released the department's regular regiments for duty elsewhere.[45]

When Congress completed action on New England, it turned its attention back to New York. British forces had massed in positions from which they could attack New York City by sea and Ticonderoga by land from Canada. Eventually three of the newly raised Continental regiments in New England and all five of the original regiments were transferred to either the Main Army at New York City or to Ticonderoga. Late in May Washington and Congress concluded that a 2 to 1 numerical superiority was needed to successfully defend both locations. On the supposition that the British would employ 10,000 men against Ticonderoga and 12,500 against New York City, Congress decided that the Northern Department should have 20,000 men and Washington's Main Army 25,000. To help achieve these totals, it called on the states for nearly

[42]Ibid., 3:379–80. Also see pp. 486–87.

[43]*R. I. Records*, 7:376, 384–86, 403–4, 410, 415, 432–38, 492–93; Rhode Island Historical Society *Collections*, 6:141–42.

[44]*JCC*, 4:311, 344–47, 355, 357, 360; Samuel Adams, *Writings*, 3:288–90; Burnett, *Letters of Congress*, 2:78–79; *R. I. Records*, 7:537–38, 554, 599–600, 606–9; Rhode Island Historical Society *Collections*, 6:154–55, 160–63, 170–73. Smith, *Letters of Delegates*, 4:3–4, 31–33, 228–29.

[45]Force, *American Archives*, 4th ser., 5:1272–74, 1288, 1296–97, 1312; 6:801–2; 5th ser., 1:3, 314, 404–5, 459–60; 2:805–6; 5th ser., 1:28–29, 48–49, 62–68, 991; 2:805–6; *Conn. Records*, 15:296–305, 416–17, 434, 485–87, 514–16; Fitzpatrick, *Writings*, 5:363, 463; Ward to Congress, 22 Nov 76, RG 360, National Archives.

THE DECLARATION OF INDEPENDENCE. *John Trumbull, a former Continental Army officer and son of Connecticut's wartime governor, completed this masterpiece while studying art in London during the late 1780's or early 1790's. The colors of the 7th Regiment of Foot, captured at St. John's in 1775, hang on the wall in the background.*

30,000 militia: 6,000 for Ticonderoga, 13,800 for New York City, and 10,000 more for a flying camp (mobile reserve).[46]

Congress' decision to turn to the militia rather than attempt to recruit more Continental regiments was based on practical and ideological reasons. Militia could take to the field quicker. Many delegates also believed that America faced a crisis which demanded the full participation of society for the Revolution to succeed. They felt that the militia, rather than the regular army, was the military institution which represented the people.[47] All of the colonies from Maryland northward responded to this and subsequent calls for militia, although few furnished their full quotas.

Pennsylvania's contribution to the Flying Camp included two special units of state troops. They contained 1,500 men organized as the Pennsylvania State Musketry Battalion and the two-battalion Pennsylvania State Rifle Regiment. (*See Table 3.*) Pennsylvania had created them in March to replace the departing continentals. The former unit was expected to defend Philadelphia from British regulars; the latter could serve also on the frontier. The Pennsylvania state troops also included an artillery contingent, but rather than going to the Flying Camp, it remained near Philadelphia to guard the Delaware River defenses. The artillery company had been established in

[46]*JCC*, 4:399–401, 410–14; Fitzpatrick, *Writings*, 5:56–58, 78n, 218–24.
[47]Burnett, *Letters*, 1:492–94; Henderson, *Party Politics*, p. 104; White, "Standing Armies," pp. 95–110; Cress, "The Standing Army, the Militia, and the New Republic," pp. 134–38.

October 1775 under Capt. Thomas Proctor with twenty-five men. By May 1776 it had increased to one hundred men, and the company volunteered as a unit to serve on the Continental Navy's ship *Hornet* in an engagement that month with the British frigate *Roebuck* in Delaware Bay. As a result of that action it was expanded to two compa- nies, and in October the state ordered the men reenlisted for the duration of the war.[48]

The militia reinforcements and the several Continental regiments that moved to New York during the summer increased the size of the Main Army. Although the militia came with their own brigadier generals, there was still a pressing need for senior officers. Congress responded on 9 August when it promoted Heath, Spencer, Sullivan, and Greene to major general and added six brigadier generals. Only Wooster of the original brigadier generals was passed over for promotion when Congress pun- ished him for his quarrelsome conduct in Canada. The new brigadier generals pri- marily replaced generals killed, promoted, or captured; in almost every case the senior colonel from the same state was promoted. Congress added several more brigadier generals in September. The additional generals enabled Washington to reorganize his brigades in August before the battle opened in New York. Eight brigades of militia and four of continentals formed three "Grand Divisions." Each division was a different size, to fit its defensive mission, but all contained both militia and continentals. This mixture continued throughout the New York campaign as other brigades were added.[49]

In mid-September the Main Army's fourteen infantry brigades contained 31,000 officers and men.[50] Over 7,000 were sick, although most were not sufficiently ill to be hospitalized. Another 3,500 were on detached duties. Fifty-seven percent of the total strength came from 36 regiments of militia and 4 regiments of state troops. The 25 Continental regiments accounted for 674 officers, 103 staff officers, 602 sergeants, 314 drummers and fifers, and 11,590 rank and file. Only slightly more than half of the rank and file were carried as present and fit for duty: 3,153 were sick and 2,356 were "on command." Nearly two-thirds of the total on special duties were conti- nentals rather than militia, a significant indication that they had better training. The regiments were reasonably complete. Half were over three-quarters full, if one in- cludes the sick and detailed personnel. The eight which fell below two-thirds all had special reasons for their status. The 1st Continental Regiment was in the process of reorganizing, and the others had suffered heavy casualties in the battle of Long Island several weeks earlier. These figures indicate that only a fraction of Washington's large army consisted of trained, reliable troops. On the other hand, his regular regiments were reasonably close to their prescribed organization and had the potential for per- forming well in battle. It is also of some note that although the Main Army still drew the majority of its men from New England, units from as far south as Virginia were present.

The expansion of the Continental Army in 1776 required enlargement of the staff serving the Main Army and the creation of staffs in the territorial departments. Other changes in staff came because individuals were promoted or resigned. Adjutant Gen- eral Gates and Mustermaster General Stephen Moylan, for example, were promoted

---

[48]Force, *American Archives*, 4th ser., 3:1819–20, 1828; 4:524, 1573–75; 6:961; 5th ser., 1:1317; 2:69, 80, 97; *Pennsylvania Archives*, 1st ser., 4:751–52, 780; 5:33; 8th ser., 8:7429–46, 7461–65.

[49]Fitzpatrick, *Writings*, 5:379–81, 422–23, 501–3; 6:3–4, 207–8; Burnett, *Letters*, 2:45–57; *JCC*, 5:597, 641; 6:898.

[50]General Return, Main Army, 14 Sep 76, RG 360, National Archives. This return does not include the Flying Camp or various regiments such as the Delaware Regiment that were not physically with their bri- gades on that day. Lesser, *Sinews*, pp. 32–35, prints another return from 28 September.

GEORGE CLINTON *(1739–1812) performed double duty in the Revolution. He was New York's first elected governor as well as a brigadier general in the militia and later in the Continental Army. He played a key role in efforts to defend the Hudson Highlands throughout the war. (Portrait by John Trumbull, 1791.)*

during the year. Joseph Reed was persuaded to accept the Adjutant General's office with the rank of colonel; his former law student, Gunning Bedford, succeeded Moylan, moving up from deputy mustermaster general. Their personal relationship ensured that the two administrative departments would work in close cooperation. At the same time, Washington instituted a more comprehensive reporting system that gave him up-to-date information on the state of his army. His British opponents did not enjoy a similar system and consequently were at a disadvantage in planning.[51]

The other major administrative section of the staff, Washington's personal aides and secretary, also experienced changes. Increases in pay and a congressional decision to give the Commander in Chief's aides the rank of lieutenant colonel (major generals' aides were majors) eased misgivings about career development. When the expanded size of Washington's army greatly increased the workload of his personal staff, Congress added a fourth aide on 24 August. New aides during 1776 were Samuel Blatchley Webb, Richard Cary, and William Grayson. The aides were supplemented by a new special unit formed on 12 March 1776, the Commander in Chief's Guard. Four men from each regiment at Boston were selected for the unit, which was commanded by Capt. Caleb Gibbs (formerly adjutant of the 14th Continental Regiment) and Lt. George Lewis, Washington's nephew. These officers served as supplemental aides, with Gibbs acting as headquarters commandant and running the household. The unit protected Washington's person, the army's cash, and official papers.[52]

Comparable expansion took place in the areas of logistical and medical support.

[51]*JCC*, 4:177, 187, 236, 311, 315; 5:419, 460; 6:933; 10:124; Force, *American Archives*, 4th ser., 6:1013–14; Fitzpatrick, *Writings*, 4:202–7, 223; Greene, *Papers*, 1:264–65; British Headquarters Papers, nos. 1894, 2443, 3320 (Charles Jenkinson to Henry Clinton, 5 Apr and 23 Nov 79 and 5 Feb 81). In 1776 reports required a ream of paper a month per regiment.

[52]*JCC*, 4:311; 5:418, 613; Fitzpatrick, *Writings*, 4:287, 369, 381, 387–88; 5:50, 125, 165, 337–38, 481; Carlos E. Godfrey, *Commander-in-Chief's Guard: Revolutionary War* (Washington: Stevenson-Smith, 1904), pp. 19, 35–38. In 1776 Washington also had an assistant secretary, Alexander Contee Harrison, and Congress appointed the French arms exporter Pierre Penet an honorary aide.

An important innovation occurred on 29 June 1776 when Washington organized a provisional artificer regiment. It was placed under the command of Col. Jonathan Brewer, the barrackmaster, and Deputy Quartermaster General John Parke. The regiment's hired or enlisted craftsmen continued to perform maintenance and construction duties, but they were now assembled into twelve companies for emergency combat duty. Each of the fifty-man companies was given a temporary captain and two lieutenants, mostly former enlisted men or civilians. Seven companies were composed of carpenters, three of smiths, and one of special nautical carpenters. The final company acted as a general maintenance organization. The regiment was dissolved in November.[53]

Although Congress attempted to provide each territorial department with competent military engineers, men with special skills remained rare. Washington brought only Rufus Putnam and Jeduthan Baldwin with him to New York. Putnam served as the Main Army's chief engineer, with assistants merely detailed from the line regiments. Baldwin went to the Northern Department where he operated at Ticonderoga under similar conditions. Both men were rewarded with the rank of engineer colonel, but the lack of special skill at designing fortifications which came only through formal education created weaknesses in the defenses at New York and Ticonderoga. Energy and resources were wasted on works too extensive to be manned adequately by the available forces.[54]

As a capstone to the creation of the larger Continental Army, Congress created a special standing committee to oversee the Army's administration and to make recommendations to Congress. On 24 January 1776 Edward Rutledge, echoing Washington's own concerns, suggested that a war office, similar to Britain's, be established. Washington's pressure and the sheer volume of military business led Congress to establish the Board of War and Ordnance on 12 June. Five delegates, assisted by a permanent secretary, Richard Peters, assumed responsibility for compiling a master roster of all Continental Army officers; for monitoring returns of all troops, arms, and equipment; for maintaining correspondence files; and for securing prisoners of war. The title reflected Congress' deliberate decision to reject the British practice of separating the artillery and engineers from the rest of their troops. The office began functioning on 21 June.[55] Washington heralded this action as "an Event of great importance [which] will be recorded as such in the Historic Page."[56]

Summary

The original plans worked out by Congress, Washington, and Schuyler in 1775 projected a small Continental Army for 1776. Twenty-six infantry, one rifle, and one artillery regiment were allocated to the Main Army and another nine infantry regiments to the Canada-New York army. Standard tables of organization ensured that the regiments would be uniform. When Great Britain committed major forces to North America and expanded the range of the conflict, however, Congress and the individ-

[53]Fitzpatrick, *Writings*, 5:197, 270; Force, *American Archives*, 5th ser., 1:765-66.
[54]*JCC*, 5:630, 732; Fitzpatrick, *Writings*, 5:5, 11, 108, 412; Baldwin, *Revolutionary Journal*, pp. 17-34, 62-63; Smith, *Letters of Delegates*, 3:38, 274, 471-72.
[55]*JCC*, 4:85, 215; 5:434, 438; Smith, *Letters of Delegates*, 3:148. Fitzpatrick, *Writings*, 5:128-29, 200-201.
[56]Fitzpatrick, *Writings*, p. 159.

ual colonies reacted by adding units beyond the number required by the initial, modest plan.

This haphazard growth eventually produced a national military institution in a geographical sense. Congress set up a network of territorial departments and added general officers and staff personnel to provide a coordinated command organization. Although many of the new regiments adopted the standard Continental regimental structure, differences in other units reflected the individual factors which had prompted their creation. Bringing these units into conformity remained a major task if the Army were to become a national institution in every sense.

The units in the north, at Charleston, and at New York City during 1776 came from a wider range of colonies than those that had assembled at Boston and in Canada in 1775. Despite some loss of internal homogeneity, the major field armies in 1776 worked well together. The need to mix militia with the Continental regulars, however, created a new set of problems that became most evident during the defense of New York City against the major British attack that opened in late August.

The American army in Canada was repulsed, but the military situation in the north stabilized after the troops withdrew to Ticonderoga. The forces in the south easily defeated Britain's small efforts to restore royal authority there. Washington's Main Army forced the British out of Boston in March but ran into serious trouble in the defense of New York. General Howe, commanding the largest British army gathered at one place in America during the war, outmaneuvered Washington's mixed force of continentals and militia, first on Long Island and then on Manhattan. The British landing at Kip's Bay on 15 September, which scattered two militia brigades in a humiliating rout, marked the lowest point of this phase of the campaign.

The next day, however, a relatively minor skirmish at Harlem Heights began to restore morale. The aggressiveness of a recently formed provisional unit, Lt. Col. Thomas Knowlton's rangers, supported by the rifle companies of the 3d Virginia Regiment and later by other troops, drove off a British force which included the elite 42d Foot (Black Watch). Other skirmishes at Pelham and Mamaroneck contributed to a restoration of confidence, at least in the Continental units. But it was a temporary resurgence, and worse defeats were still to come. To Washington the major lesson of 1776 was simply that militia could not meet British and German regulars on equal terms. Still smarting from the loss of Long Island, he wrote to the President of Congress on 2 September 1776 that

no dependence could be in a Militia or other troops than those enlisted and embodied for a longer period than our regulations heretofore have prescribed. I am persuaded, and as fully convinced, as I am of any one fact that has happened, that our Liberties must of necessity be greatly hazarded, If not entirely lost, If their defence is left to any but a permanent standing Army, I mean one to exist during the War.[57]

In this atmosphere Congress set out later that month to provide a new army to succeed the one whose enlistments expired at the end of the year.

CHAPTER 5

An Army for the War: 1777

Most Continental enlistments expired on 31 December 1776. Congress and Washington hoped to avoid a recurrence of the problems of the previous winter by beginning their preparations for reorganizing the Continental Army during the early fall of 1776. Profiting from that earlier experience, they not only started sooner but also retained the idea of developing plans in conferences between Congress and military leaders. The reorganization was applied to troops from every colony through the first comprehensive legislation to rationalize the ad hoc growth of the previous year. The central factor in the new plan was the nearly unanimous decision to recruit for the duration of the war rather than for a single year as in the past. Congress approved the proposals in September and modified them somewhat during the winter to adjust to changes that had occurred during the final phases of the 1776 campaign. Other modifications in Army organization came in 1777 when the Main Army gained its first experience in a war of maneuver rather than in a strict defense of fixed positions. The battles of 1777 would reveal the strengths and weaknesses of this planning effort.

The Eighty-Eight Battalion Resolve

The decisions made in Congress during September and early October 1776 determined the basic size and nature of the Continental Army for the rest of the war. Although delegates of various political persuasions agreed on the general outline of the new policy, there was extensive disagreement on details. The proposals first adopted by Congress settled the size of the Army, its apportionment among the several states, the conditions of enlistment, and the compensation for officers and men. Congress also approved amendments to the Articles of War.

Americans adamantly opposed long enlistments during the first year and a half of the Revolution. In addition to citing the precedent of the Provincials' one-year enlistments, politicians affirmed the ideal of a militia of citizen-soldiers rather than a standing army. Attitudes began to change during the summer of 1776, and even John Adams conceded that the newly independent nation needed "a regular Army, and the most masterly Discipline, because...without these We cannot reasonably hope to be a powerful, a prosperous, or a free People."[1] During the summer a number of new units were raised for three years' service. The lessons of the defeats in New York accelerated this change. By the fall delegates were in universal agreement that British and Ger-

---

[1] Burnett, *Letters*, 2:61.

man regulars could be opposed successfully on the battlefield only by a large body of trained and disciplined continentals.[2]

Once this agreement had been reached, Congress on 2 September 1776 directed the Board of War to draft a comprehensive plan. The board submitted its proposals on 9 September, and Congress devoted the next week to debates and amendments, settling details relating to enlistments, bounties, and state quotas. On 16 September it adopted the amended plan. Known as the eighty-eight battalion resolve, it called for eighty-eight regiments organized according to the structure approved in 1776. Congress' estimates of the population of each state governed its allocation of regiments. (*Table 4*) Quotas ranged from fifteen regiments each from Massachusetts and Virginia, to single regiments from Delaware and Georgia, the smallest states. Congress intended to retain existing regiments through reenlistment and to add additional ones only in cases where a state's quota exceeded its actual regiments. It approved cash bonuses and liberal postwar land grants to make enlisting for the duration of the war more attractive. Congress continued to commission all officers while allowing individual states to actually name the officers up to and including colonels. The states were expected to provide the arms, clothing, and other equipment for their respective regiments; they could withhold part of the men's pay to cover the cost of uniforms.[3]

Congress anticipated that the longer enlistment would increase discipline and training in the Army. No longer would there be a wholesale reorganization each winter. On 20 September Congress also modified the Articles of War. Washington had decided during the summer that the existing Articles did not sufficiently deter misbehavior, and in late July he had sent Judge Advocate William Tudor to Philadelphia to discuss a revision. Tudor and a congressional committee which included some of the finest legal minds in America produced the draft that Congress adopted. It expanded the number of articles to seventy-six, inserting material from the British Articles that had been omitted in earlier versions. The central changes added to the list of capital crimes and increased the maximum corporal punishment from 39 to 100 lashes. This version remained in effect for the rest of the war. Accompanying legislation commissioned Tudor as a lieutenant colonel and authorized deputy judge advocates to assist him in dealing with mounting casework.[4]

Before Washington learned of these September resolutions, he wrote a letter to Congress on 24 September requesting immediate action to reorganize the Army for the new year and improve discipline. His eloquent appeal overcame lingering objections and raised other issues. In particular, he asked Congress to increase the pay for officers and to furnish free uniforms to the men. Congress increased officers' salaries on 7 October and approved annual uniform allowances the next day.[5]

---

[2]Ibid., 1:319, 360–61, 505–6; 2:44–45, 57, 78–79, 98–100, 106–7; Henderson, *Party Politics*, pp., 102–5; White, "Standing Armies," pp. 128–35, 143–44; Cress, "The Standing Army, the Militia, and the New Republic," pp. 138–43.

[3]*JCC*, 5:729, 747, 749, 751, 756–57, 762–63; Burnett, *Letters*, 2:82–83, 88–89, 95–100, 102, 105–7. The system conformed to procedures laid down in the Articles of Confederation, although that document did not go into effect until 1781.

[4]*JCC*, 5:788–807; 7:265–66; Force, *American Archives*, 5th ser., 1:576; Burnett, *Letters*, 2:54–57; Fitzpatrick, *Writings*, 5:194–95; 6:91–92, 125, 147, 151. The copying was so extensive that courts-martial transcripts were required to be sent to the Secretary at War, an office which did not exist in the United States until 1781.

[5]Fitzpatrick, *Writings*, 6:106–16; *JCC*, 5:853–56.

TABLE 4—DISTRIBUTION OF REGIMENTS 1777

State	Estimated 1775 Population (in thousands)[a]	Infantry Regiment Quota 16 Sep 1776	Actual Infantry Regiments Raised Under Quota	Additional Regiments (Infantry)	Extra Regiments (Infantry)	Artillery Regiments	Light Dragoon Regiments	Total
New Hampshire	100	3	3	b	0	0	0	3
Massachusetts......	350	15	15	3	0	1	0	19
Rhode Island.......	58	2	2	$1/2$[c]	0	0	0	$2^1/2$
Connecticut........	200	8	8	$1^1/2$[d]	0	$1/2$[e]	1	11
New York.........	200	4	5	$1/2$[f]	0	$1/2$[e]	0	6
New Jersey	130	4	4	2	0	0	0	6
Pennsylvania	300	12	13[g]	$2^1/2$[h]	$1/2$[i]	1	1	18
Delaware	30	1	1	0	0	0	0	1
Maryland..........	250	8	7	0	1[j]	0	0	8
Virginia	400	15	15	3	0	1	2	21
North Carolina	200	9	9	1	0	0	0	10
South Carolina	200	6	5	0	0	1[k]	0	6
Georgia	25	1	5	0	0	0	0	5
Other	0	0	0	0	3[l]	0	0	3
Total	2,443	88	92	14	$4^1/2$	5	4	$119^1/2$

[a]Evarts B. Greene and Virginia D. Harrington, *American Population Before the Federal Census of 1790* (New York: Columbia University Press, 1935), p. 7.

[b]Scammell's Regiment planned but not raised.

[c]Half of Sherburne's raised; Cornell's planned but not raised.

[d]Webb's and half of Sherburne's.

[e]Lamb's raised half in New York and half in Connecticut.

[f]Half of Malcolm's.

[g]State Regiment subsequently 13th Pennsylvania Regiment.

[h]Includes half of Malcolm's.

[i]Half of German Battalion.

[j]Half of German Battalion; the remaining half of Maryland and Virginia Rifle Regiment.

[k]4th South Carolina Regiment remained artillery.

[l]1st and 2d Canadian Regiments and Warner's Regiment.

Washington wanted Congress to complete the reorganization before winter. At his urging, Congress requested the states to send legislative committees to Washington's headquarters and to Ticonderoga to discuss the retention of highly qualified officers. At the same time, Washington ordered the generals to compile by state lists of officers worthy of promotion or retention. When the liaison committees did not appear promptly, Congress on 4 November gave Washington and Schuyler the power to act on behalf of those states which had not yet sent committees. November also brought news that Massachusetts had promised to supplement the pay of its enlisted men and that other states were considering a similar course. Washington strongly opposed this trend. He warned that in the long run it would unbalance recruiting and foster jealousy. Congress agreed to forbid the practice on 12 November, but to overcome the reluctance of many men to enlist for an indefinite period, it allowed individuals to enlist for a fixed period of three years instead of for the duration of the war.[6]

[6]Fitzpatrick, *Writings*, 6:152–56, 186–90, 200–201, 271–73, 289–90; *JCC*, 5:854–56; 6:920–21, 944–45; Burnett, *Letters*, 2:115–16, 139–41, 143–44, 154–59.

Trenton and Princeton

In the early fall of 1776, Washington and Congress assumed that operations were about to halt for the winter. The regiments would then have ample opportunity to re- group, reenlist their men, recruit, and complete preliminary training. When General Howe continued his offensive around New York City into early December, he upset those calculations. Washington's Main Army experimented with a new internal orga- nization, won smashing triumphs at Trenton and Princeton, New Jersey, and incorpo- rated the lessons of this first real experience with a fluid battlefield situation into its basic tactical philosophy.

During the brief lull after the inconclusive battle of White Plains on 28 October 1776, Washington divided his Main Army to guard against several possible courses of action by General Howe. Maj. Gen. Charles Lee remained in Westchester County with a corps to prevent an invasion of Connecticut. Washington personally led another corps into New Jersey to bar the route to Philadelphia. A third, smaller force under Maj. Gen. William Heath moved into garrison in the Hudson Highlands to preserve the lines of communication in that strategic area. Howe's capture of Fort Washington be- fore it could be evacuated, however, not only deprived Washington of its large garri- son but also unhinged his dispositions. Lt. Gen. Charles, Earl Cornwallis, quickly drove a wedge between Washington and the other American elements and forced the conti- nentals to withdraw across the Delaware River. Howe ended the campaign on 14 De- cember and ordered his army into winter quarters.

Howe assigned Trenton, one of his most advanced outposts, to Col. Johann Gott- lieb Rall's reinforced Hessian brigade. Rall's regiments were among the best German auxiliary forces, but they were worn out, seriously short of officers, and handicapped by a cumbersome regimental organization. (*Chart 6*) Hesse-Cassel had modeled its army after Prussia's, giving each infantry regiment two 5-company battalions plus a grenadier company. The British had altered that formation before the regiments left Europe. The grenadier companies were detached to form 4-company grenadier battal- ions, and each regiment was divided into two single-battalion regiments. The new regi- ment was still large, but it had a small number of officers. It contained 5 companies for administrative purposes but fought in 8 platoons. Before it could fight, it required time to regroup into platoons. At Trenton the Hessians were billeted by company.[7]

Washington regrouped his forces behind the Delaware River. Units partially re- equipped themselves with supplies brought forward from Philadelphia. Volunteers (associators) turned out from the Pennsylvania militia, and on 20 December Conti- nental reinforcements arrived from the north. A British cavalry patrol captured Lee on 13 December, but Maj. Gen. John Sullivan took command of Lee's three brigades and marched them around the British to join Washington. As soon as Generals Schuyler and Gates learned of the fall of Fort Washington, they sent all the troops they could spare from Ticonderoga to bolster the Commander in Chief. Four regi-

[7]Carl Leopold Baurmeister, *Revolution in America: Confidential Letters and Journals, 1776–1784, of Adjutant General Major Baurmeister of the Hessian Forces*, ed. Bernard A. Uhlendorf (New Brunswick: Rutgers University Press, 1957), pp. 6–17, 72–79; Ernst Kipping, *Die Truppen von Hessian-Kassel in Amerikanischen Unabhangigkeitskrieg, 1776–1783* (Darmstadt: Wehr und Wissen Verlagsgesellchaft M. B. H., 1965), pp. 27–28; British Headquarters Papers, No. 10 (copy of treaty between Britain and Hesse- Cassel, 15 Jan 76).

CHART 6—HESSE-CASSEL INFANTRY REGIMENT 1776

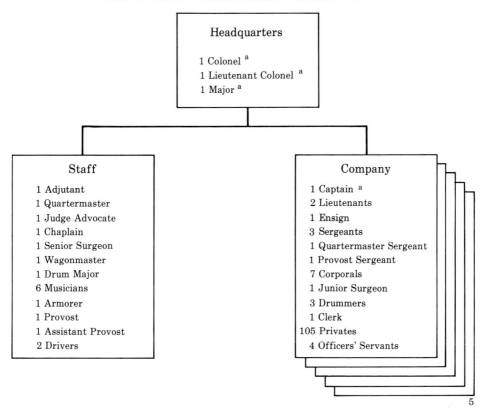

a. Each field officer was also the captain of a company; only 2 of the 5 companies actually had all 4 company officers.

ments under Brig. Gen. Arthur St. Clair proceeded directly to Pennsylvania; three others diverted to Morristown, New Jersey, to threaten the British flank.[8]

Heath's division, at Washington's specific orders, remained in the Hudson Highlands to protect critically important ferries and distract the British garrison in New York City. As early as 8 November 1775 Congress had recognized that the Highlands region was the only area between New York City and Albany where the Hudson River could be blocked to warships. The commandant of the fortifications—at first a colonel but later a brigadier general—had been the senior Continental officer in the region during most of 1776. Heath's assignment transformed the Highlands into a de facto territorial department, a status which its strategic importance preserved for the rest of the war.[9]

---

[8]Sullivan, *Letters and Papers*, 1:302; Force, *American Archives*, 5th ser., 3:1125, 1260; Gates Orderly Book (Gates' General Orders for 5–18 Nov 76); Gates Papers (Gates to Schuyler, 30 Sep 76; to Ward, 9 Nov 76; to Hancock, 27 Nov 76; to Col Joseph Vose, 8 Dec 76; to Washington, 12 Dec 76; Robert H. Harrison to Gates, 26 Nov 76; Schuyler to Gates, 26 Nov 76; St. Clair to Gates, 27 Nov 76; Heath to Gates, 14 Dec 76); Fitzpatrick, *Writings*, 6:414–16, 419.

[9]*JCC*, 3:337–38; Fitzpatrick, *Writings*, 5:10–11, 123, 138–39, 317–19, 340–41, 435–56; 6:242–45, 257–58, 284–87; 16:150–54; Robert K. Wright, Jr., "Too Little, Too Late: The Campaign of 1777 in the Hudson Highlands" (Master's thesis, College of William and Mary, 1971), pp. 30–40.

GENERAL RETURN, MAIN ARMY, 22 DECEMBER 1776. *This return of Washington's troops in eastern Pennsylvania became the basic document for evaluating the Army's ability to counterattack at Trenton, New Jersey, four days later. The 1776 version differs from the 1775 return because the later form now groups individual regiments into tactical brigades. This change was the major innovation of the Trenton and Princeton campaign. Returns in subsequent years normally listed only brigades and separate regiments.*

GEORGE BAYLOR *(1752–84) served as Washington's aide and was selected to carry dispatches to Congress announcing the Trenton victory. Baylor received command of the new 3d Continental Light Dragoon Regiment as a reward. (Miniature attributed to Charles Willson Peale, ca. 1778.)*

Washington knew that ending the year on a positive note would encourage recruiting. He also wanted to regain control of New Jersey. After exploring the possibilities and ordering the harassment of British garrisons, he decided to strike Trenton. His plan for a night attack was tailored to his available forces. The task of sealing the town off to prevent reinforcement or escape went to militia supported by a single Continental brigade. The actual assault was carried out by his other seven Continental brigades using coordinated columns. Washington shifted from the regiment to the brigade as the basic combat element for this counterattack because attrition had eroded the effective strength of most of his regiments to dangerously low levels. An additional innovation was that an artillery company directly supported each brigade.

A return of 22 December 1776 indicates that the infantry strength of the actual attack force—the seven brigades less detachments—totaled 33 field officers, 412 company officers, 368 sergeants, and 5,820 rank and file. These figures do not include St. Clair's four regiments, which did not submit a return.[10] Only two of the brigades contained substantially more than the official strength of a regiment. On the other hand, the ratio of officers and sergeants to rank and file was higher than usual, and the artillery company added materially to the firepower of each brigade, particularly in adverse weather. At Trenton, and at Princeton a week later, Washington's brigade commanders used both of these factors to advantage. Improved control paid particular dividends as brigades executed complex maneuvers at night and adjusted to rapidly changing battlefield conditions. Washington's army destroyed Rall's brigade at Trenton, severely mauled a detached British brigade at Princeton, and maneuvered the British out of all but a small toehold in New Jersey.

Thus in the space of little more than a week, Washington's small, veteran cadre shattered two enemy brigades and recovered most of New Jersey. In destroying the German auxiliaries' aura of invincibility as well, he robbed Howe of a major psychological advantage. Morale was generally restored. Washington spent the next several months digesting the lessons of this brief campaign, with its introduction to the techniques of mobile warfare. He rewarded those subordinates who had performed well under pressure with his trust, and he concluded that the campaign had demonstrated the value of a brigade composed of several infantry regiments and an artillery company. Hereafter it became the basic element of the Main Army.

Rounding Out the Army

The retreat through New Jersey had made Washington acutely aware of Howe's numerical strength and specifically his advantage in artillery and cavalry.[10] In a series of letters to Congress during December 1776, the Commander in Chief pressed for more men. Additional infantry regiments, more artillery, and a force of cavalry headed his list of needs. Congress, impressed by the December crisis, acted upon those requests within a month. As a result, the Continental Army of 1777 became a more balanced force than that envisioned on 16 September. Washington would be able to organize the Army into elements capable of competing with the British in open battle.

Washington's generals concurred with him in requesting additional strength. Central to the Army's position was a recommendation to increase the infantry battalions from the 88 called for in September to a minimum of 110. Henry Knox had submitted a plan to raise 5 artillery regiments to support the full Army. Washington transmitted the plan to Congress with a recommendation that 3 regiments of artillery would be sufficient for the Main Army and the other forces in the northern half of the country. He also favored promoting Knox to brigadier general. In addition, the Commander in Chief asked for several new staff officers, a force of cavalry, and one brigadier general for every three infantry regiments and one major general for every three brigades. He asked Congress also to confirm preliminary steps he had taken during the retreat through New Jersey to raise additional infantry companies and to accept New York's offer to raise a fifth regiment.[11]

Congress' response was slowed when the delegates fled from Philadelphia to Baltimore. It finally acted on Washington's requests on 27 December. It elected Knox brigadier general of artillery, directed Washington to establish the additional staff offices he required, and delegated to the Commander in Chief a number of emergency powers. It also ordered him to prepare a comprehensive system for promotions; Congress specified that officers should rise by seniority both within a regiment to the rank of captain and within a state's "line" through field officer grades. A state's line consisted of its quota of infantry regiments established in September. The most important element of the 27 December action, however, was contained in the following resolution:

Congress, having maturely considered the present crisis; and having perfect reliance on the wisdom, vigour, and uprightness of General Washington, do, hereby, *Resolve*, That General Washington shall be, and he is hereby, vested with full, ample, and complete powers to raise and collect together, in the most speedy and effectual manner, from any or all of these United

---

[10]RG 93, National Archives (Return of the Forces...on the Banks of Delaware, 22 Dec 76). John Chester's regiment in Paul Dudley Sargent's brigade did not participate in the attack. Lesser prints a version of this return but incorrectly identifies some of the units, *Sinews*, p. 43.

[11]Fitzpatrick, *Writings*, 6:332–33, 350–51, 379–84, 400–409; Force, *American Archives*, 5th ser., 3: 1310–14.

States, 16 battalions of infantry, in addition to those already voted by Congress; to appoint officers for the said battalions; to raise, officer, and equip three thousand light horse; three regiments of artillery, and a corps of engineers, and to establish their pay....[12]

Unlike the September regiments, the "sixteen additional regiments," the artillery regiments, and the light horse were organized directly by Continental authority rather than by the authority of the state governments and were placed completely under Washington's control. The resolution gave Washington the requested 110 regiments, for in addition to the 16 new regiments and the 88 units of the September quotas, there were 6 regiments raised by Congress the previous summer which were not explicitly tied to a single state. Actually, only 3 of these 6 regiments retained a distinct character as "extras" after the winter: Warner's (largely from the Vermont area) and the 1st and 2d Canadian Regiments. The other 3 actually were counted against state quotas. Dubois' Regiment, a predominantly New York unit, passed into that state's reorganized line when the quota was increased to five regiments. Maryland counted its portions of the German Battalion and the Maryland and Virginia Rifle Regiment as the eighth regiment of its line quota.[13]

Washington had expected Congress to accept any men raised in excess of the September quotas, and he had begun to recruit even before he learned of the new resolve. On 21 December he told Brig. Gen. William Maxwell to ask competent officers omitted from New Jersey's reorganization to recruit at least fifty men. Washington promised to make them captains with power to select their own subalterns, subject only to his final confirmation. He made the same offer on 24 December to Col. Samuel Griffin, formerly of the Flying Camp. By this time Washington had concluded that the state legislatures were retaining infantry officers on political grounds rather than on military merit. This practice and New England's reduced 1777 quotas under the September reorganization were depriving the Army of many competent leaders. The new legislation offered a way to overcome both problems, and as he settled into quarters at Morristown in January, he began organizing the new regiments. He assumed that Congress wanted them apportioned geographically, and he acted accordingly. (*See Table 4.*)[14]

Seven additional regiments were planned for New England. Henry Jackson was selected to command a regiment from Boston, which previously had not fielded a unit. Jackson had a reputation as a military expert, and he drew key officers from the town's Independent Company of Cadets. A second regiment was given to William Lee, the lieutenant colonel of the 14th Continental Regiment. The 14th had declined to reenlist as a unit under the 1777 reorganization, but sufficient members remained to justify using it as the cadre for another additional regiment from Massachusetts. Deputy Adjutant General David Henley, who earlier had served as the brigade major of Heath's Brigade, was given a third Massachusetts regiment as a reward for excellent staff service during the 1776 campaign. Washington expected Henley to be successful in recruiting because of his numerous contacts. Massachusetts' subsequent problems in filling its line quota of infantry regiments and its assigned artillery regi-

[12]*JCC*, 6:1040, 1043–46. A companion piece of legislation directed a liaison committee, left in Philadelphia when Congress departed, to establish a magazine and ammunition laboratory (factory) at Carlisle, Pennsylvania. A state's line was an administrative device rather than a tactical entity.
[13]Samuel Adams, *Writings*, 3:342–46; Fitzpatrick, *Writings*, 7:138.
[14]Fitzpatrick, *Writings*, 6:415–16, 429–30; 7:417–19.

ment, however, forced Washington to give the additional regiments from that state a low recruiting priority, and they remained at Boston during the 1777 campaign.[15]

The other four New England additional regiments suffered problems as well. Ezekiel Cornell of Rhode Island, another deputy adjutant general and a former lieutenant colonel of the 11th Continental Regiment, turned down Washington's offer of a regiment to command the brigade of state troops that Rhode Island raised in 1777. Alexander Scammell, Sullivan's protege and also a deputy adjutant general, declined a regiment to accept command of the 3d New Hampshire Regiment. No further efforts were made to raise either of these regiments. Greater success came in Connecticut. Samuel Blatchley Webb, one of Washington's aides, made substantial progress in raising a regiment there once he received support from the state government. Connecticut and Rhode Island jointly furnished the base for the last regiment; Henry Sherburne of the latter state received the command in recognition of his gallantry at The Cedars. Although the regiment took the field in 1777, it was never able to organize all its companies.[16]

The state affiliation of the five additional regiments Washington allocated to the middle portion of the country was less clear. In contrast to New England, where he had a large body of former continentals, in the middle states, Washington had to draw officers from veterans of the previous summer's militia forces. Col. William Malcolm, who had commanded a New York City militia regiment for most of 1776, was given one regiment. Brig. Gen. George Clinton and his brigade major, Albert Pawling (who became the new regiment's major), raised four of its companies in New York. Brig. Gen. John Armstrong organized the other four companies in Pennsylvania. The regiment did not assemble as a unit until October. Two veteran New Jersey militia leaders, David Forman and Oliver Spencer, raised regiments with cadres from New Jersey. In building his regiment, Forman made use of preliminary work done by Col. Samuel Griffin, who had turned down the command because he expected to become a general.[17]

The other two regiments were based primarily in Pennsylvania, although recruits came from neighboring areas as well. Following the recommendation of Richard Henry Lee, Washington gave one command to Thomas Hartley, the lieutenant colonel of the 6th Pennsylvania Battalion. Like most commanders of additional regiments, Hartley had a wide latitude in selecting his junior officers. Acting Adjutant General Morgan Connor (the major of the 1st Continental Regiment) became Hartley's lieutenant colonel when James Wilkinson, a Northern Department staff officer, declined. John Patton, who had commanded a battalion of the Pennsylvania State Rifle Regiment with distinction during operations around New York, received command of the other regiment, with Assistant Quartermaster General John Parke and Brigade Major Peter Scull as field officers.[18]

Washington was sensitive to criticism that implied he favored his native south, and he was circumspect in commissioning additional officers from that region. Georgia and the Carolinas, lying outside the sphere of his immediate command, did not appear at all. He also excused Maryland from a direct role in the regiments because of

[15]Ibid., 6:433, 499–500; 7:86–87, 136–40, 165–66.
[16]Ibid., 6:499, 505–6; 7:11, 132–33.
[17]Ibid., 6:476, 494; 7:33–34, 93, 191, 389; 9:364, 461.
[18]Ibid., 6:490, 493, 498–99; 7:60n, 374–75; *JCC*, 12:1225–26.

DAVID FORMAN *(1745–?) of New Jersey or-*
ganized Forman's Additional Continental
Regiment in 1777 after demonstrating skill
as a militia commander in the 1776 cam-
paign around New York City. (Portrait by
Charles Willson Peale, ca. 1784.)

its responsibilities for the rifle regiment and the German Battalion. Washington initially allotted only two regiments to Virginia. Both commands went to close associates:
William Grayson, one of Washington's aides, and the noted frontiersman Nathaniel
Gist. Grayson recruited in northern Virginia and in nearby Maryland, where his future brother-in-law, Brig. Gen. William Smallwood, had great influence. Gist's was a
special light infantry regiment. He was to raise four companies on the southern frontier
as rangers and then enlist up to 500 Cherokees and other southern Indians to serve
with the regiment as scouts. Their presence was intended also to ensure their tribes'
good behavior. Washington reluctantly added a third Virginia regiment two months
later. Lord Stirling had grouped three volunteer Virginia companies into a provisional
battalion under Capt. Charles Mynn Thruston, a powerful political leader in the Shenandoah Valley. When they performed well in northern New Jersey, Washington told
Thurston to recruit a regiment in the northwestern part of the state, but Thurston had
little success in filling his unit.[19]

Because of serious recruiting problems, Washington attempted to raise only 15 of
the 16 approved regiments, and 2 of those were stillborn when their colonels declined
the commands. Although some of the additional regiments were quite successful, none
could compete equally with the regiments organized under the September 1776 state
quotas. On 17 June 1777 Congress approved North Carolina's offer to raise another
regiment under Col. Abraham Sheppard. At least 300 of its men were required to report to Washington within a reasonable period, but this sixteenth additional regiment
was absorbed within a year during a reorganization of the weak North Carolina line.[20]

The three artillery regiments authorized by Congress on 27 December, like the sixteen additionals, represented an expansion requested by Washington rather than a
new departure. The September quotas had not mentioned artillery, and Washington

---

[19]Ibid., 6:491–92, 494–96; 7:6–7, 11–12, 102, 201–2, 229, 295–97, 307–8.
[20]Steuben Papers (Scammell to Frederick Steuben, 25 Sep 79); *JCC*, 8:475.

presumably was free to use one or two of the eighty-eight regiments for that purpose. During December Colonel Knox prepared a plan for five artillery regiments to properly support the enlarged Continental Army. Knox's plan called for artillery regiments for every geographical region, not just for the Main Army. On his own authority Washington ordered Knox to begin recruiting three of those regiments to support the forces in the central portion of the nation. His request to Congress, and Congress' 27 December authorization, dealt with those regiments.[21]

Like the infantry regiment, the artillery regiment of 1777 followed the same general organization which had prevailed during 1776. Congress did not change the allocation of staff and company officer positions or the division of the regiment into a dozen companies. It did make two changes. The number of field officers dropped from 5 to 3, since the total pool of artillery field officers was now large enough to allow for detachment without crippling the regiment. The second change regrouped the enlisted men in each company; the number of matrosses dropped from 32 to 28, and the specialists and noncommissioned officers now consisted of 6 sergeants, 6 corporals, 6 bombardiers, and 6 gunners. This arrangement provided balanced crews for up to six guns, plus an ammunition section within each company.

The Trenton campaign disrupted matters, but Knox was able to begin recruiting once the Main Army settled into quarters at Morristown. Continued support for the Main Army was provided by state artillery units under Maj. Thomas Proctor (two Pennsylvania companies) and Capt. Alexander Hamilton (one New York company), and by Capt. Sebastian Bauman's Continental company. The officers of the old 1776 artillery regiment set out to recruit. Two of the new regiments, commanded by majors of the 1776 regiment, relied on veterans for cadres. John Crane, a native Bostonian, raised 9 companies in Massachusetts. John Lamb, recently released by the British, recruited in the area between Connecticut and Philadelphia. Nine of his companies were new— 3 from New York, 2 from Pennsylvania, and 4 from Connecticut, where Lamb's family had moved after the fall of New York City. The other 3 companies were existing units. Bauman's Company and Hamilton's (under the command of John Doughty of New Jersey) were assigned intact. Isaiah Wool added new recruits to the remnants of Lamb's 1775 company.[22]

Washington and Knox intended to organize their third new artillery regiment from the Middle Department, using Proctor's Pennsylvania companies supplemented by companies from New Jersey and Maryland. Pennsylvania undermined this plan by expanding the Pennsylvania state artillery into a ten-company regiment under Proctor on 6 February 1777. The state then transferred the regiment to the Continental Army during the summer of 1777 with only ten companies instead of the twelve Knox had intended.[23]

Artillerymen also supported the other territorial departments. Capt. Ebenezer Stevens of Knox's regiment acted as the senior artillery officer in the Northern De-

[21]Force, *American Archives*, 5th ser., 3:1314; Fitzpatrick, *Writings*, 6:401.

[22]Fitzpatrick, *Writings*, 7:82, 138–39, 263, 467; 8:276, 460; 12:71–72; 18:303–4; John Lamb Papers (to Washington, 12 Mar 79; to Board of General Officers, 6 Aug 79; Knox to Lamb, 13 and 20 Apr 77, 24 May 77, and 17 and 22 Jan 80; Eleazur Oswald to Lamb, 16 Feb, 7 Apr, 17 Jun, and 23 Jul 77; Crane to Washington, 16 Mar 79 (copy); Report of Board of General Officers on Artillery Ranks, 8 Aug 79), New-York Historical Society.

[23]*JCC*, 8:482–83, 551, 564; 12:865; Burnett, *Letters*, 2:427; Fitzpatrick, *Writings*, 8:386, 415; 15:80–81; *Pennsylvania Archives*, 1st ser., 5:234–35, 357, 451, 455; 6:676–77; 7:121; 2d ser., 1:713.

THOMAS FORREST *(1747–1825) of Pennsylvania is typical of the talented men who served in the Continental Army. He rose from captain to lieutenant colonel in the 4th Continental Artillery Regiment and served in Congress from 1819 to 1823. (Portrait by Charles Willson Peale, 1820.)*

partment during 1776, and in November a congressional delegation directed him to reorganize that department's artillery forces for the coming year. Using veteran troops at Ticonderoga as cadres, Stevens reorganized three companies using Massachusetts recruits. He recruited a fourth company, composed of artificers to perform maintenance, at Albany from miscellaneous personnel. Stevens believed throughout 1777 that he commanded a separate corps, but in fact his companies were part of Crane's regiment, which they joined in 1778.[24] Two regiments in the Southern Department provided the total of five which Knox had contemplated. One was the 4th South Carolina Regiment. Congress had authorized the other on 26 November 1776 by expanding two existing companies in Virginia into a ten-company regiment under Col. Charles Harrison and Lt. Col. Edward Carrington. It remained in garrison in its home state throughout 1777.[25]

Knox's original proposal also encompassed the special logistical requirements of the artillery. He wanted Congress to create a company of artificers, to regroup the staff of the Commissary of Military Stores, and to establish laboratories and a foundry so that the Army could begin producing its own cannon, ammunition, and related items. He and Washington recommended that Congress import weapons from Europe until those facilities came into service. The most essential materiel, they argued, was a mobile train of brass field pieces consistent in makeup with European practice: one hundred 3-pounders, fifty 6-pounders, and fifty 12-pounders, plus a number of heavier 18- and 24-pounders for general support and sieges. Congress promised to obtain these pieces.[26]

---

[24]Lamb Papers (Oswald to Lamb, 16 Feb 77; Knox to Lamb, 20 Apr and 24 May 77); Fitzpatrick, *Writings*, 8:276.

[25]*JCC*, 6:981, 995; 8:396, 514, 655; Fitzpatrick, *Writings*, 8:117; 9:332; 10:520; *Virginia Gazette* (Dixon and Hunter), 28 Feb 77. The Virginia regiment's companies contained 4 officers, 1 sergeant, 4 corporals, 4 bombardiers, 8 gunners, and 48 matrosses.

[26]Fitzpatrick, *Writings*, 6:280–82; *JCC*, 6:963.

After some discussion Congress established a foundry at Philadelphia and laboratories at Carlisle, Pennsylvania, and Springfield, Massachusetts. The latter sites served throughout the rest of the war as ordnance depots for Army operations in the northern half of the country. Knox personally supervised the creation of the Springfield laboratory. The somewhat larger Carlisle establishment came under the authority of Lt. Col. Benjamin Flower, who had been commissary of military stores for the Flying Camp in 1776. At the same time, Flower recruited two companies of ordnance technicians and repairmen who, unlike the hired artisans of earlier years, were full-time soldiers. Capt. Isaac Coren, the "Director of the Laboratory for the United States," commanded one company, which was located at Carlisle and had a standard artillery company organization. The second company, led by a master carpenter, consisted of a full range of skilled workers to maintain the Main Army's artillery park, or general reserve.[27]

During the winter Washington and Knox addressed the problem of improving the mobility of the field artillery to furnish direct support to the infantry. During the Trenton campaign each infantry brigade had been supported by a company of artillery with two to four guns. This experiment proved so successful that the concept of a direct support company remained a fixture of the Continental Army for the remainder of the war. Other artillery companies served in the artillery park or manned the heavy garrison artillery of fixed fortifications. The brigade support company, preferably from the same state as the infantry, varied its armament according to the brigade's particular mission. The ideal armament consisted of two 6-pounders in 1777, although this weapon required the largest crew of any field piece—twelve to fifteen men including an officer. Since doctrine called for concentrated fire on enemy infantry, rate of fire and maneuverability were more important than range.[28]

During 1775 and 1776 the Continental Army relied primarily on old British artillery pieces imported during the colonial period or captured in the first actions of the war. The other source of cannon was domestic production of iron guns. The American iron industry was producing 30,000 tons of bar and pig iron in 1775, one-seventh of the world's total. It quickly turned to military production. Unfortunately, these sources contributed few weapons suitable for battlefield use. Most cannon were so heavy that they were limited to permanent fortifications. Washington counted on the foundry in Philadelphia and foreign imports to provide the lighter brass guns for the direct support companies.[29]

The imports came primarily from France. The French and, to a lesser extent, the Spanish governments furnished clandestine aid to the American colonies through the firm of Hortalez and Company in the hope of weakening Great Britain. Indirectly at

[27]Fitzpatrick, *Writings*, 6:474; 7:18–23; 8:38; *Pennsylvania Archives*, 1st ser., 5:209–10.
[28]Fitzpatrick, *Writings*, 6:364, 454; 8:100–101, 175, 235, 318–21, 396–99, 457–58; 9:290; Lamb Papers (Oswald to Lamb, 17 and 25 Jun, 23 and 25 Jul, and 14 Aug 77; Walker to Lamb, 21 Jul 77; Moodie to Lamb, 9 May 77; Knox to Lamb, 2 Dec 77). Washington similarly sought to improve the maneuverability of ammunition wagons: Fitzpatrick, *Writings*, 7:83.
[29]Force, *American Archives*, 4th ser., 4:534–35; Fairfax Downey, "Birth of the Continental Artillery," *Military Collector and Historian* 7 (1955):61–62; Keach Johnson, "The Genesis of the Baltimore Ironworks," *Journal of Southern History* 19 (1953):151–79; Irene D. Neu, "The Iron Plantations of Colonial New York," *New York History* 33 (1952):3–24; Spencer C. Tucker, "Cannon Founders of the American Revolution," *National Defense* 60 (1975):33–37; Salay, "Arming for War," pp. 202, 241–75; Fitzpatrick, *Writings*, 7:69; 8:37.

first and more openly later, the French shipped to America over 200 artillery pieces and over 100,000 1763-model Charleville muskets, as well as other supplies. The first shipment arrived at Portsmouth, New Hampshire, in April 1777. Knox judged twenty-three French 4-pounders too cumbersome for American conditions and sent them to Springfield to be melted down and recast. The other guns were sent to the Main army.[30]

The Continental Army's artillerymen turned to John Muller's *Treatise of Artillery* as a handbook for mounting these guns and casting their own. Muller's work had first appeared in 1757 as a textbook for the Royal Military Academy at Woolwich, and an American edition appeared in Philadelphia in 1779 dedicated to the Continental Artillery. His proposals were particularly important to Americans for he called for mobile iron guns and offered detailed instructions for casting them and for constructing light carriages.[31]

The emphasis on mobility extended to the third element in Congress' 27 December legislation. Unlike the additional infantry regiments and the expanded artillery, the 3,000 light horse represented a new element in the Continental Army. Most European armies still used heavy cavalry as an offensive battlefield force. During the middle of the century a renewed interest in reconnaissance and skirmishing had led to the return of some light horsemen. The terrain in America had eliminated the need for heavy cavalry during the colonial period, although some troopers had served as messengers or scouts. By the start of the Revolution a few colonies had regiments of mounted men, but they were mobile infantry rather than true cavalry. The cost of owning, feeding, and equipping a horse ensured that the men of such units came from the social elite.

The British Army's large cavalry contingent was organized for European combat. As a result, only two light cavalry regiments served in America during the Revolution. The 17th Light Dragoons arrived in Boston in May 1775 and served throughout the war; the 16th reached New York in October 1776 and remained for only two years. Each regiment consisted of six troops plus a small headquarters consisting of a titular colonel, a lieutenant colonel, a major, an adjutant, a chaplain, and a surgeon. Each troop initially contained a captain, a lieutenant, a cornet (equivalent to an infantry ensign), a quartermaster, 2 sergeants, 2 corporals, a hautboy (drummer), and 38 privates. In the spring of 1776 the establishment of a troop was increased by another cornet, a sergeant, 2 corporals, and 30 privates. General Howe was given the option of either mounting the augmentation with locally procured horses or using the men as light infantry.[32] One German cavalry regiment, the Brunswick Dragoon Regiment von Riedesel, served in Canada, but as infantry.[33]

Several times during 1775 and 1776 Congress toyed with the idea of adding mounted units to the Continental forces in the north, but it did not act since operations were largely static. The ranger regiments authorized in 1776 in the south were

[30]Force, *American Archives*, 5th ser., 1:1011–23; Burnett, *Letters*, 2:218–19, 591; Fitzpatrick, *Writings*, 8:2–3, 37, 254, 318–19.

[31]John Muller, *A Treatise of Artillery*, 3d ed. (London: John Millan, 1780; reprint, with introduction by Harold L. Peterson, Ottawa: Museum Restoration Service, 1965), pp. v–xxv; Sebastian Bauman Papers (to Lamb, 25 Jun 79; Samuel Shaw to Bauman, 17 Feb 77), New-York Historical Society.

[32]British Headquarters Papers, No. 27 (Barrington to Gage, 31 Aug 75), 114, 491 (Barrington to Howe, 29 Jan 76 and 16 Apr 77).

[33]Force, *American Archives*, 4th ser., 6:271–73. It had 4 troops, each with 3 officers and 75 men, plus a staff of 8 officers and 16 men.

mounted infantry rather than true cavalry and were intended to patrol large areas. But during the later phases of the New York campaign, Washington concluded that proper reconnaissance called for horsemen. The usefulness of a detachment of Connecticut militia troopers under Maj. Elisha Sheldon, and the intimidation of some of Washington's infantrymen by British light dragoons, prompted the Commander in Chief to ask Congress to add light horsemen to the Continental Army.[34]

Congress' initial response came on 25 November 1776 when it requested Virginia to transfer Maj. Theodorick Bland's six troops of light horse to the Continental Army. The state had raised them during the summer. Each contained 3 officers, 3 corporals, a drummer, a trumpeter, and 29 privates. Three quartermasters provided logistical support for the group. Virginia complied, and in March 1777 Bland reenlisted his troops as continentals and reorganized them into a regiment.[35] On 12 December Congress, at Washington's suggestion, directed Sheldon to raise a Continental regiment of light dragoons and appointed him lieutenant colonel commandant of cavalry, a rank equivalent to colonel of infantry. Washington gave Sheldon the same free hand in selecting junior officers that he delegated to the colonels of the additional regiments.[36]

Congress' 27 December resolve then allowed Washington to raise up to 3,000 light dragoons, and to determine how they should be organized. Washington interpreted the legislation to mean that Bland's and Sheldon's men were included in the authorized figure, and he decided to add only two more regiments. He wanted to see if he could fill them before he tried to raise others. At the request of Congress, command of one of the new units went to Washington's aide George Baylor, who had carried the news of the Trenton victory to Baltimore. Lt. George Lewis of the Commander in Chief's Guard became one of his captains. The other regiment went to Stephen Moylan, another aide, who had served as Mustermaster General and Quartermaster General.[37]

On 14 March 1777 Congress approved Washington's regimental organization for the light dragoons. (*Chart 7*) It provided 3 field officers, a staff, and 6 troops for each regiment. Every troop contained 3 officers, 6 noncommissioned officers, a trumpeter, and 34 privates. One of the sergeants specialized in logistics, and two privates, an armorer and a farrier, received higher pay. The farrier provided rudimentary veterinary care and shod the horses. The staff was similar to an infantry regiment's, with the addition of a riding instructor and a saddler to keep leather gear in repair. Four supernumeraries were cadets undergoing training who served the colonel as messengers. The Continental light dragoon regiment was comparable to the British version, but it provided more specialists on both the troop and regimental level to allow greater dispersion on reconnaissance missions.[38]

Washington believed that the light dragoons' primary mission was reconnaissance, not combat. He instructed his troopers to use inconspicuous dark horses and ordered

[34]*JCC*, 2:173, 238; 5:606–7; Smith, *Letters of Delegates*, 1:587, 590–91; Fitzpatrick, *Writings*, 5:163–64, 236–37, 242, 324; 6:39, 230–31.
[35]*JCC*, 6:980; 7:34; Burnett, *Letters*, 2:269; Fitzpatrick, *Writings*, 6:456–57; 7:103, 338–39; Henning, *Statutes at Large*; 9:135–38, 141–43; McIlwaine et al., *Journals of the Council of the State of Virginia*, 1:153, 254–55, 269, 288; Force, *American Archives*, 4th ser., 6:1531, 1556; 5th ser., 3:1270.
[36]Fitzpatrick, *Writings*, 6:350–51, 384, 386–88; *JCC*, 6:1025; Burnett, *Letters*, 2:176.
[37]*JCC*, 7:7; Fitzpatrick, *Writings*, 6:483–84; 7:51, 193–94, 304–5.
[38]Fitzpatrick, *Writings*, 12:290; *JCC*, 7:178–79; 9:869; Sullivan, *Letters and Papers*, 1:403. Sheldon's regiment operated with a slightly different configuration until 5 November 1777.

CHART 7—LIGHT DRAGOON REGIMENT 1777

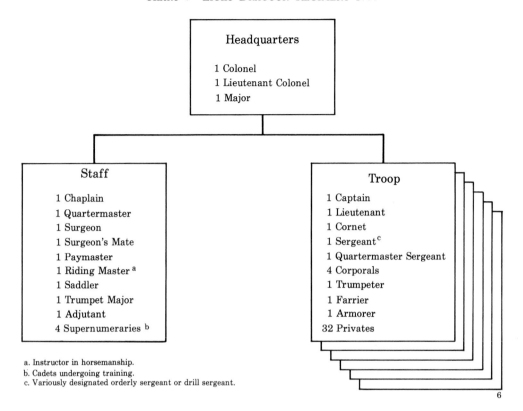

Headquarters

1 Colonel
1 Lieutenant Colonel
1 Major

Staff

1 Chaplain
1 Quartermaster
1 Surgeon
1 Surgeon's Mate
1 Paymaster
1 Riding Master [a]
1 Saddler
1 Trumpet Major
1 Adjutant
4 Supernumeraries [b]

Troop

1 Captain
1 Lieutenant
1 Cornet
1 Sergeant [c]
1 Quartermaster Sergeant
4 Corporals
1 Trumpeter
1 Farrier
1 Armorer
32 Privates

6

a. Instructor in horsemanship.
b. Cadets undergoing training.
c. Variously designated orderly sergeant or drill sergeant.

the officers to recruit native-born Americans rather than immigrants whose loyalty was less certain. The problems involved in procuring the horses and the special cavalry weapons and equipment, in training the horses for combat, and in developing high standards of individual skill contributed to the long period needed to organize the regiments. Assistance from Virginia and Connecticut, where Bland's, Baylor's, and Sheldon's regiments recruited, eased part of the difficulty, Moylan's organized at Philadelphia, where it had access to the Army's supply center. The fact that three of the four regiments came from Virginia and Connecticut, the two states noted for raising horses in the eighteenth century, indicated the importance of supply factors in Washington's allocation of the regiments.[39]

Fielding the New Army

While Washington formed his new regiments, the individual state governments reorganized their lines. Congress' 16 September 1776 resolve and supplemental instructions were clearly intended to produce uniform regiments, but particular problems and attitudes in some states led to variations in detail. During the spring these regiments, the additionals, the artillery, and the light dragoons arrived at the desig-

[39]Fitzpatrick, *Writings*, 7:123, 214–15, 219–20, 324, 368, 421; 8:53–54, 136, 264–65.

nated rendezvous according to strategic considerations. Washington and the department commanders then marshaled them into brigades and divisions. Congress and the military leaders also took this opportunity to make adjustments in the staff and support organizations of the expanded Army.

The states of the lower south had the easiest time adjusting to the new quotas because their regiments remained in their home states as the Southern Department's primary combat forces. Georgia did not reduce its force to the single regiment of the 16 September quota but retained the four infantry and one ranger units authorized during 1776. The rangers and the 1st Georgia Regiment lost strength during the spring as original enlistments expired, but the 2d and 3d reached operational strength through extensive recruiting in North Carolina and Virginia. The 4th Georgia Regiment kept enlisting men from as far away as Pennsylvania into October 1777.[40] The six South Carolina regiments adjusted to the new organizational structures by additional recruiting. The two rifle regiments (the 5th and 6th South Carolina Regiments) converted to infantry, and half of the 3d exchanged rifles for muskets. The 4th remained an artillery regiment, absorbing the separate artillery companies. Recruiting remained a major problem, and officers ranged as far as Pennsylvania in a search for volunteers.[41]

The regiments from North Carolina and Virginia did not remain at the disposal of the Southern Department commander, Brig. Gen. Robert Howe, but joined the Main Army. The 8th Virginia Regiment and various North Carolina detachments stationed in South Carolina returned to their home states during the spring to be refilled.[42] Since the current enlistment period of the six North Carolina and nine Virginia regiments lasted until 1778, they remained unchanged. North Carolina's government raised three more regiments during the spring to meet its quota, although it felt that the total was unreasonably high. All nine North Carolina regiments reached Philadelphia in early July, but only two of the regiments mustered over 200 effectives, and the nine totaled only 131 officers and 963 enlisted men. They should have contained an aggregate of about 7,000.[43]

Five Virginia regiments joined Washington in late 1776, and 10 others followed in the spring. In addition to the 9 existing units, the state raised 6 new ones following the same techniques it had employed in 1775 and 1776. Virginia was the only state that rejected the standard infantry structure and formed ten companies for each regiment. It also enlisted its men for only three-year terms, not for the duration as Congress preferred. Four of the new regiments were organized from scratch, but two contained cadres already in existence. Col. Daniel Morgan, recently released from captivity, built his 11th Virginia Regiment around the five Virginia companies from the Maryland and Virginia Rifle Regiment and the survivors of his original 1775 rifle company. Col. James Wood's 12th Virginia Regiment contained the five state frontier companies, who had reenlisted as Continental units. Maj. John Neville, their former commander, became Wood's lieutenant colonel. The state raised two infantry and one

[40]McIntosh, "Papers," 38:256–57, 266–67, 357–59, 363–67; Margaret Godley, ed., "Minutes of the Executive Council, May 7 Through October 14, 1777," *Georgia Historical Quarterly* 34 (1950):110–13; *JCC*, 9:782–83.

[41]Force, *American Archives*, 5th ser., 3:49–54, 66, 68, 72–76; Burnett, *Letters*, 2:452; Pinckney, "Letters," 58:77–79.

[42]*JCC*, 5:733–34; 6:1043–44; 7:21, 52, 90–91, 133.

[43]Force, *American Archives*, 5th ser., 1:1384; Burnett, *Letters*, 2:95–97; Gates Papers (Returns of Troops at Philadelphia, 7 and 8 Jul 77).

artillery regiment of state troops to take over the burden of local defense and, at Congress' request, added two separate Continental companies to protect the frontier. This effort exhausted the state's manpower, and for the first time officers had difficulty finding recruits.[44]

Unlike the south, the middle states were faced with a situation in which most existing enlistments expired on 31 December 1776 or shortly thereafter, and one in which regiments were on active duty outside the state. They turned to legislative liaison committees, establishing new arrangements which retained, through reenlistment, the 1776 regiments and added new ones as necessary. The new regiments depended on veterans of militia or state service, particularly with the Flying Camp, for their cadres. While this expedient created turmoil in some lines because of arguments over relative rank, it allowed each of the 1777 regiments to start with an experienced core.

Delaware's reorganization was the simplest. It merely filled vacancies in its single regiment through promotions.[45] Maryland's problems were more complex. That state argued that its quota was based on misleading total population figures and made an effort to raise only seven of its assigned eight regiments. The original 1776 regiment and attached separate companies became the 1st and 2d Maryland Regiments. The 4th through 7th formed around cadres from the four regiments sent to the Flying Camp, and the 3d assembled its officers from a variety of sources.[46]

Despite great enthusiasm among their officers for remaining in service, New Jersey and Pennsylvania took longer than Maryland to accomplish their reorganizations. Regiments at Ticonderoga got a later start in recruiting than those serving with the Main Army. New Jersey refilled its three regiments from 1776 and added a fourth built around militiamen. To free the Continental officers for recruiting duties, the state raised four temporary battalions of state troops to take up defensive responsibilities during the winter.[47] Pennsylvania also retained existing units by reenlisting the men. The 1st Continental Regiment became the 1st Pennsylvania Regiment by virtue of its seniority, with the 1st through 6th Pennsylvania Battalions becoming the 2d through 7th Pennsylvania Regiments. Col. Aneas Mackay's frontier regiment became the 8th. Sufficient personnel of the 3d and 5th battalions had escaped capture at Fort Washington to allow them to re-form as the 4th and 6th Regiments through additional recruiting. Two of the three new regiments, the 9th and 10th, drew officers from the state troops of 1776; the 11th drew its officers from various sources. William Cook's six-company frontier regiment had not yet made any substantial progress in organizing; it added two more companies and became the 12th.[48] The state also con-

[44]Henning, *Statutes at Large*, 9:179–84, 192–98, 210–11, 213–14; McIlwaine, *Journals of the Council of State*, 1:250, 270–71, 310, 321, 325, 337–40, 368; James Wood, "Correspondence of Col. James Wood," *Tyler's Quarterly Historical and Genealogical Magazine* 3 (1921):38–40.

[45]Fitzpatrick, *Writings*, 6:485; Robert Kirkwood, *The Journal and Order Book of Captain Robert Kirkwood of the Delaware Regiment of the Continental Line*, ed. Joseph Brown Turner (Wilmington: Historical Society of Delaware, 1910), pp. 4–6; *Anderson, Personal Recollections*, pp. 7, 26–29.

[46]Force, *American Archives*, 5th ser., 3:120–1, 125, 132, 163–64, 182; *Archives of Maryland*, 18:76–292; Fitzpatrick, *Writings*, 7:397.

[47]Force, *American Archives*, 5th ser., 2:1258–59; 3:1316, 1449, 1474–75; Fitzpatrick, 6:81–82; 7:27, 200–201; Gates Papers (Schuyler to Gates, 13 Nov 76).

[48]Fitzpatrick, *Writings*, 9:90; Force, *American Archives*, 5th ser., 2:92, 94; 3:195–200; *Pennsylvania Archives*, 1st ser., 5:40–41, 51, 176–77, 522–23, 545; 7:583–85; 2d ser., 1:41–42, 51–52, 717–18; 10:106–7; 4th ser., 3:656–57; Charles J. Stille, *Major-General Anthony Wayne and the Pennsylvania Line in the Continental Army* (Philadelphia: J. B. Lippincott, 1893), pp. 39–40, 43–48, 54; Gates Papers (Francis Johnston to Gates, 20 Feb 77).

solidated its enlisted state troops into a regiment with ten 100-man companies. These men were still under their original enlistments (which lasted until 1 January 1778), but on 10 June 1777 the regiment willingly transferred to the Continental Army as the 13th Pennsylvania Regiment.[49]

New York and New England units had served for two full campaigns, longer than any units from the southern or middle states. Casualties, normal attrition, and reduced quotas made it harder for these northern states to sustain the continuity of their regiments. New York faced a reduction from seven to five regiments and the loss of Manhattan and Long Island, fertile recruiting grounds. The old 1st from New York City was disbanded, and its veterans were used to fill vacancies in other units. The two Albany-area regiments, the 4th and Van Schaick's, were merged as the new 1st New York Regiment, and the old 2d and 3d were reorganized as the new 4th and 2d, respectively, reflecting the relative seniority of their new commanders. John Nicholson's regiment, which had been formed for service in Canada, disbanded, and Lewis Dubois' regiment provided the nucleus for the new 3d, although Colonel Dubois himself commanded a new 5th New York Regiment which Congress accepted on 30 November 1776.[50]

Connecticut had furnished eight regiments in 1776, and its quota in 1777 was the same. The legislature, however, completely regrouped the officer corps. Its aim was to place the best veteran officers in the most appropriate positions; it was willing to disregard prior service or considerations of unit continuity. The Connecticut Assembly made every effort to recruit rapidly, offering extra land grants and recruiting by geographical districts, but most regiments did not obtain substantial numbers until April or May.[51] Rhode Island dropped from four to two regiments by using the same device that it had employed in the 1776 reorganization. The 9th and 11th Continental Regiments became, through reenlistment, the 1st and 2d Rhode Island Regiments. The best officers from the two disbanded regiments and some of their men filled vacancies. The state also created a brigade of state troops; this effort conflicted with the work of Continental recruiters although the brigade then helped to contain the British forces in Newport.[52] New Hampshire similarly used its three existing Continental regiments as the core of its three 1777 regiments. Col. Timothy Bedel's regiment disbanded during the winter and Col. Nicholas Long's in July of 1777 when its 1776 enlistments expired. The state commissioned various veteran militia officers to fill out the three new regiments.[53]

[49]Force, *American Archives*, 5th ser., 2:80–81, 92–94; *Pennsylvania Archives*, 1st ser., 5:103–4, 107, 112–13, 318, 357; *JCC*, 8:482–83; Gates Papers (Pa. Council of Safety to Gates, 4 Mar 77, with enclosure).

[50]*JCC*, 6:994; 8:710–11; Force, *American Archives*, 5th ser., 3:206–11; 247–49, 312–20, 366–67; *Calendar of Historical Manuscripts, Relating to the War of the Revolution, in the Office of the Secretary of State, Albany, New York*, 2 vols., (Albany: Weed, Parsons, and Co., 1863–68), 2:31–53; William M. Willett, *A Narrative of the Military Actions of Colonel Marinus Willett, Taken Chiefly From his own Manuscript* (New York: C. & C. & H. Carvill, 1831), p. 39.

[51]Force, *American Archives*, 5th ser., 2:957–61; 3:799, 899–900, 1433; Hoadley et al., *Public Records of the State of Connecticut*, 1:12–16, 26, 65–70, 165–68; Charles S. Hall, *Life and Letters of Samuel Holden Parsons* (Binghamton, N.Y.: Otseningo Publishing Co., 1905), pp. 92–93; Samuel Blatchley Webb, *Correspondence and Journals of Samuel Blatchley Webb*, ed. Worthington Chauncey Ford, 3 vols. (New York: privately pub., 1893–94), 1:189–211.

[52]Fitzpatrick, *Writings*, 6:200–202, 274; 7:42–44, 349–51; Rhode Island Historical Society *Collections*, 6:175, 183–85; *R.I. Records*, 8:10–11, 20, 30–33, 103–4, 126–27, 140–41, 172–73, 192–93; Greene, *Papers*, 1:307–8, 317, 360–64.

[53]Sullivan, *Letters and Papers*, 1:317–22; Force, *American Archives*, 5th ser., 2:1175–77; 3:624–25, 646–47, 796–98, 1125.

JOHN EAGER HOWARD *(1752–1827) of Maryland is typical of the excellent regimental commanders serving in the Continental Army during the latter stages of the Revolution. He played a key role in the battle of Cowpens and went on to become a governor, congressman, and senator. (Portrait by Charles Willson Peale, 1782.)*

Massachusetts' quota of fifteen regiments reduced by two the number in service during 1776. One legislative committee traveled to New York to form seven regiments from the men on duty there in October 1776; a second went to Ticonderoga to arrange five regiments. Three others were organized within the state. Although the legislature's idea of offering additional pay was rejected by Congress, it exerted itself fully, and in April 1777 the legislature passed a bill authorizing a draft when recruiting tapered off. These efforts raised 7,816 men, mostly for the line regiments, by early July. The average number of recruits for each regiment was 470, with four above the 600-man level and only four below 400.[54]

The reorganized regiments assembled at three primary locations in the spring of 1777. Ticonderoga and Peekskill in the Hudson Highlands had obvious strategic importance. The troops at these places protected important fortifications, denied the Hudson River to British troops in Canada and New York City, and enjoyed substantial logistical support. Morristown, Washington's headquarters, served as the other rendezvous because it protected Philadelphia from British troops in New Jersey. Once the regiments reached these locations, Washington and the commanders of the Northern and Highlands Departments assembled them into brigades and divisions, the primary formations used in 1777 to maneuver the Continental Army.

In addition to the North Carolina and Virginia regiments drawn north from the Southern Department, Washington used regiments from the middle states to furnish most of the other troops for the Main Army. The infantry regiments arrived throughout the spring in company-sized increments and by May achieved operational strength. On 11 May, excluding artillery and light dragoons, the Main Army's 38 regiments of infantry (line and additional regiments from Virginia, Maryland, Dela-

[54]Force, *American Archives*, 5th ser., 3:399–400, 414–15, 494–96, 507–8, 711–13, 1030, 1083–84, 1170; Gardiner, *Warren-Gerry Correspondence*, pp. 59–60; Gates Papers (Joseph Avery's Return of Men Enlisted by Massachusetts, 10 Jul 77).

ware, Pennsylvania, and New Jersey), plus detachments, included 50 field, 532 company, and 91 staff officers; 708 sergeants; 241 drummers and fifers; and 8,378 rank and file. Two thousand men were sick, about half in hospitals, and another 400 were absent on detached duties. Only about a third of the regiments were over half strength, but recruits continued to arrive in numbers.[55]

Washington's January 1777 plans called for a brigade to have three full infantry regiments (over 2,200 men) and for a division to have three brigades. When he asked Congress to appoint additional general officers to command these formations, he also requested the appointment of three lieutenant generals as senior commanders. Many delegates considered the new rank a threat to republican virtue, and Congress rejected the idea. After considerable maneuvering by delegates to advance favorite sons, Congress eventually created six new major and fourteen new brigadier generals.[56] Washington adjusted his plans to the available number of officers and to the actual strength of the regiments, and between 11 and 22 May 1777 he established ten permanent brigades in the Main Army. Each contained four or five regiments, from the same state when possible. For example, the 3d Virginia Brigade consisted of the 3d, 7th, 11th, and 15th Virginia Regiments. Brig. Gens. Peter Muhlenberg, George Weedon, William Woodford, and Charles Scott commanded the 1st through 4th Virginia Brigades; Brig. Gens. Anthony Wayne, John DeHaas, and Thomas Conway, the 1st through 3d Pennsylvania Brigades; Brig. Gens. William Smallwood and Philippe-Hubert, Chevalier de Preudhomme de Borre, the 1st and 2d Maryland Brigades; and Brig. Gen. William Maxwell, the New Jersey Brigade. Two brigades formed a division.[57] In addition to aides, the brigade staff included a brigade major, a brigade quartermaster, and a chaplain (who replaced the regimental chaplains). The division staff included a quartermaster officer and a conductor of military stores who repaired small arms and prepared ammunition.[58]

This formation of the Main Army allowed Washington great flexibility. During the summer of 1777, divisions shifted along the main roads between Morristown and Philadelphia as the British threatened either the Hudson Highlands or the capital. He expected a division in a detached role to harass the enemy advance and to buy time for the rest of the army to concentrate.[59] In formal battle the Main Army deployed in a double line. The First Line consisted of two or more divisions in line abreast. The Second Line, or reserve, was deployed to the rear and provided depth to absorb shock. The Left Wing and Right Wing each contained portions of both lines. By December the Order of Battle of the larger Main Army had become more complex. Ten brigades deployed as the First Line and six as the Second. One additional brigade remained in

[55]RG 93, National Archives (Weekly Return, Main Army, 21 May 77; a version of this return is printed in Lesser, *Sinews*, p. 46; Fitzpatrick, *Writings*, 7:236, 278–79, 396–97, 451–52; 8:49–50.

[56]Fitzpatrick, *Writings*, 7:49–51; *JCC*, 7:90, 133, 141–42, 203, 213, 256, 323; 8:624; 9:823; Burnett, *Letters*, 2:261–63, 269–75, 287–88, 291–92, 299–301, 311–12. Robert Howe and Alexander McDougall exercised department commands during the year as brigadier generals and advanced to major generals in October.

[57]Fitzpatrick, *Writings*, 7:447–48; 8:40–41, 88–89, 97–101, 170–72; 9:103–4, 149. The senior colonel commanded in the brigadier general's absence.

[58]Ibid., 8:203–4, 337; *JCC*, 8:390, 609; Sullivan, *Letters and Papers*, 1:352.

[59]Ftizpatrick, *Writings*, 8:62–64. There is a distinct similarity between Washington's use of the division as a force capable of limited independent action and Napoleon's use of the corps as described in Steven T. Ross, "The Development of the Combat Division in Eighteenth-Century French Armies," *French Historical Studies*, 4 (1965):84–94.

general reserve. Each wing additionally used two light dragoon regiments and some supporting infantry formations, both Continental and militia, for flank security.[60]

Improved arms and training reinforced the advantages inherent in the new tactical organization of 1777. The 1763-model French Army musket, known colloquially as the Charleville, became the standard infantry weapon. This .69-caliber smoothbore, which fired a 1-ounce ball, came with a metal ramrod and a 14-inch socket bayonet. It had greater range and was more durable, reliable, and accurate than the English Brown Bess. The Charleville was an ideal weapon for the Continental Army, in which the infantry regiment's structure placed a premium on musketry rather than shock actions.[61] Spring and summer training stressed battlefield maneuvers rather than the manual of arms. New standing regulations covered the proper methods of marching and saluting, the baggage train, and guard duty. Washington told officers to "be very attentive, that their men keep their ranks always dressed, and use their feet in concert, which are equally conducive to the order, beauty, strength and expedition of a marching body."[62]

The Eastern Department did not face a serious threat from the British base at Newport and could rely, moreover, on New England's strong militia forces. Washington left it with only the three Massachusetts additional regiments for a garrison. The bulk of the New York and New England infantry regiments were assigned either to Ticonderoga or to the Hudson Highlands. In his original plan Washington instructed eighteen New Hampshire and Massachusetts regiments to go to the former, and the fifteen New York, Rhode Island, and Connecticut regiments, plus Samuel Blatchley Webb's and Henry Sherburne's additional regiments, to the latter. Slow recruiting and uncertainty over Howe's plans led Washington in time to alter this arrangement substantially. Two of the New York regiments shifted to the Northern Department while eight Massachusetts units reported to Peekskill.[63]

The Highlands remained strategically important during 1777 because troops stationed there could rapidly reinforce either the Main Army or the Northern Department. By mid-May Brig. Gen. Alexander McDougall's garrison had assumed respectable proportions. He had 18 infantry regiments: 3 from New York, 8 from Connecticut, 6 from Massachusetts, and Webb's; plus the first detachment of Rhode Islanders. The continentals included 13 field, 119 company, and 24 staff officers; 197 sergeants; 94 drummers and fifers; and 2,502 rank and file. The 400 sick and 200 detached continentals were offset by about 700 New York militia. Like the Main Army's regiments, McDougall's were still arriving by detachment.[64] Israel Putnam assumed command

[60]Fitzpatrick, *Writings*, 8:296-97; 10:94-95, 138-39.

[61]Arcadi Gluckman, *United States Muskets, Rifles and Carbines* (Harrisburg: The Stackpole Co., 1959), pp. 55-61; James E. Hicks and Fred Porter Todd, "United States Military Shoulder Arms, 1795-1935," Part 2, *Military Affairs* 2 (1938):37-42, 75-76; Harold L. Peterson, *Arms and Armor in Colonial America, 1526-1783* (Harrisburg: Stackpole Books, 1956), pp. 170-78, 190-92; Rebecca and Philip Katcher, "The Pennsylvania Division, 1780," *Military Collector and Historian* 27 (1975):120; Ernst Kipping and Samuel S. Smith, eds., *At General Howe's Side: The Diary of General Howe's Aide de Camp, Captain Friedrich von Muenchhausen* (Monmouth Beach, N.J.: Philip Freneau Press, 1974), p. 14.

[62]Fitzpatrick, *Writings*, 8:255; see also pp. 227-31, 250-51, 256, 344-49; 9:79-80.

[63]Ibid., 7:125, 272-78, 282-83, 424, 485-86; 8:6-7, 35, 43, 101-3; William Abbatt, ed., *Memoirs of Major-General William Heath*, new ed. (New York: William Abbatt, 1901), pp. 104-11; Gates *Papers* (to Hancock, 2 May 77).

[64]Alexander McDougall Papers (Weekly Returns, Highlands Department, 17 and 24 May 77), New-York Historical Society. During this single week 700 continentals arrived.

on 1 June and instituted a brigade and division organization similar to the Main Army's. By 5 August, despite numerous transfers to other departments, the Highlands force consisted of two divisions each with two brigades.[65] Philip Schuyler's Northern Department assembled brigades on the basis of Washington's instructions, ultimately forming four brigades of Massachusetts regiments and one of New Hampshire regiments. A division organization was not necessary as long as the troops were tied to the defense of Ticonderoga.[66]

While the tactical organization of the field armies was perfected during the first part of 1777, Congress and Washington improved the Army's administrative and support organizations as well. The expanded Army, dispersed over a broader area than before, made the Adjutant General's role as the central administrative figure even more important. After Col. Joseph Reed resigned at the start of the year, Washington limped along with temporary appointments until he persuaded Col. Timothy Pickering to accept the job. Through perseverance, Pickering restored order to the strength reporting system by the fall.[67] An expansion of the mustering department on 4 April assisted Pickering. A deputy was assigned to each territorial department, and a sufficient number of subordinate officials were appointed to muster every unit once a month.[68] The cross-checks established by this system and Pickering's program of separately prepared weekly and monthly returns eventually enabled Washington and Congress to have reliable and timely data on which to base their plans.

Washington reorganized his personal staff in 1777 largely as a result of personnel changes, but the new household group also assisted in improving administration. He conducted a search for influential young men with secretarial skills and a willingness to work as replacements for the aides lost to the additionals and dragoons. As a result, talented individuals such as Alexander Hamilton, Richard Kidder Meade, and John Laurens became aides during 1777.[69] The new office of Commissary General of Prisoners, created by Congress on 27 December 1776, became part of the household. Its ostensible function was supervising prisoner of war compounds and ensuring that captured Americans received proper treatment. In fact, Washington used Commissary General Elias Boudinot to coordinate intelligence activities.[70]

Changes in the logistical structure during 1777 derived from two motives. One was a desire to improve efficiency through increased specialization. The other sought modifications to provide immediate support to the field armies. The Commissary Department split into the Department of the Commissary General of Purchases and the Department of the Commissary General of Issues on 10 June 1777. The first primarily procured items, while the latter stored them and handled some distribution func-

---

[65]Israel Putnam, *General Orders Issued by Major-General Israel Putnam, When in Command of the Highlands, in the Summer and Fall of 1777*, ed. Worthington C. Ford (Brooklyn: Historical Printing Club, 1893), pp. 1, 11-12, 23-25, 46-47; Fitzpatrick, *Writings*, 7:354-55; 8:51, 234-35, 276-78, 450; 9:34-35.

[66]Fitzpatrick, *Writings*, 7:485-86; Gates Papers (Hugh Hughes to Gates; Gates to Col Van Schaick, both 19 Aug 77).

[67]*JCC*, 7:204, Sullivan, *Letters and Papers*, 1:418, 433; Fitzpatrick, *Writings*, 7:5, 67-78, 218, 336-37, 382; 8:114-16, 264.

[68]Fitzpatrick, *Writings*, 7:381, 447-48; *JCC*, 7:221-22, 253, 322.

[69]Fitzpatrick, *Writings*, 6:487; 7:41, 161, 218, 280; Douglas S. Freeman, *George Washington: A Biography*, 7 vols. (New York: Charles Scribner's Sons, 1948-57), 4:391-92.

[70]*JCC*, 8:421-22; Fitzpatrick, *Writings*, 7:383, 417-18.

JOHN LAURENS *(1754–82) was the son of South Carolina delegate and President of Congress Henry Laurens. He served as Washington's aide and carried out many diplomatic assignments until he was killed in a minor skirmish outside Charleston near the end of the war. (Posthumous miniature by Charles Willson Peale, ca. 1784.)*

tions.[71] The Quartermaster General's Department reorganized on 14 May. The department formed specialized groups to handle transportation, quarters, forage, and baking; upgrading the Army's transportation had the most immediate impact. The Quartermaster General remained directly responsible for the support of the Main Army; he had several assistants and a deputy for each division. Parallel structures were provided in each territorial department.[72] The hospital service also reorganized to improve flexible support to the territorial departments and immediate service to the troops.[73]

Congress created one new logistical department on 27 December 1776. At Washington's request, it assumed responsibility for furnishing uniforms to the troops and established a Clothier General's Department under Philadelphia merchant James Mease. His department prepared estimates, purchased and stored clothing items, and issued them to the men through the regimental quartermasters. Washington hoped to eliminate the miscellaneous nature of the clothing that the Army had been using. Such clothing, he believed, was detrimental to discipline because it "has not only an ill appearance, but it creates much irregularity; for when a soldier is convinced, that he will be known by his dress to what Corps he belongs, he is hindered from committing many faults for fear of detection."[74] Within the clothier's purview a Commissary of Hides and his subordinates turned raw hides produced by the Army's consumption of beef into needed leather goods.[75]

[71]*JCC*, 8:434–43, 452, 469–70, 610; Burnett, *Letters*, 3:3–5, 39–40; Fitzpatrick, *Writings*, 8:16, 25; 10:80–82, 183–88, 243–46.

[72]*JCC*, 5:839–41; 6:1051–52; 7:323, 355–59; 19:159.

[73]Ibid., 7:161–64, 197–200, 231–37, 244–45, 253–54; 8:626–27; Sullivan, *Letters and Papers*, 1:346.

[74]Fitzpatrick, *Writings* 7:422.

[75]Ibid., 6:109, 381, 404, 492–93; 7:127, 148, 229–30, 247–49, 420–22; 10:45–46; *JCC*, 6:880–81, 1043.

ELIAS BOUDINOT *(1740–1821) of New Jersey served in the Continental Army as the first commissary general of prisoners, a job which included intelligence responsibilities. He later became president of the Continental Congress. (Portrait by Charles Willson Peale, ca. 1782.)*

Logic indicated that the two main British armies in Canada and New York would cooperate in 1777 in a drive to capture Albany and to sever New England from the rest of the country. General Howe's troops threatened also to advance through New Jersey and to take Philadelphia. The unfolding events of the campaign of 1777 tested Congress' and Washington's winter reorganizations.

As expected, the first blow fell on the Northern Department. General St. Clair's garrison could not hold Ticonderoga against Maj. Gen. John Burgoyne's British and German regulars, and it withdrew. Burgoyne's poor transport organization and Schuyler's systematic destruction of roads leading south prevented effective pursuit. The Northern Department's forces regrouped and began receiving reinforcements from the south. Although Schuyler, with the assistance of local militia forces, developed plans that led to the defeat of British detachments at Fort Stanwix and Bennington, he had lost the confidence of most delegates in Congress. Schuyler was recalled on 31 July, and Gates was named as the new Northern Department commander on 4 August. Gate's supporters claimed that his popularity in New England would allow him to attract more militia support than Schuyler could.[76]

In addition to Continental brigades from the Highlands Department, the reinforcements dispatched to the north included one very important unit from the Main Army. Washington formed a provisional rifle corps on 13 June 1777 under Col. Daniel Morgan of the 11th Virginia Regiment. The men, primarily from Virginia and Pennsylvania regiments, were selected for their marksmanship and woodcraft. Like Thomas Knowlton's 1776 rangers, the corps served as a light infantry and skirmishing force. In the Northern Department Morgan worked closely with a provisional light infantry de-

[76]*JCC*, 7:202–3, 362–64; 8:375; 590, 596, 604; Burnett, *Letters*, 2:209–12, 336–37, 351–52, 376–77, 382–86, 424–26, 429–30, 440–41, 445, 465; Fitzpatrick, *Writings*, 9:8–9; Gates Papers (Hancock to Gates, 25 Mar and 14 Aug 77; Gates to Hancock, 20 Aug 77).

HENRY DEARBORN *(1751–1829) of New Hampshire had a career which represents the influence of the Continental Army on the subsequent United States Army. Dearborn rose from captain to lieutenant colonel and commanded the provisional light infantry battalion during the Saratoga campaign. After the Revolution he served as secretary of war (1801–1809) and eventually as the senior major general in the Army (1812–1815). (Portrait by Charles Willson Peale, ca. 1796.)*

tachment that Schuyler organized in August under Maj. Henry Dearborn; they quickly intimidated Burgoyne's Indians and drastically reduced his ability to procure accurate intelligence.[77]

Gates inflicted two defeats on Burgoyne at Bemis Heights, cut him off from Ticonderoga, and forced "Gentleman Johnny" to surrender on 17 October. Saratoga was unquestionably the greatest victory yet won by the Continental Army in terms of prisoners and captured arms and equipment. Nearly 6,000 enemy soldiers were taken, along with 42 cannon and massive quantities of stores.[78] By the time Burgoyne surrendered, Gates' forces amounted to 1,698 officers and 20,652 men, exclusive of artificers, batteauxmen, and about 700 riflemen. Over 4,000 were absent, mostly stationed to cut off any British retreat toward Ticonderoga, and slightly more than 1,000 were sick.[79]

Over two-thirds of the Northern Department's soldiers, including some artillery and cavalry troops, were militiamen from New England and New York. Only five of the thirteen brigades were Continental; these contained 3 New Hampshire, 15 Massachusetts, and 2 New York infantry regiments plus the 1st Canadian Regiment. Three of the Continental brigades also contained militia regiments. The total Continental infantry contingent, including Morgan's riflemen and Dearborn's light infantry, comprised 52 field, 457 company, and 72 staff officers; 526 sergeants; 262 drummers and fifers; and 7,644 rank and file. Only 5,000 rank and file were combat effectives.[80]

---

[77]Fitzpatrick, *Writings*, 8:156, 236–37, 246; 9:70–71, 78; Henry Dearborn, *Revolutionary War Journals of Henry Dearborn, 1775–1783*, eds. Lloyd A. Brown and Howard H. Peckham (Chicago: Caxton Club, 1939), pp. 100–13; Gates Papers (to Washington, 22 Aug and 2 Nov 77; to Morgan, 29 Aug 77).

[78]Gates Papers (State of British and State of German Troops Surrendered, both dated 17 Oct 77; James Wilkinson's return of prisoners, 31 Oct 77; Ebenezer Stevens' return of captured stores, 1 Nov 77).

[79]Ibid. (General Return, Northern Department, 16 Oct 77).

[80]In addition to the General Return cited above, the following sources in the Gates Papers were used to arrive at correct figures: State of the Army at Saratoga, 17 Oct 77; Return of Continental Troops at Van Schaick's Island, 7 Sep 77; Brigade Returns for [Brig. Gen. John] Paterson's, [Brig. Gen. John] Nixon's, and [Col. William] Shepard's [Glover's] Brigades, 25–26 Oct 77; and Richard Varick to Gates, 10 Sep 77.

Part of the Northern Department's strength had come from forces originally committed to the Hudson Highlands. When Putnam also sent three brigades to the Main Army during September, his department was left with only General Parsons' 1st Connecticut Brigade as a mobile field force, and the 5th New York Regiment, part of Lamb's artillery, and some New York militia as garrisons for the forts. Maj. Gen. Sir Henry Clinton took advantage of this weakness to attack, and on 6 October the main forts in the Highlands fell after a stubborn defense. Most of the garrisons escaped, and Clinton returned to New York when he learned of Burgoyne's surrender.[81]

General Howe had chosen not to attack the Highlands nor to move across New Jersey. Instead, he sailed by way of the Chesapeake Bay to attack Philadelphia from the rear. By the time Howe was ready to advance from his base at Head of Elk, Maryland, Washington had organized a light force under General Maxwell to harass him. The corps consisted of two provisional light infantry companies from each brigade in the Main Army, detachments of light dragoons and local militia, and a partisan unit.[82] Howe forced Washington back and defeated the continentals along Brandywine Creek, Pennsylvania, by outmaneuvering them. Washington prevented a catastrophe by shifting brigades from his unengaged flank with an adroitness that impressed professional German officers serving with Howe, and his army escaped under the cover of aggressive rearguard action.[83]

Howe moved on to capture Philadelphia on 26 September, but he had to fragment his army to hold open a supply route to the lower Delaware River. On the night of 3–4 October Washington counterattacked at Germantown, Pennsylvania. The intricate plan, similar to that used at Trenton, called for a dawn attack by concentric columns covered by diversionary attacks. Excellent march discipline and intelligence enabled the leading Continental brigades to overrun the British 2d Battalion of Light Infantry and drive back other units, leading one astonished German officer to exclaim that he had just seen "something I had never seen before, namely the English in full flight."[84] Confusion and the staunch British defense of the stone Chew House robbed the attack of its momentum, and Washington withdrew. The British spent the next month and a half dislodging the defenders of the fortifications on the Delaware River below Philadelphia.

By early November Washington's Main Army contained a dozen Continental brigades: 4 from Virginia, 3 from Pennsylvania, 2 from Maryland, and one each from North Carolina, New Jersey, and Connecticut.[85] The combined strength of 1,167 officers and 15,927 men, excluding cavalry and artillery, represented about half the Continental Army's total force. There were 82 field grade officers, 865 company officers, and 220 regimental staff personnel. Sergeants accounted for 1,009 of the enlisted men, and drummers and fifers another 523, leaving 14,395 rank and file. Some 4,500 were sick, and another 2,100 were on command, mostly in defense of the river forts.

---

[81]Wright, "Too Little, Too Late," pp. 73–88; McDougall Papers (Transcript of the Court of Inquiry Into Putnam's Conduct, 5 Apr 78).

[82]Fitzpatrick, *Writings*, 9:145, 148–49, 162–63, 172–73; John W. Wright, "The Corps of Light Infantry in the Continental Army," *American Historical Review* 31 (1926):454–55.

[83]Uhlendorf, *Revolution in America*, pp. 1–27; Kipping and Smith, *At Howe's Side*, pp. 31–32; Henry Lee, *Memoirs of the War in the Southern Department of the United States*, ed. Robert E. Lee (New York: University Publishing Co., 1869), pp. 89–90.

[84]Kipping and Smith, *At Howe's Side*, pp. 38–39; see also Uhlendorf, *Revolution in America*, pp. 5–27, and John Eager Howard "Col. John Eager Howard's Account of the Battle of Germantown," ed. Justin Winsor, *Maryland Historical Magazine* 4 (1909):314–20.

[85]RG 93, National Archives (Weekly Return, Main Army, 3 Nov 77).

Washington's actual combat strength was probably about 10,000 men, too few to continue the campaign. After calling for reinforcements from Gates, he encamped at Valley Forge on 20 December.

Summary

The Continental Army that marched into Valley Forge in December 1777 was very different in organization than the one that had retreated through New Jersey one year earlier. The regiments were now on a permanent footing and formed a larger and more balanced force. The infantry regiments, both line and additional, the artillery, and the light dragoons all contained sizable veteran cadres. Added experience, and the fact that the basic regimental organization had remained the same, had enabled the Army to quickly incorporate the lessons of open warfare learned during the Trenton campaign. Experienced field officers of earlier years now commanded the permanent brigades, which were the most important innovation of 1777. These factors and the increasing sophistication of the staff explain how the varied field armies in the Northern, Highlands, and Middle Departments, containing regiments from every state except Georgia and South Carolina, survived the defeats and crises of 1777.

Better organization, additional staff officers with special skills, and increased emphasis on transportation made the Continental Army more mobile in 1777 than in 1776. Allowing brigades and divisions to undertake limited independent action was a basic concept that made it possible to shift strategic reserves rapidly enough to offset British control of the sea. While many of the battles of 1777 ended in defeat for the Continental Army, particularly for the Main Army, most of the defeats cannot be attributed to a lack of fighting ability of individual regiments. They came from errors in judgment by generals or from inadequate resources. Better training and doctrine were needed to improve the Army's performance.

Washington was more optimistic on Christmas Day 1777 than he had been a year earlier.[86] He knew that his Army could not only fight but also even beat the British under favorable conditions. Two major concerns were to ensure that the Army won consistently and to sustain the strength that Congress had authorized. For all practical purposes, the Continental Army reached its maximum size, in terms of units, in 1777. Hereafter the states' role was not organizing new units but rather procuring individual replacements for existing regiments. This change reduced the influence of state governments and increased the military's control over its own destiny. Duration or other long-term enlistments contributed to the shift in power. The large quotas of regiments remained a particular problem, for they were overly ambitious. Nominally the 119 regiments fielded in 1777 should have contained over 90,000 officers and men. The Continental Army never came close to that total, and beginning in 1778 it faced problems of retrenchment rather than expansion.

---

[86]For the logistical situation, which was verging on total collapse, see Erna Risch, *Supplying Washington's Army* (Washington: Government Printing Office, 1981)

CHAPTER 6

Professionalism:
New Influences From Europe

The winter encampment at Valley Forge was an extremely important period in the development of the Continental Army. Despite numerous problems, for the first time in the war the Army enjoyed a winter free from the need to recruit and reorganize most of the regiments. Congress and military leaders used this time to review the campaign of 1777 and to debate reforms to improve the Army's battlefield performance. One group advocated a return to two centuries of Anglo-American experience; a second sought inspiration from European, particularly French, professional soldiers and military theory. Over the next year and a half parts of each group's program were adopted, but a preponderance of reforms came from new European ideas. This period witnessed the gradual transformation of the Continental Army into a professional fighting force.

Valley Forge

When in September 1776 Congress approved raising an army to serve for the duration of the war, it broke with the militia tradition without serious debate because the military commanders insisted that such a force was necessary to win victory. Three months later the delegates approved a larger force for the same reason. On the other hand, Congress expected such a permanent army to win victories. The Main Army did not do so in 1777, but Gates' army won a smashing victory with the assistance of large militia forces. Policy debates during the winter of 1777–78 over a number of related issues revealed two basic interpretations of the lessons of the 1777 campaign. Some delegates, supported by one contingent of army leaders, pressed for a return to the ideals of 1776. They cited Saratoga as proof that their program, which put less reliance on a large standing army, would produce results. Washington, most of the senior officers, and other delegates felt that the transformation of 1777 was correct, and they sought to improve on it. The central issues debated during the winter related to the overall direction of military affairs, the professionalization of the officer corps, and the size of the army. Neither faction won complete endorsement for its position, and tensions ran high.[1]

The first question concerned the Board of War. The original board, a standing committee of Congress, simply could not keep pace with the volume of work, and as early as April 1777 it had recommended its own replacement by a permanent administrative body. On 17 October 1777 the delegates approved a plan that called for a

---

[1]Information on the general political and ideological context is contained in Henderson, *Party Politics*, pp. 54, 102–5, 118–24; White, "Standing Armies," pp. 199–201, 207, 224–61, 277–78.

Board of War consisting of three permanent members plus a clerical staff. Congress also expanded its duties. In addition to the administrative functions of its predecessor, the new board's responsibilities included supervising recruitment, managing prisoners, and producing weapons. It was to act as Congress' sole official intermediary in dealing with the Army and the states on military affairs. On 7 November Quartermaster General Thomas Mifflin, Adjutant General Timothy Pickering, and Robert Hanson Harrison, Washington's military secretary, were elected as members, although Harrison promptly declined.[2]

Mifflin was the first to report, and he immediately took an active role. The fact that reorganizing the Quartermaster's Department was one of the Board of War's first tasks contributed substantially to Mifflin's early influence. He persuaded Congress to expand the board to five members, which it did on 24 November, and recommended Richard Peters (the permanent secretary of the old board) and Maj. Gen. Horatio Gates for the new vacancies. Congress appointed both men and named former Commissary General Joseph Trumbull to replace Harrison. At Mifflin's suggestion, Gates was named president of the board. He retained both his rank and his right to field command. These five men brought with them the staff expertise that Congress wanted the board to have, but none were members of Washington's inner circle.[3]

When Gates arrived at York, Pennsylvania, in January to take up his new duties, the memory of his victory at Saratoga remained with various delegates and Army officers.[4] He also knew that Congress had initiated investigations into the loss of forts in the Highlands and along the Delaware River and had openly criticized Washington for his failure to confiscate supplies in Pennsylvania to keep them out of enemy hands.[5] Prodded by some delegates, Mifflin, and a handful of disgruntled officers, Gates began trying to convert the Board of War into an agency with control of military operations.

In October 1777 Col. Moses Hazen had suggested to Gates that a small force could capitalize on the Saratoga victory by attacking Montreal that winter when ice would neutralize British warships on Lake Champlain; a larger force could then complete the conquest of Canada in the spring. Brig. Gen. John Stark independently convinced Congress to authorize a small raid by militia volunteers on the Lake Champlain naval base at St. John's. Gates, working through the Board of War, persuaded Congress in January to authorize an "irruption" into Canada along the lines suggested by Hazen, and to place the board in complete control of the operation. At Gates' suggestion, Congress named the Marquis de Lafayette, who had been commissioned a major general in July, to command the expedition, assisted by Maj. Gen. Thomas Conway, General Stark, and Colonel Hazen.[6]

Conway, an Irish veteran of the French Army, became known as a critic of Washington during the late fall. On 13 December Congress had promoted him, over a number of more senior brigadier generals, to major general and had named him an

[2]*JCC*, 7:241–42; 8:474n, 563; 9:809–11, 818–20, 874, 936, 971; Burnett, *Letters*, 2:52.

[3]*JCC*, 9:941, 959–63, 971–72; Burnett, *Letters*, 2:574–76; *Pennsylvania Archives*, 1st ser., 6:35.

[4]Gates Papers (James Lovell to Gates, 5 Oct and 27 Nov 77; Joseph Reed to Gates, 30 Oct 77; James Wilkinson to Gates, 4 Nov 77; Eliphalet Dyer to Gates, 5 Nov 77; Thomas Conway to Gates, 11 Nov 77; Mifflin to Gates, 17 and 27 Nov 77).

[5]*JCC*, 9:972, 975–76, 1013–15.

[6]Gates Papers (Hazen to Gates, 26 Oct 77; James Duane to Gates, 16 Dec 77; Gates to Col John Greaton, 28 Dec 77); *JCC*, 9:999–1001; 10:84–85, 87; Burnett, *Letters*, 3:124–30; Stanley J. Idzerda et al., eds., *Lafayette in the Age of the American Revolution: Selected Letters and Papers* (Ithaca: Cornell University Press, 1977–   ), 1:xxiv–xxvi, 169–72, 204–7, 213–18, 245–385.

MARIE-PAUL-JOSEPH-ROCH-YVES-GILBERT
DU MOTIER, MARQUIS DE LAFAYETTE
*(1757-1834) was only a supernumerary
cavalry captain in the French Army when
he came to America as a volunteer in 1777.
He demonstrated exceptional leadership as
a youthful Continental Army major general. (Portrait by Charles Willson Peale,
1781.)*

Inspector General. Conway planned to turn his new office into the field agency of the president of the Board of War, but Washington effectively froze him out of any role within the Main Army.[7] Gates selected Lafayette in effect to be a French figurehead for the Canadian invasion; he expected that Conway would be the de facto commander. Lafayette, however, refused to participate in any activity that might undermine Washington's authority as Commander in Chief; he insisted that Conway be removed and that orders from Congress concerning the expedition pass through Washington rather than through the board. He threatened to return to France if his demands were not met. This strong support for Washington had the desired effect, and Congress canceled the invasion on 2 March.[8]

The termination of the Canadian "irruption" and a related congressional airing and dismissal of Conway's criticisms of Washington ended the challenge to Washington's leadership of the Army. Conway submitted his resignation in a ploy to bolster his status, but Congress quickly accepted it. Gates, realizing that he lacked both the Commander in Chief's support and the strength to unseat him, abandoned the presidency of the board and returned to his field command in the north. When Mifflin was pressured into resigning on 17 August 1778, the Board of War reverted to a purely administrative role. These decisions solidified Washington's authority as the single voice of the Army on matters of policy.[9]

[7]Fitzpatrick, *Writings*, 9:387-90; 10:39, 226-28, 236-37; *JCC*, 9:1026; Gates Papers (Conway to Gates, 11 Nov 77 and 4 Jan 78).

[8]Fitzpatrick, *Writings*, 11:113-14; *JCC*, 10:107, 216-17, 253-54; Burnett, *Letters*, 3:63-65; McDougall Papers (Greene to McDougall, 5 Feb 78).

[9]Fitzpatrick, *Writings*, 10:236-37, 410-11; 11:493-94; 14:383-86; *JCC*, 10:399; 11:520, 802; Burnett, *Letters*, 3:20-25, 28-31, 39-40, 42, 48, 141-42, 209-11, 487-89; Gates Papers (Mifflin to Gates, 28 Nov 77; Gates to Washington, 8 Dec 77, 23 Jan and 17 Feb 78; to Congress, 11 Dec 77; Walter Stewart to Gates, 12 Feb 78; Pickering to Gates, 26 Aug 78); McDougall, Papers (Greene to McDougall, 25 Jan and 16 Apr 78; Varnum to McDougall, 7 Feb 78; McDougall to Greene, 14 Feb 78); S. Weir Mitchell, ed., "Historical Notes of Dr. Benjamin Rush, 1777," *Pennsylvania Magazine of History and Biography* 27 (1903):147; John Laurens, *The Army Correspondence of Colonel John Laurens in the Years 1777-78* (New York: Bradford Club, 1867), pp. 80-88, 98-101.

OATH OF ALLEGIANCE OF BENEDICT ARNOLD. *On 3 February 1778 Congress required all members of the Continental Army to sign an oath acknowledging support of national independence. This was an effort to weed Loyalist sympathizers out of the military. Maj. Gen. Benedict Arnold's oath was witnessed on 30 May 1778 by Brig. Gen. Henry Knox at the Artillery Park at Valley Forge.*

Washington asserted his restored position by answering congressional objections to improving the professional conditions of the officer corps. During the winter of 1777–78 a large number of officers were leaving the Continental Army because they could no longer afford the financial losses connected with service. An officer who wished to leave the British Army could sell his commission (under government supervision) and use the proceeds as retirement income; officers involuntarily retired in Army reductions drew half pay. Washington and his senior advisers believed that similar programs were needed in the Continental Army if it was to attract able officers in a time of inflation and other economic problems. Members of Congress with ideological objections to standing armies, however, strenuously opposed such measures as half pay, which they felt would create "a set of haughty idle imperious Scandalizers of industrious Citizens and Farmers."[10]

On 10 January 1778 Congress decided to send a Committee of Conference to Valley Forge to discuss matters relating to efficiency and economy in the Army, including the question of officers' compensation. The committee's proponents wanted it to con-

[10]Burnett, *Letters*, 3:31–33; see also 2:585–86; 3:34, 153–56; McDougall Papers (Greene to McDougall, 25 Jan 78); Albigence Waldo, "Valley Forge, 1777–78. Diary of Surgeon Albigence Waldo, of the Connecticut Line," *Pennsylvania Magazine of History and Biography* 21 (1897):314. Henderson, *Party Politics*, pp. 102–4, 120–24; White, "Standing Armies," pp. 277–78.

sist of three members of the Board of War and three delegates, but when the political tide turned against the board, the committee drew its membership exclusively from delegates. Under the leadership of Francis Dana and Gouverneur Morris, the committee held extensive discussions with Washington and his advisers between 28 January and 12 March and in effect filled the policy-setting role that Gates and Mifflin had planned for the Board of War. The committee's reports and recommendations to Congress largely echoed Washington's position and formed the basis for numerous reforms enacted during the winter and spring. On 1 April Congress rejected the committee's endorsement of half pay and peacetime sale of commissions, but it then spent six weeks attempting to find an alternative. Washington lobbied hard in support of the committee, arguing that the Army's sufferings at Valley Forge proved its loyalty to the civilian government. He won support for a compromise on 15 May. Officers serving to the end of the war were promised seven years of half pay; enlisted men, a lump-sum payment of eighty dollars.[11]

The committee at camp had a second major objective: reconciling the large size of the Army approved in the 1776 resolves with the manpower realities of the 1777 campaign. Most regiments had started that campaign below full strength, and losses had forced Washington to issue muskets to sergeants and junior officers to augment the fire of the rank and file. In contrast to the shortages of enlisted men, there were nearly full complements of officers in most regiments. Washington's suggested solution was the institution of a civilian recruiting system and a limited draft. Congress lacked the legal power to enforce such systems, but it did recommend them to the individual states. The delegates, convinced now that 110 regiments could not be filled, directed the committee at camp to look for ways to reduce quotas to realistic levels, consolidate units, and eliminate surplus officers.[12]

By the beginning of February 1778, when the committee at camp was well into its work, most of the continentals were with the Main Army. Every state except Georgia and South Carolina had sent units to Washington. The 1st Continental Artillery remained in its home state of Virginia, and the equivalent of three brigades were in the Highlands or in the Northern Department. All remaining Continental units, a force that should have numbered over 60,000 men, were at Valley Forge or its outposts. Washington had 15 brigades directly under his command at Valley Forge plus 2 others that were wintering at Wilmington, Delaware. Portions of 3 artillery regiments also were at Valley Forge, and the 4 light dragoon regiments were occupying Trenton. The infantrymen of the 15 brigades included 64 field, 720 company, and 206 staff officers; 931 sergeants; 642 drummers and fifers; and 17,491 rank and file. Only 7,600 rank and file were completely fit for duty, and a third of those were detached for various purposes. Almost 5,000 were sick, 1,100 were on furlough, and 3,700 healthy men lacked either shoes or clothes and could not participate in combat. The artillery contingent contained 117 officers and 810 men; the cavalry, 70 officers and 438 men.[13]

[11]*JCC*, 10:39–41, 67, 285–86, 300–301; 11:502–3; Burnett, *Letters*, 3:61–115, 123–24, 131, 160–63, 212–13, 219–21, 244–45, 255–56; Fitzpatrick, *Writings*, 11:285–86, 290–92, 415; Max M. Mintz, *Gouverneur Morris and the American Revolution* (Norman: University of Oklahoma Press, 1970), pp. 91–101.

[12]*JCC*, 8:593–95, 670; 9:930; 10:39–40; Fitzpatrick, *Writings*, 8:440; 9:365–67, 406–7; 10:125–26, 153, 195, 197–98, 205, 221–25; 11:236–40; "Plan for a Re-Organization of the Continental Army," *Historical Magazine*, 2d ser., 3 (1868):270–73.

[13]RG 93, National Archives (General Return, Main Army, 9 Feb 78).

The committee thus found a Main Army with only about a third of its authorized strength.

The committee members held extensive discussions with Washington and his senior advisers before reporting back to Congress. The press of other business prevented that body from implementing substantive reforms before the 1778 campaign started, although on 26 February it recommended, as an interim measure, that the states institute a recruiting program that included using nine-month drafts to fill the quotas. In a sense this decision marked a temporary retreat from the ideal of an Army composed exclusively of long-service soldiers. Congress also reduced Rhode Island's quota for the campaign to the equivalent of a single full regiment and Pennsylvania's to ten regiments.[14]

Comprehensive legislation came in May and involved a revision of the basic tables of organization for the various types of regiments. This resolve of 27 May 1778 reduced the number of regiments and especially the number of officers in each regiment, and made several other changes.[15] Perhaps the most basic of these reforms concerned the infantry regiment. After rejecting a radically different organizational model suggested by Maj. Gen. Charles Lee, Congress adopted a structure which moved toward the British regimental model.[16] (*Chart 8*) Each regiment gained a ninth company as a permanent light infantry company, but the total number of regimental officers declined from 40 to 29 and enlisted strength fell from 692 to 553. Through attrition each regiment was to eliminate its colonel and operate with only two field officers. This change would simplify prisoner of war exchanges since the British colonel was not a combat officer. Another major area of reduction was the staff, where the adjutant, quartermaster, and paymaster ceased to be separate positions. Subalterns from line companies assumed the duties of the first two offices as additional tasks, while one of the captains, elected by the unit's officers, became paymaster as well. All three received extra compensation.

Within each company one lieutenant's position disappeared, and several captains lost their positions as the field officers assumed command of companies. If a regiment still had a colonel, the senior lieutenant, as captain-lieutenant, exercised practical control over his company. Each company also lost a sergeant and a corporal from the organization approved in 1776. Privates were cut by a third, from 76 to 53. The rank and file strength, the true power of the company, fell from 80 to 56. If a regiment retained its light company, it now deployed for combat with a bayonet strength of 504 out of a total of 582. This 87 percent figure was roughly the same as in the previous structure. Normally, however, the light company was detached, and the bayonet strength then dropped to 448, roughly on a par with a British regiment.

Congress had created a regiment which would cost less than the 1776 regiment, but it was only 70 percent as strong. Its combat efficiency was even lower since 2 or 3 of the companies had only 2 officers, and the reduced staff no longer furnished a pool of spare officers to replace casualties during the heat of combat. Except for the addition

---

[14]*JCC*, 10:199–203.

[15]Ibid., 11:538–43, 570, 633–34; 12:1154–60; Burnett, *Letters*, 3:264–66, 407, 431–32; Fitzpatrick, *Writings*, 11:475–76; 12:30–35, 60–62, 274–75; Idzerda, *Lafayette*, 1:284–85.

[16]Lee, *Papers*, 2:382–89; *JCC*, 11:514–15. Lee's plan was based on the "legion" advocated by Marshal Maurice de Saxe. An earlier version of the plan is contained in Webb, *Correspondence and Journals*, 1:84–87.

CHART 8—INFANTRY REGIMENT 27 MAY 1778

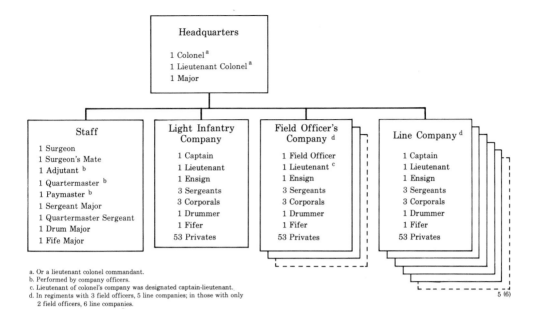

Headquarters

1 Colonel[a]
1 Lieutenant Colonel[a]
1 Major

Staff	Light Infantry Company	Field Officer's Company [d]	Line Company [d]
1 Surgeon	1 Captain	1 Field Officer	1 Captain
1 Surgeon's Mate	1 Lieutenant	1 Lieutenant [c]	1 Lieutenant
1 Adjutant [b]	1 Ensign	1 Ensign	1 Ensign
1 Quartermaster [b]	3 Sergeants	3 Sergeants	3 Sergeants
1 Paymaster [b]	3 Corporals	3 Corporals	3 Corporals
1 Sergeant Major	1 Drummer	1 Drummer	1 Drummer
1 Quartermaster Sergeant	1 Fifer	1 Fifer	1 Fifer
1 Drum Major	53 Privates	53 Privates	53 Privates
1 Fife Major			

a. Or a lieutenant colonel commandant.
b. Performed by company officers.
c. Lieutenant of colonel's company was designated captain-lieutenant.
d. In regiments with 3 field officers, 5 line companies; in those with only
   2 field officers, 6 line companies.

5 (6)

of the permanent light infantry company, the new regiment on paper was inferior to the old one as a battlefield force. Congress viewed these changes as important from a financial point of view, and also as acceptable compromises with the realities of recruiting revealed in 1777. Washington knew that the demonstrated lack of state support for a large army had negated the paper advantages of the 1776 regiment, and he grudgingly accepted the loss of tactical control, although he remained upset by Congress' insistence on using line officers to perform staff duties outside the regiment.

The artillery regiment underwent less change. It gained a third second lieutenant for each company, but lost staff officers in a change that paralleled the change in the infantry regiment's staff. Similar staff reductions took place in the light dragoon regiment. (*Chart 9*) Unlike the infantry regiment, the cavalry regiment expanded. Each troop gained 1 second lieutenant, 1 sergeant, 1 corporal, and 22 privates. On the other hand, the 4 regimental supernumeraries and the troop armorer were eliminated. The troop was now nearly double its 1777 size, with 4 officers and 64 enlisted men. The new regimental structure required 29 officers and 386 men. In Congress' eyes this increase in the ratio of enlisted men to officers gave the mounted arm a more economical organization.

Congress waited for a lull in the 1778 campaign to carry out the conversion to the new regimental organizations, but its decisions, culminating in the 27 May resolution, had modified many of the concepts embodied in the previous winter's decisions. To a certain extent its actions had simply acknowledged the practical impossibility of raising the large, long-term army that Washington had wanted. They also reflected some delegates' continuing deep-seated suspicion of a standing army. The contrast between Gates' success at Saratoga and Washington's loss of Philadelphia was still fresh in their minds. They believed that Gates' success derived from his use of a small Conti-

CHART 9—LIGHT DRAGOON REGIMENT 27 MAY 1778

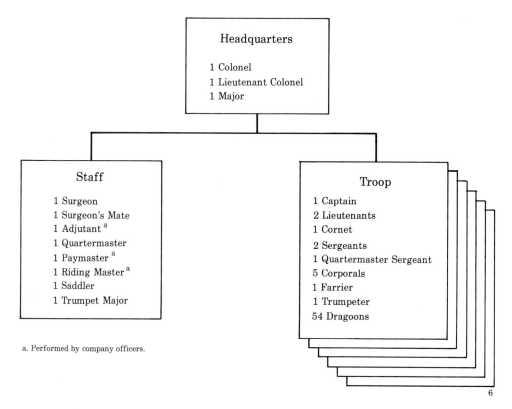

Headquarters

1 Colonel
1 Lieutenant Colonel
1 Major

Staff

1 Surgeon
1 Surgeon's Mate
1 Adjutant [a]
1 Quartermaster
1 Paymaster [a]
1 Riding Master [a]
1 Saddler
1 Trumpet Major

Troop

1 Captain
2 Lieutenants
1 Cornet
2 Sergeants
1 Quartermaster Sergeant
5 Corporals
1 Farrier
1 Trumpeter
54 Dragoons

a. Performed by company officers.

6

nental cadre combined with a large militia force called out in response to the emergency. The reconstitution of the Board of War almost certainly had stemmed from the belief that his example could be followed. Washington stood off the board's challenge to his leadership, but Congress did not accept his views on a number of issues important to his concept of a professional army. Although Congress followed his suggestion in recommending that the states institute a civilian recruiting system and a limited draft, for example, it also ordered cuts in the number of infantry units and in their size.

Foreign Advisers

The revised regimental structure adopted by Congress represented a movement toward the British model, but during the winter at Valley Forge, Washington decided to adopt certain characteristics of European military organization as well. He based his decisions not just on his reading of various military handbooks and his personal experience but also on the expert advice of a number of foreign volunteers who had joined the Army during 1777. The Continental Army's engineer corps was the first to feel this impact, followed by the mounted arm. The creation of various specialized units also reflected Washington's openness to new ideas.

Tradition in Europe allowed officers to serve in the armies of other nations to win glory, gain promotions, and taste adventure. In 1776 a number of individuals who

Louis le Begue de Presle Duportail *(1743–1802) was a skilled French engineer "loaned" to the Continental Army. He reached the rank of major general after Yorktown and is regarded as the father of the Corps of Engineers. In 1791 when France adopted the tactical reforms proposed by Guibert, Duportail was serving as minister of war. (Portrait by Charles Willson Peale, ca. 1782.)*

came to America for these reasons claimed to have technical expertise in the artillery and engineer branches. Unfortunately, many were frauds who demanded high rank. Congress' hope that Frenchmen could successfully recruit in Canada, and Germans in the German-American community, proved groundless. Since most were not fluent in English, they could not be assigned to line units. Frederick de Woedtke, a former Prussian officer, and Matthias-Alexis, Chevalier de La Rochefermoy, who both served in 1776 as brigadier generals in the Northern Department, were conspicuous failures.[17]

Silas Deane's diplomatic mission to France in the summer of 1776 included hiring skilled professional soldiers as well as soliciting material assistance. On the advice of Pierre Caron de Beaumarchais and Jean Baptiste de Gribeauval (the leading artillery expert of the century), Deane contracted with one of the latter's proteges, Philip Tronson du Coudray, to organize and lead a group of volunteers to America. Coudray, despite extravagant claims, was actually a military theorist whose rank was equivalent to that of an artillery major. Deane granted him a generous contract and the title of General of Artillery and Ordnance (with the rank of major general). The contract promised him a virtually free hand in artillery and engineer operations. His group arrived in America in the late spring of 1777. Congress commissioned two members, Thomas Conway and Philippe-Hubert, Chevalier de Preudhomme de Borre, brigadier generals; it commissioned Coudray as Inspector General of Ordnance and Military Manufactories. His accidental death on 15 September ended a controversy over rank that had erupted among American generals.[18]

[17]Idzerda, *Lafayette,* 1:68–87. Chevalier Dubuisson des Hayes, an aide to Maj. Gen. Johannes de Kalb, described the first volunteers as "officers who are deeply in debt," and added that "some of them have been discharged from their units" in Europe. He charged that the governors of the French West Indies had sent them to America with deliberately inflated credentials in order to be rid of them.

[18]Force, *American Archives,* 5th ser., 1:1011–23; 2:283–85; Jonathan R. Dull, *The French Navy and American Independence: A Study of Arms and Diplomacy, 1774–1789* (Princeton: Princeton University Press, 1975), pp. 30–49. Lafayette described Coudray as "a clever but imprudent man, a good officer but vain to the point of folly." Idzerda, *Lafayette,* 1:11.

THADDEUS KOSCIUSZKO *(1746–1817), a Pole trained as a military engineer in France, came to America in 1776 as a volunteer and became one of the most trusted members of the Corps of Engineers. He later led an unsuccessful revolution in his native land. (Portrait by Julian Rys, 1897.)*

A second group of technical experts came to America through the efforts of the French Minister of War, the Comte de Saint-Germain. He formally "loaned" four military engineers to the Continental Army. In contrast to previous volunteers, these men were given contracts that called for promotions to a grade only one step higher than their French commissions, and Saint-Germain had carefully picked them for their skills. Their leader, Louis le Begue de Presle Duportail, was commissioned a colonel on 8 July 1777, and shortly thereafter he was given command over all engineers in the Army. He and his colleagues quickly unmasked Coudray's claims to technical training as an engineer. Duportail's obvious expertise and cooperative attitude led to his promotion on 17 November to brigadier general, a status equivalent to that of General Knox.[19]

A third contingent from France reached America in 1777. Led by the Marquis de Lafayette, Gilbert du Motier, and the Bavarian-born Johannes de Kalb, they were talented proteges of the Comte de Broglie, one of France's top military commanders. Although Lafayette's military experience was limited, his powerful political connections in the French Court led Deane to offer him a major general's commission. De Kalb, an experienced officer in the French Army, received a similar offer. Deane promised them assignments in the infantry rather than in the technical services. By the time the group reached Philadelphia, however, the failure of some of the first volunteers and the controversy surrounding Coudray led to a cold reception by Congress and the Army. But Lafayette's enthusiasm, their offer to serve as unpaid volunteers, and their demonstrated competence eventually earned most of these Frenchmen commissions.[20]

[19]Elizabeth S. Kite, *Brigadier-General Louis Lebegue Duportail, Commandant of Engineers in the Continental Army, 1777–1783* (Baltimore: Johns Hopkins Press, for the Institut Francais de Washington, 1933), pp. 2–34.
[20]Idzerda, *Lafayette*, pp. xxiv–xxvi, 7–12, 17–18, 33–36, 53–56, 68–87, 145–50. Lafayette (1757–1834) held the rank in France of a cavalry captain in a reserve status, but as Kalb later commented, he was a gifted natural soldier.

The most immediate impact of foreign volunteers came in military engineering. There was no training available in America that could match that offered to British engineers at Woolwich, let alone that available in France where the science of military engineering was being perfected. Of the first foreign volunteers commissioned as engineers, only a young Polish captain, Andrew Thaddeus Kosciuszko, who had been trained in France, was qualified by European standards. Congress commissioned him a colonel of engineers on 18 October 1776.[21] Washington then included a request for an organized corps of engineers in his plans for 1777, and Congresss authorized him to form such a body on 27 December 1776. The shortage of proficient engineers, however, prevented any action. Col. Rufus Putnam chose to return to infantry duty in 1777, and a more cautious Congress halted the commissioning of untested volunteers. This decision left only Col. Jeduthan Baldwin, Kosciuszko, and a number of detailed infantry and artillery officers until Duportail's group arrived at Philadelphia.[22] With Duportail's emergence as a trusted expert, for the first time the Army now could judge Europeans solely on professional merit. He secured the services of experienced men such as Jean de Murnan, whose career in the French Army had been blocked by Court intrigue.[23]

One of the first contributions of the engineers was a bridging train. On the night of 11–12 December 1777 they constructed two bridges over the Schuylkill River at Swede's Ford. One consisted of a roadbed laid across floating rafts; the other, of thirty-six wagons placed in the shallow water of the ford with rails across them. The engineers later constructed more sophisticated flat-bottomed pontons with special wheeled carriages at Albany, and in 1781 these pontons accompanied the troops to Yorktown.[24]

A second major involvement was in the construction of permanent fortifications. After the defeats of 1777, Washington funneled available resources to the field army. He refortified only the Hudson Highlands to make the area the strategic pivot for the Main Army. From the winter of 1777–78 until the end of the war a large portion of the engineer corps worked on the fortress at West Point. Instead of a single large fort, which could be lost in one stroke, Duportail's engineers erected a modern complex of smaller, mutually supporting works for in depth defense.[25]

At Valley Forge Duportail proposed to supplement the engineer officers with companies of combat engineers. Following European custom, he called them companies of sappers and miners. Sappers dug the entrenchments (saps) for a formal siege; miners constructed underground tunnels. These companies could execute small projects or supervise infantry details in more extensive undertakings. Washington particularly

[21]*JCC*, 5:565, 614-15, 656; 6:888; Miecislaus Haiman, *Kosciuszko in the American Revolution* (New York: Polish Institute of Arts and Sciences in America, 1943), pp. 1-11.

[22]Force, *American Archives*, 5th ser., 2:549-50, 892-93; Fitzpatrick, *Writings*, 6:160-61; 7:102-6; 8:380-82; Baldwin, *Revolutionary Journal*, pp. 102-3; *JCC*, 8:380. Congress commissioned the Marquis de Fleury as a captain on 2 May 1777, but his was the only new engineer appointment made in the first half of 1777.

[23]Burnett, *Letters*, 2:417-21; Fitzpatrick, *Writings*, 10:35; *JCC*, 8:571; 9:932; 13:57-58; Kite, *Duportail*, pp. 50-52. Duportail is considered the father of the U.S. Army Corps of Engineers.

[24]Amos Perry, ed., "Dr. Albigence Waldo, Surgeon in the Continental Army," *Historical Magazine* 5 (1861):131; Enos Reeves, "Extracts From the Letter-Books of Lieutenant Enos Reeves, of the Pennsylvania Line," ed. John B. Reeves, *Pennsylvania Magazine of History and Biography* 20 (1896):458-59; James Duncan, "Captain James Duncan's Diary of the Siege of Yorktown," ed. W.F. Boogher, *Magazine of History* 2 (1905):408.

[25]Kite, *Duportail*, pp. 47-50, 60-72; Haiman, *Kosciuszko*, pp. 43-47; Fitzpatrick, *Writings*, 11:297-98.

liked Duportail's plan to train their officers as apprentice engineers, thus ensuring for the first time a steady supply of native-born engineers. Congress approved the formation of three companies on 27 May 1778, but the Army moved slowly. Washington appointed officers on 2 August 1779, after Duportail had personally interviewed the candidates, and Washington transferred carefully selected enlisted men from infantry regiments a year later. Each company was authorized a captain, 3 lieutenants, 4 sergeants, 4 corporals, and 60 privates.[26]

Congress took the final step to regularize the engineers on 11 March 1779. In response to Washington's continuing pressure, it resolved "that the engineers in the service of the United States shall be formed into a corps, styled the 'corps of engineers,' and shall take rank and enjoy the same rights, honours, and privileges, with the other troops on continental establishment."[27] This legislation gave the engineers the status of a branch of the Continental Army. They received the same pay and prerogatives as artillerymen to prevent any jealousy between the technical branches. As commandant, Duportail supervised the engineer officers and the companies of sappers and miners, functioned as a special adviser to the Commander in Chief, and assigned individual officers to specific posts before the start of each campaign.[28]

France provided a precedent for a separate topographical section. Following the Seven Years' War, France had begun rigorously training a small corps of topographical engineers, the Ingenieurs Geographes (distinct from the Corps Royal du Genie). They prepared a systematic map reference library for planning operations.[29] As a former surveyor, Washington particularly understood the value of accurate maps. On 19 July 1777 he asked for a topographical staff; six days later Congress told him to appoint a "geographer and surveyor of the roads, to take sketches of the country, the seat of war," as well as necessary subordinates. Robert Erskine accepted the job but did not report to headquarters until June 1778.

Erskine, a Scot who had migrated to New Jersey in 1771, was a civil engineer and inventor. Until he died of pneumonia on 2 October 1780, Erskine coordinated up to six survey teams from his home at Ringwood Forge near West Point. He and his successors transformed the collected raw data into a comprehensive survey of the zone of operations of the Main Army. The resulting maps equaled those of the French in accuracy and were vastly superior to anything available to British commanders.[30]

On 15 September 1777 Congress answered Washington's long-standing request for a cavalry commander on a par with Knox. He had been hoping to find another for-

[26]Fitzpatrick, *Writings*, 10:433; 11:239; 12:40, 241, 311; 14:235; 15:103, 491–92; 16:36; 17:443–45; 19:224; *JCC*, 11:541–42; 16:133; Joseph Plumb Martin, *Private Yankee Doodle: Being a Narrative of Some of the Adventures, Dangers, and Sufferings of a Revolutionary Soldier*, ed. George F. Scheer (Boston: Little, Brown and Co., 1962), pp. 194–96. The British Royal Military Artificers were not formed until 1787.

[27]*JCC*, 13:305–6.

[28]Fitzpatrick, *Writings*, 12:376–77; 14:160–61; 16:21–23, 37, 46–48; *JCC*, 14:570–71; Kite, *Duportail*, pp. 125–31.

[29]J.B. Hawley, Barbara Bartz Petchenik, and Lawrence W. Tower, eds., *Mapping the American Revolutionary War* (Chicago: University of Chicago Press, 1978), pp. 32–36, 68–75; Howard C. Rice, Jr., and Anne S. K. Brown, eds., *The American Campaigns of Rochambeau's Army: 1780, 1781, 1782, 1783*, 2 vols. (Princeton and Providence: Princeton and Brown University Presses, 1972), 1:191–219; 2:3–5, 111–20.

[30]Fitzpatrick, *Writings*, 7:65; 8:372, 443, 495–96; 11:246; 12:21; 14:182–83; 23:68–69; *JCC*, 8:580; 18:1118; 20:475–76, 738. The maps are in the Erskine-DeWitt Collection, New-York Historical Society. British Headquarters Maps are in the Henry Clinton Papers, William L. Clements Library, University of Michigan; photostatic copies are available at the New-York Historical Society. Simeon DeWitt succeeded Erskine in the north, as Thomas Hutchings did in the south.

CASIMIR PULASKI *(ca. 1748–79) was a flamboyant cavalryman from Poland who served as commander of horse at Trenton during the 1777–78 winter with the rank of brigadier general. He died of wounds received at Savannah in 1779 while leading his legion. (Portrait by Julian Rys, 1897.)*

eign volunteer who could upgrade the effectiveness of the mounted arm in the same way that Duportail was improving the engineers. Casimir Pulaski, a Pole, consequently became Commander of Horse and a brigadier general. Shortly thereafter Francois-Louis Teisseidre, the Marquis de Fleury, assumed the position of brigade major for the light dragoons, and the four regiments went into winter quarters at Trenton. Washington and Pulaski used the winter to begin transforming the troopers into an offensive force. Pulaski established a riding school to train the horses and men in European shock action, including cut-and-thrust saber tactics. The large organization approved by Congress on 27 May 1778 reflected a desire to implement this transition. Unfortunately, Pulaski clashed with his American officers and resigned as Commander of Horse on 28 March 1778. Washington never found a replacement, and the strategic changes after Monmouth led him to restore the light dragoons to a reconnaissance role.[31]

Although the light dragoons did not develop into a European-style cavalry force, the Continental Army introduced a number of other light units patterned after the European partisan corps, which had emerged in the Seven Years' War. The partisan corps, or legion, was a recent European development designed primarily to conduct raids on enemy rear areas. Maj. Nicholas Dietrich, Baron de Ottendorf, a Saxon veteran of the Prussian Army, commanded the first of these units. On 5 December 1776 Congress ordered him to recruit one company of chasseurs (light infantry) and two of jaegers (riflemen). A fourth company was added in April 1777. Most of the officers were foreign volunteers, but the enlisted men came from the German-American community. After Ottendorf deserted, Congress placed Col. Charles Armand Tuffin, the Marquis de la Rouerie (known in America as Colonel Armand), in command. It also

[31]*JCC*, 8:745; 12:897, 941; Burnett, *Letters*, 3:408; Fitzpatrick, *Writings*, 7:51, 190–91; 9:143–44, 305; 10:234–36; 11:446; 12:228, 276, 490; 13:14–15; Samuel Hay to William Irvine, 14 Nov 77, *Historical Magazine* 3 (1859):283; Gates Papers (to Washington, 23 May 78; Benjamin Tallmadge to Gates, 1 Jun 78).

told him to raise a partisan corps of 200 Frenchmen on 19 May, but he did not fill it in 1777.[32]

When General Pulaski resigned his command, Congress allowed him to raise an "independent corps." It consisted of a troop of 68 lancers and 200 light infantry organized into a legion. The cadre for the troop came from light dragoons he had trained at Trenton. Congress authorized another independent corps on 7 April 1778 to reward Capt. Henry Lee for excellent service on the lines around Philadelphia. It promoted Lee to major, withdrew his troop from the 1st Continental Light Dragoons, and expanded it first into two troops and then into three on 28 May. Lee used the small light-dragoon organization of 1777, which was appropriate for reconnaissance. Armand finally recruited his Free and Independent Chasseurs after Congress approved an organization for it on 25 June 1778. It consisted of three large companies based on Marshal Maurice de Saxe's concept of the legion. Each contained 4 officers, 8 noncommissioned officers, 2 drummers (or horn players), and 128 privates.[33]

At the end of 1778 the Main Army had three partisan corps. Lee's, an American force, was entirely mounted; Pulaski's (usually operating with the remnants of Ottendorf's companies) was a combined arms unit; and Armand's consisted entirely of infantry. Pulaski's and Armand's corps contained large foreign contingents. When Washington and Congress concluded that the most efficient partisan organization contained balanced numbers of mounted and dismounted men, Congress annexed Capt. Allen McLane's infantry company (formerly of Patton's Additional Regiment) to Lee on 13 July 1779. On 14 February 1780 it added seventy more men to form a total of three dismounted troops. The success of this experiment led Congress to rescind an earlier directive disbanding Pulaski's corps and to consolidate it with Armand's on 23 February.[34]

Congress authorized a special mounted police unit, the Marechaussee Corps, on 27 May 1778. It also had European rather than Anglo-American precedents. It consisted of 5 officers, 1 clerk, 8 noncommissioned officers, 2 trumpeters, and 47 privates (including 4 who served as executioners). The corps assisted the provost marshal in maintaining order in camp and on the march. In combat it took station behind the Second Line to secure the rear and to prevent desertion. Capt. Bartholomew Von Heer, a Prussian veteran, recruited the corps in the Pennsylvania-German communities of Berks and Lancaster Counties. It contributed to the general improvement in the Army's internal order and discipline.[35]

Another police-type unit, created in 1779, assumed responsibility for guarding prisoners of war, a function previously performed by militia. When Burgoyne surrendered, the "Saratoga Convention" stipulated that his troops had to leave North America and not return unless exchanged. When the British failed to honor some of the

---

[32]*JCC*, 6:1007; 7:186, 346; Fitzpatrick, *Writings*, 6:324; 8:91–92, 224–26; 9:162; New-York Historical Society *Collections* for 1915, pp. 566–69; Saffell, *Records of the Revolutionary War* pp. 219–21.

[33]*JCC*, 10:291, 294, 314–15, 364; 11:545, 642–45. Fitzpatrick, *Writings*, 11:80–82, 205–6, 230; 12:152–53, 470; 13:41–43. Gates Papers to Washington, 24 Jun and 13 Jul 78.

[34]Fitzpatrick, *Writings*, 14:65, 74–79; 15:233, 242, 345; 17:450–52, 496–97; *JCC*, 13:132, 143, 181; 14:822–23; 15:1418; 16:159, 187; Burnett, *Letters*, 4:45, 55, 58–59, 67; Gates Papers (Armand to Gates, 25 Jul 80).

[35]Fitzpatrick, *Writings*, 11:443; 12:26–27, 241; 13:61–63, 68–70; 19:41; *JCC*, 11:541, 729; Steuben Papers (Von Heer to Steuben, 31 Dec 79).

BENJAMIN FLOWER *(1748–81) served as commissary general of military stores and as commander of the Artillery Artificer Regiment with the rank of lieutenant colonel. He was a native of Philadelphia. (Portrait attributed to James Peale.)*

minor provisions of the agreement, Congress suspected that the regiments would in fact not be sent to Europe once they were released and therefore detained them. In the fall of 1778 they were transferred from Cambridge, Massachusetts, to Charlottesville, Virginia, for security reasons.[36] Instead of using militia guards, on 23 December 1778 Virginia decided to raise a 600-man regiment under former Continental officers. Congress modified Virginia's plan somewhat when it adopted this Regiment of Guards on 9 January 1779. It remained under the control of the governor, rather than the Southern Department. The regiment disbanded in stages between 10 April and 9 June 1781 when the "Convention Army" moved to Maryland.[37]

The Corps of Invalids was a specialized unit established in 1777. The British Army used separate companies of men not fit for field duty to garrison fortifications in the home islands. The Continental Army, reflecting its growing professionalism, turned to a similar organization to free combat units from defending depots not in immediate danger. On 20 June 1777 Congress authorized Col. Lewis Nicola, a strong proponent of the concept, to organize the corps. It had the additional mission of recruiting and training replacements. Congress directed Nicola to set up a "Military School for Young Gentlemen" within the regiment to train ensigns for ultimate assignment to line units. He recruited at Philadelphia during the summer and added a detachment at Boston the following winter. The corps never fulfilled its training function, but it performed valuable garrison duty, especially at West Point, until the end of the war.[38]

The growing sophistication of the Continental Army, inspired in part by foreign volunteers, was reflected also in improvements introduced in 1778 and 1779 in the organization of supporting troops. Following the death of General Coudray on 17 September 1777, Washington, Knox, and Commissary General of Military Stores Benjamin Flower moved to upgrade the Army's ordnance staff. On 11 November Congress approved the addition of two more artillery artificer companies. Washington and Knox hoped to group the four companies into a regiment for better administration and then to assign detachments to each division at the start of the 1778 campaign to perform small arms maintenance. On 11 February 1778 Congress consolidated responsibility for ordnance, munitions, military equipment, and repair of weapons under Flower, who also became colonel of the new Artillery Artificer Regiment. The two old and the two new companies were joined in the spring by a fifth, and the regiment later absorbed Lt. Col. Ebenezer Stevens' maintenance company when that unit joined the Main Army in August 1778. The regiment's officers held special commissions

[36]*JCC*, 9:1058-64; 10:13-17; 12:902, 1016-18; Fitzpatrick, *Writings*, 10:10,56-58; 13:131-32, 218-20, 274-75, 289-91, 308, 311-13; Smith, *Letters of Delegates*, 2:436. The British had violated a similar agreement, the Convention of Kloster Kampen, in the Seven Years' War.

[37]*JCC*, 13:42-43; Jefferson, *Papers*, 3:155-56, 191-92; 4:252-53, 565, 603-5; 5:147, 333-34, 408-9, 426-28, 661-62; 6:66-67; Henry Read McIlwaine, ed., *Official Letters of the Governors of the State of Virginia*, 3 vols., (Richmond: Virginia State Library, 1926-29), 1:347-49, 355; Burnett, *Letters*, 6:5, 99-100; Steuben Papers (Return, 1 Dec 80); Palmer, *Calendar of Virginia State Papers*, 2:574.

[38]Fitzpatrick, *Writings*, 9:28-29, 283-84; 10:11, 152; 12:69, 280; 22:121, 236-42; *JCC*, 7:288-89; 8:485-86, 554-56; RG 360, National Archives (Nicola to Congress, 2 Oct 77); Lewis Nicola, "Unpublished Letters of Colonel Lewis Nicola, Revolutionary Soldier," ed. Howard R. Marraro, *Pennsylvania History*, 13 (1946):274. Nicola had gained a national reputation as a military expert because of his translation of Chevalier de Clairac's *L'Ingenieur de Campagne; or, Field Engineer* (Philadelphia: R. Aitken, 1776) and his own *A Treatise of Military Exercise, Calculated for the Use of Americans* (Philadelphia: Styner and Cist, 1776).

which restricted their authority to the regiment; this provision was wise since they were really supervisory technicians.[39]

Congress did not make the Department of Military Stores subordinate to Knox, as Washington had wished. It remained under the Board of War's supervision. Repeated pressure produced a compromise on 18 February 1779 when Congress created the additional position of Field Commissary of Military Stores to directly support the Main Army. With ordnance officials' cooperation, artillery officers received technical training at ordnance depots. Another new office, the surveyor of ordnance, in theory allowed the artillery colonels, on a rotating basis, to make the technical service more responsive to the needs of the troops in the field. John Lamb, the colonel with the greatest technical proficiency, however, served as surveyor for the rest of the war.[40]

During the summer of 1778 Washington returned to a concept used in 1776 but discarded in 1777. The skilled workmen serving the Quartermaster General now assembled again as "companies," or work crews, under the supervision of Col. Jeduthan Baldwin. Baldwin demonstrated an aptitude for supervising construction parties, and the assignment conveniently precluded the possibility that he might quarrel with the French engineers. These artificers carried out construction at West Point, maintained wheeled vehicles, and mended roads as pioneers during marches. When the Artillery Artificer Regiment proved successful, Congress directed Washington on 11 November 1779 to arrange Baldwin's companies into a permanent Quartermaster Artificer Regiment. Its officers were under most of the same restrictions as Flower's, and the regiment ultimately contained nine companies.[41]

The foreign volunteers who arrived in America after 1776 contributed in important ways to the developing sophistication of the Continental Army. Washington and Congress began planning improvements in various areas as early as the winter of 1776–77, but they could not act until volunteers with necessary technical skills became available. The most immediate impact was the emergence of an engineer service, both combat and topographical. The former was staffed almost exclusively with foreigners; the latter was inspired by the French Army, although American experience in surveying also shaped its work. European concepts of cavalry combat did not prove successful, but foreign volunteers added several contingents of light troops to the Army. Among the special supporting units that Washington and Congress formed during 1778–79, the Marechaussee and Invalids also had foreign precedents. The greatest foreign contribution, however, came in administration and training.

The Contributions of Steuben

Foreign volunteers brought ideas recently developed by European military theorists to the attention of American officers. The volunteers thereby contributed to a professional growth already begun with the efforts of Washington and other concerned

[39]Fitzpatrick, *Writings*, 8:8; 10:277–80; *JCC*, 7:179; 9:891–92; 10:119, 144–50; 15:1398–99; Artillery Brigade Orderly Books (Artillery Brigade Orders, 25 Aug 78), New-York Historical Society. The equipment of the divisional detachments included a mobile repair shop.

[40]Fitzpatrick, *Writings*, 12:273–74; 13:489; 14:68; 15:79–80; 17:170; 20:445; *JCC*, 13:201–6; 17:724–25, 793; 18:1093; 25:540–41; John Lamb Letterbook (to Knox, 19 Jun 79), New-York Historical Society.

[41]Fitzpatrick, *Writings*, 12:246–47; 13:73; 14:212; 18:1–2; *JCC*, 15:1261–62, 1276; 16:212; Gates Papers (Baldwin to Capt [Peter] Mills, 10 Sep 78).

HENRI BOUQUET *(1719–65) was a Swiss professional soldier serving in the British Army during the French and Indian War when he helped to develop tactics of wilderness fighting that proved very influential on the later Continental Army. (Portrait by John Wollaston, ca. 1760.)*

military leaders. One volunteer, Frederick Wilhelm von Steuben, played the most important role in this regard by synthesizing military concepts for Washington, training the Main Army, and creating an administrative staff of Americans and Europeans to bring uniformity and competence to the battlefield.

European military theorists had introduced ideas during the mid-eighteenth century which under Napoleon would transform warfare. The British Army, however, remained on the periphery of these developments. Maj. Gen. Humphrey Bland's *A Treatise of Military Discipline* (first published in 1727) dominated British thinking through the French and Indian War. It was little more than a drill manual that reflected the practices of the Duke of Marlborough. A new drill book introduced in 1764 by Adjutant General Edward Harvey, and known colloquially as "The '64," replaced Bland's. The continentals used it as an unofficial manual early in the Revolutionary War. Like its predecessor, it had limited theoretical content.[42]

Two exceptional British generals exerted an important influence on American thinking during the French and Indian War. Henri Bouquet (a Swiss serving in the British Army) and John Forbes, faced with the problem of operating with a regular army in the North American wilderness, used Lancelot, Comte Turpin de Crisse's *Commentaires* and Marshal Saxe's *Reveries* for inspiration. Those French writers had argued that Roman history demonstrated that regular line infantry could function in broken terrain if they also trained as light infantry. Forbes based his 1758 campaign, in which Washington served as a brigade commander, on this concept, and Bouquet later refined it. Bouquet's "Reflections on War With the Savages of North America" appeared in 1765 as an appendix to William Smith's *A Historical Account of the Ex-*

---

[42]Fuller, *British Light Infantry*, pp. 79–86, 152–53; Ira D. Gruber, "British Strategy: The Theory and Practice of Eighteenth-Century Warfare," in Don Higginbotham, ed., *Reconsiderations on the Revolutionary War: Selected Essays* (Westport: Greenwood Press, 1978), pp. 14–31; Glover, *Peninsular Preparation*, pp. 116–22, 194–95. Few British officers pursued independent reading to compensate for Bland's weaknesses.

pedition Against the Ohio Indians in the Year MDCCLXIV and later served as a handbook for the Continental Army.[43]

Although Frederick the Great of Prussia dominated military science at mid-century, his success came from his personal genius and incredible capacity for work. His Army, trained through years of drill, resembled a machine. The widespread imitation of the Prussian Army only mimicked its external forms. Real theoretical development grew out of France's humiliating defeat in the Seven Years' War. In the aftermath, prolonged debate took place between advocates of heavy, massed infantry formations assaulting with the bayonet (the *ordre profond*) and proponents of linear tactics that maximized infantry firepower (the *ordre mince*).[44]

An important doctrinal development occurred in 1766 when the Comte de Guibert presented the French War Ministry with a memorandum introducing a compromise *ordre mixte*. This memorandum, subsequently refined and published in 1772 as the *Essai General de Tactique*, stressed flexibility and utility. Infantrymen, trained for both line and light infantry duties, deployed in line, column, or a combination of both, depending on the tactical needs of the particular situation. Guibert drew heavily on Gribeauval; artillery supported the infantry by firing on enemy troop formations, preferably from massed batteries. Although the French Army did not formally adopt Guibert's ideas until 1791, war games, particularly ones held in 1778 at Vassieux, Normandy, tested the merits of the different systems and converted many officers to the mixed order.

Americans closely followed European military developments. If European authors tended to dismiss America as atypical because of the nature of its terrain and Indian warfare, American officers in turn were selective in accepting European ideas. Nathanael Greene summarized this attitude in December 1777 when he cautioned a council of war that "experience is the best of schools and the safest guide in human affairs—yet I am no advocate for blindly following all the maxims of European policy, but where reason corresponds with what custom has long sanctified, we may safely copy their Example."[45] This insistence on filtering theory through practical experience led Washington and others to value Saxe and Guibert for their flexibility. It also contributed to the intense interest in *petite guerre*, or partisan operations, which seemed to fit the "natural genius" of Americans for ranger operations. In fact, interest in such operations led to a reprinting in 1772 of Thomas Church's *History of the Great Indian War*. First published in 1716, this account of the ranger tactics developed between 1675 and 1715 by Col. Benjamin Church in operations against New England Indians, was the only significant American military work published before the Revolution.[46]

---

[43]King Lawrence Parker, "Anglo-American Wilderness Campaign, 1754-1764; Logistical and Tactical Developments" (Ph.D. diss., Columbia University, 1970), pp. 252-342; Fuller, *British Light Infantry*, pp. 90–91, 108–10; John K. Mahon, "Anglo-American Methods of Indian Warfare, 1676-1794," *Mississippi Valley Historical Review* 45 (1958):268.

[44]This discussion is based on Robert S. Quimby, *The Background of Napoleonic Warfare: The Theory of Military Tactics in Eighteenth Century France* (New York: Columbia University Press, 1957); John Albert Lynn, "The Revolution on the Battlefield: Training and Tactics of the *Armee Du Nord*, 1792-1794" (Ph.D. diss., University of California at Los Angeles, 1973); and Stephen T. Ross, "The Development of the Combat Division in Eighteenth-Century French Armies," *French Historical Studies* 4 (1965):84-94.

[45]Worthington C. Ford, ed., *Defences of Philadelphia in 1777* (Brooklyn: Historical Printing Club, 1897), pp. 248–56.

[46]Force, *American Archives*, 4th ser., 2:385-86; Fitzpatrick, *Writings*, 4:80-81.

JEAN-BAPTISTE, CHEVALIER DE TERNANT *(1751–1816) was a French volunteer who served as the Southern Department's deputy inspector general from 1778 to 1782. After the Revolution he became a colonel in the Dutch and later French armies and briefly returned to the United States as minister of France in 1791. (Portrait by Charles Willson Peale, 1781.)*

In 1777 Washington issued standing orders directing Continental officers to use their spare time to read "military authors." Foreign observers recognized that this official policy was a sign of growing professionalism, and a number contributed their time and advice to foster the trend. Thomas-Antoine, Chevalier de Mauduit du Plessis, for example, was particularly instrumental in introducing the Army's leaders to Guibert's writings. Du Plessis, a graduate of the rigorous Grenoble artillery school, had proved his skill and gallantry at Germantown and in the defense of Fort Mifflin. He became a respected teacher at Valley Forge.[47]

Frederick von Steuben played an even more important role. "The Baron," as he came to be known, was a Prussian veteran. He had served as a junior infantry officer for ten years with responsibility for training troops. In 1757, as a reward for gallantry in action, Steuben became the principal staff officer of one of the Prussian "free corps" organized to counter Austrian light troops. This duty exposed him to a less rigid form of military organization and gave him valuable administrative experience. He progressed rapidly, and in 1762 he joined Frederick the Great's special corps of aides. This assignment provided him with the best staff training available in the eighteenth century. When Army politics forced his retirement in 1764 as a captain, he spent the next decade as the chamberlain of a minor prince.[48]

During 1777 Steuben offered his services to Benjamin Franklin, using the Comte de Saint-Germain as an intermediary. The three men prepared credentials falsely identifying Steuben as a lieutenant general. Congress accepted him as a volunteer without rank, and on 23 February 1778 he arrived at Valley Forge. After inspecting the troops

[47]Fitzpatrick, *Writings*, 8:28; Fuller, *British Light Infantry*, pp. 151–52; Sebastian Bauman Papers (George Fleming to Maj Sebastian Bauman, 6 Feb 78), New-York Historical Society; Laurens, *Army Correspondence*, pp. 98–101, 134–41; Spaulding, "Military Studies of George Washington," *American Historical Review*, 29:675–80.

[48]His claim to be a baron appears to be groundless; his family's use of the enobling "von" clearly was. Steuben himself used the French "de" in America rather than the German "von."

and conferring with senior officers, Steuben told Washington that the continentals were the finest raw material for an army he had ever seen. Washington promptly assigned Steuben to prepare a system of "discipline, maneuveres, evolutions, [and] regulations for guards."[49]

Steuben analyzed existing practices, based primarily on the 1764 British manual, and compared them to European systems. As he later wrote Franklin, "circumstances... obliged me to deviate from the Principles adopted in the European Armies....Young as We are, We have already our Prejudices as the most ancient Nations, [and] the prepossession in favor of the British service, has obliged me to comply with many Things, which are against my Principles."[50] Steuben's genius led him to develop a new system rather than to modify an existing one. He simplified the British manual of arms and slowed its prescribed tempo to improve execution. Marching in a column four abreast instead of in single file allowed more compact formations and dramatically improved battlefield deployment. He increased the marching pace from the English 60 two-foot steps per minute to 75 (the Prussian norm). He set doubletime at 120. To complement the Continental Army's excellent musketry, Steuben also emphasized bayonet training. He and Washington made officers responsible for drilling the troops. Steuben drew on many precedents, including Prussian, English, and American practices. Foreign officers recognized the uniqueness of the mixture and noted its efficiency.[51]

To speed the learning process, Washington organized a provisional "model company" as an adjunct to his guard. On 19 March, Steuben personally began to train this company. His colorful curses, delivered in a variety of languages, amused the large crowds that assembled each day to witness the spectacle. This calculated psychological effect contributed to the Baron's popularity and the smooth adoption of the drill. Members of the model company and selected officers then spent six weeks instructing all other units at Valley Forge and later extended the system to the rest of the Continental Army.[52]

Steuben produced a simple but efficient method for maneuvering on the battlefield. Like Guibert and other French theoreticians, he used both column and line to achieve tactical flexibility. Divisions and brigades marched in closed columns for speed and control and rapidly deployed into line for musket fire or bayonet charge. Skirmishers, either light infantry or details from line units, covered the columns during advance or withdrawal. They kept one hundred yards (the effective range of a musket) from the column to prevent enemy harassment of the main body. As soon as the column deployed into line, the skirmishers withdrew through gaps and re-formed. The men maintained silence when marching.[53]

In the fall of 1778 a board of generals reviewed Steuben's drill and suggested only one improvement: replacing the traditional command "Present!" with "Take Sight!" as the order immediately preceding "Fire!" Washington agreed and made the change. This emphasis indicated the Continental Army's continued reliance on marksman-

[49]Laurens, *Army Correspondence*, pp. 134–41; Fitzpatrick, *Writings*, 8:108, 255; 11:163.

[50]Steuben Papers (to Franklin, 28 Sep 79).

[51]Idzerda, *Lafayette*, 1:73–87, 91–103; Camus, *Military Music*, p. 87; Fitzpatrick, *Writings*, 11:233, 335–36, 399–401; 12:4–7; C. Fiske Harris, ed., "Diary of a French Officer, 1781 (Presumed to be that of Baron Cromot du Bourg, Aid to Rochambeau)," *Magazine of American History* 7(1881):294–95.

[52]Fitzpatrick, *Writings*, 11:163–64; 13:342; Steuben Papers (Jean Baptiste Ternant to Steuben, (20 Jan and 9 Mar 79; William Davies to Steuben, 17 Oct 78).

[53]*Pennsylvania Archives*, 2d ser., 11:290–91, 304, 320–22, 410–11.

ship.[54] Steuben polished the text. Pierre L'Enfant drew illustrations, and on 29 March 1779 Congress approved publication of the drill. Almost every officer received a copy. Washington overruled Steuben's desire to classify it as a state secret because he hoped that the militia would also adopt the drill so that replacements would be properly trained before they joined the Army.[55]

Steuben's *Regulations for the Order and Discipline of the Troops of the United States, Part I* (better known as "The Blue Book") covered all aspects of infantry service. It specified that a regiment deploy tactically in eight companies, each under its own officers. (*Chart 10*) This system prevented the type of confusion that had crippled the Hessians at Trenton. A regiment with more than 160 files (320 privates and corporals) formed as two 4-company battalions; those with less than 80 files (160 men) either temporarily combined with a second small regiment or did not take a place in the line of battle. A special 12-man color guard gave each regimental commander an emergency reserve force. Light infantry companies either deployed as skirmishers or in provisional battalions. The column became the standard maneuver formation; training emphasized movement through broken terrain and rapid deployment into line. Bayonet charges were designed to maximize their shock effect.[56] In addition, the regulations improved the efficiency of the trains so that the Army could move without encumbrance and still fight a sustained engagement immediately. The specified routine of daily life emphasized health and morale.

The *Regulations* also stressed the importance of regimental administration. An appendix clearly explained the functions of every individual in a regiment from its commander to its lowest private. Senior noncommissioned officers received training to supervise the four squads that formed each company and to act as staff officers in an emergency. The attitude that permeated the *Regulations* was summarized in the direction that a captain's "first object should be, to gain the love of his men, by treating them with every possible kindness and humanity, enquiring into their complaints, and when well founded, seeing them redressed. He should know every man of his company by name and character." This attitude put the Continental Army in the forefront of the most progressive military thinking of the period.[57]

Steuben's contributions to the Continental Army did not stop with The Blue Book, for he also served in a new staff office, that of Inspector General. Between 1778 and 1780 this office grew, and Steuben emerged as Washington's de facto chief of staff. Baron Henry D'Arendt, commander of the German Battalion, first suggested adding an inspector general to the staff. A council of war endorsed the suggestion as a way to use foreign expertise with minimum disruption. Congress altered the concept on 13 December 1777 when it authorized two inspectors general, one of whom was Gen-

[54]Fitzpatrick, *Writings*, 8:268; 12:360. Gates' notes of the 26 August 1778 board meeting are in the Gates Papers.
[55]Ibid., 14:151–52, 227–31, 369, 444–46, 488–89; 15:46–49; 16:432–33, 447, 449, 468; *JCC*, 13:384–85; Steuben Papers (Charles Thomson to Steuben, 5 Apr 79; John Jay to Steuben, 6 Apr 79; Pickering to Steuben, 26 May, 19 Jun, and 12 Jul 79; Peter Scull to Steuben, 26 Jun and 27 Jul 79; Ternant to Steuben, 29 Sep 79 and 7 Jan 80).
[56]Frederick Steuben, *Regulations for the Order and Discipline of the Troops of the United States, Part I* (Philadelphia: Styner and Cist, 1779). At least seven other editions were published by 1785, primarily to supply militia demands. Chart 10 shows the disposition prescribed for a regiment.
[57]Steuben completed a second volume, "Baron von Steuben Regulations for the Cavalry or Corps Legionaire," which closely paralleled the infantry regulations, on 22 Dec 1780, but was not published. It can be found in the Steuben Papers.

CHART 10—INFANTRY REGIMENT DEPLOYED IN TWO BATTALIONS 1779

This chart is based on Steuben, *Regulations, Chapter 4.*

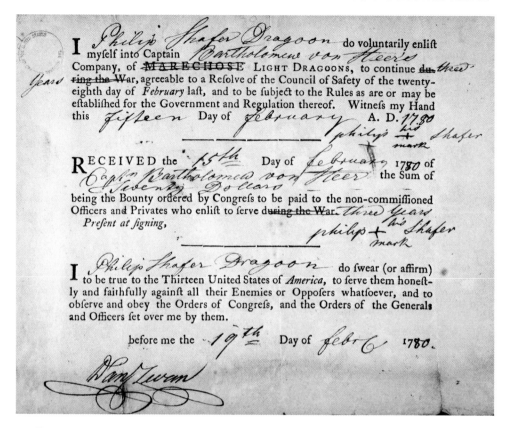

ENLISTMENT FORM OF PRIVATE PHILIP SHAFER. *By the second half of the Revolution, the Army's paperwork attained a high degree of sophistication. Private Shafer enlisted in the Marechaussee Corps on 15 February 1780. He then signed this printed form which recorded the term of his enlistment, his receipt of his enlistment bounty, and his having taken his oath of enlistment. Notice that Private Shafer was illiterate.*

eral Conway. Congress required the inspectors to see that every officer and soldier was "instructed in the exercise and manoeuvres which may be established by the Board of War." Their other duties, "agreeable to the practice of the best disciplined European Armies," related to discipline, paperwork, and investigating fraud. They reported directly to Congress, not to the Commander in Chief.[58] Washington ignored Conway and used Steuben, with his superior credentials, to regain control of this office. On 28 March 1778 he appointed Steuben as temporary Inspector General. Four subinspectors acted as division-level assistants, and one major from each brigade extended the system to that echelon. The first duty of these subinspectors and majors was implementing Steuben's drill.[59] After experience proved the utility of this arrangement,

[58]Fitzpatrick, *Writings*, 10:249-50; Laurens, *Army Correspondence*, pp. 98-101; Burnett, *Letters*, 3:20-25; *JCC*, 9:1023-26.
[59]Gates Papers (Conway to Gates, 11 Nov 77); Fitzpatrick, *Writings*, 10:226-27; 11:108, 132, 163, 173-74, 313, 335-36; 12:66-68; Laurens, *Army Correspondence*, pp. 109-12, 131-49. A fifth subinspector, the Marquis de Fleury, was added on 27 April 1778, and subsequently he instructed the Maryland division at Wilmington.

Congress approved it and on 5 May 1778 commissioned Steuben as a major general. Washington had lobbied hard for the rank.[60]

When the Main Army took the field, Washington used the subinspectors as divisional adjutants general. He also clarified the status and authority of the inspectors. Tactical command remained with the unit commanders. Inspectors simply ensured that drills followed official Army doctrine. New legislation on 18 February 1779 authorized a single Inspector General with the rank of a major general and responsibility for preparing regulations. His staff conducted inspections on the authority of the Commander in Chief or commanding officer of a territorial department and reported through those commanders to the Board of War. Brigade inspectors (majors) absorbed the functions of the brigade majors and became the senior staff officers in each brigade. The senior subinspector (a lieutenant colonel) could temporarily act for the Adjutant General. Subinspectors also served as adjutants general for wings of the Main Army or separate departments.[61]

Col. Alexander Scammell replaced Timothy Pickering as Adjutant General on 5 January 1778. Scammell, a Harvard graduate with ample command and staff experience, worked with Steuben to standardize the Army's paperwork. They developed printed forms for most of the routine regimental and brigade bookkeeping chores and even issued "blank-books" to each soldier for his personal records. Their partnership paved the way for the gradual merger of the two major staff agencies. Steuben developed policies while Scammell concentrated on routine administration. Congress agreed that consolidation made sense, and on 17 May 1779 it reduced the Adjutant General's department to the Adjutant General, two assistants, and a clerk. They operated the headquarters orderly office. The Inspector General gradually rendered the mustering department redundant as well. On 12 January 1780 Congress abolished it.[62] Consolidation was further extended on 25 September 1780. Legislation officially designated the Adjutant General as the assistant inspector general for the Main Army. It also authorized inspectors for artillery, cavalry, and militia on active duty with the Continental Army.[63]

Under Steuben the Inspector General became the Army's supreme administrator and the virtual chief of staff to the Commander in Chief. Subordinate officials in the department assumed parallel positions under territorial, division, and brigade commanders. The transformation was remarkably free of bureaucratic friction. Changes in personnel and the growth of Washington's personal staff had weakened the Adjutant General, the one official in a position to challenge Steuben's hegemony. The latter's close relationships with the final two Adjutants General, Scammell and Brig. Gen. Edward Hand, facilitated the new arrangement. In contrast to Europe, where either the Adjutant General or the Quartermaster General became paramount, the

---

[60]Fitzpatrick, *Writings*, 11:329–31, 366; *JCC*, 11:465–66, 498–500, 728–29; 12:1010. Congress appointed Chevalier de la Neuville as inspector general to Gates' northern command with the rank of brevet brigadier general. His younger brother, Noirmont de la Neuville, Conway's aide, served as his deputy. Neither made a significant contribution.

[61]*JCC*, 11:819–23; 13:111, 196–200; Burnett, *Letters*, 4:41; Fitzpatrick, *Writings*, 12:16, 66–68, 438–44; 14:444–46; 15:129–31, 288–90, 293, 475–76; Steuben Papers (Peters to Steuben, 2 Jun 78; William Davies to Steuben, 18 Jun and 21 and 26 Jul 79; subinspectors to Steuben, 20 Jun 79).

[62]Fitzpatrick, *Writings*, 10:80–82, 245, 297, 332–33; 14:120–21, 224–27, 486; 15:356–58; 16:11–13, 134–36; 17:99–100, 495–96; 18:64; *JCC*, 13:403–4; 14:600–601; 16:47; Steubens Papers (Davies to Steuben, 26 Jul 79; Scammell to Steuben, 22 Sep 79; Benjamin Walker to Steuben, 2 Feb and 10 Mar 80).

[63]*JCC*, 17:764–70; 18:855–61. The act confusingly called brigade inspectors subinspectors.

rise of the Inspector General again demonstrates the flexibility exercised in the use of European precedents. Americans borrowed where appropriate, but they were not afraid to be innovative.[64]

The Reorganization of 1778–79 in Practice

The 1778 campaign opened before Washington had an opportunity to implement the organizational changes mandated in the 27 May 1778 resolve. Steuben, Duportail, and the other foreign volunteers, however, had already begun to make their contributions. France's declaration of war on Great Britain pushed the War of American Independence into a global struggle in which North America became less important as a theater. The first impact of that change came in the British decision to evacuate Philadelphia rather than risk losing New York City. Washington set out from Valley Forge and caught up with Clinton's army on 28 June at Monmouth. Maj. Gen. Charles Lee commanded the Continental van. Recently released in a prisoner-of-war exchange, he failed to understand the changes that had taken place in the abilities of the Army since December 1776. As a result, he mishandled his troops, and Washington had to settle for a hard-fought draw. Clinton reached New York City without further incident, and Washington moved to White Plains, New York, where his Main Army joined forces with the troops from the Highlands and prepared for further action.

During the year that followed Monmouth, Washington and Congress gradually implemented the 27 May 1778 organizational changes. Action came state-by-state. Various factors influenced the timing of each reorganization and the specific arrangements: recruiting success, the initial strength of the regiments, and their geographical location. On 9 March 1779, after a careful review, Congress reduced the state lines to 80 regiments by lowering New Jersey's quota to 3, Pennsylvania's to 11, Virginia's to 11, North Carolina's to 6, and Georgia's to one.[65]

New Hampshire's three regiments made the transition to the new structure on 23 December 1778. Connecticut's eight regiments did so on 11 July 1779, and eleven days later the units of the three Massachusetts brigades stationed in the Hudson Highlands followed suit. The other Massachusetts brigade reorganized its three strongest regiments on 1 August when they returned from detached duty in Rhode Island; Bigelow's Regiment (and Alden's Regiment, which was not in the brigade) reorganized somewhat later. The Massachusetts regiments had not had numerical designations since 1776, but following the recommendation of a board of general officers, Washington numbered them on 1 August 1779 according to the relative seniority of their colonels in 1777.[66]

The New York Brigade had assembled for the first time on 22 July 1778. Washington continued to use it to defend New York's frontier, and all five of its regiments reorganized on 30 May 1779. Although Congress had allowed New Jersey to reduce its

---

[64]Ward, *Wellington's Headquarters*, pp. 130–31; David G. Chandler, *The Campaigns of Napoleon* (New York: The Macmillan Co., 1966), pp. 56, 144–61. Steuben was familiar with at least one French source; among his papers is an undated manuscript entitled "Instructions Relatives au Department des Inspecteurs de l'Armee."

[65]*JCC*, 13:108–9, 143, 298–99; Burnett, *Letters*, 4:377–79; Fitzpatrick, *Writings*, 13:485–91; 14:3–12, 26–32, 71–72, 86–87.

[66]Fitzpatrick, *Writings*, 15:342, 406, 461–62; 16:33–34, 51–53; 17:15–16; *JCC*, 15:1033; Gates Papers (Inspection Report for Glover's Brigade, 18 Aug 79).

quota to three regiments in 1778, the 4th New Jersey Regiment did not actually disband until 7 February 1779. The other three regiments then reorganized and incorporated the 4th's personnel.[67] Congress had reduced Pennsylvania's quota of regiments to ten on 26 February 1778, but on 27 March it had allotted Hartley's Additional Regiment as an eleventh Pennsylvania regiment. Washington made the reduction on 22 July 1778; Pennsylvania was thus able to adopt the new regimental organization well in advance of the other states.[68] The Maryland and Delaware regiments spent the winter of 1777–78 at Wilmington and were successful in their recruiting. They reorganized on 12 May 1779. From 16 December 1778 until 13 January 1779 the Delaware Regiment had been reinforced by the transfer of Delaware men under Capt. Allen McLane from Patton's Additional Regiment.[69]

In late 1777 Virginia loaned (until 1780) the 1st and 2d Virginia State Regiments to the Continental Army to replace that year's losses. A greater problem than replacing those losses was reenlisting the veterans in the 1st through the 9th Virginia regiments whose terms expired during the winter of 1777–78. Washington experimented with a series of provisional reorganizations, including reducing Virginia's brigades to three on 22 July 1778. The permanent reorganization came on 12 May 1779; Washington consolidated eight weak regiments into four and renumbered the line. On 5 May 1779 he had already ordered Brig. Gen. Charles Scott, in charge of recruiting in the state, to organize all available officers and recruits into three provisional regiments as reinforcements for the Southern Department. The first of these units, under Col. Richard Parker, left Petersburg in October and reached Charleston, South Carolina, on 5 December. The second, under Col. William Heth, did not arrive until 7 April. Col. Abraham Buford left the state with the third still later.[70]

When North Carolina's nine regiments joined the Main Army in 1777, they were so weak that their field officers recommended transferring all enlisted men to the three senior regiments. On 29 May 1778 Congress ordered the transfer and directed North Carolina to use the surplus officers to form four new regiments. Late in 1778 the cadres of the new units went to South Carolina in provisional formations. The 3d North Carolina Regiment had to return home in the spring of 1779 to recruit. The 1st and 2d regiments finally reorganized under the new structure on 22 July 1779 in the Hudson Highlands.[71]

Although the Georgia and South Carolina units did not serve in the north, they also declined in strength. Idleness, climate, and the expiration of enlistments took

[67]Fitzpatrick, *Writings*, 12:216; 13:264–65; 14:73–74, 414–16; 20:295–96; *JCC*, 10:361; Burnett, *Letters*, 3:109; Stirling Papers (undated 1778 return of recruiting officers).

[68]*Pennsylvania Archives*, 2d ser., 11:307–8, 336–37; Fitzpatrick, *Writings*, 12:215–18; *JCC*, 10:288, 13:298–99; Burnett, *Letters*, 3:123–24; Stille, *Anthony Wayne*, pp. 125–26, 158–59, 175–77. Hartley was a popular recruiter.

[69]*JCC*, 12:1225–26; 13:58; Fitzpatrick, *Writings*, 10:360; 15:46–47, 265–67; *Archives of Maryland*, 18:312–16; Anderson, *Personal Recollections*, pp. 53–55.

[70]*JCC*, 8:737; 9:967; Fitzpatrick, *Writings*, 9:329, 367, 481–82; 10:54–56; 153, 254–55; 12:79–81, 139, 215–17, 279; 14:72, 498–99; 15:17–19, 46; "Revolutionary Army Orders for the Main Army Under Washington, 1778–1779," *Virginia Magazine of History and Biography*, 17 (1910):417–18; George Weedon, *Valley Forge Orderly Book of General George Weedon*, ed. Samuel W. Pennypacker (New York: Dodd, Mead and Co., 1902), pp. 80, 206–7; Palmer, *Calendar of Virginia State Papers*, 1:319; Edward McCrady, *The History of South Carolina in the Revolution*, 2 vols. (New York: Macmillan Co., 1902), 1:427.

[71]*JCC*, 11:550–51; 13:14–15, 132, 385; 14:560–61; Fitzpatrick, *Writings*, 10:268–69; 12:8; 15:462; Burnett, *Letters*, 3:382–84, 426.

BENJAMIN LINCOLN *(1733–1810) joined the Continental Army in 1777 as a major general after serving at that rank in the Massachusetts militia. As commander of the Southern Department at Charleston in 1780 he presided over the worst American defeat in the war, but he was also present at the great victories of Saratoga and Yorktown and ended the Revolution as the secretary at war. (Portrait by Charles Willson Peale, ca. 1782.)*

their toll. A full company of the 1st South Carolina Regiment, serving as marines, was lost on 8 March 1778 when the frigate *Randolph* blew up during an engagement with the British ship of the line *Yarmouth* off Barbados. Georgia's troops suffered virtual annihilation during the winter of 1778–79 when the British overran that state in a new offensive. Congress finally empowered Maj. Gen. Benjamin Lincoln, who had assumed command of the Southern Department on 4 December 1778, to consolidate the two state lines and to organize them under the new regimental structure. Local political jealousies blocked action until 20 January 1780. Lincoln reorganized the Georgia units, now existing only on paper, as one infantry regiment and one regiment of mounted rangers. South Carolina's troops formed one artillery regiment and three regiments of infantry.[72]

Congress concentrated reductions and economics on separate companies and additional regiments. They generally were weaker to begin with and lacked the political support of the state lines. Congress normally consolidated units from the same or adjacent areas, retired the excess officers, and transferred the consolidated unit to a state line if possible. Patton's and Hartley's Additional Regiments, plus the four Pennsylvania companies of Malcolm's, consolidated as the 11th Pennsylvania Regiment in 1779. Spencer's Additional Regiment absorbed Malcolm's other companies. The three additional regiments from Virginia consolidated on 22 April 1779 under Col. Nathaniel Gist. Massachusetts' three additional regiments combined under Col. Henry Jackson on 24 July 1779 as the 16th Massachusetts Regiment. Col. Samuel Blatchley Webb's Connecticut regiment became the 9th Connecticut Regiment. Sherburne's Additional Regiment, on the other hand, disbanded on 1 May 1780. Its personnel transferred to Webb's or Jackson's regiments or to the 2d Rhode Island Regiment,

[72]*JCC*, 10:159–65; 12:951; 14:631; 16:26–27, 156; Burnett, *Letters*, 3:359–61; 5:34–35; Candler, *Revolutionary Records*, 2:38–39, 185–89; Moultrie, *Memoirs of the American Revolution*, 1:198–99; 2:114; Gibbes, *Documentary History*, C: 6; RG 360, National Archives (Lincoln to Congress, 19 Dec 78); Steuben Papers (Ternant to Steuben, 7 Jan 80).

depending on their native state. When New York refused to accept the 1st Canadian Regiment as an element of its state's line because of seniority issues, Washington reorganized it into five small companies. The 2d Canadian Regiment, however, continued under its special four-battalion configuration.[73]

Rhode Island's reorganization represented a unique solution to its manpower problems. At various times other states turned to their Negro inhabitants, slave and free, when recruiting lagged among whites. Most of these blacks served in integrated units, performing the same duties as other continentals, but Rhode Island followed a different pattern. In January 1778 the 1st Rhode Island Regiment transferred its privates to the 2d; the former's officers and noncommissioned officers returned home and refilled the 1st primarily with Negroes. The state government purchased slaves who wished to enlist from their owners and promised them emancipation at the end of the war. Lt. Col. John Laurens, one of Washington's aides, persuaded Congress to approve a similar plan for South Carolina on 29 March 1779, but that state refused to act on the plan.[74]

The formation of permanent light infantry companies during the reorganization simplified Washington's task of creating special strike forces. In 1779 four provisional light infantry regiments under General Wayne achieved a complete success in a night attack on Stony Point, New York. The following year six light battalions operated as a division under General Lafayette. The use of a specialized light infantry force may at first seem an exception to the European influence that had permeated other facets of the reorganization. Both Guibert and Saxe, for example, had stressed the value of training infantrymen for line as well as light infantry roles. However, every member of a regiment trained in both roles in the Continental Army, and the Light Corps itself was used in skirmishing as well as in standard linear formations.[75]

Washington and Knox found that implementing the artillery portion of the reorganization was easier than making the infantry changes. The only major impact came when three separate Maryland companies joined Col. Charles Harrison's artillery regiment, provisionally in 1778 and permanently on 9 May 1780. The large Maryland companies, each with 4 officers and 102 enlisted men, had formally transferred to the Continental Army in late 1777 to support the Maryland infantry.[76] Assigning numerical designations to the regiments completed the reorganization. Washington needed two boards of general officers to resolve seniority disputes. In August 1779 the generals decided that neither John Lamb nor John Crane could claim continuity from Knox's 1776 regiment. Harrison's regiment therefore became the 1st Continental Artillery Regiment. Col. Thomas Proctor's became the 4th because it had not transferred to the Continental Army until the summer of 1777. Lamb and Crane drew lots to deter-

[73]Fitzpatrick, *Writings*, 11:126; 13:55; 14:176, 180–81, 263, 354, 401–3, 426, 464; 16:3–4, 112–13; 18:319, 455, 462–63; 19:241–43; *JCC*, 12:1225; 13:58; Gates Papers (to Congress, Oct 1778; Hazen to Gates, 23 Jan 79; Jacques Laframboise et al. to Gates, 16 Sep 79; Gates to Washington, 24 Sep 79); Steuben Papers (Scammell to Steuben, 25 Sep 79; Hazen to Steuben, 11 Feb 80).

[74]*R.I. Records*, 8:358–61, 399, 526, 640–41; Rhode Island Historical Society *Collections*, 6:209–10; Laurens, *Army Correspondence*, pp. 114–18; Burnett, *Letters*, 4:121–24, 289; 13:386–88; David O. White, *Connecticut's Black Soldiers, 1775–1783* (Chester: Pequot Press, 1973), pp. 17–19, 29–31.

[75]Wayne Transcripts (to Irvine, 7 Jun 79), New York Public Library; Steuben Papers (Davies to Steuben, 31 May 79; Scammell to Steuben, 22 Jul 80; Hamilton to Steuben, 23 Jul 80.) In 1780 the light companies of the 1st and 3d Pennsylvania Regiments drew rifles and served as a special body within the Light Corps under Maj. James Parr.

[76]*Archives of Maryland*, 18:315–16, 571–78, 596–97; *JCC*, 9:822; 10:253; Fitzpatrick, *Writings*, 10:360, 520; 18:31–32, 277–79.

mine seniority. Lamb's became the 2d Continental Artillery Regiment; Crane's, the 3d.[77]

At Valley Forge Knox stabilized the weapons of the artillery arm. He planned to have four brass 3- or 6-pounders for each brigade. An artillery park for general support contained two 24-pounders, four 12-pounders, four 8-inch and eight 5.5-inch howitzers, and ten smaller fieldpieces. An unmanned reserve of 24-, 12-, 6-, and 3-pounders moved with the Main Army's trains, while a siege train of heavy iron guns and mortars stayed at Carlisle, Pennsylvania, and Springfield, Massachusetts. French imports, captured British guns, and pieces produced in America, all mounted on Muller-style carriages, produced a surplus of weapons by 1778. That condition forced Knox to abandon plans in 1780 to make the French 4-pounder (which most efficiently combined mobility and power) the standard fieldpiece because he could not waste the stores on hand for 6- and 3-pounders.[78] Companies rotated between brigades, large garrisons, and the artillery park for different types of training. Knox established a program of instruction and endorsed the theory that field artillery should avoid artillery duels and concentrate instead on infantry targets. During the battle of Monmouth this tactic proved so effective that Washington proudly claimed that "the Enemy have done them [the Artillery officers] the Justice to acknowledge that no Artillery could be better served."[79]

Forage problems in late 1778 forced Washington to disperse the light dragoon regiments, which never assembled as a brigade again. Serious shortages of men and horses also were factors. Washington considered, but abandoned, the idea of arming the troopers with blunderbusses in 1779 to increase their firepower. Maj. Benjamin Tallmadge of the 2d Continental Light Dragoons made a more practical suggestion. Since new recruits were easier to obtain than mount, he suggested that they be equipped temporarily as infantry. Washington ordered the 2d to implement this plan on 14 August 1779, and on 24 September he told Col. Stephen Moylan's 4th to do the same. The 1st and 3d Continental Light Dragoon Regiments transferred to the Southern Department in 1779 and operated under Lt. Col. William Washington as a composite mounted unit throughout the remaining southern campaigns.[80]

Implementing the 27 May 1778 resolve took a year and produced major changes only in the infantry regiments. Steuben's Blue Book and other improvements in training and support increased the effectiveness of both officers and men and partially compensated for the weaknesses inherent in the new regimental structure. The artillery merely improved on established practices, and the mounted arm and the partisans

[77]Fitzpatrick, *Writings*, 12:458–59; 15:170–71; 16:76, 173; Lamb Papers (Doughty to Lamb, 27 Jan 78; Oswald to Lamb, 7 Jun 78; Charles Thomson to Arnold (copy), 29 Aug 78; Lamb to Washington, 12 Mar 79; Crane to Washington (copy), 16 Mar 79; Lamb to Board of General Officers, 6 Aug 79; Board of General Officers' Report, (8 Aug 79); Ebenezer Stevens Papers (Knox to Stevens, 7 Jan 78), New-York Historical Society.

[78]Fitzpatrick, *Writings*, 10:486–87; 11:112–13; 13:317–18; 14:329; 18:244–45; 21:24; Lamb Papers (Knox to Lamb, 19 Jul 78; Lamb to Udny Hay and to George Mavins, both 1 Jun 78); Bauman Papers (to Lamb, 25 Jun 79); Steuben Papers (Knox to Board of War (copy), 1 Mar 80).

[79]Fitzpatrick, *Writings*, 12:131; see also 13:418; 15:187, 429–30; 17:215–16; Lamb Papers (to Knox, 30 Apr 78; Knox to Lamb, 11 May 78, 29 Jun 79, 31 Jul 80, 1 and 3 Aug 80; Oswald to Lamb, 7 Jun 78; Samuel Shaw to Lamb, 3 Jul 79); Artillery Brigade Orderly Books (Artillery Brigade Orders, 25 Aug 78); Uhlendorf, *Revolution in America*, pp. 189–93.

[80]Fitzpatrick, *Writings*, 13:207–8, 219–20, 284, 339–40; 14:302–3, 331, 390, 469; 15:121–22; 16:93–95, 329–30; 17:135–36, 211–13; *JCC*, 14:560.

reverted to a reconnaissance role. The permanent brigade consisting of several infantry regiments and an artillery company remained the basic tactical element of the Continental Army. Washington improved it by adding to the specialized staff serving the brigade commander. The brigade inspector, functioning as chief of staff, controlled a maintenance section under a conductor of military stores, a logistical section under a brigade quartermaster and a brigade commissary, and an administrative section. The division, less permanent, had a comparable staff.[81]

During that same period, the Army's territorial department structure stabilized.[82] Washington exercised effective control over all operations outside the south. The Main Army continued to function as the principal force in the Middle Department, although several detachments carried out missions there as well. The Northern Department and the Highlands Department remained as distinct commands but operated in close conjunction with the Main Army. The Northern Department normally contained the equivalent of a reinforced brigade; the Highlands Department, a reinforced division. The Eastern Department kept watch over the British in Newport with a field army of New England militia and state troops reinforced by one or more Continental brigades. The newest territorial department, established in 1777, was the Western Department. It protected the western frontiers of Virginia, Maryland, and Pennsylvania, but it received only two regiments in 1778 and remained a minor command.[83] Through 1778 the Southern Department contained essentially only Georgia and South Carolina units.

Summary

By July 1779 the Continental Army had achieved the status of a competent, well-trained force. Excluding the two thousand or so effectives in the Southern Department and a handful of regiments in isolated frontier garrisons in the Northern and Western Departments, Washington had about 25,000 officers and men.[84] The Main Army and the Highlands Department consisted of thirteen brigades stationed near New York and four engaged in Maj. Gen. John Sullivan's expedition against Indians in the Mohawk Valley. The infantry contingents available for combat in each of these 17 brigades averaged about 65 officers, 80 sergeants, 50 drummers and fifers, and 1,000 rank and file. The aggregate infantry strength included 107 field, 737 company, and 260 staff officers, 1,409 sergeants, and 871 drummers and fifers fit and present with their regiments. Another 78 field, 629 company, and 51 staff officers and 492 sergeants, drummers, and fifers were sick, held prisoner, or detached. Nearly 14,000 rank and file were on duty with the line companies; most of the 2,600 others "on command" served with the Light Corps. Less than 2,000 rank and file were sick. The force in Rhode Island contained 142 infantry officers and 2,255 enlisted men. Artillery with the Main Army and the Highlands and Eastern Departments accounted for another 200 or so officers and almost 2,000 men. Together, these troops represented a sizable

---

[81]Fitzpatrick, *Writings*, 15:101–3, 362–63; Idzerda, *Lafayette*, 1:193–94.

[82]Lamb Papers (Knox to Lamb, 22 Aug 80); Gates Papers (Lovell to Gates, 23 May 77).

[83]*JCC*, 7:247–49; Fitzpatrick, *Writings*, 11:439–41; 12:200–201; Reuben Gold Thwaites and Louise Phelps Kellogg, eds., *Frontier Defense on the Upper Ohio, 1777–1778* (Madison: Wisconsin Historical Society, 1912), pp. 1–3.

[84]RG 360, National Archives (Lincoln to Congress, 1 Sep 79); RG 93, National Archives (Monthly Return, Main Army, Jul 1779). Lesser, *Sinews*, pp. 124–26, prints a variation of this return.

combat force, although they probably totaled only half the authorized strength. Congress' policy of using line officers to perform staff duties at echelons above the regiment, a measure designed to cut costs, diverted 13 field and 209 company officers, a significant reduction of Washington's resources in battle. Doctrine and training maximized the usefulness of the troops that Washington and Congress did have, but quota deficiencies remained a pressing problem.

After Monmouth, units in the northern half of the country saw limited combat. Various successful engagements between portions of the Main Army and the enemy underscored the value of the professional skills that Washington and Steuben had nurtured. In 1779 operations against the Iroquois Indians by General Sullivan and a nighttime bayonet assault on Stony Point demonstrated the Army's flexibility. The battles at Springfield, New Jersey, in 1780, moreover, proved conclusively that a single brigade with a self-contained organization could successfully stand off a superior force until the rest of the Main Army could arrive.[85]

On 18 January 1778 Capt. Johann Heinrichs of the Hesse-Cassel Jaeger Corps commented in a letter to the Hessian Minister of State that the continentals were not "to be despised [for it only] requires Time and good leadership to make them formidable."[86] His observation was prophetic, for the Continental Army came of age between 1778 and 1780. Regiments trained by Washington and Steuben continued to suffer from shortages in personnel, but they fought well under a variety of conditions. The Army's organization achieved sophistication; its leadership down to the company level grew experienced, tough, and competent. The "Europeanization" of the Continental Army reflected the contributions of foreign volunteers and also the wisdom of Washington and other American leaders in selecting only those concepts that would work in America.

[85]Washington's use of the brigade in this manner was identical to the prescribed role of the division in Guibert's writings and of the corps in Napoleon's operations.

[86]Johann Heinrichs, "Extracts From the Letter-Book of Captain Johann Heinrichs of the Hessian Jaeger Corps, 1778-1780," trans Julius F. Sachse, *Pennsylvania Magazine of History and Biography* 22 (1898):137-40.

CHAPTER 7

Perseverance to Victory

The first two years of the War of American Independence witnessed the growth of the Continental Army from a nucleus of New England and New York units patterned after the Provincials of earlier wars into a force with men from every state as well as foreign volunteers. Through those volunteers, particularly Steuben and Duportail, European military theory and training merged with practical American experience. Beginning at Valley Forge this blend led to a relatively sophisticated organization that was sufficient to meet most of the battlefield problems faced by the Continental Army. During the final years of the Revolution a growing shortage of men and the general collapse of the American economy forced retrenchment. In time the Continental Army disappeared as a standing military force, but not before its triumph at Yorktown. When it disbanded, moreover, it did so in an orderly manner that reinforced the political stability of the new nation.

Economy and the 1781 Reorganization

The concern of the 27 May 1778 congressional reorganization to reduce expenses and adjust quotas to a realistic level became more acute in succeeding years. As British operations shifted emphasis to Virginia and states farther south, Washington and Congress transferred large elements of the Main Army to the Southern Department. By October 1780, when the three-year enlistments of 1777 were about to expire, the need to realign the existing military organization became intense. The major reorganization that resulted attempted to deal realistically with the limitations while still extracting maximum utility from the available resources.

Washington, Congress, and the Board of War wrestled throughout the winter of 1778–79 with the fact that the Continental Army had not achieved the strength set for it in 1778. Congress had no power to enact the national draft that Washington desired, although it did recommend that the individual states consider using a draft to meet their quotas. On the other hand, Washington and Steuben had to persuade Congress not to undertake a major reorganization of the Infantry. The next winter a similar issue arose when some delegates sought a reduction in the number of regiments in the hope of obtaining a more efficient force of full units. Washington again recommended avoiding a large-scale reorganization for the time being, arguing now that he could not undertake a major offensive until he received French naval and economic aid. He expressed particular concern over the impact that a reduction would have on the officer corps, but he also pointed out deficiencies in the 27 May 1778 reorganization. On the basis of Steuben's report that a minimum rank and file strength of 324 men per regiment was needed for anticipated operations (allowing 36 men each for the 1 light and 8 line companies), Congress on 9 February 1780 decided to establish quotas to place 35,211 men in the field for the coming campaign. No regiments were disbanded. Of this force, aside from supporting troops, the Infantry was to have a combat strength of 21,000; the Artillery, 2,000; and the Cavalry, 1,000.[1]

In January 1780 the Continental Army actually contained approximately that number of officers and men.[2] The Southern Department included all the troops from Georgia and the Carolinas, the three provisional Virginia regiments, two regiments of dragoons, and Pulaski's legion. The equivalent of a brigade of continentals served in the Eastern Department, while the Northern and Western Departments each had two regiments. Sixteen brigades plus supporting troops, the heart of the Continental Army's fighting strength, remained either with the Main Army or in the Highlands Department. Excluding the New Hampshire Brigade at Danbury, Connecticut, the fifteen brigades in New Jersey and the Highlands included an Infantry contingent of 168 field, 1,209 company, and 273 staff officers; 1,650 sergeants; 1,579 drummers and fifers; and 14,673 rank and file. The Artillery had 180 officers and 1,190 enlisted men; the Cavalry, another 64 officers and 672 men. The brigades were short 331 officers, 315 sergeants, 242 drummers and fifers, and 13,353 rank and file.

In the spring of 1780 Washington began to consider an attack on New York City if he could obtain the assistance of a French expeditionary force under Lt. Gen. Jean, Comte de Rochambeau. Efforts began to increase the effective strength of the Main Army, but when Rochambeau's troops arrived at Newport, Rhode Island, too debilitated from the sea voyage for action that year, Washington reluctantly had to abandon his plans. In September the Main Army, the Highlands Department, the Northern Department, and the Eastern Department contained a dozen Continental brigades plus supporting units and a number of regiments in detached garrisons. The Continental Infantry now included 169 field, 1,091 company, and 261 staff officers; 1,381 sergeants; 774 drummers and fifers; and 17,232 rank and file. Artillerymen from three regiments totaled another 140 officers and 1,097 men, while the Cavalry contingent numbered somewhat more than 500 of all ranks. Militia reinforcements in New York and Rhode Island amounted to 181 officers and 3,192 men.[3] There were acute shortages, particularly among ensigns, Artillery second lieutenants, and enlisted men. The Infantry force lacked 372 officers, 384 sergeants, 340 drummers and fifers, and 12,718 rank and file; the Artillery regiments, 77 officers and 652 men. Equally significant, over 200 Infantry officers were performing staff duties.

Routine recruiting problems represented only one part of the Main Army's strength problem. The deteriorating military situation in the Southern Department had robbed Washington of a substantial number of veteran regiments. To counter Britain's offensive against the southern states, Congress had ordered reinforcements sent to Charleston. Both of Washington's North Carolina regiments arrived there on 3 March 1780, joining the reorganized 3d North Carolina Regiment. The Virginia line (less the regi-

[1]*JCC*, 15:1357-59, 1369, 1376-77, 1393-96; 16:36-38, 80-83, 110, 117-20, 123, 125-28, 146-51, 178-80, 287; Fitzpatrick, *Writings*, 16:78-79; 17:172, 407-8, 431-36, 504-6; 18:202-4, 207-11; Burnett, *Letters*, 5:33, 92-93; Steuben Papers (undated 1780 memorandum).

[2]RG 93, National Archives (Monthly Return, Main Army, January 1780); Lesser, *Sinews*, pp. 148-50, prints a variant of this return.

[3]RG 93, National Archives (Monthly Return, Main Army, September 1780); Lesser, *Sinews*, pp. 180-82, prints a variant of this return.

JOHANNES DE KALB *(1721-80) was a Ba-varian-born veteran of the French Army who came to America with Lafayette. He died of wounds received at Camden where he commanded the Maryland Division as a major general. (Posthumous portrait by Charles Willson Peale based on sketches made several months before de Kalb's death.)*

ment at Fort Pitt) under Brig. Gen. William Woodford reached Charleston on 6 April 1780. The 1st, 2d, and 3d Virginia Regiments were at full strength while the other regiments had officer cadres only. Woodford's force then joined with the first two of the provisional Virginia regiments ordered raised in 1779.[4] These North Carolina and Virginia units and the Georgia and South Carolina remnants surrendered on 12 May 1780 when Charleston fell. This defeat was the worst suffered by the Continental Army during the Revolution. The sustained (42-day) defense of an inferior position, however, did demonstrate the increased fighting ability of the Army. Through the sophisticated use of artillery cross fire and ricochet techniques the Americans kept the British at bay until jaeger sniper fire silenced the guns.[5]

On 5 April 1780 the Maryland division, which included the Delaware Regiment, and the 1st Continental Artillery Regiment had received orders to transfer to the Southern Department. General de Kalb, the commander of these troops moving south, provisionally reorganized them on 15 July while en route. When Charleston fell, his became the only significant combat force in the south. De Kalb formed a division of four full eight-company regiments and sent the surplus officers home to recruit. On 24 July General Gates assumed command of the Southern Department.[6] After militia reinforcements arrived, Gates met a crushing defeat at Camden, South Carolina, on 16 August, but de Kalb's continentals fought well. The survivors of his division reas-

[4]*JCC*, 15:1087, 1256, 1347; Burnett, *Letters*, 4:322-23, 419-20, 428-29; Fitzpatrick, *Writings*, 16:360, 382, 473; 17:124, 134-35, 151, 175, 206-8, 228, 236-38, 242-43, 309; Moultrie, *Memoirs of the American Revolution*, 2:67, 114. For the provisional Virginia regiments, see above, Chapter 6.

[5]Kite, *Duportail*, pp. 172-75; Bernard A. Uhlendorf, ed., *The Siege of Charleston* (Ann Arbor: University of Michigan Press, 1938); Heinrichs, "Extracts From the Letter-Book," *Pennsylvania Magazine of History and Biography*, 22:137-70.

[6]*JCC*, 16:329, 17:508; Fitzpatrick, *Writings*, 17:228-29; 18:198-99, 204, 269; 19:78-79; Gates Papers (de Kalb to Bd of War, copy, 6 Jun 80; de Kalb to Gates, 16 Jul 80; Bd of War to Gates, 15 Jun 80; Gates to Richard Caswell, 25 Jul 80; de Kalb's division orders, 15 Jul 80; Return, 22 Jul 80).

sembled quickly, thanks to their superior training, as a provisional regiment composed of two four-company battalions and two light infantry companies.[7]

Washington's efforts to procure replacements to offset the transfer of his Virginia, Maryland, and Delaware regiments were facilitated by the prospect of a Franco-American attack on New York City and by a special congressional committee which visited headquarters in late spring. The primary mission of the committee was to investigate the logistical system, which was tottering on the brink of collapse because of rampant inflation and other problems in the American economy, and to prepare recommendations for reform. Congress especially wanted to trim expenses. The committee's secondary mission was to identify surplus regiments and to recommend revised regimental structures to achieve further savings. The committee members—Philip Schuyler, John Mathews, and Nathaniel Peabody—interpreted their mandate broadly and supported Washington's preparations for the planned operation. When Washington canceled the attack in late June, the committee returned to its basic task; the recommendations it submitted to Congress would form the basis for reforms in the various support departments in the fall.[8]

By October 1780 the Continental Army had received a series of major blows: the fall of Charleston, the debacle at Camden, and the terrible shock of Benedict Arnold's treason. The economy still verged on the brink of total collapse, and the three-year enlistments of 1777 would expire during the coming winter. As early as 15 September Washington had recommended to Congress that it centralize all military affairs under itself and resort to three-year drafts. He argued that maintaining a strong Continental Army would cost less than constantly calling out the militia, and he reminded the delegates that

no Militia will ever acquire the habits necessary to resist a regular force. Even those nearest the seat of War are only valuable as light Troops to be scattered in the woods and plague rather than do serious injury to the Enemy. The firmness requisite for the real business of fighting is only to be attained by a constant course of discipline and service.[9]

On 28 August Congress had anticipated his needs by appointing a five-man committee to prepare a reorganization plan. In addition to Samuel Adams, the committee included four staunch supporters of Washington: Joseph Jones of Virginia, Thomas McKean of Delaware, John Morin Scott of New York, and Ezekiel Cornell of Rhode Island. They consulted with Steuben and then recommended that Congress require each state to have a full complement of men in the field by 1 December. If a state could not fill its quota with men enlisted for the duration of the war, it was to furnish the balance, whether volunteers or draftees, for a period of not less than one year. The key innovation was the stipulation that the drafted men had to serve until replacements arrived. Congress adopted this plan on 21 September. Changing strategic needs, however, never allowed a thorough test of this system.[10]

[7]Steuben Papers (Otho Williams to Steuben, 12 Oct 80; Mordecai Gist to Steuben, 12 Oct 80; Return, 1 Oct 80); Gates Papers (to Washington, 3 Sep 80; Return, 23 Sep 80). The defeat caused Maryland to abandon efforts to organize an eighth regiment, the "Regiment Extraordinary."

[8]*JCC*, 16:75-79, 293-312, 332-33, 350-57, 362; 17:472, 522-23, 528, 579-80, 589-90, 604-5, 607-8, 719-20; 18:878-88, 1109-11; Fitzpatrick, *Writings*, 18:207-11, 356-58, 416-19, 425-32, 455-59; 19:2, 77-85, 118, 391-94; Burnett, *Letters*, 5:80, 89-92, 114, 126-78, 222, 343, 372-74.

[9]Fitzpatrick, *Writings*, 20:50; see also 19:402-13, 481-82. For an account of the logistical problems at this point, see Erna Risch, *Supplying Washington's Army* (Washington Government Printing Office, 1981).

[10]*JCC*, 17:786; 18:839, 844; Burnett, *Letters*, 5:378-79, 389-90. A similar system had been proposed by the Board of War in February, but Congress had declined to act on it. *JCC*, 16:248-51.

TABLE 5—1781 QUOTAS

State	Infantry Regiments	Artillery Regiments	Legionary Corps	Partisan Corps	Artificer Regiments	Total Regimental Equivalents
New Hampshire	2	.....	.....	.....	.....	2
Massachusetts	10	1	.....	.....	.....	11
Rhode Island	1	.....	.....	.....	.....	1
Connecticut	5	.....	1	.....	.....	6
New York	2	1	.....	.....	.....	3
New Jersey	2	.....	.....	.....	.....	2
Pennsylvania	6	1	1	.....	1	9
Maryland	5	.....	.....	.....	.....	5
Delaware	1	.....	.....	.....	.....	1
Virginia	8	1	2	.....	.....	11
North Carolina	4	.....	.....	.....	.....	4
South Carolina	2	.....	.....	.....	.....	2
Georgia	1	.....	.....	.....	.....	1
Unallotted	1	.....	.....	2	.....	3
Total	50	4	4	2	1	61

On 3 October 1780 congress gave preliminary approval to a comprehensive reorganization plan which attempted to balance financial constraints and Washington's wishes. As James Duane told the Commander in Chief, the plan was "submitted, as it is, to your Opinion. It is only to be considered as an Essay open to such Alterations as you may suggest." On 21 October Congress adopted verbatim the changes Washington had requested.[11]

The final plan specified that on 1 January 1781 "the regular army of the United States" was to consist of 49 infantry regiments, Moses Hazen's special Canadian infantry regiment, 4 artillery regiments, 4 legionary corps, 2 partisan corps, and a regiment of artificers. Although not mentioned in the legislation, the Corps of Engineers, the companies of sappers and miners, the Marechaussee, and the Corps of Invalids remained unchanged. All other units had to disband and transfer their enlisted men to the line regiments. Congress allotted every regiment, except Hazen's and the two partisan corps, to a single state (*Table 5*) to simplify subsistence and troop replacement. At Washington's request, it gave the Army rather than the state governments the power to decide which officers were to retire. Seniority would be the determining factor in resolving disputes.

The heart of the reorganization was the realignment of the Infantry. Congress apportioned the forty-nine regiments on the basis of realistic estimates of the men available in each state, rather than total population. A fiftieth regiment, Hazen's unallotted regiment, which now became the Canadian Regiment, continued under its four-battalion configuration. It absorbed the remaining Canadians from James Livington's old 1st Canadian Regiment plus various other men.[12] Washington did not object to the total number of infantry regiments, but he doubted that every regiment would achieve full strength. He also complained that the three regiments allotted to South Caro-

[11]*JCC*, 18:893–97, 959–62; Burnett, *Letters*, 5:404, 407, 414–15 (Duane quotation), 417–18, 422–23, 428; Steuben Papers (to Washington 23 Oct 80); Fitzpatrick, *Writings*, 20:157–67, 263–64, 277–81, 311–12, 400.

[12]*JCC*, 19:427–28; 20:711–12; RG 93 National Archives (Bd of War report, 28 Jun 81).

CHART 11—INFANTRY REGIMENT 1781

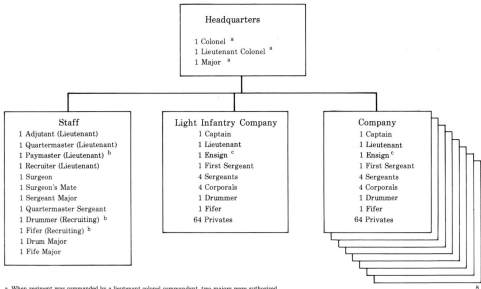

a. When regiment was commanded by a lieutenant colonel commandant, two majors were authorized.
b. One lieutenant and a fifer and a drummer were permanently on duty in the regiment's home state as a recruiting party.
c. Initially the temporary retention of a lieutenant in the ensign's position was authorized.

lina and Georgia would have to be excluded since those states were occupied by the enemy. The plan would then provide for only 18,000 infantrymen. Washington said he needed 22,000: 18,000 for mobile field forces, 2,500 for garrisons in the Hudson Highlands, and 1,500 for service on the frontiers.

The congressional plan continued the basic regimental alignment of one light and eight line companies, all equal in size. It added three enlisted men to each company and left the number of officers unchanged. Washington, however, persuaded Congress to make substantial alterations. (*Chart 11*) Each regiment's three field officers —colonel, lieutenant colonel, and major, or lieutenant-colonel commandant and two majors—now no longer served as company commanders. This change enlarged the pool of field-grade officers for special assignments and significantly increased the number of captains within each regiment. Every company could expect to have three officers present in combat. Two additional sergeants, one for the first time officially designated the first sergeant, and another corporal joined each company. The number of privates in a regiment increased from fifty-three to sixty-four. Four extra lieutenants joined the staff to fill the permanent positions of paymaster, adjutant, quartermaster, and recruiter. The regimental recruiter remained in his home state with a drummer and a fifer and worked full time to secure replacements. Extra lieutenants were available because of the reduced number of regiments; they also filled positions left vacant by the shortage of ensigns.

Washington was pleased with the new infantry regiment. The rank and file strength of each company, the true measure of unit fighting power, had increased by slightly more than 20 percent, from 56 to 68 men. Officer and sergeant strength increases promised better control. A regiment engaging in combat at full strength could deploy

CHART 12—ARTILLERY REGIMENT 1781

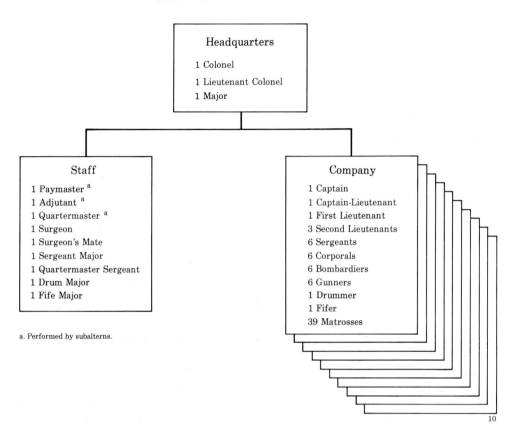

Headquarters

1 Colonel

1 Lieutenant Colonel

1 Major

Staff

1 Paymaster [a]
1 Adjutant [a]
1 Quartermaster [a]
1 Surgeon
1 Surgeon's Mate
1 Sergeant Major
1 Quartermaster Sergeant
1 Drum Major
1 Fife Major

a. Performed by subalterns.

Company

1 Captain
1 Captain-Lieutenant
1 First Lieutenant
3 Second Lieutenants
6 Sergeants
6 Corporals
6 Bombardiers
6 Gunners
1 Drummer
1 Fifer
39 Matrosses

10

544 rank and file (120 percent of the 1778 figure), 40 sergeants, 24 company officers, and 3 field officers. Although the new regiment did not regain the power of the 1776 regimental arrangement, it was substantially better organized and more efficient than the typical British regiment.

The new artillery regiment (*Chart 12*) gained eleven enlisted men, all matrosses, in each company but had fewer companies. The number of staff and company officers did not change. Congress initially planned to have 9 companies per regiment, but Washington convinced the delegates that 10 companies would simplify administration. Although the number of artillery companies in the Army dropped to 40 (in 4 regiments), the number of matrosses rose sharply from 1,344 to 1,560. Congress allotted the regiments to Virginia, New York, Massachusetts, and Pennsylvania, the states which had been their primary recruiting areas in the past. The 1st and 3d Continental Artillery Regiments converted to the new structure through attrition. Lamb's 2d, a very strong regiment, and Proctor's 4th, with only eight companies, presented more of a problem. Lamb had been engaged in a long-standing argument with Pennsylvania over controlling his men from that state. Washington consolidated the two companies of the 2d which had been raised in Pennsylvania with Gibbs Jones' separate company and Isaac Coren's company of laboratory technicians in the Regiment of Artillery Ar-

CHART 13—LEGIONARY CORPS 1781

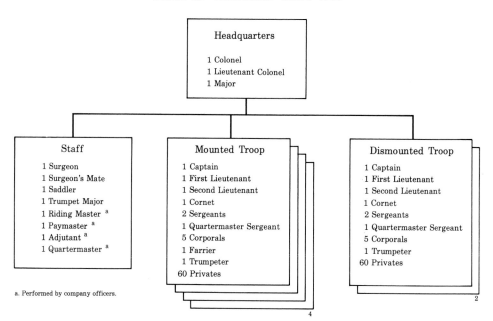

a. Performed by company officers.

tificers. The two resulting companies transferred to the 4th, bringing both regiments to the ten-company limit.[13]

In the case of the four light dragoon regiments, Congress proposed only minor changes, adding five privates to each troop. Bearing in mind current forage problems and the success of experiments of the 2d and 4th regiments, Washington countered with a very different proposal. (*Chart 13*) Under his plan each regiment would dismount two troops, thus turning the regiment into a European-style legionary corps. "I prefer Legionary Corps," he told Congress, "because the kind of Service [reconnaissance duties] we have for horse almost constantly requires the aid of Infantry."[14] The infantry contingent gave each regiment the ability to defend its quarters. The savings from eliminating over one hundred horses plus specialized equipment per regiment also argued for the change. As in the case of the artillery regiments, these legionary corps were allocated to their original recruiting areas.

Washington made one further recommendation with respect to mounted units. He stated, "Tho' in general I dislike independent Corps, I think a Partisan Corps with an Army useful in many respects. Its name and destination [mission] stimulate to enterprize."[15] Congress approved the retention of one for the Main Army and one for the Southern Army, under Lt. Col. Henry Lee and Colonel Armand, respectively. Although similar (*Chart 14*) in most respects to a legionary corps, the partisan corps had a troop organization that was quite different. Each troop had only 50 privates, and 3 of the 6

[13]Fitzpatrick, *Writings*, 18:277-79, 311; 20:344-45; 21:45-46, 411; 22:45-48; Lamb Papers (Knox to Lamb, 8 Sep, 2 and 21 Nov 80; Robert Walker to Lamb, 31 Oct 80; Ebenezer Stevens to Lamb, 3 Nov 80).
[14]Fitzpatrick, *Writings*, 20:163.
[15]Ibid., 20:163.

CHART 14—PARTISAN CORPS 1781

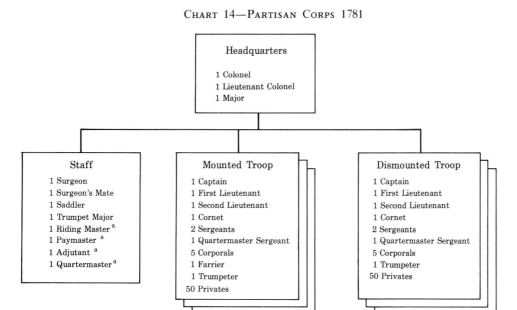

Headquarters

1 Colonel
1 Lieutenant Colonel
1 Major

Staff	Mounted Troop	Dismounted Troop
1 Surgeon	1 Captain	1 Captain
1 Surgeon's Mate	1 First Lieutenant	1 First Lieutenant
1 Saddler	1 Second Lieutenant	1 Second Lieutenant
1 Trumpet Major	1 Cornet	1 Cornet
1 Riding Master [a]	2 Sergeants	2 Sergeants
1 Paymaster [a]	1 Quartermaster Sergeant	1 Quartermaster Sergeant
1 Adjutant [a]	5 Corporals	5 Corporals
1 Quartermaster [a]	1 Farrier	1 Trumpeter
	1 Trumpeter	50 Privates
	50 Privates	

a. Performed by company officers.

troops were dismounted. The latter variation made the corps more self-reliant, allowing it to operate at a greater distance from its army than a legionary corps.

Congress reduced support troops to one regiment containing eight 60-man companies. The delegates allotted it to Pennsylvania at that state's request. The legislation did not specify which of the two existing artificer regiments would be retained, but on 29 March 1781 Congress finally directed Baldwin's Quartermaster Artificer Regiment to disband. Its men reorganized into two companies, one each in the Main and Southern Armies. Flowers' Artillery Artificer Regiment formed the regiment's other companies, but the full complement of eight companies never existed. The regiment's men served in detachments for the remainder of the war. A provisional pioneer company in the Southern Army in 1782 supplemented them.[16]

The final plan for the Continental Army in 1781 called for 61 regimental equivalents. States supporting the Southern Department furnished, on paper, 21 infantry regiments, 1 artillery regiment, 2 legionary corps, and 1 partisan corps. Washington expected the Main Army to have the services of 29 infantry regiments (including Hazen's oversized unit), 3 artillery regiments, 2 legionary corps, and 1 partisan corps, plus the companies of sappers and miners, the Marechaussee Corps, the Corps of Invalids, and his guard. The total of 61 also included the dispersed artificer regiment. The distribution of units reflected the different operations faced in each theater. Washington had more artillery, infantry, and specialist troops to attack the fortified base at New York. The Southern Army's larger cavalry force gave that army more mobility.

Implementation of the reorganization took place officially on 1 January 1781, and

[16]Ibid., 20:339–40; 21:402; 23:202–4; 24:133; *JCC*, 22:148–49; Burnett, *Letters*, 5:76–79, 462; Jefferson, *Papers*, 5:574–78. Philadelphia's urban status promised to make Pennsylvania a fertile recruiting area for "mechanics."

CHARLES TUFFIN ARMAND, MARQUIS DE LA ROUERIE *(1750–93) was a French volunteer who went by the title Colonel Armand while serving in America. He organized and commanded the 1st Partisan Corps and then returned to his native land where he died during the French Revolution as the leader of a counterrevolution in Brittany. (Portrait by Charles Willson Peale, ca. 1783.)*

by February Washington transmitted to the Board of War the new arrangement of his officers plus a list of those retired by the disbandments.[17] The Main Army implemented the reduction and reorganization in its various winter quarters. The four New England lines easily accomplished the transition by consolidating units or by disbanding high numbered ones and transferring personnel. New Hampshire chose the latter route; Rhode Island, the former, in the process ending its experiment in segregation. Massachusetts cut its regiments from 16 to 10, and Connecticut cut its regiments from 9 to 5 through consolidations. Both renumbered their lines to reflect the commanders' seniority. Because the new regiment had a larger organization, brigades required only three infantry regiments to sustain the combat power of four old ones. The region organized six brigades: 3 from Massachusetts, 2 from Connecticut, and 1 from New Hampshire. Rhode Island's regiment rounded out the 2d Connecticut Brigade, and the 10th Massachusetts Regiment served as the third element of the New Hampshire Brigade. This arrangement produced a regional force of three divisions with significant homogeneity and strength.[18]

New York's reduction from five to two regiments occurred in the Northern Department, where the New York Brigade was stationed. Consolidation produced the required enlisted strength but left a surplus of experienced officers. The state used them to organize a new corps of state troops to assume responsibility for frontier defense with Congress' financial support.[19] New Jersey simply disbanded its 3d Regiment and reorganized the remaining two regiments at Pompton. A full company of

[17]Fitzpatrick, *Writings*, 21:12–13, 38–39, 82–83, 250–51.
[18]Ibid., 20:410, 491; 21:40–41, 45, 69–70, 405.
[19]Ibid., 20:295–97, 417–18; 21:17; *JCC*, 19:339; 23:525; Burnett, *Letters*, 5:148, 157–58, 177–78, 444–45; 6:313–15, 322–23, 333–34, 337–38; Philip Van Cortlandt, *The Revolutionary War Memoir and Selected Correspondence of Philip Van Cortlandt*, ed. Jacob Judd (Tarrytown: Sleepy Hollow Restorations, 1976), pp. 57–58.

the 2d immediately marched to the Wyoming Valley to assume garrison responsibilities in that region; New Jersey troops became neutral mediators in the Connecticut-Pennsylvania jurisdictional dispute.[20] Both New York and New Jersey continued to field a brigade, although both brigades remained short a regiment.

The reorganization caused a major crisis in the Pennsylvania line, which was camped for the winter at Morristown. On the evening of 1 January, before the reorganization was actually implemented, the enlisted men mutinied over chronic shortages of food, clothing, and pay. The reorganization acted as the precipitating factor since most men believed that it released them from 1777 enlistments ambiguously recorded as "for three years or the duration of the war." Sergeants took control after an initial scuffle and marched the regiments to Princeton where they negotiated with representatives of Pennsylvania and Congress. The men turned several British agents over to the negotiators and indicated that they only wanted a redress of grievances. The settlement set up an impartial review panel which examined each man's enlistment. It released 1,250 infantrymen and 67 artillerists from Continental service by the end of January. The remaining 1,150 men were judged to have clearly enlisted for the duration, but they received furloughs until 15 March. Other terms included promises of back pay, clothing issues, and freedom from any punishment for the mutiny. The reorganization, with an effective date of 17 January, consolidated cadres on paper for six regiments and ordered them to reassemble at specific towns.[21]

The mutiny not only deprived Washington of two brigades of troops but also opened the door to future revolts. On 20 January the New Jersey regiments mutinied in an effort to obtain similar concessions. Washington reacted swiftly and asked Congress not to interfere. He sent Maj. Gen. Robert Howe from the Highlands with a detachment of New Englanders and orders to "compel the mutineers to unconditional submission" and to execute "a few of the most active and most incendiary leaders." On 27 January Howe suppressed the mutiny and ordered two ringleaders to be shot, thereby checking the spread of unrest.[22]

Washington realized that recruitment problems in the south dwarfed his own. He favored the creation of a mobile force capable of pinning the British into coastal enclaves, but the high level of military activity in that area complicated the reorganization. On 14 October 1780 he had selected Nathanael Greene to replace Gates as the department commander. Washington also sent Steuben to assist Greene in rebuilding the Southern Department's forces. After leaving Steuben in Virginia to supervise the establishment of a logistical structure and the rehabilitation of Virginia's forces, Greene arrived at Charlotte, North Carolina, on 2 December and formally relieved Gates the next day.[23]

The heart of the Southern Army remained the infantry regiments from Maryland and Delaware. After Camden these troops had formed a single provisional two-battalion

[20]Fitzpatrick, *Writings*, 21:29, 32-33, 37-38.

[21]Stille, *Anthony Wayne*, pp. 248-63; William Henry Smith, ed., *The St. Clair Papers*, 2 vols. (Cincinnati: Robert Clarke & Co., 1882), 1:532-33; Burnett, *Letters*, 5:516-33, 540-41; *Pennsylvania Archives*, 2d ser., 11:631-74; 4th ser., 3:796-99.

[22]Fitzpatrick, *Writings*, 21:124-25, 128-30, 135-37, 146-49; John Shreve, "Personal Narrative of the Services of Lieut. John Shreve of the New Jersey Line of the Continental Army," ed. S.H. Shreve, *Magazine of American History* 3 (1879):575.

[23]*JCC*, 18:906, 994-96; Gates Papers (Southern Department General Orders, 3 and 4 Dec 80); Fitzpatrick, *Writings*, 20:50, 181-82, 238-39, 321.

JOSEPH REED *(1741–85) served Washington as an aide and later became the president (governor) of Pennsylvania. In the latter capacity he negotiated the settlement of the 1781 mutiny of the Pennsylvania Line. (Portrait by Charles Willson Peale, 1783.)*

regiment. The Delaware men served in Capt. Peter Jacquette's line company and Robert Kirkwood's light infantry company. Surplus Delaware officers returned to that state to refill the rest of the regiment. They organized two more companies by mid-1781.[24] The Maryland veterans from the provisional regiment and the first reinforcements sent to Greene by the state then refilled the 1st and 2d Maryland Regiments. The 6th and 7th disbanded, and the 3d, 4th, and 5th reorganized at cadre strength in Maryland. The 5th refilled first and reached Greene by mid-February 1781; the 3d and 4th set out on 28 August and 4 September, respectively.[25]

With no organized forces from Georgia or the Carolinas, Greene had to rely on Virginia to supplement his Maryland and Delaware veterans. Civil officials in Virginia handled the actual recruiting for Steuben, who had remained in the state to supervise the rebuilding of its regiments. Washington intended to refill the Virginia units lost at Charleston by using repatriated prisoners, convalescents, and new recruits. Steuben was unable to implement this logical program because of a series of problems. Continental officers were diverted to organize a series of provisional units needed to meet specific crises or to command militia units mobilized to fend off British raiders. Another problem arose when escaped American prisoners of war claimed on their return that captivity had released them from their enlistments. By spring frustrations with these problems led to a breach between Steuben and Governor

[24]William Seymour, *A Journal of the Southern Expedition, 1780–1783* (Wilmington: Historical Society of Delaware, 1896), pp. 7–11; Kirkwood, *Journal and Order Book*, pp. 11–13; Caleb Prew Bennett, "Orderly Book of Caleb Prew Bennet at the Battle of Yorktown, 1781," ed. Charles W. Dickens, *Delaware History* 4 (1955):108–9, 113, 121, 139, 146.

[25]Gates Papers (Josiah Hall to Gates, 12 Oct 80; Gist to Gates, 26 Oct 80); Steuben Papers (Greene to Gist [copy], 10 Nov 80; Gist to Steuben, 14 Feb 81; Gist to Governor Thomas Lee, 8 Feb 81; Fitzpatrick, *Writings*, 21:82–83; Arthur J. Alexander, "How Maryland Tried To Raise Her Continental Quota," *Maryland Historical Magazine* 42 (1942):191–92. Secondary sources usually make errors in regimental numbers, most frequently mistaking Lt. Col. Benjamin Ford's 5th as the 2d Maryland Regiment.

Thomas Jefferson. The Virginia reorganization actually amounted to only a rearrangement of officers on paper. The sole exception was the 9th Virginia Regiment stationed at Fort Pitt. It regrouped as the 7th Virginia Regiment with just two companies.[26]

Without the Virginia infantry regiments Greene's army remained dangerously weak. Washington and Congress had sent him Henry Lee's 2d Partisan Corps in December 1780, and in February 1781 they decided to shift the Pennsylvania line to his department once it recovered from the mutiny. Maj. Gen. Arthur St. Clair found the reorganization of the Pennsylvania line unexpectedly difficult. To expedite matters he did not fill the permanent regiments. Instead he formed three provisional regiments, each containing eight forty-men companies. A detachment of the 4th Continental Artillery Regiment with four guns, together with one troop of the 4th Legionary Corps (containing all the men in the corps who had horses) complemented them. After overcoming major financial and logistical problems and crushing a minor mutiny, Brig. Gen. Anthony Wayne finally left York, Pennsylvania, with these units in late May. St. Clair stayed to continue recruiting.[27]

The careful plans of October 1780 for sixty-one regimental equivalents divided into two major commands thus did not materialize. Washington's Main Army and subsidiary commands in the north lost the services of the 2d Partisan Corps as well as Pennsylvania's legionary corps, artillery regiment, and 6 infantry regiments when these units moved to the badly depleted Southern Department. The latter never obtained the 7 infantry regiments projected for Georgia and the Carolinas, and it had the services of only 1 of 8 Virginia and 2 of 6 Maryland and Delaware infantry regiments. None of the Pennsylvania troops, moreover, reached the area during the first part of 1781. When they did arrive, Greene's single artillery regiment amounted to crews for just a handful of fieldpieces; his two legionary corps operated as a small cavalry regiment; and of the two partisan corps, only Lee's remained fit for combat. On the other hand, the regiments serving in the Continental Army in 1781 contained very experienced cadres. The reorganization left only the most competent officers and produced units with very efficient organizations. During 1781 those troops would engage in the war's decisive campaigns.

Triumph at Yorktown

The 1781 campaign conclusively demonstrated that the Continental Army had matured into a small but effective military force despite pay and supply problems. Washington and Greene wrested the strategic initiative from the British, adjusting their plans to take advantage of changing circumstances. With French military, naval, and financial support, they caused a major defect in British dispositions and then exploited it to the maximum.

[26]Fitzpatrick, *Writings*, 19:381–82; 20:465; 21:82; Jefferson, *Papers*, 4:17–18, 349–50, 603–4; 5:111–16, 162–63; 6:30–32; Palmer, *Calendar of Virginia State Papers*, 1:594–96; Gates Papers (Muhlenberg to Gates, 12 Oct 80; Abraham Buford to Gates, 21 Oct and 1 Nov 80; Ebenezer Stevens to Gates, 16 Nov 80; Return of Southern Army, 5 Nov 80); W. A. Irvine, ed., "Affairs at Fort Pitt in 1782," *Historical Magazine*, 1st ser. 7 (1863):306–9.

[27]*JCC*, 19:177, 275; Jefferson, *Papers*, 4:322–24; Fitzpatrick, *Writings*, 21:272–73, 294, 473–74; 22: 191–92; Smith, *St. Clair Papers*, 1:544–45, 548–49; Stille, *Anthony Wayne*, pp. 264–67; *Historical Magazine*, 1st ser. 6 (1862):337–38; RG 360, National Archives (Keene to Bd of War, 10 Apr 81; St. Clair [to Board of War], 5 Apr 81).

ARTHUR ST. CLAIR (1736–1818) served in the British Army during the French and Indian War and then settled in Pennsylvania. He raised the 2d Pennsylvania Battalion and eventually rose to the rank of major general. He was governor of the Northwest Territory and commander of the United States Army in the decade following the Revolution, suffering defeat at the hands of the Indians in Ohio in 1791. (Portrait by Charles Willson Peale, ca. 1782.)

The year's operations began in the Carolinas. General Cornwallis suffered a major setback at Cowpens on 17 January when his light troops under Lt. Col. Banastre Tarleton engaged the Southern Department's light troops under Brig. Gen. Daniel Morgan. Several experienced contingents of irregulars plus some special militia units composed primarily of Virginia Continental veterans served with Morgan, and he developed tactics which blended their talents with those of his regulars. Deploying the former in a double line of skirmishers, Morgan caused Tarleton to commit his reserve before his troops reached the Continentals. A sharp counterattack broke through the disorganized British line and destroyed Tarleton's force. Losses in this battle and in an earlier defeat on 7 October at King's Mountain deprived Cornwallis of most of his light troops.[28]

Cornwallis chased Greene across the Dan River into Virginia, but the pursuit so debilitated his regiments that they had to withdraw and refit. The pause allowed Greene time to regroup his troops, establish a supply system, and dispatch Henry Lee's 2d Partisan Corps into South Carolina to assist irregulars in harassing British outposts and lines of communications. By concentrating on quality and mobility, Greene turned the small size of his regular force into a logistical advantage. He called out large militia contingents only shortly before a battle. During the intervals the militia, Lee's 2d Partisan Corps, and Lt. Col. William Washington's composite detachment of the 1st and 3d Legionary Corps restricted British reconnaissance and freedom of movement.[29]

Greene reentered North Carolina and on 15 March fought Cornwallis at Guilford Court House. As at Cowpens, skirmish lines forced the British troops to deploy pre-

[28]Lee, Memoirs of the War in the Southern Department, pp. 230–31; [Banastre] Tarleton, A History of the Campaigns of 1780 and 1781, in the Southern Provinces of North America (London: T. Cadell, 1787), pp. 214–22; Gates Papers (Morgan to Will[iam Clajon], 26 Jan 81).
[29]Hamilton, Papers, 2:529–31; Jefferson, Papers, 4:288–89; 5:360–62; Fitzpatrick, Writings, 20:321.

maturely, and they suffered heavy casualties. The Continentals punished Cornwallis with accurate artillery and small arms fire, and the Marylanders drove back the elite Guards Brigade in a bayonet charge before Greene broke off the action. British losses of nearly 50 percent crippled Cornwallis' regiments as fighting units and ruined their morale. Greene then bypassed Cornwallis and moved against the British base at Camden, South Carolina. He gambled that operations in South Carolina would restore patriot morale and deprive the British of logistical support. Cornwallis chose not to follow, hoping to disrupt Greene's base in Virginia before his own subordinates met defeat.[30]

In a series of engagements and maneuvers Greene gradually drove Lt. Col. Francis Rawdon and Lt. Col. Alexander Stewart into coastal enclaves. On 8 September he attacked Stewart's camp at Eutaw Springs, South Carolina. Militia and irregulars led the attack, with the Continentals in reserve. The high number of relatively untrained recruits forced Greene to deploy into line too soon and the attack lost some of its momentum. When terrain and stiffening resistance slowed his advance, Greene committed his reserve in "a brisk charge with trailed Arms, through a heavy cannonade, and a shower of Musket Balls."[31] This maneuver routed the main British body. Broken terrain and casualties among key American officers, however, had disrupted many units, and Stewart was able to rally some of his men. Rather than risk defeat, Greene withdrew. Eutaw Springs left the British incapable of further offensive action in the south. Cornwallis' gamble that his subordinates could hold the Carolinas and Georgia had failed.

While Greene was beginning his spring offensive, Washington had assembled his army's light infantry companies. Each now had five sergeants and fifty rank and file. On 19 February 1781 he formed them into three battalions. Lt. Col. Elijah Vose's battalion contained the companies of the 1st through 8th Massachusetts Regiments. Lt. Col. Jean-Joseph Gimat's battalion included the remaining 2 Massachusetts companies, the 5 Connecticut companies, and the single Rhode Island company. Lt. Col. Francis Barber's battalion began with the 2 New Hampshire light companies and the single light company of Hazen's Canadian Regiment; on 22 February it gained 3 line companies and the 2 light companies from New Jersey. Lafayette took command of this Light Corps on 20 February.[32]

Benedict Arnold, in his new role as a British brigadier, had begun operating along Virginia's James River in January 1781. Washington sent Lafayette's light infantrymen south to trap him in a joint operation with French warships from Newport, Rhode Island. Shallow waters frustrated the first naval expedition, while a superior British squadron drove off a second. Lafayette's Continentals remained in Virginia, however, even as British reinforcements from New York City and Cornwallis' column from North Carolina arrived. Although Lafayette could not now defeat the British, Cornwallis lacked the mobility to catch him or to prevent the arrival in Virginia of General Wayne's Pennsylvanians. Wayne reorganized his provisional units on 14 July into two stronger regiments, and the excess officers returned to Pennsylvania to re-

[30]Tarleton, *Campaigns*, pp. 271–79; Charles O'Hara, "Letters of Charles O'Hara to the Duke of Grafton," ed. George C. Rogers, *South Carolina Historical Magazine* 65 (1964):159–66, 173–79.
[31]RG 360, National Archives (Greene to Congress, 11 Sep 81).
[32]Wright, "Corps of Light Infantry," *American Historical Review*, 31:459–61; Fitzpatrick, *Writings*, 21:169–70, 232–35, 253, 274. Lafayette had already commanded the Light Corps in 1780.

HENRY LEE *(1756–1818) was a member of Virginia's prominent Lee family who started his career in the Continental Army as a captain in the 1st Continental Light Dragoon Regiment and went on to raise the 2d Partisan Corps. He earned the nickname "Light Horse Harry" while leading the latter unit in operations in the south in 1781. His son, Robert E. Lee, also had a distinguished military career. (Portrait by Charles Willson Peale, 1782.)*

cruit.[33] Cornwallis ended the summer by selecting Yorktown as the site for a permanent naval base.

While Greene and Lafayette gradually pressed British troops in the south into a few coastal enclaves, Washington planned a Franco-American offensive to recapture New York City. By June, when he called on General Rochambeau to march his expeditionary corps from Rhode Island, the Main Army and outposts contained eight brigades, Hazen's regiment, two artillery regiments, the 2d Legionary Corps, and various special units.[34] Including the light companies with Lafayette (about 1,300 men), the infantry portion of Washington's force amounted to 61 field, 623 company, and 118 staff officers; 810 sergeants; 461 drummers and fifers; and 7,854 rank and file. The fact that the regiments remained 120 officers, 295 sergeants, 166 drummers and fifers, and 6,510 rank and file below authorized levels was discouraging. The artillery portion, with 91 officers and 711 men, was short 45 officers and 597 men; Col. Elisha Sheldon's legion had 23 of 32 officers and 303 of 423 men. Rochambeau's French corps added over 5,000 experienced, professional troops, in 4 two-battalion infantry regiments, 1 legion, 2 companies of miners, 6 artillery companies, and 1 company of bombardiers. These troops had participated in the important 1778 war games, which had tested the latest French military theories and doctrines. Washington also expected Admiral Francois, Comte de Grasse, to move up from the West Indies with additional troops and a large naval squadron.[35]

[33]John Davis, "Diary of Capt. John Davis, of the Pennsylvania Line," ed. Joseph A. Waddell, *Virginia Magazine of History and Biography* 1 (1893):5–7; Joseph M. Beatty, ed., "Letters From Continental Officers to Doctor Reading Beatty, 1781–1788," *Pennsylvania Magazine of History and Biography* 54 (1930): 159–61; Fitzpatrick, *Writings*, 21:254–56, 273–74, 421–24.

[34]RG 93, National Archives (General Return, Main Army, June 1781). Lesser, *Sinews*, pp. 204–5, prints a variant of this return.

[35]Quimby, *Background of Napoleonic Warfare*, pp. 233; Fitzpatrick, *Writings*, 22:86–87, 102–7, 109–11, 116–22, 156–58, 207–9; Ludwig Von Closen, *The Revolutionary Journal of Baron Ludwig Von Closen, 1780–1783*, trans. Evelyn N. Acomb (Chapel Hill: University of North Carolina Press, 1958), pp. 4–5, 92, 132.

WILLIAM WASHINGTON *(1752–1810) was a cousin of the commander in chief who joined the 3d Virginia Regiment as a captain in 1776 and transferred to the light dragoons in 1777. During Greene's campaign in the south he was the senior cavalry officer in the field. (Portrait by Charles Willson Peale, ca. 1781.)*

Washington and Rochambeau joined forces at Dobbs Ferry, New York, on 6 July. They were encouraged by the news that the frigate *Resolue* had reached Philadelphia with arms, clothing, medicines, and two million livres in cash. When word arrived that de Grasse intended to sail to Chesapeake Bay rather than directly to New York, Washington and Rochambeau then decided to attack Cornwallis rather than New York City. Washington took about half of the Main Army and all the French troops south. Maj. Gen. William Heath, assisted by Generals McDougall, Stirling, and Stark, remained behind to secure West Point and the northern frontier. He retained, in addition to various contingents of militia and state troops, the New Hampshire, Massachusetts, and Connecticut infantry regiments, the Corps of Invalids, the 3d Continental Artillery Regiment, and the 2d Legionary Corps. Superintendent of Finance Robert Morris and allied logistical staffs, drawing heavily on cash supplied by France, handled the largest and most complex troop movement of the war with skill and dispatch. Washington's shrewd use of deception obscured the change in plans from the British until they were powerless to intervene.[36]

De Grasse's squadron turned back a British relief fleet off the mouth of the Chesapeake Bay on 5 September, completing the isolation of Cornwallis. Washington opened his headquarters at Williamsburg ten days later and began organizing the allied troops for siege operations. Maj. Gen. Benjamin Lincoln, the senior American commander, took charge of the Right Wing of the allies. The six brigades of Continentals formed divisions under Lincoln, Lafayette, and Steuben, and formed the first line of the American wing. Virginia militia formed the second line. The Continental force amounted to 41 field, 355 company, and 66 staff officers; 547 sergeants; 272 drummers and fifers; and 6,412 rank and file. The militia contributed another 188 of-

---

[36]Burnett, *Letters*, 6:208–11; Fitzpatrick, *Writings*, 22:236–37, 395–97, 401–2, 450–51, 501–2; 23:11–12, 19–23, 25n, 33–34, 50–58, 68–72, 75–77, 104–7; RG 360, National Archives (Heath to Congress, 5 Sep 81); Victor L. Johnson, "Robert Morris and the Provisioning of the American Army During the Campaign of 1781," *Pennsylvania History* 5 (1938):7–20.

ficers and 3,426 men. Rochambeau commanded the Left Wing, consisting of his own corps and some 3,000 troops from the West Indies under Lt. Gen. Claude Anne, Marquis de Saint-Simon Maublerce.[37] The siege itself progressed rapidly and in accord with formal European procedures. Artillery fire crushed Cornwallis' defenses, and on 19 October his troops marched out of their works and laid down their arms.

Plans to continue the offensive against other British garrisons in the south ended when de Grasse announced that his fleet had to return immediately to the West Indies. Rochambeau's decision to winter in Virginia allowed the Continentals to split up. General St. Clair took part of them and reinforced Greene, arriving at Round O, South Carolina, on 4 January 1782. His troops consisted of two Delaware companies, the 3d and 4th Maryland Regiments, a provisional Virginia regiment, General Wayne's two Pennsylvania provisional regiments and a third which arrived at Yorktown after the siege, and all available mounted troopers from the 1st, 3d, and 4th Legionary Corps. Greene quickly regrouped the Pennsylvanians into two strong regiments, disbanded the 5th Maryland Regiment to fill the other four from that state, and transferred his own Delaware men to the new companies. Armand's 1st Partisan Corps had to remain behind in Virginia because it required a more time-consuming reorganization, which began with the transfer of fifty men from the light infantry corps to serve as a cadre.[38]

The rest of the Continentals, with a few exceptions, marched from Yorktown under Lincoln and joined Heath in the Highlands. On arrival, the Light Corps broke up and the individual companies returned to their regiments for the winter. Hazen's regiment escorted prisoners to Lancaster, Pennsylvania, and remained there as guards.[39] Lamb's artillerymen, initially assisted by the sappers and miners, transported the heavy guns of the siege train and over two hundred captured British pieces to Head of Elk, Maryland. The captured guns were sent to Philadelphia to be overhauled by an artificer company. The field pieces were to accompany the troops to West Point, but Lamb's regiment camped for the winter at Burlington, New Jersey, with the siege train. It did not resume its march to West Point until August.[40]

Washington spent the winter at Philadelphia in discussions with Congress. The Continental Army had successfully met the battlefield challenge during 1781. Greene's army, Lafayette's contingent, and the Franco-American force had completely altered the course of the war. Yorktown ended British hopes of overrunning the south and left the enemy with only footholds at Savannah, Charleston, and New

[37]Fitzpatrick, *Writings*, 23:134-35, 146-47; RG 93, National Archives (Weekly Return, Main Army, 13 Oct 81).
[38]Fitzpatrick, *Writings*, 23:193-95, 198, 200, 216-17, 248-50, 258, 266-67, 270, 292-99, 309-13, 317-18; RG 360, National Archives (Greene to Congress, 23 Jan 82); Steuben Papers (Abstract of Musters for the Southern Army, 1 Apr-19 Sep 82); William Irvine, "Extracts From the Papers of General William Irvine," ed. W.A. Irvine, *Pennsylvania Magazine of History and Biography* 5 (1881):268, 274-75; *Archives of Maryland*, 18:429-75; Palmer, *Calendar of Virginia State Papers*, 2:127, 241, 582-85; Kirkwood, *Journal and Order Book*, pp. 27-30; Tuffin Charles Armand, Marquis de la Rouerie, "Letters of Col. Armand," New-York Historical Society *Collections* for 1878, pp. 323-30.
[39]Fitzpatrick, *Writings*, 23:290-91, 293-94, 323-24, 374, 25:110-11; James Thacher, *Military Journal of the American Revolution. From the Commencement to the Disbanding of the American Army* (Hartford: Hurlbut, Williams & Co., 1862), pp. 302-3.
[40]Fitzpatrick, *Writings*, 25:58-59. The convoy for the 1782 move required 114 horses and 200 oxen to move the artillery park's 39 wagons, 4 traveling forges, 18 howitzers, 16 fieldpieces, and 4 twelve-pounders. Lamb Papers (Knox to Lamb, 2 Nov 81 and 31 Jul 82; Knox to Washington, 30 Jul 82 [copy].)

Jean-Baptiste-Donatien de Vimeur, Comte de Rochambeau *(1725–1807) commanded the French expeditionary corps which served in North America under Washington from 1780 to 1782. The tact and skill of this professional soldier contributed directly to the success of the Yorktown campaign and the Franco-American alliance. (Portrait by Charles Willson Peale, 1782.)*

York City. Although French naval, financial, and military aid had played a major role in achieving the final victory at Yorktown, Washington had every reason to be proud of the Continentals' battlefield prowess and superior mobility. It was not long, however, before he had to deal with new problems caused by a shrinking military force.

The Road to Newburgh

During the last two years of the Revolution, the Continental Army did not engage in any major battle. Lack of French naval support prevented assaults on the remaining British strongholds, and changed political conditions in England made it clear that a negotiated peace would come in time. Congress and the American people, weary of a long war, increased the pressure on the military establishment to reduce expenses. Washington's role in gradually dismantling the Continental Army became one of his most important contributions to the new nation.

Washington's conferences with Congress during the winter of 1781–82 quickly established that the delegates wanted to trim expenses. The latter placed a limit for the first time on the number of general officers on active duty and began reviewing staff organizations to reduce expenditures. A committee recommended cutting the number of infantry regiments and the proportion of officers since "the Class of Men who are willing to become Soldiers is much diminished by the War and therefore the Difficulties of raising an Army equal to former Establishments have increased and will continue to increase."[41] Washington countered that since 1777 the Army had proportionately reduced the number of its regiments faster than the British Army in America had, that captured documents indicated that the British Army had more Loyalists on its rolls than he had Continentals, and that combat experience had made clear that the

[41]Burnett, *Letters*, 6:177–79.

GENERAL RETURN, MAIN ARMY, 27 OCTOBER 1781. *Adj. Gen. Edward Hand compiled this return of Continental infantry present at Yorktown under Washington eight days after Cornwallis' surrender. The return reflects the actual strength of each of the six brigades in Virginia and accounts for various absences.*

ROBERT MORRIS *(1734–1806), the financial wizard of the Revolution, served during and after the war in various political roles. As a delegate in the Continental Congress he led the nationalist faction which strongly supported Washington, and as Superintendent of Finance, he contributed directly to the success of the Yorktown campaign. (Portrait by Charles Willson Peale, 1782.)*

ratio of Continental officers to men was already too low. He won his case for the time being, but on 23 April 1782 Congress overturned one of the important features of the October 1780 reorganization. In the interest of economy, the delegates ordered that three lieutenants be eliminated from each regiment and that company officers be assigned to carry out the functions of adjutant, quartermaster, and recruiter.[42]

Continuing its drive for economy, Congress concentrated in 1782 on reducing the Army's support structure. It used the permanent executive ministers which replaced standing committees as the primary means for making these changes. Robert Morris, who had become Superintendent of Finance on 20 February 1781, played a major role, just as he had in the logistical effort for the Yorktown campaign. Even more important in this effort was Benjamin Lincoln, who had become Secretary at War on 30 October 1781. Although Lincoln's statutory functions were quite similar to those of the Board of War and his English counterpart, he acted in practice as Washington's liaison with Congress and Morris. Under Lincoln, the War Office consisted of an assistant, a secretary, and two clerks. They were able to reduce the size of most staff agencies, and they replaced many remaining officials with line officers acting in a part-time capacity. When Congress insisted on eliminating many positions concerned with direct support to the field armies, Washington protested that the changes particularly impaired the Army's mobility.[43]

Washington arrived at Newburgh, New York, on 31 March 1782 and formally resumed command in the north four days later. A private's letter home written at that time reflects the conditions he found: "Times are very dubros [sic] at present for there

---

[42]*JCC*, 21:791, 1127, 1179–81, 1163–65, 1182–83; 22:211–12, 381–82; Burnett, *Letters*, 6:270–80; Fitzpatrick, *Writings*, 23:29–32, 452–56, 498–99; 24:391–92. The final return (27 April 1784) of officers forced to retire by this "reform" is in Record Group 360, National Archives.

[43]*JCC*, 19:126–28, 180; 20:662–67; 21:1030, 1087, 1173, 1186–87; 22:30–33, 36–37, 40–41, 129–31, 177–79, 216, 235, 244–45, 381, 408–15, 425–27; 23:683–86; Burnett, *Letters*, 6:11–12, 190–91, 230–31; Fitzpatrick, *Writings*, 23:410–12, 452–56; 24:98–99; 25:72–73; 26:84.

MONTHLY RETURN, MAIN ARMY, JUNE 1782. *This monthly return for Washington's force at Newburgh, New York, in June 1782 is typical of the comprehensiveness of the Army's recordkeeping by the end of the war. It accounts for all officers and men of the infantry, artillery, 2d Legionary Corps, sappers and miners, and invalids.*

is no news of Peace as yet. But the armies are all well diciplined [sic] and in wonderful good spirits and draw very good provisions."[44] By the Continental Army's standards conditions were good. Yorktown had raised morale, and the Highlands area offered long-established depots and housing as well as training programs. The Army included a high proportion of hardened veterans who knew how to make the most of their circumstances.

In June Washington and Steuben began a series of comprehensive monthly brigade inspections. They judged appearance, paperwork, maneuvers, and marksmanship. Washington approved the overall performance and competitive spirit of the exercises but warned the men that "it is the effect of the shot not the report of the Gun that can discomfort the Enemy and if a bad habit is acquired at exercise it will prevail in real Action."[45] This rigorous training program culminated on 31 August when Washington moved the Main Army down the Hudson River from Newburgh to Verplanck's Point to simplify subsistence. In the process he tested the feasibility of an amphibious attack on New York City. Five infantry brigades made the move by water, with baggage following in other boats. The individual units were assigned to boats in a manner which kept elements intact, and the flotilla maintained strict parade-ground alignment. These factors enabled the regiments to deploy promptly into line of battle as soon as the boats beached on Verplanck's Point. The experiment was a striking success. Indeed, if de Grasse's warships had been available for a real assault, Washington's veterans, with the aid of French troops, probably would have been able to seize Manhattan.[46]

Washington also established an honor system in 1782 to improve morale. He authorized a chevron worn on the left arm of the uniform coat for all enlisted men who "served more than three years with bravery, fidelity and good conduct." Two chevrons represented six years of good service. The Badge of Military Merit, a heart of purple silk edged with narrow lace bindings and worn over the left lapel, was a special decoration. Washington proudly proclaimed that "the road to glory in a patriot army and a free country is thus open to all."[47] Only three of these badges were ever granted. Sgt. William Brown (formerly of the 5th Connecticut Regiment), Sgt. Elijah Churchill of the 2d Legionary Corps, and Sgt. Daniel Bissel, Jr., of the 2d Connecticut Regiment each received one in 1783.[48]

In August 1782, when Washington practiced the amphibious landing on Verplanck's Point, his force in the northern half of the nation included eight brigades, Hazen's regiment, two artillery regiments, a legionary corps, and a variety of smaller specialist units. The infantry contingent amounted to 67 field, 475 company, and 119 staff officers; 813 sergeants; 448 drummers and fifers; and 9,210 rank and file. These figures were roughly two-thirds of the authorized full strength; Washington lacked 114 officers, 283 sergeants, 78 drummers and fifers, and 5,154 rank and file. The two artillery regiments contained 100 officers and 907 men; the Corps of Invalids, 27 offi-

[44]Sylvia J. Sherman, ed., *Dubros Times: Selected Depositions of Maine Revolutionary War Veterans* (Augusta: Maine State Archives, 1975), p. 9. Also see Fitzpatrick, *Writings*, 24:101.

[45]Fitzpatrick, *Writings*, 24:322.

[46]Ibid., 24:303, 309–10, 334, 358–59, 459–60; 25:93–96, 121.

[47]Ibid., 24:488.

[48]Ibid., 24:487–88; 25:142; 26:363–64, 481; see J. Hammond Trumbull, ed., *The Memorial History of Hartford County, Connecticut, 1623–1884*, 2 vols. (Boston: Edward L. Osgood, 1886), 2:514–15, for Bissel.

cers and 337 men; and the sappers and miners, 5 officers and 77 men. Sheldon's 2d Legionary Corps and the Marechaussee contributed 30 officers and 355 men, giving Washington a strength of about 800 officers and 12,000 men.[49]

Because of the consistent failure to secure enough recruits, Washington bowed to Congress' desire to reduce the whole Continental Army still further. On 7 August Congress ordered all states to reduce their lines by 1 January 1783 to complete regiments containing not less than 500 rank and file. Washington's suggestion that junior regiments disband and furnish men to other units became the basic method of achieving this end. On 1 January 1783 New York retained its 2 full regiments. Connecticut reduced its line to 3 regiments and Massachusetts reduced its regiments to 8; all then contained at least 500 rank and file. Because the regiments of Rhode Island, New Jersey, and New Hampshire all came close to the minimum strength, Washington obtained special permission from Congress for those states to delay their reorganization until 1 March. Ironically, they then complained that they would have to furnish a disproportionate part of the Army, and they failed to secure the necessary recruits. On 1 March the 2d New Hampshire and 2d New Jersey Regiments reduced to battalion strength. Each had four companies, two field officers, an adjutant, a quartermaster, a paymaster, and either a surgeon or mate. On 19 November 1782 Congress had restored the regimental adjutant and quartermaster positions to full staff status. The Rhode Island Regiment reorganized as a battalion with six companies.[50]

Greene faced greater problems than Washington during 1782, although the British evacuated Savannah on 11 July and Charleston on 14 December. The Southern Army only engaged in skirmishes, but the provisional regiments, less stable than Washington's units, deteriorated. Washington directed Greene to rebuild the lines allotted to the Carolinas and Georgia, but he stopped the movement of replacements from Pennsylvania and Maryland. Greene reorganized his remaining Pennsylvanians as a single provisional regiment under Lt. Col. Josiah Harmar on 4 November 1782. On 1 January Congress reduced the Pennsylvania line on paper from six to three regiments; the latter remained depot cadres in contrast to Harmar's crack combat unit. Greene handled the Maryland regiments differently. He disbanded the 3d and 4th Maryland Regiments and transferred all personnel to the 1st and 2d Regiments as of 1 January 1783. The last two companies of the Delaware Regiment went home at the end of 1782. The men received extended furlough when they reached Christiana Bridge, Delaware, on 17 January 1783.[51]

In the case of the short-term Virginia troops, Greene simply released them as their enlistments expired. The state's permanent regiments reorganized on 1 January 1783. All but two disbanded; the arrangement retained officers in proportion to the number of enlisted men remaining from the old regiments. The 1st Virginia Regiment re-

[49]RG 93, National Archives (Monthly Return, Main Army, August 1782); Lesser, *Sinews*, pp. 232-33, prints a variant of this return.

[50]Fitzpatrick, *Writings*, 24:352-55; 25:286-87, 312-13, 376, 425-26, 439-40, 456, 460-61; 26:3-4, 22, 140-42, 172; *JCC*, 22:451-53; 23:710-11, 736-39, 837; Burnett, *Letters*, 6:431-32, 537-38; 7:1-2, 11-13.

[51]RG 360, National Archives (Wayne to Greene, 12 Jul 82; Greene to Congress, 13 Aug 82); *JCC*, 23:549, 560, 837; Burnett, *Letters*, 6:446-47, 469-70, 480-81; Fitzpatrick, *Writings*, 24:409-10; 25:100, 110-11, 162-63, 193-94, 283-84, 328; 26:238; *Archives of Maryland*, 18:476-82; Seymour, *Journal*, pp. 40-42; Steuben Papers (Southern Army Returns for 9 Jan and 2 Apr 83); Southern Department Orderly Book (Greene's General Orders for 14 Sep and 2, 3, and 4 Nov 82), New-York Historical Society. A detachment of new Maryland recruits served with the Main Army in 1782 under Maj. Thomas Landsdale.

formed at the Winchester, Virginia, replacement depot. The 2d, only partially filled, contained the Virginia men on duty at Fort Pitt. Virginia's portion of the 1st Continental Artillery became a single overstrength company with Greene under Capt. William Pierce; the Maryland portion remained a single company, also with Greene. The 1st and 3d Legionary Corps formally consolidated as the 1st Legionary Corps, with five troops.[52]

Stabilized conditions in 1782 allowed North Carolina to begin raising 1,500 men for an enlistment period of eighteen months. Greene first formed them into two temporary regiments and on 2 November permanently organized them as a regiment and a battalion. The South Carolina legislature decided to reorganize two regiments, but even after the evacuation of Charleston, it made no progress. Georgia planned to form a single regiment in 1782, and on 29 July it decided to mount two of the companies. Maj. John Habersham recruited some pardoned Loyalists, but Congress took no formal action in regard to the regiment since the regiment never reached operational strength.[53]

The first months of 1783 turned into a critical period in the Revolution. As the war moved to an end, pressure mounted in Congress to reduce expenditures by dismantling the Continental Army. One group of delegates made this demand in the hope of restoring the states to the central position of government. Another element wanted a stronger central government and saw the military as an ally in their efforts to get Congress to adopt a taxation program devised by Robert Morris. At the same time, the Army, both at the officer and enlisted levels, realized that it had to secure action from Congress on its own bread-and-butter issues, particularly arrears in pay, before the war came to an end. Discontent began to mount in the Main Army's winter quarters at Newburgh, New York. Washington sympathized, but he had real fears that the troops might become rebellious. He warned Congress that he would remain in camp and "try like a careful physician to prevent if possible the disorders getting to an incurable height."[54]

Hints that Congress might renounce the promise of half-pay made earlier in the war led General McDougall, accompanied by Col. John Brooks and Col. Matthias Ogden, to carry a petition to Philadelphia in January. Unlike earlier officer protests, this petition spoke for the entire Army. Washington privately wrote to several delegates, who favored stronger central government, that the petitioners had valid claims. A committee reported favorably on the petition, but Congress defeated a resolution offering the officers a sum equal to five years' pay as commutation for their pensions. A generation that had matured listening to rhetoric about the dangers of a "standing

---

[52]*JCC*, 24:275–76; Fitzpatrick, *Writings*, 26:98, 101, 206; J. D. Eggleston, "Officers of the Virginia Line at Winchester, 1783," *William and Mary Quarterly*, 2d ser. 7 (1927):61; Katherine Glass Greene, *Winchester, Virginia, and Its Beginnings, 1743–1814* (Strasburg: Shenandoah Publishing House, 1926), pp. 241–44; *Archives of Maryland*, 18:477, 580, 596–97; Southern Department Orderly Book (Greene's General Orders for 2 and 3 Nov 82); Palmer, *Calendar of Virginia State Papers*, 2:335.

[53]Burnett, *Letters*, 6:537–38; Allen D. Candler, *Revolutionary Records*, 3:57, 79–80, 157, 161–63; RG 360, National Archives (Wayne to Greene, 12 Jul 82; Greene to Congress, 13 Aug 82); Steuben Papers ("Abstract of Musters for the Southern Army," 1 Apr–19 Sep 82; Francis Mentges to Steuben, 9 Jan and 2 Apr 83).

[54]Fitzpatrick, *Writings*, 25:269–70. Basic sources for this section discussion are the following: Henderson, *Party Politics*, pp. 318, 332–35; Richard H. Kohn, "The Inside History of the Newburgh Conspiracy: America and the Coup d'Etat," *William and Mary Quarterly*, 3d ser. 27 (1970):187–220; and Mintz, *Gouverneur Morris*, pp. 156–61.

army" then turned immediately to the Main Army to see how the Continentals would react.[55]

Alexander Hamilton, once Washington's aide and now a delegate from New York, urged Washington to use the Army's demands to push Congress toward strengthening the national government. Joseph Jones, a more moderate delegate from Virginia, gave the Commander in Chief a clearer picture of Congress' financial problems. He also warned Washington that "the ambition of some, and the pressure of distress in others; may produce dangerous combinations .... If there are men in the army who harbour wicked designs, and are determined to blow the coals of discord, they will greatly endeavour to hurt the reputation of those adverse to their projects."[56] Washington's views were closer to those of Jones than those of Hamilton. Although he decided not to become involved openly in a political matter, he prepared to counter any actions of that small group of officers within the Army who might act. This group centered around Horatio Gates, who had rejoined the Main Army on 5 October 1782.[57] In March Maj. John Armstrong, Gates' aide, prepared an anonymous address to the Continental Army, which Gates saw and approved. This document called upon the officers to plan a course of action to pressure Congress. Armstrong later explained that the purpose of the address was

to prepare their minds for some manly, vigorous Association with the other public Creditors—but the timid wretch [Walter Stewart or John Brooks] discovered it to the only man from whom he was to have kept it, and concealed it from those to whom he had expressly engaged to make it known—to be more explicit he betrayed it to the Commander in Chief—who, agreeably according to the original plan, was not to have been consulted till some later period.[58]

This First Newburgh Address appeared publicly on 10 March, followed two days later by a second. Washington reacted swiftly by calling for a general assembly of officers. Although the delay would allow time for hot heads to cool, he warned Congress on 12 March, swift congressional action was needed to alleviate the underlying problems. With dramatic flair Washington dominated the officers' meeting on 15 March. After fumbling through the first paragraph of a prepared speech, he put on a pair of glasses and murmured that not only had he grown grey in the service of his country, but now he was also going blind. The speech condemned the addresses as a call to mutiny and suggested that the author was a British agent. The officers, some in tears, quietly adopted a very moderate petition to Congress.[59]

The delegates overwhelmingly approved Washington's brilliant handling of the crisis. On 22 March, the same day that Washington's report on the officers' meeting arrived, Congress approved the commutation plan when the Connecticut delegation

[55]Fitzpatrick, *Writings*, 25:430–31; Charles Thomson, "The Papers of Charles Thomson, Secretary to the Continental Congress," New-York Historical Society *Collections* for 1878, pp. 70–80; Burnett, *Letters*, 6:405–9, 514, 528, 553; 7:13–15, 29–31, 72–74; *JCC*, 22:424–25; 24:93–95, 145–51, 154–56, 178–79; Hamilton, *Papers*, 3:290–93; Joseph Jones, *Letters of Joseph Jones of Virginia*, ed. Worthington C. Ford (Washington: Department of State, 1889), pp. 97–103.

[56]Jones, *Letters*, pp. 97–103. Also see Hamilton, *Papers*, 3:253–55.

[57]Burnett, *Letters*, 7:27–28; Fitzpatrick, *Writings*, 26:185–88; Gates Papers (George Mesam to John Armstrong, 14 Sep 80 [copy]; William Clajon to Gates, 1 Mar and [11–14] Apr 81 and 10 Mar and 13 Apr 82). Clajon fed Gates poisonous comments on Washington ("George IV") and on Washington's supporters ("the Sanhedrin").

[58]Gates Papers (Armstrong to Gates, 22 and 29 Apr 83).

[59]Fitzpatrick, *Writings*, 26:211–18, 222–27, 229–34, 323–25.

reversed its earlier opposition. In accepting commutation, the officers ended both any threat of a coup and the political controversy that had revolved around half-pay pensions. The resolution of this matter and the news on 12 March of a preliminary peace treaty cleared the way for Congress to dismantle the Army. Congress ordered an end to hostilities on 11 April and approved the preliminary treaty four days later. Washington began the armistice at noon on 19 April—eight years to the day after the first shots at Lexington.[60]

Washington and Secretary at War Lincoln promptly worked out the mechanics of disbanding the Army. Congress adopted a general resolution on 23 April that was a compromise between those members who wished a swift disbandment to reduce expenses and those who were hesitant to act until the British had evacuated their last posts. Enlistments for the duration would expire only with the ratification of a definitive treaty, but Congress allowed the Commander in Chief to furlough the troops at his discretion. He would therefore be able to recall the Army if negotiations collapsed. On 26 May Congress ordered that all men were to march home under the control of officers; at the same time, it allowed them to keep their arms as a bonus.[61]

Washington announced the furlough policy on 2 June 1783. General Heath supervised the arrangement of the men who were to remain in service. He completed this task on 15 June, and six days later they moved into garrison at West Point. The force consisted of an infantry contingent of 4 regiments from Massachusetts, 1 regiment from Connecticut, 5 companies from New Hampshire, 2 companies from Hazen's regiment, and 2 companies from Rhode Island, plus 5 artillery companies: 2 from the 2d Continental Artillery Regiment and 3 from the 3d. A provisional light corps under Lt. Col. William Hull marched into Westchester County to help restore civil government in that strife-torn region. The rest of the Army, including the troops from the Southern and Western Departments, went home on furlough.[62]

On 17 August 1783 Washington turned command of West Point over to Maj. Gen. Henry Knox and set out for Congress.[63] The previous year and a half had been trying for Washington. In 1782 he had sustained morale in the absence of military action and had honed the Main Army to a peak of training and efficiency. At Newburgh he had crushed a movement in the Army that had challenged the ideals of the Revolution. During June 1783 he had supervised the reduction of the wartime Continental Army to a small force suited to peacetime missions. Washington now turned his attention to the composition of that "peace establishment."

Peace

Objections to a Continental Army enlisted for the duration of the war had ended in late 1776 when Congress realized that single-year regiments modeled on the Provin-

[60]Fitzpatrick, *Writings*, 26:221-22, 263-64, 268-69, 285-93, 334-36; *JCC*, 24:207-10, 238-52; Burnett, *Letters*, 7:88-90, 93, 106-8, 110-11, 246-48, 378-88; Hamilton, *Papers*, 3:317-21; Christopher Collier, *Connecticut in the Continental Congress* (Chester, Conn.: Pequot Press, 1973), pp. 63-67.

[61]Fitzpatrick, *Writings*, 26:330-33, 350-52, 441-43; Burnett, *Letters*, 7:161-62, 24:253-54, 269-71, 275-76, 358-61, 364-65, 390, 496; 25:963, 966-67.

[62]Fitzpatrick, *Writings*, 26:448, 464-65, 471-75; 27:6-7, 10, 15, 19-20, 25-26, 32-34, 38-39; *JCC*, 24: 403; 2d Continental Artillery Regiment Orderly Book (Regimental Orders, 10 and 11 Jun 83), New-York Historical Society; 3d Continental Artillery Regiment Orderly Book (Regimental Orders, 8, 9, and 11 Jun 83), New-York Historical Society.

[63]Fitzpatrick, *Writings*, 27:111.

cials of the colonial period were insufficient for a long war. Those ideological arguments resurfaced, however, during the long debate over the legality of any permanent army in peacetime. These discussions in 1783 and 1784 would color the development of the United States Army for the remainder of the century.

Planning for the transition to a peacetime force had begun in April 1783 at the request of a congressional committee chaired by Alexander Hamilton. The Commander in Chief discussed the problem with key officers before submitting the Army's official views on 2 May. Significantly, there was a broad consensus of the basic framework among the officers. Washington's proposal called for four components: a small regular army, a uniformly trained and organized militia, a system of arsenals, and a military academy to train the army's artillery and engineer officers. He wanted four infantry regiments, each assigned to a specific sector of the frontier, plus an artillery regiment. His proposed regimental organizations followed Continental Army patterns but had a provision for increased strength in the event of war. Washington expected the militia primarily to provide security for the country at the start of a war until the regular army could expand—the same role it had carried out in 1775 and 1776. Steuben and Duportail submitted their own proposals to Congress for consideration.[64]

Although Congress declined on 12 May to make a decision on the peace establishment, it did address the need for some troops to remain on duty until the British evacuated New York City and several frontier posts. The delegates told Washington to use men enlisted for fixed terms as temporary garrisons. A detachment of those men from West Point reoccupied New York without incident on 25 November. When Steuben's effort in July to negotiate a transfer of frontier forts with Maj. Gen. Frederick Haldimand collapsed, however, the British maintained control over them, as they would into the 1790's. That failure and the realization that most of the remaining infantrymen's enlistments were due to expire by June 1784 led Washington to order Knox, his choice as the commander of the peacetime army, to discharge all but 500 infantry and 100 artillerymen before winter set in. The former regrouped as Jackson's Continental Regiment under Col. Henry Jackson of Massachusetts. The single artillery company, New Yorkers under John Doughty, came from remnants of the 2d Continental Artillery Regiment.[65]

Congress issued a proclamation on 18 October 1783 which approved Washington's reductions. On 2 November Washington then released his Farewell Order to the Philadelphia newspapers for nationwide distribution to the furloughed men. In the message he thanked the officers and men for their assistance and reminded them that

the singular interpositions of Providence in our feeble condition were such, as could scarcely escape the attention of the most unobserving; while the unparalleled perseverance of the Armies of the U[nited] States, through almost every possible suffering and discouragement for the space of eight long years, was little short of a standing miracle.[66]

[64]Hamilton, *Papers*, 3:317-22; Burnett, *Letters*, 7:150; Fitzpatrick, *Writings*, 26:315-16, 355, 374-98, 479, 483-96; Kite, *Duportail*, pp. 263-70; Steuben Papers (undated 1783 memorandum). Other officers submitting opinions to Washington include Armand, Heath, Knox, Jean Baptiste Obrey de Gouvion, Rufus Putnam, Ebenezer Huntington, and Governor George Clinton.
[65]Fitzpatrick, *Writings*, 26:368-69, 399-400, 480; 27:16-18, 61-63, 120-21, 221, 255-59, 278-79; *JCC*, 24:337; *Magazine of American History* 9 (1883):254-55; Bauman Papers (to George Clinton, 22 Aug 83).
[66]Fitzpatrick, *Writings*, 27:223.

THE RESIGNATION OF WASHINGTON. *John Trumbull finished his series of paintings of historic moments from the Revolution with this depiction of the moment when Washington returned his commission as commander in chief to the Continental Congress, then sitting at Annapolis, Maryland. (Painting completed between 1815 and 1822 by John Trumbull.)*

Washington believed that the blending of persons from every colony into "one patriotic band of Brothers" had been a major accomplishment, and he urged the veterans to continue this devotion in civilian life.[67]

Washington said farewell to his remaining officers on 4 December at Fraunces' Tavern in New York City. On 23 December he appeared in Congress, then sitting at Annapolis, and returned his commission as Commander in Chief: "Having now finished the work assigned me, I retire from the great theatre of Action; and bidding an Affectionate farewell to this August body under whose orders I have so long acted, I here offer my Commission, and take my leave of all the employments of public life."[68] Congress ended the War of American Independence on 14 January 1784 by ratifying the definitive peace treaty that had been signed in Paris on 3 September.[69]

Congress had again rejected Washington's concept for a peacetime force in October 1783. When moderate delegates then offered an alternative in April 1784 which scaled the projected army down to 900 men in 1 artillery and 3 infantry battalions, Congress rejected it as well, in part because New York feared that men retained from

[67]*JCC*, 25:702-5; Fitzpatrick, *Writings*, 27:167-69, 197-98, 205-8, 213, 222-30. Washington hoped the veterans would settle around the frontier posts and be a buffer between the Indians and other frontiersmen.
[68]Fitzpatrick, *Writings*, 27:285.
[69]Ibid., 27:16-18, 277-80, 284-85; *JCC*, 25:836-39; 26:23-31.

Massachusetts might take sides in a land dispute between the two states. Another proposal to retain 350 men and raise 700 new recruits also failed. On 2 June Congress ordered the discharge of all remaining men except twenty-five caretakers at Fort Pitt and fifty-five at West Point. The next day it created a peace establishment acceptable to all interests.[70]

The plan required four states to raise 700 men for one year's service. Congress instructed the Secretary at War to form the troops into 8 infantry and 2 artillery companies. Pennsylvania, with a quota of 260 men, had the power to nominate a lieutenant colonel, who would be the senior officer. New York and Connecticut each were to raise 165 men and nominate a major; the remaining 110 men came from New Jersey. Economy was the watchword of this proposal, for each major served as a company commander, and line officers performed all staff duties except those of chaplain, surgeon, and surgeon's mate. Under Josiah Harmer, the First American Regiment slowly organized and achieved permanent status as an infantry regiment of the new Regular Army.[71]

Led by Continental veterans, this small peacetime Regular Army gradually expanded over the next decade. It had inherited the rules, regulations, and traditions of the Continental Army. Steuben's Blue Book remained the official manual for the regulars, as well as for the militia of most states, until Winfield Scott in 1835 adapted the 1791 French Army Regulations for American use. At Fallen Timbers in 1794 Maj. Gen. Anthony Wayne applied the techniques of wilderness operations perfected by Sullivan's 1779 expedition against the Iroquois. The integration of ex-Continentals into the militia, coupled with the passage in 1792 of a national militia bill, improved the military responsiveness of that institution until the veterans began to age.[72]

Concluding Remarks

America's victory in the War of American Independence surprised many European observers. One Frenchman attributed it to a frontier mystique: "It may be asserted that North-America is entirely military, and inured to war, and that new levies may continually be made without making new soldiers."[73] Loyalist and some British observers suggested instead that the British did more to lose the war than the Americans did to win it.[74] Many modern historians feel that the British faced insurmountable logistical obstacles and suffered from bad leadership, particularly on the political level. Others see the militia, either as a guerrilla force or as the enforcement arm of Revolutionary government, as the most important military institution of the time since it limited

[70]*JCC*, 24:337, 492–94, 501n; 25:548–49, 722–45; 26:54–55, 201–7; 27:432–37, 486–88, 499–502, 512–24, 530–31; Burnett, *Letters*, 7:166–69, 189–91, 540–43, 546–47, 550–53, 572–73, 587–88, 604–5; Hamilton, *Papers*, 3:211, 378–97; Fitzpatrick, *Writings*, 27:140–44, 202–4; "Thomson Papers," pp. 177–79.

[71]The regiment's infantry contingent is perpetuated by the 3d Infantry, a parent regiment under the Combat Arms Regimental System, with active battalions in the Regular Army and Army Reserve; the artillery, by the 1st Battalion, 5th Field Artillery.

[72]Lyle D. Brundage, "The Organization, Administration, and Training of the United States Ordinary and Volunteer Militia, 1792–1861" (Ph.D. diss., University of Michigan, 1959), pp. 340–93; Jeffrey Kimball, "The Battle of Chippewa: Infantry Tactics in the War of 1812," *Military Affairs* 31 (1967):169–86.

[73]Marquis de Chastellux, *Travels in North-America, in the Years 1780, 1781, and 1782*, 2 vols. (London: G. G. J. and J. Robinson, 1787), 1:19. Also see Orville Theodore Murphy, Jr., "French Contemporary Opinion of the American Revolutionary Army" (Ph.D. diss., University of Minnesota, 1957).

[74]See, for example, C[harles] Stedman, *The History of the Origin, Progress and Termination of the American War*, 2 vols. (Dublin: privately printed, 1794), 2:499.

British authority to those areas physically occupied by troops. As the war became a global struggle, Britain's manpower reserves proved incapable of sustaining the effort.[75]

It is true that the militia played a very important role in the War of American Independence. Its political functions probably were indispensable, and as a military institution, supported by state troops, it continued to meets its traditional colonial responsibilities for local defense and for providing a general emergency reserve. On the other hand, it could not effectively operate as a main battle force at any distance from home or for an extended period. Congress recognized the militia's limitations from the beginning of the war and turned to full-time regular troops, the Continentals. As long as a field army of Continentals remained nearby, a British commander had to concentrate on it and leave the militia unmolested.

Britain's defeat cannot be explained by the problems of a 3,000-mile line of communications. The mother country sustained a war effort for eight years, five of them after North America became a secondary theater in a global conflict. The distance was a handicap, particularly insofar as it increased the time between a casualty and the arrival of a replacement, yet the British consistently provided their commanders with more regulars and military supplies than Washington and his subordinates had. British seapower was superior, but Washington's forces offset this advantage with better organization of land transport. American commanders used this tactical mobility to outmaneuver their opponents. When forced to flee, as in Washington's retreat through New Jersey or Greene's race to the Dan, they could always escape to a secure area and reorganize. The American ability to outdistance pursuit also robbed British battlefield victories of decisive impact. Washington's influence made American units more efficient, at least on paper, than British or German ones, particularly between 1776–78 and 1781–83. Greater line combat strength, higher ratios of officers and noncommissioned officers, and a developed regimental staff produced a powerful and responsive regiment. The British, moreover, never developed an effective echelon to match the Continental Army's permanent brigade instituted in 1777. The Continental Army's organizational concepts allowed greater control, even in semidispersed formations; the two-rank battle formation enhanced the advantages of the Army's emphasis on infantry marksmanship. Benefiting from the doctrine of aimed fire and target practice, the Continentals often inflicted heavy casualties on the British in a battle and normally dominated skirmishes.[76]

Knox's artillerymen also had a better organization and doctrine than the British. They concentrated fire on infantry targets, while the British used the more traditional and less effective counterbattery fire. As at Monmouth, tactical use of regimental headquarters as an intervening echelon of command enabled Knox to mass guns for a specific mission. More importantly, assigning a company of artillery to each permanent infantry brigade developed close teamwork between the arms. Rotating companies be-

[75]For examples of some of the most recent interpretations of the Revolution, see Stanley J. Underdal, ed., *Military History of the American Revolution: The Proceedings of the 6th Military History Symposium, United States Air Force Academy, 10–11 October 1974* (Washington: Office of Air Force History, 1976), and Don Higginbotham, ed., *Reconsiderations on the Revolutionary War: Selected Essays* (Westport: Greenwood Press, 1978).

[76]Baurmeister, *Revolution in America*, pp. 348–56; Charlotte S. J. Epping, trans., *Journal of Du Roi the Elder, Lieutenant and Adjutant in the Service of the Duke of Brunswick, 1776–1778* (New York: D. Appleton and Co., 1911), pp. 107–8.

tween garrison, general support, and direct support assignments maintained training and ensured that every company could perform any mission in an emergency. Once the Army overcame early procurement problems, Knox also tailored the armament of each company to its specific task.

The mounted arm never had the opportunity to develop into a battlefield force, although Lt. Col. William Washington's troopers gave a fine account of themselves in the later phases of southern operations. On the other hand, it did perform well in its original mission of reconnaissance. Theoretical development and practical necessity combined to produce the 1781 legion, an excellent configuration for carrying out this role in the prevailing conditions. The partisan corps, a European concept, developed into an excellent independent, long-range force that could stiffen local irregulars.

A well-rounded group of support troops backed the combat units. Unlike the British Army, the Continental Army had specialized units to perform ordnance, maintenance, quartermaster, and military police functions. Highly trained engineers, both officers and units, functioned well in offensive and defensive assignments after 1777. Combat and support units, presided over by a competent general staff, functioned by 1782 as a team equal in quality to that of any European army of the day.

The officers of the Continental Army had been selected originally on the basis of political rather than military credentials. Experience nurtured latent talents and produced a competent group of commanders, although few individual members could be called "great captains." Once trusted subordinates (Greene, Heath, Sullivan, Stirling, Lincoln, and McDougall) became commanders of territorial departments, Washington assumed a more active role in general policy. His practice of consulting with his subordinates, usually in a council of war, has frequently been misinterpreted to mean that the Army was ruled by committee. This conclusion misjudges Washington's desire to encourage each officer to state his opinions and to feel that he was participating in the war effort. Washington was Commander in Chief in every respect. He alone carried that burden, and to him is due the credit.[77]

Tradition in the United States depicts the Continental Army as a hardy group of yeoman farmers and middle-class tradesmen under amateur officers who defeated a European army of lower class troops commanded by aristocrats. Recent studies indicate that after 1776 the Continental Army did not fit this image. The long-term Continentals tended to come from the poorer, rootless elements of American society to whom the Army, despite its problems, offered greater opportunity than did civilian life. Enlisted men were young (over half were under twenty-two when they enlisted) and mostly common laborers so poor as to be virtually tax-exempt. A sizable minority were hired substitutes or not native to the place where they had enlisted.

The Continental officer corps, on the other hand, came from the upper social strata. In the deferential society of eighteenth-century America, members of the leading families naturally assumed leadership in the regular forces just as they did in the militia, in politics and law, in the church, and in business. Although it was possible for an enlisted man to become an officer, particularly during the reorganizations of 1776 and 1777, Washington's desire to maintain a distance between officers and men as a disciplinary tool kept most of the latter from rising far. In small colonies, such as New

[77]"Washington's Opinion of His General Officers," *Magazine of American History* 3 (1879):81–88; Stedman, *American War*, 2:448.

SIZE ROLL. Size rolls, such as this one of the 2d Continental Light Dragoon Regiment which that unit maintained throughout the war, differ from either muster or pay rolls. Size rolls contain much more personal information about a unit's officers and men because these rolls were for the unit commander's use rather than for the Army staff's. A commander recorded each member's name, rank, physical description, trade, home town, and enlistment data and updated the rolls throughout the war. If a man deserted, the commander could use the information on the rolls to track the offender. Notice that Cpl. Gideon Hawley ultimately received a commission as a cornet.

Jersey, a single family, reinforced by cousins, in-laws, political allies, or business associates, could dominate entire regiments.

In a force of this nature discipline posed a problem. Desertion rates were high, although few went over to the British. Washington coped by developing, in conjunction with his judge advocates, a system that adapted British military justice to the conditions of American society in the 1770's. His approach was mild by contemporary standards and extremely sophisticated. Washington did execute a few for particularly serious crimes. He preferred, however, to produce the same psychological effect on the Army by using last-second reprieves.

Washington led the Continental Army to victory in the longest war in American history before Vietnam, overcoming physical and psychological obstacles which at times appeared insurmountable. The fact that Washington not only held the Army together but also molded it into a tough professional fighting force is a tribute to his inspirational leadership and judgment. That he then disbanded this force without incident when economic considerations forced him to do so was to accomplish the nearly unthinkable in the view of his contemporaries.

THE BATTLE OF BUNKER HILL. *Howard Pyle's modern painting shows the essence of eighteenth century linear tactics. (Delaware Art Museum).*

THE DEATH OF GENERAL WARREN AT BUNKER HILL. *John Trumbull completed this stylized painting in 1786 while living in London. (Copyright Yale University Art Gallery).*

DEATH OF GENERAL MONTGOMERY IN THE ATTACK ON QUEBEC. *Two years after completing his rendering of the Bunker Hill battle site, John Trumbull produced this heroic painting of the 31 December 1775 assault on Quebec City. (Copyright Yale University Art Gallery).*

THE RETREAT THROUGH THE JERSEYS. *Howard Pyle's modern painting shows Washington's Main Army at its lowest ebb following the loss of New York City in 1776. (Delaware Art Museum).*

CAPTURE OF THE HESSIANS AT TRENTON. *Sometime between 1786 and 1797 John Trumbull finished his painting of Washington's stunning victory at Trenton on 26 December 1776. (Copyright Yale University Art Gallery).*

THE DEATH OF GENERAL MERCER AT THE BATTLE OF PRINCETON. *John Trumbull added this companion to the Trenton battle painting while living in London between 1786 and 1797. He used sketches of Brig. Gen. Hugh Mercer's son as the basis for the portrait of the general that is the focus for this work. (Copyright Yale University Art Gallery).*

ATTACK UPON THE CHEW HOUSE. *Howard Pyle's modern painting captures the heat of battle as Continentals try to batter down this stone mansion's door during the battle of Germantown. (Delaware Art Museum).*

THE SURRENDER OF GENERAL BURGOYNE AT SARATOGA. *In 1786 John Trumbull prepared his preliminary plan for this masterpiece, but the actual painting was not begun until 1816 and took several years to finish. (Copyright Yale University Art Gallery).*

THE MEETING OF GREENE AND GATES. *Howard Pyle used this modern painting to illustrate the moment in December of 1780 when Maj. Gen. Nathanael Greene relieved Maj. Gen. Horatio Gates as commander of the Southern Department. Within months the tide of the war in the south would begin to turn. (Delaware Art Museum).*

GUILFORD COURT HOUSE, 15 MARCH 1781. *The linear tactics used by Continental regulars trained in Steuben's system show up clearly in H. Charles McBarron's recent painting of Greene's third line. (Soldiers of the Revolution, Army Art Collection).*

THOMAS SHUBRICK

This miniature by John Trumbull shows a junior officer of the South Carolina Line. Miniatures were the eighteenth century equivalent of photographs and were popular with the upper classes who furnished most of the Army's officers. Shubrick served as a brigade major and aide to Generals Lincoln and Greene and was commended for gallantry at Eutaw Springs in September 1781. (Anderson House Museum, Society of the Cincinnati; photograph by Sgt. Jim Moore).

MORGAN LEWIS

Family ties were very important in the Continental Army. This miniature by an unknown artist shows the son of New York delegate Francis Lewis in the uniform he wore for most of the war as a deputy quartermaster general in his home state. Morgan Lewis achieved greater fame after the Revolution as quartermaster general of the United States Army (during the War of 1812) and later as governor of New York. (Anderson House Museum, Society of the Cincinnati; photograph by Sgt. Jim Moore).

JACOB KINGSBURY

Some officers of the Continental Army did rise through the ranks. Jacob Kingsbury of Connecticut began his service in 1775 as a private and ended it in 1783 as an ensign. In 1787 he rejoined the United States Army as a lieutenant. This miniature by an unknown artist depicts him as a colonel and inspector general at the time of his retirement in 1815. Notice he wears the badge of membership in the Society of the Cincinnati on his lapel. (Anderson House Museum, Society of the Cincinnati; photograph by Sgt. Jim Moore).

JACOB REED, JR.

This miniature by an unknown artist portrays a junior officer from New York who served in Bauman's Continental Artillery Company and in the 2d Continental Artillery Regiment. Reed's attire is typical of the time long after the war when the portrait was done. Return to civilian pursuits after the Revolution as shown here was usual for Continental Army officers and men. (Anderson House Museum, Society of the Cincinnati; photograph by Sgt. Jim Moore).

HENRY HENLEY CHAPMAN

Officers who joined the Continental Army late in the Revolution rarely rose to high rank. Chapman began service in the Maryland Line in 1781 as an ensign and finished as a lieutenant. This miniature of him, painted after the Revolution, may have been the effort of James Peale, brother of the more famous Charles Willson Peale. (Anderson House Museum, Society of the Cincinnati; photograph by Sgt. Jim Moore).

JOHN TALIAFERRO BROOKE

A Virginian, Brooke served as a lieutenant in the 1st Continental Artillery Regiment. This wartime miniature by an unknown artist doubles as excellent documentation for Continental Army uniforms. Notice particularly the unusual hat and distinctive piping on his shoulder epaulets. (Anderson House Museum, Society of the Cincinnati; photograph by Sgt. Jim Moore).

SURRENDER OF LORD CORNWALLIS AT YORKTOWN. *John Trumbull's 1797 painting shows Brig. Gen. Charles O'Hara, not Cornwallis, surrendering the garrisons of Yorktown and Gloucester to Maj. Gen. Benjamin Lincoln. Washington and his officers form the line on the right; Rochambeau and the French leaders are on the left. (Copyright Yale University Art Gallery).*

FREDERICK WILHELM AUGUSTUS VON STEUBEN. *"The Baron" (1730–1794) was the single most valuable foreign volunteer in the Continental Army, serving from 1778 on as inspector general, Washington's virtual chief of staff. Although he was a Prussian veteran, von Steuben's "Regulations" are more akin to French military theory. (Portrait by Charles Willson Peale, 1782.) (Independence National Historical Park).*

Lineages

The format of the unit lineages in this volume is adapted from that used for the official Lineage and Honors Certificates prepared by the U.S. Army Center of Military History. The data have been summarized to save space, and the format modified to fit the peculiarities of the Revolutionary War.

The 177 lineages in this volume cover every permanent unit of the Continental Army. Provisional units, such as Knowlton's Rangers of 1776 or the Light Infantry Corps, are not included nor are any units of the militia or state troops unless they later became permanent elements of the Continental Army. The lineages are grouped into eighteen sections, each of which includes a selected bibliography. Fourteen of the sections cover units raised from specific states or colonies, including Canada, which was to have become the fourteenth state. The sections also include an outline map showing county boundaries as of 4 July 1776. The remaining sections cover infantry regiments not raised from specific states (the extra and additional regiments), a miscellaneous section that includes various specialized units, artillery units, and the light dragoons and other mounted formations. The sections are arranged geographically in the order of precedence used by General George Washington: from north to south for the thirteen states and then Canada. Units are arranged within a section by numerical order, starting with the arrangement as it existed in 1777 and followed by other units listed under the designation used during the organization's most significant period of service. Readers should use the index to cross-reference any changes in designations. Those nicknames commonly used at that time are also included in the lineages. A reference note is included on those lineages whose units are perpetuated by current Army organizations, and readers should consult other volumes in the series for information concerning such units' later history. Appendix A provides a complete list of all current units that descend from organizations that existed during the American Revolution.

Engagements cited in this volume are not the same as the official named campaigns, listed in AR 672-5-1, that are shown on official Lineage and Honors Certificates. Instead, the engagements in this volume indicate the units' service and provide a guide for more detailed research. Any reader interested in such research should use the relevant sections of the bibliography dealing with combat operations. Appendix D gives the chronological and territorial limits of the various engagements designated in this volume and explains the major events of each. The lineages indicate any combat not listed in that appendix by providing the state name or topographical feature, the location of the action, and the year of the engagement. The lineages show combat against Indians by the name of the tribe and the year of the action.

Coos

Grafton

Strafford

Cheshire

Rockingham

Portsmouth

Exeter

Hillsborough

Fitzwilliam

New Hampshire

New Hampshire

1st NEW HAMPSHIRE REGIMENT

Authorized 22 May 1775 in the New Hampshire State Troops as the 1st New Hampshire Regiment. Organized 3 June 1775 at Medford, Massachusetts, to consist of ten companies from Hillsborough and Rockingham Counties. Adopted 14 June 1775 into the Continental Army and assigned to the Main Army. Assigned 22 July 1775 to Sullivan's Brigade, an element of the Main Army.

Reorganized and redesignated 1 January 1776 as the 5th Continental Regiment, to consist of eight companies. Relieved 27 April 1776 from Sullivan's Brigade and assigned to the Canadian Department. Relieved 2 July 1776 from the Canadian Department and assigned to the Northern Department. Assigned 20 July 1776 to Stark's Brigade, an element of the Northern Department. Relieved 26 November 1776 from Stark's Brigade and assigned to the Main Army (later to Sullivan's Brigade).

Reorganized and redesignated 1 January 1777 as the 1st New Hampshire Regiment, to consist of eight companies. Relieved 14 February 1777 from Sullivan's Brigade and assigned to the Northern Department. Assigned 28 April 1777 to the New Hampshire Brigade, an element of the Northern Department. (New Hampshire Brigade relieved 20 October 1777 from the Northern Department and assigned to the Main Army.) Reorganized 23 December 1778 to consist of nine companies.

(New Hampshire Brigade relieved 19 August 1781 from the Main Army and assigned to the Highlands Department; relieved 10–14 October 1781 from the Highlands Department and assigned to the Northern Department; relieved 12 November 1782 from the Northern Department and assigned to the Main Army.)

Reorganized and redesignated 1 March 1783 as the New Hampshire Regiment, to consist to nine companies. Consolidated 22 June 1783 with the New Hampshire Battalion (see 2d New Hampshire Regiment) and consolidated unit designated as the New Hampshire Battalion to consist of five companies. Disbanded 1 January 1784 at New Windsor, New York.

ENGAGEMENTS
  Siege of Boston
  Defense of Canada
  Lake Champlain
  Trenton-Princeton
  Saratoga
  Philadelphia-Monmouth
  Iroquois 1779
  Northern Department 1781

2d NEW HAMPSHIRE REGIMENT

Authorized 22 May 1775 in the New Hampshire State Troops as the 2d New Hampshire Regiment. Organized 24 May–18 June 1775 at Exeter to consist of ten companies from Strafford and Rockingham Counties. Adopted 14 June 1775 into the Continental Army and assigned to the Main Army. Assigned 22 July 1775 to Sullivan's Brigade, an element of the Main Army.

Reorganized and redesignated 1 January 1776 as the 8th Continental Regiment, to consist of eight companies. Relieved 15 April 1776 from Sullivan's Brigade and assigned to the Canadian Department. Relieved 2 July 1776 from the Canadian Department and assigned to the Northern Department. Assigned 20 July 1776 to Reed's Brigade, an element of the Northern Department. Relieved 23 July 1776 from Reed's Brigade and assigned to Stark's Brigade, an element of the Northern Department. Relieved 26 November 1776 from Stark's Brigade and assigned to the Main Army (later to Sullivan's Brigade).

Reorganized and redesignated 1 January 1777 as the 2d New Hampshire Regiment, to consist of eight companies. Relieved 14 February 1777 from Sullivan's Brigade and assigned to the Northern Department. Assigned 28 April 1777 to the New Hampshire Brigade, an element of the Northern Department. (New Hampshire Brigade relieved 20 October 1777 from the Northern Department and assigned to the Main Army.) Reorganized 23 December 1778 to consist of nine companies.

(New Hampshire Brigade relieved 19 August 1781 from the Main Army and assigned to the Highlands Departments; relieved 10–14 October 1781 from the Highlands Department and assigned to the Northern Department; relieved 12 November 1782 from the Northern Department and assigned to the Main Army.)

Reorganized and redesignated 1 March 1783 as the New Hampshire Battalion, to consist of four companies. Consolidated 22 June 1783 with the New Hampshire Regiment (see 1st New Hampshire Regiment).

ENGAGEMENTS
    Siege of Boston
    Defense of Canada
    Lake Champlain
    Trenton-Princeton
    Saratoga
    Philadelphia-Monmouth
    Iroquois 1779
    Northern Department 1781

3d NEW HAMPSHIRE REGIMENT

Authorized 22 May 1775 in the New Hampshire State Troops as the 3d New Hampshire Regiment. Organized 1–8 June 1775 at Fitzwilliam to consist of ten companies from Cheshire, Hillsborough, and Cumberland Counties. Adopted 14 June 1775 into the Continental Army and assigned to the Main Army. Assigned 22 July 1775 to Sullivan's Brigade, an element of the Main Army.

Reorganized and redesignated 1 January 1776 as the 2d Continental Regiment, to consist of eight companies. Relieved 27 April 1776 from Sullivan's Brigade and assigned to the Canadian Department. Relieved 2 July 1776 from the Canadian Department and assigned to the Northern Department. Assigned 20 July 1776 to Stark's Brigade, an element of the Northern Department. Relieved 26 November 1776 from Stark's Brigade and assigned to the Main Army (later to Sullivan's Brigade).

Reorganized and redesignated 1 January 1777 as the 3d New Hampshire Regiment, to consist of eight companies. Relieved 14 February 1776 from Sullivan's Brigade and assigned to the Northern Department. Assigned 28 April 1777 to the New Hampshire Brigade, an element of the Northern Department. (New Hampshire Brigade relieved 20 October 1777 from the Northern Department and assigned to the Main Army.) Reorganized 23 December 1778 to consist of nine companies. Disbanded 1 January 1781 at Continental Village, New York.

ENGAGEMENTS
   Siege of Boston
   Defense of Canada
   Lake Champlain
   Trenton-Princeton
   Saratoga
   Philadelphia-Monmouth
   Iroquois 1779

BEDEL'S REGIMENT

Authorized 26 May 1775 in the New Hampshire State Troops as Captain Timothy Bedel's Company of Rangers. Organized 23 June 1775 at Coos. Expanded 5–6 July 1775 as Major Timothy Bedel's Corps of Rangers, to consist of three companies. Assigned 7 August 1775 to the New York (later Northern) Department.

Expanded and reorganized in the Continental Army 8 January–12 March 1776 as Bedel's Regiment, to consist of eight companies from northwestern New Hampshire; concurrently, assigned to the Canadian Department. Relieved 2 July 1776 from the Canadian Department and assigned to the Northern Department. Disbanded 1 January 1777 at Coos.

ENGAGEMENTS
   Invasion of Canada
   Defense of Canada

LONG'S REGIMENT

Authorized 14 May 1776 in the Continental Army as a regiment to be organized in New Hampshire and assigned to the Eastern Department. Organized 16 August–25 September 1776 at Newcastle as Long's Regiment, to consist of eight companies from eastern New Hampshire. Relieved 22 November 1776 from the Eastern Department and assigned to the Northern Department. Disbanded in July 1777 in northern New York.

ENGAGEMENTS
Saratoga

WHITCOMB'S RANGERS

Authorized 15 October 1776 in the Continental Army as Whitcomb's Rangers, an element of the Northern Department. Organized in November 1776 at Fort Ticonderoga, New York, to consist of two companies from northwestern New Hampshire. Disbanded 1 January 1781 at Coos, New Hampshire.

ENGAGEMENTS
Saratoga

Bibliography

Aldrich, Edgar. "The Affair of the Cedars and the Service of Col. Timothy Bedel in the War of the Revolution." *New Hampshire Historical Society Proceedings* 3 (1891):194–231.

Batchellor, Albert S. *The Ranger Service in the Upper Valley of the Connecticut and the Most Northerly Regiment of the New Hampshire Militia in the Period of the Revolution.* Concord: Rumford Press, 1903. [Also published in *Magazine of History* 6 (1907):187–205, 249–68.]

Bouton, Nathaniel, et al., eds. *Documents and Records Relating to the Province, Towns and State of New Hampshire.* 40 vols. Concord, Nashua, and Manchester: Various publishers, 1867–1943.

Brown, Lloyd A., and Peckham, Howard H., eds. *Revolutionary War Journals of Henry Dearborn 1775–1783.* Chicago: Caxton Club, 1939.

Fletcher, Ebenezer. *The Narrative of Ebenezer Fletcher, a Soldier of the Revolution, Written by Himself.* Edited by Charles I. Bushnell. New York: Privately printed, 1866.

Fogg, Jeremiah. *Orderly Book Kept by Jeremiah Fogg, Adjutant Colonel Enoch Poor's Second New Hampshire Regiment on Winter Hill, During the Siege of Boston, October 28, 1775, to January 12, 1776.* Edited by Albert A. Folsom. Exeter: Exeter News-Letter, 1903.

Foster, John. "The Story of a Private Soldier in the Revolution." *Manchester Historic Association Collections* 3 (1902):86–96.

Gilmore, George C. "Captain John Moore's Company." *Manchester Historic Association Collections* 1 (1896):32–34.

Goodwin, William F., ed. "Colonel Alexander Scammell and His Letters, From 1768 to 1781, Including His 'Love Letters' to Miss Nabby Bishop." *Historical Magazine,* 2d ser., 8 (1870):129–46.

_____, ed. "Revolutionary Officers of New Hampshire Regiments." *Historical Magazine,* 2d ser., 4 (1868):199–201.

_____, ed. "Journal of the Congress of the Colony of New Hampshire Which Assembled at Exeter December 21st, 1775, and Adopted, January the 5th, the First Written Constitution in the United States." *Historical Magazine,* 2d ser., 4 (1868):145–54.

Hammond, Otis G., ed. *Letters and Papers of Major-General John Sullivan, Continental Army.* 3 vols. Concord: New Hampshire Historical Society, 1930–39.

Kidder, Frederick. *History of the First New Hampshire Regiment in the War of the Revolution.* Albany: Joel Munsell, 1868.

Livermore, Daniel. "Orderly Book of Capt. Daniel Livermore's Company, Continental Army." Edited by Isaac W. Hammond. *New Hampshire Historical Society Collections* 9 (1889):200–244.

Morris, George F. "Major Benjamin Whitcomb: Ranger and Partisan Leader in the Revolution." *New Hampshire Historical Society Proceedings* 4 (1903):299–320. [Reprinted in *Historical New Hampshire* 11 (1955):1–20.]

New Hampshire Committee of Safety. "Records of the Committee of Safety." *New Hampshire Historical Society Collections* 7 (1863):iii–340.

Potter, Chandler Eastman. *Military History of New Hampshire, From Its Settlement, in 1623, to the Year 1861.* 2 vols. Concord: Adjutant General's Office, New Hampshire, 1866–88.

Scammell, Alexander. "Two Letters to Col. Alexander Scammell." *Magazine of American History* 10 (1883):151–55.

Stark, Caleb, ed. *Memoir and Official Correspondence of Gen. John Stark, With Notices of Several Other Officers of the Revolution. Also, a Biography of Capt. Phinehas Stevens, and of Col. Robert Rogers, With an Account of His Services in America During the "Seven Years' War".* Concord: G. Parker Lyon, 1860.

Witcher, William F. *The Relation of New Hampshire Men to the Siege of Boston.* Concord: Rumford Printing Co., 1904.

Wheildon, William Willder. "A Remarkable Military Life [Thompson Maxwell]." *New England Historical and Genealogical Register* 45 (1891):271–78.

White, Pliny H., ed. "History of the Expedition Against the Five Nations Commanded by General Sullivan, in 1779. By Nathan Davis." *Historical Magazine,* 2d ser., 3 (1868):198–205.

Worthen, Samuel Copp. "Bedel's Rangers at the Siege of St. Johns." *Granite Monthly* 52 (1920):448–51.

_____. "Colonel Pierse Long's Regiment; Portsmouth Man's Exploits Shed Lustre on Military Annals of State During Revolution." *Granite Monthly* 57 (1925): 262–66.

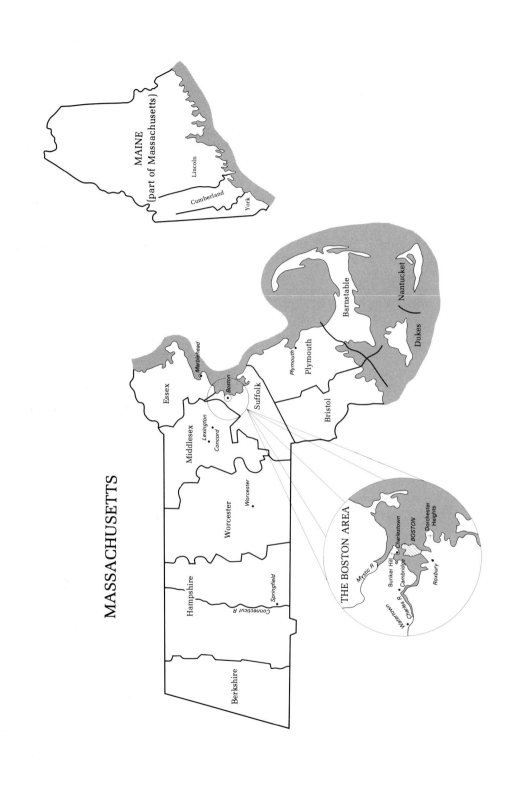

MASSACHUSETTS

MAINE
(part of Massachusetts)

Lincoln

Cumberland

York

Essex

Marblehead

Boston

Suffolk

Middlesex

Lexington

Concord

Worcester

Worcester

Hampshire

Springfield

Connecticut R

Berkshire

Plymouth

Plymouth

Bristol

Barnstable

Nantucket

Dukes

THE BOSTON AREA

Mystic R

Charlestown

Bunker Hill

Cambridge

Watertown

Charles R

Roxbury

BOSTON

Dorchester
Heights

Massachusetts

1st MASSACHUSETTS REGIMENT*

Authorized 23 April 1775 in the Massachusetts State Troops as Paterson's Regiment. Organized in spring 1775 at Cambridge to consist of eleven companies from Berkshire, Hampshire, Suffolk, Middlesex, Worcester, and York Counties, Massachusetts; and Litchfield County, Connecticut. Adopted 14 June 1775 into the Continental Army and assigned to the Main Army. Assigned 22 July 1775 to Heath's Brigade, an element of the Main Army.

Consolidated (less Morse's and Watkins' Companies) 1 January 1776 with Sayer's and Sullivan's Companies, Scammon's Regiment [see Scammon's Regiment], and consolidated unit redesignated as the 15th Continental Regiment, an element of Heath's Brigade, to consist of eight companies; (Morse's Company concurrently consolidated with Prescott's Regiment [see 7th Continental Regiment] and Watkins' Company consolidated with Phinney's Regiment [see 12th Massachusetts Regiment]). Relieved 24 January 1776 from Heath's Brigade and assigned to the Vacant Brigade, an element of the Main Army. (Vacant Brigade redesignated 16 February 1776 as Frye's Brigade.) Relieved 15 April 1776 from Frye's Brigade and assigned to the Canadian Department. Relieved 2 July 1776 from the Canadian Department and assigned to the Northern Department. Assigned 20 July 1776 to Reed's Brigade, an element of the Northern Department. (Reed's Brigade redesignated 11 August 1776 as Paterson's Brigade.) Relieved 26 November 1776 from Paterson's Brigade and assigned to St. Clair's Brigade, an element of the Main Army.

Consolidated 1 January 1777 with two companies formed from the 18th Continental Regiment [see 12th Massachusetts Regiment] and two companies formed from the 6th Continental Regiment [see 13th Massachusetts Regiment] and consolidated unit designated as Vose's Regiment, to consist of eight companies. Relieved 9 February 1777 from St. Clair's Brigade and assigned to the Northern Department. Relieved 13 March 1777 from the Northern Department and assigned to the Highlands Department. Assigned 12 June 1777 to McDougall's Brigade, an element of the Highlands Department. Relieved 15 June 1777 from McDougall's Brigade and assigned to the 2d Connecticut Brigade, an element of the Highlands Department. Relieved 10 July 1777 from the 2d Connecticut Brigade and assigned to the 2d Massachusetts Brigade, an element of the Highlands Department. (2d Massachusetts Brigade relieved 24 July 1777 from the Highlands Department and assigned to the Northern Department; relieved 7 November 1777 from the Northern Department and assigned to the Main Army; relieved 22 July 1778 from the Main Army and assigned to the Eastern Department.)

Reorganized 1 April 1779 to consist of nine companies. (2d Massachusetts Brigade relieved 7 July 1779 from the Eastern Department and assigned to the Highlands Department.) Redesignated 1 August 1779 as the 1st Massachusetts Regiment. Relieved 1 January 1781 from the 2d Massachusetts Brigade and assigned to the 1st Massachusetts Brigade, an element of the Highlands Department. Disbanded 3 November 1783 at West Point, New York.

ENGAGEMENTS
>   Siege of Boston
>   Defense of Canada
>   Lake Champlain
>   Trenton-Princeton
>   Saratoga
>   Defense of Philadelphia
>   Philadelphia-Monmouth
>   Rhode Island

*This regiment is perpetuated by the 104th Infantry, Massachusetts Army National Guard.

2d MASSACHUSETTS REGIMENT

Authorized 23 April 1775 in the Massachusetts State Troops as Thomas' Regiment. Organized in spring 1775 at Roxbury to consist of ten companies from northern Plymouth County. Adopted 14 June 1775 into the Continental Army and assigned to the Main Army. Redesignated 1 July 1775 as Bailey's Regiment. Assigned 22 July 1775 to Thomas' Brigade, an element of the Main Army.

Consolidated 1 January 1776 with Cotton's Regiment [see Cotton's Regiment] and consolidated unit redesignated as the 23d Continental Regiment, an element of Thomas' Brigade, to consist of eight companies. Relieved 24 April 1776 from Thomas' Brigade and assigned to Heath's Brigade, an element of the Main Army. Relieved 12 August 1776 from Heath's Brigade and assigned to Clinton's Brigade, an element of the Main Army. Relieved 31 August 1776 from Clinton's Brigade and assigned to Nixon's Brigade, an element of the Main Army. Relieved 14 October 1776 from Nixon's Brigade and assigned to Clinton's Brigade, an element of the Main Army.

Consolidated 1 January 1777 with the 7th Continental Regiment [see 7th Continental Regiment], Clap's Company, 21st Continental Regiment [see 21st Continental Regiment], and Peters' Company, 13th Continental Regiment [see 13th Continental Regiment], and consolidated unit redesignated as Bailey's Regiment, to consist of eight companies. Relieved 9 February 1777 from Clinton's Brigade and assigned to the Northern Department. Assigned 13 August 1777 to the 4th Massachusetts Brigade, an element of the Northern Department. (4th Massachusetts Brigade relieved 27 October 1777 from the Northern Department and assigned to the Main Army; relieved 20 November 1778 from the Main Army and assigned to the Highlands Department.)

Reorganized 12 May 1779 to consist of nine companies. Redesignated 1 August 1779 as the 2d Massachusetts Regiment. Relieved 1 January 1781 from the 4th Massachusetts Brigade and assigned to the 2d Massachusetts Brigade, an element of the Highlands Department. Disbanded 3 November 1783 at West Point, New York.

ENGAGEMENTS
  Siege of Boston
  New York City
  Northern New Jersey
  Trenton-Princeton
  Saratoga
  Defense of Philadelphia
  Philadelphia-Monmouth

3d MASSACHUSETTS REGIMENT*

Authorized 23 April 1775 in the Massachusetts State Troops as Heath's Regiment. Organized in spring 1775 at Roxbury to consist of ten companies from eastern Suffolk County. Adopted 14 June 1775 into the Continental Army and assigned to the Main Army. Redesignated 1 July 1775 as Greaton's Regiment. Assigned 22 July 1775 to Heath's Brigade, an element of the Main Army.

Consolidated 1 January 1776 with Crafts' Company, Gardner's Regiment [see 25th Continental Regiment], and consolidated unit redesignated as the 24th Continental Regiment, an element of Heath's Brigade, to consist of eight companies. Relieved 15 April 1776 from Heath's Brigade and assigned to the Canadian Department. Relieved 2 July 1776 from the Canadian Department and assigned to the Northern Department. Assigned 20 July 1776 to Arnold's Brigade, an element of the Northern Department. (Arnold's Brigade redesignated 26 October 1776 as Poor's Brigade.) Relieved 26 November 1776 from Poor's Brigade and assigned to Vose's Brigade, an element of the Main Army. (Vose's Brigade redesignated 18 December 1776 as McDougall's Brigade.)

Consolidated (less Bent's and Whiting's Companies) 1 January 1777 with the 25th Continental Regiment [see 25th Continental Regiment], and consolidated unit designated as Greaton's Regiment, to consist of eight companies; (Bent's and Whiting's Companies concurrently reorganized and redesignated as Fairfield's and Pillsbury's Companies, Wigglesworth's Regiment [see 13th Massachusetts Regiment]). Relieved 9 February 1777 from McDougall's Brigade and assigned to the Northern Department. Relieved 13 March 1777 from the Northern Department and assigned to the Highlands Department. Assigned 12 June 1777 to the 1st Massachusetts Brigade, an element of the Highlands Department. (1st Massachusetts Brigade relieved 1 July 1777 from the Highlands Department and assigned to the Northern Department; relieved 31 March 1778 from the Northern Department and assigned to the Highlands Department.)

Reorganized 12 May 1779 to consist of nine companies. Redesignated 1 August 1779 as the 3d Massachusetts Regiment. Relieved 1 January 1781 from the 1st Massachusetts Brigade and assigned to the 3d Massachusetts Brigade, an element of the Highlands Department. Relieved 12 June 1783 from the 3d Massachusetts Brigade and assigned to the 1st Massachusetts Brigade, an element of the Highlands Department. Disbanded 3 November 1783 at West Point, New York.

ENGAGEMENTS
  Siege of Boston
  Defense of Canada
  Lake Champlain
  Northern New Jersey
  Saratoga

*Elements of this regiment are perpetuated by the 182d Infantry, Massachusetts Army National Guard.

4th MASSACHUSETTS REGIMENT*

Authorized 23 April 1775 in the Massachusetts State Troops as Learned's Regiment. Organized in spring 1775 at Roxbury to consist of ten companies from southwestern Worcester County. Adopted 14 June 1775 into the Continental Army and assigned to the Main Army. Assigned 22 July 1775 to Spencer's Brigade, an element of the Main Army. Relieved 9 August 1775 from Spencer's Brigade and assigned to Thomas' Brigade, an element of the Main Army.

Consolidated 1 January 1776 with Danielson's Regiment [see Danielson's Regiment] and Wood's Company, Cotton's Regiment [see Cotton's Regiment] and consolidated unit redesignated as the 3d Continental Regiment, an element of Thomas' Brigade, to consist of eight companies. Relieved 24 April 1776 from Thomas' Brigade and assigned to Heath's Brigade, an element of the Main Army. Relieved 12 August 1776 from Heath's Brigade and assigned to Clinton's Brigade, an element of the Main Army.

Consolidated 1 January 1777 with King's Company, 21st Continental Regiment [see 21st Continental Regiment], and consolidated unit designated as Shepard's Regiment, to consist of eight companies. Relieved 9 February 1777 from Clinton's Brigade and assigned to the Northern Department. Relieved 13 March 1777 from the Northern Department and assigned to the Highlands Department. Assigned 12 June 1777 to the 1st Massachusetts Brigade, an element of the Highlands Department. Relieved 15 June 1777 from the 1st Massachusetts Brigade and assigned to the 2d Massachusetts Brigade, an element of the Highlands Department. (2d Massachusetts Brigade relieved 24 July 1777 from the Highlands Department and assigned to the Northern Department; relieved 7 November 1777 from the Northern Department and assigned to the Main Army; relieved 22 July 1778 from the Main Army and assigned to the Eastern Department.)

Reorganized 1 April 1779 to consist of nine companies. (2d Massachusetts Brigade relieved 7 July 1779 from the Eastern Department and assigned to the Highlands Department.) Redesignated 1 August 1779 as the 4th Massachusetts Regiment. Relieved 1 January 1781 from the 2d Massachusetts Brigade and assigned to the 1st Massachusetts Brigade, an element of the Highlands Department. Relieved 12 June 1783 from the 1st Massachusetts Brigade and assigned to the 2d Massachusetts Brigade, an element of the Highlands Department. Disbanded 3 November 1783 at West Point, New York.

ENGAGEMENTS
    Siege of Boston
    New York City
    Northern New Jersey
    Trenton-Princeton
    Saratoga
    Defense of Philadelphia
    Philadelphia-Monmouth
    Rhode Island

*This regiment is perpetuated by the 104th Infantry, Massachusetts Army National Guard.

5th MASSACHUSETTS REGIMENT*

Authorized 23 April 1775 in the Massachusetts State Troops as Mansfield's Regiment. Organized in spring 1775 at Cambridge to consist of ten companies from southeastern Essex County. Adopted 14 June 1775 into the Continental Army and assigned to the Main Army. Assigned 22 July 1775 to Sullivan's Brigade, an element of the Main Army.

Reorganized and redesignated 1 January 1776 as the 27th Continental Regiment, to consist of eight companies; concurrently, relieved from Sullivan's Brigade and assigned to the Vacant Brigade, an element of the Main Army. (Vacant Brigade redesignated 16 February 1776 as Frye's Brigade.) Relieved 4 April 1776 from Frye's Brigade and assigned to the Eastern Department. Relieved 11 July 1776 from the Eastern Department and assigned to the Main Army. Assigned 12 August 1776 to Mifflin's Brigade, an element of the Main Army. (Mifflin's Brigade redesignated 8 October 1776 as Stirling's Brigade.) Relieved 15 October 1776 from Stirling's Brigade and assigned to Clinton's Brigade, an element of the Main Army.

Consolidated 1 January 1777 with Walbridge's Company, 13th Continental Regiment [see 13th Continental Regiment], and consolidated unit redesignated as Putnam's Regiment, to consist of eight companies. Relieved 9 February 1777 from Clinton's Brigade and assigned to the Northern Department. Relieved 13 March 1777 from the Northern Department and assigned to the Highlands Department. Assigned 12 June 1777 to the 2d Massachusetts Brigade, an element of the Highlands Department. Relieved 15 June 1777 from the 2d Massachusetts Brigade and assigned to the 1st Massachusetts Brigade, an element of the Highlands Department. (1st Massachusetts Brigade relieved 1 July 1777 from the Highlands Department and assigned to the Northern Department; relieved 31 March 1778 from the Northern Department and assigned to the Highlands Department.)

Reorganized 12 May 1779 to consist of nine companies. Redesignated 1 August 1779 as the 5th Massachusetts Regiment. Relieved 1 January 1781 from the 1st Massachusetts Brigade and assigned to the 2d Massachusetts Brigade, an element of the Highlands Department. Furloughed 12 June 1783 at West Point, New York. Disbanded 15 November 1783.

ENGAGEMENTS
  Siege of Boston
  New York City
  Northern New Jersey
  Trenton-Princeton
  Saratoga

*This regiment is perpetuated by the 101st Engineer Battalion, Massachusetts Army National Guard.

6th MASSACHUSETTS REGIMENT

Authorized 23 April 1775 in the Massachusetts State Troops as Nixon's Regiment. Organized in spring 1775 at Cambridge to consist of ten companies from eastern Middlesex County, Essex and Lincoln Counties, Massachusetts; and Rockingham County, New Hampshire. Adopted 14 June 1775 into the Continental Army and assigned to the Main Army. Assigned 22 July 1775 to Sullivan's Brigade, an element of the Main Army.

Consolidated 1 January 1776 with Thompson's Company, Danielson's Regiment [see Danielson's Regiment], and consolidated unit redesignated as the 4th Continental Regiment, an element of Sullivan's Brigade, to consist of eight companies. Relieved 29 April 1776 from Sullivan's Brigade and assigned to Stirling's Brigade, an element of the Main Army. Relieved 12 August 1776 from Stirling's Brigade and assigned to Nixon's Brigade, an element of the Main Army.

Reorganized and redesignated 1 January 1777 as Nixon's Regiment, to consist of eight companies. Relieved 9 February 1777 from Nixon's Brigade and assigned to the Northern Department. Relieved 13 March 1777 from the Northern Department and assigned to the Highlands Department. Assigned 12 June 1777 to the 1st Massachusetts Brigade, an element of the Highlands Department. (1st Massachusetts Brigade relieved 1 July 1777 from the Highlands Department and assigned to the Northern Department; relieved 31 March 1778 from the Northern Department and assigned to the Highlands Department.)

Reorganized 12 May 1779 to consist of nine companies. Redesignated 1 August 1779 as the 6th Massachusetts Regiment. Relieved 1 January 1781 from the 1st Massachusetts Brigade and assigned to the 3d Massachusetts Brigade, an element of the Highlands Department. Furloughed 12 June 1783 at West Point, New York. Disbanded 15 November 1783.

ENGAGEMENTS
  Siege of Boston
  New York City
  Northern New Jersey
  Trenton-Princeton
  Saratoga

7th MASSACHUSETTS REGIMENT*

Constituted 16 September 1776 in the Continental Army as Alden's Regiment. Organized in spring 1777 at Boston to consist of seven companies from Worcester, Middlesex, Essex, York, Cumberland, Hampshire, Lincoln, and Suffolk Counties and Mayhew's Company, 25th Continental Regiment [see 25th Continental Regiment]. Assigned 9 February 1777 to the Northern Department. Relieved 13 March 1777 from the Northern Department and assigned to the Highlands Department. Assigned 12 June 1777 to the 2d Massachusetts Brigade, an element of the Highlands Department. Relieved 15 June 1777 from the 2d Massachusetts Brigade and assigned to the 1st Massachusetts Brigade, an element of the Highlands Department. (1st Massachusetts Brigade relieved 1 July 1777 from the Highlands Department and assigned to the Northern Department.) Relieved 31 March 1778 from the 1st Massachusetts Brigade.

Reorganized 25 September 1778 to consist of nine companies. Relieved 14 June 1779 from the Northern Department and assigned to the Main Army. Redesignated 1 August 1779 as the 7th Massachusetts Regiment. Assigned 23 August 1779 to the New Hampshire Brigade, an element of the Main Army. Relieved 14 November 1779 from the New Hampshire Brigade and assigned to the 3d Massachusetts Brigade, an element of the Highlands Department. Relieved 1 January 1781 from the 3d Massachusetts Brigade and assigned to the 1st Massachusetts Brigade, an element of the Highlands Department. Furloughed 12 June 1783 at West Point, New York. Disbanded 15 November 1783.

ENGAGEMENTS
Saratoga
Iroquois 1778
Iroquois 1779

*Elements of this regiment are perpetuated by the 182d Infantry, Massachusetts Army National Guard.

8th MASSACHUSETTS REGIMENT

Authorized 23 April 1775 in the Massachusetts State Troops as Sargent's Regiment. Organized in spring and summer 1775 at Cambridge to consist of ten companies from Essex, Bristol, Middlesex, Plymouth, Worcester, Suffolk, and Hampshire Counties, Massachusetts; and Hillsborough and Cheshire Counties, New Hampshire. Adopted 14 June 1775 into the Continental Army and assigned to the Main Army. Assigned 22 July 1775 to the Vacant Brigade, an element of the Main Army.

Reorganized and redesignated 1 January 1776 as the 16th Continental Regiment, an element of the Vacant Brigade, to consist of eight companies. Relieved 24 January 1776 from the Vacant Brigade and assigned to Heath's Brigade, an element of the Main Army. Relieved 4 April 1776 from Heath's Brigade and assigned to the Eastern Department. Relieved 11 July 1776 from the Eastern Department and assigned to the

Main Army. Assigned 12 August 1776 to Mifflin's Brigade, an element of the Main Army. Relieved 31 August 1776 from Mifflin's Brigade and assigned to Sargent's Brigade, an element of the Main Army.

Reorganized and redesignated 1 January 1777 as Michael Jackson's Regiment, to consist of eight companies. Relieved 9 February 1777 from Sargent's Brigade and assigned to the Northern Department. Assigned 13 August 1777 to the 4th Massachusetts Brigade, an element of the Northern Department. (4th Massachusetts Brigade relieved 27 October 1777 from the Northern Department and assigned to the Main Army; relieved 20 November 1778 from the Main Army and assigned to the Highlands Department.)

Reorganized 12 May 1779 to consist of nine companies. Redesignated 1 August 1779 as the 8th Massachusetts Regiment. Relieved 1 January 1781 from the 4th Massachusetts Brigade and assigned to the 2d Massachusetts Brigade, an element of the Highlands Department. Furloughed 12 June 1783 at West Point, New York. Disbanded 15 November 1783

ENGAGEMENTS
>   Siege of Boston
>   New York City
>   Northern New Jersey
>   Trenton-Princeton
>   Saratoga
>   Defense of Philadelphia
>   Philadelphia-Monmouth

9th MASSACHUSETTS REGIMENT

Authorized 23 April 1775 in the Massachusetts State Troops as Gerrish's Regiment. Organized in spring 1775 at Cambridge to consist of ten companies from Suffolk, Essex, Middlesex, and York Counties, Massachusetts; and Rockingham County, New Hampshire. Adopted 14 June 1775 into the Continental Army and assigned to the Main Army. Assigned 22 July 1775 to Heath's Brigade, an element of the Main Army.

Reorganized and redesignated 1 January 1776 as the 26th Continental Regiment, an element of Heath's Brigade, to consist of eight companies. Relieved 12 August 1776 from Heath's Brigade and assigned to Clinton's Brigade, an element of the Main Army.

Consolidated 1 January 1777 with the 21st Continental Regiment [see 21st Continental Regiment] and consolidated unit redesignated as Wesson's Regiment, to consist of eight companies. Relieved 9 February 1777 from Clinton's Brigade and assigned to the Northern Department. Assigned 13 August 1777 to the 4th Massachusetts Brigade, an element of the Northern Department. (4th Massachusetts Brigade relieved 27 October 1777 from the Northern Department and assigned to the Main Army; relieved 20 November 1778 from the Main Army and assigned to the Highlands Department.)

Reorganized 12 May 1779 to consist of nine companies. Redesignated 1 August 1779 as the 9th Massachusetts Regiment. Relieved 1 January 1781 from the 4th Massachusetts Brigade and assigned to the 3d Massachusetts Brigade, an element of the Highlands Department. Disbanded 1 January 1783 at West Point, New York.

ENGAGEMENTS
    Siege of Boston
    New York City
    Northern New Jersey
    Trenton-Princeton
    Saratoga
    Mohawk Valley
    Defense of Philadelphia
    Philadelphia-Monmouth

10th MASSACHUSETTS REGIMENT

Authorized 16 September 1776 in the Continental Army as Marshall's Regiment. Assigned 9 February 1777 to the Northern Department. Organized in spring 1777 at Boston to consist of eight companies from Middlesex, Worcester, Suffolk, Hampshire, Essex, Bristol, and Plymouth Counties, Massachusetts; and Cheshire County, New Hampshire. Assigned 13 August 1777 to the 3d Massachusetts Brigade, an element of the Northern Department. (3d Massachusetts Brigade relieved 27 October 1777 from the Northern Department and assigned to the Main Army; relieved 20 November 1778 from the Main Army and assigned to the Highlands Department.)

Reorganized 12 May 1779 to consist of nine companies. Redesignated 1 August 1779 as the 10th Massachusetts Regiment. Relieved 1 January 1781 from the 3d Massachusetts Brigade and assigned to the 1st Massachusetts Brigade, an element of the Highlands Department.

Relieved 18 June 1781 from the 1st Massachusetts Brigade and assigned to the New Hampshire Brigade, an element of the Highlands Department. (New Hampshire Brigade relieved 14 October 1781 from the Highlands Department and assigned to the Northern Department.) Relieved 12 November 1781 from the New Hampshire Brigade and assigned to the Highlands Department. Assigned 29 August 1782 to the New Hampshire Brigade, an element of the Northern Department. Relieved 26 October 1782 from the New Hampshire Brigade and assigned to the Highlands Department. Disbanded 1 January 1783 at Verplanck's Point, New York.

ENGAGEMENTS
    Saratoga
    Defense of Philadelphia
    Philadelphia-Monmouth

11th MASSACHUSETTS REGIMENT

Authorized 16 September 1776 in the Continental Army as Francis' Regiment. Assigned 9 February 1777 to the Northern Department. Organized in spring 1777 at Boston to consist of eight companies from Essex, Cumberland, York, Suffolk, and Lincoln Counties, Massachusetts; and Windham County, Connecticut. Redesignated 7 July 1777 as Tupper's Regiment.

Assigned 13 August 1777 to the 3d Massachusetts Brigade, an element of the Northern Department. (3d Massachusetts Brigade relieved 27 October 1777 from the Northern Department and assigned to the Main Army; relieved 20 November 1778 from the Main Army and assigned to the Highlands Department.)

Reorganized 12 May 1779 to consist of nine companies. Redesignated 1 August 1779 as the 11th Massachusetts Regiment. Disbanded 1 January 1781 at West Point, New York.

Engagements
    Saratoga
    Defense of Philadelphia
    Philadelphia-Monmouth

12th MASSACHUSETTS REGIMENT

Authorized 23 April 1775 in the Massachusetts State Troops as Phinney's Regiment. Organized in spring 1775 in Cumberland County to consist of ten companies from Cumberland County. Adopted 14 June 1775 into the Continental Army and assigned to the Main Army. Assigned 22 July 1775 to Heath's Brigade, an element of the Main Army.

Consolidated 1 January 1776 with Scammon's Regiment [see Scammon's Regiment] and Watkins' Company, Paterson's Regiment [see 1st Massachusetts Regiment] and consolidated unit redesignated as the 18th Continental Regiment, an element of Heath's Brigade, to consist of eight companies. Relieved 4 April 1776 from Heath's Brigade and assigned to the Eastern Department. Relieved 3 August 1776 from the Eastern Department and assigned to the Northern Department. Assigned 4 September 1776 to Paterson's Brigade, an element of the Northern Department. Relieved 18 November 1776 from Paterson's Brigade.

Reorganized and redesignated (less two companies) 1 January 1777 as Samuel Brewer's Regiment, an element of the Northern Department, to consist of eight companies; (two companies concurrently consolidated with the 15th Continental Regiment [see 1st Massachusetts Regiment]). Assigned 13 August 1777 to the 3d Massachusetts Brigade, an element of the Northern Department. (3d Massachusetts Brigade relieved 27 October 1777 from the Northern Department and assigned to the Main Army; relieved 20 November 1778 from the Main Army and assigned to the Highlands Department.)

Reorganized 12 May 1779 to consist of nine companies. Redesignated 1 August 1779 as the 12th Massachusetts Regiment. Relieved 14 November 1779 from the 3d

Massachusetts Brigade and assigned to the 1st Massachusetts Brigade, an element of the Highlands Department. Disbanded 1 January 1781 at West Point, New York.

ENGAGEMENTS
    Siege of Boston
    Lake Champlain
    Saratoga
    Defense of Philadelphia
    Philadelphia-Monmouth

13th MASSACHUSETTS REGIMENT

Authorized 23 April 1775 in the Massachusetts State Troops as Jonathan Brewer's Regiment. Organized in spring 1775 at Cambridge to consist of ten companies from Worcester, Hampshire, Middlesex, Suffolk, Bristol, Berkshire, and Barnstable Counties. Adopted 14 June 1775 into the Continental Army and assigned to the Main Army. Assigned 22 July 1775 to Greene's Brigade, an element of the Main Army.

Consolidated 1 January 1776 with Soul's Company, Fellows' Regiment [see Fellows' Regiment], and Danforth's Company, David Brewer's Regiment [see David Brewer's Regiment], and consolidated unit redesignated as the 6th Continental Regiment, an element of Greene's Brigade, to consist of eight companies. Relieved 24 January 1776 from Greene's Brigade and assigned to Thomas' Brigade, an element of the Main Army. Relieved 4 April 1776 from Thomas' Brigade and assigned to the Eastern Department. Relieved 8 August 1776 from the Eastern Department and assigned to the Northern Department.

Consolidated (less two companies) 1 January 1777 with Bent's and Whiting's Companies, 24th Continental Regiment [see 3d Massachusetts Regiment], and consolidated unit redesignated as Wigglesworth's Regiment, an element of the Northern Department, to consist of eight companies; (two companies concurrently consolidated with the 15th Continental Regiment [see 1st Massachusetts Regiment]). Relieved 13 March 1777 from the Northern Department and assigned to the Highlands Department.

Assigned 12 June 1777 to the 1st Massachusetts Brigade, an element of the Highlands Department. Relieved 15 June 1777 from the 1st Massachusetts Brigade and assigned to the 2d Massachusetts Brigade, an element of the Highlands Department. (2d Massachusetts Brigade relieved 24 July 1777 from the Highlands Department and assigned to the Northern Department; relieved 7 November 1777 from the Northern Department and assigned to the Main Army; relieved 22 July 1778 from the Main Army and assigned to the Eastern Department.)

Reorganized 1 April 1779 to consist of nine companies. (2d Massachusetts Brigade relieved 7 July 1779 from the Eastern Department and assigned to the Highlands Department.) Redesignated 1 August 1779 as the 13th Massachusetts Regiment. Disbanded 1 January 1781 at West Point, New York.

ENGAGEMENTS
    Siege of Boston
    Lake Champlain

ENGAGEMENTS—Continued
Saratoga
Defense of Philadelphia
Philadelphia-Monmouth
Rhode Island

14th MASSACHUSETTS REGIMENT

Authorized 16 September 1776 in the Continental Army as Bradford's Regiment. Assigned 9 February 1777 to the Northern Department. Organized in spring 1777 at Boston to consist of eight companies from Plymouth, Bristol, Barnstable, Suffolk, Cumberland, and Worcester Counties. Assigned 13 August 1777 to the 3d Massachusetts Brigade, an element of the Northern Department. (3d Massachusetts Brigade relieved 27 October 1777 from the Northern Department and assigned to the Main Army; relieved 20 November 1778 from the Main Army and assigned to the Highlands Department.)

Reorganized 12 May 1779 to consist of nine companies. Redesignated 1 August 1779 as the 14th Massachusetts Regiment. Disbanded 1 January 1781 at West Point, New York.

ENGAGEMENTS
Saratoga
Defense of Philadelphia
Philadelphia-Monmouth

15th MASSACHUSETTS REGIMENT

Authorized 16 September 1776 in the Continental Army as Bigelow's Regiment. Assigned 9 February 1777 to the Northern Department. Relieved 13 March 1777 from the Northern Department and assigned to the Highlands Department. Organized in spring 1777 at Boston to consist of eight companies from Worcester, Middlesex, Cumberland, Essex, Berkshire, and Bristol Counties. Assigned 12 June 1777 to the 2d Massachusetts Brigade, an element of the Highlands Department. (2d Massachusetts Brigade relieved 24 July 1777 from the Highlands Department and assigned to the Northern Department; relieved 7 November 1777 from the Northern Department and assigned to the Main Army; relieved 22 July 1778 from the Main Army and assigned to the Eastern Department; relieved 7 July 1779 from the Eastern Department and assigned to the Highlands Department.)

Redesignated 1 August 1779 as the 15th Massachusetts Regiment. Reorganized 1 November 1779 to consist of nine companies. Disbanded 1 January 1781 at West Point, New York.

ENGAGEMENTS
Saratoga
Defense of Philadelphia

ENGAGEMENTS—Continued
Philadelphia-Monmouth
Rhode Island

HENLEY'S ADDITIONAL CONTINENTAL REGIMENT

Authorized 12 January 1777 in the Continental Army as Henley's Additional Continental Regiment. Assigned 23 May 1777 to the Eastern Department. Organized in spring and summer 1777 at Boston to consist of five companies from Suffolk, Middlesex, Essex, and Worcester Counties, Massachusetts; and Hillsborough and Rockingham Counties, New Hampshire.

Relieved 18 March 1778 from the Eastern Department and assigned to the Main Army. Relieved 22 July 1778 from the Main Army and assigned to the Eastern Department. Consolidated 9 April 1779 with Henry Jackson's Additional Continental Regiment [see Henry Jackson's Additional Continental Regiment].

ENGAGEMENTS
Philadelphia-Monmouth
Rhode Island

HENRY JACKSON'S ADDITIONAL
CONTINENTAL REGIMENT*
(16th Massachusetts Regiment)

Authorized 12 January 1777 in the Continental Army as Henry Jackson's Additional Continental Regiment. Assigned 23 May 1777 to the Eastern Department. Organized in spring and summer 1777 at Boston to consist of seven companies from Suffolk and Middlesex Counties.

Relieved 7 October 1777 from the Eastern Department and assigned to the Main Army. Relieved 22 July 1778 from the Main Army and assigned to the Eastern Department. Consolidated 9 April 1779 with Lee's and Henley's Additional Continental Regiments [see Lee's and Henley's Additional Continental Regiments] and consolidated unit designated as Henry Jackson's Additional Continental Regiment, to consist of nine companies; concurrently, assigned to the 2d Massachusetts Brigade, an element of the Eastern Department. Relieved 7 July 1779 from the 2d Massachusetts Brigade. Assigned 28 September 1779 to the Rhode Island Brigade, an element of the Eastern Department. Relieved 17 November 1779 from the Rhode Island Brigade and assigned to Stark's Brigade, an element of the Main Army. Redesignated 24 July 1780 as the 16th Massachusetts Regiment. Disbanded 1 January 1781 at New Windsor, New York.

ENGAGEMENTS
Philadelphia-Monmouth
Rhode Island
New Jersey 1780

*This regiment is perpetuated by the 126th Signal Battalion, Massachusetts Army National Guard.

LEE'S ADDITIONAL CONTINENTAL REGIMENT*

Authorized 12 January 1777 in the Continental Army as Lee's Additional Continental Regiment. Assigned 23 May 1777 to the Eastern Department. Organized in spring and summer 1777 at Cambridge to consist of six companies from Essex, Middlesex, Suffolk, and Bristol Counties.

Relieved 2 October 1777 from the Eastern Department and assigned to the Main Army. Relieved 22 July 1778 from the Main Army and assigned to the Eastern Department. Consolidated 9 April 1779 with Henry Jackson's Additional Continental Regiment [see Henry Jackson's Additional Continental Regiment].

ENGAGEMENTS
Philadelphia-Monmouth
Rhode Island

*This regiment is perpetuated by the 101st Engineer Battalion, Massachusetts Army National Guard.

HENRY JACKSON'S CONTINENTAL REGIMENT

Authorized 23 October 1783 in the Continental Army as Henry Jackson's Continental Regiment. Organized 3 November 1783 at West Point, New York, to consist of nine companies of veterans of the Massachusetts Line. Disbanded 20 June 1784 at West Point, New York.

ENGAGEMENTS
None

7th CONTINENTAL REGIMENT

Authorized 23 April 1775 in the Massachusetts State Troops as Prescott's Regiment. Organized in spring 1775 at Cambridge to consist of eleven companies from northwestern Middlesex County and Hampshire County, Massachusetts; and Hillsborough County, New Hampshire. Adopted 14 June 1775 into the Continental Army and assigned to the Main Army. Assigned 22 July 1775 to Heath's Brigade, an element of the Main Army.

Consolidated 1 January 1776 with Darby's and Nowell's Companies, Scammon's Regiment [see Scammon's Regiment], and Morse's Company, Paterson's Regiment [see 1st Massachusetts Regiment], and consolidated unit redesignated as the 7th Continental Regiment, an element of Heath's Brigade, to consist of eight companies. Relieved 12 August 1776 from Heath's Brigade and assigned to Nixon's Brigade, an element of the Main Army. Relieved 31 August 1776 from Nixon's Brigade and assigned to Parsons' Brigade, an element of the Main Army. (Parsons' Brigade relieved 12 November 1776 from the Main Army and assigned to the Highlands Department.)

Consolidated 1 January 1776 with the 23d Continental Regiment and consolidated unit redesignated as Bailey's Regiment [see 2d Massachusetts Regiment].

ENGAGEMENTS
Siege of Boston
New York City
Northern New Jersey

12th CONTINENTAL REGIMENT*

Authorized 23 April 1775 in the Massachusetts State Troops as Little's Regiment. Organized in spring 1775 at Cambridge to consist of ten companies from northeastern Essex County. Adopted 14 June 1775 into the Continental Army and assigned to the Main Army. Assigned 22 July 1775 to Greene's Brigade, an element of the Main Army.

Reorganized and redesignated 1 January 1776 as the 12th Continental Regiment, an element of Greene's Brigade, to consist of eight companies. Relieved 12 August 1776 from Greene's Brigade and assigned to Nixon's Brigade, an element of the Main Army. Disbanded during February 1777 at Morristown, New Jersey; and Peekskill, New York.

ENGAGEMENTS
Siege of Boston
New York City
Trenton-Princeton
Northern New Jersey

*This regiment is perpetuated by the 101st Engineer Battalion, Massachusetts Army National Guard.

13th CONTINENTAL REGIMENT

Authorized 23 April 1775 in the Massachusetts State Troops as Read's Regiment. Organized in spring 1775 at Roxbury to consist of ten companies from southwestern Suffolk County, southeastern Worcester County, and Bristol County. Adopted 14 June 1775 into the Continental Army and assigned to the Main Army. Assigned 22 July 1775 to Spencer's Brigade, an element of the Main Army.

Consolidated 1 January 1776 with Walker's Regiment [see Walker's Regiment] and David Brewer's Regiment [see David Brewer's Regiment] and consolidated unit redesignated as the 13th Continental Regiment, an element of Spencer's Brigade, to consist of eight companies. Relieved 24 January 1776 from Spencer's Brigade and assigned to Thomas' Brigade, an element of the Main Army. Relieved 24 April 1776 from Thomas' Brigade and assigned to Heath's Brigade, an element of the Main Army. Relieved 12 August 1776 from Heath's Brigade and assigned to Clinton's Brigade, an element of the Main Army. Relieved 5 November 1776 from Clinton's Brigade and assigned to McDougall's Brigade, an element of the Main Army. Relieved 11 December 1776 from McDougall's Brigade and assigned to Sargent's Brigade, an element of the Main Army.

Disbanded (less Peters' and Walbridge's Companies) in January 1777 at Morristown, New Jersey; Peters' Company reorganized and redesignated 1 January 1777 as Warren's Company, Bailey's Regiment [see 2d Massachusetts Regiment], and Walbridge's Company reorganized and redesignated 1 January 1777 as Goodale's Company, Putnam's Regiment [see 5th Massachusetts Regiment].

ENGAGEMENTS
   Siege of Boston
   New York City
   Trenton-Princeton
   Northern New Jersey

14th CONTINENTAL REGIMENT*

Authorized 23 April 1775 in the Massachusetts State Troops as Glover's Regiment. Organized in spring 1775 at Marblehead to consist of ten companies from Marblehead in Essex County. Adopted 14 June 1775 into the Continental Army and assigned to the Main Army. Assigned 22 July 1775 to the Vacant Brigade, an element of the Main Army.

Reorganized and redesignated 1 January 1776 as the 14th Continental Regiment, an element of the Vacant Brigade, to consist of eight companies. (Vacant Brigade redesignated 16 February 1776 as Frye's Brigade.) Relieved 4 April 1776 from the Main Army and assigned to the Eastern Department. Relieved 20 July 1776 from the Eastern Department and assigned to the Main Army. Assigned 12 August to Stirling's Brigade, an element of the Main Army. Relieved 16 August 1776 from Stirling's Brigade and assigned to Fellows' Brigade, an element of the Main Army. Relieved 31 August 1776 from Fellows' Brigade and assigned to Clinton's Brigade, an element of the Main Army. Disbanded 31 December 1776 in eastern Pennsylvania.

ENGAGEMENTS
   Siege of Boston
   New York City
   Trenton-Princeton

*This regiment is perpetuated by the 101st Engineer Battalion, Massachusetts Army National Guard.

21st CONTINENTAL REGIMENT

Authorized 23 April 1775 in the Massachusetts State Troops as Ward's Regiment. Organized in spring 1775 at Roxbury to consist of ten companies from eastern

Worcester County and Middlesex and Hampshire Counties. Adopted 14 June 1775 into the Continental Army and assigned to the Main Army. Assigned 22 July 1775 to Thomas' Brigade, an element of the Main Army.

Consolidated 1 January 1776 with Fellows' Regiment [see Fellows' Regiment] and Benson's and Bradford's Companies, Cotton's Regiment [see Cotton's Regiment] and consolidated unit redesignated as the 21st Continental Regiment, an element of Thomas' Brigade, to consist of eight companies. Relieved 24 April 1776 from Thomas' Brigade and assigned to Spencer's Brigade, an element of the Main Army. Relieved 12 August 1776 from Spencer's Brigade and assigned to Parsons' Brigade, an element of the Main Army. Relieved 18 September 1776 from Parsons' Brigade and assigned to Sargent's Brigade, an element of the Main Army.

Consolidated (less Clap's and King's Companies) 1 January 1777 with the 26th Continental Regiment and consolidated unit redesignated as Wesson's Regiment [see 9th Massachusetts Regiment]; concurrently, Clap's Company reorganized and redesignated as Dunham's Company, Bailey's Regiment [see 2d Massachusetts Regiment] and King's Company reorganized and redesignated as Alvord's Company, Shepard's Regiment [see 4th Massachusetts Regiment].

ENGAGEMENTS
    Siege of Boston
    New York City
    Trenton-Princeton

25th CONTINENTAL REGIMENT*

Authorized 23 April 1775 in the Massachusetts State Troops as Gardner's Regiment. Organized in spring 1775 at Cambridge to consist of ten companies from southeastern Middlesex County and Suffolk County. Adopted 14 June 1775 into the Continental Army and assigned to the Main Army. Assigned 22 July 1775 to Greene's Brigade, an element of the Main Army.

Consolidated (less Crafts' Company) 1 January 1776 with Mayhew's Company, Cotton's Regiment [see Cotton's Regiment] and Egery's Company, Danielson's Regiment [see Danielson's Regiment], and consolidated unit redesignated as the 25th Continental Regiment, an element of Greene's Brigade, to consist of eight companies; (Crafts' Company concurrently reorganized and redesignated as Crafts' Company, 24th Continental Regiment [see 3d Massachusetts Regiment]). Relieved 15 April 1776 from the Main Army and assigned to the Canadian Department. Relieved 2 July 1776 from the Canadian Department and assigned to the Northern Department. Assigned 20 July 1776 to Arnold's Brigade, an element of the Northern Department. (Arnold's Brigade redesignated 26 October 1776 as Poor's Brigade.) Relieved 26 November 1776 from Poor's Brigade and assigned to Vose's Brigade, an element of the Main Army. (Vose's Brigade redesignated 18 December 1776 as McDougall's Brigade.)

Consolidated (less Mayhew's Company) 1 January 1777 with the 24th Continental Regiment and consolidated unit redesignated as Greaton's Regiment [see 3d Massachusetts Regiment]; Mayhew's Company concurrently reorganized and redesignated as Warren's Company, Alden's Regiment [see 7th Massachusetts Regiment].

ENGAGEMENTS
    Siege of Boston
    Defense of Canada
    Lake Champlain
    Northern New Jersey

*This regiment is perpetuated by the 182d Infantry, Massachusetts Army National Guard.

PORTER'S REGIMENT*

Authorized 19 January 1776 in the Continental Army as Porter's Regiment and assigned to the Canadian Department. Organized in early spring 1776 at Northampton and Pittsfield, Massachusetts, to consist of eight companies from Hampshire and Berkshire Counties. Relieved 2 July 1776 from the Canadian Department and assigned to the Northern Department. Assigned 20 July 1776 to Arnold's Brigade, an element of the Northern Department. (Arnold's Brigade redesignated 26 October 1776 as Poor's Brigade.)

Relieved 26 November 1776 from Poor's Brigade and assigned to Vose's Brigade, an element of the Main Army. (Vose's Brigade redesignated 18 December 1776 as McDougall's Brigade.) Disbanded in January 1777 at Morristown, New Jersey.

ENGAGEMENTS
    Defense of Canada
    Lake Champlain
    Northern New Jersey

*This regiment is perpetuated by the 104th Infantry, Massachusetts Army National Guard.

DAVID BREWER'S REGIMENT

Authorized 23 April 1775 in the Massachusetts State Troops as David Brewer's Regiment. Organized in spring 1775 at Roxbury to consist of ten companies from Berkshire, Hampshire, Worcester, Bristol, and Plymouth Counties. Adopted 14 June 1775 into the Continental Army and assigned to the Main Army. Assigned 22 July 1775 to Thomas' Brigade, an element of the Main Army.

Consolidated (less Danforth's Company) 1 January 1776 with Read's Regiment and consolidated unit redesignated as the 13th Continental Regiment [see 13th Continental Regiment]; Danforth's Company concurrently reorganized as Danforth's Company, 6th Continental Regiment [see 13th Massachusetts Regiment].

ENGAGEMENTS
    Siege of Boston

BRIDGE'S REGIMENT

Authorized 23 April 1775 in the Massachusetts State Troops as Bridge's Regiment. Organized in spring 1775 at Cambridge to consist of ten companies from northeastern Middlesex County, Essex County, and one company at large. Adopted 14 June 1775 into the Continental Army and assigned to the Main Army. Assigned 22 July 1775 to the Vacant Brigade, an element of the Main Army. Disbanded 31 December 1775 at Cambridge.

ENGAGEMENTS
  Siege of Boston

COTTON'S REGIMENT

Authorized 23 April 1775 in the Massachusetts State Troops as Cotton's Regiment. Organized in spring 1775 at Roxbury to consist of ten companies from southern Plymouth County. Adopted 14 June 1775 into the Continental Army and assigned to the Main Army. Assigned 22 July 1775 to Thomas' Brigade, an element of the Main Army.

Consolidated (less Mayhew's, Wood's, Benson's, and Bradford's Companies) 1 January 1776 with Bailey's Regiment and consolidated unit designated as the 23d Continental Regiment [see 2d Massachusetts Regiment]; Mayhew's Company concurrently reorganized and redesignated as Mayhew's Company, 25th Continental Regiment [see 25th Continental Regiment], Wood's Company reorganized and redesignated as Wood's Company, 3d Continental Regiment [see 4th Massachusetts Regiment], and Benson's and Bradford's Companies consolidated and redesignated as Clap's Company, 21st Continental Regiment [see 21st Continental Regiment].

ENGAGEMENTS
  Siege of Boston

DANIELSON'S REGIMENT*

Authorized 23 April 1775 in the Massachusetts State Troops as Danielson's Regiment. Organized in spring 1775 at Roxbury to consist of eleven companies from southern Hampshire County, Bristol and Worcester Counties, Massachusetts; and New London and Hartford Counties, Connecticut. Adopted 14 June 1775 into the Continental Army and assigned to the Main Army. Assigned 22 July 1775 to Thomas' Brigade, an element of the Main Army.

Consolidated (less Thompson's and Egery's Companies) 1 January 1776 with Learned's Regiment and consolidated unit redesignated as the 3d Continental Regiment [see 4th Massachusetts Regiment]; Thompson's Company concurrently reorganized and redesignated as Thompson's Company, 4th Continental Regiment [see 6th Massachusetts Regiment] and Egery's Company reorganized and redesignated as Egery's Company, 25th Continental Regiment [see 25th Continental Regiment].

ENGAGEMENTS
   Siege of Boston

*This regiment is perpetuated by the 104th Infantry, Massachusetts Army National Guard.

DOOLITTLE'S REGIMENT

Authorized 23 April 1775 in the Massachusetts State Troops as Doolittle's Regiment. Organized in spring 1775 at Cambridge to consist of ten companies from northwestern Worcester County and Cumberland, York, Hampshire, and Middlesex Counties. Adopted 14 June 1775 into the Continental Army and assigned to the Main Army. Assigned 22 July 1775 to Sullivan's Brigade, an element of the Main Army. Disbanded 31 December 1775 at Cambridge.

ENGAGEMENTS
   Siege of Boston

FELLOWS' REGIMENT*

Authorized 23 April 1775 in the Massachusetts State Troops as Fellows' Regiment. Organized in spring 1775 at Roxbury to consist of ten companies from central Hampshire County, southern Berkshire County, and Worcester County. Adopted 14 June 1775 into the Continental Army and assigned to the Main Army. Assigned 22 July 1775 to Thomas' Brigade, an element of the Main Army.

Consolidated (less Soul's Company) 1 January 1776 with Ward's Regiment and consolidated unit redesignated as the 21st Continental Regiment [see 21st Continental Regiment]; Soul's Company concurrently reorganized and redesignated as Soul's Company, 6th Continental Regiment [see 13th Massachusetts Regiment].

ENGAGEMENTS
   Siege of Boston

*This regiment is perpetuated by the 104th Infantry, Massachusetts Army National Guard.

FRYE'S REGIMENT*

Authorized 23 April 1775 in the Massachusetts State Troops as Frye's Regiment. Organized in spring 1775 at Cambridge to consist of ten companies from northwestern Essex County and Middlesex County. Adopted 14 June 1775 into the Continental Army and assigned to the Main Army. Assigned 22 July 1775 to the Vacant Brigade, an element of the Main Army. Disbanded 31 December 1775 at Cambridge.

ENGAGEMENTS
   Siege of Boston

*This regiment is perpetuated by the 101st Engineer Battalion, Massachusetts Army National Guard.

SCAMMON'S REGIMENT

Authorized 23 April 1775 in the Massachusetts State Troops as Scammon's Regiment. Organized in spring 1775 at Cambridge to consist of ten companies from York County. Adopted 14 June 1775 into the Continental Army and assigned to the Main Army. Assigned 22 July 1775 to Heath's Brigade, an element of the Main Army.

Consolidated (less Darby's, Nowell's, Sayer's, and Sullivan's Companies) 1 January 1776 with Phinney's Regiment and consolidated unit redesignated as the 18th Continental Regiment [see 12th Massachusetts Regiment]; Darby's and Nowell's Companies concurrently reorganized and redesignated as Darby's and Nowell's Companies, 7th Continental Regiment [see 7th Continental Regiment] and Sayer's and Sullivan's Companies reorganized and redesignated as Sayer's and Sullivan's Companies, 15th Continental Regiment [see 1st Massachusetts Regiment].

ENGAGEMENTS
    Siege of Boston

WALKER'S REGIMENT

Authorized 23 April 1775 in the Massachusetts State Troops as Walker's Regiment. Organized in spring 1775 at Roxbury to consist of ten companies from northern Bristol County. Adopted 14 June 1775 into the Continental Army and assigned to the Main Army. Assigned 22 July 1775 to Spencer's Brigade, an element of the Main Army. Consolidated 1 January 1776 with Read's Regiment and consolidated unit redesignated as the 13th Continental Regiment [see 13th Continental Regiment].

ENGAGEMENTS
    Siege of Boston

WHITCOMB'S REGIMENT

Authorized 23 April 1775 in the Massachusetts State Troops as Whitcomb's Regiment. Organized in spring 1775 at Cambridge to consist of eleven companies from northeastern Worcester County and Hampshire and Middlesex Counties. Adopted 14 June 1775 into the Continental Army and assigned to the Main Army. Assigned 22 July 1775 to Greene's Brigade, an element of the Main Army. Disbanded 31 December 1775 at Cambridge.

ENGAGEMENTS
    Siege of Boston

WOODBRIDGE'S REGIMENT*

Authorized 23 April 1775 in the Massachusetts State Troops as Woodbridge's Regiment. Organized in spring 1775 at Cambridge to consist of ten companies from northern Hampshire and Berkshire Counties and Worcester, Essex, and Bristol Counties. Adopted 14 June 1775 into the Continental Army and assigned to the Main Army. Assigned 22 July 1775 to the Vacant Brigade, an element of the Main Army. Disbanded 31 December 1775 at Cambridge.

ENGAGEMENTS
Siege of Boston

*This regiment is perpetuated by the 104th Infantry, Massachusetts Army National Guard.

Bibliography

Bates, Samual A. *Soldiers Who Served in the Revolution From the Town of Braintree.* South Braintree: Frank A. Bates, 1898.
Baxter, James Phinney, ed. *Documentary History of the State of Maine.* 20 vols. Portland: Lefavor-Tower Co., 1910–14. [*Maine Historical Society Collections,* 2d ser.]
Billias, George Athan. *General John Glover and His Marblehead Mariners.* New York: Holt, Rinehart & Winston, 1960.
Brooks, John. "A Revolutionary Letter of John Brooks." Edited by Barbara Adams Blundell. *Essex Institute Historical Collections* 112 (1976):140–148.
Clap, Caleb. "Diary of Ensign Caleb Clap, of Colonel Baldwin's Regiment, Massachusetts Line, Continental Army, March 29 Until October 23, 1776." *Historical Magazine,* 3d ser., 3 (1874–75):133–38, 247–51.
[Crafts, Benjamin.] "Crafts Journal of the Siege of Boston." Edited by Samuel P. Fowler. *Essex Institute Historical Collections* 3 (1861):51–57, 133–40, 167–74, 219–20.
Cutler, Manasseh. *Life, Journals and Correspondence.* 2 vols. Cincinnati: Robert Clarke & Co., 1888
Dodge, Abraham. "Orderly Book Kept by Capt. Abraham Dodge of Ipswich, January 1, 1776 to August 1, 1776." *Essex Institute Historical Collections* 80 (1944): 37–53, 111–30, 208–28, 368–84; 81 (1945):87–94, 152–75.
Farnsworth, Amos. *Diary Kept by Lieut Amos Farnsworth of Groton, Mass., During a Part of the Revolutionary War, April, 1775—May, 1779.* Cambridge, Mass.: John Wilson, 1898.
Fellows, George E., et al. *Maine at Valley Forge; Proceedings at the Unveiling of the Maine Marker October 17, 1907; Also Roll of Maine Men at Valley Forge.* 2d ed. Augusta: Burleigh & Flynt, 1910.
Fisher, Elijah. *Journal While in the War for Independence.* Augusta: Badger & Manley, 1880.
Gardiner, F. A. *Glover's Marblehead Regiment in the War of the Revolution.* Salem: Salem Press Co., n.d.
Glover, John. "General John Glover's Letterbook." Edited by Russell W. Knight. *Essex Institute Historical Collections* 112 (1976):1–55.
Goold, Nathan. *Colonel James Scamman's 30th Regiment of Foot 1775; Also Captain Johnson Moulton's Company.* Portland, Me.: Thurston Print, 1900.

_____. *History of Colonel Edmund Phinney's Eighteenth Continental Regiment Twelve Months' Service in 1776 With Complete Muster Rolls of the Companies.* Portland, Me.: Thurston Print, 1898.

_____. *History of Colonel Edmund Phinney's 31st Regiment of Foot Eight Months's [sic] Service Men.* Portland, Me.: Thurston Print, 1896.

Gross, Robert A. *The Minutemen and Their World.* New York: Hill & Wang, 1976.

Henshaw, William. *The Orderly Book of Colonel William Henshaw, of the American Army, April 20—September 26, 1775.* Boston: A. Williams, 1881. [Originally printed in *Proceedings of the Massachusetts Historical Society* 15 (1876):75-160.]

_____. *The Orderly Books of Col. William Henshaw, October 1, 1775, Through October 3, 1776, Reprinted From the Proceedings for April, 1947.* Worcester: American Antiquarian Society, 1948.

How, David. *Diary of David How, a Private in Colonel Paul Dudley Sargent's Regiment of the Massachusetts Line in the Army of the American Revolution.* Edited by Henry B. Dawson. Morrisania, N. Y.: Privately printed, 1865.

Ingalls, Phineas. "Revolutionary War Journal, Kept by Phineas Ingalls of Andover, Mass., April 19, 1775—December 8, 1776." Edited by M. V. B. Perley. *Essex Institute Historical Collections* 53 (1917):81-92.

Lincoln, Rufus. *The Papers of Captain Rufus Lincoln of Wareham, Mass.* Edited by James Minor Lincoln. n.p.: Privately printed, 1904.

Lincoln, William, ed. *The Journals of Each Provincial Congress of Massachusetts in 1774 and 1775, and of the Committee of Safety.* Boston: Dutton & Wentworth, 1838.

Lovell, Albert A. *Worcester in the War of the Revolution: Embracing the Acts of the Town From 1765 to 1783 Inclusive.* Worcester: Tyler & Seagrove, 1876.

Massachusetts, First Corps of Cadets. *The One Hundred and Fiftieth Anniversary of the Foundation of the First Corps of Cadets, Massachusetts Volunteer Militia.* Boston: N. Sawyer & Son, 1892.

Massachusetts, Secretary of the Commonwealth. *Massachusetts Soldiers and Sailors of the Revolutionary War; a Compilation From the Archives.* 17 vols. Boston: Wright & Potter, 1896.

Norwood, William Frederick. "Deborah Sampson, Alias Robert Shirtliff, Fighting Female of the Continental Line." *Bulletin of the History of Medicine* 31 (1957): 147-61.

Nourse, Henry S. *The Military Annals of Lancaster Massachusetts. 1740-1865. Including Lists of Soldiers Serving in the Colonial and Revolutionary Wars for the Lancastrian Towns: Berlin, Bolton, Harvard, Leominster and Sterling.* Lancaster: W. J. Coulter, 1889.

Page, Samuel. "Journal of Capt. Samuel Page, in the Campaign of 1779, With Notes." Edited by Samuel P. Fowler. *Essex Institute Historical Collections* 4 (1862):241-49; 5 (1863):1-9.

Porter, Elisha. "The Diary of Colonel Elisha Porter of Hadley, Massachusetts. Touching His March to the Relief of the Continental Forces Before Quebec, 1776." Edited by Appleton Morgan. *Magazine of American History* 30 (1893): 185-206.

Putnam, Enoch. "Orderly Book of Capt. Enoch Putnam of Danvers, 1776." *Essex Institute Historical Collections* 67 (1931):49-64, 119-36.

Reade, Philip. "Massachusetts at Valley Forge." *Magazine of History* 20 (1915):14–18, 126–33, 265–76.

_____, ed. *Dedication Exercises at the Massachusetts Military Monument Valley Forge, Pa., Erected by the Commonwealth of Massachusetts Saturday, 18 November 1911 in Grateful Memory of the Officers and Men From Massachusetts Who Served There Between 19th Dec., 1777, and 19th June, 1778 Also List of Officers in Massachusetts Organizations in the Revolutionary War and List of Officers in Massachusetts Organizations Who Served at Valley Forge.* Boston: Wright & Potter Printing Co., 1912.

Sanderson, Howard Kendall. *Lynn in the Revolution.* 2 vols. Boston: W. B. Clarke Co., 1909.

Sewall, Henry. "Diary of Captain Henry Sewall, of the Army of the Revolution, 1776–1783." *Historical Magazine,* 2d ser., 10 (1871):128–37. [Reprinted in *Bulletin of the Fort Ticonderoga Museum* 11 (1963):75–92.]

_____. "Capt. Henry Sewall." Edited by S. L. Boardman. *Historical Magazine,* 2d ser., 2 (1867):6–8.

Sherman, Sylvia J., ed. *Dubros Times: Selected Depositions of Maine Revolutionary War Veterans.* Augusta: Maine State Archives, 1975.

Shute, Daniel. "The Journal of Dr. Daniel Shute, Surgeon in the Revolution, 1781–1782." Edited by Mrs. Elno A. Carter. *New England Historical and Genealogical Register* 84 (1930):383–89.

Slocum, Joshua. *An Authentic Narrative of the Life of Joshua Slocum: Containing a Succinct Account of His Revolutionary Services.* Edited by John Slocum. Hartford: Privately printed, 1844.

Smith, Jonathan. "Two William Scotts of Peterborough, N. H." *Proceedings of the Massachusetts Historical Society* 44 (1911):495–502.

Tomlinson, Abraham, comp. *The Military Journals of Two Private Soldiers, 1758–1775. . . .* Poughkeepsie: Abraham Tomlinson, 1855.

Vose, Joseph. *Journal of Lieutenant-Colonel Joseph Vose April—July 1776.* Edited by Henry Winchester Cunningham. Cambridge, Mass.: John Wilson & Son, 1905.

Wade, F. H., ed. "Ipswich Minute Men." *Essex Institute Historical Collections* 14 (1877):237–40.

Watertown, Massachusetts. *Watertown's Military History. Authorized by a Vote of the Inhabitants of the Town of Watertown, Massachusetts.* Boston: David Clapp & Son, 1907.

Rhode Island

1st RHODE ISLAND REGIMENT

Authorized 6 May 1775 in the Rhode Island Army of Observation as Varnum's Regiment. Organized 8 May 1775 to consist of eight companies from Kings and Kent Counties. Adopted 14 June 1775 into the Continental Army. Reorganized 28 June 1775 to consist of ten companies. Assigned 22 July 1775 to Greene's Brigade, an element of the Main Army.

Reorganized and redesignated 1 January 1776 as the 9th Continental Regiment, to consist of eight companies. (Greene's Brigade redesignated 12 August 1776 as Nixon's Brigade; on 22 December 1776 as Hitchcock's Brigade.)

Reorganized and redesignated 1 January 1777 as the 1st Rhode Island Regiment. Relieved 13 January 1777 from Hitchcock's Brigade. Assigned 12 March 1777 to the Highlands Department. Assigned 10 July 1777 to the Rhode Island Brigade, an element of the Highlands Department. (Rhode Island Brigade relieved 14 September 1777 from the Highlands Department and assigned to the Main Army.)

Relieved 2 January 1778 from the Rhode Island Brigade and assigned to the Eastern Department. Reorganized in spring 1778 at Providence with Negro enlisted personnel.

Consolidated 1 January 1781 with the 2d Rhode Island Regiment [see 2d Rhode Island Regiment] and consolidated unit redesignated as the Rhode Island Regiment; concurrently, relieved from the Eastern Department and assigned to the New Hampshire Brigade, an element of the Main Army. Relieved 18 June 1781 from the New Hampshire Brigade and assigned to the 2d Connecticut Brigade, an element of the Main Army. Relieved 28 August 1781 from the 2d Connecticut Brigade and assigned to Hazen's Brigade, an element of the Main Army. Relieved 24 September 1781 from Hazen's Brigade and assigned to the New Jersey Brigade, an element of the Main Army.

Relieved 22 December 1781 from the New Jersey Brigade and assigned to the Middle Department. Relieved 15 May 1782 from the Middle Department and assigned to the Main Army. Assigned 29 August 1782 to the 2d Connecticut Brigade, an element of the Main Army. Relieved 28 October 1782 from the 2d Connecticut Brigade and assigned to the Northern Department.

Reorganized and redesignated 1 March 1783 as the Rhode Island Battalion, to consist of six companies. Reorganized 16 June 1783 to consist of two companies. Disbanded 25 December 1783 at Saratoga, New York.

ENGAGEMENTS
   Siege of Boston
   New York City
   Trenton-Princeton
   Defense of Philadelphia
   Rhode Island

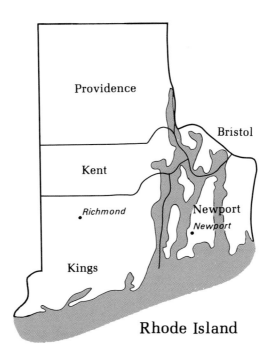

Providence

Bristol

Kent

Richmond

Newport

Newport

Kings

Rhode Island

ENGAGEMENTS—Continued
New York 1781
Yorktown

2d RHODE ISLAND REGIMENT

Authorized 6 May 1775 in the Rhode Island Army of Observation as Hitchcock's Regiment. Organized 8 May 1775 to consist of eight companies from Providence County. Adopted 14 June 1775 into the Continental Army. Reorganized 28 June 1775 to consist of ten companies. Assigned 22 July 1775 to Greene's Brigade, an element of the Main Army.

Reorganized and redesignated 1 January 1776 as the 11th Continental Regiment, to consist of eight companies. (Greene's Brigade redesignated 12 August 1776 as Nixon's Brigade; on 22 December 1776 as Hitchcock's Brigade.)

Reorganized and redesignated 1 January 1777 as the 2d Rhode Island Regiment. Relieved 13 January 1777 from Hitchcock's Brigade. Assigned 12 March 1777 to the Highlands Department. Assigned 10 July 1777 to the Rhode Island Brigade, an element of the Highlands Department. (Rhode Island Brigade relieved 14 September 1777 from the Highlands Department and assigned to the Main Army.)

Relieved 19 July 1778 from the Rhode Island Brigade and assigned to the 1st Massachusetts Brigade, an element of the Main Army. Relieved 21 July 1778 from the 1st Massachusetts Brigade and assigned to the Rhode Island Brigade, an element of the Eastern Department.

Reorganized 1 June 1779 to consist of nine companies. Relieved 17 November 1779 from the Rhode Island Brigade and assigned to Stark's Brigade, an element of the Main Army.

Consolidated 1 January 1781 with the 1st Rhode Island Regiment and consolidated unit redesignated as the Rhode Island Regiment [see 1st Rhode Island Regiment].

ENGAGEMENTS
Siege of Boston
New York City
Trenton-Princeton
Defense of Philadelphia
Philadelphia-Monmouth
Rhode Island
New Jersey 1780

CHURCH'S REGIMENT

Authorized 6 May 1775 in the Rhode Island Army of Observation as Church's Regiment. Organized 8 May 1775 to consist of seven companies from Newport and Bristol Counties. Adopted 14 June 1775 into the Continental Army. Reorganized 28 June 1775 to consist of ten companies. Assigned 22 July 1775 to Greene's Brigade, an element of the Main Army. Disbanded 31 December 1775 at Roxbury, Massachusetts.

ENGAGEMENTS
   Siege of Boston

RICHMOND'S REGIMENT

Authorized 31 October 1775 in the Rhode Island State Troops as Richmond's Regiment. Organized in November 1775 to consist of eight companies. Reorganized 8 January 1776 to consist of twelve companies. Adopted in November 1775 into the Continental Army and assigned to the Eastern Department. Disbanded 21 November 1776 at Providence.

ENGAGEMENTS
   None

LIPPITT'S REGIMENT

Authorized 8 January 1776 in the Rhode Island State Troops as Babcock's Regiment. Organized 18 January 1776 at Newport to consist of twelve companies. Redesignated 1 May 1776 as Lippitt's Regiment.

Adopted 11 May 1776 into the Continental Army and assigned to the Eastern Department. Relieved 14 September 1776 from the Eastern Department and assigned to the Main Army. Assigned 14 October 1776 to McDougall's Brigade, an element of the Main Army. Relieved 10 November 1776 from McDougall's Brigade and assigned to Nixon's Brigade (redesignated 22 December 1776 as Hitchcock's Brigade), an element of the Main Army. Disbanded 18 January 1777 at Morristown, New Jersey.

ENGAGEMENTS
   New York City
   Trenton-Princeton

Bibliography

Angell, Israel. *Diary of Colonel Israel Angell Commanding the Second Rhode Island Continental Regiment During the American Revolution 1778-1781.* Edited by Edward Field. Providence: Preston and Rounds, 1899.

Bartlett, John Russell, ed. *Records of the Colony of Rhode Island and Providence Plantations in New England.* 9 vols. Providence: Various publishers, 1856-65.

Brown, Anne S. K. "Rhode Island Uniforms in the Revolution." *Military Collector and Historian* 10 (1958):1-10.

Cohen, Joel A. "Lexington and Concord: Rhode Island Reacts." *Rhode Island History* 26 (1967):97-102.

Cowell, Benjamin. *Spirit of '76 in Rhode Island: or Sketches of the Efforts of the Government and People in the War of the Revolution.* Boston: A. J. Wright, 1850.

David, Ebenezer. *A Rhode Island Chaplain in the Revolution: Letters of Ebenezer David to Nicholas Brown 1775-1778.* Edited by Jeannette D. Black and William Greene Roelker. Providence: Rhode Island Society of the Cincinnati, 1949.

Field, Edward. *Revolutionary Defences in Rhode Island; an Historical Account of the Fortifications and Beacons Erected During the American Revolution, With Muster Rolls of the Companies Stationed Along the Shores of Narragansett Bay.* Providence: Preston and Rounds, 1896.

Gardner, Asa B. *The Rhode Island Line in the Continental Army and Its Society of Cincinnati.* Providence: Providence Press Co., 1878.

Greene, Christopher. "Orderly Book October 11, 1777, to November 20, 1777." *New Jersey Society of Pennsylvania Yearbook*:1928.

Greene, Lorenzo J. "Some Observations on the Black Regiment of Rhode Island in the American Revolution." *Journal of Negro History* 37 (1952):142-72.

Greenman, Jeremiah. *Diary of a Common Soldier in the American Revolution, 1775-1783; An Annotated Edition of the Military Journal of Jeremiah Greenman.* Edited by Robert C. Bray and Paul E. Bushnell. DeKalb: Northern Illinois University Press, 1978.

Hitchcock, Dan. "So Few the Brave (The Second Rhode Island 1777-1781)." *Military Collector and Historian* 30 (1978):18-22.

Lovell, Louise Lewis. *Israel Angell, Colonel of the 2nd Rhode Island Regiment.* [New York]: Knickerbocker Press, 1921.

Rider, Sidney S. *Historical Inquiry Concerning the Attempt To Raise a Regiment of Slaves by Rhode Island During the War of the Revolution.* Providence: S. S. Rider, 1880.

Smith, John. "Sergeant John Smith's Diary of 1776." Edited by Louise Rau. *Mississippi Valley Historical Review* 20 (1933):247-70.

Tuckerman, Henry T. *The Life of Silas Talbot, a Commodore in the Navy of the United States.* New York: J. C. Riker, 1850.

Williams, Catherine R. *Biography of Revolutionary Heroes; Containing the Life of Brigadier Gen. William Barton, and Also, of Captain Stephen Olney.* New York: Wiley & Putnam, 1839.

Litchfield

Hartford

Windham

Hartford

Wethersfield

Windham

New
Milford

Lebanon

Connecticut R.

Norwich

New Haven

New London

Danbury

New
London

New
Haven

Fairfield

Connecticut

Connecticut

1st CONNECTICUT REGIMENT

Authorized 16 September 1776 in the Continental Army as the 1st Connecticut Regiment. Organized 1 January–April 1777 at Norwich to consist of eight companies from New London, Windham, and Hartford Counties. Assigned 3 April 1777 to the 2d Connecticut Brigade, an element of the Highlands Department.

Relieved 12 June 1777 from the 2d Connecticut Brigade and assigned to the 1st Connecticut Brigade, an element of the Highlands Department. (1st Connecticut Brigade relieved 15 June 1777 from the Highlands Department and assigned to the Main Army; relieved 2 July 1777 from the Main Army and assigned to the Highlands Department.) Relieved 12 September 1777 from the 1st Connecticut Brigade and assigned to the 2d Connecticut Brigade, an element of the Highlands Department. (2d Connecticut Brigade relieved 14 September 1777 from the Highlands Department and assigned to the Main Army; relieved 1 May 1779 from the Main Army and assigned to the Highlands Department.)

Reorganized 11 July 1779 to consist of nine companies. (2d Connecticut Brigade relieved 16 November 1779 from the Highlands Department and assigned to the Main Army; relieved 27 November 1780 from the Main Army and assigned to the Highlands Department.)

Consolidated 1 January 1781 with the 8th Connecticut Regiment [see 8th Connecticut Regiment] and consolidated unit reorganized and redesignated as the 5th Connecticut Regiment, to consist of nine companies; concurrently, relieved from the 2d Connecticut Brigade and assigned to the 1st Connecticut Brigade, an element of the Highlands Department. Disbanded 1 January 1783 at West Point, New York.

ENGAGEMENTS
New York 1777
Philadelphia-Monmouth
New York 1781

2d CONNECTICUT REGIMENT

Authorized 16 September 1776 in the Continental Army as the 2d Connecticut Regiment. Organized 1 January–April 1777 at Danbury to consist of eight companies from Fairfield, Hartford, and Windham Counties. Assigned 3 April 1777 to the 1st Connecticut Brigade, an element of the Highlands Department.

Relieved 12 June 1777 from the 1st Connecticut Brigade and assigned to McDougall's Brigade, an element of the Highlands Department. Relieved 15 June 1777 from McDougall's Brigade and assigned to the 2d Connecticut Brigade, an element of the Highlands Department. Relieved 10 July 1777 from the 2d Connecticut Brigade and assigned to the 1st Connecticut Brigade, an element of the Highlands Department. Relieved 13 November 1777 from the 1st Connecticut Brigade and assigned to the Main Army (later assigned to the 2d Connecticut Brigade, an element of the Main Army). (2d Connecticut Brigade relieved 1 May 1779 from the Main Army and assigned to the Highlands Department.)

Reorganized 11 July 1779 to consist of nine companies. (2d Connecticut Brigade relieved 16 November 1779 from the Highlands Department and assigned to the Main Army; relieved 27 November 1780 from the Main Army and assigned to the Highlands Department.)

Consolidated 1 January 1781 with the 9th Connecticut Regiment [see S. B. Webb's Additional Continental Regiment] and consolidated unit reorganized and re-designated as the 3d Connecticut Regiment, an element of the 1st Connecticut Brigade, to consist of nine companies. Relieved 1 January 1783 from the 1st Connecticut Brigade and assigned to the Connecticut Brigade, an element of the Highlands Department. Furloughed 15 June 1783 at West Point, New York. Disbanded 15 November 1783.

ENGAGEMENTS
  Connecticut 1777
  New York 1777
  Hudson Highlands
  Defense of Philadelphia
  Philadelphia-Monmouth
  New York 1781

3d CONNECTICUT REGIMENT

Authorized 16 September 1776 in the Continental Army as the 3d Connecticut Regiment. Organized 1 January–April 1777 at Hartford to consist of eight companies from Hartford and Windham Counties. Assigned 3 April 1777 to the 1st Connecticut Brigade, an element of the Highlands Department. (1st Connecticut Brigade relieved 15 June 1777 from the Highlands Department and assigned to the Main Army; relieved 2 July 1777 from the Main Army and assigned to the Highlands Department; relieved 21 July 1778 from the Highlands Department and assigned to the Main Army; relieved 28 May 1779 from the Main Army and assigned to the Highlands Department.)

Reorganized 11 July 1779 to consist of nine companies. (1st Connecticut Brigade relieved 16 November 1779 from the Highlands Department and assigned to the Main Army; relieved 27 November 1780 from the Main Army and assigned to the Highlands Department.)

Consolidated 1 January 1781 with the 4th Connecticut Regiment [see 4th Connecticut Regiment] and consolidated unit reorganized and redesignated as the 1st Connecticut Regiment, an element of the 1st Connecticut Brigade, to consist of nine companies. Relieved 1 January 1783 from the 1st Connecticut Brigade and assigned to the Connecticut Brigade, an element of the Highlands Department. Reorganized and redesignated 15 June 1783 as the Connecticut Regiment, to consist of nine companies;

concurrently, relieved from the Highlands Department and assigned to the Main Army. Disbanded 15 November 1783 at West Point, New York.

ENGAGEMENTS
New York 1777
Hudson Highlands
New York 1781

4th CONNECTICUT REGIMENT

Authorized 16 September 1776 in the Continental Army as the 4th Connecticut Regiment. Organized 1 January–April 1777 at Norwich to consist of eight companies from New London, Windham, and Hartford Counties. Assigned 3 April 1777 to the 1st Connecticut Brigade, an element of the Highlands Department.

Relieved 12 June 1777 from the 1st Connecticut Brigade and assigned to the 2d Connecticut Brigade, an element of the Highlands Department. Relieved 15 June 1777 from the 2d Connecticut Brigade and assigned to McDougall's Brigade, an element of the Highlands Department. (McDougall's Brigade relieved 14 September 1777 from the Highlands Department and assigned to the Main Army.) Relieved 16 October 1777 from McDougall's Brigade and assigned to the Rhode Island Brigade, an element of the Main Army.

Relieved 21 July 1778 from the Rhode Island Brigade and assigned to the 1st Connecticut Brigade, an element of the Main Army. (1st Connecticut Brigade relieved 28 May 1779 from the Main Army and assigned to the Highlands Department.) Reorganized 11 July 1779 to consist of nine companies. (1st Connecticut Brigade relieved 16 November 1779 from the Highlands Department and assigned to the Main Army; relieved 27 November 1780 from the Main Army and assigned to the Highlands Department.)

Consolidated 1 January 1781 with the 3d Connecticut Regiment [see 3d Connecticut Regiment].

ENGAGEMENTS
Defense of Philadelphia
Philadelphia-Monmouth

5th CONNECTICUT REGIMENT

Authorized 16 September 1776 in the Continental Army as the 5th Connecticut Regiment. Organized 1 January–April 1777 at Danbury to consist of eight companies from Fairfield, Hartford, and Litchfield Counties. Assigned 3 April 1777 to the 2d Connecticut Brigade, an element of the Highlands Department.

Relieved 12 June 1777 from the 2d Connecticut Brigade and assigned to the 1st Connecticut Brigade, an element of the Highlands Department. (1st Connecticut Brigade relieved 15 June 1777 from the Highlands Department and assigned to the Main Army; relieved 2 July 1777 from the Main Army and assigned to the Highlands Department.) Relieved 10 July 1777 from the 1st Connecticut Brigade and assigned to the 2d Connecticut Brigade, an element of the Highlands Department. Relieved 12 September 1777 from the 2d Connecticut Brigade and assigned to McDougall's Brigade, an element of the Highlands Department. (McDougall's Brigade relieved 14 September 1777 from the Highlands Department and assigned to the Main Army.) Relieved 16 October 1777 from McDougall's Brigade and assigned to the 2d Connecticut Brigade, an element of the Main Army. (2d Connecticut Brigade relieved 1 May 1779 from the Main Army and assigned to the Highlands Department.)

Reorganized 11 July 1779 to consist of nine companies. (2d Connecticut Brigade relieved 16 November 1779 from the Highlands Department and assigned to the Main Army; relieved 27 November 1780 from the Main Army and assigned to the Highlands Department.)

Consolidated 1 January 1781 with the 7th Connecticut Regiment [see 7th Connecticut Regiment] and consolidated unit reorganized and redesignated as the 2d Connecticut Regiment, an element of the 2d Connecticut Brigade, to consist of nine companies. Relieved 1 January 1783 from the 2d Connecticut Brigade and assigned to the Connecticut Brigade, an element of the Highlands Department. Furloughed 15 June 1783 at West Point, New York. Disbanded 15 November 1783.

ENGAGEMENTS
 Connecticut 1777
 Defense of Philadelphia
 Philadelphia-Monmouth
 New York 1781

6th CONNECTICUT REGIMENT

Authorized 16 September 1776 in the Continental Army as the 6th Connecticut Regiment. Organized 1 January–April 1777 at New Haven to consist of eight companies from New Haven and New London Counties. Assigned 3 April 1777 to the 1st Connecticut Brigade, an element of the Highlands Department. (1st Connecticut Brigade relieved 15 June 1777 from the Highlands Department and assigned to the Main Army; relieved 2 July 1777 from the Main Army and assigned to the Highlands Department; relieved 21 July 1778 from the Highlands Department and assigned to the Main Army; relieved 28 May 1779 from the Main Army and assigned to the Highlands Department.)

Reorganized 11 July 1779 to consist of nine companies. (1st Connecticut Brigade relieved 16 November 1779 from the Highlands Department and assigned to the Main Army.) Relieved 25 September 1780 from the 1st Connecticut Brigade and assigned to the Highlands Department. Assigned 6 October 1780 to the 1st Connecticut Brigade, an element of the Main Army. (1st Connecticut Brigade relieved 27 November 1780 from the Main Army and assigned to the Highlands Department.)

Reorganized and redesignated 1 January 1781 as the 4th Connecticut Regiment, to consist of nine companies; concurrently, relieved from the 1st Connecticut Brigade and assigned to the 2d Connecticut Brigade, an element of the Highlands Department. Disbanded 1 January 1783 at West Point, New York.

7th CONNECTICUT REGIMENT

Authorized 16 September 1776 in the Continental Army as the 7th Connecticut Regiment. Organized 1 January–April 1777 at New Milford to consist of eight companies from Litchfield, Fairfield, New Haven, and New London Counties. Assigned 3 April 1777 to the 2d Connecticut Brigade, an element of the Highlands Department.

Relieved 15 June 1777 from the 2d Connecticut Brigade and assigned to the 1st Massachusetts Brigade, an element of the Highlands Department. Relieved 10 July 1777 from the 1st Massachusetts Brigade and assigned to the 2d Connecticut Brigade. (2d Connecticut Brigade relieved 14 September 1777 from the Highlands Department and assigned to the Main Army; relieved 1 May 1779 from the Main Army and assigned to the Highlands Department.)

Reorganized 11 July 1779 to consist of nine companies. (2d Connecticut Brigade relieved 16 November 1779 from the Highlands Department and assigned to the Main Army; relieved 27 November 1780 from the Main Army and assigned to the Highlands Department.)

Consolidated 1 January 1781 with the 5th Connecticut Regiment [see 5th Connecticut Regiment].

ENGAGEMENTS
Defense of Philadelphia
Philadelphia-Monmouth

8th CONNECTICUT REGIMENT

Authorized 16 September 1776 in the Continental Army as the 8th Connecticut Regiment. Organized 1 January–April 1777 at Danbury to consist of eight companies from Fairfield, Litchfield, Hartford, New Haven, and New London Counties. Assigned 3 April 1777 to the 2d Connecticut Brigade, an element of the Highlands Department.

Relieved 15 June 1777 from the 2d Connecticut Brigade and assigned to McDougall's Brigade, an element of the Highlands Department. (McDougall's Brigade relieved 14 September 1777 from the Highlands Department and assigned to the Main Army.) Relieved 16 October 1777 from McDougall's Brigade and assigned to the Rhode Island Brigade, an element of the Main Army.

Relieved 21 July 1778 from the Rhode Island Brigade and assigned to the 1st Connecticut Brigade, an element of the Main Army. (1st Connecticut Brigade relieved 28 May 1779 from the Main Army and assigned to the Highlands Department.) Reorganized 11 July 1779 to consist of nine companies. (1st Connecticut Brigade relieved 16 November 1779 from the Highlands Department and assigned to the Main Army;

relieved 27 November 1780 from the Main Army and assigned to the Highlands Department.)

Consolidated 1 January 1781 with the 1st Connecticut Regiment [see 1st Connecticut Regiment].

ENGAGEMENTS
Long Island Sound 1777
Defense of Philadelphia
Philadelphia-Monmouth

S. B. WEBB'S ADDITIONAL CONTINENTAL REGIMENT
(Decoy Regiment)
(9th Connecticut Regiment)

Authorized 11 January 1777 in the Continental Army as S. B. Webb's Additional Continental Regiment. Organized in spring 1777 at Wethersfield, Connecticut, to consist of eight companies from Hartford, New Haven, and New London Counties. Assigned 14 April 1777 to the Highlands Department. Assigned 12 June 1777 to McDougall's Brigade, an element of the Highlands Department. Relieved 10 July 1777 from McDougall's Brigade and assigned to the Rhode Island Brigade, an element of the Highlands Department. Relieved 12 September 1777 from the Rhode Island Brigade and assigned to the 1st Connecticut Brigade, an element of the Highlands Department.

Relieved 22 July 1778 from the 1st Connecticut Brigade and assigned to the Rhode Island Brigade, an element of the Eastern Department. Relieved 17 November 1779 from the Eastern Department and assigned to Stark's Brigade, an element of the Main Army.

Reorganized 9 April 1780 to consist of nine companies. Adopted 24 July 1780 by Connecticut and redesignated as the 9th Connecticut Regiment. (Stark's Brigade relieved 7 October 1780 from the Main Army and assigned to the Highlands Department.)

Consolidated 1 January 1781 with the 2d Connecticut Regiment [see 2d Connecticut Regiment].

ENGAGEMENTS
Connecticut 1777
Hudson Highlands
Rhode Island
New Jersey 1780

10th CONTINENTAL REGIMENT

Authorized 27 April 1775 in the Connecticut State Troops as the 6th Connecticut Regiment. Organized 1–20 May 1775 to consist of ten companies from New London and Windham Counties. Adopted 14 June 1777 into the Continental Army as an element of the Main Army (less one company assigned to the New York [subsequently Northern] Department). Assigned 22 July 1775 to Spencer's Brigade, an element of the Main Army.

Reorganized and redesignated 1 January 1776 (less one company disbanded 10 February 1776 in Canada) as the 10th Continental Regiment, to consist of eight companies. (Spencer's Brigade redesignated 12 August 1776 as Parsons' Brigade; Parsons' Brigade relieved 12 November 1776 from assignment to the Main Army and assigned to the Highlands Department.) Disbanded 31 December 1776 at Peekskill, New York.

ENGAGEMENTS
  Siege of Boston
  New York City
Captain Edward Mott's Company served in the following:
  Invasion of Canada
  Defense of Canada

17th CONTINENTAL REGIMENT

Authorized 1 July 1775 in the Connecticut State Troops as the 8th Connecticut Regiment. Organized 6 July 1775 to consist of ten companies from Hartford, Windham, and New London Counties. Adopted 19 July 1775 into the Continental Army and assigned to the Main Army. Assigned 9 August 1775 to Spencer's Brigade, an element of the Main Army.

Reorganized and redesignated 1 January 1776 as the 17th Continental Regiment, to consist of eight companies. (Spencer's Brigade redesignated 12 August 1776 as Parsons' Brigade; Parsons' Brigade relieved 12 November 1776 from the Main Army and assigned to the Highlands Department.) Disbanded 31 December 1776 at Peekskill, New York.

ENGAGEMENTS
  Siege of Boston
  New York City

19th CONTINENTAL REGIMENT

Authorized 1 July 1775 in the Connecticut State Troops as the 7th Connecticut Regiment. Organized 6 July 1775 to consist of ten companies from New Haven, Fairfield, New London, and Litchfield Counties. Adopted 19 July into the Continental Army and assigned to the Main Army. Assigned 9 August 1775 to Sullivan's Brigade, an element of the Main Army.

Reorganized and redesignated 1 January 1776 as the 19th Continental Regiment, to consist of eight companies. Relieved 24 January 1776 from Sullivan's Brigade and assigned to Spencer's Brigade, an element of the Main Army. Relieved 24 April 1776 from Spencer's Brigade and assigned to Sullivan's Brigade. Relieved 29 April 1776 from Sullivan's Brigade and assigned to Stirling's Brigade, an element of the Main Army. Relieved 12 August 1776 from Stirling's Brigade and assigned to McDougall's Brigade, an element of the Main Army. Relieved 5 November 1776 from McDougall's Brigade and assigned to Glover's Brigade, an element of the Main Army. Disbanded 15 February 1777 at Morristown, New Jersey.

ENGAGEMENTS
   Siege of Boston
   New York City
   Trenton-Princeton

20th CONTINENTAL REGIMENT

Authorized 27 April 1775 in the Connecticut State Troops as the 3d Connecticut Regiment. Organized 1–20 May 1775 to consist of ten companies from Windham and New London Counties. Adopted 14 June 1775 into the Continental Army and assigned to the Main Army. Assigned 22 July 1775 to the Vacant Brigade, an element of the Main Army.

Reorganized and redesignated 1 January 1776 as the 20th Continental Regiment, to consist of eight companies. (Vacant Brigade redesignated 16 February 1776 as Frye's Brigade). Relieved 24 April 1776 from Frye's Brigade and assigned to Spencer's Brigade, an element of the Main Army. (Spencer's Brigade redesignated August 1776 as Parsons' Brigade.) Relieved 12 November 1776 from Parsons' Brigade and assigned to Mercer's Brigade, an element of the Main Army. Disbanded 15 February 1777 at Morristown, New Jersey.

ENGAGEMENTS
   Siege of Boston
   New York City
   Trenton-Princeton

22d CONTINENTAL REGIMENT

Authorized 27 April 1775 in the Connecticut State Troops as the 2d Connecticut Regiment. Organized 1–20 May 1775 to consist of ten companies from Hartford County. Adopted 14 June 1775 into the Continental Army and assigned to the Main Army. Assigned 22 July 1775 to Spencer's Brigade, an element of the Main Army.

Reorganized and redesignated 1 January 1776 as the 22d Continental Regiment, to consist of eight companies. (Spencer's Brigade redesignated 12 August 1776 as Parsons' Brigade; Parsons' Brigade relieved 12 November 1776 from the Main Army and assigned to the Highlands Department.) Disbanded 31 December 1776 at Peekskill, New York.

ENGAGEMENTS
   Siege of Boston
   New York City

1st CONNECTICUT REGIMENT
(1775)

Authorized 27 April 1775 in the Connecticut State Troops as the 1st Connecticut Regiment. Organized 1–20 May 1775 to consist of ten companies from New Haven and Litchfield Counties. Adopted 14 June 1775 into the Continental Army. Assigned 25 June 1775 to the New York (subsequently Northern) Department (less two companies assigned 13 July 1775 to the Main Army). Assigned 8 January 1776 to the Canadian Department. Disbanded 1 December 1775–15 April 1776 in Canada (less two companies disbanded 20 December 1775 at Cambridge, Massachusetts).

ENGAGEMENTS
    Invasion of Canada
    Defense of Canada
Captains Bradford Steel's and Caleb Trowbridge's Companies served at
    Siege of Boston

4th CONNECTICUT REGIMENT
(1775)

Authorized 27 April 1775 in the Connecticut State Troops as the 4th Connecticut Regiment. Organized 1–20 May 1775 to consist of ten companies from Litchfield and Hartford Counties. Adopted 14 June 1775 into the Continental Army. Assigned 25 June 1775 to the New York (subsequently Northern) Department (less two companies assigned to the Main Army). Disbanded in December 1775 in Canada (less two companies disbanded 19–20 December 1775 at Cambridge, Massachusetts).

ENGAGEMENTS
    Invasion of Canada
Lieutenant Colonel Ozias Bissell's and Captain Hezekiah Parsons' Companies served at
    Siege of Boston

5th CONNECTICUT REGIMENT
(1775)

Authorized 27 April 1775 in the Connecticut State Troops as the 5th Connecticut Regiment. Organized 1–20 May 1775 to consist of ten companies from Fairfield County. Adopted 14 June 1775 into the Continental Army. Assigned 25 June 1775 to the New York (subsequently Northern) Department. Disbanded in December 1775 in Canada.

ENGAGEMENTS
    Invasion of Canada

ELMORE'S REGIMENT

Authorized 8 January 1776 in the Continental Army as a regiment to be raised from the troops in service in Canada and assigned to the Canadian Department. Organized 15 April 1776 at Quebec, Canada, as Elmore's Regiment, to consist of eight companies, primarily from Connecticut. Relieved 2 July 1776 from the Canadian Department and assigned to the Northern Department. Disbanded 10 May 1777 at Fort Schuyler, New York.

ENGAGEMENTS
    Defense of Canada

BURRALL'S REGIMENT

Authorized 8 January 1776 in the Continental Army as a regiment to be raised in Connecticut and assigned to the Canadian Department. Organized 18 January 1776 as Burrall's Regiment, to consist of eight companies.

Relieved 2 July 1776 from the Canadian Department and assigned to the Northern Department. Assigned 20 July 1776 to Arnold's Brigade, an element of the Northern Department. (Arnold's Brigade redesignated 26 October 1776 as Poor's Brigade.) Relieved 18 November 1776 from Poor's Brigade. Disbanded 19 January 1777 at Fort Ticonderoga, New York.

ENGAGEMENTS
    Defense of Canada
    Lake Champlain

WARD'S REGIMENT

Authorized 14 May 1776 in the Continental Army as a regiment to be raised in Connecticut and assigned to the Eastern Department. Organized in summer 1776 as Ward's Regiment, to consist of eight companies from Hartford, Windham, and New Haven Counties. Relieved 1 August 1776 from the Eastern Department and assigned to the Main Army. Assigned 18 September 1776 to Sargent's Brigade, an element of the Main Army. Disbanded 14 May 1777 at Morristown, New Jersey.

ENGAGEMENTS
    New York City
    Trenton-Princeton
    Northern New Jersey

WESTMORELAND INDEPENDENT COMPANIES*
(Wyoming Independent Companies)

Authorized 23 August 1776 in the Continental Army as the 1st and 2d Independent Westmoreland Companies. Organized 26 August–21 September 1776 in Westmoreland County, Connecticut, Captains Robert Durkee and Samuel Ransom commanding, and assigned to the Middle Department. Relieved 12 December 1776 from the Middle Department and assigned to the Main Army.

Relieved 15 June 1778 from the Main Army and assigned to the Western Department. Consolidated 23 June 1778 and consolidated unit redesignated as the Wyoming Independent Company, Captain Simon Spaulding commanding.

Disbanded 1 January 1781 at Fort Wyoming, Connecticut.

ENGAGEMENTS
    Northern New Jersey
    Defense of Philadelphia
    Philadelphia-Monmouth
    Iroquois 1778
    Iroquois 1779

*109th Field Artillery, Pennsylvania Army National Guard, perpetuates this unit.

Bibliography

Barber, Daniel. "Rev. D. Barber's Account of His Service in the Army of 1775-6." *Historical Magazine,* 1st ser., 7 (1863):83–88.

Bates, Albert C., ed. "Rolls and Lists of Connecticut Men in the Revolution 1775-1783." *Collections of the Connecticut Historical Society* 8 (1901).

Bill, Ledyard, ed. "Roll of Capt. Nathaniel Webb's Co., in the Fourth Connecticut Regiment—Revolutionary War—Col. John Durkee, Commanding." *New England Historical and Genealogical Register* 22 (1868):281–82.

Bostwick, Elisha. "A Connecticut Soldier Under Washington: Elisha Bostwick's Memoirs of the First Years of the Revolution." Edited by William S. Powell. *William and Mary Quarterly,* 3d ser., 6 (1949):94–107.

Brown, Ralph Adams. "Colonel Experience Storrs, Connecticut Farmer and Patriot." *Connecticut Historical Society Bulletin* 19 (1954):118–21.

Campbell, Maria. *Revolutionary Services and Civil Life of William Hull; Prepared From His Manuscripts, by His Daughter, Mrs. Maria Campbell; Together With the History of the Campaign of 1812, and Surrender of the Post of Detroit, by His Grandson, James Freeman Clarke.* New York: D. Appleton & Co., 1848.

Chittenden, Abraham. *Orderly Book of Lieut. Abraham Chittenden Adj't. 7th Conn. Reg't. August 16, 1776 to September 29, 1776.* Hartford: Privately printed, 1922.

Clark, A. H. *A Complete Roster of Colonel David Waterbury Jr.'s Regiment of Connecticut Volunteers.* New York: Privately printed, 1897.

Collier, Christopher. *Connecticut in the Continental Congress.* Chester: Pequot Press, 1973.

Connecticut Historical Society. "Lists and Returns of Connecticut Men in the Revolution 1775-1783." *Collections of the Connecticut Historical Society* 12 (1909).

_____. "Orderly Books and Journals Kept by Connecticut Men While Taking Part in the American Revolution." *Collections of the Connecticut Historical Society* 7 (1899).

Douglas, William. "Letters Written During the Revolutionary War by Colonel William Douglas to His Wife Covering the Period July 19, 1775, to December 5, 1776." *New-York Historical Society Quarterly Bulletin* 12 (1929):149-54; 13 (1929-30):37-40, 79-82, 118-22, 157-62; 14 (1930):38-42.

Fitch, Jabez. *The New-York Diary of Lieutenant Jabez Fitch of the 17th (Connecticut) Regiment from August 22, 1776 to December 15, 1777.* Edited by W. H. W. Sabine. New York: Privately printed, 1954.

Hall, Charles S. *Life and Letters of Samuel Holden Parsons, Major General in the Continental Army and Chief Judge of the Northwestern Territory 1737-1789.* Binghamton, N.Y.: Otseningo Publishing Co., 1905.

Hinman, Royal Ralph. *A Historical Collection From Official Records, Files &c., of the Part Sustained by Connecticut, During the War of the Revolution With an Appendix, Containing Important Letters, Depositions, &c. Written During the War.* Hartford: E. Gleason, 1842.

Hoadley, Charles J., et al., comps. *The Public Records of the State of Connecticut.* 11 vols. Hartford: Various publishers, 1894-1967.

Huntington, Ebenezer. *Letters Written by Ebenezer Huntington During the American Revolution.* New York: C. F. Heartman, 1914.

Huntington, Joshua, and Huntington, Jedediah. "Huntington Papers: Correspondence of the Brothers Joshua and Jedediah Huntington During the Period of the American Revolution 1771-1783." *Collections of the Connecticut Historical Society* 20 (1923).

Johnston, Henry P. "Return Jonathan Meigs: Colonel of the Connecticut Line of the Continental Army." *Magazine of American History* 4 (1880):282-92.

_____, ed. *Record of Service of Connecticut Men in the War of the Revolution, War of 1812, Mexican War.* Hartford: Case, Lockwood & Brainard Co. for the Adjutant General's Office, 1889.

Lee, Ezra. "Sergeant Lee's Experience With Bushnell's Submarine Torpedo in 1776." Edited by Henry P. Johnston. *Magazine of American History* 29 (1893):262-66.

Martin, Joseph Plumb. *Private Yankee Doodle Being a Narrative of Some of the Adventures, Dangers and Sufferings of a Revolutionary Soldier.* Edited by George F. Scheer. Boston: Little, Brown & Co., 1962.

Norton, Ichabod. *Orderly Book of Capt. Ichabod Norton of Col. Mott's Regiment of Connecticut Troops Destined for the Northern Campaign in 1776.* Edited by Robert O. Bascom. Fort Edward, N. Y.: Keating & Barnard, 1898.

Patterson, D. Williams, ed. "The Troops at Wyoming." *Historical Magazine,* 1st ser., 6 (1862):251-52.

Peters, Nathan. *The Correspondence of Captain Nathan and Lois Peters, April 25, 1775—February 5, 1777.* Edited by William H. Guthman. Hartford: Connecticut Historical Society, 1980.

Richards, Samuel. *Diary of Samuel Richards, Captain of Connecticut Line War of the Revolution 1775-1781.* Philadelphia: Privately printed, 1909.

_____. "Personal Narrative of an Officer in the Revolutionary War." *The United Service*, 3d ser., 4 (1903):235-61, 352-76.

Seymour, George Dudley. *Documentary Life of Nathan Hale Comprising All Available Official and Private Documents Bearing on the Life of the Patriot*. New Haven: Privately printed, 1941.

Squier, Ephraim. "Diary of Ephraim Squier: Sergeant in the Connecticut Line of the Continental Army." Edited by Frank Squier. *Magazine of American History* 2 (1878):685-94.

Stevens, John Austin. "Samuel Blatchley Webb: Colonel in the Connecticut Line and Brevet Brigadier General in the Continental Army." *Magazine of American History* 4 (1880):427-40.

Storrs, Experience. "Connecticut Farmers at Bunker Hill: The Diary of Colonel Experience Storrs." Edited by Wladimir Hagelin and Ralph A. Brown. *New England Quarterly* 28 (1955):72-93.

Trumbull, Benjamin. *A Complete History of Connecticut, Civil and Ecclesiastical From the Emigration of Its First Planters From England in MDCXXX, to MDCCCXIII*. 2 vols. New Haven: Maltby, Goldsmith & Co., 1818.

Trumbull, J. Hammond, ed. *The Memorial History of Hartford County Connecticut 1633-1884*. 2 vols. Boston: Edward L. Osgood, 1886.

_____ and Hoadley, Charles J., comps. *The Public Records of the Colony of Connecticut*. 15 vols. Hartford: Various publishers, 1850-90.

Trumbull, Jonathan. "The Trumbull Papers." *Massachusetts Historical Society Collections*, 5th ser., 9-10; 7th ser., 2-3 (1885-1902).

Tubbs, Charles. *The Wyoming Military Establishments: A History of the Twenty-Fourth Regiment of Connecticut Militia*. Athens, Pa.: Privately printed, 1903.

Waldo, Albigence. "Dr. Albigence Waldo, Surgeon in the Continental Army." Edited by Amos Perry. *Historical Magazine*, 1st ser., 5 (1861):104-7, 169-72. [Reprinted as "Valley Forge, 1777-1778. Diary of Surgeon Albigence Waldo, of the Connecticut Line" in *Pennsylvania Magazine of History and Biography* 21 (1897): 299-323.]

Waterbury, David, Jr. "Extracts From the Original Order Book of Colonel David Waterbury, of Stamford, Connecticut." *Magazine of American History* 12 (1884): 555-57; 15 (1885):410-11.

Webb, Samuel Blachley. *Correspondence and Journals of Samuel Blachley Webb*. Edited by Worthington Chauncey Ford. 3 vols. New York: Privately printed, 1893-94.

White, David O. *Connecticut's Black Soldiers 1775-1783*. Chester: Pequot Press, 1973.

Williams, Elisha. "Elisha Williams' Diary of 1776." Edited by W. Hyde Appleton. *Pennsylvania Magazine of History and Biography* 48 (1924):334-53; 49 (1925): 44-60.

Wyllys, George, et al. "The Wyllys Papers: Correspondence and Documents Chiefly of Descendants of Gov. George Wyllys of Connecticut 1590-1796." Edited by Albert C. Bates. *Collections of the Connecticut Historical Society* 21 (1924).

Zierdt, William H. *Narrative History of the 109th Field Artillery Pennsylvania National Guard 1775-1930*. Wilkes-Barre: Wyoming Historical & Genealogical Society, 1932.

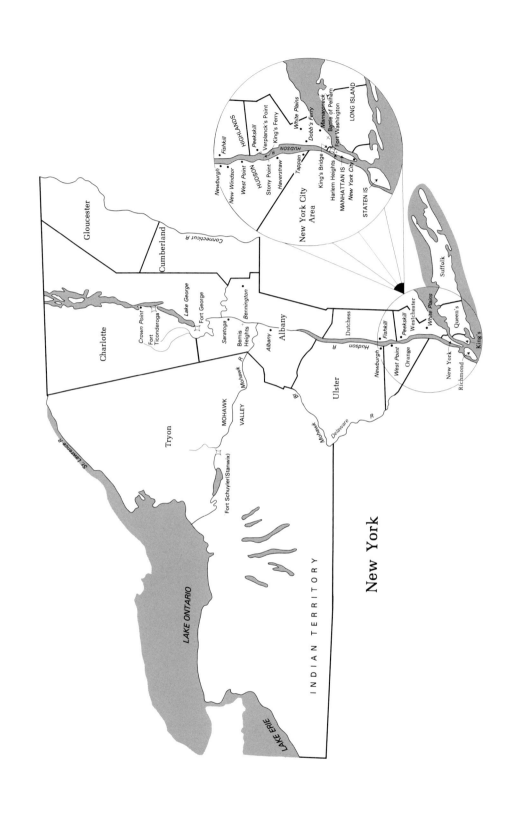

New York

New York City Area

HIGHLANDS
HUDSON

Gloucester
Cumberland
Connecticut R

Charlotte
Lake George
Fort George
Crown Point
Fort Ticonderoga
Bennington
Saratoga
Bemis Heights
Albany
Albany

Tryon
MOHAWK VALLEY
Mohawk R
Fort Schuyler(Stanwix)

Dutchess
Hudson R

Ulster
Mohawk R
Delaware R

Newburgh
West Point
Orange
Peekskill
Fishkill
Westchester
White Plains
New York
Richmond
Queen's
King's
Suffolk

LAKE ONTARIO
LAKE ERIE
St. Lawrence R

INDIAN TERRITORY

Newburgh
New Windsor
West Point
Stony Point
Haverstraw
Fishkill
Peekskill
Verplanck's Point
King's Ferry
Tappan
King's Bridge
Harlem Heights
MANHATTAN IS
New York City
STATEN IS
White Plains
Dobb's Ferry
Mamaroneck
Battle of Pelham
Fort Washington
LONG ISLAND

New York

1st NEW YORK REGIMENT

Authorized 25 May 1775 in the Continental Army as the 2d New York Regiment and assigned to the New York (subsequently Northern) Department. Organized 28 June–4 August 1775 at Albany, to consist of ten companies from Albany, Tryon, Charlotte, and Cumberland Counties.

Reorganized and redesignated 15 April 1776 as Van Schaick's Regiment to consist of eight companies; concurrently, relieved from the Northern Department and assigned to the Canadian Department. Relieved 9 June 1776 from the Canadian Department and assigned to the Northern Department.

Consolidated 26 January 1777 with the 4th New York Regiment [see *Annex*] and consolidated unit reorganized and redesignated as the 1st New York Regiment, an element of the Northern Department, to consist of eight companies. Relieved 31 March 1778 from the Northern Department and assigned to the Main Army. Assigned 31 May 1778 to the 2d Pennsylvania Brigade, an element of the Main Army. Relieved 22 July 1778 from the 2d Pennsylvania Brigade and assigned to the New York Brigade, an element of the Main Army. Relieved 4 November 1778 from the New York Brigade and assigned to the Northern Department.

Reorganized 30 May 1779 to consist of nine companies. Relieved 28 August 1780 from the Northern Department and assigned to the New York Brigade, an element of the Main Army. (New York Brigade relieved 6 November 1780 from the Main Army and assigned to the Northern Department.)

Consolidated 1 January 1781 with the 3d New York Regiment [see 3d New York Regiment] and consolidated unit designated as the 1st New York Regiment, an element of the New York Brigade. (New York Brigade relieved 16 August 1781 from the Northern Department and assigned to the Main Army.) Furloughed 2 June 1783 at Newburgh. Disbanded 15 November 1783.

Annex

Authorized 19 January 1776 in the Continental Army as the 4th New York Regiment and assigned to the New York (subsequently Northern) Department. Organized 27 April 1776 at Albany, to consist of eight companies from Albany, Tryon, and Charlotte Counties. Assigned 20 July 1776 to Stark's Brigade, an element of the Northern Department. Relieved 23 July 1776 from Stark's Brigade and assigned to Reed's Brigade, an element of the Northern Department. Relieved 10 August 1776 from Reed's Brigade but remained assigned to the Northern Department.

ENGAGEMENTS
 Invasion of Canada
 Defense of Canada

ENGAGEMENTS—Continued
  Lake Champlain
  Saratoga
  Philadelphia-Monmouth
  Iroquois 1779
  Yorktown

2d NEW YORK REGIMENT

Authorized 25 May 1775 in the Continental Army as the 4th New York Regiment and assigned to the New York (subsequently Northern) Department. Organized 28 June–4 August 1775 to consist of ten companies from Westchester, Dutchess, Kings, Queens, and Richmond Counties.

Reorganized and redesignated 12–24 April 1776 as the 3d New York Regiment to consist of eight companies; concurrently, relieved from the Northern Department and assigned to Stirling's Brigade, an element of the Main Army. Relieved 12 August 1776 from Stirling's Brigade and assigned to McDougall's Brigade, an element of the Main Army. Relieved 11 December 1776 from McDougall's Brigade and assigned to Sargent's Brigade, an element of the Main Army.

Reorganized and redesignated 26 January 1777 as the 2d New York Regiment, to consist of eight companies; concurrently, relieved from Sargent's Brigade and assigned to the Highlands Department. Assigned 12 June 1777 to McDougall's Brigade, an element of the Highlands Department. Relieved 16 August 1777 from McDougall's Brigade and assigned to the Northern Department. Assigned 22 August 1777 to the New Hampshire Brigade, an element of the Northern Department. (New Hampshire Brigade relieved 23 October 1777 from the Northern Department and assigned to the Main Army.)

Relieved 22 July 1778 from the New Hampshire Brigade and assigned to the New York Brigade, an element of the Main Army. Relieved 17 October 1778 from the New York Brigade and assigned to the Northern Department. Relieved 19 April 1779 from the Northern Department and assigned to Hand's Brigade, an element of the Main Army. Reorganized 30 May 1779 to consist of nine companies. Relieved 26 June 1779 from Hand's Brigade and assigned to the New Hampshire Brigade, an element of the Main Army. Relieved 23 August 1779 from the New Hampshire Brigade and assigned to the New York Brigade, an element of the Main Army. (New York Brigade relieved 30 May 1780 from the Main Army and assigned to the Northern Department; relieved 19 June 1780 from the Main Army and assigned to the Highlands Department; relieved 6 November 1780 from the Highlands Department and assigned to the Northern Department.)

Consolidated 1 January 1781 with the 4th and 5th New York Regiments [see 4th and 5th New York Regiments] and consolidated unit designated as the 2d New York Regiment; concurrently, assigned to the New York Brigade, an element of the Northern Department. (New York Brigade relieved 16 August 1781 from the Northern Department and assigned to the Main Army.) Furloughed 2 June 1783 at Newburgh. Disbanded 15 November 1783.

Engagements
  Invasion of Canada
  Defense of Canada
  New York City
  Trenton-Princeton
  Saratoga
  Philadelphia-Monmouth
  Iroquois 1779
  Yorktown

3d NEW YORK REGIMENT

Authorized 21 June 1776 in the Continental Army as Dubois' Regiment and as-signed to the Northern Department. Partially organized in fall 1776 in Albany pri-marily from veterans of service in Canada during 1775 and 1776.

Reorganized and redesignated 26 January 1777 as the 3d New York Regiment, to consist of eight companies from Dutchess and Ulster Counties and New York City and County; concurrently, relieved from the Northern Department and assigned to the Highlands Department. Relieved 12 May 1777 from the Highlands Department and assigned to the Northern Department. Assigned 4 November 1778 to the New York Brigade, an element of the Northern Department. (New York Brigade relieved 24 May 1779 from the Northern Department and assigned to the Main Army.)

Reorganized 30 May 1779 to consist of nine companies. (New York Brigade relieved 30 May 1780 from the Main Army and assigned to the Northern Department; relieved 19 June 1780 from the Northern Department and assigned to the Highlands Depart-ment; relieved 6 November 1780 from the Highlands Department and assigned to the Northern Department.) Consolidated 1 January 1781 with the 1st New York Regi-ment [see 1st New York Regiment].

Engagements
  New York 1777
  Mohawk Valley
  Iroquois 1779

4th NEW YORK REGIMENT

Authorized 25 May 1775 in the Continental Army as the 3d New York Regiment and assigned to the New York (subsequently Northern) Department. Organized 28 June-4 August 1775 to consist of ten companies from Ulster, Dutchess, Orange, and Suffolk Counties.

Reorganized and redesignated 27 April 1776 as the 2d New York Regiment, an element of the Northern Department, to consist of eight companies.

Reorganized and redesignated 26 January 1777 as the 4th New York Regiment, to consist of eight companies; concurrently, relieved from the Northern Department and assigned to the Highlands Department. Assigned 12 June 1777 to the 2d Connecticut

Brigade, an element of the Highlands Department. Relieved 16 August 1777 from the 2d Connecticut Brigade and assigned to the Northern Department. Assigned 22 August 1777 to the New Hampshire Brigade, an element of the Northern Department. (New Hampshire Brigade relieved 23 October 1777 from the Northern Department and assigned to the Main Army.)

Relieved 22 July 1778 from the New Hampshire Brigade and assigned to the New York Brigade, an element of the Main Army. (New York Brigade relieved 19 November 1778 from the Main Army and assigned to the Northern Department; relieved 24 May 1779 from the Northern Department and assigned to the Main Army.) Reorganized 30 May 1779 to consist of nine companies. (New York Brigade relieved 30 May 1780 from the Main Army and assigned to the Northern Department; relieved 19 June 1780 from the Northern Department and assigned to the Highlands Department.) Relieved 18 October 1780 from the New York Brigade and assigned to the Northern Department. Consolidated 1 January 1781 with the 2d and 5th New York Regiments [see 2d New York Regiment].

ENGAGEMENTS
    Invasion of Canada
    Defense of Canada
    New York 1777
    Saratoga
    Philadelphia-Monmouth
    Iroquois 1779

5th NEW YORK REGIMENT

Authorized 30 November 1776 in the Continental Army as the 5th New York Regiment. Organized 26 January 1777 to consist of eight companies from southern New York and assigned to the Highlands Department.

Relieved 22 July 1778 from the Highlands Department and assigned to the New York Brigade, an element of the Main Army. (New York Brigade relieved 19 November 1778 from the Main Army and assigned to the Northern Department; relieved 24 May 1779 from the Northern Department and assigned to the Main Army.) Reorganized 30 May 1779 to consist of nine companies. (New York Brigade relieved 30 May 1780 from the Main Army and assigned to the Northern Department; relieved 19 June 1780 from the Northern Department and assigned to the Highlands Department; relieved 6 November 1780 from the Highlands Department and assigned to the Northern Department.) Consolidated 1 January 1781 with the 2d and 4th New York Regiments [see 2d New York Regiment].

ENGAGEMENTS
    Hudson Highlands
    Iroquois 1779

1st NEW YORK REGIMENT*
(1775–1776)

Authorized 25 May 1775 in the Continental Army as the 1st New York Regiment and assigned to the New York (subsequently Northern) Department. Organized 28 June–4 August 1775 at New York City, to consist of ten companies from the City and County of New York.

Reorganized 24 February–21 May 1776 to consist of eight companies. Assigned 24 April 1776 to Stirling's Brigade, an element of the Main Army. Relieved 12 August 1776 from Stirling's Brigade and assigned to McDougall's Brigade, an element of the Main Army. Relieved 11 December 1776 from McDougall's Brigade and assigned to Sargent's Brigade, an element of the Main Army. Disbanded 26 January 1777 at Morristown, New Jersey.

ENGAGEMENTS
    Invasion of Canada
    Defense of Canada
    New York City
    Trenton-Princeton

*Company A, 1st Battalion, 69th Infantry, New York Army National Guard, perpetuates elements of this unit.

NICHOLSON'S REGIMENT

Authorized 8 January 1776 in the Continental Army as a regiment to be raised from the troops in service in Canada and assigned to the Canadian Department. Organized 15 April 1776 at Quebec, Canada, as Nicholson's Regiment, to consist of eight companies from New York. Relieved 2 July 1776 from the Canadian Department and assigned to the Northern Department. Disbanded 31 December 1776 at Albany.

ENGAGEMENTS
    Defense of Canada

Bibliography

Aimone, Alan, and Barbara. "Organizing and Equipping Montgomery's Yorkers in 1775." *Military Collector and Historian* 28 (1976):53–63.

Alexander, Arthur J. "Exemptions From Militia Service in New York State During the Revolutionary War." *New York History* 27 (1946):204–12.

Bald, F. Clever. "Colonel John Francis Hamtramck." *Indiana Magazine of History* 44 (1948):335–54.

Bleeker, Leonard. *The Order Book of Capt. Leonard Bleeker, Major of Brigade in the Early Part of the Expedition Under Gen. James Clinton, Against the Indian Set-*

tlements of Western New York, in the Campaign of 1779. New York: Joseph Sabin, 1865.

Calendar of Historical Manuscripts, Relating to the War of the Revolution, in the Office of the Secretary of State, Albany, New York. 2 vols. Albany: Weed, Parsons & Co., 1863–68.

Clinton, George. *Public Papers of George Clinton, First Governor of New York.* Edited by Hugh Hastings. 10 vols. Albany: State printers, 1899–1914.

Conover, Charles Tallmadge, ed. "Original Orderly Books Written on the Battlefields of the American Revolution." *Journal of American History* 4 (1910):341–51, 491–94; 5 (1911):105–12.

Dawson, Henry B. *Westchester-County, New York, During the American Revolution.* Morrisania: Privately printed, 1886.

Delafield, Maturin L., ed. "Colonel Henry Beekman Livingston." *Magazine of American History* 21 (1889):256–58.

Fernow, Berthold, ed. *New York in the Revolution.* Albany: Weed, Parsons & Co., 1887.

Fish, Nicholas. "Selections From the Correspondence of Major Nicholas Fish, of the Army of the Revolution." Edited by Hamilton Fish. *Historical Magazine,* 2d ser., 5 (1869):203–4.

Gano, John. "A Chaplain of the Revolution: Memoirs of the Rev. John Gano." *Historical Magazine* 5 (1861):330–35.

Gardner, Asa Bird. "The New York Continental Line of the Army of the Revolution." *Magazine of American History* 7 (1887):401–19.

Hall, William. "Colonel Rudolphus Ritzema." *Magazine of American History* 2 (1878):162–67.

Hufeland, Otto. *Westchester County During the American Revolution 1775–1783.* White Plains: Westchester County Historical Society, 1926.

Journals of the Provincial Congress, Provincial Convention, Committee of Safety, and Council of Safety, 1775–1777. 2 vols. Albany: Thurlow Weed, 1842.

Lauber, Almon W., ed. *Orderly Books of the Fourth New York Regiment, 1778–1780; the Second New York Regiment, 1780–1783 by Samuel Tallmadge and Others With Diaries of Samuel Tallmadge, 1780–1782 and John Barr, 1779–1782.* Albany: University of the State of New York, 1932.

Leggett, Abraham. *The Narrative of Major Abraham Leggett, of the Army of the Revolution, Now First Printed From the Original Manuscript.* Edited by Charles I. Bushnell. New York: Privately printed, 1865.

"List of Nominations for Officers in the N.Y. Regiments, 1775." *Historical Magazine* 7 (1863):194–95.

Livingston, Henry. "Journal of Major Henry Livingston of the Third New York Continental Line, August to December, 1775." Edited by Gaillard Hunt. *Pennsylvania Magazine of History and Biography* 22 (1898):9–33.

New York, Division of Archives and History. *The Sullivan-Clinton Campaign in 1779. Chronology and Selected Documents.* Albany: University of the State of New York, 1929.

New York, State Library. *A Guide to the Revolutionary War Manuscripts in the New York State Library.* Edited by Stefan Bielinski. Albany: New York State American Revolution Bicentennial Commission, 1976.

Poucher, J. Wilson. "Colonel Lewis Du Bois." *Proceedings of the Ulster County Historical Society for 1935–1936*:15–33.

_____. "Dutchess County Men of the Revolutionary Period—Colonel Frederick Weissenfels." *Year Book of the Dutchess County Historical Society* 27 (1942): 74–84.

Reid, W. Max, ed. "A Diary of the Siege of Fort Schuyler." *Magazine of History* 3 (1906):90–104.

Ritzema, Rudolphus. "Extract of a Letter From Colonel Rudolphus Ritzema to Captain Richard Varick." *Historical Magazine* 4 (1866):110–11.

_____. "Journal of Col. Rudolphus Ritzema of the First New York Regiment August 8, 1775 to March 30, 1776." *Magazine of American History* 1 (1877):98–107.

Shannon, Anna Madeleine. "General Alexander McDougall: Citizen Soldier, 1732–1786." Ph.D. dissertation, Fordham University, 1957.

Spaulding, Ernest W. *His Excellency George Clinton (1739–1812), Critic of the Constitution.* New York: Macmillan Co., 1938.

Sullivan, James, and Flick, Alexander C., eds. *Minutes of the Albany Committee of Correspondence, 1775–1778.* 2 vols. Albany: University of the State of New York, 1923–25.

Thomas, Howard. *Marinus Willett, Soldier Patriot, 1740–1830.* Prospect, New York: Prospect Books, 1954.

Van Cortlandt, Philip. *Philip Van Cortlandt's Revolutionary War Correspondence and Memoirs.* Edited by Jacob Judd. Tarrytown: Sleepy Hollow Restorations, 1976.

Willet, William M. *A Narrative of the Military Actions of Colonel Marinus Willett, Taken Chiefly From His Own Manuscript.* New York: G. & C. & H. Carvill, 1831.

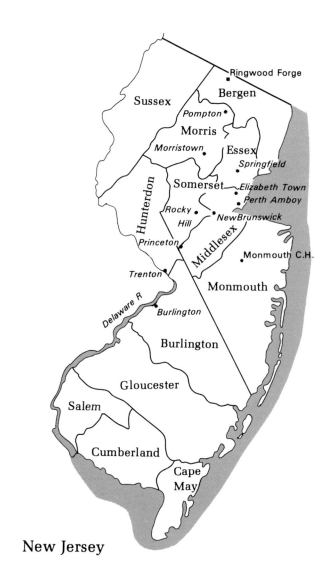

Ringwood Forge

Bergen

Sussex

Pompton

Morris

Morristown

Essex

Springfield

Somerset

Elizabeth Town

Perth Amboy

Hunterdon

Rocky
Hill

NewBrunswick

Princeton

Middlesex

Monmouth C.H.

Trenton

Monmouth

Delaware R

Burlington

Burlington

Gloucester

Salem

Cumberland

Cape
May

New Jersey

New Jersey

1st NEW JERSEY REGIMENT
(Eastern Battalion)

Authorized 9 October 1775 in the Continental Army as the 1st New Jersey Regiment and assigned to the New York (subsequently Middle) Department. Organized 26 October–15 December 1775 at Elizabethtown and Perth Amboy to consist of eight companies from Middlesex, Morris, Somerset, Monmouth, Essex, and Bergen Counties.

Assigned 24 April 1776 to Stirling's Brigade, an element of the Main Army. Relieved 27 April 1776 from Stirling's Brigade and assigned to the Canadian Department. Relieved 2 July 1776 from the Canadian Department and assigned to the Northern Department. Assigned 20 July 1776 to Stark's Brigade, an element of the Northern Department. Relieved 5 August 1776 from Stark's Brigade and assigned to St. Clair's Brigade, an element of the Northern Department.

Relieved 14 November 1776 from St. Clair's Brigade and assigned to the Main Army. Assigned 22 May 1777 to the New Jersey Brigade, an element of the Main Army. Reorganized 7 February 1779 to consist of nine companies. Reorganized and redesignated 1 March 1783 as the New Jersey Regiment. Furloughed 6 June 1783 at Newburgh, New York. Disbanded 15 November 1783.

ENGAGEMENTS
Defense of Canada
Lake Champlain
Northern New Jersey
New York 1777
Defense of Philadelphia
Philadelphia-Monmouth
Iroquois 1779
New Jersey 1780
Yorktown

2d NEW JERSEY REGIMENT
(Western Battalion)

Authorized 9 October 1775 in the Continental Army as the 2d New Jersey Regiment and assigned to the New York (subsequently Middle) Department. Organized 26 October–25 December 1775 at Burlington and Trenton to consist of eight companies from Gloucester, Hunterdon, Burlington, Salem, and Sussex Counties.

Relieved 8 January 1776 from the Middle Department and assigned to the Canadian Department. Relieved 2 July 1776 from the Canadian Department and assigned to the Northern Department. Assigned 20 July 1776 to Stark's Brigade, an element of the Northern Department. Relieved 21 October 1776 from Stark's Brigade and assigned to St. Clair's Brigade, an element of the Northern Department.

Relieved 14 November 1776 from St. Clair's Brigade and assigned to the Main Army. Assigned 22 May 1777 to the New Jersey Brigade, an element of the Main Army. Reorganized 7 February 1779 to consist of nine companies. Reorganized and redesignated 1 March 1783 as the New Jersey Battalion, to consist of four companies. Furloughed 6 June 1783 at Newburgh, New York. Disbanded 15 November 1783.

ENGAGEMENTS
Defense of Canada
Lake Champlain
Northern New Jersey
Defense of Philadelphia
Philadelphia-Monmouth
Iroquois 1779
New Jersey 1780
Yorktown

3d NEW JERSEY REGIMENT

Authorized 10 January 1776 in the Continental Army as the 3d New Jersey Regiment and assigned to the New York (subsequently Middle) Department. Organized 7 February–18 May 1776 at Elizabethtown, to consist of eight companies. Relieved 14 March 1776 from the Middle Department and assigned to the Main Army. Assigned 24 April 1776 to Stirling's Brigade, an element of the Main Army. Relieved 27 April 1776 from Stirling's Brigade and assigned to the Northern Department.

Relieved 1 March 1777 from the Northern Department and assigned to the Main Army. Assigned 22 May 1777 to the New Jersey Brigade, an element of the Main Army. Reorganized 7 February 1779 to consist of nine companies. Disbanded 1 January 1781 at Pompton.

ENGAGEMENTS
Lake Champlain
Northern New Jersey
New York 1777
Defense of Philadelphia
Philadelphia-Monmouth
Iroquois 1779
New Jersey 1780

4th NEW JERSEY REGIMENT

Authorized 16 September 1776 in the Continental Army as the 4th New Jersey Regiment. Assigned 27 December 1776 to the Main Army. Organized 28 November

1776–17 February 1777 at Morristown to consist of eight companies. Assigned 22 May 1777 to the New Jersey Brigade, an element of the Main Army. Disbanded 7 February 1779 at Elizabethtown.

ENGAGEMENTS
  Northern New Jersey
  Defense of Philadelphia
  Philadelphia-Monmouth

Bibliography

Brace, Frederic R. *Brief Sketches of the New Jersey Chaplains in the Continental Army and in the State Militia, During the War of Independence.* Paterson: The Press Printing and Publishing Co., 1909. [Originally published in *Proceedings of the New Jersey Historical Society,* 3d ser., 6 (1909):1–11.]

Dayton, Elias. "Papers of General Elias Dayton." *Proceedings of the New Jersey Historical Society,* 1st ser., 9 (1863–64):175–94.

Elmer, Ebenezer. "Extracts From the Journal of Surgeon Ebenezer Elmer of the New Jersey Continental Line, September 11–19, 1777." Edited by John Nixon Brooks. *Pennsylvania Magazine of History and Biography* 35 (1911):103–7.

_____. "Journal Kept During an Expedition to Canada in 1776 by Ebenezer Elmer, Lieutenant in the 3d Regiment of the New Jersey Troops in the Continental Service, Commanded by Colonel Elias Dayton." *Proceedings of the New Jersey Historical Society,* 1st ser., 2 (1846–47):43–50, 95–194; 3 (1848–49):21–56, 90–102.

_____. "The Lost Pages of Elmer's Revolutionary Journal." Edited by A. Van Doren Honeyman. *Proceedings of the New Jersey Historical Society,* new ser., 10 (1925): 410–24.

Ewing, George. *The Military Journal of George Ewing (1754–1824) a Soldier of Valley Forge.* Yonkers, New York: Privately printed, 1928.

Gerlach, Larry R., ed. *New Jersey in the American Revolution, 1763–1783: A Documentary History.* Trenton: New Jersey Historical Commission, 1975.

Griffith, J. H. "William Maxwell, of New Jersey, Brigadier General in the Revolution." *Proceedings of the New Jersey Historical Society,* 2d ser., 13 (1894): 109–23.

Honeyman, A. Van Doren, ed. "The Condict Revolutionary Record Abstracts." *Proceedings of the New Jersey Historical Society,* new ser., 5 (1920):236–40; 6 (1921): 89–100, 166–76; 7 (1922):25–32, 134–40, 227–32; 8 (1923):30–35, 306–13; 9 (1924):49–57; 10 (1925):182–87, 312–16.

Leiby, Adrian C. *The Revolutionary War in the Hackensack Valley: The Jersey Dutch and the Neutral Ground.* New Brunswick: Rutgers University Press, 1962.

Lender, Mark Edward. "The Enlisted Line: The Continental Soldiers of New Jersey." Ph.D. dissertation, Rutgers University, 1975.

Livingston, William. *Selections From the Correspondence of the Executive, 1776–1786.* Newark: Daily Advertiser Office, 1848.

Lundin, Leonard. *Cockpit of the Revolution: The War for Independence in New Jersey.* Princeton: Princeton University Press, 1940.

Murray, Nicholas. "A Memoir of the Rev. James Caldwell of Elizabethtown." *Proceedings of the New Jersey Historical Society* 3 (1848):77–89.

New Jersey. *Minutes of the Provincial Congress and Council of Safety 1774–1778.* 2 vols. Trenton and Jersey City: Naar, Day & J. H. Lyon, 1872–79.

New Jersey Historical Society. *Documents Relating to the Colonial, Revolutionary and Post-Revolutionary History of the State of New Jersey.* 42 vols. [*Archives of the State of New Jersey,* 1st ser.] Newark and Paterson: Various publishers, 1880–1949.

Ogden, Aaron. *Autobiography of Col. Aaron Ogden, of Elizabethtown.* Paterson: The Press Printing and Publishing Co., 1893. [Originally published in *Proceedings of the New Jersey Historical Society,* 2d ser., 12 (1892):13–31.]

Ogden, Matthias. *Journal of Major Matthias Ogden.* Morristown: Privately printed, 1928.

Shreve, S. H., ed. "Personal Narrative of the Services of Lieut. John Shreve of the New Jersey Line of the Continental Army." *Magazine of American History* 3 (1879):564–79.

"Some Unpublished Revolutionary Manuscripts." *Proceedings of the New Jersey Historical Society,* 2d ser., 13 (1894–95):17–24, 79–88, 149–60; 3d ser., 3 (1902–6): 85–92, 118–23, 180–84; 6 (1909):12–16, 79–86.

Spear, John. "The Orderly Book of Lieutenant John Spear (July 17 to December 4, 1781)." Edited by Joseph F. Folsom. *Proceedings of the New Jersey Historical Society,* new ser., 1 (1916):129–46.

Stryker, William S. *General Maxwell's Brigade of the New Jersey Continental Line in the Expedition Against the Indians, in the Year 1779.* Trenton: W. S. Sharp Printing Co., 1885.

————, comp. *Official Register of the Officers and Men of New Jersey in the Revolutionary War, Compiled Under the Orders of His Excellency Theodore F. Randolph, Governor, by William S. Stryker, Adjutant General. With Added Digest and Revision for the Use of the Society of the Cincinnati in the State of New Jersey (1911) Revised and Compiled by James W. S. Campbell.* [Original edition published in 1872.] Reprint. Baltimore: Genealogical Publishing Co., 1967.

Thompson, William Y. *Israel Shreve, Revolutionary War Officer.* Ruston, Louisiana: McGinty Trust Fund Publications, 1979.

Pennsylvania

1st PENNSYLVANIA REGIMENT

Authorized 14 June 1775 in the Continental Army as six separate companies of Pennsylvania Riflemen and assigned to the Main Army. Redesignated 22 June 1775 as the Pennsylvania Rifle Regiment. Organized 25 June–20 July 1775 to consist of nine companies from Cumberland, Lancaster, Northumberland, Northampton, Bedford, Berks, and York Counties.

Redesignated 1 January 1776 as the 1st Continental Regiment. Assigned 24 April 1776 to Sullivan's Brigade, an element of the Main Army. Relieved 29 April 1776 from Sullivan's Brigade and assigned to Greene's Brigade, an element of the Main Army. Relieved 12 August 1776 from Greene's Brigade and assigned to Nixon's Brigade, an element of the Main Army. Relieved 31 August 1776 from assignment to Nixon's Brigade and assigned to Mifflin's Brigade (redesignated 8 October 1776 as Stirling's Brigade), an element of the Main Army.

Reorganized and redesignated 1 January 1777 as the 1st Pennsylvania Regiment, to consist of eight companies. Relieved 22 May 1777 from Stirling's Brigade and assigned to the 1st Pennsylvania Brigade, an element of the Main Army. Reorganized 1 July 1778 to consist of nine companies.

Consolidated 17 January 1781 with the 10th Pennsylvania Regiment [see 10th Pennsylvania Regiment] and consolidated unit designated as the 1st Pennsylvania Regiment; concurrently, furloughed at Trenton, New Jersey, and relieved from the 1st Pennsylvania Brigade. Reorganized 1 January 1783 at Ashley Hills, South Carolina, to consist of nine companies, and assigned to the Southern Department. Relieved 1 June 1783 from the Southern Department and assigned to the Middle Department. Furloughed 11 June 1783 at Philadelphia. Disbanded 15 November 1783.

ENGAGEMENTS
Siege of Boston
New York City
Trenton-Princeton
Northern New Jersey
Defense of Philadelphia
Philadelphia-Monmouth
New Jersey 1780
Captains William Hendricks' and Mathew Smith's companies each additionally served in
Invasion of Canada

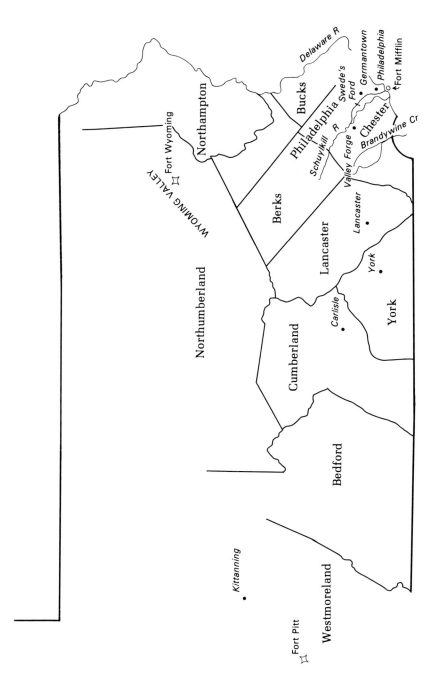

Pennsylvania

2d PENNSYLVANIA REGIMENT

Authorized 12 October 1775 in the Continental Army as the 1st Pennsylvania Battalion. Organized 25 October–26 November 1775 at Philadelphia to consist of eight companies from Philadelphia City and Philadelphia, Bucks, Berks, and Northampton Counties. Assigned 8 January 1776 to the Canadian Department. Relieved 2 July 1776 from the Canadian Department and assigned to the Northern Department. Assigned 20 July 1776 to St. Clair's Brigade, an element of the Northern Department. Relieved 14 November 1776 from St. Clair's Brigade and assigned to the Main Army.

Reorganized and redesignated 1 January 1777 as the 2d Pennsylvania Regiment, to consist of eight companies. Assigned 22 May 1777 to the 1st Pennsylvania Brigade, an element of the Main Army. Consolidated 1 July 1778 with the 13th Pennsylvania Regiment [see 13th Pennsylvania Regiment] and consolidated unit designated as the 2d Pennsylvania Regiment, to consist of nine companies. Consolidated 17 January 1781 with the 8th Pennsylvania Regiment [see 8th Pennsylvania Regiment] and consolidated unit designated as the 2d Pennsylvania Regiment; concurrently, furloughed at Trenton, New Jersey (less two companies remaining active at Fort Pitt), and relieved from the 1st Pennsylvania Brigade.

Reorganized 1 January 1783 at Lancaster to consist of seven companies in the Middle Department and two companies in the Western Department. Furloughed 11 June 1783 at Philadelphia (less two companies remaining active at Fort Pitt). Disbanded 15 November 1783.

ENGAGEMENTS
    Defense of Canada
    Lake Champlain
    Northern New Jersey
    Defense of Philadelphia
    Philadelphia-Monmouth
    New Jersey 1780

3d PENNSYLVANIA REGIMENT

Authorized 9 December 1775 in the Continental Army as the 2d Pennsylvania Battalion. Organized 2 January–17 February 1776 at Philadelphia to consist of eight companies. Assigned 8 January 1776 to the Canadian Department. Relieved 2 July 1776 from the Canadian Department and assigned to the Northern Department. Assigned 20 July 1776 to St. Clair's Brigade, an element of the Northern Department. Relieved 18 November 1776 from St. Clair's Brigade.

Reorganized and redesignated 1 January 1777 as the 3d Pennsylvania Regiment, to consist of eight companies. Relieved 24 January 1777 from the Northern Department and assigned to the Main Army. Assigned 22 May 1777 to the 3d Pennsylvania Brigade, an element of the Main Army.

Consolidated 1 July 1778 with the 12th Pennsylvania Regiment [see 12th Pennsylvania Regiment] and consolidated unit designated as the 3d Pennsylvania Regiment, to consist of nine companies. Relieved 22 July 1778 from the 3d Pennsylvania Brigade and assigned to the 2d Pennsylvania Brigade, an element of the Main Army.

Consolidated 17 January 1781 with the 11th Pennsylvania Regiment [see Hartley's Additional Continental Regiment] and consolidated unit designated as the 3d Pennsylvania Regiment; concurrently, furloughed at Trenton, New Jersey, and relieved from the 2d Pennsylvania Brigade. Reorganized 1 January 1783 at Philadelphia, to consist of nine companies, and assigned to the Middle Department. Furloughed 11 June 1783 at Philadelphia. Disbanded 15 November 1783.

ENGAGEMENTS
> Defense of Canada
> Lake Champlain
> Northern New Jersey
> Defense of Philadelphia
> Philadelphia-Monmouth
> New Jersey 1780

4th PENNSYLVANIA REGIMENT

Authorized 9 December 1775 in the Continental Army as the 3d Pennsylvania Battalion. Organized 2 January–late March 1776 at Philadelphia to consist of eight companies from eastern Pennsylvania. Assigned 27 February 1776 to the Middle Department. Relieved 11 June 1776 from the Middle Department and assigned to the Main Army. Assigned 29 June 1776 to Mifflin's Brigade (redesignated 8 October 1776 as Stirling's Brigade), an element of the Main Army.

Captured in part 16 November 1776 by the *British Army* at Fort Washington, New York; remainder of regiment reorganized and redesignated 1 January 1777 as the 4th Pennsylvania Regiment, an element of the Main Army, to consist of eight companies. Assigned 22 May 1777 to the 2d Pennsylvania Brigade, an element of the Main Army. (Captain Joshua Williams' Independent Company [*see Annex*] consolidated 6 November 1777 with the regiment.)

Reorganized 1 July 1778 to consist of nine companies. Relieved 18 July 1778 from the 2d Pennsylvania Brigade and assigned to the Northern Department. Assigned 19 April 1779 to the New York Brigade, an element of the Northern Department. (New York Brigade relieved 24 May 1779 from the Northern Department and assigned to the Main Army.) Relieved 24 August 1779 from the New York Brigade and assigned to Hand's Brigade, an element of the Main Army. Relieved 1 August 1780 from Hand's Brigade and assigned to the 1st Pennsylvania Brigade, an element of the Main Army.

Consolidated 17 January 1781 with the 7th Pennsylvania Regiment [see 7th Pennsylvania Regiment] and consolidated unit designated as the 4th Pennsylvania Regiment; concurrently, furloughed at Trenton, New Jersey. Disbanded 1 January 1783.

Annex

Authorized 15 March 1777 in the Pennsylvania State Troops as Captain Joshua Williams' Independent Company. Organized in spring 1777 at York, Pennsylvania, with personnel from York County. Consolidated 6 November 1777 with the 4th Pennsylvania Regiment.

ENGAGEMENTS
    New York City
    Northern New Jersey
    Defense of Philadelphia
    Philadelphia-Monmouth
    Iroquois 1778
    Iroquois 1779

5th PENNSYLVANIA REGIMENT

Authorized 9 December 1775 in the Continental Army as the 4th Pennsylvania Battalion. Organized 2 January–11 February 1776 at Chester to consist of eight companies from Chester, Bucks, and Lancaster Counties. Assigned 27 February 1776 to the Middle Department. Relieved 15 March 1776 from the Middle Department and assigned to the Canadian Department. Relieved 2 July 1776 from the Canadian Department and assigned to the Northern Department. Assigned 20 July 1776 to St. Clair's Brigade, an element of the Northern Department. Relieved 18 November 1776 from St. Clair's Brigade.

Reorganized and redesignated 1 January 1777 as the 5th Pennsylvania Regiment, to consist of eight companies. Relieved 24 January 1777 from the Northern Department and assigned to the Main Army. (Captain John Nelson's Independent Rifle Company [see Annex] consolidated 24 March 1777 with the regiment.) Assigned 22 May 1777 to the 2d Pennsylvania Brigade, an element of the Main Army. Reorganized 1 July 1778 to consist of nine companies.

Consolidated 17 January 1781 with the 9th Pennsylvania Regiment [see 9th Pennsylvania Regiment] and consolidated unit designated as the 5th Pennsylvania Regiment; concurrently, furloughed at Trenton, New Jersey. Disbanded 1 January 1783.

Annex

Authorized 30 January 1776 in the Continental Army as Captain John Nelson's Independent Rifle Company and assigned to the Canadian Department. Organized 7 February–17 March 1776 at Reading, Pennsylvania, with personnel from Berks County. Relieved 2 July 1776 from the Canadian Department and assigned to the Northern Department. Relieved 20 February 1777 from the Northern Department and assigned to the Main Army. Consolidated 24 March 1777 with the 5th Pennsylvania Regiment.

ENGAGEMENTS
    Defense of Canada
    Lake Champlain
    Northern New Jersey
    Defense of Philadelphia

ENGAGEMENTS—Continued
   Philadelphia-Monmouth
   New Jersey 1780

6th PENNSYLVANIA REGIMENT

Authorized 9 December 1775 in the Continental Army as the 5th Pennsylvania Battalion. Organized 2 January–late March 1776 at Philadelphia to consist of eight companies from Philadelphia City and Berks, Bucks, Chester, and Philadelphia Counties. Assigned 27 February 1776 to the Middle Department. Relieved 11 June 1776 from the Middle Department and assigned to the Main Army. Assigned 29 June 1776 to Mifflin's Brigade (redesignated 8 October 1776 as Stirling's Brigade), an element of the Main Army.

Captured in part 16 November 1776 by the *British Army* at Fort Washington, New York; remainder of regiment reorganized and redesignated 1 January 1777 as the 6th Pennsylvania Regiment, an element of the Main Army, to consist of eight companies. Assigned 22 May 1777 to the 3d Pennsylvania Brigade, an element of the Main Army.

Reorganized 1 July 1778 to consist of nine companies. Relieved 22 July 1778 from the 3d Pennsylvania Brigade and assigned to the 2d Pennsylvania Brigade, an element of the Main Army. Furloughed 17 January 1781 at Trenton, New Jersey. Disbanded 1 January 1783.

ENGAGEMENTS
   New York City
   Northern New Jersey
   Defense of Philadelphia
   Philadelphia-Monmouth
   New Jersey 1780

7th PENNSYVLANIA REGIMENT

Authorized 4 January 1776 in the Continental Army as the 6th Pennsylvania Battalion. Organized 8 January–20 March 1776 at Carlisle to consist of eight companies from Cumberland and York Counties. Assigned 27 February 1776 to the Middle Department. Relieved 14 March 1776 from the Middle Department and assigned to the Main Army. Assigned 24 April 1776 to Greene's Brigade, an element of the Main Army. Relieved 27 April 1776 from Greene's Brigade and assigned to the Canadian Department. Relieved 2 July 1776 from the Canadian Department and assigned to the Northern Department. Assigned 20 July 1776 to St. Clair's Brigade, an element of the Northern Department. Relieved 18 November 1776 from St. Clair's Brigade.

Reorganized and redesignated 1 January 1777 as the 7th Pennsylvania Regiment, to consist of eight companies. Relieved 8 February 1777 from the Northern Department and assigned to the Main Army. Assigned 22 May 1777 to the 1st Pennsylvania Brigade, an element of the Main Army. Reorganized 1 July 1778 to consist of nine companies.

Consolidated 17 January 1781 with the 4th Pennsylvania Regiment [see 4th Pennsylvania Regiment].

ENGAGEMENTS
   Defense of Canada
   Lake Champlain
   Northern New Jersey
   Defense of Philadelphia
   Philadelphia-Monmouth
   New Jersey 1780

8th PENNSYLVANIA REGIMENT

Authorized 11 July 1776 in the Continental Army as a battalion for frontier defense in the Northern Department. Designated 20 July 1776 as Mackay's Battalion. Organized 15 July–15 September 1776 at Kittanning to consist of eight companies from Westmoreland, Bedford, and Cumberland Counties. Relieved 23 November 1776 from the Northern Department and assigned to the Main Army.

Redesignated 1 January 1777 as the 8th Pennsylvania Regiment. Assigned 22 May 1777 to the 2d Pennsylvania Brigade, an element of the Main Army. Relieved 19 May 1778 from the 2d Pennsylvania Brigade and assigned to the Western Department.

Reorganized 1 July 1778 to consist of nine companies (Captain Samuel Morehead's Independent Company [see Annex] concurrently consolidated with the regiment). Consolidated 17 January 1781 with the 2d Pennsylvania Regiment [see 2d Pennsylvania Regiment].

Annex

Authorized 22 January 1777 in the Continental Army as Captain Samuel Morehead's Independent Company, an element of the Middle Department. Organized in spring 1777 at Kittanning with personnel from Westmoreland County. Relieved 9 April 1777 from the Middle Department and assigned to the Western Department. Consolidated 1 July 1778 with the 8th Pennsylvania Regiment.

ENGAGEMENTS
   Northern New Jersey
   Defense of Philadelphia
   Iroquois 1778
   Iroquois 1779
Morehead's Independent Company additionally served in
   Delawares 1777

9th PENNSYLVANIA REGIMENT

Authorized 16 September 1776 in the Continental Army as the 9th Pennsylvania Regiment. Assigned 27 December 1776 to the Main Army. Organized in spring 1777 at Philadelphia to consist of eight companies from Lancaster, Cumberland, Westmoreland, Chester, and Philadelphia Counties. Assigned 22 May 1777 to the 3d Pennsylvania Brigade, an element of the Main Army.

Reorganized 1 July 1778 to consist of nine companies. Relieved 22 July 1778 from the 3d Pennsylvania Brigade and assigned to the 2d Pennsylvania Brigade, an element of the Main Army.

Consolidated 17 January 1781 with the 5th Pennsylvania Regiment [see 5th Pennsylvania Regiment].

Engagements
    Northern New Jersey
    Defense of Philadelphia
    Philadelphia-Monmouth
    New Jersey 1780

10th PENNSYLVANIA REGIMENT

Authorized 16 September 1776 in the Continental Army as the 10th Pennsylvania Regiment. Assigned 27 December 1776 to the Main Army. Organized in spring 1777 at Philadelphia to consist of eight companies from Lancaster, York, Bucks, Northampton, and Northumberland Counties. Assigned 22 May 1777 to the 1st Pennsylvania Brigade, an element of the Main Army. (Captain Jacob Weaver's Independent Company [*see Annex*] consolidated 7 November 1777 with the regiment.)

Consolidated 1 July 1778 with the 11th Pennsylvania Regiment [see 11th Pennsylvania Regiment] and consolidated unit designated as the 10th Pennsylvania Regiment, to consist of nine companies.

Consolidated 17 January 1781 with the 1st Pennsylvania Regiment [see 1st Pennsylvania Regiment].

Annex

Authorized 18 January 1777 in the Continental Army as an independent company to guard prisoners of war at Lancaster, Pennsylvania. Organized 31 January–19 August 1777 at Lancaster as Captain Jacob Weaver's Independent Company. Consolidated 7 November 1777 with the 10th Pennsylvania Regiment.

Engagements
    Northern New Jersey
    Defense of Philadelphia
    Philadelphia-Monmouth
    New Jersey 1780

11th PENNSYLVANIA REGIMENT
(Old Eleventh)

Authorized 16 September 1776 in the Continental Army as the 11th Pennsylvania Regiment. Assigned 27 December 1776 to the Main Army. Organized in spring 1777 at Philadelphia to consist of eight companies from Philadelphia City and Berks, Chester, Northumberland, and Philadelphia Counties. Assigned 22 May 1777 to the 2d Pennsylvania Brigade, an element of the Main Army.

Consolidated 1 July 1778 with the 10th Pennsylvania Regiment [see 10th Pennsylvania Regiment].

ENGAGEMENTS
Northern New Jersey
Defense of Philadelphia
Philadelphia-Monmouth

12th PENNSYLVANIA REGIMENT

Authorized 23 August 1776 in the Continental Army as the Northampton and Northumberland Defense Battalion and assigned to the Middle Department. Redesignated 16 September 1776 as the 12th Pennsylvania Regiment. Organized 28 September–18 December 1776 at Sunbury to consist of eight companies from Northampton, Northumberland, Berks, and Cumberland Counties. Assigned 1 December 1776 to the Main Army. Assigned 22 May 1777 to the 3d Pennsylvania Brigade, an element of the Main Army.

Consolidated 1 July 1778 with the 3d Pennsylvania Regiment [see 3d Pennsylvania Regiment].

ENGAGEMENTS
Northern New Jersey
Defense of Philadelphia
Philadelphia-Monmouth

13th PENNSYLVANIA REGIMENT
(Pennsylvania State Regiment)

Authorized 6 March 1776 in the Pennsylvania State Troops as the Pennsylvania State Rifle Regiment. Organized 7 March–29 May 1776 at Marcus Hook, to consist of the 1st Battalion (six companies) from Philadelphia City and Bucks, Bedford, York, Northampton, and Northumberland Counties; and the 2d Battalion (six companies) from Berks, Lancaster, Cumberland, and Westmoreland Counties. Assigned 4 July 1776 to the Main Army. Assigned 12 August 1776 to Stirling's Brigade, an element of the Main Army. Relieved 31 August 1776 from Stirling's Brigade and assigned to Mifflin's Brigade (redesignated 8 October 1776 as Stirling's Brigade), an element of the Main Army.

Relieved in January 1777 from Stirling's Brigade. Consolidated 30 April 1777 with the Pennsylvania State Musketry Battalion [*see Annex 1*] and consolidated unit reorganized and redesignated as the Pennsylvania State Regiment of Foot, to consist of eight musket and two rifle companies. (Captain John Pugh's Independent Company [*see Annex 2*] consolidated 17 June 1777 with the regiment.) Assigned 6 July 1777 to the Main Army. Allotted 12 November 1777 to the Continental Army and redesignated as the 13th Pennsylvania Regiment.

Consolidated 1 July 1778 with the 2d Pennsylvania Regiment [see 2d Pennsylvania Regiment].

Annex 1

Authorized 6 March 1776 in the Pennsylvania State Troops as the Pennsylvania State Musketry Battalion. Organized 13 March–29 May 1776 at Chester to consist of eight companies from Philadelphia City and Bucks, Philadelphia, Chester, and Lancaster Counties. Assigned 4 July 1776 to the Main Army. Assigned 12 August 1776 to Stirling's Brigade, an element of the Main Army. Relieved 31 August 1776 from Stirling's Brigade and assigned to Mifflin's Brigade (redesignated 8 October 1776 as Stirling's Brigade), an element of the Main Army.

Relieved in January 1777 from Stirling's Brigade. Consolidated 30 April 1777 with the Pennsylvania State Rifle Regiment.

Annex 2

Authorized 8 April 1777 in the Pennsylvania State Troops as Captain John Pugh's Independent Company to guard the Powder Mill at French Creek. Organized in May 1777 at Philadelphia. Consolidated 17 June 1777 with the Pennsylvania State Regiment of Foot.

ENGAGEMENTS
    New York City
    Trenton-Princeton
    Northern New Jersey
    Defense of Philadelphia
    Philadelphia-Monmouth

CARLISLE INDEPENDENT COMPANIES

Authorized 6 October 1777 in the Continental Army as two Carlisle Independent Companies and assigned to the Middle Department. Organized 20 October–22 December 1777 at Carlisle. Disbanded 2 June 1778 at Carlisle.

ENGAGEMENTS
    None.

CAPTAIN JOHN DOYLE'S INDEPENDENT RIFLE COMPANY

Authorized 16 July 1776 in the Continental Army as Captain John Doyle's Independent Rifle Company. Organized 5 September 1776 at Lancaster with recruits from central Pennsylvania and assigned to the Main Army. Disbanded 1 July 1778 at White Plains, New York.

ENGAGEMENTS
  Northern New Jersey
  Defense of Philadelphia
  Philadelphia-Monmouth

Bibliography

Beatty, Erkuries. "Journal of Lieut. Erkuries Beatty, of the 4th Penn. Line." *Journals of the Military Expedition of Major General John Sullivan Against the Six Nations of Indians in 1779 With Records of Centennial Celebrations.* Edited by Frederick Cook. Auburn, N.Y.: Knapp, Peck & Thomson, 1887. [Originally published in *Pennsylvania Archives,* 2d ser., 15:219-53.]

Beatty, Joseph M., ed. "Letters From Continental Officers to Doctor Reading Beatty, 1781-1788." *Pennsylvania Magazine of History and Biography* 54 (1930):155-74.

_____, ed. "Letters of the Four Beatty Brothers of the Continental Army, 1774-1794." *Pennsylvania Magazine of History and Biography* 44 (1920):193-263.

Beebe, Lewis. *Journal of Lewis Beebe, a Physician on the Campaign Against Canada, 1776.* Edited by Frederick R. Kirtland. Philadelphia: Historical Society of Pennsylvania, 1935.

Bicker, Henry. "Orderly Book of the Second Pennsylvania Continental Line. Col. Henry Bicker at Valley Forge, March 29–May 27, 1778." Edited by John W. Jordan. *Pennsylvania Magazine of History and Biography* 35 (1911):333-42, 463-96; 36 (1912):30-59, 236-53, 329-45.

Clarke, William P. *Official History of the Militia and the National Guard of the State of Pennsylvania From the Earliest Period of Record to the Present Time.* Philadelphia: C. J. Hendler, 1909. [Only volume published of three projected.]

Cooper, Henrietta, ed. "Extracts From the Orderly-Book (and) Diary of Captain John Nice, of the Pennsylvania Line." *Pennsylvania Magazine of History and Biography* 16 (1892):359-62, 399-410.

Crist, Robert Grant. *Captain William Hendricks and the March to Quebec, 1775.* Carlisle: The Hamilton Library and Historical Association of Cumberland County, 1960.

Davis, Charles L., ed. "Journal of Captain John Davis of the Pennsylvania Line." *Pennsylvania Magazine of History and Biography* 5 (1881):290-311. [Also published as Joseph A. Waddell, ed. "Diary of Capt. John Davis, of the Pennsylvania Line." *Virginia Magazine of History and Biography* 1 (1893):1-16.]

Denny, Ebenezer. *Military Journal of Major Ebenezer Denny, an Officer in the Rev-*
    olutionary and Indian Wars With an Introductory Memoir. Philadelphia: J. B.
    Lippincott & Co., 1859.
Denny, William H. "Soldier of the Republic: The Life of Major Ebenezer Denny."
    Ph.D. dissertation, Miami University, 1978.
Devine, Francis E. "The Pennsylvania Flying Camp, July–November 1776." *Pennsyl-*
    vania History 46 (1979):59–78.
Fall, Ralph Emmett. "Captain Samuel Brady (1756–1795), Chief of the Rangers, and
    His Kin." *West Virginia History* 29 (1968):203–23.
Feltman, William. *The Journal of Lieut. William Feltman, of the First Pennsylvania*
    Regiment, 1781–1782, Including the March Into Virginia and the Siege of
    Yorktown. Philadelphia: Historical Society of Pennsylvania, 1853.
Frazer, Persifor. "Letters From Ticonderoga, 1776." *Bulletin of the Fort Ticonder-*
    oga Museum 10 (1961–62):386–96, 450–59.
Gratz, Simon. "Biography of General Richard Butler." *Pennsylvania Magazine of*
    History and Biography 7 (1883):7–10.
Graydon, Alexander. *Memoirs of His Own Time, With Reminiscences of the Men*
    and Events of the Revolution by Alexander Graydon. Edited by John Stockton
    Littell. Philadelphia: Lindsay and Blackiston, 1846.
Hassler, Edgar W. *Old Westmoreland: A History of Western Pennsylvania During*
    the Revolution. Pittsburgh: J. R. Weldin & Co., 1900.
[Hendricks, William.] *A Journal of the March of a Party of Provincials From Carlisle*
    to Boston, and From Thence to Quebec, Begun the 13th of July, and Ended the
    31st of December, 1775. Glasgow: R. Chapman and A. Duncan, 1776.
Henry, John Joseph. *An Accurate and Interesting Account of the Hardships and Suf-*
    ferings of That Band of Heroes, Who Traversed the Wilderness in the Campaign
    Against Quebec in 1775. Lancaster: William Greer, 1812.
Hubley, Adam, Jr. *Journal of Lieut. Col. Adam Hubley, Jr., 1779.* Edited by John
    W. Jordan. Philadelphia: J. B. Lippincott, 1909.
"Itinerary of the Pennsylvania Line From Pennsylvania to South Carolina,
    1781–1782." *Pennsylvania Magazine of History and Biography* 36 (1912):273–92.
Katcher, Rebecca, and Katcher, Philip. "The Pennsylvania Division, 1780." *Military*
    Collector and Historian 27 (1975):120–22.
Katzenberger, George A. "Major David Ziegler." *Ohio Archaeological and Historical*
    Quarterly 21 (1912):127–74.
Kyte, George W. "General Wayne Marches South, 1781." *Pennsylvania History* 30
    (1963):301–15.
Lacey, John. "Memoirs of Brigadier-General John Lacey, of Pennsylvania." *Pennsyl-*
    vania Magazine of History and Biography 25 (1901):1–13, 191–207, 341–54,
    498–515; 26 (1902):101–11, 265–70.
Linn, John Blair. "The Butler Family of the Pennsylvania Line." *Pennsylvania Mag-*
    azine of History and Biography 7 (1883):1–6.
McDowell, William. "Journal of Lieutenant McDowell of the First Pennsylvania Reg-
    iment in the Southern Campaign, 1781–1782." *Pennsylvania Archives,* 2d ser.,
    15:297–340.
McGough, Hugh. "Orderly Book of the Pennsylvania State Regiment of Foot, May
    10 to August 16, 1777." *Pennsylvania Magazine of History and Biography* 22
    (1898):57–70, 196–210, 301–20, 475–78.

McMichael, James. "Diary of Lieutenant James McMichael, of the Pennsylvania Line, 1776-1778." Edited by William P. McMichael. *Pennsylvania Magazine of History and Biography* 16 (1892):129-59.

Martin, C. H. "The Society of the Cincinnati in Lancaster." *Lancaster County Historical Society Papers* 41 (1937):93-101.

Nichols, Francis. "Diary of Lieutenant Francis Nichols, of Colonel William Thompson's Battalion of Pennsylvania Riflemen, January to September 1776." Edited by Thomas H. Montgomery. *Pennsylvania Magazine of History and Biography* 20 (1896):504-15.

Nicholson, John P., ed. "Return of the Pennsylvania Troops in the Service of the United States Commanded by Josiah Harmar, Esquire, Lieutenant Colonel Commanding." *Pennsylvania Magazine of History and Biography* 11 (1887):181-89.

"Notes and Queries [Colonel Richard Humpton]." *Historical Magazine* 5 (1861): 20-22.

"A Partial List of Pennsylvania Troops Killed, Wounded, and Captured at the Battle of Germantown, October 4, 1777." *Pennsylvania Magazine of History and Biography* 40 (1916):241-43.

Pennsylvania Archives. 9 ser. 119 vols. Philadelphia and Harrisburg: Various publishers, 1874-1935.

Pennypacker, Samuel. "Samuel J. Atlee." *Pennsylvania Magazine of History and Biography* 2 (1878):74-84.

Reed, William B. *Life and Correspondence of Joseph Reed.* 2 vols. Philadelphia: Lindsay & Blackiston, 1847.

Reeves, Enos. "Extracts From the Letter-Books of Lieutenant Enos Reeves, of the Pennsylvania Line." Edited by John B. Reeves. *Pennsylvania Magazine of History and Biography* 20 (1896):302-14, 456-72; 21 (1897):75-85, 235-56, 376-91, 466-76.

Richards, Henry M. M. *The Pennsylvania-German in the Revolutionary War, 1775-1783.* Lancaster: Pennsylvania German Society, 1908.

Rogers, Mrs. Harry, and Lane, Mrs. A. H., comp. "Pennsylvania Pensioners of the Revolution." *Pennsylvania Magazine of History and Biography* 41 (1917):468-82; 42 (1918):29-45, 156-69, 259-77.

Royer, Helen E. "The Role of the Continental Congress in the Prosecution of the American Revolution in Pennsylvania." Ph.D. dissertation, Pennsylvania State University, 1960.

St. Clair, Arthur. "Letters of General St. Clair to General Irvine." *Historical Magazine* 7 (1863):151-55.

Schaeffer, Paul N. "Pennsylvania's Draft Laws During the Revolution." *Historical Review of Berks County* 6 (1940):2-4.

Smith, Dwight L. "Josiah Harmar, Diplomatic Courier." *Pennsylvania Magazine of History and Biography* 87 (1963):420-30.

Stille, Charles J. *Major-General Anthony Wayne and the Pennsylvania Line in the Continental Army.* Philadelphia: J. B. Lippincott, 1893.

Stroh, Oscar H. *Thompson's Battalion and/or the First Continental Infantry.* Harrisburg: Graphic Services, 1975.

Thompson, William, and Armstrong, John. "Letters of Two Distinguished Pennsylvania Officers of the Revolution." *Pennsylvania Magazine of History and Biography* 35 (1911):304-7.

Tilden, John Bell. "Extracts From the Journal of Lieutenant John Bell Tilden, Second Pennsylvania Line, 1781-1782." Edited by John B. Phelps. *Pennsylvania Magazine of History and Biography* 19 (1895):51-63, 208-33.

Trussell, John B. B., Jr. *The Pennsylvania Line: Regimental Organization and Operations, 1775-1783.* Harrisburg: Pennsylvania Historical and Museum Commission, 1977.

Van Doren, Carl. *Mutiny in January: The Story of a Crisis in the Continental Army Now for the First Time Fully Told From Many Hitherto Unknown or Neglected Sources.* New York: Viking Press, 1943.

Watts, Henry Miller. "A Memoir of General Henry Miller." *Pennsylvania Magazine of History and Biography* 11 (1887):341-45; 12 (1888):425-31.

Wayne, Anthony. "Letters of General Wayne to General Irvine, 1778-1784." *Historical Magazine* 6 (1862):322-23, 336-42.

_____. "Orderly Book Fourth Pennsylvania Battalion, Col. Anthony Wayne, 1776." *Pennsylvania Magazine of History and Biography* 29 (1905):470-78; 30 (1906):91-103, 206-19.

[_____.] *Orderly Book of the Northern Army at Ticonderoga and Mt. Independence, From October 17th, 1776, to January 8th, 1777, With Biographical and Explanatory Notes and an Appendix.* Albany: J. Munsell, 1859.

Weiner, Wendy M., and Armstrong, John N., Jr. "1st Continental Regiment/1st Pennsylvania Regiment Flag." *Military Collector and Historian* 27 (1975):5-7.

Weiss, Harry B., and Zeigler, Grace M. *Colonel Erkuries Beatty, 1759-1823; Pennsylvania Revolutionary Soldier; New Jersey Judge, Senator, Farmer, and Prominent Citizen of Princeton.* Trenton: The Past Times Press, 1958.

Williams, Edward G., ed. "Muster Rolls at Fort Pitt, 1778." *Western Pennsylvania Historical Magazine* 45 (1962):179-90.

Williams, Ennion. "Journal of Major Ennion Williams, on His Journey to the American Camp at Cambridge, in New England, 1775." Edited by William Henry Engle. *Pennsylvania Archives,* 2d ser., 15:5-20.

Wright, Aaron. "Revolutionary Journal of Aaron Wright." *Historical Magazine* 6 (1862):208-12.

Young, Henry James. "The Spirit of 1775; a Letter of Robert Magaw, Major of the Continental Riflemen, to the Gentlemen of the Committee of Correspondence in the Town of Carlisle, 13 August 1775." *John & Mary's Journal* 1 (1975):6-60.

Delaware

DELAWARE REGIMENT*

Authorized 9 December 1775 in the Continental Army as the Delaware Regiment. Organized 13 January 1776 to consist of eight companies from Kent, Sussex, and New Castle Counties. Assigned 27 February 1776 to the Middle Department. Relieved 5 August 1776 from assignment to the Middle Department and assigned to the Main Army. Assigned 25 August 1776 to Stirling's Brigade, an element of the Main Army. Relieved 1 September 1776 from assignment to Stirling's Brigade and assigned to Mifflin's Brigade (redesignated 8 October 1776 as Stirling's Brigade), an element of the Main Army.

Reorganized 1 January 1777 to consist of eight companies. Assigned 22 May 1777 to the 1st Maryland Brigade, an element of the Main Army. Relieved 22 July 1778 from the 1st Maryland Brigade and assigned to the 3d Virginia Brigade, an element of the Main Army. (Captain Allen McLane's Company assigned 16 December 1778; relieved from assignment 13 January 1779—see 2d Partisan Corps.)

Reorganized 12 May 1779 to consist of nine companies; concurrently, relieved from the 3d Virginia Brigade and assigned to the 2d Maryland Brigade, an element of the Main Army. (2d Maryland Brigade relieved 5 April 1780 from assignment to the Main Army and assigned to the Southern Department.)

Reorganized 3 September 1780 to consist of two companies. Relieved 1 January 1781 from the 2d Maryland Brigade and assigned to the Maryland Brigade, an element of the Southern Department. Expanded in summer 1781 to consist of four companies by the reorganization of two companies at Christiana Bridge. Reorganized 4 January 1782 to consist of two companies.

Furloughed 17 January 1783 at Christiana Bridge. Disbanded 15 November 1783.

ENGAGEMENTS
  Chesapeake Bay
  New York City
  Northern New Jersey
  Trenton-Princeton
  New York 1777
  Defense of Philadelphia
  Philadelphia-Monmouth
  Defense of the Carolinas
  Greene's Campaign

---

*198th Signal Battalion, Delaware Army National Guard, perpetuates this regiment.

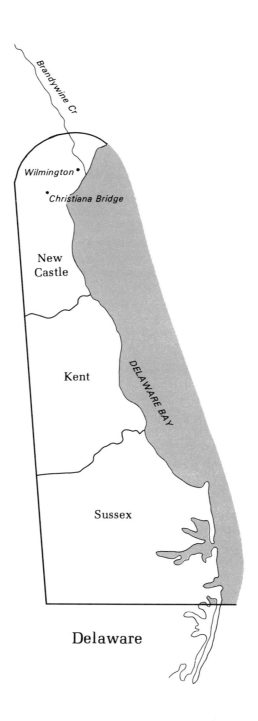

Brandywine Cr

Wilmington •
• Christiana Bridge

New
Castle

Kent

DELAWARE BAY

Sussex

Delaware

Bibliography

Anderson, Enoch. *Personal Recollections of Captain Enoch Anderson, an Officer of the Delaware Regiments in the Revolutionary War*. Edited by Henry Hobart Bellas. Wilmington: Historical Society of Delaware, 1896.

Anderson, Thomas. "Journal of Lieutenant Thomas Anderson of the Delaware Regiment 1780-1782." *Historical Magazine*, 2d ser., 1 (1867):207-11.

Bellas, Henry Hobart. *A History of the Delaware State Society of the Cincinnati From Its Organization to the Present Time. To Which is Appended a Brief Account of the Delaware Regiments in the War of the Revolution*. Wilmington: Historical Society of Delaware, 1895.

Bennett, C[aleb] P[rew]. "The Delaware Regiment in the Revolution." *Pennsylvania Magazine of History and Biography* 9 (1885):451-62.

_____. "Orderly Book of Caleb Prew Bennett at the Battle of Yorktown, 1781." Edited by Charles W. Dickens. *Delaware History* 4 (1950):105-48.

Hancock, Harold B., ed. "Revolutionary War Period Material in the Hall of Records, 1775-1787: Four Little Known Sources." *Delaware History* 17 (1976):54-85.

Kirkwood, Robert. *The Journal and Order Book of Captain Robert Kirkwood of the Delaware Regiment of the Continental Line*. Edited by Joseph Brown Turner. Wilmington: Historical Society of Delaware, 1910.

Rodney, Caesar. *Letters to and From Caesar Rodney 1756-1784*. Edited by George Herbert Ryden. Philadelphia: University of Pennsylvania Press for the Historical Society of Delaware, 1933.

Seymour, William. *A Journal of the Southern Expedition, 1780-1783*. Wilmington: Historical Society of Delaware, 1896.

Ward, Christopher. *The Delaware Continentals, 1776-1783*. Wilmington: Historical Society of Delaware, 1941.

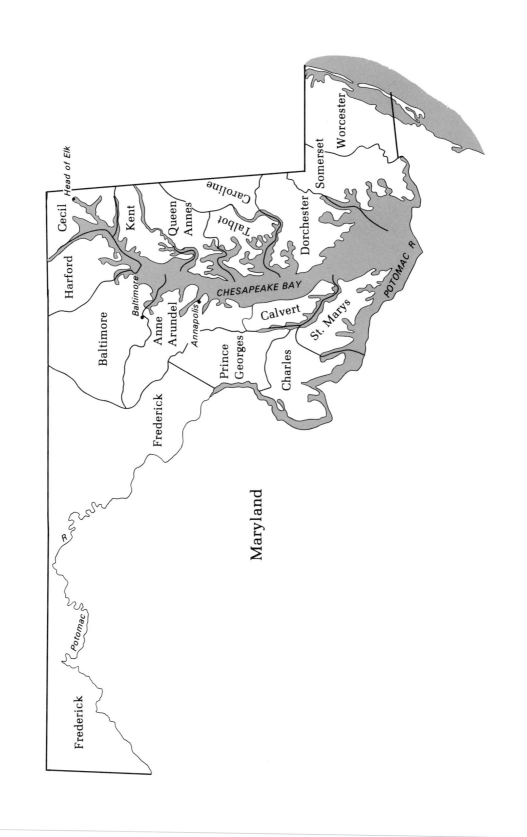

Head of Elk

Cecil

Harford

Kent

Queen Annes

Caroline

Talbot

Worcester

Somerset

Dorchester

Baltimore

Baltimore

Anne Arundel

Annapolis

CHESAPEAKE BAY

Calvert

St. Marys

POTOMAC R

Prince Georges

Charles

Frederick

Potomac R

Potomac

Frederick

Maryland

Maryland

1st MARYLAND REGIMENT*

Authorized 14 January 1776 in the Maryland State Troops as the Maryland Battalion. Organized in spring 1776 at Baltimore and Annapolis, to consist of nine companies from northern and western Maryland.

Assigned 6 July 1776 to the Main Army. Assigned 12 August 1776 to Stirling's Brigade, an element of the Main Army. Adopted 17 August 1776 into the Continental Army. Relieved 31 August 1776 from Stirling's Brigade and assigned to McDougall's Brigade, an element of the Main Army. Maryland Independent Companies (see 2d Maryland Regiment) attached 19 September 1776. Relieved 10 November 1776 from McDougall's Brigade. Assigned 10 December 1776–January 1777 to Mercer's Brigade, an element of the Main Army.

Reorganized and redesignated in January 1777 as the 1st Maryland Regiment, to consist of eight companies. Assigned 22 May 1777 to the 1st Maryland Brigade, an element of the Main Army.

Reorganized 12 May 1779 to consist of nine companies. (1st Maryland Brigade relieved 5 April 1780 from the Main Army and assigned to the Southern Department.) Relieved 1 January 1781 from the 1st Maryland Brigade and assigned to the Maryland Brigade, an element of the Southern Department.

Furloughed 27 July 1783 at Baltimore. Disbanded 15 November 1783.

ENGAGEMENTS
  New York City
  Northern New Jersey
  Trenton-Princeton
  New Jersey 1777
  Defense of Philadelphia
  Philadelphia-Monmouth
  Defense of the Carolinas
  Greene's Campaign

*175th Infantry, Maryland Army National Guard, perpetuates all seven Maryland regiments.

2d MARYLAND REGIMENT*

Authorized 14 January 1776 in the Maryland State Troops as seven Independent Companies. Organized 7–14 March 1776 at various locations on the shores of Chesapeake Bay with personnel from eastern Maryland.

Assigned 6 July–15 August 1776 to the Main Army. Adopted 17 August 1776 into the Continental Army.

Reorganized and redesignated in January 1777 as the 2d Maryland Regiment, to consist of eight companies. Assigned 22 May 1777 to the 2d Maryland Brigade, an element of the Main Army.

Reorganized 12 May 1779 to consist of nine companies. (2d Maryland Brigade relieved 5 April 1780 from the Main Army and assigned to the Southern Department.) Relieved 1 January 1781 from the 2d Maryland Brigade and assigned to the Maryland Brigade, an element of the Southern Department.

Furloughed 1 January 1783 at Charleston, South Carolina. Disbanded 15 November 1783.

ENGAGEMENTS
Chesapeake Bay
New York City
Northern New Jersey
Trenton-Princeton
New Jersey 1777
Defense of Philadelphia
Philadelphia-Monmouth
Defense of the Carolinas
Greene's Campaign

*175th Infantry, Maryland Army National Guard, perpetuates all seven Maryland regiments.

3d MARYLAND REGIMENT*

Authorized 16 September 1776 in the Continental Army as the 3d Maryland Regiment. Assigned 27 December 1776 to the Main Army. Organized 27 March 1777 to consist of eight companies from Anne Arundel, Prince Georges, Talbot, Harford, and Somerset Counties. Assigned 22 May 1777 to the 1st Maryland Brigade, an element of the Main Army.

Reorganized 12 May 1779 to consist of nine companies. (1st Maryland Brigade relieved 5 April 1780 from the Main Army and assigned to the Southern Department.) Relieved 1 January 1781 from the 1st Maryland Brigade.

Assigned 24 September 1781 to Gist's Brigade, an element of the Main Army. (Gist's Brigade relieved 27 October 1781 from the Main Army and assigned to the Southern Department.) Relieved 4 January 1782 from Gist's Brigade and assigned to the Maryland Brigade, an element of the Southern Department. Disbanded 1 January 1783 at Charleston, South Carolina.

ENGAGEMENTS
New Jersey 1777
Defense of Philadelphia
Philadelphia-Monmouth
Defense of the Carolinas
Yorktown
Greene's Campaign

*175th Infantry, Maryland Army National Guard, perpetuates all seven Maryland regiments.

4th MARYLAND REGIMENT*

Authorized 16 September 1776 in the Continental Army as the 4th Maryland Regiment. Assigned 27 December 1776 to the Main Army. Organized 27 March 1777 to consist of eight companies from Baltimore, Anne Arundel, and Somerset Counties. Assigned 22 May 1777 to the 2d Maryland Brigade, an element of the Main Army.

Reorganized 12 May 1779 to consist of nine companies. (2d Maryland Brigade relieved 5 April 1780 from the Main Army and assigned to the Southern Department.) Relieved 1 January 1781 from the 2d Maryland Brigade.

Assigned 24 September 1781 to Gist's Brigade of the Main Army. (Gist's Brigade relieved 27 October 1781 from the Main Army and assigned to the Southern Department.) Relieved 4 January 1782 from Gist's Brigade and assigned to the Maryland Brigade, an element of the Southern Department. Disbanded 1 January 1783 at Charleston, South Carolina.

ENGAGEMENTS
New Jersey 1777
Defense of Philadelphia
Philadelphia-Monmouth
Defense of the Carolinas
Yorktown
Greene's Campaign

*175th Infantry, Maryland Army National Guard, perpetuates all seven Maryland regiments.

5th MARYLAND REGIMENT*

Authorized 16 September 1776 in the Continental Army as the 5th Maryland Regiment. Assigned 27 December 1776 to the Main Army. Organized 27 March 1777 to consist of eight companies from Queen Anne, Kent, Caroline, and Dorchester Counties. Assigned 22 May 1777 to the 1st Maryland Brigade, an element of the Main Army.

Reorganized 12 May 1779 to consist of nine companies. (1st Maryland Brigade relieved 5 April 1780 from the Main Army and assigned to the Southern Department.) Relieved 1 January 1781 from the 1st Maryland Brigade and assigned to the Maryland Brigade, an element of the Southern Department.

Furloughed 1 January 1782 at Round O, South Carolina. Disbanded 1 January 1783.

ENGAGEMENTS
Defense of Philadelphia
Philadelphia-Monmouth
Defense of the Carolinas
Greene's Campaign

*175th Infantry, Maryland Army National Guard, perpetuates all seven Maryland regiments.

6th MARYLAND REGIMENT*

Authorized 16 September 1776 in the Continental Army as the 6th Maryland Regiment. Assigned 27 December 1776 to the Main Army. Organized 27 March 1777 to consist of eight companies from Prince Georges, Frederick, Cecil, Harford, Queen Anne, and Anne Arundel Counties. Assigned 22 May 1777 to the 2d Maryland Brigade, an element of the Main Army.

Reorganized 12 May 1779 to consist of nine companies. (2d Maryland Brigade relieved 5 April 1780 from the Main Army and assigned to the Southern Department.) Disbanded 1 January 1781 at Annapolis.

ENGAGEMENTS
New Jersey 1777
Defense of Philadelphia
Philadelphia-Monmouth
Defense of the Carolinas

*175th Infantry, Maryland Army National Guard, perpetuates all seven Maryland regiments.

7th MARYLAND REGIMENT*

Authorized 16 September 1776 in the Continental Army as the 7th Maryland Regiment. Assigned 27 December 1776 to the Main Army. Organized 27 March 1777 to consist of eight companies from Frederick and Baltimore Counties. Assigned 22 May 1777 to the 1st Maryland Brigade, an element of the Main Army.

Reorganized 12 May 1779 to consist of nine companies. (1st Maryland Brigade relieved 5 April 1780 from the Main Army and assigned to the Southern Department.) Disbanded 1 January 1781 at Annapolis.

ENGAGEMENTS
New Jersey 1777
Defense of Philadelphia
Philadelphia-Monmouth
Defense of the Carolinas

*175th Infantry, Maryland Army National Guard, perpetuates all seven Maryland regiments.

Bibliography

Alexander, Arthur J. "How Maryland Tried To Raise Her Continental Quota." *Maryland Historical Magazine* 37 (1942):184–96.

Balch, Thomas, ed. *Papers Relating Chiefly to the Maryland Line During the Revolution.* Philadelphia: T. K. and P. G. Collins for the Seventy-six Society, 1857.

Batt, Richard John. "The Maryland Continentals, 1780-1781." Ph.D. dissertation, Tulane University, 1974.

Beatty, William. "Correspondence of Captain William Beatty, of the Maryland Line, 1776-1781." *Historical Magazine,* 2d ser., 1 (1867):147-50.

_____. "Journal of Capt. William Beatty. 1776-1781." *Maryland Historical Magazine* 3 (1908):104-19. [Originally published in *Historical Magazine,* 2d ser., 1 (1867):79-85.]

Bedinger, Henry. "Journal of Henry Bedinger, a Sergeant From Sheperdstown." In Dorothy Dandridge, *Historic Sheperdstown* (Charlottesville: Michie Co., 1910).

Beitzell, Edwin W. *St. Mary's County, Maryland in the American Revolution: Calendar of Events.* Leonardstown: St. Mary's County, Maryland, Bicentennial Commission, 1975.

Bowie, Lucy Leigh. "Maryland Troops in the Battle of Harlem Heights." *Maryland Historical Magazine* 43 (1948):1-23.

Cassell, Frank A. *Merchant Congressman in the Young Republic; Samuel Smith of Maryland, 1752-1839.* Madison: University of Wisconsin Press, 1971.

Clark, Raymond B. *Maryland Revolutionary Records: How To Find Them & Interpret Them.* St. Michaels, Md.: Clark, 1976.

Cunz, Dieter. *The Maryland Germans: A History.* Princeton: Princeton University Press, 1948.

Dielman, Louis H., ed. "A Muster Roll of Captain Thomas Price's Company of Rifle-Men in the Service of the United Colonies." *Maryland Historical Magazine* 22 (1927):275-83.

Gunby, A. A. *Colonel John Gunby of the Maryland Line.* Cincinnati: Robert Clarke Co., 1902.

Howard, Cary. "John Eager Howard: Patriot and Public Servant." *Maryland Historical Magazine* 62 (1967):300-317.

Hoyt, William D., Jr., ed. "A List of Promotions in the Maryland Regular Troops, 1776." *Maryland Historical Magazine* 39 (1944):81-84.

Hunt, Gaillard, ed. *Fragments of Revolutionary History. Being Hitherto Unpublished Writings of the Men of the American Revolution, Collected and Edited, Under Authority of the District of Columbia Society, Sons of the Revolution.* Brooklyn: Historical Printing Club, 1892.

Jacobs, John Jeremiah. *Biographical Sketch of Captain Michael Cresap.* Edited by Otis K. Rice. Parsons, W. Va.: McClain Printing Co., 1971. [Original ed. Cumberland, Md.: J. M. Buchanan, 1826.]

Maryland Hall of Records Commission. *Calendar of Maryland State Papers.* 7 vols. Annapolis: State of Maryland, 1943-58.

Maryland Historical Society. *Archives of Maryland.* 66 vols. Baltimore: Maryland Historical Society, 1883-1954.

Papenfuse, Edward C., and Stiverson, Gregory A. "General Smallwood's Recruits: The Peacetime Career of the Revolutionary Private." *William and Mary Quarterly,* 3d ser., 30 (1973):117-32.

Peabody, Helen Lee, ed. "Revolutionary Mail Bag: Governor Thomas Sim Lee's Correspondence, 1779-1782." *Maryland Historical Magazine* 49 (1954):1-20, 122-42, 223-37, 314-51; 50 (1955):33-46, 93-108.

Read, Elizabeth. "The Howards of Maryland." *Magazine of American History* 3 (1879):239–49.

――――. "John Eager Howard: Colonel of the Second Maryland Regiment-Continental Line." *Magazine of American History* 7 (1881):276–82.

Smith, Samuel. "The Papers of General Samuel Smith." Edited by Henry B. Dawson. *Historical Magazine,* 2d ser., 7 (1870):81–92, 242–44.

Steuart, Rieman. *A History of the Maryland Line in the Revolutionary War, 1775–1783.* Towson: Society of the Cincinnati of Maryland, 1969.

Tiffany, Osmond. *A Sketch of the Life and Services of Gen. Otho Williams.* Baltimore: J. Murphy & Co., 1851.

Williams, Otho Holland. *Calendar of the Otho Holland Williams Papers in the Maryland Historical Society.* Baltimore: Historical Records Survey Project, 1940.

Virginia

1st VIRGINIA REGIMENT

Authorized 21 August 1775 in the Virginia State Troops as the 1st Virginia Regiment. Organized 21 October 1775 at Williamsburg to consist of eight companies. Adopted 1 November 1775 into the Continental Army. Reorganized 11 January 1776 to consist of ten companies.

Assigned 27 February 1776 to the Southern Department. Relieved 20 July 1776 from the Southern Department and assigned to the Main Army. Assigned 5 October 1776 to Weedon's Brigade, an element of the Main Army. Relieved 17 October 1776 from Weedon's Brigade and assigned to Stirling's Brigade, an element of the Main Army. Relieved 22 May 1777 from Stirling's Brigade and assigned to the 1st Virginia Brigade, an element of the Main Army. Reorganized 1 November 1777 to consist of eight companies.

Consolidated 12 May 1779 with the 9th Virginia Regiment [see 9th Virginia Regiment] and consolidated unit designated as the 1st Virginia Regiment, to consist of nine companies. Relieved 4 December 1779 from assignment to the 1st Virginia Brigade and assigned to the Southern Department.

Captured 12 May 1780 by the *British Army* at Charleston, South Carolina. Disbanded 15 November 1783.

ENGAGEMENTS
    Chesapeake Bay
    New York City
    Northern New Jersey
    Trenton-Princeton
    Defense of Philadelphia
    Philadelphia-Monmouth
    Charleston 1780

2d VIRGINIA REGIMENT*

Authorized 21 August 1775 in the Virginia State Troops as the 2d Virginia Regiment. Organized 21 October 1775 at Williamsburg to consist of seven companies. Adopted 1 November 1775 into the Continental Army. Reorganized 11 January 1776 to consist of ten companies.

Assigned 27 February 1776 to the Southern Department. Relieved 27 December 1776 from the Southern Department and assigned to the Main Army. Assigned 22 May 1777 to the 2d Virginia Brigade, an element of the Main Army. Reorganized 1 November 1777 to consist of eight companies.

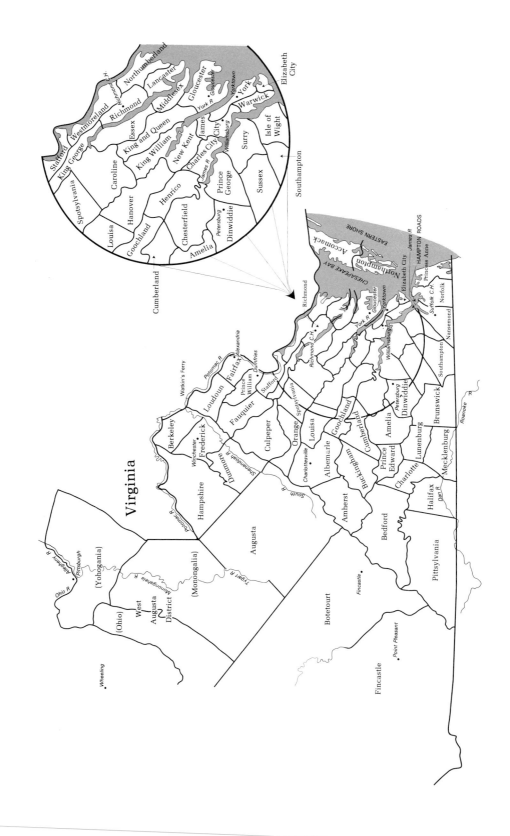

Virginia

Consolidated 12 May 1779 with the 6th Virginia Regiment [see 6th Virginia Regiment] and consolidated unit designated as the 2d Virginia Regiment, to consist of nine companies. Relieved 4 December 1779 from assignment to the 2d Virginia Brigade and assigned to the Southern Department.

Captured 12 May 1780 by the *British Army* at Charleston, South Carolina. Disbanded 15 November 1783.

ENGAGEMENTS
    Chesapeake Bay
    Northern New Jersey
    Defense of Philadelphia
    Philadelphia-Monmouth
    Charleston 1780

*The 116th Infantry, Virginia Army National Guard, perpetuates elements of this regiment.

3d VIRGINIA REGIMENT

Authorized 28 December 1775 in the Continental Army as the 3d Virginia Regiment. Assigned 27 February 1776 to the Southern Department. Organized 28 February 1776 at Alexandria and Dumfries to consist of ten companies from Prince William, Fauquier, Stafford, Louisa, Fairfax, King George, Loudoun, and Culpeper Counties.

Relieved 20 July 1776 from the Southern Department and assigned to the Main Army. Assigned 5 October 1776 to Weedon's Brigade, an element of the Main Army. Relieved 17 October 1776 from Weedon's Brigade and assigned to Stirling's Brigade, an element of the Main Army. Relieved 11 May 1777 from Stirling's Brigade and assigned to the 3d Virginia Brigade, an element of the Main Army. Reorganized 1 November 1777 to consist of eight companies. Relieved 22 July 1778 from the 3d Virginia Brigade and assigned to the 2d Virginia Brigade, an element of the Main Army.

Consolidated 12 May 1779 with the 5th Virginia Regiment [see 5th Virginia Regiment] and consolidated unit designated as the 3d Virginia Regiment, to consist of nine companies. Relieved 4 December 1779 from the 2d Virginia Brigade and assigned to the Southern Department.

Captured 12 May 1780 by the *British Army* at Charleston, South Carolina. Disbanded 1 January 1783.

ENGAGEMENTS
    Chesapeake Bay
    New York City
    Northern New Jersey
    Trenton-Princeton
    Defense of Philadelphia
    Philadelphia-Monmouth
    Charleston 1780

4th VIRGINIA REGIMENT

Authorized 28 December 1775 in the Continental Army as the 4th Virginia Regiment. Assigned 27 February 1776 to the Southern Department. Organized 28 February 1776 at Suffolk Court House to consist of ten counties from Berkeley, Charlotte, Prince Edward, Sussex, Southampton, Nansemond, Brunswick, Isle of Wight, Surry, and Princess Anne Counties and the Borough of Norfolk.

Relieved 3 September 1776 from the Southern Department and assigned to Stephen's Brigade, an element of the Main Army. Relieved 11 May 1777 from Stephen's Brigade and assigned to the 4th Virginia Brigade (redesignated 22 July 1778 as the 3d Virginia Brigade), an element of the Main Army. Reorganized 1 November 1777 to consist of eight companies.

Consolidated 12 May 1779 with the 8th Virginia Regiment [see 8th Virginia Regiment] and consolidated unit designated as the 4th Virginia Regiment, to consist of nine counties; concurrently, relieved from the 3d Virginia Brigade and assigned to 2d Virginia Brigade, an element of the Main Army. Relieved 4 December 1779 from the 2d Virginia Brigade and assigned to the Southern Department.

Captured 12 May 1780 by the *British Army* at Charleston, South Carolina. Disbanded 1 January 1783.

ENGAGEMENTS
Chesapeake Bay
Northern New Jersey
Trenton-Princeton
Defense of Philadelphia
Philadelphia-Monmouth
Charleston 1780

5th VIRGINIA REGIMENT

Authorized 28 December 1775 in the Continental Army as the 5th Virginia Regiment. Assigned 27 February 1776 to the Southern Department. Organized 28 February 1776 at Richmond County Court House to consist of ten companies from Lancaster, Richmond, Northumberland, Spotsylvania, Westmoreland, Chesterfield, Henrico, Hanover, Bedford, and Loudoun Counties.

Relieved 3 September 1776 from the Southern Department and assigned to Stephen's Brigade, an element of the Main Army. Relieved 22 May 1777 from Stephen's Brigade and assigned to the 1st Virginia Brigade, an element of the Main Army. Reorganized 1 November 1777 to consist of eight companies.

Consolidated 12 May 1779 with the 3d Virginia Regiment [see 3d Virginia Regiment].

ENGAGEMENTS
Chesapeake Bay
Northern New Jersey
Trenton-Princeton

6th VIRGINIA REGIMENT

Authorized 28 December 1775 in the Continental Army as the 6th Virginia Regiment. Assigned 27 February 1776 to the Southern Department. Organized 28 February 1776 at Williamsburg to consist of ten companies from Pittsylvania, Amherst, Buckingham, Charles City, Lunenburg, New Kent, Mecklenburg, Dinwiddie, Prince George, and Spotsylvania Counties.

Relieved 3 September 1776 from the Southern Department and assigned to Stephen's Brigade, an element of the Main Army. Relieved 22 May 1777 from Stephen's Brigade and assigned to the 2d Virginia Brigade, an element of the Main Army. Reorganized 1 November 1777 to consist of eight companies.

Consolidated 12 May 1779 with the 2d Virginia Regiment [see 2d Virginia Regiment].

ENGAGEMENTS
    Chesapeake Bay
    Northern New Jersey
    Trenton-Princeton
    Defense of Philadelphia
    Philadelphia-Monmouth

7th VIRGINIA REGIMENT

Authorized 11 January 1776 in the Virginia State Troops as the 7th Virginia Regiment. Organized 7 February–8 May 1776 at Gloucester County Court House to consist of ten companies from Halifax, Albemarle, Botetourt, Gloucester, King William, Essex, Middlesex, Cumberland, King and Queen, Orange, and Fincastle Counties. Adopted 17 June 1776 into the Continental Army and assigned to the Southern Department.

Relieved 27 December 1776 from assignment to the Southern Department and assigned to the Main Army. Assigned 11 May 1777 to the 3d Virginia Brigade, an element of the Main Army. Reorganized 1 November 1777 to consist of eight companies. Relieved 22 July 1778 from the 3d Virginia Brigade and assigned to the 2d Virginia Brigade, an element of the Main Army.

Reorganized and redesignated 12 May 1779 as the 5th Virginia Regiment to consist of nine companies. Relieved 4 December 1779 from the 2d Virginia Brigade and assigned to the Southern Department.

Captured 12 May 1780 by the *British Army* at Charleston, South Carolina. Disbanded 1 January 1783.

ENGAGEMENTS
Chesapeake Bay
Northern New Jersey
Defense of Philadelphia
Philadelphia-Monmouth
Charleston 1780

8th VIRGINIA REGIMENT*
(German Regiment)

Authorized 11 January 1776 in the Virginia State Troops as the 8th Virginia Regiment (German Regiment). Organized 9 February–4 April 1776 at Suffolk County Court House to consist of ten companies from Frederick, Dunmore [Shenandoah], Berkeley, Augusta, Hampshire, Fincastle, and Culpeper Counties and the West Augusta District. Adopted 25 May 1776 into the Continental Army and assigned to the Southern Department.

Relieved 21 January 1777 from assignment to the Southern Department and assigned to the Main Army. Assigned 11 May 1777 to the 4th Virginia Brigade (redesignated 22 July 1778 as the 3d Virginia Brigade), an element of the Main Army. Reorganized 1 November 1777 to consist of eight companies.

Consolidated 12 May 1779 with the 4th Virginia Regiment [see 4th Virginia Regiment].

ENGAGEMENTS
Chesapeake Bay
Charleston 1775–1778
Northern New Jersey
Defense of Philadelphia
Philadelphia-Monmouth

*The 116th Infantry, Virginia Army National Guard, perpetuates elements of this regiment.

9th VIRGINIA REGIMENT*

Authorized 11 January 1776 in the Virginia State Troops as the 9th Virginia Regiment. Organized 5 February–16 March 1776 on the Eastern Shore to consist of seven companies from Accomac, Northampton, Goochland, Albemarle, and Augusta Counties. Adopted 31 May 1776 into the Continental Army and assigned to the Southern Department. Reorganized 8 June 1776 to consist of ten counties.

Relieved 23 November 1776 from the Southern Department and assigned to the Main Army. Assigned 22 May 1777 to the 1st Virginia Brigade, an element of the Main Army. Reduced 7 October 1777 to a cadre in eastern Pennsylvania.

Consolidated 12 May 1779 with the 1st Virginia Regiment [see 1st Virginia Regiment].

ENGAGEMENTS
Chesapeake Bay
Northern New Jersey
Defense of Philadelphia

*The 116th Infantry, Virginia Army National Guard, perpetuates elements of this regiment.

10th VIRGINIA REGIMENT

Authorized 16 September 1776 in the Continental Army as the 10th Virginia Regiment. Assigned 27 December 1776 to the Main Army. Organized 12 February 1777 to consist of ten companies from Augusta, Amherst, Caroline, Culpeper, Cumberland, Fairfax, Fauquier, Orange, Spotsylvania, Stafford, and King George Counties.

Assigned 22 May 1777 to the 2d Virginia Brigade, an element of the Main Army. Reorganized 1 November 1777 to consist of eight companies. Relieved 22 July 1778 from the 2d Virginia Brigade and assigned to the 3d Virginia Brigade, an element of the Main Army.

Reorganized and redesignated 12 May 1779 as the 6th Virginia Regiment, to consist of nine companies. Relieved 4 December 1779 from the 2d Virginia Brigade and assigned to the Southern Department.

Captured 12 May 1780 by the *British Army* at Charleston, South Carolina. Disbanded 1 January 1783.

ENGAGEMENTS
Northern New Jersey
Defense of Philadelphia
Philadelphia-Monmouth
Charleston 1780

11th VIRGINIA REGIMENT*

Authorized 16 September 1776 in the Continental Army as the 11th Virginia Regiment. Assigned 27 December 1776 to the Main Army. Organized 3 February 1777 to consist of four companies from Loudoun, Frederick, Prince William, and Amelia Counties, Daniel Morgan's Independent Rifle Company [see *Annex*], and five companies comprising the Virginia portion of the Maryland and Virginia Rifle Regiment [see Maryland and Virginia Rifle Regiment]. (Maryland and Virginia Rifle Regiment element reorganized to consist of four companies and Captain George Rice's company [organized 18 January 1777 in the Virginia State Troops in Frederick and Augusta Counties] transferred 15 April 1777 to the regiment.)

Assigned 11 May 1777 to the 3d Virginia Brigade, an element of the Main Army. Reorganized 1 November 1777 to consist of eight companies. Relieved 22 July 1778 from the 3d Virginia Brigade and assigned to the 2d Virginia Brigade, an element of the Main Army.

Reorganized and redesignated 12 May 1779 as the 7th Virginia Regiment, to consist of nine companies. Relieved 4 December 1779 from the 2d Virginia Brigade and assigned to the Southern Department.

Captured 12 May 1780 by the *British Army* at Charleston, South Carolina. Disbanded 1 January 1781.

Annex

Authorized 14 June 1775 in the Continental Army as a Virginia Independent Rifle Company and assigned to the Main Army. Organized 22 June 1775 at Winchester, Captain Daniel Morgan commanding.

Relieved 8 September 1775 from the Main Army and assigned to the Northern Department. Captured 31 December 1775 by the *British Army* at Quebec, Canada.

Reorganized 3 February 1777 at Winchester, Captain Charles Porterfield commanding.

ENGAGEMENTS
Siege of Boston
Invasion of Canada
New York City
Trenton-Princeton
Northern New Jersey
Defense of Philadelphia
Philadelphia-Monmouth
Charleston 1780

*The 201st Field Artillery, West Virginia Army National Guard, perpetuates elements of this regiment.

12th VIRGINIA REGIMENT

Authorized 16 September 1776 in the Continental Army as the 12th Virginia Regiment. Assigned 27 December 1776 to the Main Army. Organized 12 February 1777 to consist of five companies from Hampshire, Berkeley, Botetourt, Dunmore [Shenandoah], and Prince Edward Counties and four existing companies of State Troops (organized August 1775–24 September 1776 from Botetourt, Augusta, Hampshire, and Frederick Counties and the West Augusta District) in garrison at Fort Pitt, Point Pleasant, Tyger's Valley, and Wheeling.

Assigned 11 May 1777 to the 4th Virginia Brigade (redesignated 22 July 1778 as the 3d Virginia Brigade), an element of the Main Army. Reorganized 1 November 1777 to consist of eight companies.

Reorganized and redesignated 12 May 1779 as the 8th Virginia Regiment, to consist of nine companies; concurrently, relieved from the 3d Virginia Brigade and assigned to the 2d Virginia Brigade. Relieved 4 December 1779 from the 2d Virginia Brigade and assigned to the Southern Department.

Captured 12 May 1780 by the *British Army* at Charleston, South Carolina. Disbanded 1 January 1783.

    Northern New Jersey
    Defense of Philadelphia
    Philadelphia-Monmouth
    Charleston 1780

13th VIRGINIA REGIMENT
(West Augusta Regiment)

Authorized 16 September 1776 in the Continental Army as the 13th Virginia Regiment. Assigned 27 December 1776 to the Main Army. Organized 12 February 1777 at Fort Pitt to consist of nine companies from Yohogania, Monongalia, and Ohio Counties (comprising the former West Augusta District).

Assigned 22 May 1777 to the 1st Virginia Brigade, an element of the Main Army. Reorganized 1 November 1777 to consist of eight companies. Relieved 24 May 1778 from the 1st Virginia Brigade and assigned to the Western Department.

Reorganized and redesignated 12 May 1779 as the 9th Virginia Regiment, to consist of nine companies. Reorganized and redesignated 1 January 1781 as the 7th Virginia Regiment, to consist of two companies. Disbanded 1 January 1783 at Fort Pitt, Pennsylvania.

Engagements
    Northern New Jersey
    Defense of Philadelphia
    Philadelphia-Monmouth

14th VIRGINIA REGIMENT

Authorized 16 September 1776 in the Continental Army as the 14th Virginia Regiment. Assigned 27 December 1776 to the Main Army. Organized 12 February 1777 to consist of ten companies from Halifax, Pittsylvania, Hanover, Bedford, Albemarle, Fincastle, Dinwiddie, Prince George, Goochland, Louisa, Charlotte, and Lunenburg Counties.

Assigned 22 May 1777 to the 2d Virginia Brigade, an element of the Main Army. Reorganized 1 November 1777 to consist of eight companies. Relieved 22 July 1778 from the 2d Virginia Brigade and assigned to the 1st Virginia Brigade, an element of the Main Army.

Reorganized and redesignated 12 May 1779 as the 10th Virginia Regiment, to consist of nine companies. Relieved 4 December 1779 from the 1st Virginia Brigade and assigned to the Southern Department.

Captured 12 May 1780 by the *British Army* at Charleston, South Carolina. Disbanded 1 January 1781.

ENGAGEMENTS
    Northern New Jersey
    Defense of Philadelphia
    Philadelphia-Monmouth
    Charleston 1780

15th VIRGINIA REGIMENT

Authorized 16 September 1776 in the Continental Army as the 15th Virginia Regiment. Assigned 27 December 1776 to the Main Army. Organized 12 February 1777 to consist of nine companies from Chesterfield, Brunswick, Southampton, King William, Nansemond, Princess Anne, Isle of Wight, Surry, Sussex, Westmoreland, Northumberland, and Richmond Counties and the Borough of Norfolk.

Assigned 11 May 1777 to the 3d Virginia Brigade, an element of the Main Army. Reorganized 1 November 1777 to consist of eight companies. Relieved 22 July 1778 from the 3d Virginia Brigade and assigned to the 2d Virginia Brigade, an element of the Main Army.

Reorganized and redesignated 12 May 1779 as the 11th Virginia Regiment, to consist of nine companies. Relieved 4 December 1779 from the 2d Virginia Brigade and assigned to the Southern Department.

Captured 12 May 1780 by the *British Army* at Charleston, South Carolina. Disbanded 1 January 1781.

ENGAGEMENTS
    Northern New Jersey
    Defense of Philadelphia
    Philadelphia-Monmouth
    Charleston 1780

REGIMENT OF GUARDS

Authorized 23 December 1778 in the Virginia State Troops as the Regiment of Guards. Adopted 9 January 1779 into the Continental Army and assigned to the Southern Department. Organized in January 1779 at Albemarle Barracks [Charlottesville], Virginia, to consist of nine companies from Amherst, Buckingham, Louisa, Orange, Culpeper, and Goochland Counties. Reorganized 10 December 1779 to consist of seven companies. Disbanded 10 April–9 June 1781 at Winchester and Watkin's Ferry.

ENGAGEMENTS
    None

VIRGINIA INDEPENDENT COMPANIES

Authorized 8 January 1777 in the Continental Army as two Virginia Independent Companies to garrison Fort Pitt and Fort Randolph, Pennsylvania. Organized 12 February–4 April 1777 in Yohogania and Botetourt Counties, respectively. Assigned 9 April 1777 to the Western Department. Consolidated 21 November 1779 and redesignated as Heth's Independent Company. Disbanded 1 January 1781 at Fort Pitt, Pennsylvania.

ENGAGEMENTS
    Delawares 1778
    Delawares 1779

Bibliography

Alexander, Arthur J. "A Footnote on Deserters From the Virginia Forces During the American Revolution." *Virginia Magazine of History and Biography* 55 (1947): 137–46.

Anderson, E. L. *Soldier and Pioneer; a Biographical Sketch of Lt.-Col. Richard C. Anderson of the Continental Army.* New York: G. P. Putnam's Sons, 1879.

Beale, Robert. "Revolutionary Service of a Virginia Soldier." *Southern Magazine* 17 (1875):602–7.

Boogher, William Fletcher, comp. *Gleanings of Virginia History. An Historical and Genealogical Collection, Largely From Original Sources.* Washington: Privately printed, 1903.

Boyd, Julian P., ed. *The Papers of Thomas Jefferson.* Princeton: Princeton University Press, 1950–.

Brock, R. A., ed. "Orderly Book of the Company of Captain George Stubblefield, Fifth Virginia Regiment, From March 3, 1776, to July 10, 1776, Inclusive." Virginia Historical Society *Collections,* new ser., 6 (1887):141–91.

————, ed. "Papers, Military and Political, 1775–1778, of George Gilmer, M.D., of 'Pen Park,' Albemarle County, Va." *Virginia Historical Society Collections,* new ser., 6 (1887):69–140.

Brumbaugh, Gaius Marcus. *Revolutionary War Records: Volume I, Virginia. Virginia Army and Navy Forces With Bounty Land Warrants for Virginia Military District of Ohio, and Virginia Military Script; From Federal and State Archives.* Washington: Privately printed, 1936.

Burgess, Louis A., comp. *Virginia Soldiers of 1776: Compiled From Documents on File in the Virginia Land Office Together With Material Found in the Archives Department of the Virginia State Library, and Other Reliable Sources.* 3 vols. Richmond: Richmond Press, 1927–29.

Campbell, Charles, ed. *The Orderly Book of That Portion of the American Army Stationed at or Near Williamsburg, Va., Under the Command of General Andrew Lewis From March 18th, 1776, to August 28th, 1776.* Richmond: Privately printed, 1860.

"Captain John Rogers of Caroline: An Officer in the Revolutionary Army, 1776–1782." *William and Mary Quarterly,* 1st ser., 8 (1899):100.

"Colonel Francis Taylor." *Tyler's Quarterly Historical and Genealogical Magazine* 2 (1920):335–37.

"Continental Soldiers. Abstract of Men Raised Under the Former Laws Passed for Raising Soldiers for the Continental Service—November 1782." *Tyler's Quarterly Historical and Genealogical Magazine* 9 (1928):230–45.

Decker, O. S., ed. "Virginia Soldiers at Fort Pitt, 1783." *West Virginia Historical Magazine* 3 (1903):169–71.

Edwards, William Waller. "Morgan and His Riflemen." *William and Mary Quarterly,* 1st ser., 23 (1914):73–106.

Eggleston, J. D. "Officers of the Virginia Line at Winchester, 1783." *William and Mary Quarterly,* 2d ser., 7 (1927):61.

Ethridge, Harrison M. "Governor Patrick Henry and the Reorganization of the Virginia Militia, 1784-1786." *Virginia Magazine of History and Biography* 85 (1977):427–38.

Flagg, C. A., and Waters, W. O. "A Bibliography of Muster and Pay Rolls Regimental Histories, Etc, With Introductory and Explanatory Notes." *Virginia Magazine of History and Biography* 19 (1911):402–14; 20 (1912):52–68, 181–94, 267–81; 22 (1914):57–67.

Gamble, Robert. "Orderly Book of Captain Robert Gamble of the Second Virginia Regiment, Commanded by Colonel Christian Febiger, August 21–November 16, 1779." *Virginia Historical Society Collections* 11 (1892):221–72.

Goldenberg, Joseph A.; Nelson, Eddie D.; and Fletcher, Rita Y. "Revolutionary Ranks: An Analysis of the Chesterfield Supplements." *Virginia Magazine of History and Biography* 87 (1979):182–89.

Graham, James. *The Life of General Daniel Morgan of the Virginia Line of the Army of the United States, With Portions of His Correspondence.* New York: Derby & Jackson, 1856.

Greene, Katherine Glass. *Winchester, Virginia and Its Beginnings 1743-1814.* Strasburg: Shenandoah Publishing House, 1926.

Gwathmey, John H. *Historical Register of Virginians in the Revolution: Soldiers, Sailors, Marines 1775-1783.* Richmond: Dietz Press, 1938.

Harwell, Richard Barksdale, ed. *The Committees of Safety of Westmoreland and Fincastle: Proceedings of the County Committees 1774-1776.* Richmond: Virginia State Library, 1956.

Henning, William Waller, comp. *The Statutes at Large; Being a Collection of All the Laws of Virginia, From the First Session of the Legislature, in the Year 1619.* 14 vols. Richmond: J. & G. Cochran, 1821.

Henry, William Wirt. *Patrick Henry: Life, Correspondence and Speeches.* 3 vols. New York: Charles Scribner's Sons, 1891.

Heth, William. "The Diary of Lieutenant William Heth While a Prisoner in Quebec, 1776." Edited by B. Floyd Flickinger. *Annual Papers of [the] Winchester Virginia Historical Society* 1 (1931):27–118.

_____. "Orderly Book of Major William Heth of the Third Virginia Regiment, May 15–July 1, 1777." *Virginia Historical Society Collections* 11 (1892):319–76.

Hunt, Gaillard, ed. *Fragments of Revolutionary History: Being Hitherto Unpublished Writings of the Men of the American Revolution, Collected and Edited Under Authority of the District of Columbia Society, Sons of the Revolution.* Brooklyn: Historical Printing Club, 1892.

Jackson, Luther P. "Virginia Negro Soldiers and Seamen in the American Revolution." *Journal of Negro History* 27 (1942):247-87.

Johnston, Henry P. "Christian Febiger Colonel of the Virginia Line of the Continental Army." *Magazine of American History* 5 (1881):188-203.

Joynes, Levin Smith. *A Sketch of the Life of Thomas R. Joynes of Accomack, Va.; With a Brief Notice of His Father, Col. Levin Joynes, of the Continental Army.* Columbia, S.C.: R. L. Bryan Co., 1876.

Joynes, Thomas R. "Ninth Virginia Regiment of the Revolutionary Army." *Historical Magazine* 7 (1863):172-75.

_____. "Ninth Virginia Regiment of the Revolutionary Army, With a List of Officers, January 1777." *Pennsylvania Magazine of History and Biography* 22 (1898): 122-24.

Lewis, Virgil A. *History of the Battle of Point Pleasant Fought Between White Men and Indians at the Mouth of the Great Kanawha River, (Now Point Pleasant, West Virginia) Monday, October 19th, 1774. The Chief Event of Lord Dunmore's War.* Charleston, W. Va.: Tribune Printing Co., 1909.

_____. *The Soldiery of West Virginia in the French and Indian War: Lord Dunmore's War; the Revolution; the Later Indian Wars; the Whiskey Insurrection; the Second War With England; the War With Mexico. And Addenda Relating to West Virginians in the Civil War.* Charleston, W. Va.: Third Biennial Report of the Department of Archives and History, State of West Virginia, 1911.

McAllister, J. T. "Depositions of Revolutionary Soldiers." *Virginia Magazine of History and Biography* 4 (1897):411-15; 5 (1897):153-58.

_____. "Summary of Statements Made by Soldiers Who Served in the Revolutionary War From Virginia—Either in the Continental Line or the Virginia State Line." *Virginia Magazine of History and Biography* 22 (1914):177-86.

_____. *Virginia Militia in the Revolutionary War: McAllister's Data.* Hot Springs, Va.: McAllister Publishing Co., 1913.

McBride, John David. "The Virginia War Effort; 1775-1783: Manpower Policies and Practices." Ph.D. dissertation, University of Virginia, 1977.

McIlwaine, Henry Read, ed. *Journals of the Council of the State of Virginia.* 2 vols. Richmond: Virginia State Library, 1931-52.

_____, ed. *Official Letters of the Governors of the State of Virginia.* 3 vols. Richmond: Virginia State Library, 1926-29.

Mason, George. *The Papers of George Mason 1725-1792.* Edited by Robert A. Rutland. 3 vols. Chapel Hill: University of North Carolina Press, 1970.

Morrison, Alfred J., ed. "Pay Roll of Captain John Morton's Company of Regulars, Fourth Virginia, 1776." *Virginia Magazine of History and Biography* 17 (1909):305-8.

Muhlenberg, John P. G. "Orderly Book of Gen. John Peter Gabriel Muhlenberg, [May] March 26-December 20, 1777." *Pennsylvania Magazine of History and Biography* 33 (1909):257-78, 454-74; 34 (1910):21-40, 166-89, 336-60, 438-77; 35 (1911):59-89, 156-87, 290-303.

"A Muster Roll of Captain Ambrose Madison's Company of Foot in the Regiment of Volunteer Guards at the Barracks in Albemarle County, Where Francis Taylor Esqr Is Commander to June 1st, 1779." *Virginia Magazine of History and Biography* 1 (1894):458–60.

Palmer, William P., ed. *Calendar of Virginia State Papers and Other Manuscripts.* 11 vols. Richmond: Virginia State Library, 1875–93.

Pennypacker, Samuel W., ed. *Valley Forge Orderly Book of General George Weedon of the Continental Army Under the Command of Genl. George Washington, in the Campaign of 1777–8.* New York: Dodd, Mead & Co., 1902.

Powell, Robert C. *A Biographical Sketch of Col. Levin Powell, Including His Correspondence During the Revolutionary War.* Alexandria: G. H. Ramey & Son, 1877.

"Revolutionary Army Orders for the Main Army Under Washington, 1778–1779." *Virginia Magazine of History and Biography* 13–22 (1906–14):various pages.

"Revolutionary Letters." *Tyler's Quarterly Historical and Genealogical Magazine* 8 (1927):176; 9 (1928):245–48.

Russell, T. Triplett, and Gott, John K. *Fauquier County in the Revolution.* Warrenton: Fauquier County American Bicentennial Commission, 1976.

Sanchez-Saavedra, E. M. *A Guide to Virginia Military Organizations in the American Revolution, 1774–1787.* Richmond: Virginia State Library, 1978.

Schmucker, George W., ed. "Letters of Generals Daniel Morgan and Peter Muhlenberg." *Pennsylvania Magazine of History and Biography* 21 (1897):488–92.

"Second Virginia Battalion, 1777." *Virginia Magazine of History and Biography* 6 (1898):124–27.

Sellers, John Robert. "The Virginia Continental Line, 1775–1780." Ph.D. dissertation, Tulane University, 1968.

Stephen, Adam. "Letters of General Adam Stephen to R. H. Lee." *Historical Magazine,* 1st ser., 9 (1865):118–22.

Sydnor, William. "David Griffith—Chaplain, Surgeon, Patriot." *Historical Magazine of the Protestant Episcopal Church* 44 (1975):247–56.

Tartar, Brent, ed. "The Orderly Book of the Second Virginia Regiment, September 27, 1775–April 15, 1776." *Virginia Magazine of History and Biography* 85 (1977):156–83, 302–36.

Taylor, P. Fall, ed. "Fourth Virginia Regiment in the Revolution." *Virginia Magazine of History and Biography* 1 (1893):202–7.

Tyler, Lyon G. "The Old Virginia Line in the Middle States During the American Revolution." *Tyler's Quarterly Historical and Genealogical Magazine* 12 (1930–31):1–42, 90–141, 198–203, 283–89.

Van Schreevan, William J., et al., eds. *Revolutionary Virginia: The Road to Independence.* Charlottesville: University Press of Virginia for the Virginia Independence Bicentennial Commission, 1973–.

The Virginia Gazette. Edited by John Pinkney, 1775–76. John Dixon and William Hunter, 1775–78. Alexander Purdie, 1775–78. John Clarkson and Augustus Davis, 1779–80. John Dixon and Thomas Nicholson, 1779–80. Williamsburg & Richmond.

"Virginia Officers and Men in the Continental Line." *Virginia Magazine of History and Biography* 2 (1895):241–58, 357–70.

Wallace, Lee A., Jr., ed. *The Orderly Book of Captain Benjamin Taliaferro: 2d Virginia Detachment, Charleston, South Carolina, 1780.* Richmond: Virginia State Library, 1980.

White, William E. "The Independent Companies of Virginia, 1774-1775." *Virginia Magazine of History and Biography* 86 (1978):149-62.

Williams, Edward G., ed. "Muster Rolls at Fort Pitt, 1778." *Western Pennsylvania Historical Magazine* 45 (1962):179-90.

Wilson, Samuel M., comp. *Catalogue of the Revolutionary Soldiers and Sailors of the Commonwealth of Virginia to Whom Land Bounty Warrants Were Granted by Virginia for Military Services in the War for Independence.* 1913. Reprint. Baltimore: Genealogical Publishing Co., 1967.

Wise, Barton Hextall, ed. "Memoir of General John Cropper of Accomack County, Virginia." *Virginia Historical Society Collections* 11 (1892):273-315. [Reprinted Onancock: Eastern Shore of Virginia Historical Society, 1974.]

Wood, James. "Correspondence of Col. James Wood." *Tyler's Quarterly Historical and Genealogical Magazine* 3 (1921):28-44.

Wust, Klaus. *The Virginia Germans.* Charlottesville: The University Press of Virginia, 1969.

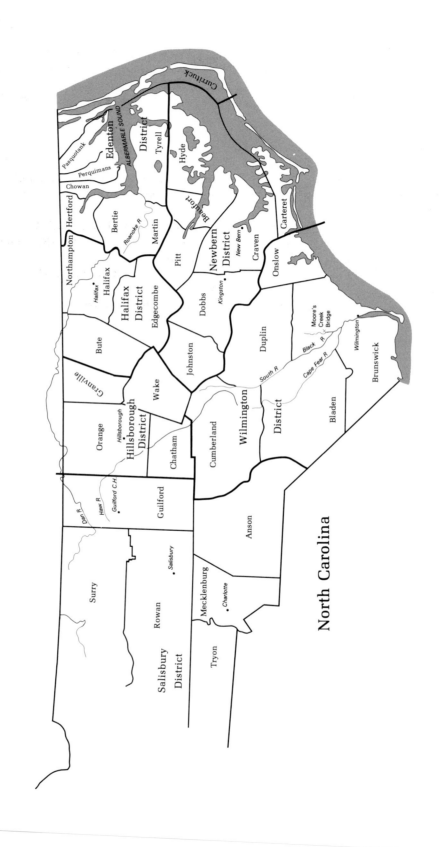

North Carolina

North Carolina

1st NORTH CAROLINA REGIMENT

Authorized 1 September 1775 in the Continental Army as the 1st North Carolina Regiment. Organized in fall 1775 at Salisbury and Wilmington to consist of ten companies. Reorganized 4 January 1776 to consist of eight companies. Assigned 27 February 1776 to the Southern Department. Relieved 5 February 1777 from the Southern Department and assigned to the Main Army.

Assigned 8 July 1777 to the North Carolina Brigade, an element of the Main Army. Reorganized 1 June 1778 to consist of nine companies. (North Carolina Brigade relieved 19 July 1779 from the Main Army and assigned to the Highlands Department; relieved 11 November 1779 from the Highlands Department and assigned to the Southern Department.) Captured 12 May 1780 at Charleston, South Carolina, by the *British Army*.

Reorganized in summer 1781 at Hillsborough and Salisbury to consist of nine companies and assigned to the North Carolina Brigade, an element of the Southern Department. Furloughed 23 April 1783 at James Island, South Carolina. Disbanded 15 November 1783.

ENGAGEMENTS
>   Southern Highlands
>   Defense of Philadelphia
>   Philadelphia-Monmouth
>   Charleston 1780
>   Greene's Campaign
> Detachments additionally served in the following:
>   Charleston 1775–1776
>   Florida

2d NORTH CAROLINA REGIMENT

Authorized 1 September 1775 in the Continental Army as the 2d North Carolina Regiment. Organized in fall 1775 at Salisbury, Edenton, and Newbern to consist of ten companies. Reorganized 4 January 1776 to consist of eight companies. Assigned 27 February 1776 to the Southern Department. Relieved 5 February 1777 from the Southern Department and assigned to the Main Army.

Assigned 8 July 1777 to the North Carolina Brigade, an element of the Main Army. Reorganized 1 June 1778 to consist of nine companies. (North Carolina Brigade relieved 19 July 1779 from the Main Army and assigned to the Highlands Department; relieved 11 November 1779 from the Highlands Department and assigned to the Southern Department.) Captured 12 May 1780 at Charleston, South Carolina, by the *British Army*.

Reorganized in summer 1781 at Hillsborough and Salisbury to consist of nine companies and assigned to the North Carolina Brigade, an element of the Southern Department. Furloughed 1 January 1783 at James Island, South Carolina. Disbanded 15 November 1783.

ENGAGEMENTS
   Chesapeake Bay
   Defense of Philadelphia
   Philadelphia-Monmouth
   Charleston 1780
   Greene's Campaign
Detachments additionally served in the following:
   Charleston 1775–1776
   Southern Highlands
   Florida
   New York 1779

3d NORTH CAROLINA REGIMENT

Authorized 16 January 1776 in the Continental Army as the 3d North Carolina Regiment. Assigned 27 February 1776 to the Southern Department. Organized in spring 1776 at Wilmington to consist of eight companies from Halifax, Edenton, and Hillsborough Districts. Relieved 5 February 1777 from the Southern Department and assigned to the Main Army.

Assigned 8 July 1777 to the North Carolina Brigade, an element of the Main Army. Reduced to a cadre 1 June 1778 at Valley Forge, Pennsylvania; concurrently relieved from the North Carolina Brigade.

Reorganized 9 July 1778 at Halifax to consist of nine companies. Relieved 7 November 1778 from the Main Army and assigned to the Highlands Department. Relieved 19 December 1778 from the Highlands Department and assigned to the Middle Department. Reduced to a cadre 17 April 1779 at Philadelphia, Pennsylvania; concurrently relieved from the Middle Department and assigned to the Southern Department.

Reorganized 5 November 1779 at Halifax to consist of nine companies. Assigned 14 February 1780 to Parker's Brigade, an element of the Southern Department. Relieved 6 March 1780 from Parker's Brigade and assigned to the North Carolina Brigade, an element of the Southern Department. Captured 12 May 1780 at Charleston, South Carolina, by the *British Army*. Disbanded 1 January 1783.

ENGAGEMENTS
   Charleston 1775–1776
   Florida
   Defense of Philadelphia
   Philadelphia-Monmouth
   Charleston 1780

4th NORTH CAROLINA REGIMENT

Authorized 26 March 1776 in the Continental Army as the 4th North Carolina Regiment and assigned to the Southern Department. Organized in spring 1776 at Wilmington to consist of eight companies from Salisbury, Edenton, and Wilmington Districts. Relieved 5 February 1777 from the Southern Department and assigned to the Main Army.

Assigned 8 July 1777 to the North Carolina Brigade, an element of the Main Army. Reduced to a cadre 1 June 1778 at Valley Forge, Pennsylvania; concurrently relieved from Main Army and assigned to the Southern Department.

Reorganized in fall 1778 at Halifax to consist of nine companies. Assigned 11 January 1779 to Sumner's Brigade, an element of the Southern Department. (Sumner's Brigade redesignated 3 June 1779 as Armstrong's Brigade.) Captured 12 May 1780 at Charleston, South Carolina, by the *British Army*. Disbanded 1 January 1783.

ENGAGEMENTS
    Defense of Philadelphia
    Philadelphia-Monmouth
    Savannah
    Charleston 1780

5th NORTH CAROLINA REGIMENT

Authorized 26 March 1776 in the Continental Army as the 5th North Carolina Regiment and assigned to the Southern Department. Organized in spring 1776 at Wilmington to consist of eight companies from Newbern, Edenton, and Hillsborough Districts. Relieved 5 February 1777 from the Southern Department and assigned to the Main Army.

Assigned 8 July 1777 to the North Carolina Brigade, an element of the Main Army. Reduced to a cadre 1 June 1778 at Valley Forge, Pennsylvania; concurrently relieved from the Main Army and assigned to the Southern Department.

Reorganized in fall 1778 at Halifax to consist of nine companies. Assigned 11 January 1779 to Sumner's Brigade, an element of the Southern Department. (Sumner's Brigade redesignated 3 June 1779 as Armstrong's Brigade.) Captured 12 May 1780 at Charleston, South Carolina, by the *British Army*. Disbanded 1 January 1781.

ENGAGEMENTS
    Defense of Philadelphia
    Philadelphia-Monmouth
    Savannah
    Charleston 1780

6th NORTH CAROLINA REGIMENT

Authorized 13 April 1776 in the North Carolina State Troops as the 6th North Carolina Regiment. Organized in spring and summer 1776 at Wilmington to consist of eight companies from Wilmington and Hillsborough Districts. Adopted 7 May 1776 into the Continental Army and assigned to the Southern Department. Relieved 5 February 1777 from the Southern Department and assigned to the Main Army.

Assigned 8 July 1777 to the North Carolina Brigade, an element of the Main Army. Reduced to a cadre 1 June 1778 at Valley Forge, Pennsylvania; concurrently relieved from the Main Army and assigned to the Southern Department.

Reorganized in fall 1778 at Halifax to consist of nine companies. Assigned 11 January 1779 to Sumner's Brigade, an element of the Southern Department. Reduced to a cadre 11 February 1779 at Purysburg, South Carolina. Disbanded 1 January 1781.

ENGAGEMENTS
   Defense of Philadelphia
   Philadelphia-Monmouth

7th NORTH CAROLINA REGIMENT

Authorized 16 September 1776 in the Continental Army as the 7th North Carolina Regiment and assigned to the Southern Department. Organized in spring 1777 at Halifax to consist of eight companies from Halifax and Edenton Districts. Relieved 5 February 1777 from the Southern Department and assigned to the Main Army.

Assigned 8 July 1777 to the North Carolina Brigade, an element of the Main Army. Disbanded 1 June 1778 at Valley Forge, Pennsylvania.

ENGAGEMENTS
   Defense of Philadelphia
   Philadelphia-Monmouth

8th NORTH CAROLINA REGIMENT

Authorized 16 September 1776 in the Continental Army as the 8th North Carolina Regiment and assigned to the Southern Department. Organized in spring 1777 at Halifax to consist of eight companies from Newbern and Wilmington Districts. Relieved 5 February 1777 from the Southern Department and assigned to the Main Army.

Assigned 8 July 1777 to the North Carolina Brigade, an element of the Main Army. Disbanded 1 June 1778 at Valley Forge, Pennsylvania.

ENGAGEMENTS
   Defense of Philadelphia
   Philadelphia-Monmouth

9th NORTH CAROLINA REGIMENT

Authorized 16 September 1776 in the Continental Army as the 9th North Carolina Regiment and assigned to the Southern Department. Organized in spring 1777 at Halifax to consist of eight companies from Hillsborough and Salisbury Districts. Relieved 5 February 1777 from the Southern Department and assigned to the Main Army.

Assigned 8 July 1777 to the North Carolina Brigade, an element of the Main Army. Disbanded 1 June 1778 at Valley Forge, Pennsylvania.

ENGAGEMENTS
  Defense of Philadelphia
  Philadelphia-Monmouth

SHEPPARD'S ADDITIONAL CONTINENTAL REGIMENT
(10th North Carolina Regiment)

Authorized 17 April 1777 in the North Carolina State Troops as Sheppard's Regiment. Organized 19 April–1 July 1777 at Kinston to consist of eight companies from the northeastern part of the state.

Adopted 17 June 1777 into the Continental Army as Sheppard's Additional Continental Regiment and assigned to the Main Army. Disbanded 1 June 1778 at Valley Forge, Pennsylvania.

ENGAGEMENTS
  Philadelphia-Monmouth

Bibliography

Angellotti, Mrs. Frank M. "The Polks of North Carolina and Tennessee." *New England Historical and Genealogical Register* 77 (1923):133–45, 213–27, 250–70; 78 (1924):33–53, 159–77, 318–30.

Ashe, Samuel A'Court. *Rutherford's Expedition Against the Indians, 1776, by Captain S. A. Ashe*. Raleigh: E. M. Uzzell & Co., 1904.

Bartholomees, James Boone, Jr. "Fight or Flee: The Combat Performance of the North Carolina Militia in the Cowpens-Guilford Courthouse Campaign. January to March 1781." Ph.D. dissertation, Duke University, 1978.

Battle, Kemp Plummer. "Career of Brigadier-General Jethro Sumner One of North Carolina's Revolutionary Officers." *Magazine of American History* 26 (1891):415–33.

Caruthers, E[li] W. *Interesting Revolutionary Incidents: and Sketches of Character, Chiefly in the 'Old North State.'* Philadelphia: Hayes & Zell, 1856.

———. *Revolutionary Incidents; and Sketches of Character, Chiefly in the 'Old North State.'* Philadelphia: Hayes & Zell, 1854.

Clark, Walter. "General Williams Richardson Davie 1756-1820." *Magazine of American History* 28 (1892):415-30.

_____, et al., eds. *The State Records of North Carolina*. 16 vols. Winston and Goldsboro: Various publishers, 1895-1907.

Davis, Charles L. *A Brief History of the North Carolina Troops on the Continental Establishment in the War of the Revolution*. Philadelphia: N.p., 1896.

Ganyard, Robert Loyal. "North Carolina During the American Revolution: The First Phase, 1774-1777." Ph.D. dissertation, Duke University, 1963.

Hay, Gertrude Sloan, ed. *Roster of Soldiers From North Carolina in the American Revolution With an Appendix Containing a Collection of Miscellaneous Records*. Durham: North Carolina Daughters of the American Revolution, 1932.

Lazenby, Mary Elinor. *Catawba Frontier, 1775-1781; Memories of Pensioners*. Washington: Privately printed, 1950.

Lefler, Hugh, and Wager, Paul, eds. *Orange County, 1752-1952*. Chapel Hill: Privately printed, 1953.

Lutz, Paul V. "A State's Concern for the Soldier's Welfare: How North Carolina Provided for Her Troops During the Revolution." *North Carolina Historical Review* 42 (1965):315-18.

McEachern, Leora H., and Williams, Isable M., eds. *Wilmington-New Hanover Safety Committee Minutes, 1774-1776*. Wilmington: Wilmington-New Hanover County American Revolution Bi-centennial Association, 1974.

McMurtrie, Douglas C. *The Proceedings of the Revolutionary Committee of the Town of Newbern, North Carolina, 1775*. Chicago: Chicago School of Printing, 1938.

Murfree, W. L. "Colonel Hardy Murfree, of the North Carolina Line." *North Carolina Booklet* 17 (1918):160-64.

Naisawald, L. Van Loan. "Major General Robert Howe's Activities in South Carolina and Georgia, 1776-1779." *Georgia Historical Quarterly* 35 (1951):23-30.

_____. "Robert Howe's Operations in Virginia, 1775-1776." *Virginia Magazine of History and Biography* 60 (1952):437-43.

Nash, Frank. "The Continental Line of North Carolina." *North Carolina Booklet* 17 (1918):105-34.

Rankin, Hugh F. *The North Carolina Continentals*. Chapel Hill: University of North Carolina Press, 1971.

Russell, Phillips. *North Carolina in the Revolutionary War*. Charlotte: Heritage Printers, 1965.

Saunders, William L., ed. *The Colonial Records of North Carolina*. 10 vols. Raleigh: Various publishers, 1886-90.

Wheeler, Earl Milton. "The Role of the North Carolina Militia in the Beginning of the American Revolution." Ph.D. dissertation, Tulane University, 1969.

_____. "Development and Organization of the North Carolina Militia." *North Carolina Historical Review* 41 (1964):307-23.

South Carolina

1st SOUTH CAROLINA REGIMENT

Authorized 6 June 1775 in the South Carolina State Troops as the 1st South Carolina Regiment. Organized in summer 1775 at Charleston to consist of ten companies from eastern South Carolina. Adopted 4 November 1775 into the Continenal Army. Assigned 27 February 1776 to the Southern Department.

Assigned 23 November 1776 to the 1st South Carolina Brigade, an element of the Southern Department. Relieved 3 January 1779 from the 1st South Carolina Brigade. Assigned 1 February 1779 to the South Carolina Brigade, an element of the Southern Department.

Consolidated 11 February 1780 with the 5th South Carolina Regiment [see 5th South Carolina Regiment] and consolidated unit designated as the 1st South Carolina Regiment, an element of the South Carolina Brigade, to consist of nine companies. Captured 12 May 1780 at Charleston by the *British Army*.

Reorganized 11 December 1782-19 March 1783 at Charleston to consist of three companies. Furloughed 1-14 May 1783 at Charleston. Disbanded 15 November 1783.

ENGAGEMENTS
    Charleston 1775-1776
    Florida 1778
    Savannah
    Charleston 1780
Captain Ioor's Company additionally served in:
    Caribbean 1778

2d SOUTH CAROLINA REGIMENT

Authorized 6 June 1775 in the South Carolina State Troops as the 2d South Carolina Regiment. Organized in summer 1775 at Charleston to consist of ten companies from eastern South Carolina. Adopted 4 November 1775 into the Continental Army. Assigned 27 February 1776 to the Southern Department.

Assigned 23 November 1776 to the 2d South Carolina Brigade, an element of the Southern Department. Relieved 26 August 1778 from the 2d South Carolina Brigade and assigned to the 1st South Carolina Brigade, an element of the Southern Department. Relieved 3 January 1779 from the 1st South Carolina Brigade. Assigned 15 June 1779 to McIntosh's Brigade, an element of the Southern Department. Relieved 14 September 1779 from McIntosh's Brigade and assigned to Huger's Brigade, an element of the Southern Department.

Consolidated 11 February 1780 with the 6th South Carolina Regiment [see 6th South Carolina Regiment] and consolidated unit designated as the 2d South Carolina

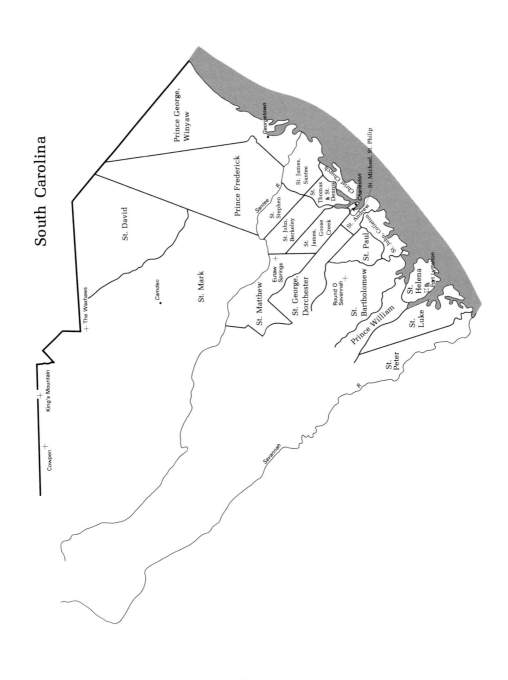

South Carolina

Regiment, to consist of nine companies; concurrently relieved from Huger's Brigade and assigned to the South Carolina Brigade, an element of the Southern Department. Captured 12 May 1780 at Charleston by the *British Army*. Disbanded 1 January 1783.

ENGAGEMENTS
    Charleston 1775–1776
    Savannah
    Charleston 1780
Detachments additionally served in:
    Florida

3d SOUTH CAROLINA REGIMENT
(South Carolina Ranger Regiment)

Authorized 6 June 1775 in the South Carolina State Troops as the South Carolina Regiment of Horse Rangers. Organized in summer 1775 at Ninety-Six Court House and other locations to consist of nine companies from western South Carolina. Redesignated 12 November 1775 as the 3d South Carolina Regiment. Adopted 24 July 1776 into the Continental Army and assigned to the Southern Department; Captain Ezekiel Polk's Independent Company (organized in summer 1775 in western South Carolina) concurrently redesignated as the 10th Company, 3d South Carolina Regiment.

Assigned 23 November 1776 to the 1st South Carolina Brigade, an element of the Southern Department. Relieved 26 August 1778 from the 1st South Carolina Brigade and assigned to the 2d South Carolina Brigade, an element of the Southern Department. Relieved 3 January 1779 from the 2d South Carolina Brigade.

Assigned 1 February 1779 to the South Carolina Brigade, an element of the Southern Department. Reorganized 11 February 1780 to consist of nine companies. Captured 12 May 1780 at Charleston by the *British Army*. Disbanded 1 January 1781.

ENGAGEMENTS
    Charleston 1775–1776
    Southern Highlands
    Savannah
    Charleston 1780
Detachments additionally served in the following:
    Cherokees 1776
    Florida
    Florida 1778

4th SOUTH CAROLINA REGIMENT
(South Carolina Artillery Regiment)

Authorized 13 November 1775 in the South Carolina State Troops as the 4th South Carolina Regiment. Organized 20 November–18 December 1775 at Charleston to consist of three companies from the greater Charleston area. Adopted 18 June 1776 into the Continental Army and assigned to the Southern Department.

Expanded 18 October 1776 to consist of six companies (Beaufort and Georgetown Independent Companies of Artillery [*see Annexes 1 and 2*] concurrently redesignated as the 4th and 5th Companies, 4th South Carolina Regiment). Captured 12 May 1780 at Charleston by the *British Army*. Disbanded 1 January 1781.

Annex 1*

Authorized 22 February 1776 in the South Carolina State Troops as the Beaufort Independent Company of Artillery. Organized in spring 1776 at Fort Lyttleton with personnel from St. Helena and Prince William Parishes. Redesignated 18 October 1776 as the 4th Company, 4th South Carolina Regiment, and adopted into the Continental Army.

Annex 2

Authorized 22 February 1776 in the South Carolina State Troops as the Georgetown Independent Company of Artillery. Organized in spring 1776 at Georgetown with personnel from Prince George, Winyah Parish. Redesignated 18 October 1776 as the 5th Company, 4th South Carolina Regiment, and adopted into the Continental Army.

ENGAGEMENTS
    Charleston 1775–1776
    Savannah
    Charleston 1780
Detachments additionally served in the following:
    Southern Highlands
    Florida
    Florida 1778

*This company is perpetuated by the 263d Air Defense Artillery and Detachment 1, Troop B, 1st Squadron, 713th Cavalry, South Carolina Army National Guard.

5th SOUTH CAROLINA REGIMENT
(1st South Carolina Rifle Regiment)

Authorized 22 February 1776 in the South Carolina State Troops as the 5th South Carolina Regiment. Organized in spring 1776 at Charleston to consist of seven companies from eastern and northern South Carolina. Adopted 25 March 1776 into the Continental Army and assigned to the Southern Department.

Assigned 23 November 1776 to the 2d South Carolina Brigade, an element of the Southern Department. Relieved 3 January 1779 from the 2d South Carolina Brigade. Assigned 1 February 1779 to the South Carolina Brigade, an element of the Southern Department. Relieved 1 May 1779 from the South Carolina Brigade. Assigned 15 June 1779 to McIntosh's Brigade, an element of the Southern Department. Relieved 14 September 1779 from McIntosh's Brigade.

Consolidated 11 February 1780 with the 1st South Carolina Regiment [see 1st South Carolina Regiment].

ENGAGEMENTS
   Charleston 1775–1776
   Savannah
Elements additionally served in:
   Florida

6th SOUTH CAROLINA REGIMENT
(2d South Carolina Rifle Regiment)

Authorized 28 February 1776 in the South Carolina State Troops as the 6th South Carolina Regiment. Organized in spring 1776 at Charleston to consist of five companies from northwestern South Carolina. Adopted 25 March 1776 into the Continental Army and assigned to the Southern Department.

Reorganized 18 October 1776 to consist of six companies (Captain Richbourg's Independent Company [organized in spring 1776 at Charleston with personnel from northwestern South Carolina] concurrently redesignated as the 6th Company, 6th South Carolina Regiment). Assigned 23 November 1776 to the 1st South Carolina Brigade, an element of the Southern Department. Relieved 3 January 1779 from the 1st South Carolina Brigade. Assigned 1 February 1779 to the South Carolina Brigade, an element of the Southern Department.

Consolidated 11 February 1780 with the 2d South Carolina Regiment [see 2d South Carolina Regiment].

ENGAGEMENTS
   Charleston 1775–1776
   Cherokees 1776
   Florida
   Florida 1778
   Savannah

Bibliography

Bass, Robert D. *Swamp Fox: The Life and Campaigns of General Francis Marion.* New York: Henry Holt & Co., 1959.

_____. *Gamecock: The Life and Campaigns of General Thomas Sumter.* New York: Holt, Rinehart & Winston, 1961.

Bennett, John, comp. "A List of Noncommissioned Officers and Private Men of the Second South Carolina Continental Regiment of Foot." *South Carolina Historical and Genealogical Magazine* 16 (1915):25–33.

Bentham, James. "Regimental Book of Captain James Bentham, 1778–1780." Edited by Robert Bentham Simons. *South Carolina Historical and Genealogical*

Magazine 53 (1952):13–18, 101–12, 161–71, 230–40; 54 (1953):37–47, 88–96, 143–55.

Cann, Marvin L. "Prelude to War: The First Battle of Ninety Six November 19–21, 1775." *South Carolina Historical Magazine* 76 (1975):197–214.

Davis, Nora M. *Fort Charlotte on Savannah River and Its Significance in the American Revolution.* Greenwood, S.C.: Star Fort Chapter, Daughters of the American Revolution, 1949.

De Saussure, Wilmot Gibbes, comp. *The Names, as far as Can Be Ascertained, of the Officers Who Served in the South Carolina Regiments on the Continental Establishment; of the Officers Who Served in the Militia; of What Troops Were Upon the Continental Establishment; and of What Militia Organizations Served; Together With Some Miscellaneous Information.* Columbia: South Carolina General Assembly, 1886.

Drayton, John. *Memoirs of the American Revolution, From Its Commencement to the Year 1776, Inclusive; as Relating to the State of South-Carolina; and Occasionally Relating to the States of North-Carolina and Georgia.* 2 vols. Charleston: A. E. Miller, 1821.

Elliott, Barnard. "Diary of Captain Barnard Elliott." *Year Book, City of Charleston for 1889*:151–262.

———. "Barnard Elliott's Recruiting Journal, 1775." Edited by Joseph W. Barnwell. *South Carolina Historical and Genealogical Magazine* 17 (1916):95–100.

Fraser, Walter J., Jr. "Reflections of 'Democracy' in Revolutionary South Carolina? The Composition of Military Organizations and the Attitudes and Relationships of the Officers and Men, 1775–1780." *South Carolina Historical Magazine* 78 (1977):202–12.

Gibbes, R. W., ed. *Documentary History of the American Revolution.* 3 vols. Columbia and New York: Banner Steam-Power Press and D. Appleton & Co., 1853–57.

Gregorie, Anne King. *Thomas Sumter.* Columbia: R. L. Bryan Co., 1931.

Grimke, John Faucheraud. "Order Book of John Faucheraud Grimke. August 1778 to May 1780." *South Carolina Historical and Genealogical Magazine* 13 (1912):42–55, 89–123, 146–53, 205–12; 14 (1913):44–57, 98–111, 160–70, 219–24; 15 (1914):51–59, 82–90, 124–32, 166–70; 16 (1915):39–48, 80–85, 123–28, 178–83; 17 (1916):26–33, 82–86, 116–20, 167–74; 18 (1917):78–84, 149–53, 175–79; 19 (1918):101–4, 181–88.

———. "Journal of the Campaign to the Southward. May 9th to July 14th, 1778." *South Carolina Historical and Genealogical Magazine* 12 (1911):60–69, 118–34, 190–206.

Harleston, John, ed. "Muster Rolls of the Sixth Regiment South Carolina Continental Troops, Made Upon 18th March, 1779." *Year Book, City of Charleston for 1895*:333–44.

Hemphill, William Edwin, and Waters, Wylma Anne, eds. *Extracts From the Journals of the Provincial Congresses of South Carolina, 1775–1776.* Columbia: South Carolina Archives Department, 1960.

———, et al., eds. *Journals of the General Assembly and House of Representatives 1776–1780.* Columbia: University of South Carolina Press, 1970.

McCrady, Edward. *The History of South Carolina in the Revolution.* 2 vols. New York: Macmillan Co., 1902.

McMaster, Fitzhugh. "The Use of South Carolina Continental Soldiers as Marines by the State Navy." *Military Collector and Historian* 32 (1980):152–54.

Marion, Francis. "Letters of General Francis Marion." *Year Book, City of Charleston for 1895*:326–32.

Moultrie, William. *Memoirs of the American Revolution, so far as It Related to the States of North and South Carolina, and Georgia. Compiled From the Most Authentic Materials, the Author's Personal Knowledge of the Various Events, and Including an Epistolary Correspondence on Public Affairs, With Civil and Military Officers of That Period.* 2 vols. New York: David Longworth, 1802.

Pinckney, Charles Cotesworth. *Life of General Thomas Pinckney.* Boston: Houghton, Mifflin, 1895.

Pinckney, Thomas. "Letters of Thomas Pinckney, 1775–1780." Edited by Jack L. Cross. *South Carolina Historical Magazine* 58 (1957):19–33, 67–83, 145–62, 224–42.

Ramsay, David. *The History of the Revolution of South-Carolina, From a British Province to an Independent State.* 2 vols. Trenton: Isaac Collins, 1785.

Rankin, Hugh F. *Francis Marion: The Swamp Fox.* New York: Thomas Y. Crowell, 1973.

Salley, A[lexander] S. *The History of Orangeburg County, South Carolina, From Its First Settlement to the Close of the Revolutionary War.* Orangeburg: R. L. Berry, 1898.

_____, comp. *Records of the Regiments of the South Carolina Line in the Revolutionary War.* Edited by Alida Moe. Baltimore: Genealogical Publishing Co., 1977. [Originally published in *South Carolina Historical and Genealogical Magazine* 5–7 (1904–6).]

_____, ed. "An Order Book of the 1st Regt., S.C. Line, Continental Establishment." *South Carolina Historical and Genealogical Magazine* 7 (1906):75–80, 130–42, 194–203; 8 (1907):19–28, 69–87.

_____, ed. *An Order Book of the 3d Regiment, South Carolina Line, Continental Establishment, December 23, 1776—May 2, 1777.* Columbia: Historical Commission of South Carolina, 1942.

Smith, Henry A. M. "General Thomas Sumter." *Magazine of History* 8 (1908): 160–67, 219–24, 277–84, 336–40; 9 (1909):17–22, 80–85, 165–68.

South Carolina, Council of Safety. "Journal of the Second Council of Safety, Appointed by the Provisional Congress, November, 1775 [November 30, 1775—26 February 1776]." *Collections of the South Carolina Historical Society* 3 (1859): 35–271.

Williams, Frances Leigh. *A Founding Family: The Pinckneys of South Carolina.* New York: Harcourt, Brace, Jovanovich, 1978.

Zahniser, Marvin R. *Charles Cotesworth Pinckney: Founding Father.* Chapel Hill: University of North Carolina Press, 1967.

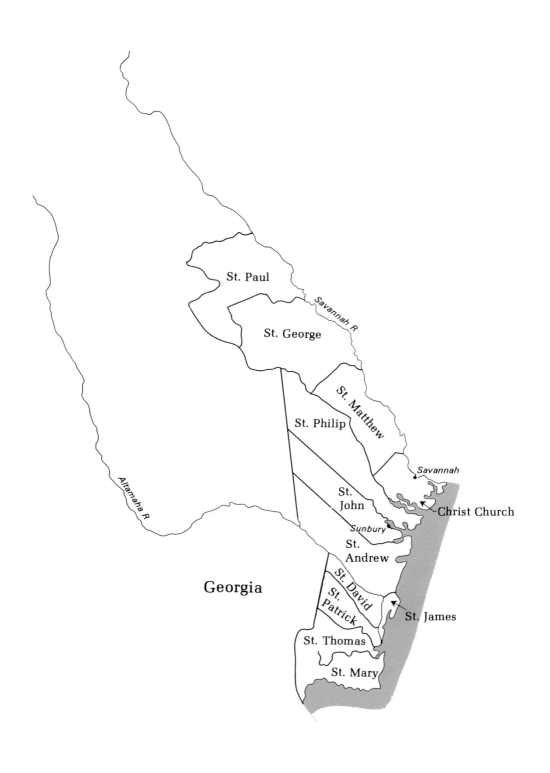

St. Paul

Savannah R

St. George

St. Matthew

St. Philip

Savannah

St. John

Christ Church

Sunbury

St. Andrew

Altamaha R

Georgia

St. David

St. Patrick

St. James

St. Thomas

St. Mary

Georgia

1st GEORGIA REGIMENT

Authorized 4 November 1775 in the Continental Army as the Georgia Regiment. Organized 20 January–28 April 1776 at Savannah to consist of eight companies. Assigned 27 February 1776 to the Southern Department. Redesignated 5 July 1776 as the 1st Georgia Regiment. Assigned 23 December 1777 to the Georgia Brigade, an element of the Southern Department.

Captured 12 May 1780 at Charleston, South Carolina, by the *British Army*. Redesignated 1 January 1781 as the Georgia Regiment. Reorganized and redesignated 1 January 1783 as the Georgia Battalion, to consist of three companies. Furloughed in summer 1783 at Charleston, South Carolina. Disbanded 15 November 1783.

ENGAGEMENTS
   Florida
   Florida 1778
   Savannah
   Charleston 1780

2d GEORGIA REGIMENT

Authorized 5 July 1776 in the Continental Army as the 2d Georgia Regiment and assigned to the Southern Department. Organized in fall and winter of 1776 at Williamsburg, Virginia, to consist of eight companies, recruited primarily in Virginia. Assigned 23 December 1777 to the Georgia Brigade, an element of the Southern Department.

Captured 12 May 1780 at Charleston, South Carolina, by the *British Army*. Disbanded 1 January 1781.

ENGAGEMENTS
   Florida
   Florida 1778
   Savannah
   Charleston 1780

3d GEORGIA REGIMENT

Authorized 5 July 1776 in the Continental Army as the 3d Georgia Regiment and assigned to the Southern Department. Organized in fall and winter of 1776 at Savannah to consist of eight companies, recruited primarily in North Carolina. Assigned 23 December 1777 to the Georgia Brigade, an element of the Southern Department.

Captured 12 May 1780 at Charleston, South Carolina, by the *British Army*. Disbanded 1 January 1781.

ENGAGEMENTS
    Florida
    Florida 1778
    Savannah
    Charleston 1780

4th GEORGIA REGIMENT

Authorized 1 February 1777 in the Continental Army as the 4th Georgia Regiment and assigned to the Southern Department. Organized in summer and fall of 1777 at Philadelphia, Pennsylvania, to consist of eight companies, recruited primarily in Pennsylvania. Assigned 23 December 1777 to the Georgia Brigade, an element of the Southern Department.

Captured 12 May 1780 at Charleston, South Carolina, by the *British Army*. Disbanded 1 January 1781.

ENGAGEMENTS
    Florida 1778
    Savannah
    Charleston 1780

GEORGIA REGIMENT OF HORSE RANGERS

Authorized in January 1776 in the Georgia State Troops as the 1st and 2d Troops of Georgia Horse. Organized in spring 1776 at Savannah. Expanded in June 1776 to consist of the 1st, 2d, 3d, and 4th Troops of Georgia Horse.

Adopted 24 July 1776 into the Continental Army; concurrently redesignated as the Georgia Regiment of Horse Rangers, assigned to the Southern Department, and expanded to consist of ten troops. Reorganized 1 January 1777 to consist of twelve troops. Captured 12 May 1780 at Charleston, South Carolina, by the *British Army*. Disbanded 1 January 1781.

ENGAGEMENTS
    Florida
    Florida 1778
    Georgia 1778
    Savannah
    Charleston 1780

Bibliography

Chandler, Allen D., ed. *The Colonial Records of the State of Georgia.* 26 vols. Atlanta: C. P. Byrd, 1904-26.

_____, ed. *The Revolutionary Records of the State of Georgia.* 3 vols. Atlanta: Franklin-Turner Co., 1908.

Coleman, Kenneth. *The American Revolution in Georgia.* Athens: University of Georgia Press, 1958.

Flippin, Percy Scott. "The Royal Government of Georgia 1752-1776: [Part] VII, Military System." *Georgia Historical Quarterly* 12 (1928):326-52; 13 (1929): 128-53.

Godley, Margaret, ed. "Minutes of the Executive Council, May 7 Through October 14, 1777." *Georgia Historical Quarterly* 33 (1949):318-30; 34 (1950):19-35, 106-25.

Harden, William, ed. "Official Letters of Governor John Martin, 1782-1783." *Georgia Historical Quarterly* 1 (1917):281-336.

[_____, ed.] "Proceedings of the Georgia Council of Safety." *Collections of the Georgia Historical Society* 5 (1901):15-127.

[_____, ed.] "Proceedings of the Georgia Provincial Congress." *Collections of the Georgia Historical Society* 5 (1901):1-13.

Jackson, Harvey H. "The Battle of the Riceboats: Georgia Joins the Revolution." *Georgia Historical Quarterly* 58 (1974):229-43.

Jones, Charles Colcock. *The Life and Services of Honorable Maj. Gen. Samuel Elbert of Georgia.* Cambridge, Mass.: Riverside Press, 1887.

_____, ed. "William Few: Lieutenant-Colonel Georgia Militia in the Revolutionary Service." *Magazine of American History* 7 (1881):340-58.

"Letters Colonial and Revolutionary." *Pennsylvania Magazine of History and Biography* 42 (1918):75-78.

McCall, Eltie Tidwell. *Roster of Revolutionary Soldiers in Georgia and Other States.* 3 vols. Baltimore: Genealogical Publishing Co., 1968-69. [Vol. I originally published n.p.: Georgia Daughters of the American Revolution, 1941.]

McIlvaine, Paul. *The Dead Town of Sunbury, Georgia.* Hendersonville, N.C.: Privately printed, 1971.

McIntosh, Lachlan. *Lachlan McIntosh Papers in the University of Georgia Libraries.* Edited by Lilla M. Hawes. Athens: University of Georgia Press, 1968.

_____. "The Papers of Lachlan McIntosh, 1774-99." Edited by Lilla M. Hawes. *Georgia Historical Quarterly* 38 (1954):148-69, 253-67, 356-68; 39 (1955):52-68, 172-86, 253-68, 356-75; 40 (1956):65-88, 152-74. [Reprinted as *Georgia Historical Society Collections* 12 (1957).]

"Muster Roll of the 1st Georgia Battalion of Continental Troops Commanded by Col. Robert Rae." *Georgia Historical Quarterly* 11 (1927):342-43.

"Muster Roll of the 4th Continental Georgia Battalion Commanded by Col. John White." *Georgia Historical Quarterly* 12 (1928):197-98.

"Muster Roll of the 3d Continental Georgia Battalion Commanded by Col. John McIntosh." *Georgia Historical Quarterly* 12 (1928):103-5.

Zlatich, Marko. "Two Georgia Revolutionary War Officers' Portraits." *Military Collector and Historian* 32 (1980):82-85.

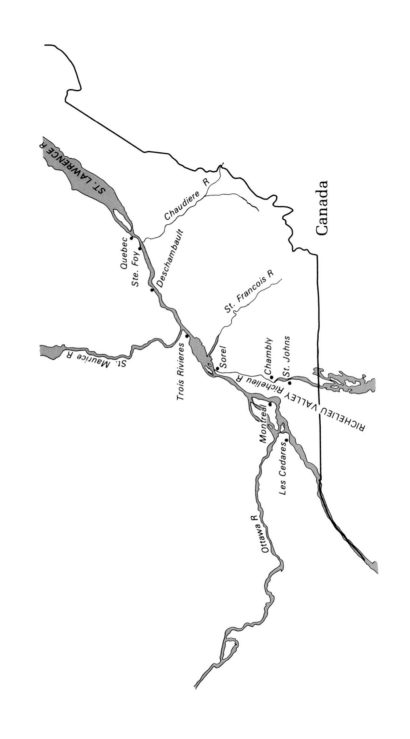

Canada

1st CANADIAN REGIMENT

Authorized 19 November 1775 in the Continental Army as the Canadian Regiment and assigned to the New York Department; concurrently organized at Pointe Olivier, Canada, to consist of eight companies. Relieved 8 January 1776 from the New York Department and assigned to the Canadian Department. Redesignated 20 January 1776 as the 1st Canadian Regiment. Relieved 2 July 1776 from the Canadian Department and assigned to the Northern Department.

Reorganized 18 December 1776 to consist of eight companies from Canada and New York. Assigned 28 December 1777 to the 1st Massachusetts Brigade, an element of the Northern Department. Relieved 4 April 1778 from the 1st Massachusetts Brigade and assigned to the Highlands Department. Relieved 22 July 1778 from the Highlands Department and assigned to the Rhode Island Brigade, an element of the Eastern Department.

Reorganized in June 1779 to consist of five companies. Relieved 17 November 1779 from the Rhode Island Brigade and assigned to Stark's Brigade, an element of the Main Army. Relieved 17 December 1779 from Stark's Brigade and assigned to Hand's Brigade, an element of the Main Army. Relieved 31 July 1780 from Hand's Brigade. Assigned 1 August 1780 to the New Jersey Brigade, an element of the Main Army. Relieved 4 August 1780 from the New Jersey Brigade and assigned to the Highlands Department. Disbanded 1 January 1781 at King's Ferry, New York.

ENGAGEMENTS
    Invasion of Canada
    Defense of Canada
    Lake Champlain
    Mohawk Valley
    Rhode Island

2d CANADIAN REGIMENT
(Congress' Own)

Authorized 20 January 1776 in the Continental Army as the 2d Canadian Regiment and assigned to the Canadian Department. Organized 10 February 1776 at Montreal, Canada, to consist of four battalions (twenty companies) from the Richelieu and St. Lawrence Valleys. Relieved 2 July 1776 from the Canadian Department and assigned to the Northern Department. Relieved 12 November 1776 from the Northern Department and assigned to the Highlands Department.

Reorganized 1 January 1777 to consist of four battalions (twenty companies) recruited at large. Relieved 8 January 1777 from the Highlands Department and assigned to the Main Army. Assigned 22 May 1777 to the 2d Maryland Brigade, an element of the Main Army.

Relieved 28 January 1778 from the 2d Maryland Brigade and assigned to the Northern Department. Relieved 4 April 1778 from the Northern Department and assigned to the Highlands Department. Relieved 22 July 1778 from the Highlands Department and assigned to the New Hampshire Brigade, an element of the Main Army. Relieved 6 March 1779 from the New Hampshire Brigade and assigned to the Northern Department. Relieved 28 August 1779 from the Northern Department and assigned to the Main Army. Assigned 25 November 1779 to Hand's Brigade, an element of the Main Army. Relieved 1 August 1780 from Hand's Brigade and assigned to the New Hampshire Brigade, an element of the Main Army.

Reorganized and redesignated 1 January 1781 as the Canadian Regiment; concurrently relieved from the New Hampshire Brigade and assigned to the Highlands Department. Relieved 5 June 1781 from the Highlands Department and assigned to the Northern Department. Relieved 10 August 1781 from the Northern Department and assigned to the Main Army. Assigned 24 September 1781 to Hazen's Brigade, an element of the Main Army.

Relieved 6 December 1781 from Hazen's Brigade and assigned to the Middle Department. Relieved 9 June 1783 from the Middle Department and assigned to the Highland's Department. Reorganized 30 June 1783 to consist of two companies. Disbanded 15 November 1783 at West Point, New York.

ENGAGEMENTS
   Defense of Canada
   Northern New Jersey
   Defense of Philadelphia
   New Jersey 1780
   New York 1781
   Yorktown

Bibliography

Boogher, W. F., ed. "Captain James Duncan's Diary of the Siege of Yorktown." *Magazine of History* 2 (1905):407–16.

Everest, Allan S. *Moses Hazen and the Canadian Refugees in the American Revolution.* Syracuse: Syracuse University Press, 1976.

Lanctot, Gustave. *Canada & the American Revolution 1774–1783.* Translated by Margaret M. Cameron. Cambridge, Mass.: Harvard University Press, 1967.

Pearce, Stewart, ed. "Extract From the Diary of Captain Andrew Lee." *Pennsylvania Magazine of History and Biography* 3 (1879):167–73.

Reed, Adela Peltier. *Memoirs of Antoine Paulint, Veteran of the Old French War 1755 to 1760, Captain in Hazen's 2nd Canadian, "Congress' Own" Regiment 1775 to 1783, Brevet Major at the Close of the Revolutionary War.* Los Angeles: Privately printed, 1940.

Schuyler, John. "Colonel James Livingston." *Magazine of American History* 21 (1889):71–74.

Stanley, George F. G. *Canada Invaded 1775–1776.* Toronto: Hakkert, 1973.

Extra and Additional Continental Regiments

Extra Regiments

MARYLAND AND VIRGINIA RIFLE REGIMENT

Authorized 14 June 1775 in the Continental Army as two Maryland and one Virginia Independent Rifle Companies and assigned to the Main Army. Captains Michael Cresap's and Thomas Price's Companies organized 21 June 1775 by the Frederick County, Maryland, Committee of Safety. Captain Hugh Stephenson's Company organized 22 June 1775 by the Berkeley County, Virginia, Committee of Safety.* [Captain Cresap died 18 October 1775 and Lieutenant Moses Rawlings promoted to command; Captain Price promoted 14 January 1776 and Lieutenant Otho Holland Williams promoted to command.]

Maryland and Virginia Rifle Regiment authorized 17 June 1776 in the Continental Army and assigned to the Main Army. Organized 27 June 1776 to consist of the three existing companies and two new companies to be raised in Maryland and four new companies to be raised in Virginia. (Captains Stephenson, Rawlings, and Williams promoted, respectively, to be Colonel, Lieutenant Colonel, and Major.) New companies organized 11–31 July 1776 in Frederick and Harford Counties, Maryland, and Fauquier, Berkeley, Frederick, and Culpeper Counties, Virginia.

Captured in part 16 November 1776 at Fort Washington, New York, by the *British Army* and regimental organization disbanded. Virginia portion transferred 3 February 1777 to the 11th Virginia Regiment [see 11th Virginia Regiment]. Maryland portion provisionally reorganized in November 1776 as a single company under Captain Alexander Lawson Smith and attached to the 4th Maryland Regiment.

Reorganized 21 March 1779 as Rawlings' Independent Corps, to consist of three companies; concurrently relieved from the Main Army and assigned to the Western Department. Disbanded 1 January 1781 at Fort Pitt, Pennsylvania.

ENGAGEMENTS
  Siege of Boston
  New York City
  Trenton-Princeton
  Northern New Jersey
  Defense of Philadelphia
  Philadelphia-Monmouth

*Perpetuated in today's 201st Field Artillery, West Virginia Army National Guard.

320 THE CONTINENTAL ARMY

WARNER'S REGIMENT
(Green Mountain Boys)

Authorized 23 June 1775 in the Continental Army as the Green Mountain Boys and assigned to the New York (subsequently Northern) Department. Organized 27 July 1775 to consist of seven companies from the New Hampshire Grants [portions of Albany and Charlotte Counties, New York, later becoming Vermont].

Reorganized in part 1 January 1776 as Major Brown's Detachment at Quebec, to consist of six companies. Expanded 12 February 1776 as Warner's Regiment, an element of the Canadian Department. Reauthorized 5 July 1776 in the Continental Army as Warner's Regiment and assigned to the Northern Department. Reorganized 16 July 1776 to consist of six companies. Disbanded 1 January 1781 at West Point, New York.

ENGAGEMENTS
Invasion of Canada
Defense of Canada
Saratoga
New York 1779

1st AND 2d CANADIAN REGIMENTS, see Canada

GERMAN BATTALION
(8th Maryland)

Authorized 25 May 1776 in the Continental Army as the German Battalion. Assigned 27 June 1776 to the Middle Department. Organized 6 July–25 September 1776 at Philadelphia, Pennsylvania, to consist of five companies from eastern Pennsylvania, two companies from Baltimore County, Maryland, and two companies from Frederick County, Maryland. Relieved 23 September 1776 from the Middle Department and assigned to the Main Army.

Assigned 22 May 1777 to the 2d Maryland Brigade, an element of the Main Army. Relieved 24 May 1777 from the 2d Maryland Brigade and assigned to the 1st Virginia Brigade, an element of the Main Army. Relieved 22 July 1778 from the 1st Virginia Brigade and assigned to the 2d Maryland Brigade, an element of the Main Army. Relieved 24 November 1778 from the 2d Maryland Brigade and assigned to Hand's Brigade, an element of the Main Army. Relieved 8 October 1779 from Hand's Brigade. Assigned 16 September 1780 to the New Jersey Brigade, an element of the Main Army. Disbanded 1 January 1781 at Morristown, New Jersey, and Baltimore, Maryland.

ENGAGEMENTS
Trenton-Princeton
Defense of Philadelphia

ENGAGEMENTS—Continued
　　Philadelphia-Monmouth
　　Iroquois 1779

DuBOIS' REGIMENT, see 3d New York Regiment

Additional Continental Regiments

FORMAN'S ADDITIONAL CONTINENTAL REGIMENT

Authorized 11 January 1777 in the Continental Army as Forman's Additional Continental Regiment and assigned to the Main Army. Organized in spring 1777 at Monmouth, New Jersey, to consist of four companies from southern New Jersey and Maryland. Consolidated 1 April 1779 with Spencer's Additional Continental Regiment [see Spencer's Additional Continental Regiment].

ENGAGEMENTS
　　Northern New Jersey
　　Philadelphia-Monmouth

GIST'S ADDITIONAL CONTINENTAL REGIMENT

Authorized 11 January 1777 in the Continental Army as Gist's Additional Continental Regiment, and assigned to the Main Army. Partially organized in spring and summer 1777 to consist of three companies from Virginia and Maryland and temporarily attached as follows: Captains John Gist's and Joseph Smith's Companies to the 3d Maryland Regiment [see 3d Maryland Regiment]; Captain Samuel Lapsley's Company to the 11th Virginia Regiment [see 11th Virginia Regiment].

Consolidated 22 April 1779 with Grayson's Additional Continental Regiment [see Grayson's Additional Continental Regiment] and Thruston's Additional Continental Regiment [see Thruston's Additional Continental Regiment] and consolidated unit designated as Gist's Additional Continental Regiment, to consist of eight companies. Assigned 12 May 1779 to the 1st Virginia Brigade, an element of the Main Army. (1st Virginia Brigade relieved 4 December 1779 from the Main Army and assigned to the Southern Department.)

Captured 12 May 1780 at Charleston, South Carolina, by the *British Army.* Disbanded 1 January 1781.

ENGAGEMENTS
　　Defense of Philadelphia
　　Philadelphia-Monmouth
　　Charleston 1780

GRAYSON'S ADDITIONAL CONTINENTAL REGIMENT

Authorized 10 January 1777 in the Continental Army as Grayson's Additional Continental Regiment and assigned to the Main Army. Organized in spring 1777 at Philadelphia, Pennsylvania, to consist of nine companies from Virginia, Maryland, and Delaware. Assigned 22 May 1777 to the 4th Virginia Brigade, an element of the Main Army. Relieved 22 July 1778 from the 4th Virginia Brigade and assigned to the 3d Virginia Brigade, an element of the Main Army.

Consolidated 22 April 1779 with Gist's Additional Continental Regiment [see Gist's Additional Continental Regiment].

ENGAGEMENTS
Northern New Jersey
Defense of Philadelphia
Philadelphia-Monmouth

HARTLEY'S ADDITIONAL CONTINENTAL REGIMENT
(11th Pennsylvania Regiment)
(New Eleventh Pennsylvania Regiment)

Authorized 12 January 1777 in the Continental Army as Hartley's Additional Continental Regiment and assigned to the Main Army. Organized in spring 1777 at Philadelphia to consist of eight companies from eastern Pennsylvania, eastern Maryland, and Delaware. Assigned 22 May 1777 to the 1st Pennsylvania Brigade, an element of the Main Army.

Relieved 8 January 1778 from the 1st Pennsylvania Brigade and assigned to the Middle Department. Allotted 27 March 1778 to the Pennsylvania Line. (Captain William Scott's Company of Thruston's Additional Continental Regiment [see Thruston's Additional Continental Regiment] consolidated 4 April 1778 with the regiment.)

Consolidated 13 January 1779 with Patton's Additional Continental Regiment [see Patton's Additional Continental Regiment] and Captain John Doyle's, Captain John Steele's, and Captain James Calderwood's Companies of Malcolm's Additional Continental Regiment [see Malcolm's Additional Continental Regiment] and consolidated unit redesignated as the 11th Pennsylvania Regiment, an element of the Middle Department, to consist of nine companies. Relieved 9 April 1779 from the Middle Department and assigned to Hand's Brigade, an element of the Main Army. Relieved 1 August 1780 from Hand's Brigade and assigned to the 2d Pennsylvania Brigade, an element of the Main Army.

Consolidated 17 January 1781 with the 3d Pennsylvania Regiment [see 3d Pennsylvania Regiment].

ENGAGEMENTS
Northern New Jersey
Defense of Philadelphia
Iroquois 1778
Iroquois 1779

HENLEY'S, JACKSON'S, AND LEE'S ADDITIONAL CONTINENTAL REGIMENTS, see Massachusetts

MALCOLM'S ADDITIONAL CONTINENTAL REGIMENT

Authorized 7 January 1777 in the Continental Army as Malcolm's Additional Continental Regiment. Assigned 27 June 1777 to the Highlands Department and organized at Ramapo, New Jersey, to consist of six companies from southern New York. Relieved 23 September 1777 from the Highlands Department and assigned to the Main Army.

Assigned 11 October 1777 to the 3d Pennsylvania Brigade, an element of the Main Army. Reorganized 13 October 1777 to consist of ten companies by consolidation with Captains John Steele's, Matthew Irvine's, Samuel Kearsley's and James Calderwood's Companies (organized in spring 1777 at Philadelphia, Pennsylvania, as elements of the Main Army with personnel from central Pennsylvania). Reorganized 3 December 1777 to consist of eight companies. Relieved 19 July 1778 from the 3d Pennsylvania Brigade and assigned to the Highlands Department.

Regiment broken up and elements consolidated as follows: the Pennsylvania companies on 13 January 1779 with Hartley's and Patton's Additional Continental Regiments to form the 11th Pennsylvania Regiment [see Hartley's Additional Continental Regiment], an element of the Middle Department; the New York companies on 1 April 1779 with Spencer's Additional Continental Regiment to form Spencer's Additional Continental Regiment [see Spencer's Additional Continental Regiment], an element of the Middle Department.

ENGAGEMENTS
    New Jersey 1777
    Defense of Philadelphia
    Philadelphia-Monmouth

PATTON'S ADDITIONAL CONTINENTAL REGIMENT

Authorized 11 January 1777 in the Continental Army as Patton's Additional Continental Regiment and assigned to the Main Army. Organized in spring 1777 at Philadelphia, Pennsylvania, to consist of seven companies from Pennsylvania, New Jersey, and Delaware. Assigned 22 May 1777 to the 4th Virginia Brigade, an element of the Main Army. Relieved 22 July 1778 from the 4th Virginia Brigade and assigned to the Highlands Department.

Consolidated 13 January 1779 (less Captain Allen McLane's Company [see 2d Partisan Corps]) with Hartley's Additional Continental Regiment [see Hartley's Additional Continental Regiment].

ENGAGEMENTS
Northern New Jersey
Defense of Philadelphia
Philadelphia-Monmouth

SHEPPARD'S ADDITIONAL CONTINENTAL REGIMENT, see North Carolina

SHERBURNE'S ADDITIONAL CONTINENTAL REGIMENT

Authorized 12 January 1777 in the Continental Army as Sherburne's Additional Continental Regiment and assigned to the Highlands Department. Organized in spring 1777 at Fishkill, New York, to consist of three companies from Rhode Island and three companies from eastern Connecticut. Assigned 12 June 1777 to the 1st Connecticut Brigade, an element of the Highlands Department. Relieved 21 June 1777 from the 1st Connecticut Brigade and assigned to the Rhode Island Brigade, an element of the Highlands Department. Relieved 14 September 1777 from the Rhode Island Brigade and assigned to the 1st Connecticut Brigade, an element of the Highlands Department.

Relieved 21 July 1778 from the 1st Connecticut Brigade and assigned to the Rhode Island Brigade, an element of the Eastern Department. Relieved 17 November 1779 from the Rhode Island Brigade and assigned to Stark's Brigade, an element of the Main Army. Disbanded 1 May 1780 at Morristown, New Jersey.

ENGAGEMENTS
Hudson Highlands
Rhode Island

SPENCER'S ADDITIONAL CONTINENTAL REGIMENT
(5th New Jersey Regiment)

Authorized 11 January 1777 in the Continental Army as Spencer's Additional Continental Regiment and assigned to the Main Army. Organized in spring 1777 at Monmouth, New Jersey, to consist of seven companies from New Jersey and one company from Pennsylvania.

Assigned 22 May 1777 to the 3d Pennsylvania Brigade, an element of the Main Army. Relieved 19 July 1778 from the 3d Pennsylvania Brigade and assigned to the Highlands Department. Relieved 16 November 1778 from the Highlands Department and assigned to the Middle Department.

Consolidated 1 April 1779 with Forman's Additional Continental Regiment [see Forman's Additional Continental Regiment] and part of Malcolm's Additional Continental Regiment [see Malcolm's Additional Continental Regiment] and consolidated unit designated as Spencer's Additional Continental Regiment, an element of the Middle Department, to consist of nine companies. Relieved 26 June 1779 from the Middle Department and assigned to the New Jersey Brigade, an element of the Main Army. Relieved 16 September 1780 from the New Jersey Brigade and assigned to the Highlands Department. Disbanded 1 January 1781 at King's Ferry, New York.

ENGAGEMENTS
    Northern New Jersey
    Defense of Philadelphia
    Philadelphia-Monmouth
    Iroquois 1779

THRUSTON'S ADDITIONAL CONTINENTAL REGIMENT

Authorized 15 March 1777 in the Continental Army as Thruston's Additional Continental Regiment, an element of the Main Army. Partially organized in spring and summer 1777 in Virginia to consist of four companies. (Captain William Scott's Company consolidated 4 April 1778 with Hartley's Additional Continental Regiment [see Hartley's Additional Continental Regiment].) Remnants attached 15 November 1778 to Grayson's Additional Continental Regiment, an element of the 3d Virginia Brigade of the Main Army.

Consolidated 22 April 1779 with Gist's Additional Continental Regiment [see Gist's Additional Continental Regiment].

ENGAGEMENTS
    Defense of Philadelphia
    Philadelphia-Monmouth

WEBB'S ADDITIONAL CONTINENTAL REGIMENT, see Connecticut

Bibliography

Extra Regiments[1]

Maryland and Virginia Rifle Regiment (Maryland and Virginia)

McGinn, Robert, and Vaden, Larry. "Michael Cresap and the Cresap Rifles." *West Virginia History* 39 (1978):341–47.
Schmitt, Dale J. "The Capture of Colonel Moses Rawlings." *Maryland Historical Magazine* 71 (1976):205–11.

[1] Also see entries under appropriate state.

Stevenson, M. Louise. "Captain Michael Cresap and the Indian Logan." *West Virginia Historical Magazine* 3 (1903):144–62.

Warner's Regiment (Vermont)

Boardman, D. S. "Reminiscences of Colonel Seth Warner." *Historical Magazine* 4 (1860):200–202.

Chipman, John. "Fort Edward, in 1779 and 1780. Orderly Book of the Captain-Commanding." *Historical Magazine,* 2d ser., 2 (1867):373–78.

Dawson, Henry B., ed. "'The Green Mountain Boys' of Vermont. Minutes of the Proceedings of Their Conventions." *Historical Magazine,* 3d ser., 1 (1872–73): 20–22, 80–85, 134–39, 206–7, 289–92; 2 (1873):93–94.

Fassett, John. "Diary of Captain John Fassett, Jr. (1743–1803), When a First Lieutenant of Green Mountain Boys, September 1, to December 7, 1775." In Henry Parker War, *The Follett-Dewey-Fassett-Safford Ancestry* (Columbus: Champlain Printing Co., 1896:211–45.)

Goodrich, John E., comp. *Rolls of the [Vermont] Soldiers in the Revolutionary War 1775 to 1783.* Rutland: State of Vermont by the Tuttle Co., 1904.

Harriman, Walter. "Memoir of Col. Seth Warner." *New England Historical and Genealogical Register* 34 (1880):363–70.

German Battalion (Maryland and Pennsylvania)

Montgomery, Thomas Lynch, ed. "The Order of March of Hand's Brigade From Wyoming to Tioga." *Pennsylvania Archives,* 6th ser., 14:67–121.

_____, ed. "Orderly Book, June 19th 1779 to July 30th, 1779." *Pennsylvania Archives,* 6th ser., 14:21–65.

_____, ed. "Orderly Book of the Lieut. Colo's Company, German Regiment, 1780." *Pennsylvania Archives,* 6th ser., 14:123–89.

_____, ed. "Orderly Book Nov. 13th, 1780, to Dec'r 9th, 1780." *Pennsylvania Archives,* 6th ser., 14:191–207.

Additional Continental Regiments[2]

Grayson's (Virginia and Maryland)

Grayson, Frederick William. "The Grayson Family." *Tyler's Quarterly Historical and Genealogical Magazine* 5 (1924):195–208.

Jackson's (Massachusetts)

Smith, Jonathan. "Two William Scotts of Petersborough, N. H." *Massachusetts Historical Society Proceedings,* 3d ser., 44 (1910–11):495–502.

Lee's (Massachusetts)

Raymond, M. D. "Colonel William S. Smith of the Revolution." *Magazine of American History* 22 (1889):74–76.

[2]Ibid.

Malcolm's (New York and Pennsylvania)

Burr, Aaron. *Memoirs of Aaron Burr With Miscellaneous Selections From His Correspondence.* Edited by Matthew L. Davis. 2 vols. New York: Harper & Brothers, 1836–37.

Lomask, Milton. *Aaron Burr: The Years From Princeton to Vice President, 1756–1805.* New York: Farrar, Straus, Giroux, 1979.

Youngs, Samuel. "Aaron Burr, as a Soldier. A Letter From Judge Young of Westchester County, New York." *Historical Magazine,* 2d ser., 9 (1871):384–87.

Sherburne's (Rhode Island and Connecticut)

Goldman, Stuart A. "A Revolutionary War Sketch." *Military Collector and Historian* 30 (1978):113–17.

Jones, Tom, and Elting, John R. "Sherburne's Additional Continental Regiment, 1779." *Military Collector and Historian* 31 (1979):19.

Spencer's (New Jersey)

Burrowes, John. "Journal of Major John Burrowes." *Journals of the Military Expedition of Major General John Sullivan Against the Six Nations of Indians in 1779 With Records of Centennial Celebrations.* Edited by Frederick Cook. Auburn, N.Y.: Knapp, Peck & Thomson, 1887.

Campfield, Jabez. "Journal of Dr. Jabez Campfield." *Journals of the Military Expedition of Major General John Sullivan Against the Six Nations of Indians in 1779 With Records of Centennial Celebrations.* Edited by Frederick Cook. Auburn, N.Y.: Knapp, Peck & Thomson, 1887:52–61. [Originally published in *New Jersey Historical Society Proceedings* 3 (1873):115–36.]

Roberts, Thomas. "Journal of Sergeant Thomas Roberts." *Journals of the Military Expedition of Major General John Sullivan Against the Six Nations of Indians in 1779 With Records of Centennial Celebrations.* Edited by Frederick Cook. Auburn, N.Y.: Knapp, Peck & Thomson, 1887:240–45.

Thruston's (Virginia)

McDonald, William Naylor, III. "The McDonald Who Turned Washington Down." *West Virginia History* 38 (1977):312–18.

Webb's (Connecticut)

Ford, Worthington Chauncey, ed. *Correspondence and Journals of Samuel Blatchley Webb.* 3 vols. New York: Privately printed, 1893–94.

McBarron, H. Charles, Jr., and Todd, Frederick P. "Webb's Continental Regiment, 1777–1781." *Military Collector and Historian* 5 (1953):100.

Miscellaneous Units

ARTILLERY ARTIFICER REGIMENT
(Flower's)

Authorized 16 January 1777 in the Continental Army as Lieutenant Colonel Benjamin Flower's Corps of Artillery Artificers and assigned to the Commissary General of Military Stores' Department. Organized in spring 1777 at Carlisle and Philadelphia, Pennsylvania, to consist of four companies from eastern and central Pennsylvania.

Expanded and redesignated 11 February 1778 as the Artillery Artificer Regiment, to consist of five companies. (Captain Noah Nichol's Artificer Company, Stevens' Provisional Artillery Battalion [see Annex] consolidated 28 August 1778 with Captain Jesse Roe's Company, Artillery Artificer Regiment to form Captain Jesse Roe's Company.)

Consolidated (less Captain Isaac Coren's Company—see 4th Continental Artillery Regiment) 1 January 1781 with the Quartermaster Artificer Regiment [see Quartermaster Artificer Regiment], and consolidated unit designated as the Artificer Regiment, to consist of six companies. Reorganized 1 January 1783 as Captains Daniel Pendleton's, Thomas Wylie's, and Jesse Roe's Separate Companies of Artificers. Disbanded 23 September 1783 at Philadelphia, Pennsylvania, and West Point, New York, respectively.

Annex

Authorized 9 November 1776 in the Continental Army as Captain Noah Nichols' Artificer Company, Stevens' Provisional Artillery Battalion, an element of the Northern Department. Organized in early 1777 at Albany, New York. (Stevens' Provisional Artillery Battalion relieved 18 May 1778 from the Northern Department and assigned to the Highlands Department; relieved 19 July 1778 from the Highlands Department and assigned to the Main Army.) Withdrawn 28 August 1778 from Stevens' Provisional Artillery Battalion and consolidated with Captain Jesse Roe's Company, Artillery Artificer Regiment.

ENGAGEMENTS
Elements of this regiment served in the following:
    Defense of Philadelphia
    Philadelphia-Monmouth
    Saratoga
    Yorktown
    Greene's Campaign

QUARTERMASTER ARTIFICER REGIMENT
(Baldwin's)

Provisionally organized 29 July 1778 in the Continental Army as Baldwin's Artificer Corps, to consist of eleven companies. Authorized 11 November 1779 in the Continental Army as the Quartermaster Artificer Regiment, reorganized to consist of ten companies, and assigned to the Quartermaster General's Department. Consolidated 1 January 1781 with the Artillery Artificer Regiment [see Artillery Artificer Regiment] to form the Artificer Regiment.

ENGAGEMENTS
  None.

CORPS OF INVALIDS
(Nicola's)

Authorized 20 June 1777 in the Continental Army as the Corps of Invalids [Colonel Lewis Nicola commanding]. Organized in summer 1777 at Philadelphia as an element of the Middle Department (less a detachment organized in winter 1777–1778 at Boston as an element of the Eastern Department). Relieved 13 June 1781 from the Middle and Eastern Departments, respectively, and assigned to the Highlands Department. Disbanded April 1783–December 1784 at West Point, New York.

ENGAGEMENTS
  Defense of Philadelphia
  Philadelphia-Monmouth

REGIMENT OF GUARDS, see Virginia

CORPS OF SAPPERS AND MINERS

Authorized 27 May 1778 in the Continental Army as the Corps of Sappers and Miners, to consist of three companies, and assigned to the Main Army. Organized 2 August 1780 at Peekskill, New York.

Relieved 24 August 1782 from the Main Army and assigned to the Highlands Department. Furloughed 11 June 1783 at West Point, New York. Disbanded 15 November 1783.

ENGAGEMENTS
  Yorktown

MARECHAUSSEE CORPS

Authorized 27 May 1778 in the Continental Army as the Marechaussee Corps and assigned to the Main Army. Organized 1 June 1778 at Valley Forge, Pennsylvania, with personnel from Pennsylvania. Disbanded 4 November 1783 at Rock Hill, New Jersey.

ENGAGEMENTS
New Jersey 1780
Yorktown

COMMANDER-IN-CHIEF'S GUARD

Authorized 11 March 1776 in the Continental Army as the Commander-in-Chief's Guard and assigned to the Main Army. Organized 12 March 1776 at Cambridge, Massachusetts. Furloughed 6 June 1783 at Newburgh, New York. Disbanded 15 November 1783.

ENGAGEMENTS
Siege of Boston
New York City
Northern New Jersey
Trenton-Princeton
Defense of Philadelphia
Philadelphia-Monmouth
New Jersey 1780
New York 1781
Yorktown

Bibliography

Artillery Artificer Regiment

Jones, James T., and Elting, John R. "The Regiment of Artillery Artificers (Flower's Artillery Regiment), 1777–1783." *Military Collector and Historian* 27 (1975):82–84.

Corps of Invalids

Marraro, Howard R. "Unpublished Letters of Colonel Nicola, Revolutionary Soldier." *Pennsylvania History* 13 (1946):274–82.

Marechaussee Corps

Chapman, Frederick T., and Elting, John R. "Provost Company of Light Dragoons, 1778–1783." *Military Collector and Historian* 11 (1959):80.

Haarman, Albert W. "The Continental Provost, 1778–1783." *Military Collector and Historian* 11 (1959):86–87.

Commander-in-Chief's Guard

Godfrey, Carlos E. *The Commander-in-Chief's Guard Revolutionary War*. Washington: Stevenson-Smith, 1904.

_____. "The Commander in Chief's Guard." *Pennsylvania Magazine of History and Biography* 38 (1914):83–88.

Lossing, Benson J. "Washington's Life Guard." *Historical Magazine* 2 (1858): 129–34.

McBarron, H. Charles, Jr., and Todd, Frederick P. "Commander-in-Chief's Guard, 1777–1783." *Military Collector and Historian* 8 (1956):74–76.

Wehmann, Howard H. "To Major Gibbs With Much Esteem." *Prologue* 4 (1972):227–32.

Corps of Sappers and Miners, Corps of Engineers, and Geographer's Department

Abbot, Henry L., comp. *The Beginnings of Modern Submarine Warfare Under Captain-Lieutenant David Bushnell, Sappers and Miners, Army of the Revolution.* 1882. Reprint. Hamden, Conn.: Archon Books, 1966.

Baldwin, Thomas Williams, ed. *The Revolutionary Journal of Col. Jeduthan Baldwin, 1775–1778.* Bangor: De Burians, 1906.

Bedini, Silvio. *Thinkers and Tinkers: Early American Men of Science.* New York: Charles Scribner's Sons, 1975.

Buell, Rowena, comp. *The Memoirs of Rufus Putnam and Certain Official Papers and Correspondence.* Boston: Houghton, Mifflin & Co., 1903.

Butterfield, L. H. "Franklin, Rush, and the Chevalier Kermorvan: An Episode of '76." *American Philosophical Society Library Bulletin for 1946*:33–44.

Caemmerer, H. Paul. *The Life of Pierre Charles L'Enfant.* Washington: National Republic Publishing Co., 1950.

Cappon, Lester Jesse. "Geographers and Map-makers, British and American, From About 1750 to 1789." *American Antiquarian Society Proceedings* 81 (1971):243–71.

Cummings, Hubertis M. "The Villefranche Map for the Defense of the Delaware." *Pennsylvania Magazine of History and Biography* 84 (1960):424–34.

De Coudray, Philippe Trouson [*sic*]. "Observations on the Forts Intended for the Defense of the Two Passages of the River Delaware, July, 1777." *Pennsylvania Magazine of History and Biography* 24 (1900):343–47.

Duportail, Louis. "Letter to Joseph Reed, 10 September 1779." *Pennsylvania Archives*, 1st ser., 7:690–91.

Gray, William. "Letter of Captain William Gray, of the Fourth Pennsylvania Regiment, With a Map of the Sullivan Expedition." Edited by William Henry Egle. *Pennsylvania Archives*, 2d ser., 15:289–93.

Guthorn, Peter J. *American Maps and Map Makers of the Revolution.* Monmouth Beach, N.J.: Philip Freneau Press, 1966.

_____. "Revolutionary War Mapmakers." *Prologue* 9 (1977):171–77.

Haiman, Mieceslaus. *Kosciuszko in the American Revolution.* New York: Polish Institute of Arts and Sciences in America, 1943.

Hall, Edward Hagaman. "Lieutenant Colonel Stephen Rochefontaine." *Twenty-Sixth Annual Report of the American Scenic and Historic Preservation Society.* Albany: J. B. Lyon, 1922:245–69.

Harley, J. B.; Petchenik, Barbara Bartz; and Towner, Lawrence W. *Mapping the American Revolutionary War*. Chicago: University of Chicago Press, 1978.

Heusser, Albert H. *George Washington's Map Maker: A Biography of Robert Erskine*. 1928. Reprinted and edited by Hubert Schmidt. New Brunswick: Rutgers University Press, 1966.

Kite, Elizabeth S. *Brigadier-General Louis Lebegue Duportail, Commandant of Engineers in the Continental Army, 1779-1783*. Baltimore: Johns Hopkins Press for the Institut Francais de Washington, 1933.

Martin, Joseph Plumb. *Private Yankee Doodle Being a Narrative of Some of the Adventures, Dangers and Sufferings of a Revolutionary Soldier*. [1830.] Edited by George F. Scheer. Boston: Little, Brown & Co., 1962.

Ollivier, Francois. "The Engineer Corps of the Revolution." *Military Engineer* 15 (1923):411-16. [Translated and reprinted from the *Revue de Genie Militaire*.]

Palmer, Dave R. "Fortress West Point: 19th Century Concept in an 18th Century War." *Military Engineer* 68 (1976):171-74.

Wagner, Frederick. *Submarine Fighter of the American Revolution: The Story of David Bushnell*. New York: Dodd, Mead & Co., 1963.

Watts, Arthur P. "A Newly Discovered Letter of Brigadier-General Duportail." *Pennsylvania History* 1 (1934):103-6.

Williams, George W. "Two Maps of Charleston in the Revolution." *South Carolina Historical Magazine* 76 (1975):49-50.

Artillery

CONTINENTAL ARTILLERY REGIMENT
(Gridley's)
(Knox's)

Authorized 10 May 1775 in the Massachusetts State Troops as the Regiment of the Train of Artillery. Organized in late May and early June 1775 at Cambridge and Roxbury to consist of ten companies with recruits from Suffolk, Middlesex, Worcester, Essex, and Hampshire Counties. Adopted 14 June 1775 into the Continental Army, assigned to the Main Army, and redesignated as the Continental Artillery Regiment. Reorganized in late June 1775 to consist of eleven companies.

Consolidated 1 January 1776 with the Rhode Island Train of Artillery [see *Annex*] and consolidated unit designated as the Continental Artillery Regiment, an element of the Main Army, to consist of twelve companies. Disbanded 1 January 1777 at Trenton, New Jersey, and Peekskill and Fort Ticonderoga, New York.

Annex

Authorized 6 May 1775 in the Rhode Island State Troops as the Rhode Island Train of Artillery. Organized 8 May–3 June 1775 at Providence with recruits from Providence County. Adopted 14 June 1775 into the Continental Army and assigned to the Main Army.

Expanded and redesignated 1 January 1776 as Captains Ebenezer Stevens' and Jotham Drury's Companies, Continental Artillery Regiment.

ENGAGEMENTS
    Siege of Boston
    New York City
    Northern New Jersey
    Trenton-Princeton
Captains Ebenezer Stevens' and Stephen Badlam's Companies additionally served in the following:
    Defense of Philadelphia
    Lake Champlain

1st CONTINENTAL ARTILLERY REGIMENT
(Harrison's)

Authorized 26 November 1776 in the Continental Army as Harrison's Continental Artillery Regiment and assigned to the Southern Department. Organized in spring and summer 1777 at Williamsburg, Virginia, to consist of ten companies, including the Virginia State Artillery Company [see *Annex 1*] and the Virginia Continental Artillery Company [see *Annex 2*].

Relieved 13 March 1778 from the Southern Department and assigned to the Main Army. Redesignated 10 August 1779 as the 1st Continental Artillery Regiment. Relieved 17 April 1780 from the Main Army and assigned to the Southern Department.

Reorganized 9 May 1780 to consist of twelve companies, including the Maryland Continental Artillery Companies [see *Annex 3*]. Reorganized 1 January 1781 to consist of ten companies. Furloughed in summer 1783 at Winchester, Virginia, and Baltimore, Maryland. Disbanded 15 November 1783.

Annex 1

Authorized 11 January 1776 in the Virginia State Troops as the Virginia State Artillery Company. Organized in spring 1776 at Williamsburg. Redesignated 26 November 1776 as a company in Harrison's Continental Artillery Regiment.

Annex 2

Authorized 19 March 1776 in the Continental Army as the Virginia Continental Artillery Company and assigned to the Southern Department. Organized in summer 1776 at Williamsburg. Redesignated 27 November 1776 as a company in Harrison's Continental Artillery Regiment.

Annex 3

Authorized 14 January 1776 in the Maryland State Troops as the 1st and 2d Maryland State Artillery Companies. Organized in spring 1776 at Baltimore and Annapolis, respectively. Reorganized 23 October 1776 to consist of the 1st, 2d, and 3d Maryland State Artillery Companies (3d Maryland State Artillery Company organized in winter 1776 at Annapolis). Adopted 22 November 1777 into the Continental Army as the 1st, 2d, and 3d Maryland Continental Artillery Companies and assigned to the Main Army. 1st Maryland Continental Artillery Company redesignated 9 May 1780 as the 11th Company, 1st Continental Artillery Regiment; 2d and 3d Maryland Continental Artillery Companies concurrently consolidated, reorganized, and redesignated as the 12th Company, 1st Continental Artillery Regiment.

ENGAGEMENTS
Elements of this regiment served in the following:
Chesapeake Bay
Philadelphia-Monmouth
Charleston 1780
Defense of the Carolinas
Yorktown
Greene's Campaign

2d CONTINENTAL ARTILLERY REGIMENT
(Lamb's)

Authorized 1 January 1777 in the Continental Army as Lamb's Continental Artillery Regiment. Organized in spring 1777 with elements in the Main Army and Highlands Department to consist of twelve companies as follows: three existing companies from New York [see *Annexes 1, 2,* and *3*] reorganized at Morristown, New Jersey, and Peekskill, New York; four new companies from Fairfield and New Haven Counties, Connecticut, organized at New Haven, Connecticut, and Peekskill, New York; three new companies from Ulster, Orange, Dutchess, Westchester, and Albany Counties and New York City and County, New York, organized at Peekskill, New York; and two new companies from Philadelphia City and County, Pennsylvania, organized at Morristown, New Jersey. Assigned 12 June 1777 (less companies with the Main Army) to the Highlands Department. Redesignated 10 August 1779 as the 2d Continental Artillery Regiment.

Reorganized 1 January 1781 to consist of ten companies [Captains Andrew Porter's and Jonas Simonds' Companies—see 4th Continental Artillery Regiment]. Relieved 28 August 1781 from the Highlands Department and assigned to the Main Army. Relieved 24 August 1782 from the Main Army and assigned to the Highlands Department. Reorganized 11 June 1783 to consist of two companies. Disbanded 1 January 1784 [less Captain John Doughty's Company* remaining in the United States Army] at West Point, New York.

Annex 1

Authorized 30 June 1775 in the Continental Army as Captain John Lamb's Company of Artillery in the New York Department. Organized 17 July–29 August 1775 at New York City. Captured in part 31 December 1775 at Quebec, Canada, by the *British Army*; remainder of the company concurrently reorganized as Captain-Lieutenant Isaiah Wool's Artillery Detachment, an element of the New York Department. Relieved 20 January 1776 from the New York Department and assigned to the Canadian Department. Relieved 2 July 1776 from the Canadian Department and assigned to the Northern Department. Reorganized and redesignated 1 January 1777 as Captain Andrew Moodie's Company, Lamb's Continental Artillery Regiment.

Annex 2

Authorized 28 October 1775 in the Continental Army as a company of artillery to be raised in New York for service in the Hudson Highlands and assigned to the New York Department. Organized 6 December 1775–27 May 1776 at New York City as Captain Sebastian Bauman's Continental Artillery Company. Relieved 13 April 1776 from the New York Department and assigned to the Main Army. Redesignated 1 January 1777 as Captain Sebastian Bauman's Company, Lamb's Continental Artillery Regiment.

Annex 3*

Authorized 6 January 1776 in the New York State Troops as the New York Provincial Company of Artillery. Organized 3 February–30 March 1776 at New York City. Assigned 17 June 1776 to the Main Army. Adopted 17 March 1777 into the Continental Army as Captain John Doughty's Company, Lamb's Continental Artillery Regiment.

ENGAGEMENTS
Elements of this regiment served in the following:
  New York City
  Trenton-Princeton
  Northern New Jersey
  Connecticut 1777
  Hudson Highlands
  Defense of Philadelphia
  Philadelphia-Monmouth
  New York 1779
  Iroquois 1779
  New Jersey 1780
  Yorktown
Lamb's Company additionally served in the following:
  New York 1775
  Invasion of Canada
  Defense of Canada
  Lake Champlain

*This company is perpetuated by today's 1st Battalion, 5th Field Artillery, Regular Army.

3d CONTINENTAL ARTILLERY REGIMENT
(Crane's)

Authorized 1 January 1777 in the Continental Army as Crane's Continental Artillery Regiment. Organized (less Stevens' Provisional Artillery Battalion—see *Annex*) in spring 1777 at Boston, Massachusetts, and Peekskill, New York, with elements in the Main Army, Highlands Department, and Northern Department, to consist of twelve companies from Massachusetts and Rhode Island (including veterans of the Continental Artillery Regiment). Redesignated 10 August 1779 as the 3d Continental Artillery Regiment.

Reorganized 1 January 1781 to consist of ten companies. Relieved 24 August 1782 from the Main Army and assigned to the Highlands Department. Reorganized 12 June 1783 to consist of four companies. Disbanded 1 January 1784 at West Point, New York.

Annex

Authorized 9 November 1776 in the Continental Army as Stevens' Provisional Artillery Battalion and assigned to the Northern Department. Organized in early 1777 at Boston, Massachusetts, and Albany and Fort Ticonderoga, New York, to consist of Captains Stephen Buckland's, Nathaniel Donnell's, and John Winslow's Companies of Crane's Continental Artillery Regiment (recruited from Massachusetts and Connecticut) and Captain Noah Nichols' Artificer Company. Relieved 18 May 1778 from the Northern Department and assigned to the Highlands Department. Relieved 19 July 1778 from the Highlands Department and assigned to the Main Army. (Captain Noah Nichols' Artificer Company withdrawn 28 August 1778 and consolidated with Captain Jesse Roe's Company, Artillery Artificer Regiment [see Artillery Artificer Regiment]). Stevens' Provisional Artillery Battalion broken up 22 December 1778 at Pluckemin, New Jersey, and companies reverted to Crane's Continental Artillery Regiment.

ENGAGEMENTS
Elements of this regiment served in the following:
    Northern New Jersey
    Saratoga
    Defense of Philadelphia
    Philadelphia-Monmouth
    Rhode Island
    New Jersey 1780

4th CONTINENTAL ARTILLERY REGIMENT
(Proctor's)

Authorized 16 October 1775 in the Pennsylvania State Troops as the Pennsylvania State Artillery Company. Organized 27 October–27 November 1775 at Philadelphia. Expanded 14 August 1776 as the Pennsylvania State Artillery Battalion, to consist of two companies. Assigned 23 September 1776 to the Main Army. Expanded 6 February 1777 as the Pennsylvania State Artillery Regiment, to consist of eight companies from eastern Pennsylvania, and relieved from the Main Army.

Adopted 10 June 1777 into the Continental Army as Proctor's Continental Artillery Regiment and assigned to the Middle Department. Relieved 14 July 1777 from the Middle Department and assigned to the Main Army. Redesignated 10 August 1779 as the 4th Continental Artillery Regiment.

Reorganized 1 January 1781 to consist of ten companies, including Captain Isaac Coren's Company, Artillery Artificer Regiment [see *Annex 1*], Captains Andrew Porter's and Jonas Simonds' Companies, 2d Continental Artillery Regiment [see *Annexes 2 and 3*], and Captain Jeremiah Freeman's Continental Artillery Company [see *Annex 4*]. Relieved 20 February 1781 from the Main Army and assigned to the Southern Department. Reorganized 1 January 1783 to consist of four companies. Relieved 24 April 1783 from the Southern Department and assigned to the Middle Department.

Furloughed 11 June 1783 at Philadelphia, Pennsylvania. Disbanded 15 November 1783.

Annex 1

Authorized 16 January 1777 in the Continental Army as Captain Isaac Coren's Laboratory Company, Lieutenant Colonel Benjamin Flower's Corps of Artillery Artificers, an element of the Commissary General of Military Stores' Department. Organized in spring 1777 at Carlisle, Pennsylvania, with recruits from central and eastern Pennsylvania. Redesignated 11 February 1778 as Captain Isaac Coren's Company, Artillery Artificer Regiment. Consolidated 1 January 1781 with Captain Andrew Porter's Company, 2d Continental Artillery Regiment, and consolidated unit designated as Captain Andrew Porter's Company, 4th Continental Artillery Regiment.

Annex 2

Authorized 1 January 1777 in the Continental Army as Captain Andrew Porter's Company, Lamb's Continental Artillery Regiment. Organized in spring 1777 at Morristown, New Jersey, with recruits from Philadelphia City and County, Pennsylvania. Redesignated 10 August 1779 as Captain Andrew Porter's Company, 2d Continental Artillery Regiment. Consolidated 1 January 1781 with Captain Isaac Coren's Company, Artillery Artificer Regiment, and consolidated unit designated as Captain Andrew Porter's Company, 4th Continental Artillery Regiment.

Annex 3

Authorized 1 January 1777 in the Continental Army as Captain James Lee's Company, Lamb's Continental Artillery Regiment. Organized in spring 1777 at Morristown, New Jersey, with recruits from Philadelphia City and County, Pennsylvania. Redesignated 10 August 1779 as Captain James Lee's Company, 2d Continental Artillery Regiment. Redesignated 12 November 1779 as Captain Jonas Simonds' Company, 2d Continental Artillery Regiment. Consolidated 1 January 1781 with Captain Jeremiah Freeman's Continental Artillery Company, and consolidated unit designated as Captain Jonas Simonds' Company, 4th Continental Artillery Regiment.

Annex 4

Authorized 20 January 1776 in the Continental Army as a company of artillery from Pennsylvania and assigned to the Canadian Department. Organized 8 February–25 March 1776 at Philadelphia as Captain Bernard Romans' Continental Artillery Company. Relieved 2 July 1776 from the Canadian Department and assigned to the Northern Department. Reorganized and redesignated 1 January 1777 as Captain Gibbs Jones' Continental Artillery Company; concurrently relieved from the Northern Department and assigned to the Main Army. Relieved 22 November 1778 from the Main Army and assigned to the Highlands Department. Redesignated 16 April 1780 as Captain Jeremiah Freeman's Continental Artillery Company. Consolidated 1 January 1781 with Captain Jonas Simonds' Company, 2d Continental Artillery Regiment, and consolidated unit designated as Captain Jonas Simonds' Company, 4th Continental Artillery Regiment.

ENGAGEMENTS
Elements of this regiment served in the following:
Delaware Bay 1776
Trenton-Princeton
Northern New Jersey
Defense of Philadelphia
Philadelphia-Monmouth
New Jersey 1778
Iroquois 1779
Yorktown
Greene's Campaign

Captain Bernard Romans' Continental Artillery Company additionally served in the following:
Defense of Canada
Lake Champlain

NORTH CAROLINA CONTINENTAL ARTILLERY COMPANY

Authorized 9 May 1776 in the North Carolina State Troops as the North Carolina Artillery Company. Organized in summer 1776 at Wilmington with recruits from eastern North Carolina. Adopted 19 July 1777 into the Continental Army as the North Carolina Continental Artillery Company and assigned to the Main Army.

Relieved 11 November 1779 from the Main Army and assigned to the Southern Department. Captured 12 May 1780 at Charleston, South Carolina, by the *British Army*. Disbanded 1 January 1781.

ENGAGEMENTS
Philadelphia-Monmouth
Charleston 1780

GEORGIA CONTINENTAL ARTILLERY COMPANIES

Authorized 5 July 1776 in the Continental Army as the 1st and 2d Georgia Continental Artillery Companies and assigned to the Southern Department. Organized in fall 1776 at Savannah and Sunbury, respectively.

Georgia Provincial Artillery Company (organized 15 May 1776 in the Georgia State Troops at Savannah) adopted 6 February 1777 into the Continental Army; concurrently redesignated as the 3d Georgia Continental Artillery Company and assigned to the Southern Department. 1st and 3d Georgia Continental Artillery Companies consolidated 19 February 1778 and consolidated unit designated as the 1st Georgia Continental Artillery Company.

1st Georgia Continental Artillery Company captured 29 December 1778 at Savannah, Georgia, by the *British Army*; 2d Georgia Continental Artillery Company captured 10 January 1779 at Sunbury, Georgia, by the *British Army*. 1st and 2d Georgia Continental Artillery Companies disbanded 29 November 1779.

ENGAGEMENTS
Florida 1778
Savannah

Bibliography

Abernethy, Thomas J. "Crane's Rhode Island Company of Artillery, 1775." *Rhode Island History* 29 (1970):46–51.

Badlam, Ezra. "Letter of Ezra Badlam." *New England Historical and Genealogical Register* 2 (1848):48–50.

Bard, Thomas R., ed. "Journal of Lieutenant Robert Parker of the Second Continental Artillery, 1779." *Pennsylvania Magazine of History and Biography* 27 (1903): 404–20; 28 (1904):12–25.

Bauman, Sebastian. *Memoirs of Colonel Sebastian Beauman and His Descendants With Selections from His Correspondence.* Edited by Mary C. Doll Fairchild. New York: Privately printed, 1900.

Birkhimer, William E. *Historical Sketch of the Organization, Administration, Materiel and Tactics of the Artillery, United States Army.* Washington: James J. Chapman, 1884.

Brooke, Francis J. *A Family Narrative Being the Reminiscences of a Revolutionary Officer Afterwards Judge of the Court of Appeals Written for the Information of His Children by Francis J. Brooke Sometime Captain in Harrison's Regiment of Artillery.* Richmond: Macfarland & Ferguson, 1849.

Brooks, Noah. *Henry Knox, A Soldier of the Revolution; Major-General in the Continental Army, Washington's Chief of Artillery, First Secretary of War Under the Constitution, Founder of the Society of the Cincinnati; 1750–1806.* New York: G. P. Putnam's Sons, 1900.

Callahan, North. *Henry Knox: General Washington's General.* New York: A. S. Barnes and Co., 1958.

Craig, Neville B. *Sketch of the Life and Services of Isaac Craig, Major in the Fourth (Usually Called Proctor's) Regiment of Artillery, During the Revolutionary War.* Pittsburgh: J. S. Davidson, 1854.

Downey, Fairfax. "Birth of the Continental Artillery." *Military Collector and Historian* 7 (1955):61–69.

Drake, Francis S. *Life and Correspondence of Henry Knox, Major-General in the American Revolutionary Army.* Boston: Samuel G. Drake, 1873.

Ford, Worthington C. "Company of Artillery Commanded by Hamilton." *New England Historical and Genealogical Register* 47 (1893):472–73.

Gardner, Asa Bird. "Henry Burbeck: Brevet Brigadier-General United States Army—Founder of the United States Military Academy." *Magazine of American History* 9 (1883):251–65.

Jones, James T., and Elting, John R. "The Regiment of Artillery Artificers (Flower's Artillery Regiment), 1777-1783." *Military Collector and Historian* 27 (1975):82-84.

Lamb, Martha J. "Major-General Ebenezer Stevens." *Magazine of American History* 24 (1890):120-22.

Leake, Isaac Q. *Memoir of the Life and Times of General John Lamb.* Albany: Munsell, 1850.

Lee, William, ed. "Record of the Services of Constant Freeman, Captain of Artillery in the Continental Army." *Magazine of American History* 2 (1878):349-60.

Meyer, Mary K., ed. "Captain John Fulford's Company February 13, 1776, to May 21, 1777." *Maryland Historical Magazine* 69 (1974):93-97.

Nash, Solomon. *Journal of Solomon Nash, a Soldier of the Revolution, 1776-1777. Now First Printed From the Original Manuscript.* Edited by Charles I. Bushnell. New York: Privately printed, 1861.

Nead, Benjamin M. "A Sketch of General Thomas Proctor." *Pennsylvania Magazine of History and Biography* 4 (1880):454-70.

Pennington, William S. "The Diary of William S. Pennington." Edited by William A. Ellis. *Proceedings of the New Jersey Historical Society* 63 (1945):199-218; 64 (1946):31-42.

Porter, William A. "A Sketch of the Life of General Andrew Porter." *Pennsylvania Magazine of History and Biography* 4 (1880):261-301.

Roof, F. H., ed. "Journal of March From Fort Schuyler Expedition Against the Onondagas by Thomas Machin, Captain in Col. Lamb's Second Regiment, N. Y. Artillery." *Magazine of American History* 3 (1879):688-89.

Shaw, Samuel. *Journals of Major Samuel Shaw, the First American Consul at Canton.* Edited by Josiah Quincy. Boston: Wm. Crosby & H. P. Nichols, 1847.

[_____]. "Captain Samuel Shaw's Revolutionary War Letters to Captain Winthrop Sargent." Edited by N. B. W. *Pennsylvania Magazine of History and Biography* 70 (1946):281-324.

Stevens, John Austin. "Ebenezer Stevens Lieut.-Col. of Artillery in the Continental Army." *Magazine of American History* 1 (1877):588-610.

Weller, Jac. "Guns of Destiny: Field Artillery in the Trenton-Princeton Campaign, 25 December 1776 to 3 January 1777." *Military Affairs* 20 (1956):1-15.

_____. "The Artillery of the American Revolution." *Military Collector and Historian* 8 (1956):61-65, 97-101.

_____. "Revolutionary War Artillery in the South." *Georgia Historical Quarterly* 46 (1962):250-73, 377-87.

Light Dragoons, Partisan Corps, and Legionary Corps

1st CONTINENTAL LIGHT DRAGOON REGIMENT
(Bland's Horse)

Authorized 8 June 1776 in the Virginia State Troops as the 1st, 2d, 3d, 4th, 5th, and 6th Troops of Light Horse. Organized 13 June–10 September 1776 at Williamsburg with recruits from eastern and northern Virginia. Redesignated 25 June 1776 as the Virginia Light Horse.

Adopted 25 November 1776 into the Continental Army, assigned to the Main Army, and redesignated as the 1st Continental Light Dragoon Regiment. (Captain Henry Lee's Troop [see 2d Partisan Corps] withdrawn 7 April 1778 and a new troop organized by Captain Addison Lewis.) Relieved 8 November 1778 from the Main Army and assigned to the Southern Department.

Reorganized and redesignated 1 January 1781 as the 1st Legionary Corps, to consist of four mounted and two dismounted troops. Consolidated 2 November 1782 with the 3d Legionary Corps [see 3d Continental Light Dragoon Regiment] and consolidated unit designated as the 1st Legionary Corps, an element of the Southern Department, to consist of five troops. Disbanded 15 November 1783 at Winchester, Virginia.

ENGAGEMENTS
   Northern New Jersey
   Defense of Philadelphia
   Charleston 1780
   Defense of the Carolinas
   Greene's Campaign

2d CONTINENTAL LIGHT DRAGOON REGIMENT
(Sheldon's Horse)

Authorized 12 December 1776 in the Continental Army as the 2d Continental Light Dragoon Regiment and assigned to the Main Army. Organized 16 December 1776–21 June 1777 at Wethersfield, Connecticut, and Middlebrook, New Jersey, to consist of four troops from Connecticut, one troop from Massachusetts, and one troop from New Jersey. (Bull's Troop assigned 9 June 1777 to the Highlands Department and de Vernejoux's Troop to the Northern Department.)

Relieved 29 May 1778 from the Main Army and assigned to the Highlands Department (Seymour's [formerly de Vernejoux's] Troop concurrently relieved from the Northern Department and assigned to the Highlands Department). Reorganized in early 1780 to consist of four mounted and two dismounted troops.

Redesignated 1 January 1781 as the 2d Legionary Corps. Furloughed 9 June 1783 at Newburgh, New York. Disbanded 20 November 1783.

ENGAGEMENTS
Northern New Jersey
Defense of Philadelphia
New York 1779
Connecticut 1779
New York 1780
New York 1781
Connecticut 1783
Captain Bull's Troop additionally served in the following:
Hudson Highlands
New York 1777
Captain de Vernejoux's Troop additionally served in:
Saratoga

3d CONTINENTAL LIGHT DRAGOON REGIMENT
(Baylor's Horse)
(Lady Washington's Horse)

Authorized 1 January 1777 in the Continental Army as the 3d Continental Light Dragoon Regiment and assigned to the Main Army. Organized in spring 1777 at Morristown, New Jersey, to consist of three troops from Virginia, two troops from Maryland, and one troop recruited at large. Relieved 5 November 1778 from the Main Army and assigned to the Middle Department. Relieved 7 May 1779 from the Middle Department and assigned to the Southern Department.

Reorganized and redesignated 1 January 1781 as the 3d Legionary Corps, to consist of four mounted and two dismounted troops. Consolidated 2 November 1782 with the 1st Legionary Corps [see 1st Continental Light Dragoon Regiment].

ENGAGEMENTS
Defense of Philadelphia
New Jersey 1778
Charleston 1780
Defense of the Carolinas
Greene's Campaign

4th CONTINENTAL LIGHT DRAGOON REGIMENT
(Moylan's Horse)

Authorized 5 January 1777 in the Continental Army as the 4th Continental Light Dragoon Regiment and assigned to the Main Army. Organized in spring 1777 at Philadelphia, Pennsylvania, and Baltimore, Maryland, to consist of six troops from Pennsylvania, Maryland, Virginia, and New Jersey.

Relieved 19 November 1778 from the Main Army and assigned to the Middle Department. Relieved 28 June 1779 from the Middle Department and assigned to the Highlands Department. Reorganized in early 1780 to consist of four mounted and two dismounted troops. Relieved 10 June 1780 from the Highlands Department and assigned to the Main Army. Relieved in December 1780 from the Main Army and assigned to the Middle Department.

Redesignated 1 January 1781 as the 4th Legionary Corps. Relieved in March 1781 from the Middle Department and assigned to the Southern Department. Reorganized 1 January 1783 to consist of one mounted troop and one dismounted troop. Furloughed 11 June 1783 at Philadelphia, Pennsylvania. Disbanded 15 November 1783.

ENGAGEMENTS
  Northern New Jersey
  Defense of Philadelphia
  New York 1779
  Connecticut 1779
  New Jersey 1780
  Yorktown
  Greene's Campaign
Captain Craig's Troop additionally served in:
  Philadelphia-Monmouth

CORPS OF NORTH CAROLINA LIGHT DRAGOONS

Authorized 13 April 1776 in the North Carolina State Troops as the Corps of North Carolina Light Dragoons. Organized in spring and summer 1776 at Wilmington to consist of the 1st, 2d, and 3d Troops. Adopted 31 July 1776 into the Continental Army and assigned to the Southern Department.

Relieved 5 February 1777 from the Southern Department and assigned to the Main Army. Relieved in fall 1777 from the Main Army and assigned to the Middle Department. (1st Troop relieved 15 May 1778 from the Middle Department and assigned to the Western Department.) Disbanded 1 January 1779 as follows: 1st Troop at Fort Pitt, Pennsylvania; 2d and 3d Troops at Halifax, North Carolina.

ENGAGEMENTS
  Defense of Philadelphia
3d Troop additionally served in:
  Charleston 1775–76

1st PARTISAN CORPS
(Armand's Legion)

Organized in winter and spring 1778 at Boston, Massachusetts, as a partisan corps under the command of Colonel Charles Armand Tuffin, recruited primarily from foreign volunteers. Adopted 25 June 1778 into the Continental Army as the Free and Independent Chasseurs, to consist of three companies, and assigned to the Highlands Department. Relieved 3 August 1778 from the Highlands Department and assigned to the Main Army.

Expanded 9 November 1778 to consist of four companies. Relieved 24 November 1778 from the Main Army and assigned to the Middle Department. Relieved 30 June 1779 from the Middle Department and assigned to the Highlands Department. Relieved 23 December 1779 from the Highlands Department and assigned to the Main Army. Consolidated 23 February 1780 with Pulaski's Legion [see Pulaski's Legion] and consolidated unit reorganized and redesignated as Armand's Legion, an element of the Southern Department, to consist of five companies.

Consolidated 1 January 1781 with Captain Henry Bedkin's Independent Troop of Light Horse [see Ottendorf's Corps] and consolidated unit reorganized and redesignated as the 1st Partisan Corps, to consist of three mounted and three dismounted troops. Relieved 11 March 1783 from the Southern Department and assigned to the Middle Department. Disbanded 25 November 1783 at York, Pennsylvania.

ENGAGEMENTS
New York 1778
New York 1779
Defense of the Carolinas
Yorktown

2d PARTISAN CORPS
(Lee's Legion)

Authorized 8 June 1776 in the Virginia State Troops as the 5th Troop of Light Horse. Redesignated 25 June 1776 as the 5th Troop, Virginia Light Horse. Organized in summer 1776 at Williamsburg with recruits from northern Virginia. (Virginia Light Horse adopted 25 November 1776 into the Continental Army, assigned to the Main Army, and redesignated as the 1st Continental Light Dragoon Regiment.)

Withdrawn 7 April 1778 from the 1st Continental Light Dragoon Regiment and expanded to form Lee's Corps of Partisan Light Dragoons, an element of the Main Army, to consist of two troops recruited at large. Expanded 28 May 1778 to consist of three troops. (Captain Allen McLane's Company [see *Annex*] assigned 13 July 1779 as the 4th Troop.)

Expanded and redesignated 14 February 1780 as Lee's Legionary Corps, to consist of three mounted and three dismounted troops. Relieved 31 October 1780 from the Main Army and assigned to the Southern Department.

Reorganized and redesignated 1 January 1781 as the 2d Partisan Corps, to consist of three mounted and three dismounted troops. Disbanded 15 November 1783 at Winchester, Virginia.

Annex

Authorized 13 January 1777 as Captain Allen McLane's Company, Patton's Additional Continental Regiment, an element of the Main Army. Organized 14 February–23

April 1777 at Dover, Delaware, with recruits from Delaware. (Patton's Additional Continental Regiment assigned 22 May 1777 to the 4th Virginia Brigade, an element of the Main Army; relieved 22 July 1778 from the 4th Virginia Brigade and assigned to the Highlands Department.)

Withdrawn 16 December 1778 from Patton's Additional Continental Regiment and assigned to the Delaware Regiment, an element of the 3d Virginia Brigade of the Main Army. Withdrawn 13 July 1779 from the Delaware Regiment and assigned to Lee's Corps of Partisan Light Dragoons as the 4th (Dismounted) Troop.

ENGAGEMENTS
  Northern New Jersey
  Defense of Philadelphia
  Philadelphia-Monmouth
  New York 1779
  New Jersey 1779
  New Jersey 1780
  Defense of the Carolinas
  Greene's Campaign
Captain McLane's Company additionally served in:
  Iroquois 1779

PULASKI'S LEGION

Authorized 28 March 1778 in the Continental Army as Pulaski's Legion and assigned to the Main Army. Organized 10 April–29 July 1778 at Baltimore, Maryland, to consist of one troop of lancers, two troops of dragoons, one company of riflemen, and two companies of light infantry, recruited primarily from Pennsylvania and Maryland. Relieved 10 November 1778 from the Main Army and assigned to the Middle Department. Relieved 2 February 1779 from the Middle Department and assigned to the Southern Department.

Consolidated 23 February 1780 with the Free and Independent Chasseurs [see 1st Partisan Corps].

ENGAGEMENTS
  New Jersey 1778
  Savannah
  Charleston 1780

OTTENDORF'S CORPS

Authorized 5 December 1776 in the Continental Army as Major Nicholas Dietrich, Baron de Ottendorf's, Corps and assigned to the Main Army. Organized 9 December 1776–1 June 1777 in eastern Pennsylvania to consist of five companies, including Captain John Paul Schott's Independent Company (authorized 6 September 1776). Redesignated 11 June 1777 as Late Ottendorf's Corps.

Corps broken up in April 1778 and its elements reorganized and redesignated as Captain Henry Bedkin's Independent Troop of Light Horse and Captains John Paul Schott's and Anthony Selin's Independent Companies, elements of the Middle Department.

Captain Henry Bedkin's Independent Troop of Light Horse relieved 3 June 1779 from the Middle Department and assigned to the Main Army. Relieved 1 January 1781 from the Main Army and assigned to the Southern Department; concurrently consolidated with Armand's Legion [see 1st Partisan Corps].

Captains John Paul Schott's and Anthony Selin's Companies relieved 1 January 1781 from the Middle Department and assigned to the Main Army; concurrently consolidated with the 2d Canadian Regiment [see 2d Canadian Regiment].

ENGAGEMENTS
    Northern New Jersey
    Defense of Philadelphia
Captain Bedkin's Troop additionally served in the following:
    New Jersey 1779
    New Jersey 1780
Captains Schott's and Selin's Companies additionally served in:
    Iroquois 1779

Bibliography

Armand, Charles Tuffin, Marquis de la Rouerie. "Letters of Col Armand." *New-York Historical Society Collections* for 1878:287–396.

Büttner, Johann Carl. *Narrative of Johann Carl Buettner in the American Revolution.* New York: C. F. Heartman, [1915].

Campbell, Charles, ed. *The Bland Papers: Being a Selection From the Manuscripts of Colonel Theodorick Bland, Jr. of Prince George County, Virginia.* 2 vols. Petersburg: E. & J. C. Ruffin, 1840–43.

Coutant, R. B. "The Action at Tarrytown, 1781: Heroism of Captain George Hurlbut." *Magazine of American History* 24 (1890):358–64.

Demarest, Thomas. "The Baylor Massacre—Some Assorted Notes and Information." *Bergen County History Annual*, 1971:29–93.

Douwes, William F. "Logistical Support of the Continental Light Dragoons." *Military Collector and Historian* 24 (1972):101–6.

Graham, A. S., and Woodhull, M. A. "Anthony Walton White, Brigadier in the Continental Army." *Magazine of History* 1 (1905):40–44; 2 (1905):394–402.

Griffin, Martin I. J. *Stephen Moylan: Muster-Master General, Secretary and Aid-de-Camp to Washington, Quartermaster-General, Colonel of Fourth Pennsylvania Light Dragoons and Brigadier-General of the War for American Independence.* Philadelphia: Privately printed, 1909.

Haarman, Albert W. "General Armand and His Partisan Corps, 1777–1783." *Military Collector and Historian* 12 (1960):97–102.

Hall, Charles S. *Benjamin Tallmadge: Revolutionary Soldier and American Businessman.* New York: Columbia University Press, 1943.

Hayes, John T. *Connecticut's Revolutionary Cavalry: Sheldon's Horse*. Chester, Conn.: Pequot Press, 1975.

Holst, Donald W., and Zlatich, Marko. "Dress and Equipment of Pulaski's Independent Legion." *Military Collector and Historian* 16 (1964):97–103.

Kieffer, Elizabeth C. "Three Caspar Schaffners." *Lancaster County Historical Society Papers* 42 (1938):181–200.

Lee, Henry. *Campaign of 1781 in the Carolinas; With Remarks Historical and Critical on Johnson's Life of Greene*. Philadelphia: E. Littell, 1824.

[_____.] "Letters of General Henry Lee." *Virginia Magazine of History and Biography* 6 (1898):153–58.

Lee, Robert E., ed. *Memories of the War in the Southern Department of the United States. By Henry Lee*. New York: University Publishing Co., 1869.

Loescher, Burt Garfield. *Washington's Eyes: The Continental Light Dragoons*. Ft. Collins, Colo.: The Old Army Press, 1977.

Montgomery, Charles B., ed. "The Case of Captain Craig." *Historical Review of Berks County* 6 (1941):119–21.

Moylan, Stephen. "Selections From the Correspondence of Col. Stephen Moylan, of the Continental Line." *Pennsylvania Magazine of History and Biography* 37 (1913):341–60.

Spencer, Richard Henry. "Pulaski's Legion." *Maryland Historical Magazine* 13 (1918):214–26.

Steiner, Edward E. "Nicholas Ruxton Moore: Soldier, Farmer and Politician." *Maryland Historical Magazine* 73 (1978):375–88.

Stutesman, John H., Jr. "Colonel Armand and Washington's Cavalry." *New-York Historical Society Quarterly* 45 (1961):5–42.

Tallmadge, Benjamin. *Memoir of Col. Benjamin Tallmadge, Prepared by Himself, at the Request of His Children*. New York: Thomas Holman, 1858.

Templin, Thomas Edwards. "Henry 'Light Horse Harry' Lee: A Biography." Ph.D. dissertation, University of Kentucky, 1975.

Ward, Townsend. "Charles Armand Tuffin, Marquis de la Rouerie." *Pennsylvania Magazine of History and Biography* 2 (1878):1–34.

Washington, Ella Bassett. "William Washington, Lieut.-Colonel Third Light Dragoons, Continental Army." *Magazine of American History* 9 (1883):94–107.

Weskerna, Eleanor, and Maurer, C. F. William. *"The Flower of the Virginian" and the Massacre Near Old Tappan: September 28, 1778*. River Vale, N. J.: Baylor's Dragoons Memorial Committee, 1978.

NEWBURGH, MAY 1783.

The striking changes which took place in the Continental Army during the Revolution are clearly shown in this modern work by H. Charles McBarron. The painting illustrates Washington's presenting the first two Badges of Military Merit to Sgts. Elijah Churchill of the 2d Legionary Corps and William Brown of the 2d Connecticut Regiment. (Soldiers of the Revolution, Army Art Collection).

Bibliography

This bibliography is not intended to be comprehensive for the War of American Independence. It is, instead, a tool for facilitating research and for introducing a reader to the massive array of sources available for this period. More extensive subject bibliographies for over 3,500 items, ranging from major manuscript collections to journal articles, are on file at the Organizational History Branch, U.S. Army Center of Military History, Washington, D.C. 20314.

The bibliographies in this section differ from those in the lineage sections. The lineage bibliographies cover an individual state's or branch's military participation. However, the subject bibliographies herein are arranged topically, with subjects pertaining to the Continental Army at large first followed by bibliographies on operations in the major theaters of the war. Later sections deal with a general background of the war and military history in the eighteenth century and also cover the other major powers which fought in North America during the Revolution.

Anyone interested in researching a specific unit should start with the appropriate state bibliography. Then the researcher should read relevant selections from the operational bibliographies relative to the engagements listed in the unit lineage. Reading should progress through material on the unit's chain of command, with particular attention to the biographies and manuscripts of brigade, division, and territorial department commanders. (*See Appendix B.*) Since the brigade was the primary combat formation in the Continental Army after 1776, many references in histories or contemporary documents end at that level.

Genealogists and historians interested in the composition of a specific unit or group of units should concentrate on the Continental Army's various personnel records. Muster rolls, payrolls, and size rolls were different types of documents compiled for different purposes, and, therefore, they contain different types of data. Unfortunately, those rolls are housed in widely dispersed repositories, and one needs diligence to compile full rosters. Every company in the Continental Army had to maintain an orderly book in which all orders were recorded down to the regimental level. All companies in a specific field force, such as the Main Army, would record the commander's orders, but differences appear in the division, brigade, and regimental orders added on at those intervening levels of command. Researchers can usually discover additional facts by reading several different units' orderly books for a single period.

Much of the interpretive material which confirms official policy on unit tactics can be found in certain primary source accounts. Diaries, official reports of senior commanders, and the correspondence of general officers are easily found but rarely tell the full story. Better sources for specific information on an engagement include the correspondence of junior officers, particularly field grade officers, the journals and letters of German or French professional soldiers written for other professional soldiers in Europe, and the official transcripts of courts-martial or courts of inquiry. The latter documents are especially valuable because they are verbatim transcripts with cross-examination of witnesses; they often include supporting documents which have since been lost; and they generally address technical military questions using very precise terminology. An officer's rank often colored his perceptions of a battle's "big picture." Any researcher should weigh the evidence in primary accounts with that caveat in mind, along with more traditional cautions about the time which had elapsed between the event and the time the document was created and about any special purpose the document's author might have had when he was writing.

Although the federal government is not the primary source of manuscript materials on the Revolution, some important federal sources do exist. The National Archives and Records Service has two significant sources. The first, the Papers of the Continental Congress (Record Group 360), includes correspondence and petitions from various officers, the records of various committees concerned with military questions, and the records of the Board of War. The second, the War Department Collection of Revolutionary War Records (Record Group 93), is strong on logistical matters and unit personnel records. The latter collection is not complete because fires in the early nineteenth century destroyed many originals, and many of the other items are merely copies of materials which are also in state collections. In addition to these Archives holdings, libraries at several National Park Service sites important during the Revolution, particularly the Morristown National Historical Park in New Jersey, contain significant collections. The other major federal repository is the Library of Congress. Key items in its collection include the George Washington Papers and the Peter Force collection of original documents and transcripts. Fortunately, the National Archives and the Library of Congress have excellent finding aids for their holdings.

Certain manuscript repositories contain fundamental records of certain New England states' units and general officers. New Hampshire materials are mainly in the Dartmouth College Library in Hanover and in the New Hampshire Historical Society, New Hampshire State Archives, and New Hampshire State Library, all of which are in Concord. The Massachusetts Historical Society in Boston includes the principal papers of Generals Ward, Thomas, Heath, Lincoln, and Knox, along with key staff officers, such as Timothy Pickering and William Tudor. Providence, Rhode Island, houses two major repositories for Rhode Island's participation: the Rhode Island Historical Society and the Rhode Island State Archives. Principal holdings for Connecticut are in the Connecticut Historical Society and Connecticut State Library in Hartford and the New Haven Colony Historical Society in New Haven. Both Hartford repositories include important logistical papers in their Trumbull Family Papers and in the Jeremiah Wadsworth Papers.

The state of New York has numerous valuable collections. The New-York Historical Society in New York, New York, is one of the most complete collections of Revolutionary War material anywhere and is superbly organized for research. Its major holdings are papers of William Alexander [Lord Stirling], James Clinton, Horatio Gates, Edward Hand, Charles Lee, Alexander McDougall, Friedrick von Steuben, Joseph Reed, and various artillery officers. It also houses one of the largest extant collections of orderly books. The New York [City] Public Library has large groups of manuscripts from this period, including Philip Schuyler's papers and the correspondence of less prominent persons of the era in the Myers and Emmet Collections. Other repositories are the New York State Historical Association in Cooperstown, the New York State Library in Albany, the Oneida Historical Society in Utica, and the Oswego Historical Society in Oswego. The Albany Institute of History and Art has some Philip Schuyler materials.

New Jersey, Pennsylvania, Delaware, and Maryland also have collections relevant to the Revolutionary War. Key repositories for information about people and units from New Jersey include the New Jersey Historical Society in Newark, the New Jersey State Library in Trenton, and the Princeton and Rutgers University Libraries in Princeton and New Brunswick, respectively. Pennsylvania materials are concentrated in the Pennsylvania Bureau of Archives and History in Harrisburg and in the Historical Society of Pennsylvania in Philadelphia. The latter collection is particularly strong in materials relating to logistics and medical support. Other significant collections in that state include the American Philosophical Society in Philadelphia and the Lancaster County Historical Society in Lancaster. Significant items for Delaware are primarily in the Delaware Hall of Records and the Historical Society of Delaware in Dover and Wilmington, respectively. Maryland materials are split between the Maryland Hall of Records in Annapolis and the Maryland Historical Society in Baltimore, except for the Mordecai Gist letterbooks in the New York Public Library.

Source materials on states south of Maryland are less accessible because they were damaged during the Revolution and the Civil War. Richmond's Virginia State Library and Virginia Historical Society hold large collections, but other Virginia materials are at the University of Virginia Library in Charlottesville; in the Draper Collection in the State Historical Society in Wisconsin in Madison; in the Febiger Papers at Harvard University in Cambridge, Massachusetts; and in the Robert Lawson Papers at Duke University in Durham, North Carolina. Key collections for North Carolina are the Southern Historical Collection at the University of North Carolina in Chapel Hill and the North Carolina Department of Archives and History in Raleigh. Columbia, South Carolina, is the home of the South Carolina Library and the South Carolina State Archives. The other important collection for that state is the South Carolina Historical Society's in Charleston. Georgia materials are most complete at the Georgia Historical Society in Savannah and the University of Georgia Library in Athens.

Resource materials relevant to certain subjects warrant special comment. Vermont was not yet a state during the Revolution, but both the Vermont Historical Society and the Vermont State Archives in Montpelier contain Revolutionary War materials. Manuscripts on artillery are well preserved. For instance, Henry Knox's papers are in the Massachusetts Historical Society and the Boston Public Library. The New-York Historical Society has the papers of John Lamb, Ebenezer Stevens, Sebastian Bauman, and Thomas Machin as well as an extensive set of orderly books for the 2d and 3d Continental Artillery Regiments. The same repository holds the Erskine-DeWitt Map Collection—the official topographical maps prepared for Washington by geographers. Mounted combat units' papers are normally found in the same repositories as the infantry units' from the same states. The Benjamin Tallmadge papers in the Litchfield Historical Society, Litchfield, Connecticut; and Henry Lee's at the University of Virginia are especially important.

Several repositories situated outside the original thirteen states hold Revolutionary War manuscripts. The Chicago Historical Society has papers of Generals Steuben and George Weedon. The Clements Library of the University of Michigan in Ann Arbor has abundant materials, especially about southern campaigns under Horatio Gates, Nathanael Greene, and Jethro Sumner. The Henry E. Huntington Library in San Marino, California, includes important Philip Schuyler papers. Rufus Putnam's manuscripts are now housed in Marietta, Ohio, at the Marietta College Library.

Documents detailing the opponent's point of view are not limited to Great Britain's repositories. Key collections of military and political materials are found, for example, in the Clements Library at the University of Michigan or in the New-York Historical Society. The most important source for this book, however, was the Headquarters Papers of the British Army in America. This collection of photostats at the Colonial Williamsburg Foundation in Virginia represents the official papers of Sir Guy Carleton, the final British commander in chief in North America. The collection contains record copies of the key items generated during his predecessors' tenures, along with other items from subordinates in semiautonomous commands. The original documents, calendared by the Historical Manuscripts Commission as the *American Manuscripts in the Royal Institution*, were returned to Great Britain in 1957 and are now in the Public Record Office (as Class 30/55). Microfilm copies of many other British and German documents are also in the Library of Congress.

GENERAL

Bibliographic Guides

Andrews, Charles McLean. *Guide to the Manuscript Materials for the History of the United States to 1783, in the British Museum, in Minor London Archives, and in the Libraries of Oxford and Cambridge*. Washington: Carnegie Institution, 1908.
_____. *Guide to the Materials for American History, to 1783, in the Public Record Office of Great Britain*. 2 vols. Washington: Carnegie Institution, 1912–14.
Clark, David Sanders. *Index to Maps of the American Revolution in Books and Periodicals: Illustrating the Revolutionary War and Other Events of the Period 1763–1789*. Westport, Conn.: Greenwood Press, 1974.
Clark, H. C. "Report on Publication of Revolutionary Military Records." *American Historical Association Annual Report* (1915): 183–99.
Deutrich, Mabel E. *Preliminary Inventory of the War Department Collection of Revolutionary War Records (Record Group 93)*. Washington: National Archives, 1962.
Gephart, Ronald M. *Periodical Literature on the American Revolution: Historical Research and Changing Interpretations, 1895–1970, a Selective Bibliography*. Washington: Library of Congress, 1971.
Higham, Robin, ed. *A Guide to the Sources of United States Military History*. Hamden, Conn.: Archon Books, 1975.
Matthews, William. *British Diaries: An Annotated Bibliography of British Diaries Written Between 1442 and 1942*. Berkeley: University of California Press, 1950.
Matthews, William, and Pearce, Roy Harvey. *American Diaries: An Annotated Bibliography of American Diaries Written Prior to the Year 1861*. Boston: J. S. Canner, 1959.
Nebenzahl, Kenneth. *A Bibliography of Printed Battle Plans of the American Revolution, 1775–1795*. Chicago: University of Chicago Press, 1975.
Peckham, Howard H. "Military Papers in the Clements Library." *Military Affairs* 2 (1938): 126–30.
Sellers, John R., et al. *Manuscript Sources in the Library of Congress for Research on the American Revolution*. Washington: Library of Congress, 1975.
Shy, John. *The American Revolution*. Northbrook, Ill.: AHM Publishing Corp., 1973.

White, J. Todd, and Lesser, Charles H. *Fighters for Independence: A Guide to the Sources of Biographical Information on Soldiers and Sailors of the American Revolution*. Chicago: University of Chicago Press, 1977.

Reference Works

Boatner, Mark Mayo, III. *Encyclopedia of the American Revolution*. New York: David McKay Co., 1966.

Cappon, Lester J., et al., eds. *The Atlas of Early American History: The Revolutionary Era, 1760-1790*. Princeton: Princeton University Press, 1976.

Greene, Evarts B., and Harrington, Virginia D. *American Population Before the Federal Census of 1790*. New York: Columbia University Press, 1932.

Heitman, Francis B. *Historical Register of Officers of the Continental Army During the War of the Revolution*. Washington: National Tribune, 1890.

Kail, Jerry, et al., eds. *Who Was Who During the American Revolution*. Indianapolis: Bobbs-Merrill Co., 1976.

Lesser, Charles H., ed. *The Sinews of Independence: Monthly Strength Returns of the Continental Army*. Chicago: University of Chicago Press, 1975.

Peckham, Howard H. *The Toll of Independence: Engagements and Battle Casualties of the American Revolution*. Chicago: University of Chicago Press, 1974.

Peterson, Clarence Stewart. *Known Military Dead During the American Revolutionary War, 1775-1783*. Baltimore: Genealogical Publishing Co., 1959.

Peterson, Harold L. *The Book of the Continental Soldier, Being a Compleat Account of the Uniforms, Weapons, and Equipment With Which He Lived and Fought*. Harrisburg: Stackpole Co., 1968.

Primary Sources

Almon, J[ohn], ed. *The Remembrancer, or, Impartial Repository of Public Events, for the Year....* London: J. Almon, published annually throughout the Revolutionary Era.

Barnard, W. T., ed. *Orderly Books of the Continental Forces, and Official Records of the Quartermaster's Department of the Revolutionary Army, 1775-1783*. Orderly Books, vol. 1. Washington, 1887. [No other volumes published.]

Beatson, Robert. *Naval and Military Memoirs of Great Britain, From 1727 to 1783*. 6 vols. London: Longman, Hurst, Rees & Orme, 1804.

Commager, Henry S., and Morris, Richard B., eds. *The Spirit of 'Seventy-Six*. New York: Harpers, 1967.

Dann, John C., ed. *The Revolution Remembered: Eyewitness Accounts of the War for Independence*. Chicago: University of Chicago Press, 1980.

Force, Peter, ed. *American Archives: A Collection of Authentic Records, State Papers, Debates, and Letters and Other Notices of Public Affairs*. 9 vols. Washington: M. St. Clair Clarke & Peter Force, 1839-53.

Gordon, William. *The History of the Rise, Progress, and Establishment of the Independence of the United States of America: Including an Account of the Late War; and of the Thirteen Colonies, From Their Origin to That Period*. 4 vols. London: Privately printed, 1788.

Hamilton, Alexander. *The Papers of Alexander Hamilton*. Edited by Harold C. Syrett and Jacob E. Cook. 26 vols. New York: Columbia University Press, 1961-79.

Kirkland, Frederick R., ed. *Letters on the American Revolution in the Library at 'Karolfred.'* 2 vols. Philadelphia: Privately printed, 1941.

Moore, Frank. *Diary of the American Revolution, From Newspapers and Original Documents.* 2 vols. New York: Charles Scribner, 1860.

New-York Historical Society. "Muster and Pay Rolls of the War of the Revolution, 1775–1783." 2 vols. *New-York Historical Society Collections* for 1914–15.

Peckham, Howard H., ed. *Sources of American Independence: Selected Manuscripts From the Collections of the William L. Clements Library.* 2 vols. Chicago: University of Chicago Press, 1978.

Ramsay, David. *The History of the American Revolution.* Dublin: William Jones, 1795.

Ryan, Dennis P., ed. *A Salute to Courage: The American Revolution as Seen Through Wartime Writings of Officers of the Continental Army and Navy.* New York: Columbia University Press, 1979.

Saffell, W. T. R. *Records of the Revolutionary War: Containing the Military and Financial Correspondence of Distinguished Officers; Names of the Officers and Privates of Regiments, Companies, and Corps, With the Dates of Their Commissions and Enlistments; General Orders of Washington, Lee, and Greene, at Germantown and Valley Forge. . . .*3d ed. Baltimore: Charles E. Saffell, 1894.

Scheer, George F., and Rankin, Hugh F., eds. *Rebels and Redcoats.* New York: World, 1957.

"Some Unpublished Revolutionary Manuscripts." *New Jersey Historical Society Proceedings,* 2d ser., 13 (1894–95): 17–24, 79–88, 149–60; 3d ser., 3 (1902, 1906): 85–92, 118–23, 180–84; 6 (1909): 12–16, 79–86.

Sparks, Jared, ed. *Correspondence of the American Revolution; Being Letters of Eminent Men to George Washington, From the Time of His Taking Command of the Army to the End of His Presidency.* 4 vols. Boston: Little, Brown & Co., 1853.

Stedman, C[harles]. *The History of the Origin, Progress and Termination of the American War.* 2 vols. Dublin: Privately printed, 1794.

Thacher, James. *Military Journal of the American Revolution, From the Commencement to the Disbanding of the American Army; Comprising a Detailed Account of the Principal Events and Battles of the Revolution, With Their Exact Dates, and a Biographical Sketch of the Most Prominent Generals.* 1823. Reprint. Hartford: Hurlbut, Williams & Co., 1862.

Secondary Sources

Adams, Charles F. *Studies Military and Diplomatic, 1775–1865.* New York: Macmillan Co., 1911.

Alden, John Richard. *The American Revolution, 1775–1783.* New York: Harper & Bros., 1954.

Barrow, Thomas C. "The American Revolution as a Colonial War for Independence." *William and Mary Quarterly,* 3d ser., 25 (1968): 452–64.

Belcher, Henry. *The First American Civil War; First Period, 1775–1778.* 2 vols. London: Macmillan & Co., 1911.

Carrington, Henry B. *Battles of the American Revolution, 1775–1781: Historical and Military Criticism, With Topographical Illustration.* New York: A. S. Barnes & Co., 1871.

Cress, Lawrence Delbert. "Radical Whiggery on the Role of the Military: Ideological Roots of the American Revolutionary Militia." *Journal of the History of Ideas* 40 (1979): 43-60.

Crow, Jeffrey J., and Tise, Larry E., eds. *The Southern Experience in the American Revolution*. Chapel Hill: University of North Carolina Press, 1978.

Durand, John. *New Materials for the History of the American Revolution*. New York: Henry Holt & Co., 1889.

Fox, Dixon Ryan. "Culture in Knapsacks." *Quarterly Journal of the New York State Historical Association* 11 (1930): 31-52.

Graham, Gerald S. "Considerations on the War of American Independence." *Institute for Historical Research Bulletin* 22 (1949): 22-34.

Greene, Francis Vinton. *The Revolutionary War and the Military Policy of the United States*. New York: Charles Scribner's Sons, 1911.

Hatch, Louis C. *The Administration of the American Revolutionary Army*. New York: Longmans, Green, & Co., 1904.

Higginbotham, Don. "American Historians and the Military History of the American Revolution." *American Historical Review* 70 (1964): 18-34.

_____. *The War of American Independence: Military Attitudes, Policies, and Practice, 1763-1789*. New York: Macmillan Co., 1971.

_____, ed. *Reconsiderations on the Revolutionary War: Selected Essays*. Westport, Conn.: Greenwood Press, 1978.

Higgins, W. Robert, ed. *The Revolutionary War in the South: Power, Conflict, and Leadership: Essays in Honor of John Richard Alden*. Durham: Duke University Press, 1979.

Johnson, Elmer Douglass. "David Ramsay: Historian or Plagiarist?" *South Carolina Historical Magazine* 57 (1956): 189-98.

Jones, E. Alfred. "English Convicts in the American Army in the War of Independence." *New Jersey Historical Society Proceedings*, new ser., 7 (1922): 286-91.

Libby, Orin Grant. "A Critical Examination of William Gordon's History of the American Revolution." *American Historical Association Annual Report for 1899*: 367-88.

Loring, James S. "Our First Historian of the American Revolution." *Historical Magazine* 6 (1862): 41-49, 78-83.

Lossing, Benson J. *The Pictorial Field-Book of the Revolution; or Illustrations, by Pen and Pencil, of the History, Biography, Scenery, Relics, and Traditions of the War for Independence*. 2 vols. New York: Harper & Bros., 1859.

Mackesy, Piers. *The War for America, 1775-1783*. Cambridge: Harvard University Press, 1964.

Middleton, Richard D. "British Historians and the American Revolution." *Journal of American Studies* 5 (1971): 43-58.

Mitchell, Broadus. *The Price of Independence: A Realistic View of the American Revolution*. New York: Oxford University Press, 1974.

Mitchell, Joseph B. *Decisive Battles of the American Revolution*. New York: G. P. Putnam's Sons, 1962.

_____. *Discipline and Bayonets: The Armies and Leaders in the War of the American Revolution*. New York: G. P. Putnam's Sons, 1967.

Montross, Lynn. *Rag, Tag and Bobtail*. New York: Harper & Row, 1952.

Morris, Richard B. *The American Revolution, a Short History*. New York: Van Nostrand, 1955.

_____. *The American Revolution Reconsidered*. New York: Harper & Row, 1967.

Nevins, Allan. *The American States During and After the Revolution, 1775–1789*. New York: Macmillan Co., 1924.

Newmyer, R. Ken. "Charles Stedman's *History of the American War*." *American Historical Review* 63 (1958): 924–34.

Palmer, Dave Richard. *The Way of the Fox: American Strategy in the War for America, 1775–1783*. Westport, Conn.: Greenwood Press, 1975.

Palmer, John McAuley. *America in Arms, the Experience of the United States With Military Organization*. New Haven: Yale University Press, 1941.

Peckham, Howard H. *The War for Independence: A Military History*. Chicago: University of Chicago Press, 1958.

Proctor, Donald John. "From Insurrection to Independence: The Continental Congress and the Military Launching of the American Revolution." Ph.D. dissertation, University of Southern California, 1965.

Robson, Eric. *The American Revolution in Its Political and Military Aspects, 1763–1783*. New York: Oxford University Press, 1955.

Shy, John. *A People Numerous and Armed: Reflections on the Military Struggle for American Independence*. New York: Oxford University Press, 1976.

Trevelyan, George O. *The American Revolution*. 3 vols. in 4. New York: Longmans, Green, 1899–1907.

Underdal, Stanley J., ed. *Military History of the American Revolution: The Proceedings of the 6th Military History Symposium, United States Air Force Academy, 10–11 October 1974*. Washington: Office of Air Force History, 1976.

Upton, Emory. *The Military Policy of the United States*. Washington: Government Printing Office, 1912.

Wallace, Willard M. *Appeal to Arms: A Military History of the American Revolution*. New York: Harper & Bros., 1951.

Ward, Christopher. *The War of the Revolution*. Edited by John R. Alden. 2 vols. New York: Macmillan Co., 1952.

Ward, Harry M. *The Department of War, 1781–1795*. Pittsburgh: University of Pittsburgh Press, 1962.

Weigley, Russell F. *The American Way of War; a History of the United States Military Strategy and Policy*. New York: Macmillan Co., 1973.

_____. *History of the United States Army*. New York: Macmillan Co., 1964.

Special Studies

D'Auberteuil, Hillard. "List of French Officers Who Served in the American Armies With Commissions From Congress Prior to the Treaties Made Between France and the Thirteen United States of America." *Magazine of American History* 3 (1879): 364–69.

Dawson, Henry B., ed. "Plan for a Re-organization of the Continental Army by Brigadier-General Mordecai Gist." *Historical Magazine*, 2d ser., 3 (1868): 270–73.

Echevarria, Durand, and Murphy, Orville T. "The American Revolutionary Army: A French Estimate in 1777." *Military Affairs* 27 (1963): 1–7, 153–62.

Gottschalk, Louis. "The Attitude of European Officers in the Revolutionary Armies Toward General George Washington." *Journal of the Illinois State Historical Society* 32 (1939): 20-50.

Jameson, Hugh. "The Organization of the Militia of the Middle States During the War for Independence, 1775-1781." Ph.D. dissertation, University of Michigan, 1936.

Merritt, Elizabeth. "The Lexington Alarm, April 19, 1775: Messages Sent to the Southward After the Battle." *Maryland Historical Magazine* 41 (1946): 89-114.

Murphy, Orville Theodore, Jr. "The American Revolutionary Army and the Concept of the *Levee en Masse*." *Military Affairs* 23 (1959): 13-20.

_____. "French Contemporary Opinion of the American Revolutionary Army." Ph.D. dissertation, University of Minnesota, 1957.

_____. "The French Professional Soldier's Opinion of the American Militia in the War of the Revolution." *Military Affairs* 32 (1969): 191-98.

Nelson, Paul David. "Citizen Soldiers or Regulars: The Views of American General Officers on the Military Establishment, 1775-1781." *Military Affairs* 43 (1979): 126-32.

Paret, Peter. "Colonial Experience and European Military Reform at the End of the Eighteenth Century." *Institute for Historical Research Bulletin* 37 (1964): 47-59.

Prelinger, Catherine M. "Less Lucky Than Lafayette: A Note on the French Applicants to Benjamin Franklin for Commissions in the American Army, 1776-1785." *Western Society for French History Proceedings* 4 (1976): 263-70.

Quarles, Benjamin. *The Negro in the American Revolution*. Chapel Hill: University of North Carolina Press, 1961.

Royster, Charles W. *A Revolutionary People at War: The Continental Army and American Character, 1775-1783*. Chapel Hill: University of North Carolina Press, 1980.

White, John Todd. "Standing Armies in Time of War: Republican Theory and Military Practice During the American Revolution." Ph.D. dissertation, George Washington University, 1978.

Wright, John W. "The Corps of Light Infantry in the Continental Army." *American Historical Review* 31 (1926): 454-61.

_____. "Notes on the Continental Army." *William and Mary Quarterly*, 2d ser., 11 (1931): 81-105, 185-209; 12 (1932): 79-104, 229-49; 13 (1933): 85-97.

GENERAL OFFICERS

Collected Biographies

Billias, George A[than], ed. *George Washington's Generals*. New York: Morrow, 1964.

Heitman, Francis B. *Historical Register of Officers of the Continental Army During the War of the Revolution, April, 1775, to December, 1783*. rev. ed. Washington: The Rare Book Shop Publishing Co., 1914.

Nelson, Paul David. "Lee, Gates, Stephen and Morgan: Revolutionary War Generals of the Lower Shenandoah Valley." *West Virginia History* 37 (1976): 185-200.

Washington, George. "Washington's Opinion of His General Officers." *Magazine of American History* 3 (1879): 81-88.

Alexander, William (Lord Stirling)

Danforth, George Henry. "The Rebel Earl." Ph.D. dissertation, Columbia University, 1955.

Duer, William Alexander. *William Alexander, Earl of Stirling, Major General in the Army of the United States During the Revolution. New Jersey Historical Society Collections*, vol. 2. New York: Wiley & Putnam, 1847.

Valentine, Alan C. *Lord Stirling*. New York: Oxford University Press, 1969.

Armand, Charles Tuffin, Marquis de la Rouerie

Armand, Charles Tuffin, Marquis de la Rouerie. "Letters of Col. Armand." *New-York Historical Society Collections* for 1878: 287-396.

Ward, Townsend. "Charles Armand Tuffin, Marquis de la Rouerie." *Pennsylvania Magazine of History and Biography* 2 (1878): 1-34.

Whitridge, Arnold. "The Marquis de la Rouerie, Brigadier General in the Continental Army." *Massachusetts Historical Society Proceedings* 79 (1968): 47-63.

Armstrong, John

Armstrong, John. "Letters of General John Armstrong of Kittaning to Gen. Wm. Irvine." *Historical Magazine*, 1st ser., 8 (1864): 16-21.

Darlington, William M. "Major-General John Armstrong." *Pennsylvania Magazine of History and Biography* 1 (1877): 183-87.

Arnold, Benedict

Arnold, Issac N. *The Life of Benedict Arnold; His Patriotism and His Treason*. Chicago: Jansen, McClurg & Co., 1880.

Proceedings of a General Court Martial of the Line, Held at Raritan, in the State of New-Jersey, by Order of His Excellency George Washington, Esq., General and Commander in Chief of the Army of the United States of America, for the Trial of Major General Arnold, June 1, 1779; Major General Howe, President; Published by Order of Congress. Philadelphia: F. Bailey, 1780.

Sellers, Charles Coleman. *Benedict Arnold, the Proud Warrior*. New York: Minton, Balch & Co., 1930.

Wallace, Willard M. *Connecticut's Dark Star of the Revolution: General Benedict Arnold*. Hartford: American Revolution Bicentennial Commission of Connecticut, 1978.

_____. *Traitorous Hero: The Life and Fortunes of Benedict Arnold*. New York: Harper, 1954.

Clinton, George

Clinton, George. *Public Papers of George Clinton, First Governor of New York*. Edited by Hugh Hastings and James Austin Holden. 10 vols. Albany: State Printers, 1899-1914.

Pagano, Francis B. "An Historical Account of the Military and Political Career of George Clinton, 1739-1812. Ph.D. dissertation, St. John's University, 1956.

Spaulding, Ernest Wilder. *His Excellency George Clinton (1739-1812), Critic of the Constitution*. New York: Macmillan Co., 1938.

Dayton, Elias

Dayton, Elias. "Papers of General Elias Dayton." *New Jersey Historical Society Proceedings* 9 (1864): 175-94.

Elbert, Samuel

Elbert, Samuel. "Order Book of Samuel Elbert, Colonel and Brigadier General in the Continental Army." Edited by William Harden. *Georgia Historical Society Collections*, pt. 2, 5 (1905): 5-191.
Jones, Charles Colcock. *The Life and Services of Honorable Maj. Gen. Samuel Elbert of Georgia*. Cambridge, Mass.: Riverside Press, 1887.
Simms, William Gilmore. "Major-General Samuel Elbert, of Georgia." *Historical Magazine*, 2d ser., 3 (1868): 34-37.

Gadsden, Christopher

Gadsden, Christopher. *The Writings of Christopher Gadsden, 1746-1805*. Edited by Richard Walsh. Columbia: University of South Carolina Press, 1966.

Gates, Horatio

Nelson, Paul David. *General Horatio Gates: A Biography*. Baton Rouge: Louisiana State University Press, 1976.
Patterson, Samuel White. *Horatio Gates: Defender of American Liberties*. New York: Columbia University Press, 1941.
Saltzman, Martin, et al. *The Horatio Gates Papers, 1726-1828: A Guide to the Microfilm Edition*. Sanford, N.C.: Microfilming Corporation of America, 1979.

Glover, John

Billias, George Athan. *General John Glover and His Marblehead Mariners*. New York: Holt, Rinehart & Winston, 1960.
Glover, John. "General John Glover's Letterbook." Edited by Russell W. Knight. *Essex Institute Historical Collections* 112 (1976): 1-55. [Reprinted as *General John Glover's Letterbook, 1776-1777*. Salem: Essex Institute, 1976.]
Sanborn, Nathan Perkins. *Gen. John Glover and His Marblehead Regiment in the Revolutionary War*. Marblehead, Mass.: Marblehead Historical Society, 1903.

Greene, Nathanael

Greene, Francis Vinton. *General Greene*. New York: D. Appleton, 1893.
Greene, George W[ashington]. *The Life of Nathaniel Greene, Major-General in the Army of the Revolution*. 3 vols. New York: Hurd & Houghton, 1867-71.
Greene, Nathanael. *The Papers of General Nathanael Greene*. Edited by Richard K. Showman, et al. Chapel Hill: University of North Carolina Press for the Rhode Island Historical Society, 1976.
Johnson, William. *Sketches of the Life and Correspondence of Nathaniel Greene, Major General of the Armies of the United States, in the War of the Revolution, Compiled Chiefly From Original Materials*. 2 vols. Charleston: A. E. Miller, 1822.
Thane, Elswyth. *The Fighting Quaker: Nathaniel Greene*. New York: Hawthorne Books, 1972.

Thayer, Theodore. *Nathaniel Greene: Strategist of the American Revolution*. New York: Twayne Publishers, 1960.

Hand, Edward

Forry, Richard Reuben. "Edward Hand: His Role in the American Revolution." Ph.D. dissertation, Duke University, 1976.

Hand, Edward. "Orderly Book of General Edward Hand, Valley Forge, January, 1778." Edited by William B. Read. *Pennsylvania Magazine of History and Biography* 41 (1917): 198-223, 257-73, 458-67.

_____. *The Unpublished Revolutionary Papers of Major General Edward Hand of Pennsylvania, 1777-1784*. Edited by A. J. Bowden. New York: Privately printed, 1907.

Heath, William

Dolan, Graham Philip. "Major General William Heath and the First Years of the American Revolution." Ph.D. dissertation, Boston University, 1966.

Heath, William. "The Heath Papers." *Massachusetts Historical Society Collections*, 5th ser., 4 (1878): 1-285; 7th ser., 4 (1904) and 5 (1905).

_____. *Memoirs of Major-General William Heath by Himself, to Which Is Added the Accounts of the Battle of Bunker Hill by Generals Dearborn, Lee and Wilkinson*. Edited by William Abbatt. new ed. New York: William Abbatt, 1901.

Hogun, James

Clark, Walter. "Career of General James Hogun: One of North Carolina's Revolutionary Officers." *Magazine of American History* 28 (1892): 284-87.

Howe, Robert

Bellamy, John D. *Sketch of Maj. Gen. Robert Howe, of the American Revolution*. Wilmington, N.C.: S. G. Hall, 1882.

"Proceedings of a General Court Martial, Held at Philadelphia, in the State of Pennsylvania, by Order of His Excellency General Washington, Commander in Chief of the Army of the United States of America for the Trial of Major General Howe, December 7, 1781; Major General Baron Steuben, President. *New-York Historical Society Collections* for 1879: 215-311. [Originally published Philadelphia: Hall & Sellers, 1782].

Huntington, Jedediah

Huntington, Joshua, and Huntington, Jedediah. "Huntington Papers: Correspondence of the Brothers Joshua and Jedediah Huntington During the Period of the American Revolution, 1771-1783." *Connecticut Historical Society Collections* 20 (1923).

Irvine, William

Irvine, William. "Extracts From the Papers of General William Irvine." Edited by William A. Irvine. *Pennsylvania Magazine of History and Biography* 5 (1881): 259-75.

_____. "Selections From the Military Papers of Brig. Gen. William Irvine." *Pennsylvania Magazine of History and Biography* 40 (1916): 108-12.

Wainwright, Nicholas B. *The Irvine Story*. Philadelphia: Historical Society of Pennsylvania, 1964.

Kalb, Johannes (or Jean), Baron de Kalb

Colleville, Ludovic, Comte de. *Les Missions secretes du general-major Baron de Kalb
et son role dans la guerre de l'Independance Americaine*. Paris: E. Perrin, 1885.

Kapp, Friedrich. *Life of John Kalb*. New York: Holt, 1884. [Originally published as
Leben des amerikanischen Generals Johann Kalb. Stuttgart: Gottaschen Verlag,
1862.]

Smith, John Spear. *Memoir of the Baron de Kalb*. Baltimore: J. D. Toy, 1858.

Zucker, A. E. *General De Kalb, Lafayette's Mentor*. Chapel Hill: University of North
Carolina Press, 1966.

Knox, Henry

Brooks, Noah. *Henry Knox, a Soldier of the Revolution; Major-General in the Conti-
nental Army, Washington's Chief of Artillery, First Secretary of War Under the
Constitution, Founder of the Society of the Cincinnati; 1750–1806*. New-York:
G. P. Putnam's Sons. 1900.

Callahan, North. *Henry Knox: General Washington's General*. New York: A. S.
Barnes & Co., 1958.

Drake, Francis S. *Life and Correspondence of Henry Knox, Major-General in the
American Revolutionary Army*. Boston: Samuel G. Drake, 1873.

Lafayette, Marie du Motier, Marquis de

Bill, Shirley A., and Gottschalk, Louis. "Silas Deane's 'Worthless' Agreement With
Lafayette." *Prologue* 4 (1972): 219–23.

Charaway, Etienne. *Le General La Fayette, 1757–1834: Notice bibliographique*. Paris:
Au siege de la Societe de l'histoire de la Revolution francaise, 1898.

Chinard, Gilbert, ed. *When Lafayette Came to America, an Account From the Dubois
Martin Papers in the Maryland Historical Society*. Easton, Pa.: American Friends
of Lafayette, 1948.

Gottschalk, Louis. *Lafayette and the Close of the American Revolution*. Chicago: University of Chicago Press, 1942.

_____. *Lafayette Comes to America*. Chicago: University of Chicago Press, 1935.

_____. *Lafayette Joins the American Army*. Chicago: University of Chicago Press,
1937.

Kite, Elizabeth S. "Lafayette and His Companions on the 'Victoire.' " *American Catholic Historical Society Records* 45 (1934): 1–32, 144–78, 212–45, 275–311.

Lafayette, Marie du Motier, Marquis de. *Lafayette in the Age of the American Revolution: Selected Letters and Papers 1776–1790*. Edited by Stanley J. Idzerda et al.
Ithaca: Cornell University Press, 1977–.

_____. *Memoirs, Correspondence and Manuscripts of General Lafayette Published
by His Family*. 3 vols. London: Saunders & Otley, 1837. [6 vols., Paris: H. Fournier
aine, 1837–38.]

Loveland, Ann C. *Emblem of Liberty; the Image of Lafayette in the American Mind*.
Baton Rouge: Louisiana State University Press, 1971.

Tower, Charlemagne. *The Marquis de La Fayette in the American Revolution, With Some Account of the Attitude of France Toward the War of Independence*. 2 vols. Philadelphia: J.B. Lippincott, 1895.

Lee, Charles

Alden, John R. *General Charles Lee, Traitor or Patriot?* Baton Rouge: Louisiana State University Press, 1951.

Lee, Charles. "The Lee Papers." 4 vols. *New-York Historical Society Collections* for 1871–74.

Patterson, Samuel W. *Knight Errant of Liberty; the Triumph and Tragedy of General Charles Lee*. New York: Lantern Press, 1958.

Lincoln, Benjamin

Cavanagh, John Carroll. "The Military Career of Major General Benjamin Lincoln in the War of the American Revolution, 1775–1781." Ph.D. dissertation, Duke University, 1969.

McDougall, Alexander

Champagne, Roger J. *Alexander McDougall and the American Revolution in New York*. Schenectady: New York State American Revolution Bicentennial Commission, 1975.

McDougall, William L. *American Revolutionary: A Biography of General Alexander McDougall*. Westport, Conn.: Greenwood Press, 1977.

McIntosh, Lachlan

Jackson, Harvey Hardaway, III. *Lachlan McIntosh and the Politics of Revolutionary Georgia*. Athens: University of Georgia Press, 1979.

Lawrence, Alexander A. "General Lachlan McIntosh and His Suspension From Continental Command During the Revolution." *Georgia Historical Quarterly* 38 (1954): 101–41.

McIntosh, Lachlan. *Lachlan McIntosh Papers in the University of Georgia Libraries*. Edited by Lilla M. Hawes. Athens: University of Georgia Press, 1968.

_____. "The Papers of Lachlan McIntosh." Edited by Lilla M. Hawes. *Georgia Historical Society Collections* 12 (1957). [Originally published in the *Georgia Historical Quarterly* 38 (1954): 148–69, 253–67, 356–68; 39 (1955): 52–68, 172–86, 253–68, 356–75; 40 (1956): 65–88, 152–74.]

Maxwell, William

Griffith, J. H. "William Maxwell, of New Jersey, Brigadier General in the Revolution." *New Jersey Historical Society Proceedings*, 2d ser., 13 (1894): 109–23.

Maxwell, William. "General William Maxwell Correspondence." Edited by A. Van Doren Honeyman. *New Jersey Historical Society Proceedings*, new ser., 10 (1925): 176–80.

Mercer, Hugh

Waterman, Joseph M. *With Sword and Lancet: The Life of General Hugh Mercer*. Richmond: Garrett & Massie, 1941.

Mifflin, Thomas

Rossman, Kenneth R. *Thomas Mifflin and the Politics of the American Revolution*. Chapel Hill: University of North Carolina Press, 1952.

Montgomery, Richard

Cullum, George W. "Major-General Richard Montgomery." *Magazine of American History* 11 (1884): 273–99.

Hunt, Louise Livingston. *Biographical Notes Concerning General Richard Montgomery Together With Hitherto Unpublished Letters*. Poughkeepsie: Book & Job Printing House, 1876.

Montgomery, Richard. *Major General Richard Montgomery: A Contribution Toward a Biography From the Clements Library*. Ann Arbor: University of Michigan, 1970.

Robinson, Thomas P. "Some Notes on Major-General Richard Montgomery." *New York History* 37 (1956): 388–98.

Morgan, Daniel

Edwards, William Waller. "Morgan and His Riflemen." *William and Mary Quarterly*, 1st ser., 23 (1914): 73–106.

Graham, James. *The Life of General Daniel Morgan of the Virginia Line of the United States, With Portions of His Correspondence*. New York: Derby & Jackson, 1856.

Higginbotham, Don. *Daniel Morgan: Revolutionary Rifleman*. Chapel Hill: University of North Carolina Press, 1961.

Moultrie, William

Hartley, Cecil B. *Heroes and Patriots of the South; Comprising Lives of General Francis Marion, General William Moultrie, General Andrew Pickens, and Governor John Rutledge, With Sketches of Other Distinguished Heroes and Patriots Who Served in the Revolutionary War in the Southern States*. Philadelphia: G. G. Evans, 1860.

Moultrie, William. *Memoirs of the American Revolution, So Far as It Related to the States of North and South Carolina, and Georgia, Compiled From the Most Authentic Materials, the Author's Personal Knowledge of Various Events, and Including Epistolary Correspondence on Public Affairs, With Civil and Military Officers, at That Period*. 3 vols. New York: David Longworth, 1802.

Muhlenberg, John Peter Gabriel

Hocker, Edward W. *The Fighting Parson of the American Revolution: A Biography of General Peter Muhlenberg, Lutheran Clergyman, Military Chieftan, and Political Leader*. Philadelphia: Privately printed, 1936.

Muhlenberg, Henry A. *A Life of Major-General Peter Muhlenberg of the Revolutionary Army*. Philadelphia: Carey & Hart, 1849.

Nash, Francis

Waddell, Alfred M. *Gen. Francis Nash; an Address by Hon. A. M. Waddell, Delivered at the Unveiling of a Monument to General Nash, Voted by Congress, at the Guilford Battle Ground, July 4, 1906*. Greensboro: Guilford Battle Ground Co., 1906.

Nixon, John

Merriam, John McKinstry. *Five Framingham heroes of the American Revolution; a Paper Read Upon Invitation of the Framingham Chapter of the Daughters of the American Revolution*. Framingham: Lakeview Press, 1925.

Parsons, Samuel Holden

Hall, Charles S. *Life and Letters of Samuel Holden Parsons, Major General in the Continental Army and Chief Justice of the Northwestern Territory, 1737–1789*. Binghamton, N.Y.: Otseningo Publishing Co., 1905.

Paterson, John

Egleston, Thomas. *The Life of John Paterson: Major-General in the Revolutionary Army*. 2d ed. New York: G. P. Putnam's Sons, 1898.

Poor, Enoch

Akerman, Amos T. *Sketch of the Military Career of Enoch Poor, Brig. Gen. in the Revolutionary War*. Manchester, N. H.: T. H. Tuson, 1878.
Ames, Ellis. "The Duel Between General Poor and Major Porter. *Massachusetts Historical Society Proceedings* 19 (1882): 256–61.
Beane, Samuel Collins. "General Enoch Poor." *New Hampshire Historical Society Proceedings* 3 (1895–99): 435–72.

Pulaski, Casimir (Kazimierz)

Bentalou, Paul. *A Reply to Judge Johnson's Remarks on an Article in the North American Review Relating to Count Pulaski*. Baltimore: J. D. Toy, 1826.
[Girardin, Louis Hue]. *Pulaski Vindicated From an Unsupported Charge Inconsiderately or Malignantly Introduced in Judge Johnson's Sketches of the Life and Correspondence of Major Gen. Nathaniel Greene*. [Erroneously attributed to Paul Bentalou.] Baltimore: John D. Toy, 1824.
Gordon, William W. "Count Casimir Pulaski." *Georgia Historical Quarterly* 13 (1929): 169–227.
Konopczynski, Wladylsaw. *Casimir Pulaski*. Translated by Irena Makarewicz. Chicago: Polish Roman Catholic Union of America, 1947. [Originally published as *Kazimierz Pulaski; zyciorys*. Krakow: Sk. g. w ksieg. Gebenthnera i Wolfa, 1931.]
Kopczewski, Jan Stanislaw. *Kazimierz Pulaski*. Warsaw: Interpress, 1973.
Manning, Clarence A. *Soldier of Liberty*. New York: Philosophical Library, 1945.
Pulaski, Casimir. *Correspondence du general Casimir Pulaski avec Claude de Rulhiere, 1774–1778*. Paris: Societe historique et litteraire polonaise, 1948.
Wayda, Wladyslaw. *Pulaski w Ameryce*. Warsaw: Nakl. F. Hoesicka, 1930.
Zielinski, Ryszard. *Kazimierz Pulaski, 1747–1779*. Warsaw: Wydown. Ministerstwa Obrony Narodowej, 1967.

Putnam, Israel

Humphreys, David. *An Essay on the Life and Times of the Honorable Major-General Israel Putnam*. Hartford: Hudson & Goodwin, 1788.
Niven, John. *Connecticut's Hero: Israel Putnam*. Hartford: American Revolution Bicentennial Commission of Connecticut, 1977.

Tarbox, Increase N. *Life of Israel Putnam ("Old Put"), Major-General in the Continental Army.* Boston: Lockwood, Brooks & Co., 1876. Reprint. Port Washington, N.Y.: Kennikat Press, 1970.

Putnam, Rufus

Cone, Mary. *Life of Rufus Putnam, With Extracts From His Journal and an Account of the First Settlement in Ohio.* Cleveland: W. W. Williams, 1886.

Hoar, George Frisbie. *Rufus Putnam, Founder and Father of Ohio.* Worcester: Press of C. Hamilton, 1898.

Putnam, Rufus. *Journal of Gen. Rufus Putnam Kept in Northern New York During Four Campaigns of the Old French and Indian War, 1757–1760.* Edited by E. C. Dawes. Albany: Joel Munsell's Sons, 1886.

———. *The Memoirs of Rufus Putnam and Certain Official Papers and Correspondence.* Edited by Rowena Buell. Boston: Houghton, Mifflin & Co., 1903.

Reed, James

Blake, Amos J. "Gen. James Reed." *New Hampshire Historical Society Proceedings* 1 (1872–88): 109–15.

Garfield, James F. D. "General James Reed." *Fitchburg Historical Society Proceedings and Papers* 4 (1908): 112–24.

St. Clair, Arthur

Beals, Ellis, "Arthur St. Clair, Western Pennsylvania's Leading Citizen, 1764–1818." *Western Pennsylvania Historical Magazine* 12 (1929): 75–96, 175–96.

"Proceedings of a General Court Martial, Held at White Plains, in the State of New-York, by Order of His Excellency General Washington, for the Trial of Major General St. Clair, August 25, 1778. Major General Lincoln, President." *New-York Historical Society Collections* for 1880: 1–172. [Originally published Philadelphia: Hall & Sellers, 1778.]

St. Clair, Arthur. *The St. Clair Papers: The Life and Public Services of Arthur St. Clair, Soldier of the Revolutionary War, President of the Continental Congress, and Governor of the North-Western Territory With His Correspondence and Other Papers.* Edited by William Henry Smith. 2 vols. Cincinnati: Robert Clarke & Co., 1882.

Schuyler, Philip John

Bush, Martin. *Revolutionary Enigma: A Re-appraisal of General Philip Schuyler of New York.* Port Washington, N.Y.: Ira J. Friedman, 1969.

Gerlach, Don R. *Philip Schuyler and the American Revolution in New York, 1733–1777.* Lincoln: University of Nebraska Press, 1964.

Lossing, Benson J. *The Life and Times of Philip Schuyler.* 2 vols. New York: Sheldon & Co., 1873.

"Proceedings of a General Court Martial Held at Major General Lincoln's Quarters, Near Quaker-Hill, in the State of New York, by Order of His Excellency General Washington, Commander in Chief of the Army of the United States of America, for the Trial of Major General Schuyler, October 1, 1778; Major General Lincoln,

President." *New York Historical Society Collections* for 1879: 5–211. [Originally published Philadelphia: Hall & Sellers, 1778.]

Schuyler, George L. *Correspondence and Remarks Upon Bancroft's History of the Northern Campaign of 1777, and the Character of Major-Gen. Philip Schuyler.* New York: David G. Francis, 1867.

Scott, Charles

Smucker, Isaac. "General Charles Scott." *Historical Magazine*, 3d ser., 3 (1874): 88–90.

Spencer, Joseph

Whittelsey, Charles Barney. "Historical Sketch of Joseph Spencer, Major-General of the Continental Troops." *Decennial Register of the Society of the Sons of the Revolution in the State of Connecticut, 1893–1913*: 117–29.

Stark, John

Gould, Sylvester C. "Bibliography on Major-General John Stark." *Manchester Historic Association Collections* 1 (1898–1900): 205–11, 295.

Stark, Caleb, ed. *Memoir and Official Correspondence of Gen. John Stark, With Notices of Several Other Officers of the Revolution; Also a Biography of Capt. Phinehas Stevens, and of Col. Robert Rogers, With an Account of His Services in America During the "Seven Years' War."* Concord: G. Parker Lyon, 1860.

Stephen, Adam

Stephen, Adam. "Letters of General Adam Stephen to R. H. Lee." *Historical Magazine*, 1st ser., 9 (1865): 118–22.

Steuben, Friedrich (Frederick) Wilhelm von

Chase, Philander D. "Baron von Steuben in the War of Independence." Ph.D. dissertation, Duke University, 1973.

Cronau, Rudolf. *The Army of the American Revolution and Its Organizer; a Thrilling Story of the Times That Tried Men's Souls.* New York: Privately printed, 1923.

Doyle, Joseph B. *Frederick William von Steuben and the American Revolution.* Steubenville, Ohio: H. C. Cook Co., 1913.

Kapp, Friedrich. *Life of Major General Frederick William von Steuben.* New York: Mason, 1859. [Originally published as *Leben des amerikanischen generals Friedrich Wilhelm von Steuben.* Philadelphia: Schafer & Koradi, 1858.]

Palmer, John McAuley. *General von Steuben.* New Haven: Yale University Press, 1937.

Rothenberg, Gunther E. "Steuben, Washington, and the Question of 'Revolutionary' War." *Indiana Military History Journal* 3 (1978): 5–11.

Sullivan, John

Amory, Thomas C. *The Military Services and Public Life of Major-General John Sullivan of the American Revolutionary Army.* Boston: Wiggin & Lunt, 1868.

Rising, Oscar E. *A New Hampshire Lawyer in General Washington's Army: A Biographical Sketch of the Hon. John Sullivan, Major General in the Continental Army, and an Account of the Expedition Under His Command Against the Six Indian Nations in 1779.* Geneva, N.Y.: W. F. Humphry, 1915.

Sullivan, John. *Letters and Papers of Major-General John Sullivan, Continental Army.* Edited by Otis G. Hammond. Vols. 13-15. *New Hampshire Historical Society Collections.* Concord: New Hampshire Historical Society, 1930-39.

Whittemore, Charles P. *A General of the Revolution: John Sullivan of New Hampshire.* New York: Columbia University Press, 1961.

Sumner, Jethro

Battle, Kemp P. "Career of Brigadier-General Jethro Sumner: One of North Carolina's Revolutionary Officers." *Magazine of American History* 26 (1891): 415-33.

Thomas, John

Coffin, Charles. *The Lives and Services of Major General John Thomas, Colonel Thomas Knowlton, Colonel Alexander Scammell, Major General Henry Dearborn.* New York: Egbert, Hovey & King, 1845.

Varnum, James Mitchell

Gardner, Asa Bird. "General James M. Varnum of the Continental Army." *Magazine of American History* 18 (1887): 185-93.

Varnum, James Mitchell (1848-1907). *A Sketch of the Life and Public Services of James Mitchell Varnum of Rhode Island.* Boston: D. Clapp & Son, 1906.

Ward, Artemas

Allis, Frederick S., Jr., and Pruitt, R. Bruce, comps. *Guide to the Microfilm Edition of the Artemas Ward Papers.* Boston: Massachusetts Historical Society, 1967.

Martyn, Charles. *The Life of Artemas Ward, the First Commander-in-Chief of the American Revolution.* New York: A. Ward, 1921.

Washington, George

Cunliffe, Marcus. *George Washington: Man and Monument.* Boston: Little, Brown & Co., 1957.

Flexner, James T. *George Washington.* 4 vols. Boston: Little, Brown & Co., 1965-72.

Freeman, Douglas S. *George Washington: A Biography.* 7 vols. Vol. 7 With John A. Carroll and Mary Wells Ashworth. New York: Charles Scribner's Sons, 1948-57.

Frothingham, Thomas G. *Washington: Commander in Chief.* Boston: Houghton Mifflin Co., 1930.

Knox, Dudley W. *The Naval Genius of George Washington.* Boston: Houghton Mifflin Co., 1932.

Nettles, Curtis P. *George Washington and American Independence.* Boston: Little, Brown & Co., 1951.

Sparks, Jared. "Was Washington a Marshal of France?" *Massachusetts Historical Society Proceedings* 7 (1863): 283-91.

Spaulding, Oliver L. "The Military Studies of George Washington." *American Historical Review* 29 (1924): 675-80.

Washington, George. *The Writings of George Washington.* Edited by Jared Sparks. 12 vols. Boston: Charles C. Little & James Brown, 1834-37.

_____. *The Writings of George Washington From the Original Manuscript Sources,*

1745-1799. Edited by John C. Fitzpatrick. 39 vols. Washington: Government Printing Office, 1931–44.

Wright, Esmond. *Washington and the American Revolution.* New York: Macmillan Co., 1957.

Wayne, Anthony

Dunn, Frederick S. "The Classical Origin of 'Mad Anthony' Wayne's Sobriquet." *Pennsylvania History* 2 (1935): 172–77.

Moore, H[oratio] N[ewton]. *Life and Services of Gen. Anthony Wayne.* Philadelphia: Leary, Getz & Co., 1859.

Stille, Charles J. *Major-General Anthony Wayne and the Pennsylvania Line in the Continental Army.* Philadelphia: J. B. Lippincott, 1893. Reprint. Port Washington, N.Y.: Kennikat Press, 1968.

Wayne, Anthony. *Anthony Wayne, a Name in Arms: Soldier, Diplomat, Defender of Expansion Westward of a Nation; the Wayne-Knox-Pickering-McHenry Correspondence.* Edited by Richard C. Knopf. Pittsburgh: University of Pittsburgh Press, 1959.

Weedon, George

Ward, Harry M. *Duty, Honor of Country: General George Weedon and the American Revolution.* Philadelphia: American Philosophical Society, 1979.

Weedon, George. "Calendar of the Correspondence of Brigadier-General George Weedon, U.S.A., With Celebrated Characters of the American Revolution; in the Library of the American Philosophical Society." *American Philosophical Society Proceedings* 38 (1899): 81–114.

Williams, Otho Holland

Tiffany, Osmond. *A Sketch of the Life and Services of Gen. Otho Williams.* Baltimore: J. Murphy & Co., 1851.

Williams, Otho Holland. *Calendar of the Otho Holland Williams Papers in the Maryland Historical Society.* Baltimore: Historical Records Survey Project, 1940.

Woodford, William

Stewart, Mrs. Catesby Willis. *The Life of Brigadier General William Woodford of the American Revolution.* 2 vols. Richmond: Whittet & Shepperson, 1973.

Woodford, William. "Unpublished Letters of General Woodford of the Continental Army, 1776–1779." Edited by John W. Jordon. *Pennsylvania Magazine of History and Biography* 23 (1899): 453–63.

Wooster, David

Deming, Henry Champion. *An Oration Upon the Life and Services of Gen. David Wooster, Delivered at Danbury, April 27th, 1854 When a Monument Was Erected to His Memory.* Hartford: Case, Tiffany & Co., 1854.

Wooster, David. *Genealogy of the Woosters in America, Descended From Edward Wooster of Connecticut; Also an Appendix Containing a Sketch Relating to the Author, and a Memoir of Rev. Hezekia Calvin Wooster, and Public Letters of General David Wooster.* San Francisco: M. Weiss, 1885.

HEADQUARTERS ACTIVITIES

Alexander, Arthur J. "Judge John Laurance: Successful Investor in New York State Lands." *New York History* 25 (1944): 35-45.

Bast, Hormer. "Tench Tilghman—Maryland Patriot." *Maryland Historical Magazine* 42 (1947): 71-94.

Baxter, William T. *The House of Hancock: Business in Boston, 1724-1775.* New York: Russell & Russell, 1965.

Bill, Shirley A., and Gottschalk, Louis. "Silas Deane's 'Worthless' Agreement With Lafayette." *Prologue* 4 (1972): 219-23.

Bowling, Kenneth R. "New Light on the Philadelphia Mutiny of 1783: Federal-State Confrontation at the Close of the War for Independence." *Pennsylvania Magazine of History and Biography* 101 (1977): 419-50.

Brenneman, Gloria E. "The Conway Cabal: Myth or Reality." *Pennsylvania History* 40 (1973): 169-77.

Davies, Wallace E. "The Society of Cincinnati in New England, 1783-1800." *William and Mary Quarterly*, 3d ser., 5 (1948): 3-25.

Dollot, Rene. "A Companion of La Fayette: Count de More, 1758-1837." *Legion d'Honneur Magazine* 10 (1940): 463-68.

DuPonceau, Peter Stephen. "Autobiography of Peter Stephen DuPonceau." Edited by J. L. Whitehead. *Pennsylvania Magazine of History and Biography* 63 (1939): 189-227, 311-43.

Fernow, Berthold. "Washington's Military Family." *Magazine of American History* 7 (1881): 81-103.

Griffin, Martin I. J. *Stephen Moylan: Muster-Master General, Secretary and Aide-de-Camp to Washington.* Philadelphia: Privately printed, 1909.

Hendrickson, Robert. *Hamilton I (1757-1789).* New York: Mason/Charter, 1976.

Humphreys, Frank Landon. *Life and Times of David Humphreys: Soldier-Statesman-Poet.* 2 vols. New York: G. P. Putnam's Sons, 1917.

Jacobs, James Ripley. *Tarnished Warrior: Major-General James Wilkinson.* New York: Macmillan Co., 1938.

Jaffe, Irma B. *John Trumbull: Patriot-Artist of the American Revolution.* Boston: New York Graphic Society, 1975.

Kaplan, Sidney. "Rank and Status Among Massachusetts Continental Officers." *American Historical Review* 56 (1951): 318-26.

———. "Veteran Officers and Politics in Massachusetts, 1783-1787." *William and Mary Quarterly*, 3d ser., 9 (1952): 29-57.

Kimball, Le Roy Elwood. *Fleury in the American Revolution.* Franco-American Pamphlet Series, no. 6, New York, 1935.

Knollenberg, Bernhard. *Washington and the Revolution, a Reappraisal: Gates, Conway and the Continental Congress.* New York: Macmillan Co., 1940.

Kohler, Max J. "Colonel David S. Franks." *Magazine of History* 4 (1906): 63-72.

Kohn, Richard H. "The Inside History of the Newburgh Conspiracy: America and the Coup d'Etat." *William and Mary Quarterly*, 3d ser., 27 (1970): 187-220.

Laurens, John. *The Army Correspondence of Colonel John Laurens in the Years 1777-78, Now First Printed From Original Letters Addressed to His Father Henry*

Laurens, President of Congress, With a Memoir by Wm. Gilmore Simms. New York: Bradford Club, 1867.

Lawrence, Alexander A. "General Lachlan McIntosh and His Suspension From Continental Command During the Revolution." *Georgia Historical Quarterly* 38 (1954): 101-41.

McHenry, James. "The Battle of Monmouth Described by Dr. James McHenry, Secretary to General Washington." Edited by Thomas H. Montgomery. *Magazine of American History* 3 (1879): 355-63.

_____. *A Sidelight on History: Being the Letters of James McHenry, Aide-de-Camp of the Marquis de Lafayette to Thomas Sim Lee, Governor of Maryland, Written During the Yorktown Campaign, 1781.* Southampton, N.Y.: Privately printed, 1931.

Mitchell, Broadus. *Alexander Hamilton.* 2 vols. New York: Macmillan Co., 1957-62.

[More, Charles Albert], Chevalier de Pontgibaud. *A French Volunteer of the War of Independence.* Translated and edited by Robert B. Douglas. Paris: Charles Carrington, 1898.

Nelson, Paul David. "Horatio Gates at Newburgh, 1783: A Misunderstood Role." With rebuttal by Richard H. Kohn. *William and Mary Quarterly*, 3d ser., 29 (1972): 143-58.

Pickering, Octavius, and Upham, Charles Wentworth. *The Life of Timothy Pickering.* 4 vols. Boston: Little, Brown & Co., 1867-73.

Proctor, Donald John. "From Insurrection to Independence: The Continental Congress and the Military Launching of the American Revolution." Ph.D. dissertation, University of Southern California, 1965.

Reed, William B. *Life and Correspondence of Joseph Reed.* 2 vols. Philadelphia: Lindsay & Blackiston, 1847.

Rossie, Jonathan Gregory. *The Politics of Command in the American Revolution.* Syracuse: Syracuse University Press, 1975.

Rossman, Kenneth. "Conway and the Conway Cabal." *South Atlantic Quarterly* 41 (1942): 32-38.

Rush, Benjamin. *An Account of the Life and Character of Christopher Ludwick, Late Citizen of Philadelphia, and Baker-General of the Army of the United States During the Revolutionary War.* 1801. rev. ed. Philadelphia: Garden & Thompson, 1831.

Steiner, Bernard C. *The Life and Correspondence of James McHenry, Secretary of War Under Washington and Adams.* Cleveland: Burrows Bros., 1907.

Tilghman, Tench. *Memoir of Lieut. Col. Tench Tilghman, Secretary and Aide to Washington, Together With an Appendix, Containing Revolutionary Journals and Letters, Hitherto Unpublished.* Albany: Joel Munsell, 1876.

Townsend, Sara B. *An American Soldier: The Life of John Laurens.* Raleigh: Edwards & Broughton Co., 1958.

Trumbull, John. *The Autobiography of Colonel John Trumbull, Patriot-Artist, 1756-1843, Containing a Supplement to the Works of Colonel John Trumbull.* Edited by Theodore Sizer. New Haven: Yale University Press, 1953. [Original edition New Haven: B. L. Hamlen; New York: Wiley & Putnam, 1841.]

Turner, Harriot Stoddert. "Memoirs of Benjamin Stoddert, First Secretary of the United States Navy." *Columbia Historical Society Records* 20 (1917).

Wilkinson, James. *Memoirs of My Own Times.* 2 vols. Philadelphia: Abraham Small, 1816.

Zitt, Hersch L. "David Salisbury Franks, Revolutionary Patriot (c. 1740-1793)." *Pennsylvania History* 16 (1949): 77-95.

LOGISTICS

Anspach, Peter. *Day Book of Peter Anspach, Paymaster to the Quartermaster General's Department, September 10, 1781 to May 17, 1782.* Edited by Nellie P. Waldenmaier. Washington: National Genealogical Society, 1941.

Aylett, William. "Correspondence of Col. William Aylett, Commissary General of Virginia." *Tyler's Quarterly Historical and Genealogical Magazine* 1 (1919-20): 87-110, 145-61.

Bradford, S. Sydney. "Hunger Menaces the Revolution, December, 1779-January, 1780." *Maryland Historical Magazine* 61 (1966): 1-21.

Burnett, Edmund C. "The Continental Congress and Agricultural Supplies." *Agriculture History* 2 (1928): 111-28.

Colles, Christopher. *A Study of the Roads of the United States of America, 1789.* Edited by W. W. Rostow. Cambridge: Harvard University Press, 1961.

Destler, Charles McArthur. "Colonel Henry Champion, Revolutionary Commissary." *Connecticut Historical Society Bulletin* 36 (1971): 52-64.

Ferguson, E. James. *The Power of the Purse: A History of American Public Finance, 1776-1790.* Chapel Hill: University of North Carolina Press, 1961.

Heydinger, Earl J. "The Schuylkill, Lifeline to Valley Forge." *Bulletin of the Historical Society of Montgomery County, Pennsylvania* 9 (1954): 159-70.

Huston, James A. "The Logistics of Arnold's March to Quebec." *Military Affairs* 32 (1968): 110-24.

_____. *The Sinews of War: Army Logistics, 1775-1953.* Washington: Government Printing Office, 1966.

Jameson, Hugh. "Equipment for the Militia of the Middle States, 1775-1781." *Military Affairs* 3 (1939): 26-38.

_____. "Subsistence for Middle States Militia, 1776-1781." *Military Affairs* 30 (1966): 121-34.

Johnson, Victor L. *The Administration of the American Commissariat During the Revolutionary War.* Philadelphia: University of Pennsylvania Press, 1941.

_____. "Robert Morris and the Provisioning of the American Army During the Campaign of 1781." *Pennsylvania History* 5 (1938): 7-20.

Leonard, Eugenie Andruss. "Paper as a Critical Commodity During the American Revolution." *Pennsylvania Magazine of History and Biography* 74 (1950): 488-99.

Pinkett, Harold T. "Maryland as a Source of Food Supplies During the American Revolution." *Maryland Historical Magazine* 46 (1951): 157-72.

Ridgely, Ruxton M., ed. "Provisioning the Continental Army." *Maryland Historical Magazine* 9 (1914): 241-49.

Risch, Erna. *Quartermaster Support of the Army: A History of the Corps, 1775-1939.* Washington: Quartermaster Historian's Office, Office of the Quartermaster General, 1962.

_____. *Supplying Washington's Army.* Washington: Government Printing Office, 1981.

Salay, David Lewis. "Arming for War: The Production of War Material in Pennsylvania for the American Armies of the Revolution." Ph.D. dissertation, University of Delaware, 1977.

Stewart, Charles. "Supplies for General Sullivan: The Correspondence of Colonel Charles Stewart, May–September, 1779." Edited by Marion Brophy and Wendell Tripp. *New York History* 60 (1979): 245–81, 439–67; 61 (1980).

Svejda, George J. *Quartering, Disciplining, and Supplying the Army at Morristown, 1779-1780.* Washington: Department of the Interior, 1970.

Van Tyne, C. H. "French Aid Before the Alliance of 1778." *American Historical Review* 31 (1925): 20-40.

MILITARY TECHNOLOGY

Artz, Frederick B. *The Development of Technical Education in France, 1500–1850.* Cleveland: Society for the History of Technology, 1966.

Boehret, Paul C. *The Committee of Safety Musket.* Privately printed, 1956.

Boudriot, Jean. *Armes a feu francaises.* 2 vols. Paris, 1961.

Crout, Robert Rhodes. "Pierre-Emmanuel de la Plaigne and Georgia's Quest for French Aid During the War of Independence." *Georgia Historical Quarterly* 60 (1976): 176–84.

Esper, Thomas. "The Replacement of the Longbow by Firearms in the English Army." *History and Technology* 6 (1965): 382–93.

Gluckman, Arcadi. *United States Muskets, Rifles and Carbines.* Harrisburg: Stackpole Co., 1959.

Hecht, Arthur. "Lead Production in Virginia During the Seventeenth and Eighteenth Century." *West Virginia History* 25 (1964): 173–83.

Hicks, James E. *Notes on French Ordnance, 1717 to 1936.* Mt. Vernon, N.Y.: Privately printed, 1938.

_____. "United States Military Shoulder Arms, 1795-1935." Part II With Fred Porter Todd. *Military Affairs* 1 (1937): 23–33, 75–79; 2 (1938): 37–42; 175–76.

Hughes, B. P. *British Smooth-Bore Artillery: The Muzzle Loading Artillery of the 18th and 19th Centuries.* London: Arms & Armour Press, 1969.

Jackson, Melvin H., and De Beer, Carel. *Eighteenth Century Gunfounding.* Washington: Smithsonian Institution Press, 1974.

Johnson, Keach. "The Genesis of the Baltimore Ironworks." *Journal of Southern History* 19 (1953): 157–79.

Johnston, Henry P., ed. "Sergeant Lee's Experience With Bushnell's Submarine Torpedo in 1776." *Magazine of American History* 29 (1893): 262–66.

Mauncy, Albert. *Artillery Through the Ages: A Short Illustrated History of Cannon, Emphasizing Types Used in America.* Washington: National Park Service, 1949.

Muller, John A. *A Treatise of Artillery*, 3d ed. London: John Millan, 1780. Reprint with introduction by Harold L. Peterson. Ottawa: Museum Restoration Service, 1965.

Neu, Irene D. "The Iron Plantations of Colonial New York." *New York History* 33 (1952): 3-24.

Nuxoll, Elizabeth M. "Congress and the Munitions Merchants: The Secret Committee of Trade During the American Revolution, 1775-1777." Ph.D. dissertation, City University of New York, 1979.

Peterson, Harold L. *Arms and Armor in Colonial America, 1526-1783*. Harrisburg: Stackpole Books, 1956.

_____. *Round Shot and Rammers*. Harrisburg: Stackpole Books, 1969.

Pleasants, Henry, Jr. "Contraband From Lorient." *Military Affairs* 7 (1943): 123-32.

Reynolds, Donald E. "Ammunition Supply in Revolutionary Virginia." *Virginia Magazine of History and Biography* 73 (1965): 56-77.

Rome, Adam Ward. *Connecticut's Cannon: The Salisbury Iron Furnace in the American Revolution*. Hartford: American Revolution Bicentennial Commission of Connecticut, 1977.

Rosen, Howard. "Le Systeme Gribeauval et la guerre moderne." *Revue historique des armees* 2 (1975): 28-36.

Salay, David Lewis. "Arming for War: The Production of War Material in Pennsylvania for the American Armies of the Revolution." Ph.D. dissertation, University of Delaware, 1977.

Stephenson, Orlando W. "The Supply of Gunpowder in 1776." *American Historical Review* 30 (1925): 271-81.

Tucker, Spencer C. "Cannon Founders of the American Revolution." *National Defense* 60 (1975): 33-37.

Wright, John W. "The Rifle in the American Revolution." *American Historical Review* 29 (1924): 293-99.

York, Neil L. "Clandestine Aid and the American Revolutionary War Effort: A Re-Examination." *Military Affairs* 43 (1979): 26-30.

MEDICAL DEPARTMENT

Applegate, Howard L. "The Medical Administration of the American Revolutionary Army." *Military Affairs* 25 (1961): 1-10.

Beardsley, Ebenezer. "Remarks on the Effects of Stagnant Air." *Memoirs of the American Academy of Arts and Sciences* 1 (1785): 542-43.

Bell, Whitfield J., Jr. *John Morgan, Continental Doctor*. Philadelphia: University of Pennsylvania Press, 1965.

Blanco, Richard L. "The Development of British Military Medicine, 1793-1814." *Military Affairs* 38 (1974): 4-10.

_____. *Physician of the American Revolution: Jonathan Potts*. New York: Garland STPM Press, 1979.

Cash, Philip. "The Canadian Military Campaign of 1775-1776: Medical Problems and Effects of Disease." *Journal of the American Medical Association* 236 (1976): 52-56.

_____. *Medical Men at the Siege of Boston, April, 1775-April, 1776: Problems of the Massachusetts and Continental Armies*. Philadelphia: American Philosophical Society, 1973.

Cochrane, John. "Medical Department of the Revolutionary Army." *Magazine of American History* 12 (1884): 241-60.

Gibson, J. E. *Dr. Bodo Otto and the Medical Background of the American Revolution.* Springfield, Mass.: Charles C. Thomas, 1937.

Griffenhagen, George B. "Drug Supplies in the American Revolution." *Contributions From the Museum of History and Technology* [Smithsonian Institution] 225 (1961): 109-33.

Hawke, David Freeman. *Benjamin Rush; Revolutionary Gadfly.* Indianapolis: Bobbs-Merrill, 1971.

Jordan, John W. "The Military Hospitals at Bethlehem and Lititz During the Revolution." *Pennsylvania Magazine of History and Biography* 20 (1896): 137-57.

_____, ed. "Continental Hospital Returns, 1777-1780." *Pennsylvania Magazine of History and Biography* 23 (1899): 35-50, 210-23.

_____, ed. "Return of the Sick at Lititz Hospital, August 23, 1778 ." *Pennsylvania Magazine of History and Biography* 36 (1912): 379-81.

Rush, Benjamin. "Benjamin Rush's Directions for Preserving the Health of Soldiers, With a Note Upon Surgeon Ebenezer Alden." Edited by Henry Pelorize de Forest. *Military Surgeon* 22 (1908): 182-90.

Saffron, Morris H. *Surgeon to Washington: Dr. John Cochran, 1730-1807.* New York: Columbia University Press, 1977.

Sproat, James. "Extracts From the Journal of Rev. James Sproat, Hospital Chaplain of the Middle Department, 1778." Edited by John W. Jordan. *Pennsylvania Magazine of History and Biography* 27 (1903): 441-45.

Stevenson, Isobel. "Medical Literature Produced During the War of Independence." *Ciba Symposia* 2 (1940): 520-28.

Thursfield, Hugh. "Smallpox in the American War of Independence." *Annals of Medical History*, 3d ser., 2 (1940): 312-18.

Tilton, James. *Economical Observations on Military Hospitals and the Prevention of Disease Incident to an Army.* Wilmington: Wilson, 1813.

Van Swieten, Baron. *The Diseases Incident to the Armies With the Method of Cure.* Translated by John Ranby. Philadelphia: Bell, 1776.

MORALE AND DISCIPLINE

Applegate, Howard Lewis. "Constitutions Like Iron: The Life of the American Revolutionary War Soldiers in the Middle Department, 1775-1783." Ph.D. dissertation, Syracuse University, 1966.

Berlin, Robert H. "The Administration of Military Justice in the Continental Army During the American Revolution, 1775-1783." Ph.D. dissertation, University of California at Santa Barbara, 1976.

Bolton, Charles Knowles. *The Private Soldier Under Washington.* New York: Charles Scribner's Sons, 1902.

Bowman, Allen. *The Morale of the American Revolutionary Army.* Washington: American Council on Public Affairs, 1943.

Bradford, S. Sidney. "Discipline in the Morristown Winter Encampments." *New Jersey Historical Society Proceedings* 80 (1962): 1–30.

Edmonson, James Howard. "Desertion in the American Army During the Revolutionary War." Ph.D. dissertation, Louisiana State University, 1971.

Maurer, Maurer. "Military Justice Under General Washington." *Military Affairs* 28 (1964): 8–16.

Stadelman, Bonnie Sue Shelton. "The Amusements of the American Soldiers During the Revolution." Ph.D. dissertation, Tulane University, 1969.

Thomas, David Y. "How Washington Dealt With Discontent." *South Atlantic Quarterly* 32 (1933): 63–73.

FLAGS AND UNIFORMS

Davis, Gherardi. *Regimental Colors in the War of the Revolution.* New York: Privately printed, 1907. With supplements in 1908 and 1910.

Elting, John R. "The Thompson Westcott Descriptions of Military Dress During the American Revolution." *Military Collector and Historian* 12 (1960): 1–5.

_____, ed. *Military Uniforms in America: The Era of the American Revolution, 1755–1795.* San Rafael, Calif.: Presidio Press, 1974.

F., P. "Badge of Military Merit." *Historical Magazine* 3 (1859): 1–3.

Finke, Detmar H. "Insignia of Rank in the Continental Army, 1775–1783." *Military Collector and Historian* 8 (1956): 71–73.

Finke, Detmar H., and McBarron, H. Charles, Jr. "Continental Army Uniforms and Specifications, 1779–1781." *Military Collector and Historian* 14 (1962): 35–41.

Gardner, Asa Bird. "The Uniforms of the American Army." *Magazine of American History* 1 (1877): 461–91.

Holst, Donald W. "Regimental Colors of the Continental Army." *Military Collector and Historian* 20 (1968): 69–73.

Holst, Donald W., and Zlatich, Marko. "A Return of Some Continental Army Regimental Colors of 1778." *Military Collector and Historian* 19 (1967): 109–15.

Jaffe, Irma B. *John Trumbull: Five Paintings of the Revolution.* Hartford: Wadsworth Athenaeum, 1975.

Lefferts, Charles. *Uniforms of the American, British, French & German Armies in the War of the American Revolution, 1775–1783.* New York: New-York Historical Society, 1926.

Schermerhorn, Frank Earle. *American and French Flags of the Revolution, 1775–1783.* Philadelphia: Pennsylvania Society of Sons of the Revolution, 1948.

Schubert, Frank N. *Soldiers of the American Revolution—a Sketchbook.* Washington: Government Printing Office, 1976.

Sellers, Charles Coleman. *Charles Willson Peale.* New York: Charles Scribner's Sons, 1969.

_____. "Portraits and Miniatures by Charles Willson Peale." *American Philosophical Society Transactions*, new ser., 42 (1952): 1–371.

Sizer, Theodore. *The Works of Colonel John Trumbull, Artist of the American Revolution.* rev. ed. New Haven: Yale University Press, 1967.

CHAPLAINS

Griffin, Martin I. J. *Catholics and the American Revolution.* 3 vols. Philadelphia: Privately printed, 1907-11.

Headley, Joel T. *The Chaplains and Clergy of the Revolution.* New York: Scribner, 1864.

Honneywell, Roy J. *Chaplains of the United States Army.* Washington: Office of the Chief of Chaplains, 1958.

Metzger, Charles H. "Chaplains in the American Revolution." *Catholic Historical Review* 31 (1945): 31-79.

Williams, Eugene Franklin. "Soldiers of God: Chaplains of the Revolutionary War." Ph.D. dissertation, Texas Christian University, 1972.

MUSIC

Anderson, Simon Vance. "American Music During the War for Independence, 1775-1783." Ph.D. dissertation, University of Michigan, 1965.

Camus, Raoul F. *Military Music of the American Revolution.* Chapel Hill: University of North Carolina Press, 1976.

INTELLIGENCE AND ESPIONAGE

Bakeless, John. *Turncoats, Traitors and Heroes.* Philadelphia: J. B. Lippincott Co., 1960.

Bemis, Samuel F. "British Secret Service and the French-American Alliance." *American Historical Review* 29 (1924): 474-95.

Bennett, Gordon, ed. "Trial of Joshua Hett Smith, for Complicity in the Conspiracy of Benedict Arnold and Major Andre." *Historical Magazine* supps. 1-5 (1866): 1-5, 33-38, 65-73, 97-105, 129-38.

Burnett, Edmund Cody. "Ciphers of the Revolutionary Period." *American Historical Review* 22 (1917): 329-34.

Butterfield, Lyman H. "Psychological Warfare in 1776: The Jefferson-Franklin Plan to Cause Hessian Desertion." *American Philosophical Society Proceedings* 94 (1950): 233-41.

Crary, Catherine S. "The Tory and the Spy: The Double Life of James Rivington." *William and Mary Quarterly*, 3d ser., 16 (1959): 61-72.

Dawson, Henry B., ed. "Capture of Major Andre, Statements of Williams and Van Wart." *Historical Magazine* 9 (1865): 177-80.

Deane, James E. "Enoch Crosby Not a Myth." *Magazine of American History* 18 (1887): 73-75.

Delancey, Edward F., ed. "Sir Henry Clinton's Original Secret Record of Private Daily

Intelligence." *Magazine of American History* 10 (1883): 327–42, 409–19, 497–507; 11 (1884): 53–70, 156–67, 247–57, 342–51, 433–44, 533–44; 12 (1884): 72–79, 162–75.

Flexner, James T. *The Traitor and the Spy, Benedict Arnold and John Andre.* New York: Harcourt, Brace & Co., 1953.

Ford, Corey. *A Peculiar Service.* Boston: Little, Brown & Co., 1965.

Hatfield, Guy. "Harvey Birch and the Myth of Enoch Crosby." *Magazine of American History* 17 (1887): 431–33.

_____. "Harvey Birch Not Enoch Crosby." *Magazine of American History* 18 (1887): 341.

Heron, William. "Sir Henry Clinton's Original Secret Record of Private Daily Intelligence: Unpublished Letter From W. Heron to Sir Henry Clinton." Edited by William Evarts Benjamin. *Magazine of American History* 20 (1888): 329–32.

Johnston, Henry P. "Colonel Varick and Arnold's Treason." *Magazine of American History* 8 (1882): 717–33.

_____. "The Secret Service of the Revolution." *Magazine of American History* 8 (1882): 95–105.

Lawson, John L. "The 'Remarkable Mystery' of James Rivington, 'Spy.' " *Journalism Quarterly* 35 (1958): 316–23, 394.

Norwood, Mary E., ed. "Arnold the Traitor, and Andre the Sufferer: Correspondence Between Josiah Quincy, Jared Sparks and Benjamin Tallmadge." *Magazine of American History* 3 (1879): 747–59.

Paltsits, Victor Hugo. "The Use of Invisible Ink for Secret Writing During the American Revolution." *New York Public Library Bulletin* 39 (1935): 361–64.

Pennypacker, Morton. *George Washington's Spies on Long Island and in New York.* Brooklyn: Long Island Historical Society, 1939.

Pickering, James H., ed. "Enoch Crosby, Secret Agent of the Neutral Ground: His Own Story." *New York History* 47 (1966): 51–73.

Seed, Geoffrey. "A British Spy in Philadelphia, 1775–1777." *Pennsylvania Magazine of History and Biography* 85 (1961): 3–37.

Smith, Joshua Hett. *An Authentic Narrative of the Causes Which Led to the Death of Major Andre, Adjutant-General of His Majesty's Forces in North America.* London: Mathews & Leigh, 1808.

Stone, William L. "Schuyler's Faithful Spy: An Incident in the Burgoyne Campaign." *Magazine of American History* 2 (1878): 414–19.

Van Doren, Carl. *Secret History of the American Revolution.* New York: Viking Press, 1941.

Walker, Warren S. "The Prototype of Harvey Birch." *New York History* 37 (1956): 399–413.

PRISONERS OF WAR

Alexander, John K. "Forton Prison During the American Revolution: A Case Study of British Prisoner of War Policy and the American Prisoner Response to That Policy." *Essex Institute Historical Collections* 103 (1967): 365–89.

Anderson, Olive. "The Treatment of Prisoners of War in Britain During the American

War of Independence." *Bulletin of the Institute of Historical Research* 28 (1955): 63–83.

Boudinot, Elias. "Colonel Elias Boudinot's Notes of Two Conferences Held by the American and British Commissioners To Settle a General Cartel for the Exchange of Prisoners of War, 1778." *Pennsylvania Magazine of History and Biography* 24 (1900): 291–305.

————. *Journal or Historical Recollections of American Events During the Revolutionary War.* Philadelphia: Frederick Bourquin, 1894.

Bowie, Lucy L. "German Prisoners in the American Revolution." *Maryland Historical Magazine* 40 (1945): 185–200.

Bowman, Larry G. *Captive Americans: Prisoners During the American Revolution.* Athens: Ohio University Press, 1977.

Boyd, George A. *Elias Boudinot: Patriot and Statesman, 1740–1821.* Princeton: Princeton University Press, 1952.

Clark, Barbara Louise. *E. B.: The Story of Elias Boudinot IV, His Family, His Friends, and His Country.* Philadelphia: Dorrance, 1977.

Clark, Jane, ed. "The Convention Troops and the Perfidy of Sir William Howe." *American Historical Review* 37 (1932): 721–23.

Dixon, Martha W. "Divided Authority: The American Management of Prisoners in the Revolutionary War, 1775–1783." Ph.D. dissertation, University of Utah, 1977.

Edmonson, James Howard. "Desertion in the American Army During the Revolutionary War." Ph.D. dissertation, Louisiana State University, 1971.

Egleston, N. H. "The Newgate of Connecticut: The Simsbury Copper Mines." *Magazine of American History* 15 (1885): 321–34.

Ford, W[orthington] C., ed. "British and American Prisoners of War, 1778." *Pennsylvania Magazine of History and Biography* 17 (1893): 159–74, 316–24.

Hyde, West, and Andre, John. "Exchange of Prisoners, 1779." *Historical Magazine* 8 (1864): 200–207.

Jordan, Helen, ed. "Colonel Elias Boudinot in New York City, February, 1778." *Pennsylvania Magazine of History and Biography* 24 (1900): 453–66.

Knepper, George W. "The Convention Army, 1777–1783." Ph.D. dissertation, University of Michigan, 1954.

Lingley, Charles R. "The Treatment of Burgoyne's Troops Under the Saratoga Convention." *Political Science Quarterly* 22 (1907): 440–59.

Nichols, Francis. "Diary of Lieutenant Francis Nichols, of Colonel William Thompson's Battalion of Pennsylvania Riflemen, January to September 1776." Edited by Thomas H. Montgomery. *Pennsylvania Magazine of History and Biography* 20 (1896): 504–15.

Prelinger, Catherine M. "Benjamin Franklin and the American Prisoners of War in England During the American Revolution." *William and Mary Quarterly*, 3d ser., 32 (1975): 261–92.

Van Dyke, John. "Narrative of Confinement in the Jersey Prison Ship, by John Van Dyke, Captain in Lamb's Regiment, N.Y.S.A." *Historical Magazine* 7 (1863): 147–51.

White, Herbert H. "British Prisoners of War in Hartford During the Revolution." *Connecticut Historical Society Bulletin* 19 (1954): 65–81.

OPERATIONS

New England Theater

Ahlin, John Howard. "New England Rubicon: A Study of Eastern Maine During the American Revolution." Ph.D. dissertation, Boston University, 1962.

Alden, John R. "Why the March to Concord?" *American Historical Review* 49 (1944): 446-54.

Allen, John. *Military Operations in Eastern Maine and Nova Scotia During the Revolution, Chiefly Compiled From the Journals and Letters of Colonel John Allen, With Notes and a Memoir of Col. John Allen.* Compiled by Frederick Kidder. Albany: Joel Munsell, 1867.

Allyn, Charles. *The Battle of Groton Heights.* rev. ed. New London: Charles Allyn, 1882.

Case, James Royal. *An Account of Tryon's Raid on Danbury in April, 1777, Also the Battle of Ridgefield and the Career of Gen. David Wooster, With Much Original Matter Hitherto Unpublished.* Danbury: [Danbury Printing Co.], 1927.

Clark, William B. *George Washington's Navy: Being an Account of His Excellency's Fleet in New England Waters.* Baton Rouge: Louisiana State University Press, 1960.

Coburn, Frank. *The Battle of April 19, 1775.* 2d ed. Lexington: Lexington Historical Society, 1922. [1st ed. Lexington: Privately printed, 1912.]

Collins, James F. "Whaleboat Warfare on Long Island Sound." *New York History* 25 (1944): 195-201.

Dawson, Henry B. "Bunker's Hill." *Historical Magazine*, 2d ser., 3 (1868): 321-442.

Dearborn, Henry. *An Account of the Battle of Bunker Hill, Written for the Port Folio, at the Request of the Editor.* Philadelphia: Harrison Hall, 1818.

Drake, Samuel Adams. *Bunker Hill: The Story Told in Letters From the Battle Field by British Officers Engaged.* Boston: Nichols & Hall, 1875.

Fisher, Horace N., ed. "Letters on the Siege of Boston." *Magazine of History* 15 (1912): 47-52.

Fleming, Thomas J. *Now We Are Enemies: The Story of Bunker Hill.* New York: St. Martin's Press, 1960.

Ford, Worthington C., ed. *General Orders Issued by Major General William Heath When in Command of the Eastern Department, 23 May 1777-3 October 1777, With Some Fragmentary Orders of Major General Putnam and Lt. Col. William S. Smith.* Brooklyn: Historical Printing Club, 1890.

French, Allen. *The First Year of the American Revolution.* Boston: Houghton Mifflin Co., 1934.

Frothingham, Richard. *History of the Siege of Boston, and of the Battles of Lexington, Concord and Bunker Hill.* 4th ed. Boston: Little, Brown & Co., 1873.

Greene, Christopher. "Crisis on the Sparkling Bay (Revolution in Rhode Island, April 1775-April 1776)." *Military Collector and Historian* 29 (1977): 52-61.

Henshaw, William. *The Orderly Book of Colonel William Henshaw, of the American Army, April 20-Sep. 26, 1775, Including a Memoir by Emory Washburn, and Notes by Charles C. Smith; With Additions by Harriet E. Henshaw.* Boston: A. Williams & Co., 1881.

Ketchum, Richard. *The Battle for Bunker Hill.* Garden City, N.Y.: Doubleday, 1962. [Revised as *Decisive Day: The Battle for Bunker Hill,* Garden City: Doubleday, 1974.]

Knollenberg, Bernhard. "Bunker Hill Re-viewed: A Study in the Conflict of Historical Evidence." *Massachusetts Historical Society Proceedings* 72 (1957-60): 84-100.

McDevitt, Robert F. *Connecticut Attacked: A British Viewpoint, Tryon's Raid on Danbury.* Chester, Conn.: Pequot Press, 1974.

Manders, Eric L. "Notes on Troop Units in the Cambridge Army, 1775-1776." *Military Collector and Historian* 23 (1971): 69-74.

Massachusetts-Bay Provincial Congress. *A Narrative of the Excursions and Ravages of the King's Troops Under the Command of General Gage, on the Nineteenth of April, 1775, Together With the Depositions Taken by Order of Congress, To Support the Truth of It.* Worcester: Isaiah Thomas, 1775.

Mott, Frank Luther. "The Newspaper Coverage of Lexington and Concord." *New England Quarterly* 17 (1944): 489-505.

Murdock, Harold. *Bunker Hill: Notes and Queries on a Famous Battle.* Boston: Houghton Mifflin Co., 1927.

_____. *The Nineteenth of April, 1775.* Boston: Houghton Mifflin Co., 1923.

_____. "The Remarkable Story of the Rev. John Martin." *Massachusetts Historical Society Proceedings* 58 (1925): 201-14.

_____, ed. *Late News of the Excursions and Ravages of the King's Troops on the Nineteenth of April 1775 as Set Forth in the Narrative of Lt. William Sutherland of His Majesty's 38th Regiment of Foot and of Richard Pope of the 47th Regiment.* Cambridge: Harvard University Press, 1927.

Muzzey, A[rtemas] B[owers]. *The Battle of Lexington; With Personal Recollections of Men Engaged in It.* Boston: Williams, 1877.

Phinney, Elias. *History of the Battle of Lexington on the Morning of the 19th April, 1775.* Boston: Phelps & Farnham, 1825.

Rathbun, Jonathan. *The Narrative of Jonathan Rathbun of the Capture of Fort Griswold, the Massacre That Followed, and the Burning of New London, Conn., September 6, 1781, With the Narratives of Rufus Avery and Stephen Hempstead, Eye Witnesses; New and Revised Edition, Including the Narrative of Thomas Herttell, 1832.* New York: William Abbatt, 1911. [Original ed. New London, 1840.]

Reed, Silvanus. "Orderly Book of Adjutant Silvanus Reed." Edited by Isaac W. Hammond. *New Hampshire Historical Society Collections* 9 (1889): 364-414.

Rider, Sidney S., ed. *The Centennial Celebration of the Battle of Rhode Island, at Portsmouth, R.I., August 29, 1878.* Providence: Sidney S. Rider, 1878.

Seybolt, Robert Francis. "A Note on the Casualties of April 19, and June 17, 1775." *New England Quarterly* 4 (1931): 525-28.

Todd, Charles Burr. "The Massacre at Fort Griswold, September 6th, 1781." *Magazine of American History* 7 (1881): 161-75.

_____. "Whale-Boat Privateersmen of the Revolution." *Magazine of American History* 8 (1882): 168-81.

Tourtellot, Arthur B. *A Bibliography of the Battles of Lexington and Concord.* New York: Privately printed, 1959.

_____. *William Diamond's Drum.* Garden City: Doubleday & Co., 1959.

Townshend, Charles H. *The British Invasion of New Haven, Connecticut, Together*

With Some Account of Their Landing and Burning of the Towns of Fairfield and Norwalk, July 1779. New Haven: Privately printed, 1879.

Trevett, John. "The Despot's Heel Is on Thy Shore." *Military Collector and Historian* 30 (1978): 158–72.

Tyler, J. E., ed. "An Account of Lexington in the Rockingham Mss. at Sheffield." *William and Mary Quarterly*, 3d ser., 10 (1953): 99–107.

Waller, J. "Letter of J. Waller on Bunker Hill, 1775." Edited by Harold Murdock. *Massachusetts Historical Society Proceedings* 58 (1924): 84–87.

Northern Theater

Ainsley, Thomas. *Canada Preserved: The Journal of Captain Thomas Ainsley.* Edited by Sheldon S. Cohen. New York: New York University Press, 1968.

Anbury, Thomas. *With Burgoyne From Quebec: An Account of the Life at Quebec and of the Famous Battle of Saratoga.* Edited by Sydney Jackman. Toronto: Macmillan of Canada, 1963. [Originally published as *Travels Through the Interior Parts of North America*, vol. 1, London: W. Lane, 1789.]

Arndt, Karl J. R. "New Hampshire and the Battle of Bennington: Colonel Baum's Mission and Bennington Defeat as Reported by a German Officer Under Burgoyne's Command." *Historical New Hampshire* 32 (1977): 198–227.

Arnold, Benedict. *Benedict Arnold's Regimental Memorandum Book Written While at Crown Point and Ticonderoga, 1775.* Philadelphia: Collens, 1884. [Originally published in *Pennsylvania Magazine of History and Biography* 3 (1884): 363–76.]

Atkinson, C. T., ed. "Some Evidence for the Burgoyne Expedition." *Journal of the Society for Army Historical Research* 26 (1948): 132–42.

Baxter, James Phinney, ed. *The British Invasion From the North: The Campaigns of Generals Carleton and Burgoyne From Canada, 1776–1777; With the Journal of Lieut. William Digby, of the 53d, or Shropshire Regiment of Foot.* Albany: Joel Munsell's Sons, 1887.

Beebe, Lewis. *Journal of Lewis Beebe, a Physician on the Campaign Against Canada, 1776.* Edited by Frederick R. Kirkland. Philadelphia: Historical Society of Pennsylvania, 1935. [Originally published in *Pennsylvania Magazine of History and Biography* 59 (1935): 321–61.]

Bowler, R. Arthur. "Sir Guy Carleton and the Campaign of 1776 in Canada." *Canadian Historical Review* 55 (1974): 131–40.

Burgoyne, John. *A State of the Expedition From Canada as Laid Before the House of Commons, by Lieutenant-General Burgoyne, and Verified by Evidence, With a Collection of Authentic Documents, and an Addition of Many Circumstances Which Were Prevented From Appearing Before the House by the Prorogation of Parliament.* 2d ed. London: J. Almon, 1780.

Carroll, Charles. *Journals of Charles Carroll of Carrollton, During His Visit to Canada in 1776, as One of the Commissioners From Congress, With a Memoir and Notes.* Edited by Brantz Mayer. Baltimore: Maryland Historical Society, 1876.

Clark, Jane. "Responsibility for the Failure of the Burgoyne Campaign." *American Historical Review* 35 (1935): 542–59.

Coburn, Frank W. *The Centennial History of the Battle of Bennington, Compiled From the Most Reliable Sources, and Fully Illustrated With Original Documents and Entertaining Anecdotes.* Boston: G. E. Littlefield, 1877.

Da Costa, B. F. "The Fight at Diamond Island." *Magazine of History* 2 (1905): 265-72.

Danford, Jacob. "Quebec Under Siege, 1775-1776: The 'Memorandums' of Jacob Danford." Edited by John F. Roche. *Canadian Historical Review* 50 (1969): 68-85.

Dawson, Henry B. "The Battle of Bennington." *Historical Magazine*, 2d ser., 7 (1870): 289-305.

Dupuy, R. Ernest. *The Battle of Hubbardton: A Critical Analysis.* Vermont Historic Sites Commission, 1960.

French, Allen. *The Taking of Ticonderoga in 1775: The British Story, a Study of Captors and Captives.* Cambridge: Harvard University Press, 1928.

Gerlach, Don R. "Philip Schuyler and 'The Road to Glory': A Question of Loyalty and Competence." *New-York Historical Society Quarterly* 44 (1965): 341-86.

Hadden, James M. *Hadden's Journal and Orderly Books: A Journal Kept in Canada and Upon Burgoyne's Campaign in 1776 and 1777, by Lieut. James M. Hadden, Roy. Art.* Edited by Horatio Rogers. Albany: Joel Munsell's Sons, 1884.

Haskell, Caleb. *Caleb Haskell's Diary, May 5-May 30, 1776: A Revolutionary Soldier's Record Before Boston and With Arnold's Quebec Expedition.* Edited by Lothrop Withington. Newburyport, Mass.: W. H. House & Co., 1881.

Hellman, Florence S., comp. *The Saratoga Campaign, 1777: A Biographical List.* Washington: Library of Congress, 1940.

Henry, John Joseph. *Account of Arnold's Campaign Against Quebec and of the Hardships and Sufferings of That Band of Heroes Who Traversed the Wilderness of Maine From Cambridge to the St. Lawrence in the Autumn of 1775.* Albany: Joel Munsell, 1877.

Holden, James A. "Influence of the Death of Jane McCrea on the Burgoyne Campaign." *New York State Historical Association Proceedings* 12 (1913): 249-310.

Huot, Lucien. *Le Siege du Fort de St. Jean en 1775.* Saint Jean, P.Q.: Des presses a vapeur du franco-canadien, 1889.

Irvine, William. "Gen. Irvine's Journal of the Canadian Campaign, 1776." Edited by W. A. I[rvine]. *Historical Magazine* 6 (1862): 115-17.

Johnson, John. *Orderly Book of Sir John Johnson During the Oriskany Campaign, 1776-1777.* Edited by William L. Stone. Albany: Joel Munsell's Sons, 1882.

Jones, Charles Henry. *History of the Campaign for the Conquest of Canada in 1776, From the Death of Montgomery to the Retreat of the British Army Under Sir Guy Carleton.* Philadelphia: Porter & Coates, 1882.

Kirtland, Samuel. "Journal of the Reverend Samuel Kirtland, Missionary Among the Oneidas." Edited by E. B. O'Callaghan. *Historical Magazine*, 2d ser., 3 (1868): 37-39.

Lanctot, Gustave. *Canada and the American Revolution, 1774-1783.* Translated by Margaret M. Cameron. Cambridge: Harvard University Press, 1967.

Lansing, Amy E. "Baum's Raid." *Quarterly Journal of the New York State Historical Association* 9 (1928): 45-56.

Lutnick, Solomon. "The American Victory at Saratoga: A View From the British Press." *New York History* 44 (1963): 103-27.

Luzader, John F. "The Arnold-Gates Controversy." *West Virginia History* 27 (1966): 75-84.

Montgomery, Richard. "Original Letter of General Montgomery." *Historical Magazine* 6 (1862): 175–76.

Morison, George. "An Account of the Assault on Quebec, 1775." *Pennsylvania Magazine of History and Biography* 14 (1890): 434–39.

Napier, Francis. "Lord Francis Napier's Journal of the Burgoyne Campaign." Edited by S. Sydney Bradford. *Maryland Historical Magazine* 57 (1962): 285–333.

Neilson, Charles. *An Original, Compiled and Corrected Account of Burgoyne's Campaign; and the Memorable Battles of Bemis' Heights, Sept. 19, and Oct. 7, 1777, From the Most Authentic Sources of Information, Including Many Interesting Incidents Connected With the Same.* Albany: J. Munsell, 1844.

Nelson, Paul David. "The Gates-Arnold Quarrel, September 1777." *New-York Historical Society Quarterly* 55 (1971): 235–52.

————. "Guy Carleton Versus Benedict Arnold: The Campaign of 1776 in Canada and on Lake Champlain." *New York History* 57 (1976): 339–66.

————. "Legacy of Controversy: Gates, Schuyler, and Arnold at Saratoga, 1777." *Military Affairs* 37 (1973): 41–47.

Nelson, Peter. "The Battle of Diamond Island." *Quarterly Journal of the New York State Historical Association* 3 (1922): 36–53.

————. "Learned's Expedition to the Relief of Fort Stanwix." *Quarterly Journal of the New York State Historical Association* 9 (1928): 380–85.

Nickerson, Hoffman. *The Turning Point of the Revolution; or, Burgoyne in America.* Boston: Houghton Mifflin Co., 1928.

Porterfield, Charles. "Memorable Attack on Quebec, December 21 [*sic*], 1775: Diary of Colonel Charles Porterfield." Edited by Marcus J. Wright. *Magazine of American History* 21 (1889): 318–19.

"Proceedings of a General Court Martial Held at Major General Lincoln's Quarters, Near Quaker-Hill, in the State of New York, by Order of His Excellency General Washington, Commander in Chief of the Army of the United States of America, for the Trial of Major General Schuyler, October 1, 1778; Major General Lincoln, President." *New-York Historical Society Collections* for 1879: 5–211.

Robbins, Ammi Ruhumah. *Journal of Reverend Ammi R. Robbins, a Chaplain in the American Army, in the Northern Campaign of 1776.* New Haven: Hamlen, 1850.

Roberts, Ellis H. *Memorial of the Centennial Celebration of the Battle Oriskany, August 6, 1877.* Utica: Ellis H. Roberts & Co., 1878.

Roberts, Kenneth, comp. *March to Quebec: Journals of the Members of Arnold's Expedition.* 4th ed. New York: Doubleday & Co., 1940. [1st ed. 1938.]

Schoolcraft, Henry R. *Historical Considerations on the Siege and Defense of Fort Stanwix in 1777.* New York: New-York Historical Society, 1846.

Schuyler, Philip, et al. "Evacuation of Ticonderoga, 1777." *Magazine of American History* 8 (1882): 566–73.

Smith, Justin H. *Arnold's March From Cambridge to Quebec; a Critical Study, Together With a Reprint of Arnold's Journal.* New York: G. P. Putnam's Sons, 1903.

————. *Our Struggle for the Fourteenth Colony; Canada in the American Revolution.* 2 vols. New York: G. P. Putnam's Sons, 1907.

Standing, Percy Cross. "Burgoyne's Defeat and Surrender: An Inquiry From an English Standpoint." *Magazine of American History* 24 (1890): 40–44.

Stanley, George Francis Gilman. *Canada Invaded, 1775–1776.* Toronto: Hakkert, 1973.

Stone, William Leete. *The Campaign of Lieut. Gen. John Burgoyne, and the Expedition of Lieut. Col. Barry St. Leger.* Albany: Joel Munsell, 1877.

Washington, Ida H., and Washington, Paul A. *Carleton's Raid.* Canaan, N. H.: Phoenix, 1977.

Willcox, William B. "Too Many Cooks: British Planning Before Saratoga." *Journal of British Studies* 2 (1962): 56–91.

Wurtele, Fred C., ed. *Blockade of Quebec in 1775–1776 by the American Revolutionists (Les Bastonnais).* 1906. Reprint. Port Washington, N.Y.: Kennikat Press, 1970.

New York Theater

Abbatt, William. *The Battle of Pell's Point (or Pelham), October 18, 1776, Being the Story of a Stubborn Fight.* New York: William Abbatt, 1901.

Babcock, H. G., ed. *The Great Chain: The Original Copies of the Bills for the Work of Obstructing the Navigation of the Hudson River Near West Point, 1777 and 1778, Under the Direction of Capt. Thomas Machin, Engineer.* Little Falls, N.Y.: Privately printed, 1891.

Billias, George A[than]. "Pelham Bay: A Forgotten Battle." *New-York Historical Society Quarterly* 42 (1958): 20–38.

Bolton, Reginald Pelham. "The Defense of Croton River in the Revolution." *New-York Historical Society Quarterly* 8 (1924): 35–39.

_____. "The Defenses of the Hudson River." *Quarterly Journal of the New York State Historical Association* 12 (1931): 360–65.

_____. *Fort Washington.* New York: Empire State Society, 1902.

Cadwalader, Lambert. "Letter of Lambert Cadwalader to Timothy Pickering on the Capture of Fort Washington." *Pennsylvania Magazine of History and Biography* 25 (1901): 259–62.

Calderhead, William L. "British Naval Failure at Long Island: A Lost Opportunity in the American Revolution." *New York History* 57 (1976): 321–38.

Clark, Donald F., ed. *Fort Montgomery and Fort Clinton: Several Contemporary Accounts of the Battle, Monday, 6 October 1777.* Fort Montgomery, N.Y.: Town of Highlands, 1952.

Clarke, Samuel C., ed. "Capture of Stony Point, July, 1779, by Major William Hull." *Magazine of American History* 28 (1892): 182–85.

Collier, George. " 'To My Inexpressible Astonishment': Admiral Sir George Collier's Observations on the Battle of Long Island." Edited by Louis L. Tucker. *New-York Historical Society Quarterly* 48 (1964): 293–306.

Dawson, Henry B., ed. "The Battle of Springfield, N.J.: *Historical Magazine*, 2d ser., 8 (1870): 55–56.

DeLancy, Edward Floyd. *The Capture of Mount Washington, November 16th, 1776, the Result of Treason.* New York: New-York Historical Society, 1877.

De Voe, Thomas F. "The Massacre of the Stockbridge Indians, 1778." *Magazine of American History* 5 (1880): 187–95.

Dornfest, Walter T. "British, Hessian and Provincial Troops at Paulus Hook, 18th–19th August, 1779." *Journal of the Society for Army Historical Research* 45 (1967): 177–82.

Doughty, Joshua, Jr. "Washington's March From Princeton to Morristown." *New Jersey Historical Society Proceedings*, new ser., 5 (1920): 240-46.

Emmet, Thomas Addis. "The Battle of Harlem Heights." *Magazine of History* 4 (1906): 125-34.

Field, Thomas W. *The Battle of Long Island, With Connected Preceding Events, and the Subsequent American Retreat.* Vol. 2. *Long Island Historical Society Memoirs.* Brooklyn: Long Island Historical Society, 1869.

Fleming, Thomas. *The Forgotten Victory: The Battle for New Jersey—1780.* New York: E. P. Dutton & Co., 1973.

Irvine, William. "Letters of Gen. Irvine to His Family." Edited by William Irvine. *Historical Magazine* 7 (1863): 81-83.

Johnston, Henry P. *Battle of Harlem Heights, September 16, 1776.* New York: Macmillan Co., 1897.

———. *Campaign of 1776 Around New York and Brooklyn Including a New and Circumstantial Account of the Battle of Long Island and the Loss of New York, With a Review of Events to the Close of the Year.* Brooklyn: Long Island Historical Society, 1876.

———. *The Storming of Stony Point on the Hudson, Midnight, July 15, 1779: Its Importance in the Light of Unpublished Documents.* New York: James T. White, 1900.

Kemp, Franklin W. *"A Nest of Rebel Pirates."* Egg Harbor City, N.J.: Laureate Press, 1966.

Koke, Richard J. "Forcing the Hudson River Passage, October 9, 1776." *New-York Historical Society Quarterly* 36 (1952): 459-66.

———. "The Struggle for the Hudson: The British Naval Expedition Under Captain Hyde Parker and Captain James Wallace, July 12-August 18, 1776." *New-York Historical Society Quarterly* 40 (1956): 114-75.

Koke, Richard J., and Carr, William H. "Twin Forts of the Popolopen." *Palisades Interstate Park Commission Historical Bulletin* 1 (1937).

Maxwell, William. "The Battle of Springfield." *Historical Magazine* 3 (1859): 211.

Palmer, Dave Richard. *The River and the Rock: The History of Fortress West Point, 1775-1783.* New York: Greenwood Publishing Co., 1969.

Pennypacker, Samuel W. "The Capture of Stony Point." *Pennsylvania Magazine of History and Biography* 26 (1902): 360-69.

Putnam, Israel. *General Orders Issued by Major-General Israel Putnam, When in Command of the Highlands, in the Summer and Fall of 1777.* Edited by Worthington C. Ford. Brooklyn: Historical Printing Club, 1893.

Roosevelt, Franklin D., ed. "Events on Hudson's River in 1777, as Recorded by British Officers in Contemporary Reports." *Dutchess County Historical Society Yearbook* 20 (1935).

Ruttenber, E. M. *Obstructions to the Navigation of Hudson's River.* Albany: J. Munsell, 1860.

Simms, W. Gilmore, ed. "Revolutionary Letters." *Historical Magazine* 2 (1858): 321-24.

Sklarsky, I. W. *The Revolution's Boldest Venture: The Story of "Mad Anthony" Wayne's Assault on Stony Point.* Port Washington, N.Y. Kennikat Press, 1965.

Stevens, John Austin. "The Battle of Harlem Plains." *Magazine of American History* 4 (1880): 351-75.

_____. "The New Version of the Battle of Harlem Plains." *Magazine of American History* 6 (1881): 260–63.

_____. "The Operations of the Allied Armies Before New York, 1781." *Magazine of American History* 4 (1880): 1–45.

Stowe, Gerald C., and Weller, Jac. "Revolutionary West Point: 'The Key to the Continent.' " *Military Affairs* 19 (1955): 81–98.

Stryker, William S. *The Affair at Egg Harbor, New Jersey, October 15, 1778.* Trenton: Naar, Day & Naar, 1894.

Ten Broeck, Cornelius, and Ten Broeck, Peter. "News From Camp: Letters Received by Cornelius Ten Broeck of Rocky Hill, New Jersey, From His Sons Cornelius and Peter, Serving in the Continental Army, 1779–1780." Edited by George C. Beekman. *Magazine of American History* 2 (1878): 168–75.

Thomas, William S. "Revolutionary Camps of the Hudson Highlands." *Quarterly Journal of the New York State Historical Association* 2 (1921): 1–45.

Winfield, Charles H. "The Affair at Block-House Point, 1780." *Magazine of American History* 5 (1880): 161–86.

Wright, Robert K., Jr. "Too Little, Too Late: The Campaign of 1777 in the Hudson Highlands." Master's thesis, College of William and Mary, 1971.

Pennsylvania Theater

Balderston, Marion. "Lord Howe Clears the Delaware." *Pennsylvania Magazine of History and Biography* 96 (1972): 326–45.

Bell, Andrew. "Copy of a Journal by Andrew Bell, Esq., at One Time Confidential Secretary of General Sir Henry Clinton. Kept During the March of the British Army Through New-Jersey in 1778." *New Jersey Historical Society Proceedings,* 1st ser., 6 (1851): 15–19.

Brackenridge, Hugh Montgomery, ed. "The Siege of Fort Mifflin." *Pennsylvania Magazine of History and Biography* 11 (1887): 82–88.

D'Arendt, Baron Henry. "The Attack on Fort Mifflin, 1777: Two Unpublished Letters of the Baron D'Arendt." Translated by T. Bailey Myers. *Historical Magazine,* 3d ser., 1 (1872): 77–79.

Dawson, Henry B. "Mr. Bancroft and Colonel Reed." *Historical Magazine,* 2d ser., 5 (1869): 45–50.

Ford, Worthington C., ed. *Defences of Philadelphia in 1777.* Brooklyn: Historical Printing Club, 1897.

Hamilton, Alexander, and Irvine, William. "The Battle of Monmouth." *Pennsylvania Magazine of History and Biography* 2 (1878): 139–48.

Holmes, Asher. "Letter Concerning the Battle of Germantown, 1777." Edited by A. Van Doren Honeyman. *New Jersey Historical Society Proceedings,* new ser., 7 (1922): 34–35.

Howard, John Eager. "Col. John Eager Howard's Account of the Battle of Germantown." Edited by Justin Winsor. *Maryland Historical Magazine* 4 (1909): 314–20.

Jackson, John W. *The Pennsylvania Navy, 1775–1781: The Defense of the Delaware.* New Brunswick: Rutgers University Press, 1974.

Laurens, John. "Letter of John Laurens, November, 1777." Edited by Frederick R. Kirtland. *Pennsylvania Magazine of History and Biography* 65 (1941): 353–62.

McHenry, James. "The Battle of Monmouth Described by Dr. James McHenry, Secretary to General Washington." Edited by Thomas H. Montgomery. *Magazine of American History* 3 (1879): 355–63.

Moomaw, William H. "The Denouement of General Howe's Campaign of 1777." *English Historical Review* 79 (1964): 498–512.

Pickering, Timothy. "Col. Timothy Pickering's Account of the Battles of Brandywine and Germantown." *Historical Magazine* 7 (1866): 218–20.

Pinckney, Charles Cotesworth. "The Battles of Brandywine and Germantown." Edited by Henry B. Dawson. *Historical Magazine* 10 (1866): 202–4.

Pleasants, Henry, Jr. "The Battle of Paoli." *Pennsylvania Magazine of History and Biography* 72 (1948): 44–53.

Potts, William J., ed. "Battle of Germantown From a British Account." *Pennsylvania Magazine of History and Biography* 11 (1887): 112–14.

Reed, John F. *Campaign to Valley Forge, July 1, 1777–December 19, 1777.* Philadelphia: University of Pennsylvania Press, 1965.

————. *Valley Forge: Crucible of Victory.* Monmouth Beach, N.J.: Philip Freneau Press, 1969.

Reed, Joseph. "General Joseph Reed's Narrative of the Movements of the American Army in the Neighborhood of Trenton in the Winter of 1776–77." *Pennsylvania Magazine of History and Biography* 8 (1884): 391–402.

Rosengarten, Joseph G., trans. "The Battle of Germantown Described by a Hessian Officer." *Pennsylvania Magazine of History and Biography* 16 (1892): 197–201.

Sheldon, Richard N. "Editing a Historical Manuscript: Jared Sparks, Douglas Southall Freeman, and the Battle of Brandywine." *William and Mary Quarterly*, 3d ser., 36 (1979): 255–63.

Stacker, H. Fitz M. "Princeton." *Journal of the Society for Army Historical Research* 13 (1934): 214–28.

Stryker, William S. *The Battle of Monmouth.* Edited by William Starr Myers. Princeton: Princeton University Press, 1927.

————. *Battles of Trenton and Princeton.* Boston: Houghton, Mifflin & Co., 1898.

Sullivan, Thomas. "The Battle of Princeton." *Pennsylvania Magazine of History and Biography* 32 (1908): 54–57.

————. "Before and After the Battle of Brandywine: Extracts From the Journal of Sergeant Thomas Sullivan of H. M. Forty-Ninth Regiment of Foot." *Pennsylvania Magazine of History and Biography* 31 (1907): 406–18.

Thayer, Theodore. *The Making of a Scapegoat: Washington and Lee at Monmouth.* Port Washington, N.Y.: Kennikat Press, 1976.

Tompkins, Hamilton B., ed. "Contemporary Account of the Battle of Germantown." *Pennsylvania Magazine of History and Biography* 11 (1887): 330–32.

Wayne, Anthony. "Letter of General Anthony Wayne." Edited by Henry Day. *Pennsylvania Magazine of History and Biography* 11 (1887): 115–16.

Virginia Theater

Adams, Randolph G. "A View of Cornwallis' Surrender at Yorktown." *American Historical Review* 37 (1931): 25–49.

Anderson, D. R., ed. "The Letters of Col. William Woodford, Col. Robert Howe and Gen. Charles Lee to Edmund Pendleton, President of the Virginia Convention." *Richmond College Historical Papers* 1 (1915): 96–163.

Burne, A. H. "Cornwallis at Yorktown." *Journal of the Society for Army Historical Research* 17 (1938): 71–76.

Butler, Richard. "General Richard Butler's Journal of the Siege of Yorktown." *Historical Magazine* 8 (1864): 102–12.

Carrington, Henry B. "Lafayette's Virginia Campaign, 1781." *Magazine of American History* 6 (1881): 340–52.

Chadwick, French Ensor, ed. *The Graves Papers and Other Documents Relating to the Naval Operations of the Yorktown Campaign, July to October 1781.* New York: Naval Historical Society, 1916.

Clinton, Henry. *Narrative of the Campaign in 1781 in North America.* London: J. Debrett, 1783.

_____. *Observations on Earl Cornwallis' Answer.* London: J. Debrett, 1783.

Devereux, Eugene, ed. "Extracts From Original Letters Relating to the War of Independence and Cornwallis' Capitulation at Yorktown." *Pennsylvania Magazine of History and Biography* 11 (1887): 333–37.

Eckenrode, H. J. *The Story of the Campaign and Siege of Yorktown.* Washington: Government Printing Office, 1931.

Gallatin, Gaspard de. *Journal of the Siege of York-town.* Translated by the French Department of the College of William and Mary. Washington: Government Printing Office, 1931.

Hatch, Charles E., Jr. "The 'Affair Near James Island' (or, 'The Battle of Green Spring'), July 6, 1781." *Virginia Magazine of History and Biography* 53 (1945): 172–96.

_____. "Gloucester Point in the Siege of Yorktown, 1781." *William and Mary Quarterly*, 2d ser., 20 (1940): 265–84.

Hatch, Charles E., Jr., and Pitkin, Thomas M., eds. *Yorktown, Climax of the Revolution.* Washington: Department of the Interior, National Park Service, 1941.

Johnston, Henry P. *The Yorktown Campaign and the Surrender of Cornwallis, 1781.* New York: Harper & Bros., 1881.

Kyte, George W. "A Projected British Attack Upon Philadelphia in 1781." *Pennsylvania Magazine of History and Biography* 76 (1952): 379–93.

_____. "Strategic Blunder: Lord Cornwallis Abandons the Carolinas." *Historian* 22 (1960): 129–44.

Landers, H. L. *The Virginia Campaign and the Blockade and Siege of Yorktown, 1781.* Washington: Government Printing Office, 1931.

Larrabee, Harold A. *Decision at the Chesapeake.* New York: Clarkson N. Potter, 1964.

Lutnick, Solomon N. "The Defeat at Yorktown: A View From the British Press." *Virginia Magazine of History and Biography* 72 (1964): 471–78.

Luykx, John M. "Fighting for Food: British Foraging Operations at St. George's Island." *Maryland Historical Magazine* 71 (1976): 212–19.

Moomaw, William Hugh. "The Naval Career of Captain Hammond, 1775–1779." Ph.D. dissertation, University of Virginia, 1955.

Naisawald, Louis Van Loan. "Robert Howe's Operations in Virginia, 1775–1776." *Virginia Magazine of History and Biography* 60 (1952): 437–43.

Newsome, A. R., ed. "A British Orderly Book, 1780–1781." *North Carolina Historical Review* 9 (1932): 57–78, 163–86, 273–98, 366–92.

Stevens, Franklin Benjamin, ed. *The Campaign in Virginia, 1781: An Exact Reprint of Six Rare Pamphlets on the Clinton-Cornwallis Controversy With Very Numerous Important Unpublished Manuscript Notes by Sir Henry Clinton, K. B., and the Omitted and Hitherto Unpublished Portions of the Letters in Their Appendixes Added From the Original Manuscripts.* 2 vols. London: Privately printed, 1888.

Stevens, John Austin. "The Allies at Yorktown, 1781." *Magazine of American History* 6 (1881): 1–55.

Trusty, Lance. "War by the Book: The Defense of Yorktown, 1781." *Indiana Academy of the Social Sciences Proceedings* 11 (1976): 111–25.

Tucker, St. George. "St. George Tucker's Journal of the Siege of Yorktown, 1781." Edited by Edward M. Riley. *William and Mary Quarterly*, 3d ser., 5 (1948): 375–95.

———. "The Southern Campaign, 1781, From Guilford Court House to the Siege of York Narrated in the Letters From Judge St. George Tucker to His Wife." Edited by Charles Watson Coleman, Jr. *Magazine of American History* 7 (1881): 36–46, 201–16.

Wayne, Anthony. "Anthony Wayne at Green Spring, 1781: His Account of the Action." *Magazine of American History* 15 (1886): 201–2.

Wright, John W. "Notes on the Siege of Yorktown in 1781 With Special Reference to the Conduct of a Siege in the Eighteenth Century." *William and Mary Quarterly*, 2d ser., 12 (1932): 229–49.

Southern Theater

Adams, Randolph G. "Cartography of the British Attack on Fort Moultrie in 1776." In *Essays Offered to Herbert Putnam.* Edited by W. W. Bishop and A. Keough. New Haven: Yale University Press, 1929.

Barnwell, Joseph W. "The Evacuation of Charleston by the British in 1782." *South Carolina Historical and Genealogical Magazine* 11 (1910): 1–26.

Bulger, William Thomas, Jr. "The British Expedition to Charleston, 1779–1780." Ph.D. dissertation, University of Michigan, 1957.

Cann, Marvin L. "Prelude to War: The First Battle of Ninety–Six, November 19–21, 1775." *South Carolina Historical Magazine* 76 (1975): 197–214.

Cashin, Edward J. "Nathanael Greene's Campaign for Georgia in 1781." *Georgia Historical Quarterly* 61 (1977): 43–58.

Clinton, Henry. "Sir Henry Clinton's 'Journal of the Siege of Charleston, 1780.' " Edited by William Thomas Bulger, Jr. *South Carolina Historical Magazine* 66 (1965): 147–74.

Cruger, John Harris. "The Siege of Savannah, 1779, as Related by Colonel John Harris Cruger." Edited by Henry C. Van Schaack. *Magazine of American History* 2 (1878): 489–92.

Davidson, Chalmers. *Piedmont Partisan: The Life and Times of Brigadier General William Lee Davidson.* Davidson, N.C.: Davidson College, 1951.

Draper, Lyman C. *King's Mountain and Its Heroes: History of the Battle of King's Mountain, October 7th, 1780, and the Events Which Led to It.* Cincinnati: Peter G. Thomson, 1881.

Estaing, Comte Jean Baptiste Charles Henri Hector d'. "Siege of Savannah, 1779: General Orders of the Count D'Estaing for the Attack by the Allied Forces, 8th and 9th October." Edited by Frank Moore. *Magazine of American History* 2 (1878): 548-51.

Gates, Horatio. "Orders Issued by Major Genl. Gates While Commanding the Southern Army, July 26th to August 31st, 1780." Edited by Thomas Addis Emmett. *Magazine of American History* 5 (1880): 310-20.

_____. "The Southern Campaign, 1780. Letters of Major General Gates From 21st June to 31st August." Edited by Thomas Addis Emmett, *Magazine of American History* 5 (1880): 281-310.

Gray, Robert. "Colonel Robert Gray's Observations on the War in Carolina." *South Carolina Historical and Genealogical Magazine* 11 (1910): 139-59.

Habersham, John. "Habersham's Indian Expedition: Georgia—1782." *Historical Magazine* 4 (1860): 129-31.

Harden, William, ed. "Account of the Siege of Savannah, From a British Source." *Georgia Historical Society Collections* 5 (pt. I, 1901): 129-39.

Horry, [Peter]. "Battle of Fort Moultrie." *Historical Magazine* 3 (1859): 249.

Hough, Franklin B., ed. *The Siege of Charleston by the British Fleet and Army Under the Command of Admiral Arbuthnot and Sir Henry Clinton Which Terminated With the Surrender of That Place on the 12th of May, 1780.* Albany: J. Munsell, 1867.

_____, ed. *The Siege of Savannah by the Combined American and French Forces, Under the Command of Gen. Lincoln and the Count D'Estaing, in the Autumn of 1779.* Albany: J. Munsell, 1866.

Johnson, Joseph. *Traditions and Reminiscences Chiefly of the American Revolution in the South.* Charleston: Walker & James, 1851.

Jones, Charles C., Jr., ed. "Memorandum of the Route Pursued by Colonel Campbell and His Column of Invasion in 1779, From Savannah to Augusta; With a Narrative of Occurrences Connected With His March, and a Record of Some of the Military Events Which Transpired in That Portion of the Province of Georgia During the War of the Revolution." *Magazine of American History* 18 (1887): 256-58, 342-48.

_____, ed. *The Siege of Savannah, in 1779, as Described in Two Contemporary Journals of French Officers in the Fleet of Count D'Estaing.* Albany: Joel Munsell, 1874.

Kennedy, Benjamin, ed. *Muskets, Cannon Balls and Bombs.* Savannah: Beehive Press, 1973.

Kepner, Francis Reece, ed. "A British View of the Siege of Charleston, 1776." *Journal of Southern History* 11 (1945): 93-103.

Kyte, George W. "The British Invasion of South Carolina in 1780." *Historian* 14 (1952): 149-72.

_____. "General Greene's Plans for the Capture of Charleston 1781-1782." *South Carolina Historical Magazine* 61 (1961): 96-106.

_____. "Victory in the South: An Appraisal of General Greene's Strategy in the Carolinas." *North Carolina Historical Review* 37 (1960): 321-47.

Lawrence, Alexander A. "General Robert Howe and the British Capture of Savannah in 1778." *Georgia Historical Quarterly* 36 (1952): 303-27.

_____. *Storm Over Savannah: The Story of Count d'Estaing and the Siege of the Town in 1779.* Athens: University of Georgia Press, 1951.

Lee, Henry. *Campaign of 1781 in the Carolinas; With Remarks Historical and Critical on Johnson's Life of Greene.* Philadelphia: E. Littell, 1824.

_____. "Letters of H. Lee, Jr., to R. H. Lee." *Historical Magazine* 9 (1865): 281–83.

_____. *Memoirs of the War in the Southern Department of the United States, by Henry Lee.* Edited by Robert E. Lee. New York: University Publishing Co., 1869.

"Letters to General Lewis Morris." *New-York Historical Society Collections* for 1875: 433–514.

McCowen, George Smith, Jr. *The British Occupation of Charleston, 1780–82.* Columbia: University of South Carolina Press, 1972.

Morgan, Daniel. *Cowpens Papers: Being the Correspondence of General Morgan and Prominent Actors.* Edited by Theodoras Baily Myers. Charleston: News and Courier Book Presses, 1881.

Murdoch, Richard K., trans. "A French Account of the Siege of Charleston, 1780." *South Carolina Historical Magazine* 67 (1966): 138–54.

Naisawald, L. Van Loan. "Major General Robert Howe's Activities in South Carolina and Georgia, 1776–1779." *Georgia Historical Quarterly* 35 (1951): 23–30.

Nelson, Paul David. "Horatio Gates in the Southern Department, 1780: Serious Errors and a Costly Defeat." *North Carolina Historical Review* 50 (1973): 256–72.

Pinckney, Thomas. "General Gates' Southern Campaign." *Historical Magazine* 10 (1866): 244–53.

Prevost, Augustine. "Papers Relating to the Allied Attack on Savannah in 1779." *Historical Magazine* 8 (1864): 290–97.

"Proceedings of a General Court Martial, Held at Philadelphia, in the State of Pennsylvania, by Order of His Excellency General Washington, Commander in Chief of the Army of the United States of America for the Trial of Major General Howe, December 7, 1781; Major General Baron Steuben, President." *New-York Historical Society Collections* for 1879: 215–311.

Pugh, Robert Coplin. "The Cowpens Campaign and the American Revolution." Ph.D. dissertation, University of Illinois, 1951.

Rankin, Hugh F. "The Moore's Creek Bridge Campaign, 1776." *North Carolina Historical Review* 30 (1953): 23–60.

Roberts, Kenneth. *The Battle of Cowpens: The Great Morale-Builder.* Garden City: Doubleday & Co., 1958.

Robertson, Heard. "The Second British Occupation of Augusta, 1780–1781." *Georgia Historical Quarterly* 58 (1974): 442–46.

Robson, Eric. "The Expedition to the Southern Colonies, 1775–1776." *English Historical Review* 66 (1951): 535–60.

Saint-Marc, Meyronnet de. "Meyronnet de Saint-Marc's Journal of the Operations of the French Army Under D'Estaing at the Siege of Savannah, September, 1779." Edited by Roberta Leighton. *New-York Historical Society Quarterly* 36 (1952): 255–87.

Schenck, David. *North Carolina, 1780–'81: Being a History of the Invasion of the Carolinas by the British Army Under Lord Cornwallis. . . .* Raleigh: Edwards & Broughton, 1889.

Searcy, Martha C. "The Georgia-Florida Campaigns in the American Revolution: 1776, 1777, and 1778." Ph.D. dissertation, Tulane University, 1979.

Skelly, Francis. "Demonstration Against Charleston, South Carolina, in 1779: Journal of Brigade Major F. Skelly." Edited by Charles C. Jones, Jr. *Magazine of American History* 26 (1891): 152–54, 392–93.

Smith, W. Calvin. "Mermaids Riding Alligators: Divided Command on the Southern Frontier, 1776–1778." *Florida Historical Quarterly* 54 (1976): 443–64.

Stevens, John Austin. "The Southern Campaign, 1780: Gates at Camden." *Magazine of American History* 5 (1880): 241–81, 425–26.

Tarleton, [Banastre]. *A History of the Campaigns of 1780 and 1781, in the Southern Provinces of North America.* London: T. Cadell, 1787.

Walton, George. "Two Interesting Letters of Hon. George Walton. Edited by Charles C. Jones, Jr. *Magazine of American History* 23 (1890): 502–3.

Weigley, Russell F. *The Partisan War: The South Carolina Campaign of 1780–1782.* Columbia: South Carolina Tricentennial Commission, 1970.

Weller, Jac. "Irregular but Effective: Partisan Weapons and Tactics in the American Revolution, Southern Theater." *Military Affairs* 21 (1957): 119–31.

———. "The Irregular War in the South." *Military Affairs* 24 (1960): 124–36.

Wilson, John. "Lieutenant John Wilson's 'Journal of the Siege of Charleston.' " Edited by Joseph Ioor Waring. *South Carolina Historical Magazine* 66 (1965): 175–82.

Indians and the West

Almeida, Dierdre. "The Stockbridge Indian in the American Revolution." *Historical Journal of Western Massachusetts* 4 (1975): 34–39.

Badders, Hurley E. *Broken Path: The Cherokee Campaign of 1776.* [Pendleton?]: Pendleton District [S.C.] Historical and Recreational Commission, 1976.

Ballard, Edward, ed. "Attack on Cherry-Valley." *Historical Magazine*, 2d ser., 5 (1869): 276–77.

———, ed. "Letters of Gen. Stark and Others Relative to Operations in Cherry Valley in 1778." *Historical Magazine* 10 (1866): 172–76.

Bast, Homer. "Creek Indian Affairs, 1775–1778." *Georgia Historical Quarterly* 33 (1949): 1–25.

Bleeker, Leonard. *The Order Book of Capt. Leonard Bleeker, Major of Brigade in the Early Part of the Expedition Under Gen. James Clinton, Against the Indian Settlements of Western New York, in the Campaign of 1779.* New York: Joseph Sabin, 1865.

Brady, William Young. "Brodhead's Trail up the Allegheny, 1779." *Western Pennsylvania Historical Magazine* 37 (1954): 19–31.

Buckley, Thomas J., ed. "Attempt on Oswego, 1783." *Historical Magazine* 3 (1859): 186–87.

Butler, Zebulon. "Correspondence of Col. Zebulon Butler, Wyoming, June–December 1778." *Wyoming Historical and Geological Society Proceedings and Collections* 7 (1902): 131–50.

———. "Orderly Book of Col. Zebulon Butler, at Wyoming, August–December 1778." Edited by Horace Edwin Hayden. *Wyoming Historical and Geological Society Proceedings and Collections* 7 (1902): 106–30.

Butterfield, Consul Willshire, ed. *Washington-Irvine Correspondence; the Official Letters Which Passed Between Washington and Brigadier General William Irvine, and Between Irvine and Others Concerning Military Affairs in the West From 1781 to 1783.* Madison, Wis.: D. Atwood, 1882.

Cook, Frederick, ed. *Journals of the Military Expedition of Major General John Sullivan Against the Six Nations of Indians in 1779 With Records of Centennial Celebrations.* Auburn, N.Y.: Knapp, Peck & Thomson, 1887.

Craft, David. "The Expedition of Col. Thomas Hartley Against the Indians in 1778, To Avenge the Massacre of Wyoming." *Wyoming Historical and Geological Society Proceedings and Collections* 9 (1905): 189–216.

Darlington, Mary Carlson, ed. *Fort Pitt and Letters From the Frontier.* Pittsburg: J. R. Welden & Co., 1892.

Davis, Andrew McFarland. "The Employment of Indian Auxiliaries in the American War." *English Historical Review* 2 (1887): 709–28.

Dendy, John Oliver. "Frederick Haldimand and the Defense of Canada, 1778–1784." Ph.D. dissertation, Duke University, 1972.

Edson, Obed. "Brodhead's Expedition Against the Indians of the Upper Allegheny, 1779." *Magazine of American History* 3 (1879): 649–75.

Flick, Alexander C. "The Sullivan-Clinton Campaign in 1779." *New Jersey Historical Society Proceedings*, new ser., 15 (1930): 64–72.

———, ed. "New Sources on the Sullivan-Clinton Campaign in 1779." *Quarterly Journal of the New York State Historical Association* 10 (1929): 185–224, 265–317.

Ganyard, Robert L. "Threat From the West: North Carolina and the Cherokee, 1776–1778." *North Carolina Historical Review* 45 (1968): 47–66.

Gerlach, Don R. "Philip Schuyler and the New York Frontier in 1781." *New-York Historical Society Quarterly* 53 (1969): 148–81.

Gore, Obadiah, Jr. *The Revolutionary War Diary of Lieut. Obadiah Gore, Jr.* Edited by R. W. G. Vail. New York: New York Public Library, 1929.

Graham, Louise E. "Fort McIntosh." *Western Pennsylvania Historical Magazine* 15 (1932): 93–119.

Grant, Thomas. "Gen. Sullivan's Expedition to the Genesee Country, 1779: A Journal of General Sullivan's Army After They Left Wyoming." *Historical Magazine* 6 (1862): 233–37, 272–76.

Graymont, Barbara. *The Iroquois in the American Revolution.* Syracuse: Syracuse University Press, 1972.

Hand, Edward. "Correspondence of General Edward Hand of the Continental Line, 1779–1781." *Pennsylvania Magazine of History and Biography* 33 (1909): 353–60.

Hough, Franklin Benjamin, ed. *The Northern Invasion of October, 1780: A Series of Papers Relating to the Expeditions From Canada Under Sir John Johnson and Others Against the Frontiers of New York, Which Were Supposed To Have Connection With Arnold's Treason; Prepared From Originals.* New York: Bradford Club, 1866.

Hubley, Adam, Jr. "Adam Hubley, Jr., Lt. Col., Comdt., 11th Penna. Regt., His Journal, Commencing at Wyoming, July 30th, 1779." Edited by John W. Jordan. *Pennsylvania Magazine of History and Biography* 33 (1909): 129–46, 279–302, 409–22.

Irvine, W. A., ed. "Affairs at Fort Pitt in 1782." *Historical Magazine*, 1st ser., 7 (1863): 306–9.

Kellogg, Louise Phelps, ed. *Frontier Advance on the Upper Ohio, 1778–1779.* Madison: Wisconsin Historical Society, 1916.

_____, ed. *Frontier Retreat on the Upper Ohio, 1779–1781.* Madison: Wisconsin Historical Society, 1917.

McAdams, Donald R. "The Sullivan Expedition: Success or Failure." *New-York Historical Society Quarterly* 54 (1970): 53–81.

Massay, Glenn F. "Fort Henry in the American Revolution." *West Virginia History* 24 (1963): 248–57.

New York Division of Archives and History. *The Sullivan-Clinton Campaign in 1779: Chronology and Selected Documents.* Albany: University of the State of New York, 1929.

O'Donnell, James H., III. *Southern Indians in the American Revolution.* Knoxville: University of Tennessee Press, 1972.

Pastore, Ralph T. "Congress and the Six Nations, 1775–1778." *Niagara Frontier* 20 (1973): 80–95.

Rockwell, E. F., ed. "Parallel and Combined Expeditions Against the Cherokee Indians in South and North Carolina in 1776." *Historical Magazine*, 2d ser., 2 (1867): 212–20.

Rogers, William. *The Journals of a Brigade Chaplain in the Campaign of 1779 Against the Six Nations, Under the Command of Major General John Sullivan.* Providence: S. S. Rider, 1879.

Rossie, Jonathan G. "The Northern Indian Department and the American Revolution." *Niagara Frontier* 20 (1973): 52–65.

Russell, E. L. "The Lost Story of the Brodhead Expedition." *Quarterly Journal of the New York State Historical Association* 11 (1930): 252–63.

Sosin, Jack M. *The Revolutionary Frontier, 1763–1783.* New York: Holt Rinehart & Winston, 1967.

_____. "The Use of Indians in the War of the American Revolution: A Re-assessment of Responsibility." *Canadian Historical Review* 46 (1965): 101–21.

Stone, Rufus B. "Brodhead's Raid on the Senecas: The Story of a Little Known Expedition in 1779 From Fort Pitt To Destroy the Indian Villages on the Upper Allegheny." *Western Pennsylvania Historical Magazine* 7 (1924): 88–101.

Stone, William L. *Border Wars of the American Revolution.* 2 vols. New York: Harper & Bros., 1845.

Stryker, William S. *General Maxwell's Brigade of the New Jersey Continental Line in the Expedition Against the Indians, in the Year 1779.* Trenton: W. S. Sharp Printing Co., 1885.

Thwaites, Reuben Gold, and Kellogg, Louise Phelps, eds. *Frontier Defense on the Upper Ohio, 1777–1778.* Madison: Wisconsin Historical Society, 1912.

_____, eds. *The Revolution on the Upper Ohio, 1775–1777.* Madison: Wisconsin Historical Society, 1908.

Vivian, James F., and Vivian, Jean H. "Congressional Indian Policy During the War for Independence: The Northern Department." *Maryland Historical Magazine* 63 (1968): 241–74.

Williams, Edward G. *Fort Pitt and the Revolution on the Western Frontier.* Pittsburgh: Historical Society of Western Pennsylvania, 1978.

_____, ed. "A Revolutionary Journal and Orderly Book of General Lachlan McIntosh's Expedition, 1778." *Western Pennsylvania Historical Magazine* 43 (1960): 1-17, 157-77, 267-88.

Williams, Richmond D. "Col. Thomas Hartley's Expedition of 1778." *Now and Then* 12 (1960): 258-60.

Other Theaters

Beer, William. "The Capture of Fort Charlotte, Mobile." *Publications of the Louisiana Historical Society* 1 (1896): 31-34.

_____, ed. "The Surrender of Fort Charlotte, Mobile, 1780." *American Historical Review* 1 (1896): 696-99.

Begnaud, Allen Eustis. "British Operations in the Caribbean and the American Revolution." Ph.D. dissertation, Tulane University, 1966.

Buker, George E., and Martin, Richard Apley. "Governor Tonyn's Brown-Water Navy: East Florida During the American Revolution, 1775-1778." *Florida Historical Quarterly* 58 (1979): 58-71.

Bullen, Ripley P. "Fort Tonyn and the Campaign of 1778." *Florida Historical Quarterly* 29 (1951): 253-60.

Conover, Bettie James. "British West Florida's Mississippi Frontier Posts, 1763-1779." *Alabama Review* 29 (1976): 177-207.

Cubberly, Fred. "Fort George (St. Michael), Pensacola." *Florida Historical Quarterly* 6 (1928): 220-34.

Dart, Henry P., ed. "West Florida—the Capture of Baton Rouge by Galvez, September 21, 1779, From Reports of the English Officers." *Louisiana Historical Quarterly* 12 (1929): 255-65.

Farmar, Robert. "Bernardo de Galvez's Siege of Pensacola in 1781 (as Related in Robert Farmar's Journal)." Edited by James A. Padgett. *Louisiana Historical Quarterly* 26 (1943): 311-29.

Galvez, Bernardo de. "Bernardo de Galvez's Combat Diary for the Battle of Pensacola, 1781." Edited by Murray Baker and Margaret Bissler Haas. *Florida Historical Quarterly* 56 (1977): 176-99.

Glascock, Melvin Bruce. "New Spain and the War for America, 1779-1783." Ph.D. dissertation, Louisiana State University, 1969.

Haarmann, Albert W. "The Siege of Pensacola: An Order of Battle." *Florida Historical Quarterly* 44 (1966): 193-99.

_____. "The Spanish Conquest of British West Florida, 1779-1781." *Florida Historical Quarterly* 39 (1960): 107-34.

Holmes, Jack D. L. "Alabama's Bloodiest Day of the American Revolution: Counterattack at the Village, January 7, 1781." *Alabama Review* 29 (1976): 208-19.

_____. "The Historiography of the American Revolution in Louisiana." *Louisiana History* 19 (1978): 309-26.

Killion, Howard Ray. "The Suffren Expedition: French Operations in India During the War of American Independence." Ph.D. dissertation, Duke University, 1972.

Lackey, Robert J., ed. "The Siege of Pensacola in 1781." *Historical Magazine* 4 (1860): 166-72.

McGuffie, Tom Henderson. *The Siege of Gibraltar, 1779-1783.* London: B. T. Batsford, 1965.

McLarty, Robert Neil. "The Expedition of Major General John Vaughan to the Lesser Antilles, 1779-1781." Ph.D. dissertation, University of Michigan, 1951.
_____. "Jamaica Prepares for Invasion, 1779." *Caribbean Quarterly* 4 (1955): 62-67.
Miranda, Francisco. "Miranda's Diary of the Siege of Pensacola, 1781." Translated by Donald E. Worcester. *Florida Historical Quarterly* 29 (1951): 163-96.
Osborn, George C. "Major General John Campbell in British West Florida." *Florida Historical Quarterly* 27 (1949): 317-39.
Patterson, A[lfred] Temple. *The Other Armada: The Franco-Spanish Attempt To Invade Britain in 1779*. Manchester: Manchester University Press, 1960.
Rush, N[ixon] Orwin. *The Battle of Pensacola, March 9 to May 8, 1781: Spain's Final Triumph Over Great Britain in the Gulf of Mexico*. Tallahassee: Florida State University, 1966.
Scott, Kenneth, ed. "Britain Loses Natchez, 1779: An Unpublished Letter." *Journal of Mississippi History* 26 (1964): 45-46.
Starr, J. Barton. "Tories, Dons and Rebels: The American Revolution in British West Florida." Ph.D. dissertation, Florida State University, 1971.
Villebeuvre, Juan de la. "Fort Panmure, 1779, as Related by Juan Delavillebeuvre to Bernardo de Galvez." Translated by Anna Lewis. *Mississippi Valley Historical Review* 18 (1932): 541-48.
Wright, J. Leitch, Jr. *Florida in the American Revolution*. Gainesville: University Presses of Florida, 1976.

BACKGROUND

Military Theory

Bernath, Stuart L. "George Washington and the Genesis of American Military Discipline." *Mid-America* 49 (1967): 83-100.
Caples, William Goff. "George Washington's Military Guide." *Military Engineer* 19 (1927): 244-47.
Church, Thomas. *The History of the Great Indian War of 1675 and 1676, Commonly Called Philip's War; Also, the Old French and Indian Wars, From 1689 to 1704*. Edited by Samuel G. Drake. Hartford: Silas Andrus & Son, 1854.
Glover, Richard. *Peninsular Preparation: The Reform of the British Army, 1795-1809*. Cambridge: Cambridge University Press, 1963.
Gruber, Ira D. "British Strategy: The Theory and Practice of Eighteenth-Century Warfare." In *Reconsiderations on the Revolutionary War: Selected Essays*, edited by Don Higginbotham, pp. 14-31. Westport, Conn.: Greenwood Press, 1978.
Hyatt, A. M. J. "The Origin of Napoleonic Warfare: A Survey of Interpretations." *Military Affairs* 30 (1966): 177-85.
Lane, William Coolidge. *A Catalogue of the Washington Collection in the Boston Athenaeum*. Boston: Boston Athenaeum, 1897.
Lynn, John Albert. "The Revolution on the Battlefield: Training and Tactics of the *Armee Du Nord*, 1792-1794." Ph.D. dissertation, University of California at Los Angeles, 1973.
Paret, Peter. "Colonial Experience and European Military Reform at the End of the Eighteenth Century." *Institute of Historical Research Bulletin* 37 (1964): 47-59.

_____. "The Relationship Between the Revolutionary War and European Military Thought and Practice in the Second Half of the Eighteenth Century." In *Reconsiderations on the Revolutionary War: Selected Essays*, edited by Don Higginbotham, pp. 144–57. Westport, Conn.: Greenwood Press, 1978.

[Philadelphia Associators]. "Directions for Manouvres, To Be Performed by the Brigade Composed of the Three City Battalions, on Tuesday, the Fourteenth of November, 1775." *Historical Magazine* 8 (1864): 343–44.

Phillips, Thomas R., ed. *Frederick the Great: Instructions for His Generals*. Harrisburg: Stackpole Co., 1944.

"Plan for a Re-organization of the Continental Army." *Historical Magazine*, 2d ser., 3 (1868): 270–73.

Quimby, Robert S. *The Background of Napoleonic Warfare: The Theory of Military Tactics in Eighteenth Century France*. New York: Columbia University Press, 1957.

Ross, Stephen. "The Development of the Combat Division in Eighteenth-Century French Armies." *French Historical Studies* 4 (1965): 84–94.

Saxe, Maurice de. *Reveries on the Art of War*. Translated and edited by Thomas R. Phillips. Harrisburg: Military Service Publishing Co., 1944.

Smith, George. *An Universal Military Dictionary*. London: J. Milan, 1779.

Spaulding, Oliver L., Jr. "The Military Studies of George Washington." *American Historical Review* 29 (1924): 675–80.

Spaulding, Oliver L., Jr.; Nickerson, Hoffman; and Wright, John Womack. *Warfare: A Study of Military Methods From the Earliest Times*. New York: Harcourt, Brace & Co., 1925.

Spaulding, Thomas M. "Early Military Books in the Folger Library." *Military Affairs* 1 (1937): 91–100.

Spaulding, Thomas M., and Karpinski, Louise C. *Early Military Books in the University of Michigan Libraries*. Ann Arbor: University of Michigan Press, 1941.

Wright, John Womack. "Pickering's Letter on Washington." *Tyler's Quarterly Historical and Genealogical Magazine* 7 (1925): 16–45.

Colonial Military Background

Aimone, Alan C., and Aimone, Barbara. "New Netherland Defends Itself." *Military Collector and Historian* 32 (1980): 52–57.

Aldridge, Frederick Stokes. "Organization and Administration of the Militia System of Colonial Virginia." Ph.D. dissertation, American University, 1964.

Anderson, Niles. *The Battle of Bushy Run*. Harrisburg: Pennsylvania Historical and Museum Commission, 1966.

Archer, Christian Irving. *The Army in Bourbon Mexico, 1760–1810*. Albuquerque: University of New Mexico Press, 1978.

Axtell, James. "The Scholastic Philosophy of the Wilderness." *William and Mary Quarterly*, 3d ser., 29 (1972): 335–66.

Boucher, Ronald L. "The Colonial Militia as a Social Institution: Salem, Massachusetts, 1764–1775." *Military Affairs* 37 (1973): 125–30.

Braddock, Edward. *Major General Edward Braddock's Orderly Books, From February 26 to June 17, 1755, From the Originals, in the Congressional Library*. Cumberland: Will H. Lowdermilk, 1880.

Branch, E. Douglas. "Henry Bouquet: Professional Soldier." *Pennsylvania Magazine of History and Biography* 62 (1938): 41-51.

Breen, Timothy. "English Origins and New World Development: The Case of the Covenanted Militia in Seventeenth-Century Massachusetts." *Past & Present* 57 (1972): 74-96.

Campbell, John, 4th Earl of Loudoun. *General Orders of 1757; Issued by the Earl of Loudoun and Phineas Lyman in the Campaign Against the French*. New York: Dodd, Mead, 1898.

Campbell, Leon G. *The Military and Society in Colonial Peru, 1750-1810*. Philadelphia: American Philosophical Society, 1978.

Champagne, Roger. "The Military Association of the Sons of Liberty." *New-York Historical Society Quarterly* 44 (1957): 338-50.

Church, Thomas. *The History of the Great Indian War of 1675 and 1676, Commonly Called Philip's War; Also, the Old French and Indian Wars, From 1689 to 1704*. Edited by Samuel G. Drake. Hartford: Silas Andrus & Son, 1854.

Cole, David William. "The Organization and Administration of the South Carolina Militia System, 1670-1783." Ph.D. dissertation, University of South Carolina, 1953.

Cuneo, John R. *Robert Rogers of the Rangers*. New York: Oxford University Press, 1959.

De Valinger, Leon. *Colonial Military Organization in Delaware, 1638-1776*. Wilmington: Historical Society of Delaware, 1938.

Eccles, W[illiam] J[ohn]. "The Social, Economic, and Political Significance of the Military Establishment in New France." *Canadian Historical Review* 52 (1971): 1-22.

Esbenshade, Ranz E. "Sober, Modest Men of Confined Ideas: The Officer Corps of Provincial New Hampshire." Master's thesis, University of New Hampshire, 1976.

Foote, William Alfred. "The American Independent Companies of the British Army, 1664-1764." Ph.D. dissertation, University of California at Los Angeles, 1966.

Forbes, John. *Letters of General John Forbes Relating to the Expedition Against Fort Duquesne in 1758*. Edited by Irene Stewart. Pittsburgh: Colonial Dames of America, 1927.

_____. *Writings of General John Forbes Relating to His Service in North America*. Edited by Alfred Proctor James. Menasha, Wis.: The Collegiate Press, 1938.

Gates, Stewart Lewis. "Disorder and Social Organization: The Militia in Connecticut Public Life, 1660-1860." Ph.D. dissertation, University of Connecticut, 1975.

Gipson, Lawrence Henry. *The British Empire Before the American Revolution*. 15 vols. New York: Alfred A. Knopf, 1936-70.

Grant, Charles S. "Pontiac's Rebellion and the British Troop Moves of 1763." *Mississippi Valley Historical Review* 40 (1953): 75-88.

Hadlock, Wendell Stanwood. "War Among the Northeastern Woodland Indians." *American Anthropologist* 49 (1947): 204-21.

Hamilton, Edward Pierce, ed. *Braddock's Defeat; the Journal of Captain Robert Chomley's Batman; the Journal of a British Officer; Halkett's Orderly Book*. Norman: University of Oklahoma Press, 1959.

Henderson, Susan Wright. "The French Regular Officer Corps in Canada, 1755-1760: A Group Portrait." Ph.D. dissertation, University of Maine, 1975.

Hunt, George T. *The Wars of the Iroquois: A Study in Intertribal Relations*. Madison: University of Wisconsin Press, 1940.

Hunter, William A. *Forts on the Pennsylvania Frontier, 1753-1758*. Harrisburg: Pennsylvania Historical and Museum Commission, 1960.

Ivers, Larry E. *British Drums on the Southern Frontier: The Military Colonization of Georgia, 1733-1749*. Chapel Hill: University of North Carolina Press, 1974.

Jabbs, Theodore Harry. "The South Carolina Militia, 1663-1733." Ph.D. dissertation, University of North Carolina at Chapel Hill, 1973.

Jones, E. Alfred. "The American Regiment in the Carthagena Expedition." *Virginia Magazine of History and Biography* 30 (1922): 1-20.

Kenny, Robert W. "The Beginnings of the Rhode Island Train Bands." *Rhode Island Historical Society Collections* 33 (1940): 25-38.

Lanctot, Gustave. "Les Troupes de la Nouvelle France." *Canadian Historical Association Annual Report* for 1926: 40-60.

Larrabee, Edward Conyers McMillan. "New Jersey and the Fortified Frontier System of the 1750's." Ph.D. dissertation, Columbia University, 1970.

Leach, Douglas Edward. *Arms for Empire: A Military History of the British Colonies in North America, 1607-1763*. New York: Macmillan Co., 1973.

_____. *Flintlock and Tomahawk: New England in King Philip's War*. New York: W. W. Norton, 1958.

_____. "The Military System of Plymouth Colony." *New England Quarterly* 24 (1951): 342-64.

McAlister, Lyle N. *The "Fuero Militar" in New Spain, 1764-1800*. Gainesville: University Presses of Florida, 1978.

_____. "The Reorganization of the Army of New Spain, 1763-1766." *Hispanic American Historical Review* 33 (1953): 1-32.

McCorison, Marcus A. "Colonial Defense of the Upper Connecticut Valley." *Vermont History*, new ser., 30 (1962): 50-62.

Mahon, John K. "Anglo-American Methods of Indian Warfare, 1676-1794." *Mississippi Valley Historical Review* 45 (1958): 254-75.

Malone, Patrick Mitchell. "Indian and English Military Systems in New England in the Seventeenth Century." Ph.D. dissertation, Brown University, 1971.

Marcus, Richard Henry. "The Connecticut Valley: A Problem in Intercolonial Defense." *Military Affairs* 33 (1969): 230-42.

_____. "The Militia of Colonial Connecticut, 1639-1775: An Institutional Study." Ph.D. dissertation, University of Colorado, 1965.

Middleton, C.R. "A Reinforcement for North America, Summer 1757." *Bulletin of the Institute for Historical Research* 41 (1968): 58-72.

Millar, David Richard. "The Militia, the Army, and Independency in Colonial Massachusetts." Ph.D. dissertation, Cornell University, 1967.

Morton, Louis. "The Origins of American Military Policy." *Military Affairs* 22 (1958): 75-82.

Pargellis, Stanley M. *Lord Loudoun in North America*. New Haven: Yale University Press, 1933.

_____, ed. *Military Affairs in North America, 1748-1765: Selected Documents From the Cumberland Papers in Windsor Castle*. New York: D. Appleton-Century Co., 1936.

Parker, King Lawrence. "Anglo-American Wilderness Campaigning, 1754-1764: Logistical and Tactical Developments." Ph.D. dissertation, Columbia University, 1970.

Peckham, Howard H. *The Colonial Wars, 1689–1762*. Chicago: University of Chicago Press, 1964.

_____. *Pontiac and the Indian Uprising*. Princeton: Princeton University Press, 1947.

_____. "Speculations on the Colonial Wars." *William and Mary Quarterly*, 3d ser., 17 (1960): 463–72.

Peterson, Harold L. "The Military Equipment of the Plymouth and Bay Colonies: 1620–1690." *New England Quarterly* 20 (1947): 197–208.

Radabaugh, Jack Sheldon. "The Military System of Colonial Massachusetts, 1690–1740." Ph.D. dissertation, University of Southern California, 1965.

Rawlyk, G. A. *Yankees at Louisbourg*. Orono: University of Maine, 1967.

Rogers, Alan. *Empire and Liberty: American Resistance to British Authority, 1755–1763*. Berkeley: University of California Press, 1974.

Rogers, Robert. *Journals of Major Robert Rogers*. Edited by Howard H. Peckham. New York: Corinth Books, 1961.

Russell, Peter E. "Redcoats in the Wilderness: British Officers and Irregular Warfare in Europe and America, 1740 to 1760." *William and Mary Quarterly*, 3d ser., 35 (1978): 629–52.

Rutman, Darrett B. "A Militant New World, 1607–1640: America's First Generation, Its Martial Spirit, Its Tradition of Arms, Its Militia Organization, Its Wars." Ph.D. dissertation, University of Virginia, 1959.

Sanders, George Earl. "The Spanish Defense of America 1700–1763." Ph.D. dissertation, University of Southern California, 1973.

Sargent, Winthrop. *The History of an Expedition Against Fort Duquesne in 1755; Under Major-General Edward Braddock, Generalissimo of H.B.M. Forces in America*. Philadelphia: Lippincott, Grambo & Co., 1855.

Scisco, Louis Dow. "Evolution of Colonial Militia in Maryland." *Maryland Historical Magazine* 35 (1940): 166–77.

Sharp, Morrison. "Leadership and Democracy in the Early New England System of Defense." *American Historical Review* 50 (1945): 244–60.

Shea, William Lee. "To Defend Virginia: The Evolution of the First Colonial Militia, 1607–1677." Ph.D. dissertation, Rice University, 1975.

Shy, John W. "A New Look at Colonial Militia." *William and Mary Quarterly*, 3d ser., 20 (1963): 175–85.

Stacey, C. P. *Quebec, 1759: The Siege and the Battle*. New York: Macmillan Co., 1959.

Stanley, George F. G. "The Canadian Militia During the Ancien Regime." *Journal of the Society for Army Historical Research* 22 (1943): 157–68.

Sulte, Benjamin. "The Captains of Militia." *Canadian Historical Review* 1 (1920): 241–45.

_____. Histoire de la Milice canadienne-francaise, 1760–1897. Montreal: Desbarats & Cie., 1897.

Syrett, David. "American Provincials and the Havana Campaign of 1762." *New York History* 49 (1968): 375–90.

Thwaites, Reuben Gold, and Kellogg, Louise Phelps, eds. *Documentary History of Dunmore's War, 1774*. Madison: Wisconsin Historical Society, 1905.

Vaughan, Alden T. *New England Frontier: Puritans and Indians, 1620–1675*. Boston: Little, Brown & Co., 1965.

Washburn, Wilcomb E. *The Governor and the Rebel: A History of Bacon's Rebellion in Virginia*. Chapel Hill: University of North Carolina Press, 1957.

Wheeler, E. Milton. "Development and Organization of the North Carolina Militia." *North Carolina Historical Review* 61 (1964): 307-23.

Williams, Edward G., ed. *Bouquet's March to the Ohio: The Forbes Road (From the Original Manuscripts in the William L. Clements Library)*. Pittsburgh: Historical Society of Western Pennsylvania, 1975.

European Military Background

Berthaut, Henri. *Les Ingenieurs geographes militaires, 1624-1831: Etude historique*. 2 vols. Paris: Imprimerie du Service geographique, 1902.

Blanchard, Anne. " 'Ingenieurs de Sa Majeste Tres Chretienne a l'etranger,' ou l'ecole francaise de fortifications." *Revue d'histoire moderne et contemporaine* 20 (1973): 25-36.

Chandler, David G. *The Campaigns of Napoleon*. New York: Macmillan Co., 1966.

Chartier, Roger. "Un Recrutement scolaire au XVIIIe siecle: L'Ecole royale du genie de Mezieres." *Revue d'histoire moderne et contemporaine* 20 (1973): 351-75.

Colin, Jean Lambert Alphonse. *The Transformations of War*. Translated by L. H. R. Pope-Hennessy. London: Hugh Rees, 1912. [Originally published as *Les Transformations de la guerre*, Paris: E. Flammarion, 1911.]

_____. *L'Infanterie au XVIIIe siecle: La Tactique*. Paris: Berger-Levrault, 1907.

_____. *L'Education militaire de Napoleon*. Paris: R. Chapelot, 1900.

Corvissier, Andre. *L'Armee francaise de la fin du XVIIe siecle au ministere de Choiseul: Le Soldat*. 2 vols. Paris: Presses universitaires de France, 1964.

Coste, Gabriel. *Les Anciennes Troupes de la marine (1622-1792)*. Paris: L. Baudoin, 1893.

Covington, Samuel Anderson. "The *Comite militaire* and the Legislative Reform of the French Army, 1789-1791." Ph.D. dissertation, University of Arkansas, 1976.

Desbriere, Edouard, and Sautai, Maurice. *La Cavalerie de 1740 a 1789*. Paris: Berger-Levrault, 1906.

Devos, Jean Claude, and Waksman, Pierre. "Les Compagnies d'ordonnance, de la guerre de Sept Ans a leur dissolution (1788)." *Revue d'histoire moderne et contemporaine* 20 (1973): 37-57.

Duffy, Christopher. *The Army of Frederick the Great*. New York: Hippocrene Books, 1974.

_____. *The Army of Maria Theresa*. New York: Hippocrene Books, 1977.

_____. *Fire and Stone: The Science of Fortress Warfare, 1660-1860*. New York: Hippocrene Books, 1975.

_____. *Siege Warfare: The Fortress in the Early Modern World, 1495-1660*. Boston: Routledge & Kegan Paul, 1979.

France, Ministere de la Guerre. *Reglement concernant l'exercise et les manoeuvres de l'infanterie du 1er aout 1791*. Paris: Bureau du journal militaire, 1792.

Gribeauval, Jean Baptiste Vaquette de. *Tables des constructions des principaux attirails de l'artillerie, proposees ou approuvees depuis 1764 jusqu'en 1789, par M. de Gribeauval, executees et recueillees par M. de Manson et par plusieurs autres officiers du corps royal de l'artillerie de France*. 3 vols. in 4. Paris: Imprimerie royale, 1792.

Hennebert, Eugene. *Gribeauval, lieutenant-general des armees du Roy, premier inspecteur-general du Corps royal de l'artillerie (1715-1789)*. Paris: Berger-Levrault, 1896.

Kennett, Lee. *The French Armies in the Seven Years' War: A Study in Military Organization and Administration*. Durham: Duke University Press, 1967.

Lynn, John Albert. "The Revolution on the Battlefield: Training and Tactics of the *Armee Du Nord*, 1792-1794." Ph.D. dissertation, University of California at Los Angeles, 1973.

Margerand, J. *Armement et equipment de l'infanterie francaise du XVIe au XXe siecle*. Paris: Editions militaires illustrees, 1945.

Nickle, Barry Harold. "The Military Reforms of Prince Maurice of Orange." Ph.D. dissertation, University of Delaware, 1975.

Paret, Peter. *Yorck and the Era of Prussian Reform, 1807-1815*. Princeton: Princeton University Press, 1966.

Quimby, Robert S. *The Background of Napoleonic Warfare: The Theory of Military Tactics in Eighteenth Century France*. New York: Columbia University Press, 1957.

Ross, Stephen T. "The Development of the Combat Division in Eighteenth-Century French Armies. *French Historical Studies* 4 (1965): 84-94.

Rothenberg, Gunther Erich. *The Austrian Military Border in Croatia, 1522-1747*. Urbana: University of Illinois Press, 1960.

_____. *The Military Border in Croatia, 1740-1881*. Chicago: University of Chicago Press, 1966.

_____. "The Habsburg Army in the Napoleonic Wars." *Military Affairs* 37 (1973): 1-5.

Scott, Samuel F. *The Response of the Royal Army to the French Revolution: The Role and Development of the Line Army, 1787-1793*. New York: Oxford University Press, 1978.

_____. "The Regeneration of the Line Army During the French Revolution." *Journal of Modern History* 42 (1970): 307-30.

Shanahan, William O. *Prussian Military Reforms, 1786-1813*. New York: Columbia University Press, 1945.

Van Crevald, Martin. *Supplying War: Logistics From Wallenstein to Patton*. New York: Cambridge University Press, 1977.

White, Jon Manchip. *Marshal of France: The Life and Times of Maurice, Comte de Saxe (1692-1750)*. London: Hamish Hamilton, 1962.

Wilkinson, Spencer. *The French Army Before Napoleon*. Oxford: Clarendon Press, 1915

Wrong, Charles John. "The French Infantry Officer at the Close of the Ancien Regime." Ph.D. dissertation, Brown University, 1968.

_____. "The Officiers de Fortune in the French Infantry." *French Historical Studies* 9 (1976): 400-31.

Causes

Ammerman, David. *In the Common Cause: American Reponse to the Coercive Acts of 1774*. Charlottesville: University Press of Virginia, 1974.

Bailyn, Bernard. *Ideological Origins of the American Revolution*. Cambridge: Harvard University Press, 1967.

Colburn, H. Trevor. *The Lamp of Experience: Whig History and the Intellectual Origins of the American Revolution*. Chapel Hill: University of North Carolina Press, 1965.

Dickerson, Oliver M. *The Navigation Acts and the American Revolution*. Philadelphia: University of Pennsylvania Press, 1951.

Gerlach, Larry R. "Soldiers and Citizens: The British Army in New Jersey on the Eve of the Revolution." *New Jersey History* 93 (1975): 5–36.

Gipson, Lawrence Henry. *The Coming of the Revolution, 1763–1775*. New York: Harper & Row, 1954.

Greene, Jack P. "The Plunge of Lemmings: A Consideration of Recent Writings on British Politics and the American Revolution." *South Atlantic Quarterly* 67 (1968): 141–75.

———. "The South Carolina Quartering Dispute, 1757–1758." *South Carolina Historical Magazine* 60 (1959): 193–204.

Kurtz, Stephen G., and Hutson, James H., eds. *Essays on the American Revolution*. Chapel Hill: University of North Carolina Press, 1973.

Labaree, Benjamin Woods. *The Boston Tea Party*. New York: Oxford University Press, 1964.

Maier, Pauline. *From Resistance to Revolution: Colonial Radicals and the Development of an Opposition to Britain 1765–1776*. New York: Alfred A. Knopf, 1972.

Main, Jackson Turner. *The Upper House in Revolutionary America, 1763–1788*. Madison: University of Wisconsin Press, 1967.

Marshall, Peter. "Colonial Protest and Imperial Retrenchment: Indian Policy, 1764–1768." *Journal of American Studies* 5 (1971): 1–17.

Morgan, Edmund S. "The American Revolution: Revisionists in Need of Revising." *William and Mary Quarterly*, 3d ser., 14 (1957): 3–15.

Morris, Richard B. *The American Revolution Reconsidered*. New York: Harper & Row, 1967.

Mott, Frank Luther. "The Newspaper Coverage of Lexington and Concord." *New England Quarterly* 17 (1944): 489–505.

Namier, Lewis. *England in the Age of the American Revolution*. 2d ed. New York: St. Martin's Press, 1961.

Nelson, William H. "The Revolutionary Character of the American Revolution." *American Historical Review* 70 (1965): 998–1014.

Page, Elwin L. "The King's Powder, 1774." *New England Quarterly* 18 (1945): 83–92.

———. "What Happened to the King's Powder?" *Historical New Hampshire* 19 (1964): 28–33.

Rogers, Alan. *Empire and Liberty: American Resistance to British Authority, 1755–1763*. Berkeley: University of California Press, 1974.

Shy, John. *Toward Lexington: The Role of the British Army in the Coming of the American Revolution*. Princeton: Princeton University Press, 1965.

Ubbelohde, Carl. *The Vice-Admiralty Courts and the American Revolution*. Chapel Hill: University of North Carolina Press, 1960.

Wentworth, John. "John Wentworth's Narrative of the Raids on Fort William and Mary." Edited by Paul Wilderson. *Historical New Hampshire* 32 (1977): 228–36.

Wickwire, Franklin B. *British Subministers and Colonial America, 1763–1783*. Princeton: Princeton University Press, 1966.

Wilderson, Paul, ed. "The Raids on Fort William and Mary: Some New Evidence." *Historical New Hampshire* 30 (1975): 178–202.

Wood, Gordon S. *The Creation of the American Republic, 1776–1787*. Chapel Hill: University of North Carolina Press, 1969.

_____. "Rhetoric and Reality in the American Revolution." *William and Mary Quarterly*, 3d ser., 23 (1966): 3-32.

Zobel, Hiller B. *The Boston Massacre*. New York: W. W. Norton Co., 1970.

Political Aspects

Adams, John. *Adams Family Correspondence*. Edited by Lyman H. Butterfield et al. Cambridge: Harvard University Press, 1963-.

_____. *Diary and Autobiography of John Adams*. Edited by Lyman H. Butterfield et al. Cambridge: Harvard University Press, 1961-.

Adams, Samuel. *The Writings of Samuel Adams*. Edited by Harry Alonzo Cushing. 4 vols. New York: G. P. Putnam's Sons, 1907.

Burnett, Edmund C. *The Continental Congress*. New York: Macmillan Co., 1941.

_____, ed. *Letters of Members of the Continental Congress*. 8 vols. Washington: Carnegie Institution of Washington, 1921-36.

Cometti, Elizabeth. "The Civil Servants of the Revolutionary Period." *Pennsylvania Magazine of History and Biography* 75 (1951): 159-69.

Dangerfield, George. *Chancellor Robert R. Livingston of New York, 1746-1813*. New York: Harcourt, Brace & World Co., 1960.

Ellery, William. "Diary of the Hon. William Ellery of Rhode Island." Edited by Henrietta C. Ellery. *Pennsylvania Magazine of History and Biography* 11 (1887): 318-29, 476-81.

Ferguson, E. James. "The Nationalists of 1781-1783 and the Economic Interpretation of the Constitution." *Journal of American History* 56 (1969): 241-61.

Ford, Worthington C., ed. *Journals of the Continental Congress, 1774-1789*. 34 vols. Washington: Government Printing Office, 1904-37.

Gardiner, C. Harvey, ed. *A Study in Dissent: The Warren-Gerry Correspondence, 1776-1792*. Carbondale: Southern Illinois University Press, 1968.

Gerlach, Larry R. "A Delegation of Steady Habits: The Connecticut Representatives to the Continental Congress, 1774-1789." *Connecticut Historical Society Bulletin* 32 (1967): 33-39.

Haskett, Richard C. "Prosecuting the Revolution." *American Historical Review* 59 (1954): 578-87.

Henderson, H. James. *Party Politics in the Continental Congress*. New York: McGraw-Hill Book Co., 1974.

Hunt, Agnes. *Provincial Committees of Safety of the American Revolution*. Cleveland: Western Reserve University, 1904.

Jensen, Merrill. *The Articles of Confederation: An Interpretation of the Social-Constitutional History of the American Revolution, 1774-1781*. Madison: University of Wisconsin Press, 1948.

Jones, Joseph. *Letters of Joseph Jones of Virginia*. Edited by Worthington C. Ford. Washington: Department of State, 1889.

Jones, Robert F. "William Duer and the Business of Government in the Era of the American Revolution." *William and Mary Quarterly*, 3d ser., 32 (1975): 393-416.

Kenyon, Cecilia M. "Republicanism and Radicalism in the American Revolution: An Old Fashioned Interpretation." *William and Mary Quarterly*, 3d ser., 19 (1962): 153-82.

Ketcham, Ralph L. "France and American Politics, 1763-1793." *Political Science Quarterly* 78 (1963): 198-223.

McDonald, Forrest. *E Pluribus Unum: The Formation of the American Republic, 1776-1790.* Boston: Houghton Mifflin, 1965.

MacMillan, Margaret Burnham. *The War Governors in the American Revolution.* New York: Columbia University Press, 1943.

Main, Jackson T. *Political Parties Before the Constitution.* Chapel Hill: University of North Carolina Press, 1973.

Martin, James Kirby. *Men in Rebellion: Higher Governmental Leaders and the Coming of the American Revolution.* New Brunswick: Rutgers University Press, 1973.

Mintz, Max M. *Gouveneur Morris and the American Revolution.* Norman: University of Oklahoma Press, 1970.

Rolater, Fred S. "Charles Thomson, 'Prime Minister' of the United States." *Pennsylvania Magazine of History and Biography* 101 (1977): 322-48.

Rossie, Jonathan Gregory. *The Politics of Command in the American Revolution.* Syracuse: Syracuse University Press, 1975.

Rush, Benjamin. "Historical Notes of Dr. Benjamin Rush, 1777." Edited by S. Weir Mitchell. *Pennsylvania Magazine of History and Biography* 27 (1903): 129-50.

Smith, Paul H., et al., eds. *Letters of Delegates to Congress, 1774-1789.* Washington: Library of Congress, 1976-.

Taylor, Robert J. "Trial at Trenton." *William and Mary Quarterly*, 3d ser., 26 (1969): 521-47.

Thomson, Charles. "The Papers of Charles Thomson, Secretary to the Continental Congress." *New-York Historical Society Collections* for 1878: 1-286.

Wood, Gordon S. *The Creation of the American Republic.* Chapel Hill: University of North Carolina Press, 1969

Diplomacy

Auger, Helen. *The Secret War of Independence.* New York: Duell, Sloan & Pierce, 1955.

Bemis, Samuel Flagg. *The Diplomacy of the American Revolution.* Bloomington: Indiana University Press, 1957.

Corwin, Edward. *French Policy and the American Alliance of 1778.* Princeton: Princeton University Press, 1916.

Deane, Silas. "Correspondence of Silas Deane, Delegate to the First and Second Congress at Philadelphia, 1774-1776." *Connecticut Historical Society Collections* 2 (1870): 127-368.

_____. "The Deane Papers; Correspondence Between Silas Deane, His Brother, and Their Business and Political Associates, 1771-1795." *Connecticut Historical Society Collections* 23 (1930): 1-277.

_____. "The Deane Papers, 1774-1790." Edited by Charles Isham. 5 vols. *New-York Historical Society Collections* for 1887-90.

Dull, Jonathan Romer. *The French Navy and American Independence: A Study of Arms and Diplomacy, 1774-1787.* Princeton: Princeton University Press, 1975.

Kite, Elizabeth. *Beaumarchais and the War of American Independence.* 2 vols. Boston: R. G. Badger, 1918.

_____. *Conrad Alexandre Gerard and American Independence*. [Philadelphia], 1921.

Meng, John J. *The Comte de Vergennes; European Phases of His American Diplomacy (1774-1780)*. Washington: Catholic University of America, 1932.

_____, ed. *Dispatches and Instructions of Conrad Alexandre Gerard, 1778-1780: Correspondence of the First French Minister to the United States With the Comte de Vergennes*. Baltimore: Johns Hopkins University Press, 1939.

Morris, Richard B. *The Peacemakers: The Great Powers and American Independence*. New York: Harper & Row, 1965.

Stevens, Franklin Benjamin, comp. *F. B. Stevens's Facsimilies of Manuscripts in European Archives Relating to America, 1773-1783, With Descriptions, Editorial Notes, Collations, References and Translations*. 24 vols. London: Malby & Sons, 1889-95.

Stinchcombe, William C. *The American Revolution and the French Alliance*. Syracuse: Syracuse University Press, 1969.

Stourzh, Gerald. *Benjamin Franklin and American Foreign Policy*. Chicago: University of Chicago Press, 1954.

Van Tyne, C. H. "French Aid Before the Alliance of 1778." *American Historical Review* 31 (1925): 20-40.

OTHER PARTICIPANTS

Crown Forces

Adams, Randolph Greenfield. *British Headquarters Maps and Sketches Used by Sir Henry Clinton While in Command of the British Forces Operating in North America*. Ann Arbor: William L. Clements Library, 1928.

Alden, John R. *General Gage in America: Being Principally a History of His Role in the American Revolution*. Baton Rouge: Louisiana State University Press, 1948.

Alexander, Arthur J. "Deserters: A British Source of Information During the American Revolution." *Journal of the Society for Army Historical Research* 27 (1949): 12-18.

Anderson, Troyer S. *The Command of the Howe Brothers During the American Revolution*. New York: Oxford University Press, 1936.

Andre, John. *Major Andre's Journal: Operations of the British Army Under Lieutenant Generals Sir William Howe and Sir Henry Clinton, June 1977 to November 1778; Recorded by Major John Andre, Adjutant General*. Edited by C. DeWitt Willcox. Tarrytown: William Abbatt, 1930.

Atkinson, Christopher T. "British Forces in North America, 1774-1781: Their Distribution and Strength. *Journal of the Society for Army Historical Research* 16 (1937): 3-23; 19 (1940-41): 163-66, 190-92.

_____. "The Highlanders in Westphalia, 1760-1762, and the Development of Light Infantry." *Journal of the Society for Army Historical Research* 20 (1941): 208-23.

_____. *Marlborough and the Rise of the British Army*. London: G. P. Putnam's Sons, 1921.

_____. "Material for Military History in the Reports of the Historical Manuscripts Commission." *Journal of the Society for Army Historical Research* 21 (1942): 17-34.

Baker, Norman. *Government and Contractors: The British Treasury and War Supplies, 1775-1783*. London: University of London, 1971.

Balderston, Marion, and Syrett, David, eds. *The Lost War: Letters From British Officers During the American Revolution*. New York: Horizon Press, 1975.

Barker, John. *The British in Boston, Being the Diary of Lieutenant John Barker of the King's Own Regiment From November 15, 1774 to May 31, 1776*. Edited by Elizabeth Ellery Dana. Cambridge: Harvard University Press, 1924.

Bass, Robert D. *The Green Dragoon: The Lives of Banastre Tarleton and Mary Robinson*. New York: Henry Holt & Co., 1957.

Baurmeister, Carl Leopold. *Revolution in America: Confidential Letters, 1776-1784, of Adjutant General Major Baurmeister of the Hessian Forces*. Edited by Bernard A. Uhlendorf. New Brunswick: Rutgers University Press, 1957.

Beers, Henry P. "The Papers of the British Commanders in Chief in North America, 1754-1783." *Military Affairs* 13 (1949): 79-94.

Benton, William Allen. *Whig-Loyalism: An Aspect of Political Ideology in the American Revolutionary Era*. Rutherford, N.J.: Fairleigh Dickinson University Press, 1969.

Billias, George A., ed. *George Washington's Opponents*. New York: William Morrow, 1969.

Bowler, R. A. *Logistics and the Failure of the British Army in America, 1775-1783*. Princeton: Princeton University Press, 1975.

Bowman, Larry. "The Court-Martial of Captain Richard Lippincot." *New Jersey History* 89 (1971): 23-36.

Boynton, Lindsey. *The Elizabethan Militia, 1558-1638*. London: Routledge & Kegan Paul, 1967.

Bradford, S. Sydney, ed. "A British Officer's Revolutionary War Journal, 1776-1778." *Maryland Historical Magazine* 56 (1961): 150-75.

Brown, Gerald S. *The American Secretary: The Colonial Policy of Lord George Germain, 1775-1778*. Ann Arbor: University of Michigan Press, 1963.

Brown, Wallace. *The Good Americans: The Loyalists in the American Revolution*. New York: William Morrow, 1969.

_____. *The King's Friends: The Composition and Motives of the American Loyalist Claimants*. Providence: Brown University Press, 1965.

_____. "The View at Two Hundred Years: The Loyalists of the American Revolution." *American Antiquarian Society Proceedings*, new ser., 80 (1970): 25-47.

Burns, R. E. "Ireland and British Military Preparations for War in America in 1775." *Cithara* 2 (1963): 42-61.

Burt, Alfred L. "The Quarrel Between Germain and Carleton: An Inverted Story." *Canadian Historical Review* 11 (1930): 202-20.

Carter, Clarence E. "The Significance of the Military Office in America, 1763-1775." *American Historical Review* 28 (1923): 475-88.

Chandler, David. *The Art of War in the Age of Marlborough*. New York: Hippocrene Books, 1976.

Chapman, Frederick T., and Elting, John R. "The Brunswick Regiment of Dragoons, 1776-1783." *Military Collector and Historian* 12 (1960): 17-18.

Clark, Dora Mae. "The British Treasury and the Administration of Military Affairs in America, 1754-1774." *Pennsylvania History* 2 (1935): 197-204.

Clark, Jane. "The Command of the Canadian Army for the Campaign of 1777." *Canadian Historical Review* 10 (1929): 129-35.

Clayton, Robert. "Extracts From the Orderly Book of Major Robert Clayton, of the Seventeenth Regiment, British Foot, 1778." Edited by John W. Jordan. *Pennsylvania Magazine of History and Biography* 25 (1901): 100-103.

Clinton, Henry. *The American Rebellion: Sir Henry Clinton's Narrative of His Campaigns, 1775-1782, With an Appendix of Original Documents.* Edited by William B. Willcox. New Haven: Yale University Press, 1954.

Clode, Charles M. *The Military Forces of the Crown: Their Administration and Government.* 2 vols. London: John Murray, 1869.

Copeland, Peter F., and Haarmann, Albert W. "The Provisional Chasseur Companies of Hesse-Cassel During the Revolutionary War." *Military Collector and Historian* 18 (1966): 11-13.

Cornwallis, Charles. *Correspondence of Charles, 1st Marquis Cornwallis.* Edited by Charles Ross. 3 vols. London: J. Murray, 1859.

Corsar, Kenneth Charles, ed. "Letters From America, 1780 and 1781." *Journal of the Society for Army Historical Research* 20 (1941): 130-35.

Cruickshank, C. G. *Elizabeth's Army.* 2d ed. New York: Oxford University Press, 1966.

Cruickshank, E. A. "The King's Royal Regiment of New York." *Ontario Historical Society Papers and Records* 27 (1931): 193-323.

Cuneo, John R. "The Early Days of the Queen's Rangers, August 1776-February 1977." *Military Affairs* 22 (1958): 65-74.

Curtis, Edward E. *Organization of the British Army in the American Revolution.* New Haven: Yale University Press, 1926.

_____. "The Recruiting of the British Army in the American Revolution." *American Historical Association Annual Report* for 1922: 311-22.

De Fonblanque, Edward B. *Political and Military Episodes in the Latter Half of the Eighteenth Century Derived From the Life and Correspondence of the Rt. Hon. John Burgoyne, General Statesman, Dramatist.* London: Macmillan & Co., 1876.

Dippel, Horst. "Sources in Germany for the Study of the American Revolution." *Quarterly Journal of the Library of Congress* 33 (1976): 199-217.

Dohla, Johann Conrad. *Tagebuch eines Bayreuther Soldaten, des Johann Conrad Dohla, aus dem nordamerikanischen Freiheitskrieg von 1777 bis 1783.* Bayreuth: Burger, 1913.

Dornfest, Walter T. "The Royal Garrison Battalion, 1778-1784." *Journal of the Society for Army Historical Research* 47 (1969): 55-69; 51 (1973): 124-25.

Du Roi, August Wilhelm. *Journal of Du Roi the Elder, Lieutenant and Adjutant, in the Service of the Duke of Brunswick, 1776-1778.* Translated by Charlotte S. J. Epping. New York: D. Appleton & Co., 1911.

East, Robert A., and Judd, Jacob, eds. *The Loyalist Americans: A Focus on Greater New York.* Tarrytown: Sleepy Hollow Restorations, 1975.

Eelking, Max von. *German Allied Troops in the North American War.* Translated by J. G. Rosengarten. Albany: Joel Munsell's Sons, 1893.

[Egli, Clara, trans.] "Diary of a Voyage From Stade in Hanover to Quebec in America of the Second Division of Ducal Brunswick Mercenaries." *Quarterly Journal of the New York State Historical Association* 8 (1927): 323-51.

Evelyn, W. Glanville. *Memoir and Letters of Captain W. Glanville Evelyn, of the 4th Regiment ("King's Own"), From North America, 1774-1776.* Edited by G. D. Scull. Oxford: James Parker & Co., 1879.

Ewald, Johann. *Diary of the American War: A Hessian Journal.* Translated by Joseph P. Tustin. New Haven: Yale University Press, 1979.

Fann, Willerd R. "On the Infantryman's Age in Eighteenth Century Prussia." *Military Affairs* 41 (1977): 165-70.

Fellows, Jo-Ann, ed. "A Bibliography of Loyalist Source Material in Canada." *American Antiquarian Society Proceedings* 82 (1972): 67-270.

Ferling, John E. "Joseph Galloway's Military Advice: A Loyalist's View of the Revolution." *Pennsylvania Magazine of History and Biography* 98 (1974): 171-88.

Firth, C. H. *Cromwell's Army: A History of the English Soldier During the Civil Wars, the Commonwealth and the Protectorate.* 1902. Reprint (4th ed.). London: Methuen & Co., 1962.

Ford, Worthington C., comp. *British Officers Serving in the American Revolution 1774-1783.* Brooklyn: Historical Printing Club, 1897.

Fortescue, John W. *A History of the British Army.* 13 vols. and 6 atlases. London: Macmillan & Co., 1899-1935.

French, Allen. *General Gage's Informers: New Material Upon Lexington and Concord; Benjamin Thompson as Loyalist and the Treachery of Benjamin Church, Jr.* Ann Arbor: University of Michigan Press, 1932.

Fuller, J. F. C. *British Light Infantry in the Eighteenth Century (an Introduction to "Sir John Moore's System of Training").* London: Hutchinson & Co., 1925.

_____. "The Revival and Training of Light Infantry in the British Army, 1757-1806." *Journal of the Royal United Service Institution* 57 (1913): 1187-1214.

_____. *Sir John Moore's System of Training.* London: Hutchinson & Co., 1924.

Gage, Thomas. *The Correspondence of General Thomas Gage With the Secretaries of State, 1763-1775.* Edited by Clarence E. Carter. 2 vols. New Haven: Yale University Press, 1931-33.

Gee, Olive. "The British War Office in the Later Years of the American War of Independence." *Journal of Modern History* 26 (1954): 123-36.

George III (George William Frederick). *The Correspondence of King George the Third From 1760 to December 1783.* Edited by John W. Fortesque. 2d ed. 6 vols. London: Frank Cass & Co., 1967.

Glover, Richard. *Peninsular Preparation: The Reform of the British Army, 1795-1809.* Cambridge: Cambridge University Press, 1963.

Godfrey, Carlos E. "Muster Rolls of Three Troops of Loyalist Light Dragoons Raised in Pennsylvania, 1777-1778." *Pennsylvania Magazine of History and Biography* 34 (1910): 1-8.

Gradish, Stephen F. "The German Mercenaries in North America During the American Revolution: A Case Study." *Canadian Journal of History* 4 (1969): 23-46.

Graham, Samuel. "An English Officer's Account of His Services in America—1779-1781." *Historical Magazine* 9 (1865): 241-49, 267-74, 301-8, 329-35.

Gruber, Ira D. *The Howe Brothers and the American Revolution.* Chapel Hill: University of North Carolina Press, 1972.

Guthorn, Peter J. *British Maps of the American Revolution.* Monmouth Beach, N.J.: Philip Freneau Press, 1972.

_____. "A Hessian Map From the American Revolution: Its Origin and Purpose." *Quarterly Journal of the Library of Congress* 33 (1976): 219-31.

Haarmann, Albert W. "American Provincial Corps Authorized by Lord Dunmore, 1775." *Journal of the Society for Army Historical Research* 52 (1974): 254-55.

_____. "Contemporary Observations on the Hesse-Cassel Troops Sent to North America, 1776–1781." *Journal of the Society for Army Historical Research* 54 (1976): 130–34.

_____. "The Hessian Army and the Corps in North America, 1776–1783." *Military Collector and Historian* 14 (1962): 69–75.

_____. "Notes on the Brunswick Troops in British Service During the American War of Independence, 1776–1783." *Journal of the Society for Army Historical Research* 48 (1970): 140–43; 51 (1973): 123.

_____. "Printed German Army Lists, 1775–1783." *Journal of the Society for Army Historical Research* 51 (1973): 182–83.

_____. "The Roman Catholic Volunteers, 1777–1778." *Journal of the Society for Army Historical Research* 49 (1971): 184–85.

_____. "The 3d Waldeck Regiment in British Service, 1776–1783." *Journal of the Society for Army Historical Research* 48 (1970): 182–85.

Hayes-McCoy, G. A. "Strategy and Tactics in Irish Welfare, 1593–1601." *Irish Historical Studies* 2 (1941): 255–79.

Heinrichs, Johann. "Extracts From the Letter-Book of Captain Johann Heinrichs of the Hessian Jager Corps, 1778–1780." Translated by Julian F. Sachse. *Pennsylvania Magazine of History and Biography* 22 (1898): 137–70.

Herbert, Charles. "Coxheath Camp, 1778–1779." *Journal of the Society for Army Historical Research* 14 (1967): 129–48.

[Heusler, Captain, ed.] "The Brunswick Contingent in America, 1776–1783." *Pennsylvania Magazine of History and Biography* 15 (1891): 218–24.

Higham, Robin, ed. *A Guide to the Sources of British Military History.* Berkeley: University of California Press, 1971.

Historical Manuscripts Commission. *Report on American Manuscripts in the Royal Institution of Great Britain.* 4 vols. London: His Majesty's Stationery Office, 1904–9.

_____. *Report on the Manuscripts of Mrs. Stopford-Sackville, of Drayton House, Northamptonshire.* 2 vols. London: His Majesty's Stationery Office, 1904–10.

Howe, William. *General Sir William Howe's Orderly Book at Charlestown, Boston and Halifax, June 17, 1775 to 1776, 26 May; to Which Is Added the Official Abridgement of General Howe's Correspondence With the English Government During the Siege of Boston, and Some Military Returns, and Now First Printed From the Original Manuscripts.* Edited by Franklin Benjamin Stevens. 1890. Reprint. Port Washington, N.Y.: Kennikat Press, 1970.

Hughes, Thomas. *A Journal by Thos. Hughes for His Amusement, and Designed Only for His Perusal by the Time He Attained the Age of 50 If He Lives So Long (1778–1789).* Edited by E. A. Benians. Cambridge: Cambridge University Press, 1947.

Huth, Hans. "Letters From a Hessian Mercenary." Translated by C. V. Easum. *Pennsylvania Magazine of History and Biography* 62 (1938): 488–501.

Inman, George. "Losses of the Military and Naval Forces Engaged in the War of the American Revolution." *Pennsylvania Magazine of History and Biography* 27 (1903): 176–205.

Ippel, Henry Peter. "Jeffrey, Lord Amherst, British Commander-in-Chief, 1778–1782." Ph.D. dissertation, University of Michigan, 1957.

Johnston, S. H. F. "The Irish Establishment." *Irish Sword* 1 (1949): 33–36.

Kapp, Frederick, ed. "Report of the Court-Martial for the Trial of the Hessian Officers Captured by Washington at Trenton." *Pennsylvania Magazine of History and Biography* 7 (1883): 45–49.

Katcher, Philip R. N. "Loyalist Militia in the War of American Independence." *Journal of the Society for Army Historical Research* 54 (1976): 136–39.

_____. "The Provincial Corps of the British Army, 1775–1783." *Journal of the Society for Army Historical Research* 54 (1976): 164–71.

Kelby, William, ed. *Orderly Book of the Three Battalions of Loyalists Commanded by Brigadier-General Oliver De Lancey, 1776–1778.* New York: New-York Historical Society, 1917.

Kellogg, Louise Phelps, ed. "Journal of a British Officer During the American Revolution." *Mississippi Valley Historical Review* 7 (1920): 51–58.

Kemble, Stephen. "Journal of Lieut.-Col. Stephen Kemble, 1773–1789; and British Army Orders: Gen. Sir William Howe, 1775–1778; Gen. Sir Henry Clinton, 1778; and Gen. Daniel Jones, 1778." *New-York Historical Society Collections* for 1884.

Kipping, Ernst. *Die Truppen von Hessian-Kassel im amerikanischen Unabhangig-keitskrieg, 1776–1783.* Darmstadt: Wehr & Wissen Verlagsgesellchaft M. B. H., 1965.

Krafft, John Charles Philip von. "Journal of Lieutenant John Charles Philip von Krafft." *New-York Historical Society Collections* for 1882.

Kyte, George W. "Introduction to the Periodical Literature on Middle Colony Loyalists in the American Revolution." *Pennsylvania History* 18 (1951): 104–18.

Lamb, R. *An Original and Authentic Journal of Occurrences During the Late American War, From Its Commencement to the Year 1783.* Dublin: Wilkinson & Courtney, 1809.

LeRoy, Percy Eugene. "Sir Guy Carleton as a Military Leader During the American Invasion and Repulse in Canada, 1775–1776." Ph.D. dissertation, Ohio State University, 1960.

Lowell, E. J. *The Hessians and Other German Auxiliaries of Great Britain in the Revolutionary War.* New York: Harper & Bros., 1884.

McAnally, Henry. *The Irish Militia, 1793–1816; a Social and Military Study.* Dublin: Clonmore & Reynolds, 1949.

McDonald, Alexander. "Letter-Book of Captain Alexander McDonald, 1775–1779." *New-York Historical Society Collections* for 1882: 203–498.

MacKenzie, Frederick. *Diary of Frederick MacKenzie, Giving a Daily Narrative of His Military Service as an Officer of the Regiment of Royal Welch Fusileers During the Years 1775–1781 in Massachusetts, Rhode Island and New York.* 2 vols. Cambridge: Harvard University Press, 1930.

Mackesy, Piers. "British Strategy in the War of American Independence." *Yale Review* 71 (1963): 539–57.

Marshall, Douglas W. "The British Military Engineers, 1741–1783: A Study of Organization, Social Origin, and Cartography." Ph.D. dissertation, University of Michigan, 1976.

Mathew, Edward. "Mathew's Narrative." Edited by Thomas Balch. *Historical Magazine* 1 (1857): 102–6.

Melsheimer, F[rederick] V[alentine]. *Journal of the Voyage of the Brunswick Auxiliaries From Wolfenbeutel to Quebec.* Edited by William Wood and William L. Stone. Quebec: Morning Chronicle Steam Printing Establishment, 1891.

Meyer, Mary K., and Bachman, Virginia B. "The First Battalion of Maryland Loyalists." *Maryland Historical Magazine* 68 (1973): 199-210.

Miller, E. Arnold. "Some Arguments Used by English Pamphleteers, 1697-1700, Concerning a Standing Army." *Journal of Modern History* 18 (1946): 306-13.

Montressor, John. "Journal of Captain John Montressor, July 1, 1777, to July 1, 1778." Edited by G. D. Scull. *Pennsylvania Magazine of History and Biography* 5 (1881): 393-417; 6 (1882): 34-57, 189-206, 284-99.

Moody, James. *Lieut. James Moody's Narrative of His Exertions and Sufferings in the Cause of Government, Since the Year 1776; Authenticated by Proper Certificates.* 2d ed. London: Richardson & Urquhart, 1783.

Mowat, Charles L. "The Southern Brigade: A Sidelight on the British Military Establishment in America, 1763-1775." *Journal of Southern History* 10 (1944): 59-77.

Muenchhausen, Friedrich von. *At General Howe's Side: The Diary of General Howe's Aide de Camp, Captain Friedrich von Muenchhausen.* Edited and translated by Ernst Kipping and Samuel S. Smith. Monmouth Beach, N.J.: Philip Freneau Press, 1974.

Murdock, Harold. *Earl Percy Dines Abroad: A Boswellian Episode.* Boston: Houghton Mifflin Co., 1924.

Nelson, Paul David. "British Conduct of the American Revolutionary War: A Review of Interpretations." *Journal of American History* 65 (1978): 623-53.

Nelson, William H. *The American Tory.* London: Oxford University Press, 1961.

O'Hara, Charles. "Letters of Charles O'Hara to the Duke of Grafton." Edited by George C. Rogers, Jr. *South Carolina Historical Magazine* 65 (1964): 158-80.

Oliver, Peter. *Origin and Progress of the American Rebellion.* Edited by Douglas Adair and John Schutz. San Marino, Calif.: Huntington Library, 1961.

Olson, Gary D. "Thomas Brown, Loyalist Partisan, and the Revolutionary War in Georgia, 1777-1782." *Georgia Historical Quarterly* 54 (1970): 1-19, 183-208.

Omond, J. S. *Parliament and the Army, 1642-1904.* Cambridge: Cambridge University Press, 1933.

O'Snodaigh, Padraig. "Some Police and Military Aspects of the Irish Volunteers." *Irish Sword* 13 (1978-79): 217-29.

Parfitt, G. Archer. "91st Foot or Ackland's Loyal Shropshire Regiment, Otherwise Known as the Shropshire Volunteers, 1779-1783." *Journal of the Society for Army Historical Research* 47 (1969): 225-32.

Partridge, Bellamy. *Sir Billy Howe.* London: Longmans, Green & Co., 1932.

Pattison, James. "Official Letters of Major General James Pattison." *New-York Historical Society Collections* for 1875: 1-432.

Pausch, Georg. *Journal of Captain Pausch, Chief of the Hanau Artillery During the Burgoyne Campaign.* Translated by William L. Stone. Albany: Joel Munsell's Sons, 1886.

Peckham, Howard H. "Sir Henry Clinton's Review of Simcoe's *Journal.*" *William and Mary Quarterly*, 2d ser., 21 (1941): 360-70.

Pell, Joshua, Jr. "Diary of Joshua Pell, Junior, an Officer of the British Army in America, 1776-1777." Edited by James L. Onderdonk. *Magazine of American History* 2 (1878): 43-47, 107-12.

Percy, Hugh. *Letters of Hugh Earl Percy From Boston and New York, 1774-1776.* Edited by Charles Knowles Bolton: Charles L. Goodspeed, 1902.

Popp, Stephen. *A Hessian Soldier in the American Revolution: The Diary of Stephen Popp.* Translated by Reinhart Pope, Jr. Privately printed, 1953.

Public Record Office. *Alphabetical Guide to War Office and Other Military Records Preserved in the Public Record Office.* London: His Majesty's Stationery Office, 1931.

――――. *List of War Office Records.* London: His Majesty's Stationery Office, 1908.

Rainsford, Charles. "Transactions as Commissary for Embarking Foreign Troops in the English Service From Germany With Copies of Letters Relative to It, for the Years 1776–1777." *New-York Historical Society Collections* for 1879: 313–543.

Riedesel, Frederick Augustus von. *Memoirs, and Letters and Journals, of Major General Riedesel, During His Residence in America, Translated From the Original German of Max von Eelking.* Translated by William L. Stone. 2 vols. Albany: J. Munsell, 1868.

Riedesel, Frederika von. *Baroness von Riedesel and the American Revolution: Journal and Correspondence of a Tour of Duty, 1776–1783.* Edited by Marvin L. Brown. Chapel Hill: University of North Carolina Press, 1965.

Robson, Eric. "British Light Infantry in the Mid-Eighteenth Century: The Effect of American Conditions." *Army Quarterly* 63 (1952): 209–22.

――――. "Purchase and Promotion in the British Army in the Eighteenth Century." *History*, new ser., 36 (1951): 57–72.

――――. "The Raising of a Regiment in the War of American Independence." *Journal of the Society for Army Historical Research* 27 (1949): 107–15.

Robertson, Archibald. *Archibald Robertson, Lieutenant-General, Royal Engineers: His Diaries and Sketches in America, 1762–1780.* Edited by Harry Miller Lydenberg. New York: New York Public Library, 1930.

Russell, Peter. "The Siege of Charleston: Journal of Captain Peter Russell, December 25, 1779, to May 2, 1780." Edited by James Bain, Jr. *American Historical Review* 4 (1899): 478–501.

Sabine, Lorenzo. "The Tory Contingent in the British Army in America in 1781." *Historical Magazine* 8 (1864): 321–26, 354–59, 389–92.

Savory, Reginald. *His Britannic Majesty's Army in Germany During the Seven Years' War.* Oxford: Clarendon Press, 1966.

Schmidt, H. D. "The Hessian Mercenaries: The Career of a Political Cliche." *History* 43 (1958): 207–12.

Schwoerer, Lois G. *"No Standing Armies!": The Antiarmy Ideology in Seventeenth-Century England.* Baltimore: Johns Hopkins University Press, 1974.

Scouller, R. E. *The Armies of Queen Anne.* Oxford: Clarendon Press, 1966.

Searle, Ambrose. *The American Journal of Ambrose Searle, Secretary to Lord Howe, 1776–1778.* Edited by Edward H. Tatum, Jr. San Marino, Calif.: Huntington Library, 1940.

Seumes, J. G. "Memoirs of a Hessian Conscript: J. G. Seumes' Reluctant Voyage to America." Translated by Margarete Woelfel. *William and Mary Quarterly*, 3d ser., 5 (1949): 533–70.

Shy, John. *Toward Lexington: The Role of the British Army in the Coming of the American Revolution.* Princeton: Princeton University Press, 1965.

Siebert, Wilbur Henry. "The Loyalist Troops of New England." *New England Quarterly* 4 (1931): 108–47.

Simcoe, John Graves. *Simcoe's Military Journal: A History of the Operations of a Partisan Corps, Called the Queen's Rangers, Commanded by Lieut. Col. J. G. Simcoe, During the War of the American Revolution.* New York: Bartlett & Welford, 1844.

Slagle, Robert Oakley. "The Von Lossberg Regiment: A Chronicle of Hessian Participation in the American Revolution." Ph.D. dissertation, American University, 1965.

Smith, Paul H. *Loyalists and Redcoats: A Study in British Revolutionary Policy.* Chapel Hill: University of North Carolina Press, 1964.

Spector, Margaret M. *The American Department of the British Government, 1768-1782.* New York: Columbia University Press, 1940.

Stevens, Enos. "A Fragment of the Diary of Lieutenant Enos Stevens, Tory, 1777-1778." Edited by Charles Knowles Bolton. *New England Quarterly* 11 (1938): 374-88.

Stone, William L., trans. *Letters of Brunswick and Hessian Officers During the American Revolution.* Albany: Joel Munsell's sons, 1891.

Stryker, William S. *"The New Jersey Volunteers" (Loyalists) in the Revolutionary War.* Trenton: Naar, Day & Naar, 1887.

Sullivan, Thomas. "The Common British Soldier—From the Journal of Thomas Sullivan, 49th Regiment of Foot." Edited by S. Sydney Bradford. *Maryland Historical Magazine* 62 (1967): 219-53.

Tarleton, Banastre. "New War Letters of Banastre Tarleton." Edited by Richard M. Ketchum. *New-York Historical Society Quarterly* 51 (1967): 61-81.

Tebbenhoff, Edward H. "The Associated Loyalists: An Aspect of Militant Loyalism." *New-York Historical Society Quarterly* 63 (1979): 115-44.

Uhlendorf, Bernard A., ed. *The Siege of Charleston With an Account of the Province of South Carolina: Diaries and Letters of Hessian Officers From the von Jungkenn Papers in the William L. Clements Library.* Ann Arbor: University of Michigan Press, 1938.

Valentine, Alan. *Lord George Germain.* New York: Oxford University Press, 1962.
_____. *Lord North.* 2 vols. Norman: University of Oklahoma Press, 1967.

Waldeck, Philipp. *Philipp Waldeck's Diary of the American Revolution.* Edited by Marion Dexter Learned. Philadelphia: Americana Germanica Press, 1907.

Walton, Clifford. *History of the British Standing Army, A.D.1660 to 1700.* London: Harrison & Sons, 1894.

Ward, S. G. P. *Wellington's Headquarters: A Study of the Administrative Problems in the Peninsula, 1809-1814.* Oxford: Oxford University Press, 1957.

Webb, Henry J. "Elizabethan Field Artillery." *Military Affairs* 19 (1955): 197-202.
_____. *Elizabethan Military Science: The Books and the Practice.* Madison: University of Wisconsin Press, 1965.

Weinmeister, Oscar K., Jr. "The Hessian Grenadier Battalions in North America, 1776-1783." *Military Collector and Historian* 27 (1975): 148-53.

Western, John R. *The English Militia in the Eighteenth Century: The Study of a Political Issue, 1660-1802.* London: Routledge & Kegan Paul, 1965.

White, A. S. *Bibliography of Regimental Histories of the British Army.* London: Society for Army Historical Research, 1965.

Whitworth, Rex. *Field Marshal Lord Ligonier: A Story of the British Army 1702–1770.* New York: Oxford University Press, 1958.

Wickwire, Franklin, and Wickwire, Mary. *Cornwallis: The American Adventure.* Boston: Houghton Mifflin Co., 1970.

Wiederhold, Andreas. "The Capture of Fort Washington, New York, Described by Captain Andreas Wiederhold, of the Hessian 'Regiment Knyphausen.' " *Pennsylvania Magazine of History and Biography* 23 (1899): 95–97.

_____. "Colonel Rall at Trenton." *Pennsylvania Magazine of History and Biography* 22 (1898): 462–67.

Willcox, William B. "The British Road to Yorktown: A Study in Divided Command." *American Historical Review* 52 (1946): 1–35.

_____. "British Strategy in America, 1778." *Journal of Modern History* 19 (1947): 97–121.

_____. *Portrait of a General: Sir Henry Clinton in the War of Independence.* New York: Alfred A. Knopf, 1964.

_____. "Rhode Island in British Strategy, 1780–1781." *Journal of Modern History* 17 (1945): 304–31.

_____. "Too Many Cooks: British Planning Before Saratoga." *Journal of British Studies* 2 (1962): 56–90.

French Forces

Balch, Elise Willing. "Marquis de Fleury, Lieutenant-Colonel in the Continental Army." *Magazine of American History* 1 (1877): 724–26.

Balch, Thomas. *The French in America During the War of Independence.* 2 vols. Philadelphia: Porter & Coates, 1891–95.

Blanchard, Claude. *The Journal of Claude Blanchard, Commissary of the French Auxiliary Army Sent to the United States During the American Revolution, 1780–1783.* Translated by William Duane and edited by Thomas Balch. Albany: Joel Munsell, 1876.

Bodinier, Gilbert. "Les Officiers du corps expeditionnaire de Rochambeau et la Revolution francaise. *Revue historique des armees* 3 (1976): 139–63.

Chastellux, Marquis de. *Travels in North-America, in the Years 1780, 1781, and 1782; Translated From the French by an English Gentleman, Who Resided in America at That Period.* 2 vols. London: G. G. J. and J. Robinson, 1787.

Cilleuls, J. des. "Jean-Francois Coste (1741–1819), medecin en chef de l'armee de Rochambeau; premier maire de Versailles (1790–1792)." *Revue historique des armees* 4 (1977): 2–27.

Constantini, A. "Le Corps Rochambeau face aux difficultes economiques de royaume et des Etats-Unis d'Amerique (1780–1782)." *Revue historique des armees* 3 (1976): 107–37.

Contenson, Ludovic. *La Societe des Cincinnati de France et la guerre d'Amerique, 1778–1783.* Paris: Auguste Picard, 1934.

Dawson, Warrington. "Les 2,112 Francais morts aux Etats-Unis de 1777 a 1783 en combattant pour l'independance americaine." *Journal de la Societe des americanistes,* new ser., 28 (1936): 1–154.

Deux-Ponts, Count Guillaume de. *My Campaigns in America: A Journal Kept by*

Count William De Deux-Ponts, 1780–81. Translated and edited by Samuel Abbott Green. Boston: J. K. Wiggin & Wm. Parsons Lunt, 1868.

[du Bourg, Baron Cromot?] "Diary of a French Officer, 1781 (Presumed To Be That of Baron Cromot du Bourg, Aide to Rochambeau)." Edited by C. Fiske Harris. *Magazine of American History* 4 (1880): 204–14, 293–308, 376–85, 441–52; 7 (1881): 283–95.

Dull, Jonathan R. *The French Navy and American Independence, 1774–1789.* Princeton: Princeton University Press, 1975.

Edmunds, Albert J., trans. "Letters of a French Officer, Written at Easton, Penna., in 1777–1778." *Pennsylvania Magazine of History and Biography* 35 (1911): 90–102.

Fersen, Hans Axel von. "Letters of De Fersen, Aide-de-Camp to Rochambeau, Written to His Father in Sweden." *Magazine of American History* 3 (1879): 300–309, 369–76, 437–48.

Fonteneau, le General. "La Periode francaise de la guerre d'Independance (1776–1780)." *Revue historique des armees* 3 (1976): 47–85.

France. Ministere des Affaires Etrangeres. *Les Combattants Francaises de la guerre americaine, 1778–1783; listes establie d'apres les documents deposes aux Archives nationales et aux Archives du ministere de la Guerre; publiees par les soins du ministere des Affaires Etrangeres.* Paris: Ancienne Maison Quantin, 1903; Washington: Government Printing Office, 1905.

Gardner, Asa Bird. *The Order of the Cincinnati in France.* Rhode Island State Society of the Cincinnati, 1905.

Kennett, Lee. *The French Forces in America, 1780–1783.* Westport, Conn.: Greenwood Press, 1977.

Lauzun, Armand Louis de Gontaut, Duc de. *Memoirs of the Duc de Lauzun.* Translated by C. K. Scott Moncreiff. London: George Routledge & Sons, 1928.

Lewis, Charles L. *Admiral de Grasse and American Independence.* Annapolis: United States Naval Institute, 1945.

Merlant, Joachim. *Soldiers and Sailors of France in the American War of Independence.* Translated by Mary Bushnell Coleman. New York: Charles Scribner's Sons, 1920.

Montmort, Roger, Comte de. *Antoine Charles du Houx, Baron de Viomenil, Lieutenant-General of the Armies of the King, Second in Command Under Rochambeau.* Translated by John Francis Gough. Baltimore: Johns Hopkins University Press, 1935.

Moran, Charles. "D'Estaing, an Early Exponent of Amphibious Warfare." *Military Affairs* 9 (1945): 314–32.

Murphy, Orville Theodore, Jr. "French Contemporary Opinion of the American Revolutionary Army." Ph.D. dissertation, University of Minnesota, 1957.

Noailles, Amblard-Marie-Raymond Amedee, Vicomte de. *Marins et soldats francaises en Amerique pendant la guerre de l'independance des Etats-Unis, 1778–1783.* Paris: Perrin & Cie., 1903.

Rice, Howard C., Jr., and Brown, Anne S. K., eds. *The American Campaigns of Rochambeau's Army, 1780, 1781, 1782, 1783.* 2 vols. Princeton: Princeton University Press; Providence: Brown University Press, 1972.

Rochambeau, Jean Baptiste Donatien de Vimeur, Comte de. *Memoirs of the Marshal*

Court de Rochambeau, Relative to the War of Independence of the United States. Translated by M. W. E. Wright (from the original edition of 1808). Paris: French, English, & American Library, 1838.

_____. "Rochambeau's 'Memoire de la guerre en Amerique.' " Edited by Claude C. Sturgill. *Virginia Magazine of History and Biography* 78 (1970): 34–64.

Saint-Marc, Meyronnet de. "Meyronnet de Saint-Marc's Journal of the Operations of the French Army Under D'Estaing at the Siege of Savannah, September, 1779." *New-York Historical Society Quarterly* 36 (1952): 255–87.

Stone, Edward Martin. *Our French Allies; Rochambeau and His Army, Lafayette and His Devotion, D'Estaing, DeTernay, Barras, De Grasse and Their Fleets in the Great War of the American Revolution From 1778 to 1782, Including Military Operations in Rhode Island, the Surrender of Yorktown Sketches of French and American Officers, and Incidents of Social Life in Newport, Providence, and Elsewhere.* Providence: Providence Press Co., 1884.

Von Closen, Baron Ludwig. *The Revolutionary Journal of Baron Ludwig Von Closen, 1780–1783.* Translated and edited by Evelyn M. Acomb. Chapel Hill: University of North Carolina Press, 1958.

Wheelen, Jean-Edmond. *Rochambeau, Father and Son; a Life of the Marechal de Rochambeau and the Journal of the Vicomte de Rochambeau (Hitherto Unpublished).* Translated by Lawrence Lee. New York: Holt, 1936.

Whitridge, Arnold. *Rochambeau.* New York: Macmillan Co., 1965.

Spanish Forces

Bobb, Bernard E. *The Viceregency of Antonio Maria Bucareli in New Spain, 1771–1779.* Austin: University of Texas Press, 1962.

Caughey, John Walton. *Bernardo de Galvez in Louisiana, 1776–1783.* Berkeley: University of California Press, 1934.

Cummins, Light Townsend. "Spanish Agents in North America During the Revolution, 1775–1779." Ph.D. dissertation, Tulane University, 1977.

Holmes, Jack D. L. *A Guide to Spanish Louisiana, 1762–1806.* New Orleans: Louisiana Collection Series, 1970.

Lewis, James Allen. "New Spain During the American Revolution, 1779–1783: A Viceroyalty at War." Ph.D. dissertation, Duke University, 1975.

Nasatir, Abraham P. *Borderland in Retreat: From Spanish Louisiana to the Far Southwest.* Albuquerque: University of New Mexico Press, 1976.

NAVAL ASPECTS

Allard, Dean C. "The Potomac Navy of 1776." *Virginia Magazine of History and Biography* 84 (1976): 411–30.

Allen, Gardner Weld. *A Naval History of the American Revolution.* 2 vols. Boston: Houghton, Mifflin, 1913.

Barrington, Samuel. *Letters and Papers of Admiral the Hon. Samuel Barrington.* Edited by D. Bonner-Smith. 2 vols. London: Naval Records Society, 1937–41.

Besson, Maurice. *Le Comte d'Estaing, colonel aux Indes, gouveneur de Saint-Domingue, vice-admiral sous la guerre d'Independance, 1729–1794.* Paris: Larousse, 1931.

Bolton, Reginald Pelham. "The British Navy in the Revolution." *Magazine of History* 2 (1905): 223-27.

Brewington, Marion V. "The Design of Our First Frigates." *American Neptune* 8 (1948): 11-25.

Brisout de Barneville, Nicolas Francois Denis. "Journal de guerre de Brisout de Barneville, mai 1780—octobre 1781." *French-American Review* 3 (1950): 217-78.

Calmon-Maison, Jean J. *L'Admiral d'Estaing (1729-1794)*. Paris: Calmann-Levy, 1910.

Clark, William Bell. "American Naval Policy, 1775-1776." *American Neptune* 1 (1941): 26-41.

———. *George Washington's Navy: Being an Account of His Excellency's Fleet in New England Waters*. Baton Rouge: Louisiana State University Press, 1960.

Clark, William Bell, et al., eds. *Naval Documents of the American Revolution*. Washington: Department of the Navy, 1964-.

Dawson, Francis Warrington, ed. "The Chevalier d'Ancteville and His Journal of the 'Chesapeake Campaign.'" *Legion d'honneur* 2 (1931): 83-96.

Dull, Jonathan R. *The French Navy and American Independence: A Study of Arms and Diplomacy, 1774-1787*. Princeton: Princeton University Press, 1975.

Everett, Sidney. "The Chevalier de Ternay." *New England Historical and Genealogical Review* 27 (1873): 404-18.

Fowler, William M., Jr. "James Nicholson and the Continental Frigate *Virginia*." *American Neptune* 24 (1974): 135-41.

———. "The New York Frigates." *American Neptune* 38 (1978): 15-27.

———. *Rebels Under Sail: The American Navy During the Revolution*. New York: Charles Scribner's Sons, 1976.

Gardiner, Robert. "The Frigate Designs of 1755-1757." *Mariner's Mirror* 63 (1977): 51-69.

Grasse, Comte Alexandre Francois Auguste de. *Notice biographique sur l'amiral comte de Grasse (Francois-Joseph-Paul), de'apres les documents inedits communiques par M. le comte Alexandre-Francois-Auguste de Grasse, son fils*. Paris: Imprimerie de E.-J. Bailly, 1840.

Green, William. *The Memoranda of William Green, Secretary to Vice-Admiral Marriot Arbuthnot in the American Revolution*. Edited by Henry S. Fraser. Providence: Rhode Island Historical Society, 1924.

Jackson, John W. *The Pennsylvania Navy, 1775-1781: The Defense of the Delaware*. New Brunswick: Rutgers University Press, 1974.

James, William. *The British Navy in Adversity: A Study of the War of American Independence*. London: Longmans, Green & Co., 1926.

Jarvis, John. "Letters of Captain Sir John Jarvis to Sir Henry Clinton, 1774-1782." Edited by Marie Martel Hatch. *American Neptune* 7 (1947): 87-106.

Keith, George Keith Elphinstone, Viscount. *The Keith Papers, Selected From the Letters and Papers of Admiral Viscount Keith*. Edited by W. G. Perrin and Christopher Lloyd. 3 vols. London: Navy Records Society, 1927.

Kerallain, Rene Prigent de. *Bougainville a l'armee de cte. de Grasse, guerre d'Amerique, 1781-1782*. Paris: Maisonneuve freres, 1930.

———. *Bougainville a l'escadre du cte. d'Estaing, guerre d'Amerique, 1778-1779*. Paris: Maisonneuve freres, 1927.

Lacour-Gayet, Georges. *La marine militaire de la France sous le regne de Louis XVI.* Paris: Honore Champion, 1905.

Lavery, Brian. "The Origins of the 74-Gun Ship." *Mariner's Mirror* 63 (1977): 335–47.

Lewis, Charles L. *Admiral de Grasse and American Independence.* Annapolis: United States Naval Institute, 1945.

Lincoln, Charles H. *Naval Records of the American Revolution, 1775–1788.* Washington: Government Printing Office, 1906.

Linyer de la Barbee, Maurice. *Le Chevalier de Ternay; vie de Charles Henry Louis d'Arsac de Ternay, chef d'escadre des armees navales, 1723–1780.* 2 vols. Grenoble: Editions des 4 Seigneurs, 1972.

Lynch, Barbara A., comp. *The War at Sea: France and the American Revolution, a Bibliography.* Washington: Department of the Navy, 1976.

Mahan, Alfred T. *The Major Operations of the Navies in the American War of Independence.* Boston: Little, Brown & Co., 1913.

Manwaring, George Ernest. *A Bibliography of British Naval History; a Biographical and Historical Guide to Printed and Manuscript Sources.* London: G. Routledge & Sons, 1930.

Marcus, G[eoffrey] J. *Hearts of Oak: A Survey of British Sea Power in the Georgian Era.* Oxford: Oxford University Press, 1975.

Mason, George C. "British Fleet in Rhode Island." *Rhode Island Historical Society Collections* 7 (1885): 301–25.

Maurer, Maurer. "Coppered Bottoms for the Royal Navy: A Factor in the Maritime War of 1778–1783." *Military Affairs* 14 (1950): 57–61.

Mervine, William M., ed. "Excerpts From the Master's Log of His Majesty's Ship *Eagle*, Lord Howe's Flagship, 1776–1777." *Pennsylvania Magazine of History and Biography* 38 (1914): 211–26.

Mevers, Frank Clement. "Congress and the Navy: The Establishment and Administration of the American Revolutionary Navy by the Continental Congress, 1775–1784." Ph.D. dissertation, University of North Carolina at Chapel Hill, 1972.

Miller, Nathan. *Sea of Glory; the Continental Navy Fights for Independence, 1775–1783.* New York: McKay, 1974.

Moomaw, William Hugh. "The Naval Career of Captain Hammond, 1775–1779." Ph.D. dissertation, University of Virginia, 1955.

Mouzon, Harold A. *"Defence,* A Vessel of the Navy of South Carolina." *American Neptune* 13 (1953): 29–50.

[O'Beirne, Thomas Lewis.] *A Candid and Impartiall Narrative of the Transactions of the Fleet. . . .* 2d ed. London: J. Almon, [1779].

Paullin, Charles O. *Navy of the American Revolution: Its Administration, Its Policy, and Its Achievements.* Cleveland: Burroughs Bros., 1906.

Revel, Gabriel Joachim du Perron, Comte de. *Journal particulier d'une compagne aux Indes occidentales (1781–1782).* Paris: H. Charles-Lavauzelle, 1898.

Roelker, William G., ed. "Patrol of Narragansett Bay (1774–1776)." *Rhode Island History* 7 (1948): 12–19, 90–95; 8 (1949): 45–63, 77–83; 9 (1950): 52–58.

Roland, Alex. "Bushnell's Submarine: American Original or European Import?" *Technology and Culture* 18 (1977): 157–74.

Rowbotham, W. B. "The West Indies Hurricanes of October 1780." *Journal of the Royal United Service Institution* 106 (1961): 573–84.

Sherman, Constance D., ed. "Journals of the 1781, 1782, and 1783 Campaigns on the Royal Ship *Hercule.*" *New-York Historical Society Quarterly* 61 (1977): 6–48.

Shuldham, Molyneux. *The Dispatches of Molyneux Shuldham, Vice-Admiral of the Blue and Commander-in-Chief of His Britannic Majesty's Ships in North America, January–July, 1776.* Edited by Robert W. Neeser. New York: Naval History Society, 1913.

Smith, Charles R. *Marines in the Revolution: A History of the Continental Marines in the American Revolution, 1775–1783.* Washington: United States Marine Corps, 1975.

Smith, Myron J., Jr. *Navies in the American Revolution: A Bibliography.* Metuchen, N.J.: Scarecrow Press, 1973.

Stout, Neil R. *The Royal Navy in America, 1760–1775: A Study of Enforcement of British Colonial Policy in the Era of the American Revolution.* Annapolis: Naval Institute Press, 1973.

Syrett, David. "H. M. Armed Ship *Vigilant*, 1777–1780." *Mariner's Mirror* 64 (1978): 57–62.

———. "Lord George Germain and the Protection of Military Storeships, 1775–1778." *Mariner's Mirror* 60 (1974): 395–405.

———. *Shipping and the American War, 1775–83: A Study of British Transport Organization.* London: University of London, 1970.

Town, Ithiel, comp. *A Detail of Some Particular Services Performed in America During the Years 1776, 1777, 1778, and 1779, Compiled From Journals and Original Papers, Supposed To Be Chiefly Taken From the Journal Kept on Board the Ship Rainbow, Commanded by Sir George Collier, While on the American Station During That Period: Giving a Minute Account of Many Important Attacks on Towns and Places, Expeditions Sent up Rivers, Skirmishes, Negotiations, etc.* New York, 1835.

Wagner, Frederick. *Submarine Fighter of the American Revolution, the Story of David Bushnell.* New York: Dodd, Mead & Co., 1963.

Yerxa, Donald A. "Vice-Admiral Samuel Graves and the North American Squadron, 1774–1776." *Mariner's Mirror* 62 (1976): 371–85.

POSTWAR DEVELOPMENTS

Brown, Alan S. "The Role of the Army in Western Settlement: Josiah Harmar's Command, 1785–1790." *Pennsylvania Magazine of History and Biography* 93 (1969): 161–78.

Brundage, Lyle D. "The Organization, Administration and Training of the United States Ordinary and Volunteer Militia, 1792–1861." Ph.D. dissertation, University of Michigan, 1959.

Cress, Lawrence D. "The Standing Army, the Militia, and the New Republic: Changing Attitudes Toward the Military in American Society, 1768 to 1820." Ph.D. dissertation, University of Virginia, 1976.

Cunliffe, Marcus. *Soldiers and Civilians: The Martial Spirit in America, 1775–1865.* Boston: Little, Brown & Co., 1968.

Gaines, William H. J. "The Forgotten Army: Recruiting for a National Emergency." *Virginia Magazine of History and Biography* 56 (1948): 267-79.

Godfrey, Carlos E. "Organization of the Provisional Army of the United States in the Anticipated War With France, 1798-1800." *Pennsylvania Magazine of History and Biography* 38 (1914): 129-82.

Jacobs, James R. *The Beginning of the U.S. Army, 1783-1812.* Princeton: Princeton University Press, 1947.

Kimball, Jeffrey. "The Battle of Chippewa: Infantry Tactics in the War of 1812." *Military Affairs* 31 (1967): 169-86.

Kohn, Richard H. *The Eagle and the Sword: The Federalists and the Creation of the Military Establishment in America, 1783-1802.* New York: Free Press, 1975.

Lofgren, Charles A. "Compulsory Military Service Under the Constitution: The Original Understanding." *William and Mary Quarterly,* 3d ser., 33 (1976): 61-88.

Mahon, John K. *The American Militia: Decade of Decision, 1789-1800.* Gainesville: University of Florida Press, 1960.

Smith, Carlton B. "Congressional Attitudes Toward Military Preparedness During the Monroe Administration." *Military Affairs* 40 (1976): 22-25.

_____. "The United States War Department, 1815-1842." Ph.D. dissertation, University of Virginia, 1967.

Tevis, Raymond Harry. "American Opinions and Attitudes Toward British Retention of the Western Posts and American Attempts To Obtain the Western Posts, 1783-90." Ph.D. dissertation, St. Louis University, 1976.

Appendixes

APPENDIX A—U.S. ARMY UNITS DATING FROM THE REVOLUTION

Current Designation	Component	Initial Organization	Designation(s) During the Revolution
182d Infantry	Massachusetts Army National Guard	1636	25th Continental Regiment 3d and 7th Massachusetts Regiments 1st Middlesex Regiment, Massachusetts Militia
101st Engineer Battalion	Massachusetts Army National Guard	1636	Frye's Regiment 12th, 14th Continental Regiments 5th Massachusetts Regiment Lee's Additional Continental Regiment Essex County Brigade, Massachusetts Militia
772d Military Police Company	Massachusetts Army National Guard	1639	1st Company, 3d Bristol Regiment, Massachusetts Militia
104th Infantry	Massachusetts Army National Guard	1662	Danielson's Fellows', and Woodbridge's Regiments Porter's Regiment 1st, 4th Massachusetts Regiments Hampshire and Berkshire County Brigades, Massachusetts Militia
169th Infantry	Connecticut Army National Guard	1672	1st Regiment, Connecticut Militia
102d Infantry	Connecticut Army National Guard	1672	2d Regiment, Connecticut Militia 4th Regiment, Connecticut Militia
192d Field Artillery	Connecticut Army National Guard	1672	3d, 4th, 8th, 9th, 16th, and 20th Regiments, Connecticut Militia
201st Field Artillery	West Virginia Army National Guard	1735	Maryland and Virginia Rifle Regiment 11th Virginia Regiment Berkeley County Regiment, Virginia Militia
Service Battery, 2d Battalion, 214th Field Artillery	Georgia Army National Guard	1736	Light Horse Troop, 1st Regiment, Georgia Militia
126th Signal Battalion	Massachusetts Army National Guard	1741	Jackson's Additional Continental Regiment Independent Company of Cadets, Massachusetts Militia
116th Infantry	Virginia Army National Guard	1742	2d, 8th, and 10th Virginia Regiments Augusta County Regiment, Virginia Militia
111th Infantry	Pennsylvania Army National Guard	1747	Associators of the City and Liberties of Philadelphia (Philadelphia Brigade, Pennsylvania Militia)

APPENDIX A—U.S. ARMY UNITS DATING FROM THE REVOLUTION (CONTINUED)

Current Designation	Component	Initial Organization	Designation(s) During the Revolution
Headquarters and Head-quarters Battery, 118th Field Artillery Brigade	Georgia Army National Guard	1751	1st Regiment, Georgia Militia
169th Military Police Company	Rhode Island Army National Guard	1755	Artillery Company of Westerly, Charlestown and Hopkinton, Rhode Island Militia
263d Air Defense Artillery	South Carolina Army National Guard	1756	Artillery Battalion of Charleston, South Carolina Militia Beaufort Independent Artillery Company
295th and 296th Infantry	Puerto Rico Army National Guard	1765	Milicias disciplinadas de la Isla de San Juan de Puerto Rico
175th Infantry	Maryland Army National Guard	1774	1st–7th Maryland Regiments
Troop A, 1st Squadron, 104th Cavalry	Pennsylvania Army National Guard	1774	Light Horse of the City of Philadelphia
Company A, 2d Special Forces Battalion, 19th Special Forces Group, 1st Special Forces	Rhode Island Army National Guard	1774	North Providence Rangers, Rhode Island Militia 2d Company, Rhode Island State Artillery Regiment
Battery B, 3d Battalion, 197th Field Artillery	New Hampshire Army National Guard	1775	Minute Company of Dover, New Hampshire Militia
Headquarters and Head-quarters Detachment, 192d Engineer Battalion	Connecticut Army National Guard	1775	Norwich Light Infantry, 20th Regiment, Connecticut Militia
109th Field Artillery	Pennsylvania Army National Guard	1775	Westmoreland (Wyoming) Independent Companies 24th Regiment, Connecticut Militia
Company A, 1st Battalion, 69th Infantry	New York Army National Guard	1775	8th Company, 1st New York Regiment (1775)
Battery A, 1st Battalion, 156th Field Artillery	New York Army National Guard	1775	Poughkeepsie Invincibles, 4th Dutchess County Regiment, New York Militia
Service Battery, 1st Battalion, 156th Field Artillery	New York Army National Guard	1775	Captain Hendrick Schoonmaker's Company, 1st Ulster County Regiment, New York Militia
198th Signal Battalion	Delaware Army National Guard	1775	Delaware Regiment
1st Battalion, 5th Field Artillery	Regular Army	1776	New York Provincial Company of Artillery
Detachment 1, Troop B, 1st Squadron, 713th Cavalry	South Carolina Army National Guard	1776	Beaufort Independent Artillery Company
103d Engineer Battalion	Pennsylvania Army National Guard	1777	The Artillery Battalion, Pennsylvania Militia
1st Squadron, 150th Armored Cavalry	West Virginia Army National Guard	1778	Greenbrier County Regiment, Virginia Militia

APPENDIX B—DEPARTMENT COMMANDERS

Department	Commander	Dates of Command
Main Army	George Washington	Duration of war
Eastern Department	Artemas Ward	4 Apr 1776–20 Mar 1777
	William Heath	20 Mar 1777–7 Nov 1778
	Horatio Gates	7 Nov 1778–Nov 1779
Northern Department (initially New York Department)	Philip Schuyler	25 Jun 1775–19 Aug 1777
	Horotio Gates	19 Aug 1777–17 Apr 1778
	John Stark	17 Apr 1778–19 Oct 1778
	Edward Hand	19 Oct 1778–20 Nov 1778
	James Clinton	20 Nov 1778–25 Jun 1781
	John Stark	25 Jun 1781–15 Oct 1781
	William Alexander (Stirling)	15 Oct 1781–21 Nov 1781
	John Stark	21 Nov 1781–29 Aug 1782
	William Alexander (Stirling)	29 Aug 1782–15 Jan 1783
Southern Department	Charles Lee	1 Mar 1776–9 Sep 1776
	Robert Howe	9 Sep 1776–25 Sep 1778
	Benjamin Lincoln	25 Sep 1778–13 Jun 1780
	Horatio Gates	13 Jun 1780–31 Oct 1780
	Nathanael Greene	31 Oct 1780–end of war
Western Department	Edward Hand	10 Apr 1777–26 May 1778
	Lachlan McIntosh	26 May 1778–20 Feb 1779
	Daniel Brodhead	5 Mar 1779–24 Sep 1781
	William Irvine	24 Sep 1781–end of war
Highlands Department	William Heath	12 Nov 1776–21 Dec 1776
	Alexander McDougall	21 Dec 1776–12 May 1777
	Israel Putnam	12 May 1777–16 Mar 1778
	Alexander McDougall	16 Mar 1778–20 May 1778
	Horatio Gates	20 May 1778–24 Nov 1778
	Alexander McDougall	24 Nov 1778–27 Nov 1779
	William Heath	27 Nov 1779–21 Feb 1780
	Robert Howe (acting)	21 Feb 1780–21 Jun 1780
	Alexander McDougall	21 Jun 1780–3 Aug 1780
	Benedict Arnold	3 Aug 1780–25 Sep 1780
	George Washington	25 Sep 1780–28 Sep 1780
	Alexander McDougall	28 Sep 1780–5 Oct 1780
	Nathanael Greene	5 Oct 1780–17 Oct 1780
	William Heath	17 Oct 1780–11 May 1781
	John Paterson (acting)	11 May 1781–24 Jun 1781
	Alexander McDougall	24 Jun 1781–18 Jan 1782
	William Heath	18 Jan 1782–24 Aug 1782
	Henry Knox	24 Aug 1782–end of war
Canadian Department	Richard Montgomery (provisional)	9 Dec 1775–31 Dec 1775
	David Wooster (provisional)	31 Dec 1775–6 Mar 1776
	Charles Lee	17 Feb 1776–1 Mar 1776 (never served)
	John Thomas	6 Mar 1776–1 Jun 1776
	John Sullivan	1 Jun 1776–2 Jul 1776
	Horatio Gates	Appointed 17 Jun 1776 but never served due to withdrawal of troops from department area

APPENDIX C—PRINCIPAL STAFF OFFICERS

Office	Name	Dates
Adjutant General	Horatio Gates	17 Jun 1775–5 Jun 1776
	Joseph Reed	5 Jun 1776–13 Jan 1777
	Vacant	14 Jan 1777–17 Jun 1777
	Timothy Pickering	18 Jun 1777–5 Jan 1778
	Alexander Scammell	5 Jan 1778–8 Jan 1781
	Edward Hand	8 Jan 1781–end of war
Paymaster General	James Warren	27 Jul 1775–19 Apr 1776
	William Palfrey	27 Apr 1776–14 Dec 1780
	John Pierce	17 Jan 1781–end of war
Mustermaster General	Stephen Moylan	11 Aug 1775–7 Jun 1776
	Gunning Bedford	18 Jun 1776–10 Apr 1777
	Joseph Ward	10 Apr 1777–1 Mar 1780
Judge Advocate	William Tudor	30 Jul 1775–10 Apr 1777
	John Laurance	10 Apr 1777–3 Jun 1782
	Vacant	4 Jun 1782–1 Oct 1782
	Thomas Edwards	2 Oct 1782–end of war
Inspector General	Thomas Conway (nominal)	13 Dec 1777–28 Apr 1778
	Frederick Steuben	28 Mar 1778–end of war
Quartermaster General	Thomas Mifflin	14 Aug 1775–7 Jun 1776
	Stephen Moylan	7 Jun 1776–28 Sep 1776
	Thomas Mifflin	28 Sep 1776–7 Nov 1777
	Vacant	8 Nov 1777–1 Mar 1778
	Nathanael Greene	2 Mar 1778–5 Aug 1780
	Timothy Pickering	5 Aug 1780–end of war
Commissary General of Purchases	Joseph Trumbull	19 Jul 1775–18 Jun 1777
	Joseph Trumbull	18 Jun 1777–5 Aug 1777
	William Buchanan	5 Aug 1777–9 Apr 1778
	Jeremiah Wadsworth	9 Apr 1778–2 Dec 1779
	Ephraim Blaine	2 Dec 1779–Nov 1781
Commissary General of Issues	Charles Stewart	18 Jun 1777–Nov 1781
Director General of Hospital Department	Dr. Benjamin Church	27 Jul 1775–4 Oct 1775
	Dr. John Morgan	17 Oct 1775–9 Jan 1777
	Vacant	10 Jan 1777–9 Apr 1777
	Dr. William Shippen	10 Apr 1777–3 Jan 1781
	Dr. John Cochran	17 Jan 1781–end of war

Appendix D—Engagements

Engagement	Time Period	Area	Explanation
Siege of Boston	20 Apr 1775–17 Mar 1776	Eastern Massachusetts	Operations relating to the British occupation of Boston
Invasion of Canada	4 Sep–31 Dec 1775	Canada	Operations by Montgomery and Arnold through assault on Quebec
Chesapeake Bay	15 Sep 1775–31 Aug 1776	Chesapeake Bay and adjacent coastline regions	Engagements with Lord Dunmore's land and naval forces
Charleston 1775–1776	15 Sep 1775–28 Jun 1776	Coastal portions of the Carolinas and Georgia	Engagements with land and naval forces of Royal governors and repulse of Clinton's expedition
Southern Highlands	15 Sep 1775–24 Feb 1776	Interior portions of the Carolinas and Georgia	Engagements with loyalist forces
Defense of Canada	1 Jan–2 Jul 1776	Canada	Siege of Quebec after repulse of the assault and withdrawal from Canada
New York City	3 Apr–16 Nov 1776	Southern New York and Bergen County, New Jersey	Operations relating to the British capture of Long, Staten, and Manhattan Islands
Lake Champlain	2 Jul–3 Nov 1776	Charlotte County, New York	Carleton's attack on Ticonderoga
Florida	1 Aug 1776–31 May 1777	Georgia south of Ossawba Sound and East Florida	American invasions of East Florida and British counterattacks
Northern New Jersey	20 Nov 1776–26 Jun 1777	Staten Island and northern New Jersey	Engagements from capture of Fort Lee to British withdrawal to start the invasion of Pennsylvania
Trenton-Princeton	8 Dec 1776–6 Jan 1777	Southern New Jersey	Engagements from Washington's retreat across the Delaware River to his encampment at Morristown
Rhode Island	26 Dec 1776–25 Oct 1779	Rhode Island	Operations relating to the British occupation of Newport
Saratoga	18 Jun–17 Oct 1777	Albany and Charlotte Counties, New York	Operations relating to Burgoyne's campaign
Mohawk Valley	25 Jun–24 Aug 1777	Albany and Tryon Counties, New York	Operations relating to St. Leger's campaign
Defense of Philadelphia	25 Aug–19 Dec 1777	Eastern Pennsylvania, Maryland, and Delaware	Engagements from British landing at Head of Elk to Washington's encampment at Valley Forge
Hudson Highlands	1–31 Oct 1777	Southern New York	Operations relating to Clinton's relief expedition
Philadelphia-Monmouth	20 Dec 1777–10 Jul 1778	Pennsylvania, Delaware, and New Jersey	Operations relating to the British occupation of Philadelphia and withdrawal to Sandy Hook

APPENDIX D—ENGAGEMENTS (CONTINUED)

Engagement	Time Period	Area	Explanation
Savannah	28 Nov 1778–15 Oct 1779	Georgia and South Carolina	Operations relating to the British capture and defense of Savannah and coastal South Carolina
Charleston 1780	10 Feb–29 May 1780	South Carolina	Siege of Charleston and related occupation of South Carolina through the battle of Waxhaws
Defense of the Carolinas	30 May 1780–14 Feb 1781	The Carolinas	Operations under Gates and Greene to the withdrawal across the Dan
Yorktown	30 Dec 1780–19 Oct 1781	Virginia	Siege of Yorktown and preliminaries beginning with Arnold's Raid
Greene's Campaign	15 Feb 1781–14 Dec 1782	The Carolinas and Georgia	Greene's reconquest of the South

Glossary

Agent	In the British Army, a civilian appointed by the colonel of a regiment to handle the unit's financial accounts.
Adjutant	The regimental staff officer responsible for a unit's administrative paperwork and for supervising daily details, such as guards and work parties.
Adopt	To place a unit organized by state authority on the rolls of the Army as an element of the Continental Line.
Aide-major	Archaic term for adjutant.
Allot	To assign a unit to the Continental Line of a state or states. This action provided a unit with needed legal and administrative support to secure replacements, clothing, and financial resources. Units allotted to a specific state, remained so for the rest of their existence. Those not allotted were directly responsible to the Continental Congress.
Assign	To make a unit part of a larger organization and to place it under the larger unit's command and control until relieved. Units were assigned to territorial departments and brigades.
Authorize	To place the designation of a new unit on the official rolls of the Continental Army. Only done by action of the Continental Congress.
Batmen	Hired servants who cared for an officer's baggage and personal effects. The term was also used to describe privates detailed to perform these jobs.
Battalion	The basic tactical unit of eighteenth century warfare composed of a group of companies or platoons and usually commanded in combat by a lieutenant colonel. In both the British and Continental Armies, most regiments had only a single battalion, and the terms battalion and regiment were virtually synonymous.
Bombardier	An artillery specialist rank given to privates who were specialists in preparing ammunition and in firing mortars. During times of hazardous duty, bombardiers merited supplemental pay.
Brigadier	A rank held in the British Army only during wartime. The officer commanding a brigade received this rank which fell between lieutenant colonel and colonel. The brigadier was not a general officer.

Camp-colour-men	A duty detail consisting of about one man per company to assist the regimental quartermaster in preparing a new camp site. The camp colours were small pennants used to mark the outline of the regimental area.
Captain	A company's or troop's commanding officer.
Captain-lieutenant	In infantry or cavalry units in which field officers also served as captains of specific companies, the lieutenant who actually commanded the colonel's company. This lieutenant was the senior in his rank within the regiment. In artillery companies, the captain-lieutenant was the second ranking officer.
Colonel	A regiment's commanding officer. In the British Army this was a titular rank, and the colonel attended only to financial matters. In the Continental Army, the colonel was the actual commander responsible for tactical leadership and administration.
Commissary	A civil officer who performed various logistical duties.
Commissioned officer	One who exercised authority under a commission from the king or the Continental Congress. Officers ranging from ensign to general received commissions. Those issued in the British Army were a form of property and could be bought and sold under governmental supervision.
Company	The smallest administrative unit of infantry or artillery. Both British and Continental Army companies could be either separate entities or parts of a regiment. Also, in both armies, the company was virtually synonymous with the tactical platoon.
Company-grade officer	Officers who served in company-sized units: captains, captain-lieutenants, lieutenants, ensigns, and cornets.
Conductor	A member of the civil staff who supervised depots, magazines, or groups of wagons.
Consolidate	To merge or combine two or more units into one. The new unit might have retained the designation of one of the originals or might have a new designation. However, the new unit inherits the lineage of all units affected by the merger. In the eighteenth century, consolidation frequently merged several understrength units into one full-strength unit.
Continental Army	Those units of regular soldiers enlisted for full-time service, generally for extended periods, and for whom the ultimate authority for their organizations, maintenance, administration, and discipline remained with the Continental Congress. Each unit of this Army was cited explicitly by a Resolution of the Continental Congress.

Cornet
: The most junior officer in a cavalry troop. Equivalent to an ensign in an infantry company.

Corporal
: A noncommissioned officer who was usually responsible for supervising a squad. In combat, corporals served in the line of battle with privates.

Disband
: To remove the designation of a unit from the official rolls of the Continental Army.

Ensign
: The lowest-ranking commissioned officer in an infantry company. In the Continental Army, a regiment's ensigns carried the regimental colors on a rotating basis and were particularly responsible for the dress and cleanliness of the company.

Field officer
: Officers concerned with a regiment's overall operations. These officers were colonels, lieutenant colonels, and majors.

Fireworker
: The rank of the youngest lieutenants in the artillery. They were particularly responsible for preparing ammunition.

Furlough
: To place a unit on leave and, therefore, to remove the government's obligation to pay or feed the men, and yet to keep the unit subject to recall for duty. Used as a preliminary to disbanding.

General
: The category of officer responsible for commanding large units. The British Army had three ranks of general officer: major general, lieutenant general, and general. (A still higher rank, field marshal, was not used in North America.) The Continental Army had two ranks: brigadier general (normally who commanded a brigade) and major general (division). Washington's rank as "General and Commander-in-Chief" was unique.

Gunner
: An artillery private who had special status because of his responsibility for loading and aiming an artillery piece. This private received higher pay than a matross.

Lance corporal
: An acting corporal. In eighteenth century European armies, future officers receiving on-the-job training received this rank. However, the British and Continental Armies preferred to designate future officers as "cadet" or "volunteer" and not to give them official standing in the army until they were commissioned.

Lieutenant
: The middle rank of company-grade officers. When organizations had more than one lieutenant per company, distinctions were established between first, second, and third lieutenants.

Lieutenant colonel	The second in command of a regiment. In the British Army this person actually commanded the regiment in the field. In the Continental Army, when a lieutenant colonel was the senior officer of the regiment, he was called a lieutenant colonel commandant.
Line	That portion of the Continental Army under the auspices of a specific state. This term was also used to refer to the aggregate of the light dragoon regiments or the artillery regiments. However, it applied to combat units only. In battlefield dispositions, the "line" was that segment of the Army deployed in linear formation.
Major	The lowest ranking field officer in a regiment, particularly responsible for administration. Infantry majors were the only officers who went into battle mounted and who were responsible for rallying the regiment if its line became broken.
Matross	The term used for artillery privates. Matrosses performed the semi-skilled tasks in firing a cannon.
Militia	The basic military force of each state or colony, nominally composed of its total male population capable of bearing arms. State governments always exercised final authority over militia even when militia forces served with the Continental Army. Because the militia was essentially a local defense organization, provisional units did most extended service.
Miner	Special troops used to construct tunnels during siege operations.
Minutemen	A part of the militia tasked with responding immediately to an emergency. Minutemen units received additional training and some monetary compensation. However, the minuteman organization was used in 1775 and 1776 only.
Noncommissioned officers	Sergeants, corporals, drum majors, and fife majors appointed by a regimental commander to command privates. Only the regimental commander or a court-martial could remove noncommissioned officers from their rank.
Organize	To fill a unit with personnel and to issue it arms and equipment to allow it to perform its mission.
Paymaster	The officer formally charged with the care of a regiment's funds and with paying the troops.
Pioneer	Troops responsible for repairing roads and occasionally preparing fortifications.

Platoon	The smallest tactical unit in the eighteenth century. Normally a battalion would deploy in eight platoons. In European armies platoons were often temporary formations for a specific battle; in the British and Continental Armies, companies and platoons were virtually synonymous.
Quartermaster	An officer responsible for housing, feeding, equipping, and moving troops.
Rank and file	A unit's privates and corporals. This classification represented a unit's actual combat strength as deployed for linear combat. Also referred to as a unit's "bayonet strength."
Redesignate	To change a unit's official name, number, or both. Redesignation is changing title only; the lineage remains the same.
Regiment	The basic administration unit of eighteenth century armies. British and Continental Army regiments normally had only one battalion, so the terms regiment and battalion were synonymous.
Reorganize	To change the structure of a unit according to a new organizational plan.
Sapper	Special troops who dug entrenchments ("saps") during sieges.
Sergeants	Noncommissioned officers armed with a halberd who enforced discipline and acted as file closers during battle.
State troops	Regular forces, often for full-time service, raised under state or colonel governments' authority. State troops, unlike those of the Continental Army, remained under state governments' authority. In addition, they sometimes operated with the Continental Army for extended periods.
Subaltern	Company-grade officer below the rank of captain—lieutenant, ensign, or cornet.
Warrant officer	An officer who exercised authority through a warrant rather than a commission, and who was usually assigned to staff duty. Warrants, like commissions, were issued by the Continental Congress or the king. However, lesser authorities, such as commanders of staff or territorial departments, could also issue warrants.

Index